ENCYCLOPEDIA OF RELIGIOUS CONTROVERSIES IN THE UNITED STATES

ENCYCLOPEDIA OF RELIGIOUS CONTROVERSIES IN THE UNITED STATES

Edited by GEORGE H. SHRIVER
and BILL J. LEONARD

GREENWOOD PRESS
Westport, Connecticut • London

Library of Congress Cataloging-in-Publication Data

Encyclopedia of religious controversies in the United States / edited
by George H. Shriver and Bill J. Leonard.
    p.   cm.
   Includes bibliographical references and index.
   ISBN 0–313–29691–X (alk. paper)
   1. Church controversies—Encyclopedias. 2. United States—Church
history—Encyclopedias. 3. United States—Religion—Encyclopedias.
I. Shriver, George H. II. Leonard, Bill.
BR515.E53   1997
273'.9'0973—dc21   97–8781

British Library Cataloguing in Publication Data is available.

Library of Congress Catalog Card Number: 97–8781
ISBN: 0–313–29691–X

First published in 1997

Greenwood Press, 88 Post Road West, Westport, CT 06881
An imprint of Greenwood Publishing Group, Inc.

Printed in the United States of America

The paper used in this book complies with the
Permanent Paper Standard issued by the National
Information Standards Organization (Z39.48–1984).

10 9 8 7 6 5 4 3 2 1

This book is dedicated to faculty members at the Southern Baptist Theological Seminary, Louisville, Kentucky, and the Southeastern Baptist Theological Seminary, Wake Forest, North Carolina (1970–1990), most of whom are no longer at these institutions because of controversy and conscience.

CONTENTS

ACKNOWLEDGMENTS

Edited volumes have numerous and unusual problems, but we must pay high tribute and sincere appreciation to the more than fifty writers who have joined us in this worthy project. We have been a team and a community at work together.

The mechanics of putting things together has been made easier by the help of Brandi Scott at Georgia Southern University, Thelma Heywood and Jonathan S. Speegle at Samford University, and Betsy Clement at Wake Forest University. Our spouses, Cathy and Candyce, have endured our sometimes rough temperaments and special friends have shared ideas and prodding remarks. Alicia Merritt and Bridget M. Austiguy-Preschel of Greenwood Press have been especially helpful and creatively encouraging.

And, finally, without the thousands of religious controversies in the United States this book would not exist. However, we would finally urge better understanding and ecumenism as one result of reading about fragmentations and contentiousness. May some cosmos emerge from the apparent chaos.

INTRODUCTION

Alfred North Whitehead once observed that "the clash of doctrines is not a disaster, it is an opportunity." No religion on the face of the earth is devoid of controversy. In fact, is it not true that to be completely harmonious is to be devoid of process and structure? Or, to put it another way, there is no heresy (controversy) in a dead religion. Further, as Lewis Coser cogently observed in his excellent *The Functions of Social Conflict*, "Intensity of conflict is related to closeness of the relationship," and in such closely knit groups, if conflict occurs, it will be intense and passionate. Religious bodies are always closely knit, and their conflicts are always "intense and passionate."

This being the case, where else in the world would there be more religious controversy and conflict than in the United States, where the opening of Pandora's box of religious liberty and separation of church and state has resulted in more than 1,700 different religious bodies, the most dominant of which are Christian groups? Religious controversy is part of the warp and woof of religious bodies in the United States. This can be very discouraging and depressing at times, but it is at least illustrative of lively and creative process and structure. A multiplicity of religious controversies crisscross our society on every fresh day. One has only to read the dailies to see this. Many religious bodies were conceived and born in controversy. They are "struggle" groups and continuously select and reselect those they consider to be "worthy leaders" at a given point in their pilgrimage. Some of these groups are more elastic than others and experience less conflict; on the other hand, some of them are more rigid and undergo greater conflict and sometimes even schism. Even the perception of threat to a religious group will result in conflict.

Values, claims, history, doctrinal essence, and ideals often result in controversy. Those who fight hard for the ideals of the religious body of which they are a part can be so intense in their commitment that the controversy sometimes tears the group apart, and controversy is duplicated many times over as history continues. On the other hand, if controversy is not so intense, there is an opportunity for "antagonistic cooperation," as Coser called it. There are less serious controversies from which the group profits internally, but the more serious ones may cause rifts and even schism, producing yet another religious body on the American scene.

The present volume cannot be all-inclusive. Since religion is the truly interdisciplinary subject that touches on virtually every aspect of living in a society, there are thousands of controversies touching on religion. When one adds the more than one thousand bodies in the United States, the controversies rise to the tens of thousands. We have included in these alphabetically arranged entries the major persons, themes, terms, institutions or groups, books (a limited number), and secular topics that lend themselves to religious controversy. Every historian's list would differ slightly, but we are optimistic enough to think that 98 percent of these entries would be on everyone's list. Our discussions from a wide range of scholars have concentrated on the "controversy" aspect of these entries without omitting other important information. Cross-references are noted in the text with an asterisk, and the brief bibliographies for each entry can lead the reader to far more involved and detailed discussions of the entry topic.

It is our hope that this reference volume will be useful to those interested in religious controversy in the United States. It will definitely not be definitive; it is meant to be useful. One who reads here will find useful parts of the whole story, since the whole story cannot really be told. On the other hand, this book does stand as a first attempt to bring together the major pieces of the jigsaw puzzle of religious controversy in the United States. Personally, we would like to affirm the tremendous benefit this project has brought to us. Our own knowledge of the subject has been greatly enlarged by the numerous and creative contributions by our colleagues from across the United States. This project is a continuing pilgrimage. We invite the reader to join us on the journey, using significant knowledge already discovered as well as pushing on toward the discovery of even more knowledge on the horizon of religious controversy in the United States.

ENCYCLOPEDIA OF RELIGIOUS CONTROVERSIES IN THE UNITED STATES

A

Abernathy, Ralph David. An African-American Baptist pastor, civil rights* leader, and close colleague of Martin Luther King, Jr.,* Ralph David Abernathy was born on March 11, 1926, in Linden, Alabama and the grandson of a former slave. In 1948 he announced his call to the Baptist ministry and received a B.S. degree from Alabama State College in 1950 and a master's from Atlanta University in 1951.

In 1950 Abernathy became pastor of the historic First (Colored) Baptist Church in Montgomery, in which the National Baptist Foreign Mission Convention, a precursor to the National Baptist Convention (NBC), was founded in 1880. Along with King, Abernathy helped to start the Montgomery bus boycott immediately after Rosa Parks's* arrest for refusing to give up her seat to a white person on December 1, 1955. In the aftermath, Abernathy's home and church were bombed, with the church having to be completely rebuilt. The boycott lasted for 381 days, and the Supreme Court decision against segregation was delivered on November 13, 1956. In the light of the boycott, King, along with Abernathy, and the nonviolent passive resistance philosophy received national acclaim. In January 1957 King, along with Abernathy, organized the Southern Christian Leadership Conference* (SCLC), which was primarily an organization of black southern ministers committed to the nonviolent methodology. Under King's leadership and with Abernathy's help, SCLC became one of the leading civil rights organizations in the nation, and the nonviolent passive resistance philosophy rivaled the more conservative civil rights philosophy of the National Association for the Advancement of Colored People (NAACP*).

In celebration of the first anniversary of the bus boycott in December 1956, Abernathy invited Joseph H. Jackson, president of the National Baptist Convention (NBC), to speak at First Baptist. The NBC was the largest black organization in the world, with over seven million members. As president, Jackson would be returning to the site where the NBC had been first organized seventy-six years earlier. The Montgomery boycott had been modeled after one led two years earlier by the Reverend Theodore J. Jemison in Baton Rouge, whose father, David V. Jemison, had been president of the NBC before Jackson. However, in his sermon Jackson never mentioned the bus boycott. By 1959 Jackson had publicly taken a position against nonviolent passive resistance. In part, the situation led to a split in the NBC in 1961 and the organizing of the Progressive National Baptist Convention the same year.

Regardless, throughout the history of the civil rights movement, from Montgomery in 1955 to Memphis in 1968, Abernathy was King's closest friend and civil rights associate. As in the case of the Jackson scenario, seemingly their thoughts remained essentially the same, and Abernathy remained at King's side. Like King a year earlier, in 1961 Abernathy moved to Atlanta, the headquarters of SCLC, and assumed the pastorate of West Hunter Street Baptist Church, where he served until 1983.

With the assassination of King on April 4, 1968, Abernathy assumed the presidency of SCLC. His leadership was contested by SCLC staff members who believed him to be a second fiddle. After years of silence, however, Abernathy authored a controversial book, *And the Walls Came Tumbling Down* (1989), in which he accused King of plagiarism and sexual indiscretions. Evidently, Abernathy was not happy with history's presentation of his role in the civil rights movement as King's subordinate. In response, Abernathy said that it was important for the record to be set straight. King was human: he had problems with women, especially black women, and regularly took the ideas of others, using them as his own. Abernathy contended that many of the ideas presented as King's own were actually his ideas. To be sure, Abernathy stated that King had insisted that he succeed him as SCLC president, for this would guarantee the continued implementation of King's program. Abernathy's book caused quite a reaction, with some critics accusing him of character assassination. Abernathy died in Atlanta on April 17, 1990.

Bibliography. Abernathy, R. D., *And the Walls Came Tumbling Down* (New York: Harper and Row 1989); Jackson, J. H., "National Baptist Philosophy of Civil Rights," in *Afro-American Religious History*, ed. M. C. Sernett (Durham: Duke University Press, 1985); Murphy, L. G., ed., *Encyclopedia of African American Religions* (New York: Garland Publishing, 1993); Sawyer, M. R., *Black Ecumenism* (Valley Forge, PA: Trinity Press International, 1994).

Thomas J. Davis

Abolitionism. Abolitionism was the nineteenth-century movement to abolish the practice of slavery in the United States, which eventually resulted in political schism and ultimately in war between North and South. Abolitionists first created schism in America's religious institutions. Most historians have seen the beginnings of antislavery thought in America in Puritan cleric Samuel Sewall's 1700 treatise "The Selling of Joseph" or the "Inner Light" ideology of the Quakers, often considered the first religious group in America to reject slavery. In reality, African Americans were the first "abolitionists," even though they did not use the term. This becomes obvious when one notes the degree to which the "official" abolitionist movement had its beginnings in black churches or homes such as that of Philadelphia dentist James C. McCrummell, where the American Antislavery Society was founded. Still, initial antislavery rumblings deriving from the egalitarianism of the Great Awakenings and the American Revolution came to be subordinated to political pragmatism and compromise necessary to post-Revolution nation building.

In the early national period, however, revivalism* and its concomitant emphasis (at least in the North) on benevolence or social reform, Christian perfectionism, postmillennialism, and the growing hunger for freedom among African-American Christians contributed to the rise of abolitionism as an identifiable movement. Free blacks in the North organized to protest colonization, a giant step toward antislavery agitation. Slavery was barred in the northern states carved out of the Louisiana territory by the 1820 Missouri Compromise, which an aging Thomas Jefferson called a "firebell in the night" for fear that it had reintroduced slavery into Congress as a politically divisive issue. In the same decade black Christians like Denmark Vesey* and David Walker attempted or advocated insurrection by the slaves. In their "war against proslavery religion," these black and white abolitionists called upon clergy and denominations to denounce slavery as a sin and to bar slaveholders from church membership.

Further stimulated by the founding of William Lloyd Garrison's journal the *Liberator* and the slave rebellion of Nat Turner* in 1831, the movement developed an institutional center with the formation of the American Antislavery Society in December 1833. Through the postal service and in stump speeches, abolitionists bore down most heavily on the churches who shied away from denouncing slavery. In 1843 one writer published an incendiary pamphlet called "The Brotherhood of Thieves, or, A True Picture of the American Church and Clergy," and later Frederick Douglass, the best-known black abolitionist of the day, bitterly contrasted "Slaveholding Christianity" with "the Christianity of Christ." Other black abolitionists like Samuel Ringgold Ward, Harriet Tubman, and Sojourner Truth* became the most sought-after speakers on the antislavery circuit. Some, like Henry Highland Garnet, even advocated violent insurrection by the slaves, on the grounds that to submit to an earthly master was to deny the lordship of Christ. Eventually the increase of this kind of rhetoric polarized the nation's evangelical denominations. In 1845, even though their denominations were far from committed to "immediate emancipation," the southern wings of both the Methodist and Baptist denominations felt enough opprobrium on their compromise with slaveholding that they withdrew to form their own

Southern branches. Many unionists lamented these schisms as the precursors of America's later political division after 1860. Abolitionist fervor continued with the publication of *Uncle Tom's Cabin* (1852) by Harriet Beecher Stowe,* whom Abraham Lincoln once greeted as "the lady who started this war." Given the connections between the antislavery movement and the Civil War, abolitionism could arguably be the bloodiest controversy in American religious history.

Bibliography. Mathews, Donald G., ed., *Agitation for Freedom: The Abolitionist Movement* (New York: John Wiley and Sons, 1972); McKivigan, John R., *The War against Proslavery Religion: Abolitionism and the Northern Churches, 1830–1865* (Ithaca: Cornell University Press, 1984); Quarles, Benjamin, *Black Abolitionists.* (New York: Oxford University Press, 1969); Stewart, James Brewer, *Holy Warriors* (New York: Hill and Wang, 1976).

Andrew M. Manis

Abortion. The earliest abortifacient recipe is thought to be over 4,500 years old; and induced abortion was employed for birth control long before the Christian era. Such legal restraints as there were existed, not for the protection of nascent life, but for safeguarding maternal life and guaranteeing that husbands would not be deprived of children by wives who were vain, fearful, or otherwise unwilling to become mothers. Orthodox Judaism teaches that a fetus is not a juridical person and therefore is not protected from dismemberment by drug or by hand until crowning (head presentation) or the greater part of the body is visible at birth. The prevailing Jewish view nevertheless limits abortion to cases that involve a hazard (whether physical or psychological) to the pregnant woman's life; the preference, moreover, is that these pregnancies be terminated "within the first forty days or at least within the first three months." Initial Christian objection to both abortion and infanticide was grounded in speculation about the soul—its origin, its existence in time, and its eventual destiny. The principal alternative theories consisted of generationism (each soul comes into existence coincident with its body as a biological transmission), creationism (each soul is immediately and directly created by God), and quickening (when the mother-to-be first detects stirrings of life in her womb). Although no definitive position had been generally accepted by the Middle Ages, St. Thomas Aquinas formulated the presiding view: the soul (*anima*) is not created at conception but at the time when it is "infused" into the body (which he reckoned at about the fortieth day in male, and about the eightieth day in female, embryos).

The current Roman Catholic teaching on the inviolability of nascent human life began to take definite doctrinal shape in the seventeenth century under Innocent XI; it was solidified by Pius XI in his 1930 encyclical *Casti Connubii*. Theoretical uncertainty regarding when animation occurs was resolved into practical certainty by asserting that since we cannot truly know when God establishes his never-to-be-severed relationship with one of us, practically we should act as though we know that animation has occurred at conception. Direct and voluntary abortion is therefore a moral offense of the gravest sort since it is the deliberate destruction of an ensouled and innocent life. The Vatican Council II* declared (*Gaudium et Spes*, paragraph 51) that "from the moment of conception life must be guarded with the greatest care, while abortion and infanticide are unspeakable crimes." This has similarly been the position of Greek Orthodoxy over the centuries, that the taking of unborn life is morally wrong.

Protestant Christian positions, where they have been taken, range across a broad spectrum from prohibition to reluctant and qualified approval to straightforward affirmation of a woman's "right to choose." (1) The Mennonite General Assembly has asserted that "abortion violates the biblical principles of the sanctity and value of human life"; and both American Baptists and Southern Baptists have expressed their opposition to abortion. "The Assemblies of God is unashamedly pro-life" and affirms "the long-standing Christian view that aborting the life of a developing child is evil"; and the Presbyterian Church in America has declared, "Because Scripture affirms the sanctity of human life and condemns its arbitrary destruction, we affirm that the intentional killing of an unborn child between conception and birth, for any reason at any time, is clearly a violation of the Sixth Commandment." (2) The Presbyterian Church, USA, asserts that while "abortion ought to be an option of the last resort," there are "possible justifying circumstances" for abortion; the Moravian Church advocates "that abortion be regarded as a serious matter of responsible personal decision on the part of Christians to be considered only after sincere exploration of all alternatives, counselling, and prayer"; and the Episcopal Church, believing that "all human life is sacred from its inception until death," regards abortion as having "a tragic dimension" and "believes strongly" that if the legal right to abortion is exercised, "it should be used only in extreme situations." The Lutheran Church–Missouri Synod holds "firmly to the clear biblical truths that the living but unborn are persons in the sight of God from conception . . . since abortion takes a human life, abortion is not a moral option, except as a tragically unavoidable byproduct of medical procedures necessary to prevent the death of another human being, viz., the mother." The United Methodist Church has declared that "our belief in the sanctity of unborn human life makes us reluctant to approve abortion. But we are equally bound to respect the sacredness of the life and well-being of the mother." (3) The Disciples of Christ "reaffirms our historic commitment to reproductive freedom for women"; the Evangelical Lutheran Church in America "recognizes that there can be sound reasons for ending a pregnancy"; and the United Church of Christ "affirms a woman's right to choose." So long as religious bodies in North America cannot or will not commit to common sources of religious authority and shared notions of when life is human life, so long will abortion remain an intractable religious controversy.

Bibliography. Judicatory position papers are typically available through the appropriate church commission or headquarters. See also the following: Feldman, David M., *Birth Control in Jewish Law* (New York: New York University Press, 1968); Jakobovits, Immanuel, *Jewish Medical Ethics* (New York: Bloch Publishing Co., 1975); Pojman, Louis P., *Life and Death: A Reader in Moral Problems* (Boston: Jones and Bartlett, 1993), 267–329; Rosner, Fred, *Modern Medicine and Jewish Law* (New York: Yeshiva University, 1972); Smith, Harmon L., *Ethics and the New Medicine* (Nashville: Abingdon Press, 1970).

Harmon L. Smith

Academic Freedom. Though definitions of academic freedom are somewhat ambiguous, the numerous threats to and violations of academic freedom in the history of education in the United States have been completely unambiguous. Religious issues have been involved in many of these threats and violations that have resulted in numerous controversies.

The most contributive organization in the United States to the concept and defense of academic freedom is the American Association of University Professors (AAUP). It was founded in 1915 in the context of concern for professors who had been dismissed for political views as well as for religious views. Though from the start the AAUP recognized that academic freedom could not be completely unlimited, by 1940 a widespread consensus had evolved concerning academic freedom and the organization adopted its famous 1940 statement that has since been virtually canonized. The critical phrases of this statement are worthy of repetition:

> Institutions of higher education are conducted for the common good [which involves the religious sphere] and not to further the interest of either the individual teacher or the institution as a whole. The common good depends upon the free search for truth and its free exposition.
>
> Academic freedom is essential to these purposes and applies to both teaching and research. Freedom in research is fundamental to the advancement of truth. Academic freedom in its teaching aspect is fundamental for the protection of the rights of the teacher in teaching and of the student to freedom in learning. It carries with it duties correlative with rights. . . .
>
> The teacher is entitled to full freedom in research and in the publication of the results. . . . The teacher is entitled to freedom in the classroom in discussing his subject, but he should be careful not to introduce into his teaching controversial matter which has no relation to his subject. Limitations of academic freedom because of religious or other aims of the institution should be clearly stated in writing at the time of appointment. (*AAUP Policy Documents and Reports*, 3)

Though margins of vagueness remained, discussion of the issue took on greater cogency and clarity than had been present earlier. In relation to religiously related institutions, the most debated section of the AAUP statement is the "limitations" sentence. When originally written, the statement was probably a reluctant permission to limit rather than an encouragement to limit. By the mid-1960s, however, there was certainly a greater need to clarify the meaning of the limitations clause, because by then it was apparent that some institutions by unreasonable self-restriction were on the verge of removing themselves from the community of higher education. Later in the decade a special committee of the AAUP, chaired by a religionist, urged that ''religious privilege not be employed to provide a sanctuary in which to avoid the full responsibilities of higher education.''

By the 1980s there existed three different kinds of religiously affiliated institutions in relation to academic freedom. All such schools had definitely entered the ecumenical age—some affirming the age and others opposing it. First was the ''nonaffirming'' school. It might once have had denominational affiliation and might indeed have continued a commitment to moral and spiritual values, but in terms of curriculum, teaching, and an understanding of academic freedom, it could hardly be distinguished from a secular institution. At the other end of the spectrum was the ''defender of the faith'' school where so-called academic freedom was boxed in by an often rigid orthodoxy to which the school was committed. In between these two types was the free Christian or Jewish school. Such a school had a definite religious commitment but also strove for a free play of the mind. Such a school strove to further religious interests as well as allowing academic freedom.

Presently, this description is helpful but not conclusive. More recently, other schools have been strung out on a linear construct somewhere between these three types. For example, on the far right, with no real interest in academic freedom, tenure, or faculty governance, would be numerous fundamentalist schools. Other ''evangelical'' schools are not as separatistic and would be interested in traditional accreditation. These schools want religious commitment as well as academic status in the larger academic community. A genuine possibility for these schools is a unique contribution in religious as well as intellectual vitality to American higher education.

Academic freedom abounds and flourishes in numerous religiously oriented institutions of several types; academic freedom is violated in a comparatively few religiously oriented institutions, generally of fundamentalist outlook. Where this latter happens, there is really a denial of what an educational seat of higher learning in the Western world is all about. William May has succinctly stated the main issues in these words:

> The problem that remains, if we accept the argument about pluralism and the contribution of church-related institutions to our society, is where to draw the line on the limitations to academic freedom. There is no question that institutions have the right to define themselves as they wish. However, if they want to be identified and accredited as institutions of higher education, they must meet the standard of free inquiry that higher education demands. Clearly that standard, which has evolved in the last fifty years, places the burden on the institutions to justify any limitation on free expression of the results of sound scholarship. (*Academe*, July–August 1988, 28)

Bibliography. *AAUP Policy Documents and Reports* (Washington, DC: AAUP, 1990); May, William, "Academic Freedom in Church-related Institutions," *Academe*, July–August 1988, 23–28; Metzger, Walter, *Academic Freedom in the Age of the University* (New York: Columbia University Press, 1961); Poch, Robert K., *Academic Freedom in American Higher Education* (Washington, DC: ASHE-ERIC Higher Education Report no. 4, 1993).

George H. Shriver

Adventism. Various groups focus on the imminent advent (coming) of Jesus. Many of these groups, particularly the Seventh-Day Adventists, are descendants of the Millerite movement. William Miller* was a lay Baptist preacher from the revivalistic-prone area of upper New York State now called the Burned-over District. Throughout the 1830s Miller preached, lectured, and wrote about the imminent return of Jesus. In 1836 he published *Evidences from Scripture and History of the Second Coming of Christ, about the Year 1843*. Joshua Himes, a Boston minister, helped extend Miller's influence onto a national scale through skillful promotion of Miller's "midnight cry." Himes set up conferences and camp meetings and created a journal, the *Signs of the Times* (1840).

By 1843 Miller's opposition from mainstream churches had become intense, as had the internal pressure from followers to more closely specify the date of Jesus' coming. In January 1843 Miller complied, asserting that the advent would occur between March 21, 1843, and March 21, 1844. When that prediction failed, Miller revised the date to October 22, 1844. After the second failure, he refused further date setting. Some of the estimated 50,000 committed followers were disillusioned and returned to their former churches; others who had "come out" of the old denominations in preparation for the end time developed new Adventist groups.

Adventists came to refer to Miller's failures as "the Great Disappointment." The largest number of Adventists coalesced around the leadership of Ellen G. Harmon White and developed into the Seventh-Day Adventist Church. They affirmed White's prophecies and visions (over two thousand in all) and began to revere her writings. Her prophecies are still published. White and other Adventists still affirmed the imminent return of Jesus; Miller's prediction of 1844 was spiritualized to mean that Jesus began blotting out sins in the heavenly sanctuary, not the earthly one, on that date. As adventism grew, new important and distinctive doctrines included the observance of the Sabbath (Saturday worship; White was influenced by Seventh-Day Baptists) and the idea of conditional immortality. Some Adventists have advocated pacifism, and many follow the dietary laws of the Old Testament. White is known for setting up a sanitarium in Battle Creek, Michigan, that emphasized health and a vegetarian diet (John Kellogg was its superintendent). Miller's Baptist roots can be seen in the Adventists' practice of these ordinances: baptism by immersion, the Lord's Supper, and footwashing.

Other, smaller Adventist groups developed from the Millerite movement. Some observe Sunday worship, like the Advent Christian Church. Other groups that can be called Adventist, emphasizing the imminent return of Christ, abound in American religion. They include the Worldwide Church of God and the Jehovah's Witnesses.*

Adventism created controversy in American religion. Date setting of the end time using the biblical books of Daniel and Revelation has continued since Miller's time. Many opponents criticize this practice as an escapist and "otherworldly" orientation that fails to deal with pressing societal problems in this world. Some adventism, as in Millerism, led to religious fanaticism, with people leaving their homes and churches to wait for the coming of Jesus. Seventh-Day Adventists have been criticized for excessively venerating the writings of White and in conservative Christian circles are often described as a cult. Saturday worship and the accompanying refusal to work that day have resulted in job discrimination for some Adventists. Other Christians have also harshly criticized the Adventist focus on the dietary laws of the Old Testament.

Bibliography. Butler, J. M., "From Millerism to Seventh Day Adventism: Boundlessness to Consolidation," *Church History* 55 (1986): 50–64; Land, Gary, ed., *Adventism in America: A History* (Grand Rapids, MI: William B. Eerdmans, 1986); Melton, J. Gordon, *The Encyclopedia of American Religions* (Detroit: Gale Research Co., 1978).

Douglas Weaver

AIDS. Like other fearsome epidemics throughout history, AIDS has been interpreted as a punishment or judgment from God for the wrongdoings of its victims and their society. When the condition was first identified in the United States in 1981 among the male homosexual population, it was called Gay-related immune deficiency (GRID), and antigay judgments righteously declared that "the wages of sin" were now being paid. When hemophiliacs and prisoners developed the same symptoms, authorities at the Centers for Disease Control sought a more accurate name and decided on acquired immune deficiency syndrome, and the acronym AIDS stuck. "The word 'acquired' separated the immune deficiency syndrome from congenital defects or chemically induced immune problems, indicating the syndrome was acquired from somewhere even though nobody knew from where" (Shilts, 171).

Controversy, both scientific and ethical, has followed this devastating epidemic from the beginning. Scientists have tested various theories of its origins and modus operandi. As the epidemic has gained momentum, knowledge about sexual and drug-use transmission of the virus has led to further controversy about the most effective means of prevention. The recommendations of health authorities that distribution of condoms and clean needles can slow the spread of the virus have been condemned and politically opposed as contributing to the moral delinquency behind the problem, an issue further complicated by efforts to institute AIDS-awareness and condom-distribution programs in secondary schools. Those opposing these preventive measures advocate self-discipline and celibacy outside of marriage as the only moral solution.

In the minds of certain moralists, where people acquire the human immuno-deficiency virus (HIV) has become the fulcrum separating its "innocent" victims—first hemophiliacs and then children born to HIV-infected mothers—from the guilty or deserving victims, those whose sins—perverse or promiscuous sex and drug use—earned them their just due. "The sexual transmission of the illness, considered as a calamity one brings on oneself, is judged more harshly than other means—especially since AIDS is understood as a disease not only of sexual excess, but of perversity" (Sontag, 26). Thus, for those to whom homosexuality* is anathema, and who are willing to overlook the international and heterosexual dimensions of the disease, including fundamentalist Protestants like Jerry Falwell* and Pat Robertson* as well as conservative Roman Catholics like Archbishop John Kroll and political aspirant Patrick Buchanan, "AIDS is God's judgment on a society that does not live by his rules" (Sontag, 61).

Such severe judgment is the exception rather than the rule, however. Roman Catholic Archbishop John R. Quinn proclaimed that the church "must not contribute to breaking the spirit of the sick and weakening their faith by harshness." The United Methodist Board of Discipleship has called on Christians to "accept people as they are, relate them to God's healing grace, and empower them to undertake ministries of compassion and hope."

Many people of faith nearly affected by the epidemic, in fact, have been inspired to love rather than judge, believing that "ironically, and in the long run, it will be AIDS that judges the churches," rather than the reverse (Quoted in Kayal, 25) These people have seen in AIDS a call to compassion, an opportunity for bearing witness, for "taking on the cross or the suffering of others as if it were one's own" (Kayal, xviii).

The United Fellowship of Metropolitan Community Churches cites the example of Christ explaining to the disciples in John 9:1–3 that the man's blindness was not the result of his own or his parents' sin. Rather, it was "so that God's works might be revealed in him." A similar explanation for the presence of illness and pain in the world informs Harold Kushner's *Why Bad Things Happen to Good People*. However catastrophic, AIDS is no more than a natural event, without moral meaning except that which it inspires in those who live and die with it.

Bibliography. *HIV/AIDS: Is It God's Judgment?* (Dallas: United Fellowship of Metropolitan Community Churches, 1994); Kayal, Philip M., *Bearing Witness* (Boulder, CO: Westview Press, 1993); Kushner, Harold, *When Bad Things Happen to Good People* (New York: Schocken Books, 1981); Shilts, Randy, *And the Band Played On* (New York: St. Martin's Press, 1987); Sontag, Susan, *AIDS and Its Metaphors* (New York: Farrar, Straus and Giroux, 1989).

Fred Richter

Alien Immersion. In the 1840s among some Baptists* who eventually were involved in Landmarkism* and in the fledgling Churches of Christ* movement, later to become a distinct denomination, there evolved the thinking that only a particular kind of Christian baptism was valid. Landmarkism began to teach that the only pure Christian churches were Baptist churches and that, therefore, only baptism administered by a Baptist church was valid. Baptists were, of course, immersionists, but these Landmarkers also believed that only baptism by immersion carried out by a local Baptist church was valid. Thus they considered all immersion by non-Baptist churches as invalid and named it "alien immersion." Landmarkism never founded a denomination, but there are still a vast number of Baptists, especially in the Southern Baptist Convention,* who believe that all other forms of baptism but their own are invalid and "alien" to the Christian tradition. This has often led to controversy among Baptists themselves and is an obviously antiecumenical viewpoint.

Also emerging in the nineteenth century from the teachings of Alexander Campbell* was a new denomination on the American scene, the Churches of Christ. Like the Landmark position, these Churches of Christ looked upon themselves as the only valid followers of the ancient and original Christian church and, therefore, as the only authentically Christian church. Unlike the Baptists, this tradition believed that baptism was necessary for salvation and that the adult believer's immersion was the proper way to do it. Though the phrase "alien immersion" was never popularly used by this tradition, it did believe that alien immersion was invalid and not Christian. Needless to say, both these traditions are separationist to the extreme and antiecumenical.

Bibliography. Dayton, A. C., *Pedobaptist and Campbellite Immersions* (Nashville: Southwestern Publishing House, 1858); Graves, J. R., *Old Landmarkism: What Is It?* (Memphis: Baptist Book House, 1880); Hudson, W. S., *Baptist Concepts of the Church* (Chicago: Judson Press, 1959); Shurden, Walter, *Not a Silent People* (Nashville: Broadman Press, 1972).

George H. Shriver

Allen, Richard. Late in the eighteenth century, African Americans struggled to take control of their own churches. One of the movements for independence was led by Richard Allen in Philadelphia. Allen, Absalom Jones, and other African Americans were members of St. George's Methodist Episcopal Church. When the church restricted where they could sit, they did not comply and were forcibly removed from the church, never to return.

In 1787 Allen and his friends established the Free African Society, which, according to the society's preamble, was to be ecumenical and was to respond not only to religious needs of the community but also to social and economic needs. The founders were interested in responding to the everyday concerns of the African Americans within the context of a simple but intense spirituality.

The Free African Society received immediate support from the African-American community and became the prototype for similar groups throughout the area. These groups functioned as protest organizations against white intolerance and included abolitionist activities. While the Society had secular interests, it did sponsor regular religious services, giving the appearance of being a church without actually being one. Allen stressed independence from the white community and from the limitations of specific creedal statements.

When the society became influenced by the Quaker style of religious expression instead of the original Methodism,* Allen and some of his supporters formed the independent Mother Bethel Church in the summer of 1794. This African Methodist Episcopal (AME) Church, strongly opposed to slavery, supported the Denmark Vesey* rebellion in Charleston in 1822 and was a vital link in the Underground Railroad movement during the antebellum years. Allen was elected bishop of the AME Church and served in that capacity until his death in 1831.

Bibliography. Allen, Richard, *The Life Experience and Gospel Labors of the Rt. Rev. Richard Allen* (1873. Reprint. New York: Abingdon Press, 1960); George, Carol V. R., *Segregated Sabbaths: Richard Allen and the Emergence of Independent Black Churches, 1760–1840* (New York: Oxford University Press, 1973); Wesley, Charles Harriss. *Richard Allen: Apostle of Freedom.* (Washington, DC: Associated Publishers, 1969); Wilmore, Gayraud, *Black Religion and Black Radicalism*, 2d rev. ed. (Maryknoll: Orbis Books, 1983).

Coleman Markham

Alliance of Baptists. An organization of moderate Southern Baptists organized as a result of controversies in the denomination. The Alliance of Baptists was founded as the Southern Baptist Alliance in 1986. The name was changed to the Alliance of Baptists in 1992. It was one of the first groups established by Southern Baptist moderates after a decade-long struggle for control of America's largest Protestant denomination, the Southern Baptist Convention* (SBC). In 1979 SBC fundamentalists began a successful effort to gain control of convention agencies by electing a series of conservative presidents who would appoint trustees to convention agencies who were sympathetic with fundamentalist agendas. Fundamentalists charged that denominational institutions were controlled by persons who were moving the convention away from conservative doctrines such as biblical inerrancy (the belief that the Bible is infallible in all matters it discusses, whether theological, historical, sociological, or biological) and other traditional dogmas. Moderates responded by charging that fundamentalists were simply attempting a political takeover of the denomination. Each group sought to get enough votes to elect specific candidates to the presidency of the denomination in order to dominate the appointive powers of the office. After a decade of fundamentalist success and the redirecting of convention agencies in more rightward directions (fundamentalists called it a "course correction"), some moderates were ready to invest their energies elsewhere, founding a new organization that would move away from confrontation and toward more creative endeavors. The founding documents declared, "The Southern Baptist Alliance is an alliance of individuals and churches dedicated to the preservation of historic Baptist principles, freedoms and traditions and the continuance of our ministry and mission within the Southern Baptist Convention." By 1991 the phrase "within the Southern Baptist Convention" was dropped as the organization sought to minimize its relationship to the convention and expand its network to other Baptist bodies. Thus the alliance was born of controversy but sought to move beyond it.

Alliance members faced another controversy in the proposal to found a new Baptist theological seminary. While some opposed the effort, insisting that attempts should be made to sustain existing schools and keep them from fundamentalist control, others thought that it was time to begin a new endeavor. As a result of this impetus, the meeting of the alliance in Greenville, South Carolina, in 1989 led to the formation of a committee to study the feasibility of a new school. In 1991 Baptist Theological Seminary, Richmond, Virginia, was founded, one of the first of a series of schools to be established by moderate Southern Baptists. Classes began in the fall semester of 1991. The alliance continued to provide funding for the seminary after it opened.

Another controversy developed over the relationship of alliance churches to the Southern Baptist Convention itself. While some churches wanted to break all ties to the parent body, others preferred to retain membership in the SBC but minimize participation. The alliance itself did not require that member churches break with the Southern Baptist Convention, leaving the final decision on such matters with the individual congregation. Under the leadership of Stan Hastey, the organization's first executive director, the alliance developed extensive dialogues and cooperative efforts with other Baptist denominations, especially American Baptist Churches in the USA and the Progressive National Baptist Convention.

Bibliography. Bill J. Leonard, ed., *Dictionary of Baptists in America* (Downers Grove: InterVarsity Press, 1995); Shurden, Walter B., ed., *The Struggle for the Soul of the SBC* (Macon: Mercer University Press, 1993).

Bill J. Leonard

Altizer, Thomas. Thomas Altizer was the leader of the "death of God"* theology of the 1960's. Born in Cambridge, Massachusetts, on September 28, 1927, Altizer received bachelor's, master's, and doctoral degrees from the University of Chicago. He began teaching at Emory University in 1956 in the Department of Religious Studies.

In 1961 Altizer and William Hamilton of Colgate Rochester Divinity School began writing independently on the question "Is it possible to conceive of a form of Christianity coming to expression without a belief in God?" (Altizer and Hamilton, *Radical Theology and the Death of God*, 9). While Paul Van Buren of Temple University and Gabriel Vahanian of Syracuse University were also associated with this movement, Altizer and Hamilton, working together, spearheaded it. They addressed the widespread perception that God was irrelevant to modern Western culture. In the social upheaval of the 1960s, the sacred was absent in daily life. Christian churches had lost their meaning.

In response to this crisis, Altizer and Hamilton proclaimed the death of God. They declared that to accommodate modernity, theologians must jettison outdated categories—like deity. Christianity must stress secularism over supernaturalism. Rather than despairing about the church's future, they believed that this new, transformative theology, which they called "a mood or a tendency" rather than a movement, would enable the church to thrive in a post-Christian culture. (Altizer and Hamilton, *Radical Theology and the Death of God*, 9).

By 1965 these ideas sparked national controversy. A famous *Time* magazine cover queried, "Is God dead?" World political and religious leaders were asked about the demise of deity. Shock value captured headlines, but Altizer and Hamilton continued their work despite the furor. In 1966 a national conference was held on radical theology, Altizer and Hamilton collected their essays in *Radical Theology and the Death of God*, and Altizer published *The Gospel of Christian Atheism*.

Altizer emerged as the primary exponent of the meaning of God's death for Christian theology. He argued that it was a historical event analogous to the incarnation and the resurrection. According to Altizer, "God dies in the Crucifixion: therein he fulfills the movement of the Incarnation by totally emptying himself of his primordial sacrality" (*Gospel of Christian Atheism*, 113). God's death was an eschatological and apocalyptic kenosis, an existential paradox: the sacred was embodied by radically affirming the profane. Influenced by Hegel, Nietzsche, Kierkegaard, Tillich, and Eastern mysticism, Altizer posited a radical disjuncture between the Christian tradition and the theology of "Christian atheism." He stated, "If there is one clear portal to the twentieth century, it is a passage through the death of God, the collapse of any meaning or reality lying beyond the newly discovered radical immanence of modern man, an immanence dissolving even the memory or the shadow of transcendence" (*Gospel of Christian Atheism*, 22).

Provocative and poetic, Altizer was reprimanded by the Methodist bishops of the Southeastern Jurisdiction in 1966. In 1968 he left Emory under pressure to teach English and religious studies at the State University of New York at Stony Brook. In his subsequent work, he continued to stress the death of God as a metaphor for exploding traditional theological categories and reinfusing them with meaning.

The death-of-God theology splashed momentarily on the national scene and was forgotten; it did not herald the transformation that Altizer had hoped. Yet to dismiss his work as a blip on theological radar underestimates his influence on later theologians. Theologians of the 1970s, 1980s, and 1990s are indebted to his insistence that the Christian church reckon with its relevance in a post-Christian age.

Bibliography. Altizer, Thomas J. J., *The Gospel of Christian Atheism* (Philadelphia: Westminster Press, 1966); Altizer, Thomas J. J., and William Hamilton, *Radical Theology and the Death of God* (Indianapolis: Bobbs-Merrill, 1966); Bent, Charles N., *The Death-of-God Movement* (New York: Paulist Press, 1967); Cobb, John B., Jr., ed., *The*

Theology of Altizer: Critique and Response (Philadelphia: Westminster Press, 1970); Ogletree, Thomas W., *The Death of God Controversy* (Nashville: Abingdon Press, 1966).

Evelyn A. Kirkley

American Baptist Association. The American Baptist Association (ABA) was formed in 1905 as a Landmark denomination representing churches in twelve states. Most notable of the several small Landmark groups that merged to form the ABA were the Baptist Missionary Association* (BMA), a split from the Baptist General Convention of Texas, and the General Association of Arkansas Baptists, a split from the Arkansas State Baptist Convention. The emergence of the ABA (originally named the Baptist General Association) was the direct result of Landmark controversies within Southern Baptist state conventions. When the state conventions refused to reform according to Landmark thought and practice, the Landmark leaders and their churches had little choice but to form new associations based on the tenets of their ecclesiology.

The ABA has its headquarters in Texarkana, Arkansas. It operates a seminary, colleges, Bible institutes, and a publishing house. It has missionaries in the United States and other countries. The ministries of the ABA are focused primarily in Texas and Arkansas. In 1950 the ABA itself split, with a splinter group forming the North American Baptist Association.

Baptist historians understand Landmarkism* as (1) a reaction to the Campbell movement and (2) an expression of the need for identity during the formative decades of the Southern Baptist Convention,* especially in frontier states where Baptists did not have a long history. According to Landmarkism, Baptist churches may trace their lineage back to Jerusalem, to the first century, and even to John the Baptist. Baptist churches assumed an identity that afforded both heritage and primacy. At the same time, the strong identity assumed by Landmarkism had its weaknesses. First, Landmarkism's notion of "ecclesiological successionism" had little basis in history, theology, or the Bible. Second, the spirit of Landmarkism was antithetical to the desire to create a cooperative denomination. Third, even though the splits in Texas and Arkansas involved significant numbers of churches and membership, most Baptists in these states rejected the myopic vision of Landmarkism.

Even though Landmarkism separated from these state conventions, Landmark thought and practice are still evident in Baptist churches of the mid-South and Southwest. Landmark ideas include a narrow interpretation of baptism* and Communion, Baptist successionist history, and a near-total disregard for ecumenical relationships.

Bibliography. *Dictionary of Christianity in America* (Downers Grove, IL: InterVarsity Press, 1990); McBeth, Leon, *The Baptist Heritage* (Nashville: Broadman Press, 1987).

Bill J. Leonard

Americanism. Americanism is a name given to certain doctrines condemned by Pope Leo XIII in his apostolic letter *Testem Benevolentiae*, January 22, 1899.

The doctrines censured were in five areas: the rejection of external spiritual direction as unnecessary, the exaltation of natural over supernatural virtues, the preference of the active over the passive virtues, rejection of religious vows as not compatible with Christian liberty, and the adoption of new methods of apologetics to attract non-Catholics to the faith. In this last error, the pontiff rejected the idea that the church should adapt its beliefs to modern societies in order to win converts to Catholicism. All of the condemned doctrines were contained within a French translation of a biography of Isaac Hecker* written by an American Paulist priest, Father Walter Elliott. Although the controversy was primarily within the French church, its roots were within American Catholicism.

The dispute arose from the divisions within the hierarchy and priests in the United States over Catholic participation in American life. Some bishops, notably Archbishop John Ireland of St. Paul and Bishop John J. Keane of Richmond, desired greater acceptance of American public life, particularly movements for social and economic reform. The other group, headed by Archbishops Michael Corrigan of New York and Frederick Katzer of Milwaukee, thought that American society was basically Protestant and tainted with the liberalism condemned in 1864 by the "Syllabus of Errors" of Pope Pius IX. Cardinal James Gibbons of Baltimore basically supported those who favored more Catholic participation, but he tried to mediate between both groups.

In France, Catholic liberals admired the work and writings of Cardinal Gibbons and Archbishop Ireland, and they backed Pope Leo XIII's call in 1892 for a *ralliement* between the French Republic and the church. Archbishop Ireland visited Paris in 1892, where he praised American democracy and the activities of Catholics. Ireland's speeches were then collected and translated by Father Felix Klein of the Institut Catholique and published in 1894. Father Klein then translated Elliott's 1891 biography of Hecker, and the French edition appeared in 1897. Father Klein wrote an enthusiastic preface for the book praising Father Hecker as the priest of the future and lauding the American church for its acceptance of democracy. This theme was taken up by Father Denis O'Connell, rector of the North American College in Rome, who in August 1897 praised the "Americanism" in the life of Father Hecker, stressing his acceptance of separation of church and state* and democracy.

Jesuits and others in France who opposed such *ralliement* with the French Republic began attacking Hecker and this "L'Americanisme mystique." Father Charles Maignen of the Brothers of St. Vincent de Paul published in 1898 *Études sur l'Americanisme: Le Père Hecker, est-il un Saint?* As the battle raged through the French Catholic press during 1898, there was the backdrop of the American victory in the Spanish-American War. In France, Spain, and Italy, the Catholic press overwhelmingly condemned what it considered to be an American imperialistic intervention. This furor soon caught the attention of the pontiff, who rejected requests to put the Hecker biography on the Index of Forbidden Books. Instead, he gave the work to a committee of cardinals to study. They recommended a censure of certain doctrines now termed Americanism. Pope

Leo XIII complied with this request, but softened the condemnation somewhat by stating that no person was accused of holding such doctrines. His letter stated explicitly that it was in no way an attack on the U.S. government or the "honor of the people of America."

Archbishop Ireland, Bishop Keane, and Father Klein all submitted to the declaration, while also denying that they held the doctrines. Archbishop Corrigan wrote to the Holy Father to thank him for saving the American Catholic Church from this "specious" and "false Americanism." Cardinal Gibbon responded to the pontiff by submitting to the declaration, claiming that such "Americanism" had nothing in common with "the views, the aspirations, the doctrines, and the conduct of Americans." French conservatives immediately claimed victory, and the issue within the American church would remain dormant for more than six decades. The writings of American Jesuit John Courtney Murray and the declarations of the Vatican Council II* would also address many of the same concerns of this "affaire Americanisme."

Bibliography. McAvoy, Thomas T., *The Great Crisis in American Catholic History, 1895–1900* (Chicago: Henry Regnery, 1957), reissued as *The Americanist Heresy in Roman Catholicism, 1895–1900* (Notre Dame, University of Notre Dame Press Paperbacks, 1963).

James M. Woods

Antiliquor. Also called "temperance," antiliquor was a major avenue in social reform among American Protestants that began in the late eighteenth and early nineteenth centuries. Temperance reform in America began in the late eighteenth century when New England Protestants began to decry the mounting social problems associated with the consumption of distilled liquors. During the period between 1790 and 1830, Americans drank more alcohol per capita than has been consumed before or since: In 1790 an estimated three gallons of absolute alcohol (the total alcohol content in a beverage) per capita were consumed—about half again as much pure alcohol as Americans consume today; by 1810 that figure had reached four gallons per capita.

The social consequences of such mass consumption began to attract the attention of religious, civic, and medical leaders, but the reaction took place in the context of the Second Great Awakening* in the early nineteenth century and the social reform that accompanied it. Temperance reform was second only to the abolition of slavery on the religious social reform agenda. At first, temperance advocates opposed only the consumption of distilled spirits, urging people to sign pledges promising to abstain from the imbibing of "ardent spirits." Soon, however, the temperance movement began to entreat people to sign a pledge promising to abstain from all alcoholic beverages. The pledge against ardent spirits became known as the "Old Pledge," or "O.P.," whereas the new pledge was known as the "T" pledge—"T for total" (hence the origin of the word "teetotaler").

The antiliquor movement became controversial in American churches when local churches and eventually entire Protestant denominations began to excommunicate individuals who drank alcohol in any form. Soon temperance advocates moved from this position to the excommunication of anyone involved in the traffic of liquor. By the early 1850s the temperance movement was gaining success in antiliquor legislation, the most notable of which was the "Maine Law" of 1851, which "provided for the effectual arrest, seizure, and destruction of all existing alcoholic liquors in the state. . . . Not only were violators to be fined or imprisoned, but liquors illegally held were to be taken and destroyed (Maine Law of 1851)." The most notable change the antiliquor movement made in church practice in the nineteenth century was the move from fermented wine to grape juice in the service of the Lord's Supper.

After the Civil War the temperance and prohibition movements gained still more momentum. As part and parcel of the social reform agenda, temperance advocates deemed the outlawing of alcoholic beverages as important a battle as the battle against slavery they had just won. Incidentally, the temperance movement did not engender as much support in the South as it did in the North. Exemplary of this are the southern Free Will Baptists,* who maintained an antitemperance stance until as late as 1913, despite the fact that their New England counterparts, the Freewill Baptists, were leaders in the northern temperance crusade.

As mid-nineteenth-century social reform evolved into the "Social Gospel"* of the late nineteenth and early twentieth centuries, prohibition of alcoholic beverages was an issue that had the support of both liberals and fundamentalists. In fact, some fundamentalists shied away from the temperance crusade because of its overt "Social Gospel" overtones.

The temperance movement reached its culmination on January 17, 1920, when the Eighteenth Amendment, prohibiting "the manufacture, sale, or transportation of intoxicating liquors," took effect. This victory was short-lived, however, and the amendment was repealed in 1933.

Antiliquor still exerts great influence in American Protestantism—in mainline Baptist and Methodist circles as well as in fundamentalist and evangelical circles. Curious differences of opinion prevail in contemporary fundamentalist circles, with some insisting that the wine Christ made in his first miracle at the wedding at Cana was unfermented. Other groups, like some Primitive Baptists,* insist that only fermented wine should be used in communion, while its social use should be discouraged. Antiliquor attitudes have had less influence on nineteenth-century immigrant Protestant groups like the Missouri Synod Lutherans,* and more on traditional American Protestants, both white and black.

Bibliography. Blocker, Jack S. Jr., *American Temperance Movements: Cycles of Reform* (Boston: Twayne Publishers, 1989); Marsden, George M., *Fundamentalism and American Culture* (New York: Oxford University Press, 1980); Pinson, James Matthew, "Religious Social Reform in the Antebellum North: Abolition and Temperance Reform among the Northern Freewill Baptists, 1800–1860" (M.A. thesis, University of West

Florida, 1993); Rorabaugh, W. J., *The Alcoholic Republic: An American Tradition* (New York: Oxford University Press, 1979).

J. Matthew Pinson

Anti-Masonry. Anti-Masonry is the belief that the Masons, with their rituals and ideology, are really a secret aristocracy trying to control the American Republic. Anti-Masonry dates back to the 1790s when certain New England ministers accused the Masonic Order of fomenting the French Revolution, with its terrorism, atheism, and anarchy. Such sentiment had quieted after the start of the nineteenth century, but it sprang to life suddenly in the late 1820s as a political force in certain states. The Anti-Masonic party was America's first third party.

The Anti-Masonic party started over the mysterious disappearance of William B. Morgan in western New York during the fall of 1826. Morgan arrived in Rochester, New York, in 1822 as a stonemason. There he joined the local Masonic lodge and then moved on to nearby Batavia in hopes of a new job. He soon discovered that he could find no work or join the local lodge of Freemasonry. Rebuffed and out for revenge, Morgan wrote a treatise "exposing this secret order." He then went looking for a publisher and found one in Batavia. When word leaked out of Morgan's plans, he soon discovered that he was in trouble with the law. Abducted and taken to Canandaigua, New York, he was charged with some minor crimes. Released from jail on September 12, he was just as quickly kidnapped, was taken to confinement in Fort Niagara, and from there disappeared. Outraged citizens in Batavia and Canandaigua started investigations concerning his disappearance, and the investigation spread to Rochester, where Thurlow Weed, then a local newspaper editor, headed the inquiry. Impatient with the local authorities, many pious and sincere citizens came to believe that the political and legal elites in western New York, who were almost all Masons, were involved in Morgan's disappearance and were covering this up. What started out as an investigation of one crime soon turned into a campaign against Freemasonry itself, its secret rituals, oaths, obligations, and its control over society and politics in western New York.

The indignation over the circumstances of Morgan's disappearance spawned a new political movement that blazed quickly for a time. After ousting several Masons from political power in Rochester and other areas of western New York, its followers started a newspaper in Rochester in February 1828 called the *Anti-Masonic Enquirer*; a month later the Anti-Masonic party of New York was formed. The organization soon spread into New England, Ohio, Pennsylvania, and Michigan. Anti-Masonry held real power in just three states, Rhode Island, Vermont, and Pennsylvania. Within the latter two states its followers elected governors in 1831 and 1835; in New York and Massachusetts they won some local races and held the balance of power between the Whigs and Democrats. Future political leaders like Thurlow Weed, William Seward, and Thaddeus Stevens all started their long political careers within the Anti-Masonic movement. William Lloyd Garrison, before he became an abolitionist, edited the Anti-

Masonic paper in Massachusetts. Since President Andrew Jackson and his 1832 opponent, Henry Clay, were both prominent Masons, the party was forced to run its own candidate. Anti-Masonic delegates from eleven states met in Philadelphia in September 1831 to nominate William Wirt of Maryland, a distinguished jurist, evangelical Christian, and former U.S. attorney general, for the presidency. Amos Ellmaker of Pennsylvania was his running mate. Wirt carried about 3 percent of the national vote and won only Vermont's seven electoral votes. Anti-Masonry has left its mark on American political tradition with its invention of the national political party convention, a vehicle the major parties quickly copied. By 1834 the Anti-Masonic movement was running out of steam and was slowly assimilated into the Whig party over the next decade, giving that organization a strong evangelical Christian base in the Northeast.

Anti-Masonry has been long regarded as a movement of the religiously zealous and socially discontent, yet there were also some wealthy attorneys and up-and-coming politicians who made the movement important in several states. Like other American third-party movements, anti-Masonry had a short life span and was absorbed into one of the two major parties.

Bibliography. Cross, Whitney, *The Burned-over District: The Social and Intellectual History of Enthusiastic Religion in Western New York, 1800–1850,* (Ithaca: Cornell University Press, 1950); Formisano, Ronald P., and Kathleen S. Kutolowski, ''Antimasonry and Masonry: The Genesis of Protest, 1826–1827,'' *American Quarterly* 29 (Summer 1977): 139–65; Goodman, Paul, *Towards a Christian Republic: Antimasonry and the Great Transition in New England, 1826–1836* (New York: Oxford University Press, 1988); Kutolowski, Kathleen S., ''Antimasonry Reexamined: Social Bases of the Grass Roots Party,'' *Journal of American History* 71 (September 1984): 269–93; Vaughn, William P., *The Antimasonic Party in the United States, 1826–1843* (Lexington: University Press of Kentucky 1983).

James M. Woods

Antimissions. Most forms of Christianity have favored some type of evangelical outreach, usually justifying the impulse by reference to Matthew 28:19–20. Over the years only a small minority of voices have opposed such activities, and in American religious experience this proportion has held true as well. Among the factors accounting for those who express little concern for missions, one must recognize that mere lethargy is a constant reality. Some people simply do not care about those beyond their limited circle of acquaintances. For those who do care, many wish to support missions only in local areas. This is not antimission sentiment as much as it is a statement of priorities, a preference to expend efforts on the nearby and familiar rather than on the foreign and unknown. Another basic attitude militating against specialized evangelical work touches on financial priorities. Some refuse to support mission agencies because they are suspicious of bureaucratic mismanagement and want to control monetary allocations instead of trusting others to do it for them.

On slightly more principled grounds antimission attitudes have derived from a philosophical determinism that is usually associated with Calvinist thought.

Some individuals reason that if God is truly a sovereign who has already decided the ultimate fate of every living soul, then the Almighty's wishes will eventually be served regardless of human effort. Missions to the unconverted are unnecessary for those already slated to experience salvation, and they are a waste of time regarding those predestined to hell. The ultimate fate of human souls will eventuate according to divine intentions, not evangelical activities, and so it is futile and possibly blasphemous to pursue missionary programs. Such thinking subsided as Calvinism itself passed its heyday, certainly in the mid-nineteenth century and thereafter. In the current century antimission principles have derived from another rationale, namely, concern for the integrity of host cultures. After reviewing the impact of missionary activities that were often forced on numerous civilizations, some observers have concluded that the lasting effect brought too much destruction to a variety of languages, material cultures, ethics, rituals, and art. They oppose missions because they decry the imperialism and aggressive cultural arrogance that they say lies at the heart of any attempt to change human cultures from one orientation to another.

These motifs are perennial and will remain so. In the first decades of the nineteenth century, however, an antimission movement took on a more tangible form. Men of some prominence such as John Leland, Elias Smith, Ransom Gates, and Alexander Campbell* spoke out strongly against national missionary agencies. They and other individuals associated particularly with Baptists,* Methodists, Quakers, Unitarians, and Disciples of Christ perceived a threat in large evangelical associations. To them an American Board of Commissioners for Foreign or Home Missions was a menace that could curtail private judgment and suppress personal initiative. Bible and tract societies, and especially the 1828 General Union for Observance of the Sabbath, smacked of reestablishing a union of church and state along the lines of a Congregationalist-Presbyterian frame of reference. Therefore in the name of denominational liberty and individual freedom of thought, this antimissionary coalition protested evangelical efforts to control national policy. They also fed on frontier wariness of salaried ministers and bureaucratic centers located on the Atlantic seaboard. But such sentiments notwithstanding, missionary outreach flourished, particularly when it was conceived and pursued within separate denominational frameworks.

Bibliography. Beaver, R. Pierce, ed., *American Missions in Bicentennial Perspective* (South Pasadena, CA: Carey Press, 1977); Goodsell, Fred F., *You Shall Be My Witnesses* (Boston: ABCFM, 1959).

Henry Warner Bowden

Anti-Mormonism. There has been opposition to Mormons since before the Church of Jesus Christ of Latter-Day Saints (hereafter LDS) was organized in 1830. For almost a century Mormons exhibited a striking capacity to arouse enmity among their gentile (non-Mormon) neighbors, and they interpreted such hostility as satanic attempts to frustrate God's plan for restoring a righteous order on earth.

Most early controversies centered on Joseph Smith, Jr.,* whom adherents accepted as a prophet and revelatory, but whom critics considered a charlatan and a fraud. To begin with, his claim that the Book of Mormon had been translated from golden plates shown him by an angel strained the credulity of most observers. Angry charges of financial misdeeds caused him and his followers to leave Ohio in 1837. A year later disputes over land possession and views on slavery led to vigilante action and pitched battles in Missouri. In Illinois (1839) Smith made the town of Nauvoo the centerpiece of his efforts to reinstate God's law in human society. He also stirred up storms of controversy by appearing to set himself up as ruler of an independent government where he dominated the courts, denied freedom of the press, and controlled his own armed militia. Personal jealousies, political fears, and religious antagonisms all came to a head on June 27, 1844, when a gentile mob connived with local magistrates and murdered the prophet while he was temporarily incarcerated at Carthage, Illinois.

Smith's death did not bring an end to the LDS organization or to many disputes surrounding it. For purposes of convenient summary, these controversies may be seen as touching upon questions of authority, status, ritual practices, and social integration.

Mormons view other forms of Christianity as failed remnants of truth gone awry. They find these earlier institutions inadequate for nurturing salvation, but God has restored authority, they believe, through Joseph Smith and successive presidents of the LDS church. Prophecy, angelic visitations, and new revelations provide insights for better understanding of the Bible and for additional divine wisdom over the course of time. Enemies of this perspective claim that the traditional Bible has been sufficient as God's word for centuries; any reference to further revelation is deluded at best, blasphemous at worst.

Following the view that a more complete awareness of God's will is possible again under LDS auspices, Mormons consider their church to be the only one with valid sacraments and leadership. A new dispensation now makes it possible to reinstate God's earlier work in ancient priesthoods and the primitive church. The true church exists again, making salvation a vivid reality in contemporary experience, but churches other than LDS lack the proper capacity to help those who seek God's full message. Opponents decry this exclusivist claim as unwarranted arrogance and presumption. As critics refuse to accept the idea of continuing, postbiblical revelation, so they also reject the idea that any institution stemming from nineteenth-century personnel can be superior to those of longer heritage. Foes of LDS denounce the church's notion of exclusive status for the same reason as they deny its alleged supernatural authority.

Of many distinctive practices found among LDS believers, outsiders have been particularly vociferous against two. Late in his career Smith introduced the concept of polygamy or plural marriages that were sealed for eternity. Many followers resisted this practice, but it survived the prophet's death and remained a bone of contention for more than half a century. Another controversial practice was baptism performed in the name of someone deceased. Critics held that such a vicarious acceptance of the gospel was impossible and flew in the face of individual responsibility for one's soul. To add further ill feeling, these ordinances and many others took place within an LDS temple that barred all gentiles. Adherents monopolized an authoritative status and liturgical prerogatives, leading those excluded to speculate resentfully about secret rituals.

The way Mormon leaders supervised believers' lives also caused many to oppose the spread of this religion. Believers reasoned that if God's will were administered through chosen servants, then the best form of government would be a theocracy, with no separation of church and state. Critics pointed out that this amalgam of religious and civil power was contrary to American constitutional liberty and that LDS influence was a direct threat to democratic freedoms. In 1846 Mormons began moving to Utah in order to escape persecution and follow their own way of life. In 1850 the United States made Utah a territory, and federal officials harassed Mormons for decades as misfits in a republican system. Authoritarian social control and continuing polygamy were what gentiles found most objectionable in the burgeoning western population. But in 1890 Mormons complied with national law by discontinuing plural marriage, and in 1896 Utah became a state in the federal union. Since then controversies have subsided considerably. Claims about uniqueness are muted, and rebuttals are more polite. Issues of revelation and exclusiveness as well as doctrine and liturgy remain basic, but today's exchanges occur amid a spirit of mutual tolerance rather than the previous hostility.

Bibliography. Allen, James B., and Glen M. Leonard, *The Story of the Latter-Day Saints* (Salt Lake City: Deseret Books, 1976); Arrington, Leonard J., and Davis Bitton, *The Mormon Experience: A History of the Latter-Day Saints* (New York: Alfred A. Knopf, 1979); Hansen, Klaus J., *Mormonism and the American Experience* (Chicago: University of Chicago Press, 1981); Shipps, Jan, *Mormonism: The Story of a New Religious Tradition* (Urbana: University of Illinois Press, 1985).

Henry Warner Bowden

Antinomian Crisis. A pivotal event in the shaping of religion, gender, and government in early America, the Antinomian Crisis of 1636–1638 pitted preacher against preacher, man against woman, and town against town in a battle over theological doctrine, ecclesiastical authority, and social uniformity. The two primary figures were Anne Marbury Hutchinson* and her renowned pastor, John Cotton. Before arriving in New England in 1634, Anne Hutchinson had already absorbed from Cotton's ministry in Boston, Lincolnshire, her position on the Covenant of Grace, creating an antipathy within her toward those ministers who were preaching what she considered a Covenant of Works. Hutchinson saw Cotton as espousing a doctrine of "free grace" in which the believer's assurance of salvation came not from the outward performance of "good works" but the inward seal of the Spirit. Emphasizing an "inward experience" of grace was by no means un-Puritan for the seventeenth century. What made Hutchinson a radical (and Cotton problematic) to many Puritan divines and lay leaders was the degree to which she used this experience to satisfy the demands of sanctification. To Hutchinson, both election and sanctification were governed by "free grace." Anything else involved works, and that she could not accept. The Puritan divines in New England would not have argued about the inability of human works to ensure one's election, but they did insist on the presence of "good works" *after* salvation as evidence of one's election. Otherwise, how could one know a true "visible" saint from a hypocrite? Both Hutchinson and Cotton were convinced that by placing so much emphasis on works as a mark of sanctification the clergy were creating great confusion among the people, leading many to rely on a mere keeping of the law as their assurance of election. Hutchinson termed these ministers "legalists": they were denying the true role of the Spirit, both in salvation and sanctification. The ministers, on the other hand, called Hutchinson an "antinomian" for not allowing the law any role whatsoever in sanctification. (It should be noted that no member of either party ever acknowledged being an "antinomian" or a "legalist.") To experience anxiety by striving for outward signs of election as a means of gaining assurance was unscriptural to the antinomians, the work of the anti-Christ himself. Anxiety marked the absence of grace; the solution was to "rest" in Christ and his "free grace." To the New England ministers, however, anxiety generally signaled the presence of grace, for to make one's election "sure" required constant activity. The "rest" the antinomians proposed was but an easy way out for the lax saint or sinner to ignore the demands of the law, the ministers argued.

What separated Hutchinson even more from the New England ministers was her insistence that the Holy Spirit did not merely "come upon" believers but that it dwelt within each believer by means of private illumination and direct revelation. In essence, Hutchinson was claiming for herself the radical position of prophetess, a claim that even Cotton eventually could not accept. She began holding meetings twice weekly in her home, both to reinforce the doctrine of "free grace" coming from Cotton's Sunday sermon (he was now the teaching elder at the Boston church) and to demonstrate her own capacity as a teacher. Her biblical insights about grace found fertile ground in a populace burdened by an overly "precise" attention to biblical law and lack of assurance. As her meetings began to attract large crowds (as many as sixty to one hundred people) and her criticism of the clergy of New England as "legalists" grew sharper, the authorities, both civil and ecclesiastical, feared that the "Hutchinsonians," as they were later called, would soon take over the colony. With the election of her friend Henry Vane as governor and her brother-in-law John Wheelwright as assistant pastor to Cotton in the Boston church, the antinomians occupied positions of power in the community as well as the church. But the Puritan leaders of New England were not about to allow their "city upon a hill" to become a center for antinomian activity. They used a fast-day sermon delivered by Wheelwright in January 1637 as a sufficient reason for bringing charges of "sedition" and "contempt" against him. Though the charges were bitterly contested by the Hutchinsonians, Wheelwright was found guilty and banished from the colony. This led to a bitter election in May in which Vane was ousted as governor and replaced by former governor John Winthrop, who seemed commissioned now to stamp out all antinomianism in New England.

The first step in that process was the convening of a synod (New England's first) on August 30, 1637, ostensibly to deal with the colony's spiritual condition as a consequence of the Pequot War. Since the colony had enjoyed peace and prosperity before Anne Hutchinson arrived, and since it had experienced much turmoil since (even God's judgment by way of the Pequot War, which the Hutchinsonians did not support), Winthrop and others saw no reason to search any further than the nearly ninety "errors" held by the antinomians. On September 7, 1637, they resolved that a woman acting "in a prophetical way" and criticizing the ministers before a large assembly in her home each week was "disorderly, and without rule" (Winthrop, *History,* 234). Hutchinson did not heed this warning from the synod, and consequently charges against her and her followers were brought before the General Court in early November of that year, a court dominated now by the Winthrop party. Many of her followers (fifty-eight men from Boston alone, seventeen from surrounding towns) were stripped of their colonial authority, disarmed, fined, and even banished (mostly for signing a petition supporting John Wheelwright). Both hatred and fear drove the proceedings. Hutchinson was charged with having "troubled the peace of the commonwealth and the churches" by speaking in a manner "prejudicial to the honour of the churches and ministers thereof." The court had no choice but to "reduce" her in order that she might become "a profitable member" of the community (Hutchinson, 366). If she would not repent, she would be banished. Hutchinson defended herself well, entering into detailed discussions of the Covenant of Grace and Works, as well as a woman's role in the church and community. She might have escaped banishment had she not admitted on the second day of the hearing that her spiritual insight came directly from God "by an immediate revelation" (Hutchinson, 384). Outraged by what they saw as rank "pride, insolency, [and] contempt of authority" (Winthrop, *Short Story,* 211), Winthrop and his supporters (only two members of the court supported Hutchinson) voted that she be "banished . . . as being a woman not fit for our society" (Hutchinson, 391).

The court postponed her banishment until the next spring. Since the November General Court was only a civil proceeding, some felt that ecclesiastical action should be taken as well against Hutchinson. As a result, a church court was convened on March 15, 1638, for the purpose of trying Hutchinson not only for antinomianism, but also for mortalism and familism, combining beliefs against the resurrection of the body and rejection of law with the promotion of free love, leading her former friend, now turned critic, John Cotton to predict that "more dangerous evils and filthy uncleanness and other sins will follow than you do not imagine or conceive" (Dexter, 178). Hutchinson defended herself against these allegations, but to no avail. Her final condemnation concerned her gender more than her theology. As Hugh Peter warned her, "you have stepped out of your place, you have rather been a husband than a wife, a preacher than a hearer, a magistrate than a subject" (Dexter, 186). Excommunicated on March 22, within six days Anne Hutchinson and her family were on their way to resettlement in Rhode Island, and "order" was restored once again in Massachusetts.

Was Anne Hutchinson an "American Jesabel" (Winthrop, *Short Story*, 310), or were the New England elders and rulers extremely misogynistic? Was she a rebellious woman who refused to submit to proper (male) authority, or were the male rulers overreacting to her assertiveness with fear, anger, jealousy, and wounded pride? Were she and her followers disrupting the "peace" of the community, or were the leaders of church and state violating her "freedom of conscience"? Was she a "free spirit" seeking some means (as a woman) to validate what she considered to be her personal experience with God and her spiritual gifts in the church, or were the elders "sound believers" bent on applying what they perceived to be the laws of God and correct theology to all concerns of life—social, ecclesiastical, and personal? Did the Antinomian Crisis prove the triumph of English Congregationalism, or did it reveal an inherent weakness in the New England Way? At various points historians have answered all these questions in the affirmative, but the truth is much more difficult to ascertain, for in the profound ambiguities of the Antinomian Crisis, in its dangers and attractiveness, rests its very Americanness. To Anne Hutchinson and the antinomians, much like Thomas Morton and the maypolers at Merry-Mount, a vision of seventeenth-century New England as a refuge for freedom of conscience and individual expression was simply not to be, yet in their confrontation with the authorities they established a quintessentially American situation: a lone individual challenging the dictates of society, finding his or her essence in expression, not submission. The evolution of American society has turned many such "rebels" into heroes; the same fate, no doubt, holds true for Anne Hutchinson and the antinomians.

Bibliography. Battis, Emory, *Saints and Sectaries: Anne Hutchinson and the Antinomian Controversy in the Massachusetts Bay Colony* (Chapel Hill: University of North Carolina Press, 1962); Dexter, Franklin B., ed., "A Report of the Trial of Mrs. Anne Hutchinson before the Church in Boston, 1638," *Massachusetts Historical Society Proceedings,* 2nd ser. 4 (1889): 159–91; Hall, David D., *The Antinomian Controversy, 1636–1638: A Documentary History,* 2nd ed. (Durham, NC: Duke University Press, 1990); Hutchinson, Thomas, *The History of the Colony and Province of Massachusetts-Bay,* Vol. 2 (1767. Reprint. Cambridge: Harvard University Press, 1936); Stoever, William K. B., *"A Faire and Easie Way to Heaven": Covenant Theology and Antinomianism in Early Massachusetts* (Middletown, CT: Wesleyan University Press, 1978); Winthrop, John, *Winthrops' Journal: "History of New England,"* 1630–49. vol. 1, ed. James Kendall Hosmer (New York: Barnes and Noble, 1959); Winthrop, John, *A Short Story of the Rise, Reign,* *and Ruine of the Antinomians, Familists, and Libertines* (London, 1644), in Hall, *The Antinomian Controversy*, 199–310.

Timothy D. Whelan

Anti-Semitism. The term *anti-Semitism* was coined in 1879 by Wilhelm Marr, generally recognized as a racist and an anti-Jewish German agitator. Marr used the term in referring to the anti-Jewish campaigns in Europe in his own time. But anti-Semitism, in Marr's sense of the word, has existed from ancient times. The controversies surrounding the term are many.

There is little agreement regarding a working definition of the term. The term itself is more than a little problematic, since Semitic has become a technical term for a linguistic family, including not only Hebrew but Arabic, Aramaic, and Amharic, plus other related languages. Thus the word is certainly not neatly racial, since many races use Semitic languages, especially Hebrew and Arabic. But thanks to Hitler and the Holocaust, anti-Semitism has become a general term used to denote anti-Jewish attitudes and behaviors of all kinds. While there is a movement to replace the term with the more accurate ''anti-Jewish'' or ''anti-Judaism,'' anti-Semitism will probably continue to be the most commonly used designation. Other areas of controversy surround the questions of its origins, its nature and causes, and its relationship to Christianity.

Whether in its political, theological, social, psychological, economic, or ''racial'' form, anti-Semitism has existed at least since pre-Christianity classical times. Greek and Roman writers provide abundant examples of anti-Jewish sentiments. With the emergence of a Christianized Roman Empire in the fourth century, the foundations for the anti-Semitism of the Third Reich were forged. But drawing a neat cause-and-effect relationship between historic Christian anti-Semitism and the Holocaust ignores the complexity of the nature and causes of modern anti-Semitism.

There is controversy among scholars regarding the degree to which the anti-Christianity attitudes and actions of the Judaism—or, more accurately, the Judaisms—of the first century of Christianity's existence may have contributed to Christian anti-Semitism, especially once Christianity gained imperial power and was in a position to retaliate. But recent Jewish and Christian scholarship seems to be in agreement that Judaisms' (in the sense of the multiple parties claiming Hebraic roots) treatment of Christians and Christianity in antiquity must be taken into account, while it certainly does not justify the retaliation.

The controversies surrounding ''justification'' for later Christian anti-Semitism—the exclusiveness of Jewish communities, the role of Jews in financial affairs, the political influence of some Jews—appear to be subsiding as historians and theologians recognize that most of these ''characteristics'' of medieval and early modern Jews in the predominantly Christian societies were the result of laws (civil and ecclesiastical) that the majority culture imposed on the Jewish communities rather than of the free choices made by the Jews themselves. Careful reading of the history of the church's statements and actions results in the resolving of some controversies regarding the culpability of Christianity, while generating some new controversies, especially in the context of the Holocaust of the Third Reich. The story of the church's official positions and efforts vis-à-vis the unofficial and often popular attitudes and actions is a perplexing account still being unraveled by Christian and Jewish scholars, but it is becoming more and more clear that the answers to the questions concerning the nature and the causes of anti-Semitism, whether in its Christian or more general expressions, will not be found in the many simple explanations often given. Thus there does not appear to be much room for controversy when scholars in general declare that anti-Semitism is rooted in a multiplicity of causes, and that recognizing this complexity and taking steps to address these multiple causes would be an important step toward understanding and dealing with the phenomena of genocide that continue to capture headlines as the twentieth century comes to a close.

Bibliography. Monographs abound and are usually written to prove a point. Even the more balanced account presented in *The New Catholic Encyclopedia* (N.Y.: McGraw-Hill, 1967) falls victim to some begging of the question. Not surprisingly, so does the very complete and important account in *Encyclopadia Judaica* (Jerusalem, NY: Macmillan Co., 1971–1972). Nonetheless, it is recommended that readers start with these two accounts before turning to some of the classics in the field such as Jules Isaac, *The Teaching of Contempt* (New York: Holt, Rinehart and Winston, 1964), and Gavin I. Langmuir, *History, Religion, and Antisemitism* (Berkeley: University of California Press, 1990).

Robert L. VanDale

Arminianism. Arminianism is the designation given to a theological position held by a wide variety of Christian denominations, groups within denominations, and individuals. Their commonality is often found in what they reject ("strict Calvinism") as well as what they mutually affirm ("universal atonement" and "free grace").

The controversies surrounding Arminianism serve as a paradigm for understanding many theological disputes in general. While Arminianism traces its origins to Jacobus Arminius (1560–1609), as Calvinism traces its origins to John Calvin (1509–1564), the Arminian-Calvinist disputes are found, at points, to misrepresent their namesakes. Centuries of controversy between Calvinists and Arminians, with their appeals to their respective "founders," tend to give the impression that Calvin and Arminius were themselves holders of the positions presented by their later followers. Recent studies suggest that Calvinists outstrip Calvin and Arminians outstrip Arminius in their passion for defending their positions and in characterizing their opponents. In short, Calvin was probably not a "Calvinist," nor was Arminius an "Arminian," in the context of these disputes among their followers. It is good to keep in mind that Arminius himself carried on his debates within the context of the Calvinist-Reformed tradition—in fact, as a one-time defender of "Calvinism." Therefore, it is helpful to view the emergence of these disputes in the context of the political-cum-theological concerns in Holland at the time Arminianism emerged. A careful study of the issues of that time—theological, political, ecclesiastical, and personal—is instructive for understanding the continuation of the debates between Calvinists and Arminians into our own day. The basics include the following.

As Holland strove to establish and consolidate its identity and unity in the sixteenth century, many influential scholars and politicians saw that identity and unity best served by a rather strict version of Calvinism with its Five Points (TULIP—total depravity, unconditional election, limited atonement, irresistible grace, and perseverance/preservation of the saints). The Arminian position most pointedly locked horns with this version of Calvinism in the Arminian Remonstrance of 1610, which stated: "That . . . Jesus Christ, the Saviour of the world, died for all men and for every man, so that he has obtained for them all, by his death on the cross, redemption and the forgiveness of sins; yet that no one actually enjoys the forgiveness of sins, except the believer, according to the word of the Gospel of John 3:16—'God so loved the world that he gave his only begotten Son, that whosoever believeth in him should not perish, but have everlasting life': and in the First Epistle of John 2:2—'And he is the propitiation for our sins; and not for ours only, but also for the sins of the whole world' " (Article II). This highlights the Arminian-Calvinist flash points of universal vis-à-vis limited atonement intended by God and accomplished by Jesus, and the role of human decision in experiencing the grace of God (along with the durability of saving grace in the life of the Christian). As the literature from both camps in this ongoing theological warfare demonstrates, the overarching controversy incorporates many subcontroversies: interpretations of key biblical passages and attitudes regarding the ecclesiastical—as well as the eternal—status of those "on the other side," with Arminians tending to be inclusive, Calvinists tending to be exclusive.

The major Arminian denominational family is Methodism,* with many Arminian adherents in Baptist, Lutheran, and Anglican churches as well as a vast array of other, smaller denominations. Even the main Calvinist denominational family—Presbyterians—contains numerous crypto-Arminians as well as many overt advocates of a modified Calvinism that could qualify as Arminian.

Bibliography. Readers are encouraged to start with the articles on Arminianism and Arminius in a good encyclopedia, for example, *The New Catholic Encyclopedia* (New York: McGraw-Hill, 1967) before reading works of adherents such as Gerald McCulloh, ed., *Man's Faith and Freedom: The Theological Influence of Jacobus Arminius* (New York: Abingdon Press, 1962) as well as critics such as Rienk Kuiper, *For Whom Did Christ Die? A Study of the Divine Design of the Atonement* (Grand Rapids, MI: Eerdmans, 1959). Also recommended is Alan P. Sell, *The Great Debate: Calvinism, Arminianism, and Salvation* (Grand Rapids, MI: Baker Book House, 1982).

Robert L. VanDale

Artificial Insemination. The history of experimentation with artificial insemination (AI) is relatively brief. The earliest recorded discussion of AI probably occurs in a second-century C.E. Talmudic text that hypothesizes the moral status of a woman who alleged that she had been accidentally impregnated in bathwater previously used by a man. Thereafter, Arab horse breeders are said to have impregnated brood mares by AI as early as the fourteenth century; Ludwig Jacobi successfully fertilized fish in 1742; and Lazario Spallanzani achieved fecundation in a spaniel bitch (which bore three puppies) in 1780. The first successful AI in humans, with the wife of a London draper, is credited to John Hunter in the late eighteenth century; and in 1909 a donor AI, performed twenty-five years earlier, was reported by an American doctor.

Presently AI is a procedure that consists of depositing semen, with the aid of instruments, into the vagina, cervical canal, or uterus with the intention of causing pregnancy that, by ordinary sexual union, is deemed unlikely or impossible (e.g., in cases of oligospermia). It is basically of two sorts: homologous, or AIH (by husband); and heterologous, or AID (by donor). Typically more for emotional than biological reasons, a third type, designated AIHD or CAI (combined AI), is sometimes undertaken. Roughly half a dozen religious bodies in the United States have adopted official statements regarding this technology, some prohibiting AI in all its forms, some affirming AIH, and none approving AID or AIHD.

If deemed necessary to achieve conception within marriage, AIH is generally permitted by Judaism. Although AID is not regarded as constituting ''an adulterous relationship or a child so conceived as suffering the serious disability of bastardy,'' Jewish authorities strongly object to donor insemination. Both AI and in vitro fertilization and embryo transfer are addressed by the Roman Catholic Congregation for the Doctrine of the Faith, which echoes the teachings of Pope Pius XII and takes the position that ''heterologous insemination is contrary to the unity of marriage, to the dignity of the spouses, to the vocation proper to parents, and to the child's right to be conceived and brought into the world in marriage and from marriage.'' Homologous AI is similarly condemned: ''From the moral point of view a truly responsible procreation vis-à-vis the unborn child must be the fruit of marriage. . . . the act of conjugal love is considered in the teaching of the Church as the only setting worthy of human procreation.'' A like position is taken by Greek Orthodoxy: ''The sacramental unity of marriage . . . excludes all intrusions such as if a third party joins one of the spouses in sexual relations, but also when the seal of marriage is broken by an outside party contributing genetic material (whether semen or ovum) towards the creation of a child who ought to belong to not one but both marriage partners.''

Protestant Christian bodies have generally not addressed AI, but those that have adopted positions tend to affirm AIH outright or with qualifications. The Presbyterian Church USA ''affirms the use of artificial insemination by husband as a responsible means of overcoming certain fertility problems'' and ''affirms *in vitro* fertilization as a responsible alternative for couples for whom there is no other way to bear children.'' The Evangelical Lutheran Church in America statement focuses on AID because ''AIH presents few legal, social, or ethical problems''; conversely, AID ''has to do with the very nature of marriage and parenthood,'' so much so that ''AID is not an ethically acceptable alternative to childlessness in the case of male fertility.'' The Lutheran Church–Missouri Synod insists that ''the joining of mutual love with procreation is an essential element in the mystery of our created humanity'' and cautiously approves AIH while condemning AID.

The minority religious view holds that humans should and can be ''co-laborers with God'' in the generation and development of their families. The greater weight of evidence in ecclesial pronouncements, however, insists that baby making cannot be sundered from lovemaking; and that the procreative and unitive functions of marriage must be united; that AI, either in fact or tendency, separates procreation from love in the measure to which it occurs within a matrix in which neither donor nor recipient posits his or her act within the sphere of a love that unites them.

Bibliography. Judicatory position papers are typically available from the appropriate commission or headquarters. Feldman, David M., *Birth Control in Jewish Law* (New York: New York University Press, 1968); Jakobovits, Immanuel, *Jewish Medical Ethics,* new ed. (New York: Bloch Publishing Co., 1975); Kardimon, Samson, ''Artificial Insemination in the Talmud,'' *Hebrew Medical Journal* 2 (1942): 164; *The Pastoral Constitution on the Church in the Modern World,* in *The Documents of Vatican II,* Walter M. Abbott, ed. (New York: Guild Press, Association Press, and American Press, 1966); Rosner, Fred, *Modern Medicine and Jewish Law* (New York: Yeshiva University, 1972); Smith, Harmon L., *Ethics and the New Medicine* (Nashville: Abingdon Press, 1970).

Harmon L. Smith

Auburn Affirmation. In the 1890s the Northern Presbyterian Church became locked in controversy over the historical-critical interpretation of the Bible. During that crucial decade the church tried Charles A. Briggs* of Union Theological Seminary* and Henry Preserved Smith* of Lane Seminary* for heresy and convicted them. Other noted Presbyterians, including A. C. McGiffert* of Union Seminary, later left the denomination due to the pressure of the dispute.

The Presbyterians were not content with these trials. The denomination's General Assembly, the church's highest governing body, passed the Portland Deliverance,* a summary of doctrinal truths, in 1892 and reaffirmed its action in 1893, 1894, 1899, and 1910. The Portland Deliverance affirmed that the Bible was without error, as it had come from God. Under this act, the church required every minister to affirm that the Bible was the only infallible guide to faith and practice at his ordination. In 1910 Presbyterian conservatives, still deeply worried about the church's orthodoxy, led the General Assembly to pass the Five Points Deliverance. The Five Points required all ministers to agree with biblical inspiration and inerrancy, the Virgin Birth* of Christ, Christ's death as a sacrifice, the bodily Resurrection, and the historicity of Jesus' miracles. In other circles, these affirmations became known as the five fundamentals.* The General Assembly reaffirmed the Five Points in 1916 and in 1923.

World War I occupied most Presbyterians' attention from 1914 to 1919. Once this battle had cleared, however, the battle over the Bible resumed. The First Presbyterian Church of New York called a young Baptist minister, Harry Emerson Fosdick,* to serve as its pulpit minister. Deeply worried about the worsening controversy among Presbyterians, Fosdick preached his famous sermon "Shall the Fundamentalists Win?" in 1922. The sermon was an impassioned plea for a Presbyterianism that was open to new theological directions. In the sermon, Fosdick explicitly identified biblical inerrancy, the Virgin Birth, and the Second Coming of Christ as teachings that many modern Christians believed not essential to the gospel.

The resultant dispute led to a resolution calling on Fosdick to transfer his ministerial standing to the Presbyterian Church. Had Fosdick accepted the invitation, Presbyterian conservatives might have charged him with heresy in the church courts. Unwilling to subject himself to such discipline, Fosdick resigned his pulpit in 1924 and accepted the pulpit of the Fifth Avenue Baptist Church.

The controversy over Fosdick served as a wake-up call for the denomination's theological liberals. Liberal ministers adopted the Auburn Affirmation in 1924 at a meeting at upstate New York's Auburn Seminary. They chose the place carefully. New School Presbyterian ministers had adopted an earlier declaration of principles at Auburn (the Auburn Declaration*) in 1837. In time, more than a thousand ministers signed the statement. The main thrust of the affirmation was that the Five Points were not essential doctrines of the Word of God. Conservatives continued to insist that the church, not the individual, had the right to determine the content of Presbyterian doctrine. But the affirmation did lead to a 1926 affirmation of the diversity within the denomination and the end of the Five Points as a condition for ordination.

In retrospect, the Auburn Affirmation was the crucial turning point in the fundamentalist-modernist battle in the Northern Presbyterian Church. Although Presbyterians have continued to debate the issue of biblical authority, the battle for toleration within the denomination had ended. When the denomination revised its theological standards, the Confession of 1967 used language that transcended the earlier controversies while retaining the denomination's biblical basis. In order to make clear the diversity within the denomination, the Presbyterian Church also adopted a Book of Confessions that contained other traditional Reformed theological standards. When the Northern and Southern Presbyterian churches merged in 1983, the resultant denomination retained this broad understanding of the church's theological heritage.

Bibliography. Balmer, Randall, and John R. Fitzmier, *The Presbyterians* (Westport, CT: Greenwood Press, 1993); Loetscher, Lefferts, *The Broadening Church: A Study of Theological Issues in the Presbyterian Church since 1869* (Philadelphia: University of Pennsylvania Press, 1972); Longfield, Bradley, *The Presbyterian Controversy: Funda-*

mentalists, Modernists, and Moderates (New York: Oxford University Press, 1991); Nash, Arnold S., *Protestant Thought in the Twentieth Century: Whence and Whence* (New York: Macmillan, 1951).

Glenn Miller

Auburn Declaration. Almost from its founding, the American Presbyterian Church was unstable. The Adopting Act that created the original synod in 1729 marked an uneasy truce between two parties. One faction represented Puritans who had migrated south and settled in New Jersey and on Long Island. The other represented Scotch-Irish immigrants. While both parties were broadly Calvinistic, the Puritan faction placed less emphasis on the Westminster Confession of Faith than the more formal Scotch-Irish. The two parties divided into Old and New Side churches during the Great Awakening,* with many members of the Puritan party supporting the new revivalism and many of the Scotch-Irish distrusting it. Although the two churches reunited in 1758, the church had not resolved many of the questions that had divided it. These questions returned later.

After 1800 a Second Great Awakening* swept the new nation. The new revival included two related movements: a fervent evangelism and a decision to organize New World Christians for the work of missions. Both affected the Presbyterian Church. In 1801 the Presbyterian General Assembly and the Congregationalist Consociation of Connecticut agreed to the Plan of Union. Despite its somewhat grandiose title, the plan was actually an alliance between the two denominations to evangelize the West. Under the terms of the agreement, new western congregations could retain membership in both denominations. When these churches called a minister, they could select a pastor from either denomination. In turn, that minister would have standing in the councils of both churches. The plan had no provision for what would happen when these western churches matured, because its framers believed that the westward expansion of the United States would be a slow process.

The Plan of Union was part of a larger effort at organizing American Christians. As with fellow believers in Great Britain, the world seemed to offer an invitation to missions. In 1810 concerned Protestants, mainly Congregationalists, created the American Board of Commissioners for Foreign Missions. Many Presbyterians became strong supporters of this organization as well. The American Board was quickly followed by other Congregational and Presbyterian organizations: the American Sunday School Union, the American Home Missionary Society, the American Educational Society, and the American Bible Society. While each of these had its own elective officers, the same people often served several societies. Shared leadership made meetings at the same time and place convenient and practical.

The Baptists* and Methodists spearheaded the evangelistic advance. Although most Baptists were Calvinists and most Methodists Arminians, both churches stressed a simple gospel that urged people to respond emotionally to Christ, repent, and live a moral life. The revivals sparked by the Baptists and Methodism* varied in size. Most were small meetings of less than one hundred persons that often led to the formation of new congregations. In addition to Baptist and Methodist revivals, less emotional revivals also occurred among Presbyterians and Congregationalists. In New England Asahel Nettleton was noted for his revivals. In a Nettleton revival, the evangelist would preach for a number of Sundays and would gather a "harvest" of those who wanted to join the church.

Although Nettleton was rigorously orthodox, it was inevitable that some of the popular methods and doctrines of the Baptists and Methodists would spread to Congregational and Presbyterian ranks. In northern New York, Charles Grandison Finney* underwent a powerful religious conversion in 1821. The experience convinced him that he needed to preach the gospel. After a brief period of study, the former law clerk began an itinerant ministry among the Plan of Union churches in his region. Finney's revivals were different from anything known among Presbyterians or Congregationalists. The evangelists described his methods as the "new measures." The new measures were often adaptations of Methodist practices. The anxious bench was a pew at the front where those who were under conviction (considering conversion) might come for special prayer. During the services, Finney or a member of the congregation often prayed for individuals by name, often mentioning the sinner's most serious vice aloud. The evangelist often asked women to lead these prayers. Finney believed that music was particularly effective in leading people to faith. He traveled with his own music director, and the first thing that he did when he arrived in town was to organize a large choir from among the sponsoring congregations. Perhaps because few western New Yorkers had formal musical training, Finney's services featured "gospel music" with easily remembered words and tunes.

Theologically, Finney held doctrines similar to those held by the Methodists. Finney's formal theology was not, however, as important as his American frame of reference. Like many other Americans, Finney believed that what made human life meaningful was an individual's right to choose his or her own destiny. The American Republic invited people to make meaningful choices politically, and the nation's aggressive capitalism likewise encouraged them to control their economic life. In much the same way, Finney urged them to subject their religious and moral life to their own will. Finney's belief in the importance of human choice was one reason that he believed slavery to be wrong. By definition, a slave was a person whose will belonged to another.

Both the new organizations and the new theology troubled conservative Presbyterians. One of the central premises of Presbyterian polity was that Christian activities ought to be subject to the church and its duly established forms of ecclesiastical government. Whatever might be true of the missionary societies, conservative Presbyterians believed that they were not sufficiently ecclesiastical. In their place, they proposed that the church take these missions directly under its control and organize them in a way that would subject them to the General

Assembly. Practically speaking, what they wanted was to replace the ecumenical societies with mission boards.

The societies were not the only organizational concern. Much of Presbyterian church government took place in local presbyteries. These church courts, composed of both teaching and ruling elders, had the power to examine candidates for the ministry. In addition, any process against a particular minister for heresy had to begin in that cleric's home presbytery. Ordinarily, presbyteries served a particular location. In an effort to handle disagreements in the church, the General Assembly permitted the formation of some presbyteries on a voluntary or elective basis. In most cases, revivalists who supported the voluntary societies formed these "elective affinity" presbyteries in order to gain some freedom from the oversight of more conservative, geographically defined bodies. Conservatives believed (perhaps rightly) that the primary function of these presbyteries was to ordain or install persons who were unacceptable to the larger body.

Concern about elective-affinity presbyteries was closely linked to worries about the western Plan of Union presbyteries. Conservative Presbyterians noted that many ministers who were less than orthodox by Presbyterian standards entered the Presbyterian Church through New England Congregationalism. In many ways, Lyman Beecher* typified their concerns. Beecher was an energetic pastor who served congregations in Connecticut and Massachusetts before accepting a concurrent call as president of Lane Seminary in Cincinnati, Ohio, and pastor of the Second Presbyterian Church in that city. Beecher was deeply influenced by the theology of Nathaniel Taylor, professor of theology in the Divinity Department of Yale College. Although Taylor's system retained much of the language of traditional New England theology, his thought had moved far from the traditional doctrines of original sin and election. For instance, Taylor interpreted original sin primarily in terms of the inevitability of human sin and did not dwell on whether original sin implied the damnable guilt of every unconverted person. In a similar way, Taylor moved from the dreadful mysteries of predestination* to a less strenuous theism that worked with—not against—human will. God did not so much stop sinners in their tracks as God provided the needed religious encouragement for a person to turn to Christ. While Taylor's theology was similar in some respects to Wesley's, his work lacked the vibrant sense of the Holy Spirit that enlivened the English evangelical's theology. Although Beecher had originally opposed Charles Finney's revivalism, he came to recognize (probably correctly) that he and the controversial awakener had much in common. Not surprisingly, the conservative Presbytery of Cincinnati tried Beecher for heresy in 1835. Although the court did not convict him, the trial greatly increased tensions between revivalistic Presbyterians and their conservative opponents.

At almost the same time as Beecher's trial, conservative Presbyterians in Philadelphia struggled with the theology of Albert Barnes. In 1829 Barnes published a sermon, "The Way of Salvation," that highlighted the sinner's decision to accept Christ. The sermon was widely read, and it may have contributed to

Barnes's selection as pastor of the prestigious First Presbyterian Church of Philadelphia. The Presbytery of Philadelphia brought charges against Barnes in 1830 that the General Assembly finally adjudicated at the 1831 General Assembly. Although the General Assembly believed Barnes not guilty of heresy, it cautioned him to be more circumspect in the future. Barnes was not. In 1835 he published a commentary on Romans that stressed the human role in conversion. Conservatives again brought Barnes before the church courts, with his case dragging from presbytery to synod to assembly. Although the assembly again eventually found Barnes not guilty, conservatives were not satisfied with the outcome. If someone as far from the Westminster Standards as Barnes was still Presbyterian, they asked, what did the standards mean as a practical matter?

Until 1836 the prorevivalist faction seemed to be dominant. Although the conservatives had charged the many prominent supporters of the revival with heresy, various church courts had acquitted them. Presbyterian support for the ecumenical societies also seemed to have survived the various challenges brought by the conservatives. In 1836, for instance, the General Assembly approved the American Board of Commissioners. Further, the assembly that same year approved New York's Union Seminary, a school whose name bore eloquent witness to its founder's commitment to the Plan of Union. Union's charter also clearly stated the school's commitment to the reformist program of the prorevival party.

Yet the conservatives had a strong majority in the assembly of 1837. They used their dominance to excise (expel) the prorevival party. At the same time, they moved to establish their own missionary boards to replace the voluntary societies. The conservatives had conducted an ecclesiastical revolution that reversed the position of the two parties to the controversy. By expelling their opponents, they guaranteed their own future power by weakening the revivalists' potential support. Although the remaining prorevival delegates contested the 1838 assembly, the issue was not in doubt.

In August 1837 representative prorevival Presbyterians met at Auburn Seminary in upstate New York to affirm their orthodoxy. In a series of carefully drawn statements, they sought to show that their theology was in harmony with the Westminster Confession and Catechisms. While the document affirmed the basic tenets of revivalism, it was more cautious than earlier expressions of prorevival thought and more attentive to the careful distinctions found in classical Calvinism. Although its supporters hoped that the document might persuade the 1838 assembly, it did not have that effect. Instead, the Auburn Declaration helped to shape the New School Presbyterian Church that the prorevivalists created in the wake of their political defeat. In this regard, the declaration pointed toward an ecclesiastical body that would take its Presbyterian heritage with the same seriousness as its contemporary situation. Following this lead, the New School gradually developed its own missionary boards and agencies that were separate from the various "American" societies. Equally important, the New School changed theologically. To be sure, earlier New School stalwarts, including Albert Barnes, continued to teach and write in the older manner. Yet a new spirit was afoot. Such theologians as Henry Preserved Smith* of Union Theological Seminary* (New York) turned toward the new learning and romanticism that had become common in Europe. Using these elements and a deep and resolute devotion to scholarship, they shaped a theology that looked forward to the intellectual problems of the post–Civil War era. Old and New School Presbyterians united in 1868, with the New School becoming the liberal party and the Old School the conservative faction. The Auburn Declaration began as a statement of conscience and concern; as it was used, it became a statement of direction.

Bibliography. Balmer, Randall, and John R. Fitzmier, *The Presbyterians* (Westport, CT: Greenwood Press, 1993); Cross, Whitney, *The Burned-over District: The Social and Intellectual History of Enthusiastic Religion in Western New York, 1800–1850* (Ithaca: Cornell University Press, 1950); Hambrock-Stowe, Charles, *Charles G. Finney and the Spirit of American Evangelicalism* (Grand Rapids, MI: Eerdmans, 1996); Marsden, George, *The Evangelical Mind and the New School Presbyterian Experience: A Case Study of Thought and Theology in Nineteenth-Century America* (New Haven: Yale University Press, 1970).

Glenn Miller

Azusa Street. The modern Pentecostal* movement is dated to the Azusa Street revival, which took place in Los Angeles under the leadership of William Joseph Seymour from 1906 to 1909. Earlier Seymour, an African American, had been a part of the Apostolic Faith movement, under the leadership of Charles F. Parham,* a former Methodist minister. Regardless of race, all Pentecostals are indebted to Seymour and Azusa Street for bringing Pentecostalism, especially speaking in tongues, to national attention. African Americans call him the Apostle and Pioneer, believing that American Pentecostalism initially started at Azusa Street as a black movement, and that whites later joined.

At the crux of Seymour's teachings was speaking in tongues as an evidence of having received the Holy Spirit. He taught that sanctification was only the second work of grace, and faith healing was a part of atonement. But the third experience was the baptism of the Holy Ghost and fire, which was totally separate from the second experience. In other words, "sanctification cleansed and purified the believer, but the baptism of the Holy Spirit brought great power for service." Biblically, this doctrine was based upon Acts 2:1–4, in which on the day of Pentecost the 120 disciples spoke in tongues. Seymour taught that any other interpretation of the meaning of baptism was not in accordance with the New Testament, and that speaking in tongues was the only proof of having received the Holy Spirit.

Described as a short and stocky, poverty-stricken man with one eye, Seymour had earlier been a Baptist preacher. He had come to the Houston area from his native Louisiana and accepted the second blessing of sanctification, becoming a Holiness minister. Although this was a period of rank segregation, in 1905 he was allowed to enroll in the white Holiness Bible School, taught by Parham. For several months Parham taught him the new Pentecostal doctrine, and Seymour carried the new doctrine to Los Angeles and Azusa Street.

In early April 1906 Seymour came to Los Angeles as minister of a small black Holiness mission that was affiliated with the Church of the Nazarene. The mission's members had been dismissed from Second Colored Baptist Church for practicing Holiness doctrine. When Seymour preached the baptism of the Holy Spirit with tongues, disgruntled members padlocked the church. While conducting a nightly meeting on the front porch of a house on Bonnie Brae Street, Seymour himself received for the first time the gift of speaking in tongues.

The need for larger quarters caused Seymour to rent an abandoned Methodist Church building on Azusa Street. Although the building was in a state of physical disarray, large crowds came from near and far, and many received the Holy Spirit, speaking in tongues. Newspapers carried reports throughout the country and to foreign countries. There was no formal order of worship or robed choir. Everything happened spontaneously and "in the spirit." Whenever one felt compelled to preach or sing, it was done. There were nine services taking place in one day, around the clock. Seymour acted as moderator, teacher, and preacher, but usually he sat with his head bowed "inside the shoe-box pulpit." People came from all races and worshipped together—blacks, whites, Chinese, Jews, Armenians. However, some critics were appalled. They accused the services of being too emotional, with too much interracial mingling and too many sexual overtones, such as kissing between the sexes and races.

In October 1906 Parham arrived at Azusa Street and denounced the revival. He was shocked by the emotionalism and holy-rolling worship atmosphere. He had heard of whites "imitating unintelligent, crude negroisms . . . , and laying it on the Holy Ghost." He was told that all the stunts common in old camp meetings among colored folks "were being performed in the service." After preaching several times, Parham was told to leave by Seymour's supporters. The situation led to a breach between the two that was never resolved, and for the remainder of his life, Parham denounced the Azusa Street revival.

However, many of the hundreds and thousands who came to Azusa Street between 1906 and 1909 believed the event to be genuine. Whites and blacks came together in worship at the height of the period of racial segregation. Foreigners also participated and, having received the gift of the Holy Spirit and tongues, left to start new and segregated Pentecostal denominations throughout North America and Europe. But practices sanctioned by Seymour came to be frowned upon by whites, who referred to the emotionalism and holy dancing as "crude negroisms."

Bibliography. "The Azusa Street Mission and its Influential Newsletter: A Reprint of the first Issue of *The Apostolic Faith*," September 1906, in *North American Religion* ed. T. A. Robinson and M. Greenshields (Lewiston, NY: Center for the Study of North American Religion at the University of Lethbridge and Edwin Mellen Press, 1992);

Nickel, T. R., *Azusa Street Outpouring* (Hanford, CA: Great Commission International, 1979); Synan, V., *The Holiness-Pentecostal Movement in the United States* (Grand Rapids, MI: William B. Eerdmans Publishing Company, 1971).

Lawrence H. Williams

B

Bakker, James (Jim) Orsen. Prominent television evangelist and founder of PTL, Jim Bakker, a native of Michigan, was born in 1940 and raised in the Pentecostal milieu. Bakker attended an Assemblies of God college, North Central Bible College in Minneapolis, Minnesota, and there met and married Tammy Faye LaValley in 1961. Because of the marriage the school expelled the couple; Bakker obtained no further formal education.

The Bakkers served as itinerant ministers in North Carolina, emphasizing a children's puppet ministry. In 1964 Bakker was ordained by the Assemblies of God. The next year Pat Robertson of the Christian Broadcasting Network (CBN) named Bakker his cohost on the "700 Club" as well as featuring the Bakkers on "The Jim and Tammy Show," a children's radio and television show. The Bakkers' televangelistic success continued as he cofounded the Trinity Broadcasting Network in 1973 and began the PTL Club (Praise the Lord; later People That Love), a Christian talk show originating out of Charlotte, North Carolina.

The Bakkers and PTL experienced phenomenal success during the 1970s and 1980s. By 1987 Bakker had a $172-million religious empire, a popular cable television program, and a Christian theme park, Heritage USA. He preached a charismatic prosperity "feel good" gospel and lived an opulent lifestyle.

Bakker's empire self-destructed in 1987 as PTL was rocked by sexual and financial scandals. A 1980 affair with a church secretary, Jessica Hahn, and subsequent hush money were revealed, and Bakker's $1.6-million salary and bonuses from 1986–1987, despite a PTL debt of $70 million, were exposed. After an investigation of PTL finances, Bakker was convicted of fraud in 1989. He was released from prison in 1995; Tammy Faye had divorced him while he was in prison. Bakker's extravagant lifestyle, prosperity gospel, and lack of financial accountability demonstrated the controversial nature of televangelism in American religion.

Bibliography. Burgess, Stanley, and Gary B. McGee, eds. *Dictionary of Pentecostal and Charismatic Movements* (Grand Rapids, MI: Zondervan, 1988); "Heaven Can Wait," *Newsweek,* June 8, 1987, 58–65; "The Rise and Fall of Holy Joe," *Time,* August 3, 1987, 54–55.

Douglas Weaver

Baptism. Religious communities in America have long debated the meaning and importance of Christian baptism for the church and the individual. Controversies have erupted over the proper candidate, the mode of baptism, and the theological significance of this most Christian ritual. The earliest religious establishments in the New World were founded by traditions—Roman Catholic, Anglican, and Puritan—that practiced infant baptism. Protestants challenged the Catholic idea that baptism was necessary to wash away the curse of original sin. In seventeenth-century New England, Puritans retained the practice of baptizing infants but required a confession of personal faith for those who would receive full membership in the church. Baptism was administered to the children of professing church members as a sign of the covenant of grace extended to the "seed" of the elect. For many, infant baptism was the New Testament counterpart to Old Testament circumcision. Controversy over infant baptism developed when the Baptist presence took shape in New England. Roger Williams* (1603–1683), John Clarke (1609–1676), and other colonial Baptists* declared that infant baptism was not compatible with the teaching of Holy Scripture nor with the idea of a church of believers only. In their view, baptism was to follow, not precede, the necessary profession of faith. For these and other antiestablishment views Roger Williams was expelled from Massachusetts. He founded Rhode Island, which became a haven for Baptists and other dissenters. The controversy did not end in Massachusetts, where Henry Dunster (1612–1659), the first president of Harvard College, was removed from office in 1654 for refusing to have his infant child baptized.

For New Englanders, the famous Half-way Covenant* of 1662 was precipitated by another baptismal controversy. The covenant was a response to a familial and theological dilemma created when persons baptized in infancy but unconverted as adults requested baptism for their own children. It permitted the baptism of these second-generation Puritans but granted full church membership—Communion and voting privileges—only when they made the required profession of faith. The Half-way Covenant received mixed response from individual churches. Some rejected it completely, others used it, and others went beyond it, extending Communion to all baptized persons, converted or not. Jonathan Edwards* (1703–1758) and other revivalist preachers condemned the covenant and reemphasized the need for a completely regenerated church membership.

By the nineteenth century debates over baptism accompanied churches as they moved west toward the frontier. Controversies over the mode and meaning of baptism divided Protestants, with Methodists and Presbyterians defending the sprinkling of infants against the Baptist and "Christian" call for total immersion of adult believers. Peter Cartwright (1785–1872), the Methodist circuit rider, once suggested that "Baptists make so much ado about baptism by immersion that the uninformed would suppose that heaven was an island and the only way to get there was by swimming or diving." Baptists responded with sentiments expressed in this frontier doggerel:

> Not at the Jordan River, but in that flowing stream,
> stood John the Baptist preacher when he baptized Him.
> John was a Baptist preacher when he baptized the Lamb,
> So Jesus was a Baptist and thus the Baptists came.

The "Christian" or "Disciples" movement, fostered by Barton W. Stone* (1772–1844) and Alexander Campbell* (1788–1866), claimed to have restored the true New Testament practices, including immersion baptism. Campbell also created controversy, especially with the Baptists, by insisting that faith and baptism were inseparable elements of Christian belief and practice. Baptists responded that baptism was simply a symbol of the necessary faith and charged Campbell with promoting "baptismal regeneration," not unlike Roman Catholics. Debates on these issues were held across the frontier, attracting great crowds who came to support their favorite preacher and doctrine.

One Baptist response to these questions came from the Old Landmark movement, an effort to trace Baptist churches in an unbroken line to Jesus and his baptism by John the Baptist, thereby proving that they were the one true church. Taking their name from Proverbs 22:28: "Remove not the ancient landmark which thy fathers have set," Landmarkers believed that Baptist churches alone had the true baptism. They rejected infant baptism as well as the "alien immersion"* administered in other non-Baptist traditions. All persons who had not received baptism in a proper Baptist church were required to be rebaptized. Landmarkers also promoted "closed Communion" by which the Lord's Supper was given only to members of the specific congregation in which it was celebrated. Landmark attempts to impose such dogmas on the Southern Baptist Convention* created controversy and schism within that denomination. In 1905 the American Baptist Association was formed by former Southern Baptists who were dissatisfied with the convention's failure to require Landmark doctrines of all its member churches.

During the twentieth century many Baptist churches, black and white, North and South, and associations (regional church organizations) divided over the acceptance of baptism from other denominations. Some churches received all professing Christians into membership on the basis of any previous baptism. Others accepted the earlier baptism of those who had received immersion regardless of the tradition, while still others required immersion in Baptist churches only. Some Baptists rejected immersion administered in Baptist congregations whose theology of baptism was considered questionable. For example, during the 1970s certain Southern Baptist congregations in Indiana required the rebaptism of persons who came from General Baptist churches since those churches believed in falling from grace. Baptist churches that advocated an open baptismal policy, receiving those baptized in other traditions without requiring rebaptism, were frequently disciplined or even dismissed from their local associations. Local Baptist churches themselves often split over such policies. By the latter twentieth century debates continued over the meaning of baptism itself as sacrament, symbol, or sign, the relationship between faith and baptism, and the significance of the ritual for both infants and adults.

Bibliography. *Baptism, Eucharist and Ministry* (Geneva: World Council of Churches, 1982); Beasley-Murray, G. R., *Baptism in the New Testament* (Grand Rapids, MI: Eerdmans, 1981); Moody, Dale, *Baptism: Foundation for Christian Unity* (Nashville: Broadman Press, 1967).

Bill J. Leonard

Baptism of the Holy Spirit. A phrase common in the Holiness, Pentecostal,* and charismatic traditions, variously interpreted but referring to the reception of the Holy Spirit by believers. The term is based on the preaching of John the Baptist that Jesus would baptize with the Holy Spirit. Other key passages found in Acts (chapters 2, 8, 9, 10, 19) are seen as initiation-type experiences of the Holy Spirit.

In American Christianity, the phrase "baptism of the Holy Spirit" first received widespread use during the Holiness movement of the nineteenth century. In the antebellum era Wesleyan theology and the Oberlin perfectionism of Charles Finney* and Asa Mahan emphasized sanctification and Christian perfection, a "second blessing"* subsequent to conversion that provided instantaneous cleansing of the heart from inbred sin. As in the writings of John Wesley, the second blessing was described in Christocentric terms (having the mind of Christ in you). After midcentury, amidst Holiness revivalism, advocates like Mahan, along with influential Methodist revivalists such as Phoebe Palmer,* began using the Pentecostal imagery of the baptism of the Holy Spirit to describe the second blessing of sanctification.

Others in the growing Holiness movement, like Reuben Torrey, did not equate the two. Adopting the theology of the Keswick movement of England, these leaders argued that sanctification began at conversion and was a gradual process of cleansing that was never finished. The purpose of the second blessing of the baptism of the Holy Spirit was not cleansing but an enduement of power for witnessing. Still others used the language of successive "fillings" of the Holy Spirit for the renewal of the Spirit's power in the life of a believer.

How did one know whether one really had received the Holy Spirit baptism? Torrey said that one received the Spirit by fulfilling the commands of God. Others said, "Only believe." Still others searched for a more specific answer, yearning for some tangible evidence. In 1901 Charles Parham,* the "father" of Pentecostalism, read the story of Pentecost in Acts 2 to mean that speaking in tongues was the "initial evidence" of the reception of the baptism of the Holy Spirit. Parham's view became the primary distinctive of the Pentecostal movement.

As Pentecostal denominations developed, some followed the Keswick view of progressive sanctification, and thus the baptism of the Holy Spirit evidenced by "tongues" was properly called the second blessing (Assemblies of God, International Church of the Foursquare Gospel). Others, primarily those with Wesleyan roots, affirmed three separate (temporal and logical) religious experiences: conversion, sanctification, and baptism of the Holy Spirit (Church of God, Church of God in Christ). For all Pentecostals, the purpose of Holy Spirit baptism is an immersion in the Spirit's power for witness, service, and mighty works. The baptism is received by faith, while prayer, obedience, and surrender are essential characteristics of that faith. Early Pentecostals had "tarrying meetings" to seek the baptism.

Charismatic theology also emphasizes the centrality of the baptism of the Holy Spirit. Many charismatics view it as a second rather than third distinct work of grace; most do not insist on glossolalia* as the only "initial evidence" of the baptism's reception. Catholic charismatics usually see the baptism of the Holy Spirit sacramentally; it is an actualization of what has already been given in the sacrament of water baptism.

Non-Pentecostals have often suspected the Pentecostal emphasis on receiving a special Spirit baptism as, at best, a license for spiritual pride and, at worst, an implication that only Pentecostals really are Christian. Pentecostal theology disavows these criticisms but admits that some radical believers hold them. Most non-Pentecostals follow a traditional Protestant view that affirms that the Holy Spirit is received at conversion and believers do not have to wait for another separate blessing. Some "Reformed" critics elaborate that the language of being baptized with the Holy Spirit in the New Testament refers to the giving of the Spirit at the birth of the church and thus is a historical event that is not necessary nor possible to repeat.

Bibliography. Bruner, Frederick D., *A Theology of the Holy Spirit* (Grand Rapids, MI: William B. Eerdmans, 1970); Burgess, Stanley, and Gary B. McGee, eds. *Dictionary of Pentecostal and Charismatic Movements* (Grand Rapids, MI: Zondervan, 1988); Dayton, Donald, *Theological Roots of Pentecostalism* (Grand Rapids, MI: Francis Asbury Press, 1987).

Douglas Weaver

Baptist Bible Fellowship. Possibly the most prolific movement among Baptist fundamentalism* in the twentieth century, the Baptist Bible Fellowship (BBF) began in May 1950 at the Texas Hotel in Fort Worth, Texas, the result of a sharp division between the two prominent leaders of the then World Fundamental Baptist Missionary Fellowship (WFBMF) and its school, the Bible Baptist Seminary—J. Frank Norris* and George Beauchamp Vick.* Norris, the controversial pastor of the huge First Baptist Church of Fort Worth, Texas, along with his Bible teacher and administrator Louis Entzminger, had founded the WFBMF in the 1930s after the demise of the Bible Baptist Union, of which Norris had been a cofounder. The WFBMF, an alternative "independent" fellowship for pastors dissatisfied with the drift toward modernism in both the Northern and Southern Baptist Conventions (Norris had been voted out of the Texas Baptist convention in the 1920s), became a powerful vehicle, along with Norris's paper the *Searchlight* (later named the *Fundamentalist*), for promoting his brand of local church government, mass evangelism, flamboyant pulpiteering, indigenous Sunday school literature, and autocratic control of the church by the pastor. All of these innovations created an intense spirit of independence among the many pastors and students studying at the seminary, attending meetings of the WFBMF, and faithfully reading the *Fundamentalist*, at the same time that it fostered one of the most intense loyalties to one leader any movement has ever seen. George Beauchamp Vick, who in the early 1920s had been one of Norris's most successful Sunday school administrators, was asked by Norris in 1936 to become general superintendent (essentially de facto pastor) of his newly acquired pastorate at Temple Baptist Church in Detroit, Michigan. By 1948 the two churches had a combined membership of over 25,000. The tremendous size of these two churches, along with the hundreds of pastors and students affiliated with the WFBMF and the Bible Baptist Seminary, placed Norris and Vick at the front of a formidable independent Baptist empire.

In 1948 all allegiances were still with Norris, but a growing discontent over Norris's handling of the finances of the seminary (located on the property of First Baptist in Fort Worth and controlled almost exclusively by Norris) led many members of the WFBMF to waver in their monetary support of the seminary, at this point some $250,000 in debt. To alleviate the discontent and reestablish the financial stability of the seminary, Norris uncharacteristically stepped down as head of the school and persuaded Vick to take over as president in 1948. Vick proceeded to turn the school around academically, financially, and organizationally. In doing so he developed a strong appreciation among the pastors and students, an appreciation not unnoticed by the domineering Norris. Not accustomed to being upstaged or sharing power, Norris more and more perceived the growing allegiance to Vick as a direct criticism of his previous efforts and a threat to his continued position as leader of the WFBMF. What many thought was Norris's plan for an orderly succession of power (he was seventy-three at the time and had suffered a significant stroke the year before) proved to be premature. Consequently, in May 1950 he decided to reassert himself as head of the seminary once again, dismissing two faculty members without Vick's approval, instituting a new set of bylaws that gave full authority of the school to himself and the church, and replacing Vick as president with the Scottish evangelist Jack Group. Vick demanded a full hearing on this matter, as did many others in the WFBMF, at the annual meeting of the fellowship in

Fort Worth in late May 1950. After being harangued by Norris for over an hour at the meeting, Vick proceeded to rebut Norris point by point with full documentation. The majority of the WFBMF met the next day at the Texas Hotel and after some deliberation decided that the best response to Norris would be a complete break. Thus the Baptist Bible Fellowship was born, with Vick, a man who owed so much to Norris, who had worked with him for almost thirty years under some very trying circumstances and who yet had been so vilified the day before by Norris himself, reluctantly but resolutely casting the first vote. Vick requested that Norris come to Detroit and present his side to the deacons of Temple Baptist, which he did, after which a motion was made to remove Norris as copastor in favor of Vick, a motion that the congregation passed by a vote of 3,000 to 7. Humiliated, Norris returned to Fort Worth and began a vicious smear campaign in the *Fundamentalist,* part of a last-ditch effort to discredit Vick and the new movement and regain his power and reputation, in one issue alone accusing the various leaders of the BBF of adultery, theft, fraud, and perjury. The BBF responded, of course, in its own periodical, the *Baptist Bible Tribune,* edited by Norris's former editor, the brilliant and often caustic Noel Smith. For many of these men, the rift was never healed.

Vick was elected president of the new Baptist Bible College, the educational arm of the new Fellowship, and W. E. Dowell, then pastor of High Street Baptist Church in Springfield, Missouri, and previously president of the WFBMF, was elected president of the BBF, with both the headquarters of the fellowship and the school located in Springfield. Vick served as president until his death in 1975, presiding over a phenomenal growth in the school (from 107 students in 1950 to over 2,400 at the time of his death), in the fellowship (from 150 churches in 1950 to more than 2,300 in 1975), in missions (from 17 to over 430 missionaries), and in the number of church members in fellowship churches (from under 100,000 to over 1,500,000). Though the BBF reached its apex in terms of churches and members in the early 1980s, it is still a formidable force in American fundamentalism today.

Bibliography. Bartlett, Billy Vick, *The Beginnings: A Pictorial History of the Baptist Bible Fellowship,* vol. 1 (Springfield, MO: Baptist Bible College, 1975); Bartlett, Billy Vick, *A History of Baptist Separatism* (Springfield, MO: Rourk and Son, 1972); Bartlett, Billy Vick, "Roots and Origins of Baptist Fundamentalism: The Baptist Bible Fellowship: The First Twenty-Five Years," *Baptist Bible Tribune,* December 23, 1983 8–9; Combs, James O., "Roots and Origins of Baptist Fundamentalism, 1950—The Baptist Bible Fellowship Begins," *Baptist Bible Tribune,* January 20, 1984, 8; Dowell, W. E., *The Birthpangs of the Baptist Bible Fellowship* (Springfield, MO: Temple Press, 1977); Randall, Mike, *G. B. Vick* (Springfield, MO: Baptist Bible College, 1987).

Timothy D. Whelan

Baptist Joint Committee on Public Affairs. In 1936 the Southern Baptist Convention* (SBC) reformed its Committee on Chaplains to be the Committee on Public Relations, a standing committee of the convention. This Southern

Baptist committee soon affiliated with similar committees from other Baptist groups, and in 1946 a full-time office was opened in Washington, D.C. Thus began the Joint Conference Committee on Public Relations. In 1950 the name was changed to the Baptist Joint Committee on Public Affairs (BJC). As the structure of the BJC evolved, so did its mission as a watchdog agency for religious liberty.

It might be assumed that the mission of the BJC would invite controversy: seeking to represent different bodies of Baptists* on issues of religious liberty and church-state separation that are prone to be controversial. However, in its first thirty years the BJC benefited from the fact that Baptist groups were fairly unanimous on their positions related to religious liberty and church-state separation. Two minor controversies did arise. First, during the time that James E. Wood, Jr., was its executive director, he led the BJC to adopt a prochoice position on abortion.* When the fundamentalist takeover of the SBC began in the 1980s, fundamentalists seized on this fact in an attempt to discredit the BJC. The fundamentalists demanded that the BJC adopt a strict prolife position on abortion. The BJC stated that it was to deal with issues regarding the First Amendment only. Abortion was an ethical issue so it came under the purview of the Christian Life Commission of the SBC. The second minor controversy was also related to the attempt of fundamentalists to control the SBC. BJC executive director James M. Dunn was forced to resign from participation in the organization People for the American Way. Fundamentalists argued that Dunn's choice to associate with People for the American Way was an indication of the liberal leanings of the BJC.

Since the 1980s the unanimity of Baptists on religious liberty issues has fragmented, making the work of the BJC more difficult. Specifically, a major controversy arose in 1982. Fundamentalist leaders of the SBC supported President Ronald Reagan's proposed constitutional amendment for prayer in public schools. The BJC opposed the proposed amendment. Now the BJC and the fundamentalist leadership of the SBC were in open and direct conflict. SBC leaders concluded that the BJC must come under the direct control of the SBC, or a new office should be started in Washington, D.C., that would more accurately reflect the positions of what they considered to be the majority of Southern Baptists.

The controversy played out between 1987 and 1992. There were recurring attempts to defund the BJC at annual meetings of the SBC and an unsuccessful attempt to create a new agency for religious liberty issues. In one last grasp for power, the SBC sought to use its majority status (in funding and representation) on the BJC's board to exercise control over the BJC. Finally, in 1992 the SBC voted to defund the BJC and shifted both the BJC's budget allocation and its responsibilities for addressing First Amendment issues to the Christian Life Commission, which then opened an office in Washington, D.C. Thus ended more than fifty years of relationship between the SBC and the BJC.

Baptist groups that currently support and participate in the BJC include American Baptist Churches in the USA, Baptist General Conference, National Baptist Convention of America, National Baptist Convention, USA, Inc., National Missionary Baptist Convention, North American Baptist Conference, Progressive National Baptist Convention, Inc., Religious Liberty Council, and Seventh Day Baptist General Conference. Even though the SBC stopped all funding, various Southern Baptist state conventions, associations, and churches have chosen to fund the BJC directly. The BJC celebrated its sixtieth anniversary in 1996 and continues to defend what it regards as the historic Baptist concepts of religious liberty and church-state separation.

Bibliography. Hastey, S. L., "A History of the Baptist Joint Committee on Public Affairs, 1946–1971" (Th.D. diss., Southern Baptist Theological Seminary, 1974); Parry, Pamela, *On Guard for Religious Liberty: Securing Religious Liberty for Six Decades of the Baptist Joint Committee* (Macon: Smyth and Helwys, 1996).

Andrew Pratt

Baptist Missionary Association. Formed in 1899 as a schism of the Baptist General convention of Texas (BGCT), the Baptist Missionary Association (BMA) represented the first state organization of Landmark Baptist churches. The term "Landmarkism"* was first used in the 1850s by J. R. Graves* and J. M. Pendleton to designate a particular view of Baptist ecclesiology that upheld the absolute primacy of the local church based upon its direct succession from the New Testament church. Landmarkism had a direct effect on how the church preached, administered the ordinances, and conducted missionary work. While Graves and Pendleton developed and disseminated the ideas of Landmarkism, persons such as Samuel A. Hayden and Benjamin M. Bogard* undertook the task of institutionalizing these ideas within existing Baptist state conventions and the Southern Baptist Convention.*

Samuel A. Hayden, Dallas pastor and editor of the *Texas Baptist Herald*, was the dominant personality behind the BMA. Beginning in 1879, Hayden aggressively promoted Landmark ideas among Texas Baptists and sought to make them the recognized ecclesiology of the state convention. Hayden's efforts, as well as his rancorous spirit, created division among Texas Baptists. In an effort to bring peace to the state convention, Texas Baptist leaders refused to seat Hayden as a messenger to the annual meetings of the state convention in 1897 and 1898. This decision, supported by the convention's messengers, signified the final rejection of Hayden's agenda and the narrow-minded ecclesiology of Landmarkism.

Defeated in their attempts to reform the state convention according to Landmark thought and practice, Hayden and his followers separated from the BGCT to form the Baptist Missionary Association. In 1905 the BMA merged with other small Landmark groups in Arkansas and neighboring states to form the American Baptist Association.* A joint committee was formed in 1933 in an attempt to restore unity among Texas Baptists. The BGCT voted to accept the committee's principles for reunification, but the BMA rejected the plan. Even though those who advocated Landmark ecclesiology were unable to convert the state conventions to their views, the spirit and ideas of Landmarkism continue to permeate Baptist churches in the mid-South and Southwest.

Bibliography. McBeth, H. L., *The Baptist Heritage* (Nashville: Broadman Press, 1987): *Encyclopedia of Baptists in America* (Downers Grove: InterVarsity Press, 1995).

Andrew Pratt

Baptists. Controversy and dissent characterized the Baptist tradition from its beginnings in seventeenth-century Holland and England. Such controversies are evident in (1) the Baptist response to political issues; (2) their confrontations with other religious groups; and (3) their own theological and organizational debates. Political controversies existed from the beginning. The earliest British Baptists, led by John Smyth (c. 1570–1612) and Thomas Helwys (c. 1550–1615), founded a church in Amsterdam in 1609. They immediately advocated a radical religious liberty, insisting that God alone was judge of conscience. The state could not punish the heretic or the atheist for incorrect belief or no belief at all. Naturally, such views produced frequent persecution from the state, with imprisonment by the British crown on charges of both heresy and treason.

Controversy with the state continued in the American colonies. Roger Williams* (1603–1683), founder of the first Baptist church in America, challenged the Puritan establishment of New England almost on arrival in 1634. He declared that the Native Americans, not the British monarchs, were the sole owners of the new land and should be justly compensated for it. Williams questioned the idea of a Christian commonwealth, challenging the right of a political entity to protect and promote genuine faith without corrupting it. Banished from Massachusetts, Williams bought land from the Indians and founded Providence, Rhode Island, a colony offering complete religious liberty for its citizens. He also participated in founding the first Baptist church in America around 1639. The quintessential dissenter, Williams left the Baptists in quest of a new revelation from God.

As Baptists spread throughout the colonies, they continued to challenge religious establishments. Many were fined, jailed, and otherwise harassed for declaring their views. By the 1700s Massachusetts preacher Isaac Backus (1724–1806) was appointed by New England Baptists as a lobbyist to the Continental Congress in behalf of religious liberty. In Virginia, many Baptists were incarcerated for their refusal to pay church taxes or to secure preaching licenses from the state. John Leland* (1754–1841) influenced James Madison and Thomas Jefferson in behalf of religious liberty in Virginia and in the American Constitution.

As with other American Protestants, controversy also erupted among Baptists over the politics and ethics of slavery. During the late eighteenth and early nineteenth centuries, many Baptists, North and South, deplored the keeping of slaves and urged gradual manumission of some type. With the rise of abolitionism* in the North, the growth of the cotton empire in the South, and the increased polarization over sectional differences, the scene was set for schism. While the Triennial Convention, the national missionary organization linking Baptist churches in the North and South, sought to remain neutral on the slavery question, a controversy finally erupted in 1845 over the appointment of slaveholding missionaries. Georgia Baptists submitted the name of a known slaveholder as a candidate for missionary service. When the board refused to accept his appointment, Southerners reacted by founding a new denomination, the Southern Baptist Convention.*

Race remained a powerful political issue for Baptists throughout the twentieth century. In the early 1950s African-American Baptist churches became the center of the civil rights* movement, North and South. Martin Luther King, Jr.* (1929–1968), pastor of Dexter Avenue Baptist Church* in Montgomery, Alabama, was propelled into leadership of the effort to secure an end to racial segregation in the South. Many African-American Baptist churches were bombed, including the Sixteenth Street Baptist Church* in Birmingham, Alabama, where in 1963 a blast killed four young women as they participated in Sunday school.

In the 1980s and 1990s many Independent Baptist churches encouraged their members to participate in antiabortion, school-prayer, and antipornography movements as a way of reclaiming traditional values in an increasingly secularized America. Jerry Falwell* (1933–   ), pastor of the Thomas Road Baptist Church in Lynchburg, Virginia, helped to found the Moral Majority* and other organizations to help bring conservative ideals into the public square. Their criticisms of secularism, big government, and the loss of public morality brought these Baptists into conflict with others who charged that they were imposing sectarian views on the pluralistic environment of American life. Other Baptists challenged their right-wing political orientation as promoting a new establishment mentality while undermining religious liberty and soul freedom.

In their response to other Christian groups, Baptists have often created controversy. When the followers of Barton W. Stone* (1772–1844) and Alexander Campbell* (1788–1866) began to promote the idea that they had "restored" the true New Testament church, Baptists responded that they had never lost the truth but could trace it all the way to Jesus' baptism in the River Jordan. Thus Baptist Landmarkism* became a means of distinguishing Baptists from other "man-made" denominations.

As the Catholic presence expanded in America, many Baptists responded by challenging Catholic ideas of papal authority and church government. Baptists also expressed serious opposition to any effort to use government funds to subsidize Catholic parochial schools. Many Baptists were active in the opposition to Catholics serving in public office, particularly during the presidential races of Catholics Al Smith and John F. Kennedy.

Baptists have also experienced significant controversy within their own ranks. One of the earliest began in the 1700s regarding the implications of Calvinism for missions and evangelism. Daniel Parker* (1781–1844), a Baptist preacher in Crawford County Illinois, questioned the need for mission activities and the formation of mission boards to send out mission volunteers. Parker's Calvinism led him to believe that missions were a form of "works" for salvation. God would save the elect in God's own time and plan. Missionary activity was a form of human effort to accomplish what only God could do. Parker also opposed the use of mission societies or boards for funding missionary endeavors. Parker saw these boards as a form of church hierarchy that undermined the authority of the local congregation. The Primitive Baptist Churches with their staunch Calvinist views are heirs of the Parker controversy.

Another theological debate among Baptists involved the relationship between social action and evangelism. Some Baptists believed that the primary impetus of the church is evangelism, the saving of souls to faith in Christ and away from sin and eternal punishment. Others emphasize the church's calling to respond to the needs of the poor and oppressed, feeding the hungry, clothing the naked, and addressing the sins of the social order. As a German Baptist pastor in Hell's Kitchen, New York, Walter Rauschenbusch (1861–1918), sometimes known as the father of the Social Gospel in the United States, worked to provide for both the spiritual and physical needs of the poor. Baptist educator and activist Clarence Jordan* (1912–1969) established Koinonia Farm* in Americus, Georgia, to address racial and economic divisions in the region. His project led to controversy and even to violence against the community in the 1950s and 1960s.

Perhaps no other controversy so divided Baptists as the fundamentalist-liberal debates of the twentieth century. Issues involved the methods of interpreting Holy Scripture, the meaning of Christ's death and Resurrection, and the application of reason to theological dogmas. Conservatives and fundamentalists pressed for more precise doctrinal statements on Scripture, atonement, evangelism, and education, while moderates and liberals warned that Baptists were not a creedal people, insisting that traditional ideals of the priesthood of believers and soul liberty prevail. Such divisions among Baptists in the North led to the formation of several new conservative or fundamentalist groups, including the Conservative Baptist Association of America* and the General Association of Regular Baptist Churches.* Divisions among Baptists in the South over these issues became more pronounced in the latter half of the twentieth century. Fundamentalists gained control of the Southern Baptist Convention, forcing more liberal churches and individuals to develop new entities such as the Alliance of Baptists,* the Cooperative Baptist Fellowship,* and a variety of new theological schools. Baptists remain a people given to debate over polity, theology, and practice at every level of their ecclesiastical life.

Bibliography. Ammerman, Nancy, *Baptist Battles* (New Brunswick, NJ: Rutgers University Press, 1990); Brackney, William, *The Baptists* (Westport, CT: Greenwood Press, 1991); McBeth, H. Leon, *The Baptist Heritage* (Nashville: Broadman Press, 1987); Torbet, Robert, *A History of the Baptists*, 3rd ed. (Valley Forge, PA: Judson Press, 1973).

Bill J. Leonard

Beecher, Henry Ward. The son of of nineteenth-century Congregationalist preacher Lyman Beecher,* Henry Ward Beecher (1813–1887) went on to become one of America's best-known preachers in his own right. Beecher was born in Litchfield, Connecticut, in 1813 and migrated to Cincinnati with his family in 1832 when his father became president of Lane Theological Seminary* in that city. After attending Lane Seminary, Beecher pastored churches in Lawrenceburg, Indiana, and Indianapolis before accepting a call to the pulpit of Plymouth Congregational Church in Brooklyn. From Brooklyn Beecher involved himself in virtually every major public issue from 1855 until his death in 1887.

Beecher supported the Union cause in the Civil War despite his rather late and comparatively lukewarm adoption of abolitionist sentiments. His support of President Abraham Lincoln evolved as well. Initially cool, if not outright hostile, toward Lincoln in the early years of the war, Beecher fully warmed to Lincoln after the election of 1864. Beecher preached a sermon on the occasion of the occupation of Fort Sumter by federal troops in April 1865. He also offered a celebratory eulogy of Lincoln after his assassination.

After the war Beecher moved into his role as a "Prince of the Pulpit" with great zeal. No public issue escaped his comment, and parishioners flocked to Brooklyn to hear him hold forth. Speaking on public issues invited public criticism, and Beecher relished the notoriety his outspokenness brought him. He preached an accommodating gospel of love over against a more rigorous creedal expression of Christianity. As a consequence, many critics labeled his preaching heretical. He espoused a form of evangelical liberalism and became an early champion of efforts to ensure the vitality of Christianity in a modernizing world.

Beecher's reputation suffered a direct blow in 1874 when a parishioner, Theodore Tilton, accused him of seducing Mary Tilton, his wife. Beecher ultimately won acquittal in a sensational trial, but not without public speculation about his sexual habits. That speculation had existed before the trial, but it reached a fever pitch after the charges arose. The speculation heightened when "free love" advocate Barbara Clafin Woodhull championed his cause.

The trial for criminal conversation injured Beecher's standing in the public mind, but only a little. To the chagrin of his critics, Beecher emerged from the Tilton episode still revered by the public. Indeed, by 1880 many believed Beecher a viable candidate for the Republican nomination for the presidency. The outpouring of public grief and approbation at his death testified to the powerful hold this eloquent and forceful preacher had over the hearts and minds of a wide segment of the American public.

Bibliography. Beecher, Henry Ward, *Patriotic Addresses*, ed. J. R. Howard (New York: Scribner's, 1887); Beecher, Henry Ward, "Progress of Thought in the Church," *North American Review* 135 (August 1882): 99–117; Caskey, Marie, *Chariot of Fire: Religion and the Beecher Family* (New Haven: Yale University Press, 1978); Clark, Clifford E., Jr., *Henry Ward Beecher: Spokesman for a Middle-Class America* (Urbana: University of Illinois Press, 1978); McLoughlin, William G., *The Meaning of Henry Ward Beecher* (New York: Alfred A. Knopf, 1970).

Russell Congleton

Beecher, Lyman. Lyman Beecher (1775–1863) was a Presbyterian and Congregationalist minister, a controversialist, and a leading revivalist of the Second Great Awakening.* Born at New Haven, Connecticut, on October 12, 1775, Beecher was the son of a blacksmith, David Beecher, and his wife, Esther Lyman. Because his mother died shortly after his restless, rather undisciplined adolescence, he entered Yale College, where he came under the religious influence of the new president, Timothy Dwight. Converted to evangelical Christianity by Dwight, he remained for an additional year to study for the ministry. Theologically, he was influenced at this time both by Dwight and by Samuel Hopkins* (1721–1803), who had significantly modified the received Calvinism of New England in the direction of an Arminian emphasis on human ability. In 1799 Beecher married Roxana Foote, with whom he had nine children, one of whom died in infancy. Several of these children became famous in their own right, notably Catharine (1800–1878), Edward (1803–1895), Harriet Beecher Stowe* (1811–1896), Henry Ward Beecher* (1813–1887), and Charles (1815–1900). Beecher's first church was the Presbyterian Church at East Hampton, Long Island, which he as a Congregationalist served under the terms of the Plan of Union between the two denominations. In 1810 he became pastor of the Congregationalist church at Litchfield, Connecticut, where he established himself as one of the leading revivalist preachers of his time, doing battle with every form of infidelity (especially Deism, Unitarianism, and Roman Catholicism) and unbelief. In 1817, after the death of Roxana, he married Harriet Porter; they had four children, one of whom died in infancy. Best known of Harriet's children were Isabella Beecher Hooker (1822–1907) and Thomas (1824–1900). In 1826 Beecher moved to Boston, where he crusaded against Unitarianism from the pulpit of the Hanover Street Church. By this time his theology was basically identical to that of his good friend Nathaniel William Taylor (1786–1858), first professor of the Yale Divinity School. Taylor, even more than Hopkins, stressed the initiative of sinners in the process of conversion, while continuing to assert the sinfulness of humankind and the sovereignty of God. In 1832 Beecher moved to Cincinnati, where he became president of the newly founded Lane Seminary* and pastor of the Second Presbyterian Church. Conflict, which heretofore had largely been with those outside his own household of faith, now came with his own students and fellow ministers. The Lane students broke with Beecher over the issue of abolitionism,* which they favored but he did not; the result was the famous ''Lane Rebellion'' of 1834 in which almost all of the students left the seminary. At this time, several ''Old School'' Presbyterian ministers of Cincinnati found Beecher untrustworthy in matters of doctrine because his ''Taylorism'' was similar to ''New School'' Presbyterian teachings that they despised. In 1834 they brought formal charges of heresy. Acquitted at every level of the Presbyterian judicial system, Beecher pleaded his case to a larger public in his *Views in Theology* (1836). He also published his famous *Plea for the West* (1835) during this period; this anti-Catholic, anti-immigrant tract pleaded for evangelical Protestant hegemony in the western regions, lest the nation be lost to Roman despotism. After the double blow of the Lane Rebellion and the heresy trial, Beecher slowly rebuilt both the seminary and his somewhat tarnished reputation. In 1836, after the death of Harriet Porter, he married Mrs. Lydia Jackson; they had no children. Surviving an Old School attempt to oust him as president of Lane in 1846, he retired from the presidency in 1851; he had earlier left the pulpit of Second Presbyterian Church after a dispute with the congregation. After retirement he moved to Boston, near his son Edward. He there began his sprawling *Autobiography* (1864), which was completed later by several of his children under the leadership of Charles. In 1856 he moved to Brooklyn to be near Henry Ward Beecher. He died on January 10, 1863.

Bibliography. Harding, Vincent, *A Certain Magnificence: Lyman Beecher and the Transfomation of American Protestantism, 1775–1863* (Brooklyn, NY: Carlson Publishing, 1991); Henry, Stuart, *Unvanquished Puritan: A Portrait of Lyman Beecher* (Grand Rapids, MI: Eerdmans, 1973).

Donald L. Huber

The Berrigans. Daniel (1921–   ) and Philip (1923–   ) Berrigan were the first Roman Catholic priests to receive federal sentences for peace activities in the United States. Daniel is an accomplished poet and Jesuit priest; Philip was a Josephite priest ministering in black ghettoes before marrying in 1969 and being laicized. They are the youngest of six sons of Thomas Berrigan, who was a militant Socialist party and Catholic trade-union activist in Syracuse, New York.

Daniel Berrigan spent a final year of Jesuit formation in study and ministry at Lyons, France, in 1953–1954, where he was influenced by the "worker-priest" movement. In 1957 he won the Lamont Prize for his first collection of poetry, *Time without Number*. From 1957–1963 he taught the New Testament at Le Moyne College in Syracuse, where he also formed students in pacifist, civil rights, and radical social issues. One of his students, David Miller, became the first convicted draft-card burner during the antiwar protests of the 1960s. He and his brother Philip were instrumental in anti–Vietnam War activity with the formation of the Catholic Peace Fellowship (1964) and the interdenominational Clergy and Laymen Concerned about Vietnam (1965).

Philip Berrigan served as a parish priest for six years (1955–1961) in the New Orleans ghettoes before taking up ministry at St. Peter Claver Church, a black inner-city parish in Baltimore. He chronicled his nontraditional collaboration with black leaders such as Stokely Carmichael (of the Student Nonviolent Coordinating Committee) in the 1960s in his first book, *No More Strangers,* where he examined the psychology of racism. He linked racial and economic oppression in the United States with the escalation of American military policy in Indochina.

The Berrigans' concern with the Cold War arms race and the threat of nuclear war led Philip and three others to enter the Selective Service office in the Baltimore Customs House on October 27, 1967, and to open Selective Service draft files, pour blood on them in protest of the killings in Vietnam, and wait to be arrested. Catholic church officials reacted by claiming that the action was liable to alienate sincere people seeking a just peace. While Phillip was awaiting sentencing for his crimes, the brothers began planning a second prophetic protest involving seven others. On May 17, 1968, the group that came to be known as the Catonsville Nine chose a draft-board office (Selective Service Board 33) in Catonsville, Maryland, because it was housed in a Knights of Columbus hall and, they claimed, showed the church's complicity with "the warfare state." The protesters emptied files containing hundreds of 1-A draft records, burned them with homemade napalm in the parking lot, and again awaited arrest. Following their sentencing—Philip to three and a half years to run concurrently with the six-year sentence he had begun serving, and Daniel to three years— Philip was free on bail and awaited, along with Daniel, their appeal for a year and four months until the Supreme Court refused to reconsider the verdict.

On April 9, 1970, the date set for serving their sentences, the two brothers and three other of the convicted went underground. On April 21 Philip was captured by FBI agents at St. Gregory the Great Church in Manhattan and sent to federal prison in Lewisburg, Pennsylvania. While in prison, Philip was indicted on charges growing from details in clandestine correspondence between him and Sister Elizabeth McAlister, whom he had secretly married the previous year. He had been spied on by the FBI informer who gained his confidence and carried their letters when leaving the prison to attend classes at Bucknell University. The two correspondents and other draft resisters in Rochester, New York (including Daniel, who was captured as a result of details in the correspondence), were arrested as the Harrisburg Seven. In January 1972 the seven were defended by a distinguished team of lawyers including former Attorney General Ramsey Clark; following a deadlocked jury, a mistrial was declared, and a circuit court of appeals subsequently overturned the smuggling convictions because of entrapment by the government informer. Philip meanwhile was transferred to Danbury, Connecticut, federal prison and paroled on December 20, 1972, having served thirty-nine months of prison sentences.

In September 1980 the Berrigan brothers and six others entered the secret nuclear factory of General Electric in King of Prussia, Pennsylvania, and damaged two unarmed nuclear warheads and threw their blood on them. The "Ploughshares Eight" were tried and convicted in 1981 in Norristown, Pennsylvania, and sentenced to terms of from three to ten years.

In more recent activities, Philip Berrigan and three other antiwar activists known as the Pax Christi–Spirit of Life Ploughshares were sentenced for vandalizing a U.S. Air Force fighter-bomber on December 7, 1993, at a Goldsboro,

North Carolina, military base. The attack with blood and hammers on the high-tech weapon resulted in $27,000 in damages. This event marked more than one hundred arrests since Philip Berrigan began protesting the Vietnam War. In the mid-1980s Daniel Berrigan began ministering to AIDS patients at St. Vincent's Hospital in Greenwich Village. On October 26, 1991, he was arrested as a member of the "Fervent Five" in Rochester, New York, for an antiabortion protest against the announced opening of an abortion clinic. He and four others were sentenced to forty hours of community service for blocking an entrance to a Planned Parenthood facility.

Bibliography. Berrigan, Daniel, *To Dwell in Peace: An Autobiography* (San Francisco: Harper and Row, 1987); Berrigan, Philip, *Widen the Prison Gates: Writing from Jails, April 1970–December 1972.* (New York: Simon and Schuster, 1973); Dear, John, ed., *Apostle of Peace: Essays in Honor of Daniel Berrigan* (Maryknoll, NY: Orbis, 1996).

George Kilcourse

Bible Societies. Bible societies are nonprofit organizations whose purpose is the distribution of copies of the Bible and "good books." Early groups in Great Britain were the Society for the Promotion of Christian Knowledge (1698), the Society for the Propagation of the Gospel in Foreign Parts (1701), the Society in Scotland for Propagating Christian Knowledge (1709), the Society for Promoting Religious Knowledge among the Poor (1750), the Bible Society (1780), and the Society for the Support and Encouragement of Sunday Schools (1785). The Canstein Bible Institute was begun in Halle, Germany (1710), to make the Scriptures available.

In 1804 the British and Foreign Bible Society was organized with the sole purpose of making Bibles available in various languages, not only to the British Isles, but to the various countries of the world. The first Bible society formed in the United States was the Philadelphia Bible Society (1808). Its example was followed in Connecticut, Massachusetts, New York, and New Jersey (1809). At the time of the creation of the American Bible Society (1816), there were already 123 state, auxiliary, and associated Bible societies in the United States. Concurrently, Bible societies were initiated in the Netherlands, France, Russia, Switzerland, and other countries.

Presently the American Bible Society works in at least 150 countries distributing the Scriptures in at least 1,300 different languages and dialects. Much of the work is done by missionaries in the field working with Christian nationals. Bibles are supplied for the blind in braille, and "Talking Bible" records are distributed. To avoid theological controversy or rivalry, the American Bible Society limits its Bibles to the text alone, without notes or comment. This is consistent with the tradition of Bible societies in general that welcome persons of all religious persuasions to become members.

In 1932 the British and Foreign Bible Society and the American Bible Society began to coordinate their efforts. By 1946 the United Bible Societies attracted cooperation from other national Bible societies. From 1816 to 1970 the American Bible Society distributed more than 800 million complete or partial Bibles; by 1985 it had dispensed an additional 725 million Bible selections. The 1993 *American Bible Society Annual Report* stated that the society shared 287 million copies of the Scriptures.

Bibliography. "Bibles for Millions," *America* 129 (1973): 269–70; Ferris, I., *Jubilee Memorial of the American Bible Society* (New York: American Bible Society, 1867); Howsam, L., *Cheap Bibles: Nineteenth-Century Publishing and the British and Foreign Bible Society* (Cambridge: Cambridge University Press, 1991); Lacy, C., *The Word-carrying Giant: The Growth of the American Bible Society, 1816–1966.* (South Pasadena, CA: William Carey Library, 1977); Strickland, W. P., *History of the American Bible Society* (New York: Harper and Brothers, 1856).

Frederick V. Mills, Sr.

Bible Translations. Since the earliest British settlement of North America, American publishers have issued more than 2,500 Bible translations, often amidst intense controversy. The very first English book printed in North America, the Bay Psalm Book, was compiled because of Puritan dissatisfaction with the metrical psalters of Stehnhold and Hopkins (1562) and Henry Ainsworth (1612). Their debates were only the beginning of several centuries of American contention over various translations by individuals or committees, including biblical condensations or ideological translations.

Bible translations by individuals have often been poorly received. John Eliot's 1663 Algonquin translation was the first entire Bible printed in British North America, but most copies were soon destroyed by the Algonquins themselves. In 1808 Charles Thomson published the first English translation in America, but critics berated his reliance on the Greek Septuagint for his Old Testament text. Lexicographer Noah Webster called his 1833 translation "the most important enterprise of my life," but most of his Bibles remained unsold. In 1923 Edgar J. Goodspeed published his New Testament and then traveled throughout thirteen states to defend his translation in 125 lectures. James Moffatt published his best-selling translation in its final form in 1935, but he himself preferred the King James Version for public reading.

Committee translations and revisions have often provoked great controversy. The American public castigated the British translators of the 1885 Revised Version for their high-handed treatment of their auxiliary American Committee, which subsequently published its own translation as the 1901 American Standard Version. In 1952 one North Carolina pastor burned the Revised Standard Version (RSV) and mailed the ashes to its translators, who had replaced the King James "virgin" with "young woman" in Isaiah 7:14, largely eliminated "thee" and "thou," dropped the word "begotten" from the "only begotten Son" of John 3:16, and relegated several passages to footnotes; a U.S. Air Force training manual later warned of the RSV's Communist influences. In 1968 the American Bible Society's Good News for Modern Man was denounced as "the devil's masterpiece" by South Carolina bumper stickers, symbolically buried in a funeral service by a North Carolina pastor, and burned as fuel for a marshmallow roast in Denver, Colorado. The 1989 New Revised Standard Version was banned from liturgical use by the Vatican for its inclusive language, even as others criticized its retention of masculine references to God.

Attempts to condense or edit the Bible have not been well received. Thomas Jefferson compiled two different versions of the "Life and Morals of Jesus of Nazareth," although the "Jefferson Bible" remained unpublished until 1928. One 1861 edition of the New Testament condensed Romans to seven chapters and Revelation to three chapters and omitted Hebrews altogether. Edgar J. Goodspeed edited his 1933 condensation, *The Short Bible: An American Translation*, in chronological order. The 1982 Reader's Digest Bible condensed the Revised Standard Version, shortening the New Testament by one-fourth and the Old Testament by half, although such classic passages as the Twenty-third Psalm and 1 Corinthians remained intact.

Some revisions of the Bible have been attacked for their ideological bias. Beginning with an 1826 version edited by Disciples of Christ founder Alexander Campbell,* several "immersionist" Bibles preferred to "translate" the Greek "βαπτίζω" as "immerse" rather than "transliterating" it as "baptize," splitting the American Bible Society over the issue in 1836. The 1852 Olive Pell Bible removed sex, violence, and "carnivorous references." The Jewish cantor Isaac Leeser published his scholarly translation in 1853, avoiding christological interpretations of the Old Testament, just as the Jewish Publication Society sought to eliminate Christian biases in its 1917 Jewish Version and 1985 New Jewish Version. Several late-twentieth-century "Jewish" versions use "El," "Elohim," and "Yahweh" for "God," or translate "Jesus" as "Yeshua" and transliterate proper names in Jewish form. In the Jehovah's Witnesses* 1961 New World Translation, "the Lord" becomes "Jehovah," "church" becomes "congregation," and John 1:1 becomes "The Word was with God, and the Word was a god." Reviewers panned Kenneth Taylor's 1971 Living Bible paraphrase as theologically impoverished, anachronistic, distorted, inaccurate, anti-Semitic, and "zealously fundamentalist," often citing such tendentious paraphrases as "a way to heaven" instead of "salvation," yet the public purchased more than 30 million copies in its first fourteen years. In 1993 the Jesus Seminar published its translation of the Five Gospels (including the noncanonical Gospel of Thomas), color-coding the words of Jesus to represent their presumed authenticity; after a Gary, Indiana, newspaper ran a front-page review of the book, protesters burned their copies of the newspaper and canceled their subscriptions.

Women's suffrage and feminism have inspired new translations. In 1876 Julia E. Smith, who had learned Greek to evaluate William Miller's* millennial predictions, became the first woman to translate the entire Bible. Her translation, featuring the Old Testament in Hebrew canonical order and an "immersionist" New Testament, was criticized for its stilted "literal" English and its odd verb tenses. From 1895 to 1898 Elizabeth Cady Stanton* and a Revising Committee of twenty women published the two-volume Woman's Bible, comprising about one-tenth of the Bible (closely following the King James text) accompanied by extensive commentaries. The first volume went through seven printings in six months, but one typical clergyman condemned it as "the work of women, and the devil." Even the National American Woman Suffrage Association feared that the Woman's Bible would do more harm than good for its cause and censured both Stanton and the book in 1896. From 1983 to 1985 the National Council of Churches* published the Inclusive Language Lectionary, amending the RSV by eliminating masculine language for God and humanity and by recasting pejorative language about slavery, darkness, and (in subsequent revisions) Judaism. In many instances (such as the translation of ἄνθρωπος as "person") its translation was more faithful to the original texts, but inelegant renderings such as "the Human One" for the "Son of Man" and "God the Father [and Mother]" for "God the Father" prompted one early critic of the inclusive-language movement to warn, "Keep your clumsy, meddling hands off the Holy Bible!" Several recent translations, including the New Jerusalem Bible, the Revised English Bible, and the New Revised Standard Version, have also been sensitive to gender issues.

The continuing evolution of language and the ever-increasing knowledge of biblical texts and their world assures the proliferation of new Bible translations. Amidst the great diversity of American religious thought, new translations will inevitably provoke new controversy.

Bibliography. Frerichs, Ernest S., ed, *The Bible and Bibles in America* (Atlanta: Scholars Press, 1988); Lewis, Jack P., *The English Bible from KJV to NIV: A History and Evaluation* (Grand Rapids, MI: Baker Book House, 1982); Orlinsky, Harry M., and Robert G. Bratcher, *A History of Bible Translation and the North American Contribution* (Atlanta: Scholars Press, 1991); Roy, Ralph Lord, *Apostles of Discord: A Study of Organized Bigotry and Disruption on the Fringes of Protestantism* (Boston: Beacon Press, 1953).

David B. McCarthy

Biblical Criticism. Biblical criticism has generated a flurry of insights as well as controversies as scholars have approached biblical texts with new methods of engagement. The centuries following the Renaissance, particularly the eighteenth and nineteenth, were a time of considerable ferment as new texts and versions of the Bible became available for study. Further, a new sophistication in reading led to questions concerning authority, inspiration, and textual differences. The ideological and social roots of biblical criticism were of one piece with the large-scale cultural movement throughout Europe, which must be set alongside the Reformation as a critical influence in the formation of the modern world.

Biblical criticism was in its early stages characterized as "higher" and "lower"; higher (or historical) criticism dealt with the idea that the Pentateuch and the Synoptic Gospels were composed by drawing on previous documents or sources, while lower criticism dealt with issues of textual integrity, that is, establishing the best manuscripts. More recent approaches have moved beyond this kind of evaluative distinction to affirm the constructive use of varying representative methodologies such as form criticism, which delineates the oral sources behind the written text; literary criticism, which takes seriously the contribution of contemporary literary theology as it relates to narrative world, plotted time, characterization, implied author, and other matters; rhetorical criticism, which probes the elements, types, and goals of classical rhetoric; redaction criticism, which seeks to ascertain the editing processes that shape the final form of a text; and feminist criticism, which seeks both historical retrieval of the buried women's history in the Bible and the particular contributions of women to its theological tapestry.

The chief objection to biblical criticism has been that it did not recognize Scripture's distinctive character as sacred literature sufficiently. Thus methods that were used with other writings were deemed inappropriate for the Holy Bible because of its special status. Its human character cannot be gainsaid, however, as persons rooted in particular historical circumstances and worldviews functioned as Spirit-inspired authors. The revelation of God always comes to humans in mediated form; hence it is entirely appropriate to surmise that the humanity of the discrete biblical authors was not an impediment to the divine disclosure, but was rather the chosen means of spiritual reflection and communication.

Biblical criticism has served the church well in that it has addressed the questions of persons of faith and reason. The methods of biblical criticism demand careful attention to contextual issues, social location, and the dimensions of religious experience as it seeks to allow the distinctive insights of the biblical material to gain fresh hearing today. It has awakened a sense of the remarkable continuity of biblical history, theological development, and faithful interpretation.

Bibliography. Barr, James, *Holy Scripture: Canon, Authority, Criticism* (Philadelphia: Westminster Press, 1983); Reventlow, Henning Graf, *The Authority of the Bible and the Rise of the Modern World*, trans. John Bowden (Philadelphia: Fortress Press, 1985); Trible, Phyllis, *Rhetorical Criticism: Context, Method, and the Book of Jonah* (Minneapolis: Fortress Press, 1994).

Molly Marshall

Birth Control. Interest in the control of pregnancy and, conversely, opposition to birth control, or contraception, are ancient and varied. Contraceptive methods have ranged from crocodile-dung preparations, according to Egyptian papyrus records, to contemporary use of the "pill," condoms, the IUD, or the "morning-after" pill. The chief controversy in recent years has involved Catholic rejection of any physical impediment to the possibility of conception, as opposed to Protestant acceptance of such methods, by and large.

Early on, both Catholics and Protestants rejected the prevention of conception as an article of faith. For both, the justification for their opposition derived from a literal reading and application of limited but significant biblical sources. On the positive side, God's commandment to Adam and Eve in the initial creation narrative was viewed as a clear imperative: "Be fruitful and multiply and fill the earth" (Genesis 1:28)

A negative conclusion regarding contraception has resulted from a literal interpretation of Genesis 38:8–10. Here Onan was commanded by his father, Judah, to perform his duty according to the custom of levirate marriage and raise up a male heir by his deceased brother's widow. However, Onan "spilled the semen on the ground," that is, practiced coitus interruptus, and frustrated the Levitical law. The judgment of a displeased God was severe and swift: God "slew him."

Though Catholic teaching, following Augustine, concluded that Onan's death was due to the sin of contraception, this has been a matter of some debate in biblical scholarship. No commandments exist in any biblical code condemning contraception, a practice that, however crude and unreliable in its ancient form, was surely known to the Hebrews. Moreover, "Onanism" has erroneously been interpreted to mean masturbation, a secondary term listed in *Webster's Unabridged Dictionary* (3rd edition), when the meaning is clearly withdrawal during sexual intercourse.

In addition to perceived biblical proscriptions regarding contraception, the Thomistic concept of "natural law" became a pivotal factor in Catholic thought. The purpose of sexual intercourse, by its "nature," is to produce offspring. Contraception is "unnatural" and, therefore, reprehensible. Moreover, Augustine had earlier held that the primary nature and purpose of marriage is procreation.

In the early decades of the twentieth century negative attitudes toward contraception within Protestantism generally were exemplified by official Anglican and Episcopalian statements of condemnation. In the face of changing medical and religious opinion, however, the Lambeth Conference of Anglican bishops in 1930 passed a resolution cautiously allowing contraceptive methods based "on Christian principle." Partly in response to such perceived apostasy from historic Christian principles, the encyclical *Casti Connubi* by Pope Pius XI on December 31, 1930, attempted to reinforce and clarify the Catholic position. He declared:

> Assuredly no reason, even the most serious, can make congruent with nature and decent what is intrinsically against nature. Since the act of the spouses is by its own nature ordered to the generation of offspring, those who, exercising it, deliberately deprive it of its natural force and power, act against nature and effect what is base and intrinsically indecent. (Noonan, *Contraception*, 507)

At the beginning of the twentieth century the emerging birth-control movement had become international in scope. In America advocacy of birth control resulted both from concerns regarding Malthusian projections of worldwide population problems and from a growing commitment to promote individual freedom of choice. The work of Margaret Sanger is most associated with efforts to advance the cause of contraceptive freedom in the United States.

In Connecticut a law passed by a conservative Protestant majority in 1879 provided penalties of a fine and/or imprisonment for the use of any contraceptive device or for counseling such use. Kept on the books later by a Catholic majority, the law had been under continuing assault by the Planned Parenthood League of Connecticut. In 1965 the United States Supreme Court declared such laws unconstitutional in a landmark case, *Griswold v. Connecticut* (381 U.S. 479). The *Griswold* decision prevented majority opposition to the use of birth-control devices or information from being imposed upon an unwilling minority and made freedom of choice in the matter of contraception the law of the land.
Bibliography. Gunther, Gerald, and N. T. Dowling, *Cases and Material on Constitutional Law*, 8th ed. (Mineola, NY: Foundation Press, 1970); Noonan, J. T., Jr., *Contraception* (New York: Mentor-Omega Books, 1967); Raab, Earl, *Religious Conflict in America* (Garden City, NY Anchor Books, 1964).

Bernard H. Cochran

Black Ministerial Protest Leadership. There has been a long history of black ministerial protest leadership in America, dating from the days of slavery through the contemporary civil rights* movement. Such leadership is related in part to the fact that the black church has been the only black-owned and operated institution in America. Likewise, the belief in individual salvation and a local democratic church polity, especially as espoused by Baptists* and Methodists, has been a major factor. The situation allowed for the nurturing and developing of a black ministerial protest leadership class.

In the seventeenth century the bishop of London decreed that it was possible to be simultaneously a slave and a Christian. The missionary arm of the Anglican Church, the Society for the Propagation of the Gospel in Foreign Parts, made a concerted effort to Christianize slavery. During the Great Awakenings in America slaves joined by throngs the white dissenting sects of the Baptists and Methodists, which emphasized heartfelt religion as an experience of conversion instead of the Anglican catechism. This new religious expression was very similar in form to the traditional religions of the African past. According to W.E.B. Du Bois, the most important person in African traditional religion was the river priest and obeah man, who emerged on American soil as the black preacher. He became the head of the most important institution for blacks in America, the black church, which because of this African influence did not become fully Christian until well into the twentieth century.

Another factor in the development of this black ministerial protest leadership was that the Baptists and Methodists also gave slaves the opportunity to preach. Carter G. Woodson has called this opportunity "the dawn of a new day." The oldest black church on record in America is the Silver Bluff Baptist Church in Aiken County, South Carolina, which according to its cornerstone dates from 1750. There were a number of independent all-black Baptist churches across the South, pastored by slaves and free blacks. The Bible served as the primary tool of leadership, in part, because of its inherent relationship to the ability to read and write. It also was a definite advantage when the preacher could master a body of literature possessed by whites. Some all-black churches were members of white Baptist associations, but they did not have voting privileges.

The three major slave revolts in the United States were led by black church leaders. The Gabriel Prosser revolt occurred in Richmond, Virginia, in 1800. Citing the Bible as a source of freedom, the conspirators compared their plight to that of the children of Israel. According to various estimates, there were a thousand to three thousand participants. In the Denmark Vesey* plot in 1822, the leaders were members of the African Methodist Church in Charleston, South Carolina, who quoted Zechariah 14:3, believing that they were called by God to strike a blow for freedom. Often church meetings provided the opportunity for planning revolts. Vesey's church was one of the black congregations that had broken from the white denomination earlier that year. All leaders were members of the new independent church, and Morris Brown, later a bishop in the African Methodist Episcopal Church, was a secret counselor. The best-known slave plot was led in 1831 by Nat Turner,* a Baptist lay preacher in Southampton, Virginia. Turner's plot was conceived in what E. Franklin Frazier has called the "invisible institution [the Negro Church]," the clandestine church that met in the woods, beyond the master's eye.

The greatest opposition to slavery was led by the new black denominations taking shape in the North. In 1786 Richard Allen* and other black members protested racial segregation in St. George's Methodist Episcopal Church in Philadelphia. The situation led to the founding of the African Methodist Episcopal Church (AME) in 1816, and Allen becoming bishop. In 1821 a similar situation in the John Street Methodist Episcopal Church in New York City led to the founding of the African Methodist Episcopal Zion Church. In both cases the white Methodist Episcopal churches engaged the blacks in a bitter fight. Both new all-black denominations strongly opposed slavery. Allen's parsonage was a station on the Underground Railroad, and Frederick Douglass was a lay minister in the Zion Church.

An alternative method of protesting slavery was through emigration, and black church leaders led the way. As early as 1815 blacks in Richmond, Virginia, formed the Richmond African Baptist Missionary Society and, along with the American Colonization Society and the Triennial Baptist convention, sent Lott Carey and Colin Teague, former slaves, to Sierra Leone in 1821. They founded Liberia in 1822. In the late 1850s the Southern Baptist Convention* (SBC) appointed nineteen missionaries to Liberia; all were blacks. During this period a common belief was that blacks were physically better able to withstand tropical diseases than whites. But by the 1880s there were numerous complaints by black missionaries of inequity in pay and racism. By this time there was an improvement in the cure of tropical diseases, which enabled whites to better survive in tropical Africa. For these reasons, all African-American missionaries were released.

As a protest, in 1880 William W. Colley, a dismissed black SBC missionary, organized the all-black Baptist Foreign Mission Convention in Montgomery, Alabama. In 1882, along with three African-American missionaries, Colley worked among the Vai people in Liberia creating the Bendoo mission. Likewise, in 1898 Bishop Henry M. Turner* of the AME Church visited South Africa and added 10,800 members to the AME Church. Two years earlier the AME Zion Church had appointed John Bryan Small as bishop for Africa, who primarily worked in what is present-day Ghana. These were the first fruits of modern black nationalism and pan-Africanism. Black denominations in the United States and former black members of colonial churches in Africa formed a loose organization known as the Ethiopian movement. The movement took its name from Psalm 68:31, which extols the previous glories of the Ethiopian and Egyptian civilizations.

Problems of racism and paternalism led to the founding of the all-black National Baptist convention in 1895. More militant blacks tired of racism and condescension among whites of the Northern Baptist and Southern Baptist Conventions. Graduates of American Baptist Home Mission Society schools for blacks were denied administrative and faculty positions. When Southern Baptist ministers protested the American Baptist Publication Society's offer for black scholars to write articles in society journals, the offer was withdrawn. So black Baptist ministers started their own separate all-black convention, which grew to be the largest black Christian organization in the world. They also established their own independent publishing house, under the leadership of Richard H. Boyd, and their own independent black schools.

The modern civil rights* movement also was led by black ministers. In 1955 the Montgomery bus boycott was led by Martin Luther King, Jr.,* and Ralph Abernathy,* both Baptist ministers. In 1957 they started the Southern Christian Leadership Conference,* a protest organization of black ministers across the South that adhered to a philosophy of nonviolence. The organization's activism culminated in the passing of the Civil Rights Act in 1964, the Voting Rights Act in 1965, and the Civil Rights Act of 1968. The success of the civil rights movement caused the development of a new kind of black leader. Unlike in the King era, this new black leader will no longer be clergy based.

Bibliography. Lincoln C. E., "The Development of Black Religion in America," in *African American Religious Studies*, ed. G. S. Wilmore (Durham: Duke University Press, 1989); Lincoln, C. E., and L. H. Mamiya, *The Black Church in the African-American Experience* (Durham: Duke University Press, 1990); Wilmore, G. S. *Black Religion and Black Radicalism* (Maryknoll, NY: Orbis Books, 1983); Woodson, C. G., *The History of the Negro Church*, 2nd. rev. ed. (Washington, DC: The Associated Publishers, 1972).

Lawrence H. Williams

Black Muslims. The term "Black Muslims" was coined during the late 1950s by the scholar C. Eric Lincoln to refer to the Nation of Islam.* At the time, the term was not unjustified, because the evidence supported the conclusion that most African-American Muslims were in fact members of the Nation of Islam. Over the years, however, the term has become problematic when used in the original sense. The leadership of the Nation of Islam has never formally approved the term, and with the passage of time African-American Muslim groups have become far more numerous than they were in the 1950s. It is now estimated that one-third of the three to four million Muslims in North America are black, but only a small minority of them belong to the Nation of Islam. Moreover, the term "Black Muslim" is disturbing to most Muslims, for whom one's Islamic identity transcends and makes irrelevant one's racial, ethnic, linguistic, sexual, or other identity. As Malcolm X* himself discovered near the end of his life, Islam is a universalist faith.

With these caveats in mind, it is meaningful to use the term "Black Muslim" with regard to certain developments within the African-American community. During the early twentieth century hundreds of thousands of African Americans migrated from southern farms to the industrial cities of the North, only to become bitterly disillusioned by economic difficulties and discrimination. Numerous cults and sectarian groups emerged in response to their despair; some of them had Christian trappings, but others sought to emphasize an African identity for American blacks. These included black nationalist groups, such as Marcus Garvey's* Universal Negro Improvement Association, and sectarian associations that professed affiliation with Islam, such as the Moorish Science Temple* and the Nation of Islam. Affiliation with Islam, the religion of perhaps one-third of the slaves who were brought to this country, served to reestablish ties with Africa and to stigmatize Christianity as the white man's religion.

The African-American Islamic groups have tended to be political, social, and economic, movements as much as religious ones. Because they believe that in a predominantly white society they will never obtain justice, they have stressed themes of separation from white institutions of justice and economics and have striven to achieve self-reliance through hard work and self-discipline. Often they have denied an afterlife and have insisted that salvation consists in the achieving of economic and social goals in this world.

When the Nation of Islam grew to prominence during the 1960s, several other African-American Islamic groups sprang up. Some, like the Ansaar Allah and the Five Percenters, were Islamically inspired, but Sunni Islamic groups did not consider their tenets and practice to accord with authentic Islam. Others, such as the Hanifi Movement, the Islamic Party of North America, the Islamic Brotherhood, Inc., and the Dar ul-Islam, have been accepted by Sunni Muslims as authentic. In addition, when Elijah Muhammad* died in 1975, his son Wallace Deen Muhammad began transforming the Nation of Islam into a Sunni organization, which eventually disbanded so that no barriers would exist between these Muslims and the world Muslim community. In 1977 Louis Farrakhan* led a minority secessionist movement from Wallace Deen Muhammad's group and reestablished the Nation of Islam.

By the end of the century, the term "Black Muslim" has thus become problematic as a meaningful term. Some African-American groups still remain on the fringe of what many Muslims would consider orthodox, whereas a majority are fully accepted into the world community of Islam. The latter do not emphasize the racial factor in their having chosen to embrace Islam and resent the rubric "Black Muslim." Moreover, an increasing number of blacks in the United States are recent Muslim African immigrants, for whom issues of identity are quite different from those that prompted the growth of groups such as the Nation of Islam.

Bibliography. Haddad, Y. Y. and J. I. Smith, *Mission to America* (Gainesville: University Press of Florida, 1993); Haddad, Y. Y., and J. I Smith, *Muslim Communities in North America* (Albany: State University of New York Press, 1994); Lincoln, C. E., *The Black Muslims in America* (Boston: Beacon Press, 1961; rev. ed. 1973); Washington, J. R., Jr., *Black Sects and Cults* (Garden City, NY: Doubleday, 1972); Wilmore, G. S. *Black Religion and Black Radicalism* (Garden City: Doubleday and Company, Inc., 1973).

Vernon Egger

Black Theology. Black theology was an attempt to indigenize theology, making it serve in the struggle for black liberation. In 1966 a split occurred in the civil rights* movement, with the more militant wing taking a position favoring black power. However, Martin Luther King, Jr.,* and leaders of the Southern Christian Leadership Conference,* consisting primarily of southern black ministers, refused to endorse black power, believing that the concept was too nihilistic and negative. King believed that the concept divided the races and therefore was unchristian. However, the National Committee of Black Churchmen (later the National Conference of Black Christians), a caucus of black ministers who served primarily in white denominations, went on record endorsing black power and calling for the development of an accompanying black theology.

Several black scholars undertook the task of developing a new black theology. In 1967 historian Vincent Harding, a lay Mennonite minister, wrote an apology called "Black Power and the American Christ" in which he called black power the judgment of God on Christian America. He argued that historically, American Christianity was not the religion of the Suffering Servant of God, but one of American culture. Rather than demonize Stokely Carmichael and other black power supporters, Americans should view black power as a type of pluralism which provided acceptance for blacks. Likewise, in 1968 Albert Cleage* (later Jaramogi Abebe Agyeman), a Detroit Congregationalist pastor, also took a position favoring black power and began writing a black theology. He fathered a movement that was called black Christian nationalism. Using black icons, he changed the name of his church to the Shrine of the Black Madonna and Child and wrote two books, *The Black Messiah* (1969) and *Black Christian Nationalism* (1972), explaining his position. He compared the contemporary struggle of blacks to that of the ancient Hebrews and that of Jesus and his disciples.

Moving away from the concept of universal love, he contended that Jesus was on the side of black power. But Cleage's work was by no means a systematic study; it primarily consisted of sermons and conference papers.

Black theology really came to maturation under the leadership of James H. Cone,* who wrote *Black Theology and Black Power* (1969). A Union Theological Seminary* professor, Cone labeled traditional theology as a white theology, which was not racially neutral, but on the side of the white status quo. It was not biblically based and was more concerned with theological abstractions such as the theodicy problem. So Cone called for a black theology based upon the Bible, black culture, and liberation. He concluded that God was in the ghetto and fighting on the side of black people. Actually Cone was taking a position that was similar to the one taken by black literary scholars earlier, such as Le Roi Jones (Amiri Baraka) and Don L. Lee (Haki R. Madhubuti), who were members of the black arts movement. They called for overturning so-called universal literary standards in favor of those that were didactic and serving the black struggle. Cone also was taking a position held by earlier black nationalists such as Henry M. Turner* and Marcus M. Garvey.* Turner had argued that "God is a Negro," and Garvey that God needed to be created in the image of black people.

More moderate positions in relation to black theology were taken by other black theologians and philosophers. J. Deotis Roberts wrote *Liberation and Reconciliation* (1971) and argued that there could be no liberation without reconciliation, for reconciliation between whites and blacks was the final stage of liberation. Then William R. Jones wrote *Is God A White Racist?* (1973). A black Unitarian Universalist minister, Jones used a humanocentric theology to investigate the theodicy problem as it related to the black struggle.

In his second work, *A Theology of Black Liberation* (1970), Cone put his black theology into systematic categories. However, critics accused him of building a black theology on the theological discourse of white theologians. Regardless of being called black theology, it was still white theology. In his third book, *The Spirituals and the Blues* (1972), Cone developed an indigenous black theology based on folk tales and folk songs. Cone argued that the spirituals and the blues were concrete and historically important to the black community. He suggested that spirituals were struggles for freedom in this world, not simply in the next. Likewise, blues songs were similar. They came from the depths of black life and survival. For the blues were simply "secular spirituals" that were related to problems caused by the Hayes-Tilden Compromise of 1877, when federal troops were withdrawn from the South, causing open season upon black folks. They related to the separate-but-equal doctrine of 1896 that relegated blacks to a legal status of inferiority. For Cone, the blues reflected the suffering of blacks. A true theology of liberation came only from these materials.

To be sure, in the 1960s and 1970s Cone and other African-American scholars elaborated black theology into a fully developed theology of black liberation.

Black theology also served as a catalyst for the development of other theologies of oppressed groups, including women and people in the Third World.

Bibliography. Cone, J. H., *Black Theology and Black Power* (New York: Seabury Press, 1969); Cone, J. H., *The Spirituals and the Blues* (New York: Seabury Press, 1972); Harding, V., "Black Power and the American Christ," in *Black Theology*, ed. G.S. Wilmore and J. H. Cone (Maryknoll, N.Y.: Orbis Books, 1979); Jones, W. R., *Is God a White Racist?* (Garden City, NY: Anchor Press, 1973).

Lawrence H. Williams

Blackwell, Antoinette Brown. The first American woman to be fully ordained to the Christian ministry, Antoinette Brown Blackwell (1825–1921) was called to the Congregational Church of South Butler, New York, in 1853. As a child in upstate New York, Blackwell felt drawn to the ministry, and she attended Oberlin College in order to pursue the proper course of study. When professors tried to dissuade her from theological studies, she remained in their classes without official recognition. Ironically, Blackwell's desire for ordination was as unpopular among her feminist friends as it was among the male ministers who believed that the apostle Paul commanded women in the church to be silent.

Blackwell's closest friend at Oberlin, feminist and future suffragist leader Lucy Stone, questioned her attachment to the church, which Stone deemed oppressive and hierarchical. Instead, Stone encouraged Blackwell's friendship with proponents of women's rights—including Susan B. Anthony and Elizabeth Cady Stanton*—who came to value Blackwell as a platform speaker while never fully sympathizing with her religious commitments. After her marriage to Samuel Blackwell, Antoinette Brown Blackwell resigned from her Congregational pastorate to concentrate on public speaking, scientific studies, and raising a family.

In later years Blackwell was wary of identifying with any church lest her increasingly liberal convictions be compromised. But in 1878 she applied for membership in the Unitarian Fellowship. Although she had hoped to pastor a church—unlike the situation in the 1850s, there were now almost two hundred ordained women—she could not find a position. Alternatively, Blackwell began writing a series of books, sketching her philosophy of life, that sought to harmonize science with religion. Affirming that God could be experienced through all of the created world—including nature, humanity, and culture, she preached a positive vision of interdependence. By the time of her death, Blackwell's reputation as a trailblazer—standing firm against both the church establishment and its feminist critics—was part of the historical record. Those who followed in her wake celebrated Antoinette Brown Blackwell's life as a testament to women's rights and to the struggle for women's equality.

Bibliography. Cazden, Elizabeth, *Antoinette Brown Blackwell: A Biography* (Old Westbury, NY: Feminist Press, 1983); Stone, Lucy, *Friends and Sisters: Letters between Lucy Stone and Antoinette Brown Blackwell, 1846–93* (Urbana: University of Illinois Press, 1987); Stone, Lucy, *Soul Mates: The Oberlin Correspondence of Lucy Stone and Antoi-*

nette Brown, 1846–1850, ed. Carol Lasser and Marlene Merrill (Oberlin, OH: Oberlin College, 1983).

Diane Winston

Bloody Monday. A name that designates the anti-immigrant and anti-Catholic riots in Louisville, Kentucky, on August 6, 1855. Along with events in Charlestown, Massachusetts, in 1834, and Philadelphia in 1844, the Bloody Monday riots stand among the most explosive evidences of opposition to Catholicism in antebellum America.

At the time of the riots, Louisville was amongst the twelve largest cities in the United States—its population growth reflecting the inflow of Germans and Irish into the nation. In the era after the Monroe Doctrine of 1823 that proclaimed the western hemisphere off-limits to European interference, Catholic allegiance to the Pope was seen as a point of confrontation. American Catholics maintained that they were friendly to national liberties and that they followed the Pope in religious matters only, not political ones.

Their critics maintained that the Pope remained a temporal sovereign ruling over the Papal States that stretched across central Italy. Along with suspicions and distrusts stretching back to the European Reformation of the sixteenth century, these critics also suspected Catholicism in America for its hierarchical structure, for what was then the ''foreign'' language of its worship (Latin), and for its rapid national growth.

Anti-immigrant and anti-Catholic intensity found political expression in the Know-Nothing party of the 1850's. By the time of the riots, Louisville had selected a Know-Nothing, John Barbee, as its mayor. George Prentice, editor of the influential *Louisville Journal*, was a former Whig who had turned Know-Nothing in his sympathies. His editorials the week before the civic eruptions were full of inflammatory commentary and election advice for his readers: ''Rally to put down an organization of . . . priests and other papists, who aim by secret oaths and horrid midnight plottings, to sap the foundations of all our political edifices'' (*Louisville Journal,* August 5, 1855).

The riots began when attempts were made on election day, August 6, to keep naturalized immigrant citizens from voting. By the day's end, over twenty people were dead from violence in the streets, most of them Irish immigrants from a residence known as Quinn's Row in the city's near West End. The recently dedicated Cathedral of the Assumption (1852) was threatened but spared. Catholic Bishop Martin John Spalding pleaded for the people to turn away from ''bloody feuds and civic strife'' as did a committee of Protestant ministers. Peace was soon restored, but some hundreds of immigrants are believed to have moved away from the city.

Bibliography. Crews, Clyde F., *An American Holy Land* (Wilmington: Michael Glazier Press, 1987); McGann, Agnes Geralding, *Nativism in Kentucky to 1860* (Washington:

Catholic University of American Press, 1944); Yater, George, *Two Hundred Years at the Falls of the Ohio* (Louisville: Pinaire, 1987).

Clyde F. Crews

The Bloudy Tenent of Persecution. Polemical work by New England separatist Roger Williams* presenting his arguments for religious liberty and against religious theocracy. The foil of Williams's work was Boston pastor and Puritan divine John Cotton. The book was published in London in 1644, where Williams had gone to secure a charter for the colony of Rhode Island.

Educated at Cambridge and ordained in the Church of England, Williams moved through Puritanism and separatism to a radical separatism that embraced religious liberty through the separation of church and state.* From the time he arrived in Boston in 1631, Williams consistently advocated a more complete separation for the churches of New England: complete separation from the corrupt Church of England and complete separation from the civil government. The crux of Williams's argument was that the civil magistrate had authority to enforce only the second table of the law (the last six commandments) but no authority over the first table (the four commandments that govern a person's relationship to God). Governance of this realm belongs to conscience alone.

The Bloudy Tenent of Persecution was Williams's most complete and forceful statement of his views on liberty of conscience. The work has three prefaces: the first very general, the second addressed to the houses of Parliament, and the third addressed to "Every Courteous Reader." Williams then began the work by juxtaposing a letter supposedly written by an Anabaptist being held in Newgate Prison and a response to said letter written by John Cotton. The book proper is posed as a dialogue between "Peace" (arguing Cotton's perspective as those who would keep the peace at the cost of conscience) and "Truth" (representing Williams's perspective that there should be no coercion of conscience). In the first half of the book Peace and Truth discuss the main points of Cotton's response to the Anabaptist letter. In the second half Truth and Peace discuss the document "A Model of Church and Civil Power" from the church at Salem, Massachusetts.

The immediate significance of this work is related to the debate within New England Puritanism regarding the structure of New England society, specifically the relationship between civil government and the church. Still, the essence of Williams's argument for separation, that the most infamous persecution is that against the cause of conscience, had far-reaching implications. First, early Baptists* in the colonies were deeply influenced by Williams' ideas and made religious liberty the central tenet of Baptist identity. Second, when the U.S. Constitution was being written (almost one hundred years after his death), it was Williams's vision for society that became the constitutional vision.

Bibliography. Gaustad, E. S., *Liberty of Conscience: Roger Williams in America* (Grand Rapids, MI: Eerdmans, 1991); Miller, Perry, *Roger Williams: His Contribution to Amer-*

ican Culture (New York: Atheneum, 1962); Williams, Roger, *Complete Writings* (New York: Russell and Russell, 1963).

Andrew Pratt

Bogard, Benjamin Marcus. Benjamin Bogard (1868–1951) was involved in the ''anti–corresponding secretary'' controversy at the annual meeting of the Arkansas Baptist State convention held in Paragould in 1901. Bogard and those in sympathy with him asserted that even though it had been present in the state convention for twenty years, the position of corresponding secretary was leading to greater centralization and less autonomy for local churches. Their opposition was based on Landmarkism,* which emphasizes the absolute primacy of local church autonomy. Bogard was successful in having the Executive Board report, which included the reelection of the corresponding secretary, sent back to the Executive Committee for revision, but a revised report was later accepted that did not in any way accede to Landmark demands. When the effort to reform the state convention according to Landmark thought and practice proved unsuccessful, Bogard led in the formation of the General Association of Baptist Churches in 1902. Three years later the General Association merged with the Baptist Missionary Association* (Texas) and several other small Landmark groups. The General Association changed its name to the American Baptist Association* (ABA) in 1924. Bogard also mounted an unsuccessful attempt to institute Landmarkism in the Southern Baptist Convention.*

Born on March 9, 1868, near Elizabethtown, Kentucky, Bogard was the son of Nancy and M. L. Bogard. He attended college in Georgetown, Kentucky, and Bethel College, Russellville, Kentucky. He married Linnie Onida Meacham Owen on August 18, 1891. Bogard was a pastor in Kentucky and Missouri before being called to First Baptist Church, Searcy, Arkansas, in 1899. He was the author of two books: *Pillars of Orthodoxy, or, Defenders of the Faith* (1901) and *The Baptist Way-Book: A Manual Designed for Use in Baptist Churches* (1945); founded the Sunday school literature arm of the ABA; served as editor of the *Missionary Baptist Searchlight*; was a pioneer radio minister in Arkansas; and was founder and president of the Missionary Baptist Seminary. In 1920 Bogard became pastor of Antioch Missionary Baptist Church, Little Rock, where he remained for twenty-seven years. Bogard died May 29, 1951, in Little Rock, Arkansas.

Bibliography. Hinson, E. G., *A History of Baptists in Arkansas* (Little Rock, Arkansas State Convention, 1979).

Andrew Pratt

Bowne, Borden Parker. Born during the bleak winter of 1847, on January 14, Bowne spent his boyhood on the family farm near Leonardville, New Jersey. At seventeen he went to live with friends in Brooklyn and three years later matriculated at New York University, from which he graduated Phi Beta Kappa and valedictorian of his class in 1871. Having been licensed to preach in 1867, he entered the New York East Conference of the Methodist Episcopal Church in 1872 and was ordained deacon. After one year at the church in Whitestone, Long Island, he departed for study and travel in Europe. Bowne was called to Boston University in 1876, and remained there until his death on April 1, 1910.

Six years before his death, two actions were brought against Bowne; a third was instituted in 1908—all initiated by a fellow Methodist minister, George A. Cooke. Of these, there is no substantive record of the first and third set of charges, although we know that the second set of allegations were introduced after the first action was unsuccessful, and that the Conference unanimously refused to entertain the third action. It was reported that the stenographic report of the trial for the second set of charges would make a book of two hundred forty pages; but the transcript is missing. The transcript was available eighteen years after the trial when portions of it were excerpted for an article in *The Methodist Review*. Those excerpts are the *only* basis for any reconstruction of the trial and the Conference's decision.

Overall Bowne was charged with teaching doctrines which are contrary to the Methodist Episcopal Church's Articles of Religion and doctrines which are contrary to the established standards of the Methodist Episcopal Church. Specifically, it was alleged: (1) that Bowne denied the doctrine of the Trinity and the moral attributes of the Deity as these are described in the first and fourth Articles of Religion; (2) that his teachings on miracles tended to weaken if not destroy faith in large portions of the Old and New Testaments, and that his views on the inspiration of the Bible contradict both the Bible and the fifth Article of Religion; (3) that he repudiated penal and substitutionary theories of the Atonement; (4) that he embraced universal salvation, and rejected the future punishment of the wicked and reward of the righteous; and (5) finally that his teaching on the Christian life did not represent the views of the Methodist Episcopal Church.

A careful review of such evidence as there is, which includes Bowne's publications, suggests: (1) that while Bowne's writings accentuated the unity of God, he insisted that this emphasis was sponsored by a commitment to make it impossible to think of God at all except by thinking at once of Father, Son, and Spirit; (2) that Bowne repudiated biblical literalism and advocated instead the view that the truth of revelation is not truth *about* God but encounter with the very God himself, and that methodological issues associated with hermeneutics were his principal concern, neither of which is at variance with the fifth Article of Religion; (3) that Bowne did reject substitution and ransom Atonement theories in favor of simply becoming "disciples of our Lord, trusting in his promises and the Father whom he revealed . . . (with which) we shall receive all the benefits of the Savior's work without any theory . . . (for) without this discipleship we are lost, whatever our theory"; (4) that there is no direct reference in any of Bowne's writings, cited in the allegation as proof, to universalism or impersonally conceived divine sovereignty; and (5) that the citations from Bowne's *Theism* and *The Christian Life* only show that he advanced what is essentially an evolutionary view of Christian experience.

While Bowne was surely in advance of the popular theological constructions of his own time, he was clearly within traditional limits at four of the five points on which he stood accused. He could have been challenged more forcefully on the doctrine of Atonement; but his innocence overall and his acquittal appears to have been warranted. He was plainly a liberal churchman and a forward-thinking theologian; and while these traits in and of themselves have often been taken to be sufficient reason for accusations of heresy, that claim is far from demonstrated fact in the case of Bowne, who is the most recent American Methodist to have been subjected to this allegation.

Bibliography. Bowne's principal works include *The Atonement* (Cincinnati: Curts and Jennings, 1989); *The Christian Revelation* (Cincinnati: Jennings and Pye, 1900); *Studies in the Christian Life* (Boston: Christian Witness, 1900); *Theism* (New York and Cincinnati: American Book Co., 1902). See also Buckley, James M., "The Acquittal of Professor Bowne," *The Christian Advocate* lxxix (April 14, 1904): 571–573; McConnell, Francis John, *Borden Parker Bowne: His Life and His Philosophy* (New York: Abingdon Press, 1929); Smith, Harmon L., "Borden Parker Bowne: Heresy at Boston," in *American Religious Heretics*, ed. George H. Shriver (Nashville–New York: Abingdon Press, 1966).

Harmon L. Smith

Boyd, Malcolm. Since his parents divorced shortly after his birth in Buffalo, New York, on June 8, 1923, Malcolm Boyd spent most of his formative years with his mother in Connecticut. He majored in journalism at the University of Arizona (1944) and moved to Hollywood, soon gaining some success as a television and motion-picture executive. But even the presidency of the TV Producers Association could not fill his inner needs, and by 1951 he decided to study for the ministry. Graduating from Church Divinity School of the Pacific in 1954, Boyd studied at Oxford during the following year and obtained an S.T.M. in 1956 under the tutelage of Reinhold Niebuhr at Union Theological Seminary.* After ordination as an Episcopal priest in 1955, he served as rector of a church in Indianapolis, Indiana. There, between 1957 and 1959, he said that he became more sharply aware of racial tensions that festered in urban centers. Naming other influences in his increasingly restive outlook, Boyd cited a Church of England slum mission in Sheffield and a summer's experience as a worker-priest at Taizé, France.

Continuing the old Social Gospel* impulses, Boyd represented in clerical garb much of the unrest voiced in the turbulent 1960s. He deliberately embraced the label of "secular clergyman" and strove to shock people out of their complacency while ministering to an alienated generation. During stints as college chaplain (Colorado State University, 1959–1961; Wayne State University, 1961–1965), he tried to reach students by going to their favorite meeting places, especially coffeehouses, instead of just inviting them to church. This avant-garde approach was too brashly modern for conventional church leaders, and Boyd had difficulty with various bishops until he found refuge in national church bureaucracy. In 1965 he became a field representative of the Episcopal agency concerned with cultural and racial unity. After placement as resident fellow at Yale in 1968, he functioned as something like a chaplain-at-large to American colleges, lecturing on hundreds of campuses over the years.

One of Boyd's strongest convictions was that the church had to break out of its self-satisfied ghetto and take its place on the battlefront of contemporary causes. He demonstrated that impulse by participating in freedom rides, voter-registration campaigns, and civil rights* protests. Since he thought that some of the best sermons were conveyed through novels and theater, he wrote several plays about racial prejudice, with *Boy* and *Study in Color* making the greatest impact. In another departure he stood on the steps of Washington's National Cathedral in 1966, reading prayers with guitar accompaniment. This style temporarily made him a pop star, culminating at the hungry i nightclub in California. Those who criticized Boyd said that he trivialized sacred matters. Even granting a passion to connect with people on urgent issues, his manner was just too precious, a pose of being hippier-than-thou. His glib populism did its thinking in slogans, they charged, its speaking in clichés.

In 1976 Boyd added another feature to an already-controversial career by revealing publicly that he was gay. Since then he has written much on the question of homosexuality and on its legitimacy among the clergy and in society at large. He is still active in his seventies; his current office associated with the Episcopal Peace Fellowship is located in Santa Monica, California.

Bibliography. Boyd has written more than twenty books and plays. Among his most popular and self-revelatory are *Are You Running with Me, Jesus? Prayers* (New York: Holt, Rinehart and Winston, 1965); *As I Live and Breathe: Stages of an Autobiography* (New York: Random House, 1970); *Gay Priest: An Inner Journey* (New York: St. Martin's Press, 1986); *Human like Me, Jesus: Prayers with Notes on the Humanistic Revolution* (New York: Simon and Schuster, 1971).

Henry Warner Bowden

Branch Davidians. The Branch Davidians are a religious sect that gained worldwide attention in February 1993 when their compound outside of Waco, Texas, was invaded by over one hundred heavily armed agents of the Bureau of Alcohol, Tobacco, and Firearms (ATF) in search of suspected illegal weapons. The Branch Davidians resisted with automatic weapons, and the ensuing battle left four ATF agents and six Branch Davidians dead. There followed a fifty-one-day siege in which efforts to secure a peaceful surrender failed. On April 19 an effort was made to drive them out with tear gas, but they responded by igniting the compound. The resulting fire consumed the compound and sixty-one of its inhabitants, including seventeen children.

The original Davidians were organized in 1929 by Victor T. Houteff. An immigrant from Bulgaria, he joined the Seventh-Day Adventist Church but broke with it when it branded some of his teachings as heretical. He and his followers moved in 1935 from California to an isolated area outside of Waco, Texas, to await Christ's Second Coming.

After Houteff's death in 1955, his widow, Florence, assumed leadership. Her failed prophecy that Christ's Second Coming would occur on April 22, 1959, led to the fracturing of the Davidian community but not to the death of the dream that had originally prompted it. The community split into a number of Davidian communities that can be found today around the world.

One of the splinter groups, named the Branch Davidians, led by Benjamin Roden, remained near Waco. After his death in 1978 there was a struggle for leadership between his widow, Lois, and his son, George. Lois, seeking to strengthen her leadership claim, described a vision in which the femininity of the Holy Spirit was revealed to her. In 1981 a young man from east Texas named Vernon Howell joined the group. Mrs. Roden was immediately attracted to his charismatic persona and his ability to memorize and quote the Scriptures. There is strong evidence that Howell became her consort as she groomed him as her successor. The struggle between George Roden and Howell took many forms, including gun fights and court battles. In 1988 Howell took control of Mt. Carmel and the Branch Davidians.

Howell's leadership soon took on new dimensions. He renamed himself David Koresh, after Israel's King David and Persia's King Cyrus. He married a four-teen-year-old member of the community and began promoting the importance of producing offspring from his divine seed. All the women of the compound were claimed by Koresh, and several children were born to these relationships. Some of the Branch Davidians began frequenting gun shows and collecting weapons. Charges of child abuse and possession of an illegal arms cache began to be made. These charges and ensuing investigations led to the ATF invasion of February 1993. The publicity surrounding this event focused attention not only on this little-known religious group but also on the question of how the government should relate to dissident groups, religious and otherwise, in a free society.

Bibliography. Bailey, Brad and Bob Darden, *Mad Man in Waco* (Waco, TX: WRS Publishing, 1993); Lewis, James R. ed., *From the Ashes: Making Sense of Waco* (London: Rowman and Littlefield, 1994); Tabor, James D., and Eugene V. Gallagher, *Why Waco? Cults and the Battle for Religious Freedom in America* (Berkeley: University of California Press, 1995); Wright, Stuart A., ed., *Armageddon in Waco* (Chicago: University of Chicago Press, 1995).

Daniel B. McGee

Briggs, Charles Augustus. Charles Augustus Briggs (1841–1913) was perhaps the foremost Presbyterian advocate of the historical-critical method of biblical study in the late nineteenth century. He was frequently at the center of storms of controversy about the character of biblical authority and the nature of the biblical writings.

Briggs was cofounder and coeditor of the *Presbyterian Review*, a scholarly journal that attempted to bridge the divide between conservatives and liberals in the Presbyterian Church by presenting both sides on various issues. With Archibald Alexander Hodge* of Princeton Seminary, Briggs, having begun his career as a professor at Union Theological Seminary* in New York, tried to use the journal to present fairly the divergent views of the two institutions, which represented the two camps in Presbyterianism. The *Presbyterian Review* soon became one of the leading theological journals in the United States, but the tensions between the two sides (and between Briggs and his coeditors) continued to build. The question of revision of the Westminster Confession of Faith finally provided the straw that broke the camel's back, and harsh disagreements between Briggs and coeditor B. B. Warfield* led the Union Seminary faculty to discontinue the *Review*.

Briggs's views on Scripture continued to arouse opposition, particularly through his inaugural address when he was named the Edward Robinson Professor of Biblical Theology in 1890. In the address Briggs rejected the concept of the inerrancy of the biblical materials and advocated a reasonable approach to biblical study using the historical-critical method. The address created storms of protest, and a number of presbyteries pushed for action against Briggs.

The Presbytery of New York condemned certain views held by Briggs, and the General Assembly of 1891 rejected his new appointment. In defiance of the assembly's veto, the seminary's Board of Directors supported Briggs and voted to separate the seminary from the Presbyterian Church's authority in 1892. In addition, the Presbytery of New York, given the responsibility of preparing the formal proceedings against Briggs, heard his arguments and explanations and voted to dismiss the case. Pushed to retry the case, the Presbytery of New York formally acquitted Briggs in 1893.

That was not the end of the battle, however, for those unsatisfied with the decision of the presbytery brought the case again to the General Assembly of 1893. After much debate and political maneuvering, the assembly voted to suspend Briggs from the Presbyterian ministry for heretical beliefs. Briggs retained his post at Union and eventually was ordained by the Episcopal Church.

Bibliography. Handy, Robert T., *A History of Union Theological Seminary in New York* (New York: Columbia University Press, 1987); Loetscher, Lefferts A., *The Broadening Church: A Study of Theological Issues in the Presbyterian Church since 1869* (Philadelphia: University of Pennsylvania Press, 1954); Shriver, George H., ed., *American Religious Heretics: Formal and Informal Trials* (Nashville: Abingdon Press, 1966).

Stephen R. Graham

Broadman Commentary Controversy. The Broadman Commentary controversy erupted among Southern Baptists in 1969–1971 over a commentary on Genesis in The Broadman Bible Commentary series, published by the denomination's official publishing house. G. Henton Davies, author of the Genesis portion of the commentary and an English Baptist, was charged with a liberal interpretation of Genesis, specifically Genesis 22:1–19, God's call to Abraham to sacrifice Isaac. Davies insisted that God would not have made such a demand upon Abraham.

Opposition to the commentary was led by Ross Edwards, editor of the *Word and Way*, a Baptist paper in Missouri, and by M. O. Owens, a pastor in North Carolina. Critics charged the Sunday School Board and Broadman Press with doctrinal laxity and lack of respect for the authority of the Bible. Supporters rushed to support Broadman and to encourage freedom of inquiry.

In 1970 Edwards and several former presidents of the Southern Baptist Convention* called for an "Affirming the Bible Conference" to precede the annual convention meeting in Denver, Colorado. Messengers to the convention then voted to instruct the Sunday School Board to recall the volume and revise it.

At the 1971 Southern Baptist Convention session in St. Louis, Kenneth Barnette, a messenger from Oklahoma, expressed his displeasure over the Sunday School Board's failure to revise the volume and called for the board to obtain another writer. His motion passed. At the Philadelphia Southern Baptist Convention in 1972, messengers defeated a motion to rewrite the entire series. The Sunday School Board then hired H. Leo Eddleman, the president of New Orleans Baptist Theological Seminary, as a theological editor for the series to ensure its conformity to the theology of conservatives in the Southern Baptist Convention. Clyde T. Francisco, professor of Old Testament interpretation at Southern Baptist Theological Seminary,* was then hired to rewrite the volume.

Bibliography. Fletcher, Jesse C., *The Southern Baptist Convention: A Sesquicentennial History* (Nashville: Broadman and Holman, 1994); Leonard, Bill J., *God's Last and Only Hope: The Fragmentation of the Southern Baptist Convention* (Grand Rapids, MI: Eerdmans, 1990). Shurden, Walter B., *Not a Silent People: Controversies That Have Shaped Southern Baptists* (Nashville: Broadman Press, 1972).

Robert N. Nash, Jr.

Brownson, Orestes Augustus. Orestes Augustus Brownson (September 16, 1803–April 17, 1876) was a New England–born writer and editor who ran a gamut of theological views before his admission to the Catholic Church in 1844. Strongly influenced by Methodism* in his youth, Brownson served ministerial roles at times among the Presbyterians, Universalists, and Unitarians. He was influenced in particular by the writings of William Ellery Channing and was for a time in the mid-1830s a member of Ralph Waldo Emerson's circle, the Transcendentalist Club. He disputed some thinkers in that movement, though, as being too individualistic and subjective.

Brownson was founding editor of the *Boston Quarterly Review* in 1838 and after its closing in 1842 wrote for the *Democratic Review*. In 1844 he began publication of his own review, *Brownson's Quarterly*. His political views were summarized in his 1866 work *The American Republic*. Other titles by Brownson include *New Views of Christianity: Society and the Church* (1836) and *The Convert* (1857).

In 1840 Brownson's long essay *The Laboring Classes* established his name among those considered by many to be socially radical. Yet, he increasingly maintained that social justice was to be attained not only through political solidarity, but spiritual solidarity as well. This position in part led him to adherence, at the age of forty-one, to the Catholic Church.

Within the fold of American Catholicism, Brownson became perhaps the best-known, most outspoken lay intellectual of his age. But within that tradition, too, he remained a controversial figure. He quarreled with the developmental views of another famous convert of his era, John Henry Newman. He urged immigrant Catholics to embrace American institutions but also maintained that the pope was supreme not only in spiritual matters, but at times in temporal matters touching on the spiritual as well. This position put him at odds with more liberal Catholics of midcentury. After Pope Pius IX's 1864 Syllabus of Errors, Brownson became increasingly theologically conservative. Near his life's end, he published *Essay in Refutation of Atheism*. He died in Detroit in 1876 and was buried at the University of Notre Dame.

Bibliography. Carey, Patrick W., ed., *Orestes A. Brownson: Selected Writings* (New York: Paulist Press, 1991); Maynard, Theodore, *Orestes Brownson: Yankee, Radical, Catholic* (New York: Macmillan, 1943); Ryan, Thomas, *Orestes A. Brownson: A Definitive Biography* (Huntington, IN: Our Sunday Visitor Press, 1976); Schlesinger, Arthur, Jr., *A Pilgrim's Progress: Orestes A. Brownson* (Boston: Little, Brown and Co., 1966).

Clyde F. Crews

Bryan, William Jennings. Politician and antievolutionary fundamentalist leader William Jennings Bryan (1860–1925) was born and raised in Illinois in a broadly evangelical home. Educated at Illinois College and Union Law College (Chicago), he practiced as an attorney before entering politics. Bryan served in the House of Representatives, ran three times as the Democratic candidate for president of the United States, and was secretary of state under Woodrow Wilson from 1913 to 1915.

In the wake of World War I, Bryan became convinced that the war and German military atrocities were rooted in a Darwinist "might-makes-right" philosophy. Such a philosophy, he insisted, was diametrically opposed to Christianity and threatened all efforts at moral and economic reform and social progress. Bryan, the best-known layman in the Presbyterian Church and a seasoned speaker on the Chautauqua lecture circuit, thus took the lead in fundamentalist opposition to the teaching of biological evolution in public schools. In lectures and print he lambasted evolutionary thought, warning that Darwinism was undermining Christian civilization. Taking the battle to his church, he ran for moderator of the General Assembly of the Presbyterian Church in 1923 and tried unsuccessfully to convince that assembly to forbid funding to any Presbyterian school that taught biological evolution. The assembly adopted a milder statement allowing room for the teaching of theistic evolution.

Bryan's efforts came to a head in the summer of 1925 at the trial of John T. Scopes* in Dayton, Tennessee. Scopes, a high-school science teacher, was accused of violating the state's law prohibiting the teaching of biological evolution in the public schools. At the trial, which became a national spectacle, Bryan, serving as counsel for the prosecution, squared off against the prominent agnostic lawyer, Clarence Darrow.* At the height of the trial Darrow called Bryan as a witness for the defense, and Bryan, revealing his shallow background in scientific and religious subjects, withered under Darrow's examination. Though Scopes was convicted (the ruling was later overturned on a technicality), Bryan's performance and Dayton's rural setting left the widespread impression that fundamentalism was a rural, anti-intellectualistic phenomenon. Bryan's death five days after the trial left interdenominational fundamentalism without a clear, visible leader, contributing to the decline of the movement in the following years. **Bibliography.** Coletta, Paolo E., *William Jennings Bryan*, 3 vols. (Lincoln: University of Nebraska Press, 1964–1969); Levine, Lawrence, *Defender of the Faith: William Jennings Bryan, the Last Decade, 1915–1925* (New York: Oxford University Press, 1965); Marsden, George M., *Fundamentalism and American Culture: The Shaping of Twentieth-Century Evangelicalism, 1870–1925* (New York: Oxford University Press, 1980).

Bradley J. Longfield

Buchman, Frank N. Frank N. Buchman (1878–1961) was the founder of so-called Buchmanism,* which he successively named "a First Century Christian Fellowship," then "the Oxford Group," and finally "Moral Re-Armament" (MRA). Born at Pennsburg, Pennsylvania, on June 4, 1878, Buchman grew up in a traditionally pietistic Lutheran home. He studied for the ministry at the Lutheran Theological Seminary at Philadelphia (Mt. Airy), graduating in 1902. After a year of study abroad, spent mostly at Cambridge and working with the Inner Mission in Germany, he became a parish pastor at Overbrook, Pennsylvania. From 1905 to 1908 he directed a hospice for young men in Philadelphia. In June 1908 he attended a Keswick Conference in England, where he became convicted of sin and had a vision of Christ; he was now convinced that he was called to minister to a parish much broader than the ones he had previously served. From 1909 to 1915 he served as YMCA student secretary at Pennsylvania State College, where he began to implement the evangelistic techniques that would make him famous. After spending a year with missionaries in India, Korea, and Japan, he became extension lecturer in personal evangelism at Hartford Seminary. After several years of friction with the faculty, who found his piety and scholarship simplistic, he left Hartford in 1922. Thereafter he was essentially an independent evangelist, heading up a movement on several eastern campuses that was soon dubbed "Buchmanism." His ambitions were global from an early date; the first "House Party" was held in China in 1918. In the early 1920s he worked mostly on American campuses, although contacts had already been made in England and other countries. After 1927 the center of Buchman's operations shifted to England, from which evangelistic campaigns were launched in Canada, the United States, Holland, South Africa, and other countries. Buchman retained personal control of the ensuing movement, refusing to enroll "members" and claiming that he never asked for money. In spite of this, he lived well, depending on the generosity of wealthy friends and supporters. Never married, he long lived a peripatetic life; in later years he spent much of his time at his London headquarters or at the MRA center at Caux, Switzerland. He died on August 6, 1961, at Freudenstadt, Germany.

Bibliography. Lean, Garth, *On the Tail of a Comet: The Life of Frank Buchman* (Colorado Springs: Helmers and Howard, 1988).

Donald L. Huber

Buchmanism. A parachurch movement begun by Frank N. Buchman,* a former Lutheran pastor and YMCA student secretary. Buchman experienced a vision of Christ while attending a Keswick Conference in England in 1908; his subsequent evangelistic efforts were idiosyncratic but successful. Beginning in the early 1920s he worked independently of the YMCA on college campuses, developing the techniques that would become the trademarks of "Buchmanism": informal "House Parties" for sharing both religious insights and a good time, the practice of personal meditation (which he called "Quiet Time"), the interpretation through the group of God's will for each individual ("Guidance"), and the public confession of sins ("Sharing"). The object was to challenge young men and women to live "the Changed Life," which was said to be reached through a process of "confidence, confession, conviction, conversion, and continuance" ("the Five C's"). After conversion, one would live according to "the Four Absolutes": perfect honesty, purity, unselfishness, and love.

Buchmanism was controversial from the outset. Critics argued that the movement was doctrinally vapid, ethically naïve, psychologically dangerous, and too centered on the charismatic personality of "Frank," as Buchman was known to his followers. The irony of Buchman's penchant for lavish living while leading a movement that for a while called itself "a First Century Christian Fellowship" was obvious. Church leaders and college officials were concerned about the graphic confession of sexual sins during "Sharing." The practice of "Guidance" seemed manipulative to many. On the other hand, Buchman had strong supporters, such as the Reverend Samuel M. Shoemaker, Jr., rector of Calvary Episcopal Church in New York City, whose church was practically the headquarters of the movement for many years.

The peripatetic Buchman soon took his movement overseas. By the late 1920s he had followers at Oxford University; beginning in 1928 the movement was renamed "the Oxford Group," a name that Buchman seems to have liked both because of its elite cachet and because it implied an international perspective that he was anxious to claim.

Controversy continued to dog the movement during its Oxford phase. In addition to religious concerns, Buchman's perceived political radicalism became an issue. In 1936 Buchman told an interviewer:

> I thank heaven for a man like Adolf Hitler, who built a front line of defense against the Anti-Christ of Communism. Think what it would mean to the world if Hitler surrendered to the control of God. Or Mussolini. Or any dictator. Through such a man God could control a nation overnight and solve every last bewildering problem.

Although his more generous critics conceded that Buchman was thereby exposing his political naïveté more than any strong attachment to fascism, this statement continued to be used against the movement for many years.

As his international emphasis grew, Buchman tended to downplay the specifically Christian elements of the Oxford Group. He believed that the spiritual maxims that he was advocating were equally applicable to the devotees of all religions. By the late 1930s he usually spoke of the group's "ideology," the core of which was its increasingly anti-Communist perspective. In line with this change, which many Christian critics saw as a move toward religious syncretism, Buchman renamed the movement again. After 1938 it became widely known as "Moral Re-Armament" (MRA) and began to concentrate on larger conferences that were held at its centers at Mackinac Island, Los Angeles, and Caux, Switzerland. Just before and after World War II, several World Assemblies for Moral Re-Armament were held at Caux and elsewhere that for a time attracted national leaders as well as Oxford Group faithful from the four corners of the globe.

Although written off by many of its critics as a spent force even before the death of Buchman in 1961, Buchmanism in the form of MRA has continued to appeal to many. Sympathetic observers have attributed this to its idealism, to its nondogmatic emotional and moralistic messages, and to the fact that many persons have experienced significant betterment of their personal lives as a result of their involvement. (Related to the last point is the positive role the movement played in the early history of Alcoholics Anonymous.) Critics have continued to challenge its religious syncretism, its political naïveté, its penchant for elitism, its frequent exaggeration of its impact on individuals and nations, and its lack of accountability to its followers (leadership has resided in a self-perpetuating oligarchy of full-time workers and their wealthy supporters).

Bibliography. Clark, Walter H., *The Oxford Group: Its History and Significance* (New York: Bookman Associates, 1951); Lean, Garth, *On the Tail of a Comet: The Life of Frank Buchman* (Colorado Springs: Helmers and Howard, 1988); Williamson, Geoffrey, *Inside Buchmanism: An Independent Inquiry into the Oxford Group Movement and Moral Re-armament* (New York: Philosophical Library, 1955).

Donald L. Huber

Burroughs, Nannie Helen. Nannie Helen Burroughs (1879–1961) was perhaps the most outstanding African-American female Baptist leader during the first six decades of the twentieth century. She waged a life-long struggle for women's rights within the male-clergy–dominated leadership of the National Baptist Convention (NBC). Almost through her efforts alone the Women's Convention of the NBC was formed in 1900, and in 1909 the National Training School for

Women and Girls was founded in Washington, D.C. But the Women's Convention remained an auxiliary of the NBC, with no voting privileges in the NBC at large. Although Burroughs had been the primary force behind organizing the National Training School, the NBC attempted to bring it under its control, along with the Women's Convention. The situation led to a battle between the male-dominated NBC and the Women's Convention, and between the National Training School, Burroughs, and the NBC. The struggle was not only between religious organizations within the NBC, but also was related to sexism.

In 1900 Burroughs gave a speech, "How the Sisters Are Hindered from Helping," at the annual meeting of the NBC in Richmond, Virginia, that brought her to national prominence. The speech also registered what Evelyn Brooks Higginbotham has called "the righteous discontent of women in the black Baptist church." Although women were the backbone of most local Baptist churches, they had no voice or organization. Burroughs's speech provided the impetus for the founding of the Women's Convention that same year. She served as corresponding secretary from 1900 to 1948 and president from 1948 until her death in May 1961.

Burroughs was born on May 2, 1879, in Orange, Virginia. Moving to Washington, D.C., at an early age, she graduated from Colored High School and was an active member of the Nineteenth Street Baptist Church. Then she served as bookkeeper and editorial secretary to Lewis G. Jordon, corresponding secretary of the NBC Foreign Mission Board in Louisville, Kentucky. It was while working for the Foreign Mission Board that she made the profound speech leading to the founding of the Women's Convention, which became the largest organization of African-American women in the United States, with 1.5 million members by 1907.

Undoubtedly, Burroughs's greatest work was the founding of the National Training School in 1909. In its first twenty-five years the school had over two thousand students. Using primarily the domestic science philosophy, the school included both high school and junior college. It trained missionaries and taught secretarial skills and black history. By 1938 the school was worth $200,000.

But a controversy in relation to control by the NBC developed from the very beginning. The school had been financially successful because of the personal fund-raising efforts of Burroughs, and the school's trustee board had been chartered as an independent entity. By 1916 the attempted takeover also related to the controversy over the ownership of the NBC publishing house, which led to a lawsuit and the splitting of the NBC in 1915. Calling for consolidation of all its boards, including the Women's Convention and the National Training School, the NBC became incorporated. In 1916 an audit of the school's records showed financial discrepancies. However, the charges were later proven false. The situation led to a dispute between the NBC and the school that lasted for thirty years. From 1938 to 1947 NBC and Women's Convention support were completely withdrawn from the school.

In her 1938 address to the Women's Convention, Burroughs responded by referring to the NBC as a "man's organization." She stated that black Baptist women deserved a parallel national organization with equal powers, not the present and unequal arrangement where women would have no vote or control over the Training School. For these reasons, she refused to relent. According to a biographer, Opal V. Easter, Burroughs had not only worked hard for the school, but she often called it "God's School." It was the only school in the country operated by black women, and perhaps the only one in the world. In 1939 there was a concerted effort by the NBC leadership to get Burroughs voted out of the Women's Convention, but the women refused to cooperate. Finally, peace came in 1941 with the election of David V. Jemison as president of the NBC. Today, the school is called the Nannie Helen Burroughs School and is an elementary school. The Howard University School of Divinity has a scholarship named in her honor, which has assisted female students.

Bibliography. Easter, O. P., *Nannie Helen Burroughs* (New York: Garland Publishing, 1995); Hammond, L. H., *In the Vanguard of a Race* (New York: Council of Women for Home Missions and Missionary Education Movement of the United States and Canada, 1922); Higginbotham, E. B., "Burroughs, Nannie Helen," *Black Women in America*, ed. D.C. Hine (Brooklyn, NY: Carlson Publishing, 1993); Lindley, S., " 'Neglected Voices' and Praxis in the Social Gospel," *Journal of Religious Ethics*, Spring 1990.

Lawrence H. Williams

Bushnell, Horace. Known as the "Father of Modern Liberalism" and the "American Schleiermacher," Horace Bushnell (1802–1876) was no stranger to controversy throughout his career. At the same time, he was one of America's most influential theologians.

As a young pastor, Bushnell rejected what he viewed as the overly rationalistic theology that characterized many of his New England peers. He became convinced that religious experience was a more reliable basis for faith than logic, since human modes of communication were seriously limited and unable to convey completely or accurately the depth or nuances of theology.

His theory of language led him to insist that poetic language could often convey truth more fully than rationalistic prose. Bushnell had his first book, *Christian Nurture* (1847), withdrawn by the publisher after it drew a storm of criticism. In contrast to the growing emphasis among many American Christians on the necessity of a dramatic conversion experience, Bushnell instead advocated nurture of children within Christian homes and churches to the point that the young person would never recall a time when he or she was not Christian.

Bushnell's theology was shaped by a mystical experience in 1848 he described as his "spiritual birthday." He believed that he had discovered a fuller gospel that he expressed in *God in Christ*, published in 1849. True knowledge of God, he insisted, came not through rational speculation, but through an experience of God. Bushnell was accused of reviving ancient heresies such as Apollinarianism, Sabellianism, and Eutycheanism, as well as espousing the modern "heresies" of Friedrich Schleiermacher. Bushnell dismissed the charges, saying that his theology was, in fact, more ancient and more true to the theology of the Bible and the early church than the theology of the "dialectical rationalists" who attacked him.

A number of ministers attempted to bring Bushnell up on charges of heresy, but again and again he was exonerated by the Hartford Central Association of the Congregational Church. The flames of controversy were fanned higher by the appearance of *Christ in Theology* in 1851. Many ministers urged action against Bushnell by the General Association, but that body, while rejecting some of Bushnell's ideas, refused to overturn the opinion of the Hartford Central Association. For four consecutive years various groups and associations tried to convince the General Association formally to condemn Bushnell, but each time the polity of the Congregational Church protected Bushnell from censure as long as his local association, Hartford Central, continued to support him.

Though Bushnell was never formally condemned by the Congregational Church, accusations of heresy dogged him throughout his career. He consistently stretched the boundaries of New England Congregational orthodoxy and perplexed opponents by both his theological method and his ideas.

Bibliography. Bushnell, Horace, *Christ in Theology* (Hartford: Brown and Parsons, 1851); Bushnell, Horace, *Christian Nurture* (New York: Scribner's, 1847); Bushnell, Horace, *God in Christ* (New York: Scribner's, 1849); Smith, David L., *Symbolism and Growth: The Religious Thought of Horace Bushnell* (Chico, CA: Scholars Press, 1981); Smith, H. Shelton, ed., *Horace Bushnell* (New York: Oxford University Press, 1965).

Stephen R. Graham

C

Campbell, Thomas and Alexander. Thomas Campbell came to America in May 1807 from Ireland, where he had been a Scotch-Irish Presbyterian minister of an Old Light Anti-burgher Seceder Presbyterian Church. In his new country he assumed preaching responsibilities through the Presbyterian Church in southeast Pennsylvania.

Campbell was soon accused of inviting non-Presbyterians to the Lord's Supper. He withdrew from the presbytery and began preaching independently. In 1809 he and a few others formed the Christian Association of Washington (Pennsylvania), and he published his *Declaration and Address*, one of the seminal documents of the founding years of the movement. In his document the group proclaimed its independence from any established authority, asserting that each person had to think for oneself in religious matters. A return to evangelical Christianity was essential to the reformation of Christianity in America. Using the Bible as the pattern, each person could discover for oneself the essence of Christianity free from confusing human opinions.

While the Campbell family was waiting to join Thomas in America, his son Alexander was studying at the University of Glasgow, Scotland. There he was influenced by a few ministers of the area who urged the establishment of a church on the basis of primitive Christianity. When the family arrived in America in 1809, father and son discovered that they had arrived at the same ideas about the Bible and the church although they had been separated by an ocean.

The Christian Association organized itself into the Brush Run Church, which ordained Alexander to the ministry in 1812. The church was constituted as an autonomous body, observing the Lord's Supper weekly and using the Bible as the definitive authority for faith and practice. When the church began practicing immersion of adult believers, it associated with the Baptist Association in the area, but by 1830 the two groups discontinued their cooperation. The Campbell group became known as "Disciples." The movement quickly spread, with Campbell using the newspaper format to express his ideas, first with the *Christian Baptist* and after 1830 with the *Millennial Harbinger*. Popular journalism contributed greatly to the success of the reforming movement. After Campbell's movement merged with Barton Stone's* "Christians" in 1832, the new church established its place in mainstream American Christianity, between the emotional and rational extremes within Protestantism.

Bibliography. Campbell, Thomas, and Barton Stone, *Declaration and Address and Last Will and Testament of the Springfield Presbytery* (St. Louis: Mission Messenger, 1978); Dunnavant, Anthony L., and Richard L. Harrison, Jr., eds., *Explorations in the Stone-Campbell Traditions* (Nashville: Disciples of Christ Historical Society, 1995); Garrison, Winfred E., *Alexander Campbell's Theology: Its Sources and Historical Setting* (St. Louis: Christian Publishing Company, 1900); Lawrence, Kenneth, ed., *Classic Themes of Disciples Theology* (Fort Worth: Texas Christian University Press, 1986); McAllister, Lester G., and William E. Tucker, *Journey in Faith: A History of the Christian Church (Disciples of Christ)* (St. Louis: Bethany Press, 1975); Toulouse, Mark G., *Joined in Discipleship* (St. Louis: Chalice Press, 1992).

Coleman Markham

Campbell, Will D. Will D. Campbell is best known for his work against racial segregation and racist attitudes within southern Protestantism, specifically among Baptists* of the South. Born in rural Mississippi in 1926 and educated at Wake Forest University (A.B., 1948) and Yale Divinity School (B.D., 1952), Campbell came to prominence in 1954 as director of religious life at the University of Mississippi in the immediate wake of the U.S. Supreme Court's landmark decision in *Brown v. Board of Education*. Campbell was an open and active supporter of integration and the work of Martin Luther King, Jr.* Because of his actions, Campbell had to leave the University of Mississippi, and from 1956 to 1963 he directed the Southern Office of the Department of Racial and Cultural Relations for the National Council of Churches,* located in Nashville, Tennessee.

In 1964 Campbell founded the Committee of Southern Churchmen (CSC) as a vehicle of expression for his unique ministry. The Nashville-based CSC existed as a network of persons who were active in the pursuit of racial justice and social reform. The organization published a journal, *Katallagete: Be Reconciled* from 1975 to 1983. Through the journal, Campbell and the CSC promulgated the idea that Christianity is rooted in a theology of reconciliation (see 2 Corinthians 5:15–20) in which Christians are ambassadors of God's universal reconciliation. Campbell experienced conflict with the institutions of society (religious, academic, and political) because they not only did not embrace reconciliation but actually used their structures to preserve segregation. These experiences led Campbell to be skeptical of institutions and iconoclastic. He has spoken and written not only against racism,* but also against civil religion, the electronic church,* theological education,* liberalism, and abortion.* He advocates for prisoners, farm workers, and the poor. For Campbell, the Christian life consists in doing deeds of compassion for the neighbor.

Campbell lives on a farm near Mt. Juliet, Tennessee, where he whittles, chews "Beechnut," and raises guinea hens. He is the author of several books, including: *Brother to a Dragonfly* (New York: Seabury, 1977), *The Glad River 3* (Holt, Rinehart, and Winston, 1982), and *Forty Acres and a Goat* (San Francisco: Harper and Row, 1986).

Bibliography. Connelly, Thomas L., *Will Campbell and the Soul of the South* (New York: Continuum, 1982); *Encyclopedia of Religion in the South* (Macon: Mercer University Press, 1984).

Andrew Pratt

Capital Punishment. There are twenty-three offenses in the Hebrew Bible—ranging from murder to proselytizing to cursing or hitting a parent—that are punishable by death, but modern Judaism, in its several expressions, repudiates capital punishment. As early as 1959 the Union of American Hebrew Congregations unanimously resolved, "We believe there is no crime for which the taking of human life by society is justified." Later, the Synagogue Council of America declared its opposition "as a matter of principle to the imposition of the death penalty and support of its abolition"; and in 1972, the American Jewish Committee went on record "as favoring the abolition of the death penalty." Contrary to the popular view that Jewish law (as an outgrowth of Torah) favored capital punishment, the rabbis have historically shunned the practice and almost never resorted to it.

On the other hand, chiefly among Christians, capital punishment has a long and sometimes painful history. Some have exhorted the eye-for-an-eye, tooth-for-a-tooth, quid pro quo of the Old Testament; others have cited Jesus' forgiveness of the adulteress in John 8:3–11 and other New Testament admonitions to turn the other cheek and to love and forgive our enemies. There appears to be no undifferentiated biblical theological ground for either unqualified endorsement or unconditional condemnation of capital punishment. Together with just-war theory, capital punishment has been widely believed to be an exception to the general Christian prohibition against killing. While St. Thomas Aquinas put forward a defense of the death penalty, St. Augustine opposed it. Over time the Roman Catholic Church has consistently declined to take a direct stand on this issue, most often on the ground that this is a matter traditionally reserved to the temporal power. A statement from the U.S. Catholic Conference suggests, however, that an abolitionist view is gaining support: "In 1974 . . . the Catholic bishops of the United States declared their opposition to capital punishment. We continue to support this position. . . . Past history . . . shows that the death penalty in its application has been discriminatory with respect to the disadvantaged, the indigent and the socially impoverished. Furthermore, recent data . . . definitely question the effectiveness of the death penalty as a deterrent to crime.'' The Greek Orthodox Church has similarly opposed the death penalty in principle and has denied that religious grounds support it; it has nevertheless recognized that the state may consider the death penalty necessary: "[Capital punishment] was not seen as . . . a desireable thing, but as an unfortunate necessary evil. In no case was it ever argued that capital punishment . . . ever fitted very well with the Christian idea.''

Most Protestant church bodies have called for the abolition of capital punishment. The Disciples of Christ has resolved to "support a permanent moratorium on capital punishment whether undertaken for deterrence or redress''; the Episcopal Church recorded "its conviction that the death penalty ought to be abolished''; and the United Methodist Church "oppose[s] capital punishment and urge[s] its elimination from all criminal codes.'' The United Church of Christ "reaffirm[s] opposition to the death penalty''; the American Baptist convention "recommends the abolition of capital punishment''; the Evangelical Lutheran Church in America "urge[s] the abolition of the death penalty''; and the Presbyterian Church USA declares that "capital punishment cannot be condoned by an interpretation of the Bible based upon the revelation of God's love in Jesus Christ.'' To these voices could be added those of the Church of the Brethren, the American Friends Service Committee, the Mennonite General Conference, the Reformed Church in America, and the Unitarian Universalist Association. The minority view is represented by the Lutheran Church–Missouri Synod, which declares that although "Christians should exert a positive influence on the government's exercise of its responsibility of bearing the sword . . . capital punishment is in accord with the Holy Scriptures and the Lutheran Confessions.'' "Opinion in the Assemblies of God on capital punishment is mixed. However, more people associated with the Assemblies of God probably favor capital punishment for certain types of crimes . . . than those who would oppose capital punishment without reservation. . . . Even though the Bible permits capital punishment . . . restraint should be exercised in imposing the death penalty.''

Religious controversy about capital punishment appears likely to continue; and any temporary moratorium is typically followed by intermittent revival of execution. The arguments of modern religious groups increasingly appeal less to biblical texts and antiquarian philosophical tenets than to civic and cultural concerns for justice, for fairness and equality in application, for the purposes of punishment, and for alternative penalties.

Bibliography. Positions taken by particular religious groups can be obtained from their respective commissions or national headquarters. Additional information is available from the National Council of Churches of Christ in the USA, 475 Riverside Drive, New York, NY 10027. For an overview of the death penalty, see Hugo A. Bedau and Chester Pierce, eds., *Capital Punishment in the United States* (New York: AMS Press, 1976); and Karl Menninger, *The Crime of Punishment* (New York: Viking Press, 1968).

Harmon L. Smith

Capitalism. The seeds of capitalism can be found in the Middle Ages as Europe moved toward a commercial economy. This new economy was more open and less controlled by guilds and feudal lords. By the eighteenth century the classic version of capitalism had emerged. Although it is difficult to provide a precise definition of capitalism because of the many different shapes that it has taken at different times and in different societies, there are some common features that set it apart from socialism or Marxism.

As capitalism's name implies, the primary factor in a capitalist economic system is capital, not labor or skills. In contrast to a "command system" where a single authority, such as government, controls the economy, a free and competitive "market system" determines production and distribution of goods and services. This leads to the dominance of private property rather than any form of communal or public ownership. Pursuit of profits is the appropriate motivation to drive and direct economic activity. Therefore, individual happiness or success in life is generally measured by the amount of wealth amassed. Correspondingly, at the societal level, economic goals and values take precedence over other interests.

The defining defense and description of capitalism is found in Adam Smith's 1776 work *The Wealth of Nations*. Here Smith argued that economic success of some nations is attributed to the freedom and competition in their economic systems. Here each person pursued his or her individual interest, and an "invisible hand" guided these efforts to the service of the common good. In this model Smith seemed to assume an inherent goodness in humanity that mutes any social damage emerging from these selfish acts.

Many historical factors have been identified as contributors to the development of capitalism. The breakdown of the medieval synthesis left all social systems (religious, political, economic, and so on) open for reformulation. Karl Marx pointed to how the emerging role of the machine reduced the value of the laborer in the process of production. Utilitarianism, a dominant value system of this era that promoted the greatest good for the greatest number, was congenial with capitalism's penchant for efficiency and concern for the bottom line. Capitalism's embrace of competition as the ruling order in economics was fostered by social Darwinism's claim that the survival of the fittest was not only the law of nature but also the law of the social order. Then there is the well-known claim of Max Weber in *The Protestant Ethic and the Spirit of Capitalism* (1920) that Calvinism's doctrine of predestination* encouraged people to seek to demonstrate their salvation by working hard and amassing wealth.

The capitalist system and ideology were challenged by the ideologies of socialism and Marxism and the hardships that many suffered in the industrial system. In the United States labor rebelled and organized. The economic depression of the 1930s drove the government into the game of economic planning and the distribution of economic resources. The result is that pure laissez-faire capitalism has been replaced by a mixed economy or what some call "democratic capitalism."

Bibliography. Benne, Robert, *The Ethic of Democratic Capitalism* (Philadelphia: Fortress Press, 1981); Bennett, John C., ed., *Christian Values and Economic Life* (New York: Harper and Brothers, 1954); Friedman, Milton, *Capitalism and Freedom* (Chicago: University of Chicago Press, 1962); Galbraith, John Kenneth, *American Capitalism* (Boston: Houghton Mifflin, 1956); Tawney, R. H., *Religion and the Rise of Capitalism* (New York: Harcourt, Brace and Co., 1926).

Daniel B. McGee

Catholic Anti-Intellectualism. The classic critique of anti-intellectualism in American Catholic life is the 1955 article of Monsignor John Tracy Ellis, "American Catholics and the Intellectual Life," *Thought* 30 (Autumn 1955): 351–88. The article had a profound impact because the author, a professor at the Catholic University of America in Washington, D.C., was the dean of American Catholic historians and was also a highly respected churchman. His article, reprinted in book form the following year with a preface by Bishop (later Cardinal) John J. Wright of Pittsburgh, provoked a major debate in the American Catholic community about the condition of Catholic higher education and Catholic scholarly activity.

Ellis took as his starting point the comment in 1941 of Cambridge political scientist Sir Denis Brogan that "in no Western society is the intellectual prestige of Catholicism lower than in the country where, in such respects as wealth, numbers and strength of organization, it is so powerful." More in sorrow than in anger, Ellis said, "No well-informed American Catholic will attempt to challenge that statement." Ellis attributed American Catholic intellectual backwardness partially to causes beyond the control of American Catholics, such as the general American lack of interest in the intellectual life, the poverty of American Catholic immigrants, and the inhibiting effect of anti-Catholic prejudice in academic circles.

However, Ellis directed most of his fire at his fellow Catholic academics and castigated them for "the absence of a love of scholarship for its own sake" and a tendency to emphasize the value of Catholic schools mainly as an "agency for moral development." He was especially critical of the tendency to multiply the number of small and academically weak Catholic colleges and graduate schools. "The result," he lamented, "is a perpetuation of mediocrity and the draining away from each other of the strength that is necessary if really superior achievements are to be attained." Several other American Catholic scholars such as Thomas F. O'Dea, Walter J. Ong, S.J., Gustave Weigel, S.J., and John J. Cavanaugh, C.S.C., published their own critiques, inaugurating a debate among American Catholics that has continued to the present day.

Ellis was at pains to point out that there was a rich Catholic intellectual heritage that stretched back to ancient times, and for that reason he criticized American Catholic scholars for "what might be called a betrayal of that which is peculiarly their own." Ellis deplored the lack of a Catholic intellectual tradition in the United States. He explained that such a tradition might have developed from such roots as the European-educated members of the colonial Maryland Catholic gentry, or the cultivated émigré clergy who fled to the United States during the French Revolution, or intellectual converts such as Orestes Brownson* and Isaac Hecker* who entered the Catholic Church in the early nineteenth century. Instead, the Catholic Church concentrated its attention on providing a basic education for millions of poor Catholic immigrants. At the Third Plenary Council of Baltimore in 1884, the American bishops committed themselves to establishing a parochial school in every parish within two years, a goal that they were never able to attain but that stretched their limited educational resources to the breaking point. Catholic colleges were usually founded under the auspices of religious communities who prized their autonomy, with the result that there were several hundred small and academically weak Catholic colleges instead of a few large, strong institutions.

In the 1880s and 1890s there were signs of a modest but real intellectual awakening among the American Catholic clergy, the most notable example of which was the establishment of the Catholic University of America in 1887, spearheaded by such progressive prelates as John Ireland, John Keane, and John Lancaster Spalding. However, the papal condemnation of modernism* in 1907 crushed this promising development and dealt a withering blow to Catholic intellectual life both in Europe and in America. Catholic seminaries reverted to the system of rote memorization of Latin theological manuals. At one Catholic graduate school in the 1930s a faculty member disparaged research in favor of "contemplation," since Catholics had already attained true wisdom.

The quality of American Catholic intellectual life improved after World War II due to such factors as the GI Bill of Rights, which enabled millions of American Catholics to obtain a college education for the first time, and a more open intellectual atmosphere in the Catholic Church, especially after Vatican Council II.* In Scripture studies and ethics American Catholic scholars achieved national and international recognition. The quality of Catholic higher education has improved in many respects, but a major concern now is how to achieve academic excellence while still retaining Catholic identity.

Bibliography. Ellis, John Tracy, *American Catholics and the Intellectual Life* (Chicago: Heritage Foundation, 1956); Gannon, Michael V., "Before and after Modernism: The Intellectual Isolation of the American Priest," in *The Catholic Priest in the United States: Historical Investigations,* ed. John Tracy Ellis (Collegeville, MN: Liturgical Press, 1971), 293–384; Gleason, Philip, *Keeping the Faith: American Catholicism: Past and Present* (Notre Dame: University of Notre Dame Press, 1987); "The Intellectual Life: Essays in Memory of John Tracy Ellis," *U.S. Catholic Historian* 13:1–2 (Winter 1995).

Thomas J. Shelley

Celibacy, Roman Catholic Priesthood. Celibacy is an ecclesiastical discipline limiting the ordained ministry to those who are unmarried. While the ancient Eastern churches forbid marriage after ordination and insist that bishops must be celibate, most controversy in America over clerical celibacy has centered on the Latin rite of the Catholic Church, in which ordained men may not marry, and under normal conditions married men may not be ordained as priests.

A spiritual ideal with roots in ancient Christian experience, the expectation of priestly celibacy came to dominate the medieval West, receiving the sanction of the Catholic Church's canon law in the Gregorian Reform (c. 1050–1150). Even so, in the following centuries the rule was challenged by occasional theological debates and the disobedience of many clergymen who continued to take wives or concubines.

Traditional arguments for a celibate clergy have drawn on notions of its apostolic origin, ritual purity, the spiritual superiority of celibacy over marriage, and its value as a sign of the unmarried state in the life to come. A more pragmatic concern is that pastors must be free from domestic concerns to care for their flocks. The Protestant Reformers and their successors, however, denounced vows of celibacy as unbiblical and unnatural, a burden on Christian liberty that leads to sexual temptation. These condemnations have been frequently repeated over the last two centuries in America's Protestant-dominated culture and in recent years have been heard from some Catholic leaders as well.

The Catholic magisterium has vigorously defended clerical celibacy in such documents as Vatican Council II's* *Decree on the Ministry and Life of Priests* (1965) and Pope Paul VI's encyclical *Sacerdotalis Caelibatus* (1967). Yet the Vatican II pronouncement noted that celibacy is not "demanded by the very nature of the priesthood," affirmed the married clergy tradition of the Eastern churches, and provided for married men to be ordained to a restored permanent diaconate. American Catholic opponents of mandatory celibacy were pleased by these conciliar developments. They received additional encouragement when, beginning in 1971, a small number of married clergymen from other Christian communions who had become Catholic converts received papal dispensations to be ordained. Reform sentiment eventually crystallized in several advocacy groups such as the Corps of Reserve Priests United for Service (CORPS, founded in 1974), which claims thousands of married priests in its membership.

Catholic critics of celibacy have condemned it as a denial of the basic human right to marry. Many blame the celibacy rule for the decline in the number of American priests since the 1960s, noting the disillusionment of married ex-priests and suggesting that contemporary youth are less willing to give up sex. Citing highly publicized cases of deviant sexual behavior among priests, many also conclude that celibacy hinders psychosexual maturity. Opinion polls suggest that the majority of American Catholics join them in calling for change.

Supporters of the celibacy rule respond that contemporary cultural attitudes devaluing the priesthood are the more obvious reason for the declining number of priests. At the same time, little evidence suggests that today's young men are more desirous of sex than those of fifty years ago. In any case, in a divorce-ridden society, allowing marriage among the clergy is not likely to solve many problems. Celibacy actually provides an important countercultural statement in a sexually saturated society.

Meanwhile, say celibacy proponents, sexually deviant behavior also appears among married men and the clergy of all denominations. In fact, several scientific studies show that priests as a group demonstrate a level of psychosocial maturity, personal happiness, and work satisfaction comparable to that of married men of similar age and education. Surveys also suggest that dissatisfaction with celibacy is not the prime motivator for most of those who have left the priesthood and married.

In the end, theological and sociological arguments may prove to be less decisive than concrete pastoral concerns in particular settings. By allowing for a handful of married priests, the Vatican maintains the option of welcoming more if it should find that circumstances warrant a change.

Bibliography. Greeley, A., "In Defense of Celibacy?" *America* 171, no. 6 (Sept 10, 1994): 10–15. Groeschel, B. J., *The Courage to Be Chaste* (New York: Paulist Press, 1985); Schillebeeckx, E., *Celibacy* (New York: Sheed and Ward, 1968); Sipe, A.W.R., *A Secret World: Sexuality and the Search for Celibacy* (New York: Brunner/Mazel, 1990).

T. Paul Thigpen

Charismatic Movement. Also known as Neopentecostalism, the charismatic movement refers to the spread of Pentecostal* distinctives to Protestant and Catholic Christians. Charismatics affirm the spiritual gifts of 1 Corinthians 12: 8–10, especially glossolalia,* prophecy, and healing. Whereas classical Pentecostals see speaking in tongues as the initial evidence of their central doctrine, the baptism of the Holy Spirit,* charismatics usually suggest that glossolalia is only a sign of this second work of grace.

Before 1960 Pentecostal beliefs reached some non-Pentecostals through the post–World War II healing revivals of Oral Roberts* and others. The Full Gospel Business Men's Fellowship International, founded in 1951, also extended the Pentecostal message. The traditional origin of the charismatic movement was the announcement on April 3,1960, by Episcopalian priest Dennis J. Bennett of Van Nuys, California, that he had been baptized in the Spirit and had spoken in tongues. Conflict erupted, Bennett resigned from his church, and *Time* and *Newsweek* gave the story national publicity.

In the early 1960s, the charismatic experience made inroads into practically every Protestant denomination and the Catholic Church. Gradually, charismatic organizations, conferences, and literature abounded. Independent ministries and megachurches developed. Charismatic faith was integral to the development of the "electronic church."* Television ministries, especially the Christian Broadcasting Network of Pat Robertson and the Trinity Broadcasting Network, grew rapidly.

Conflict has followed the charismatic movement. Southern Baptists and the Lutheran Church–Missouri Synod have been the most resistant denominations, state conventions sometimes ousting charismatic churches. In the 1970s the shepherding/discipleship movement created a furor over its reported dictatorial authoritarian leadership teachings.

Financial and sex scandals have rocked several television ministries, the case of Jim Bakker* and PTL being the most famous. Pat Robertson's 1987 presidential candidacy drew media criticism of charismatic religion.

Since the 1980s the "signs and wonders" emphasis of the ministry of John Wimber and his Vineyard Fellowship has flourished. In the 1990s the "Toronto Blessing," the gift of holy laughter and barking, captivated some charismatics but was denounced by Wimber. Conflict continues to surround the ministries of the faith-healing evangelists like Kenneth Hagin, Kenneth Copeland, and Benny Hinn who emphasize a gospel of health and prosperity. Despite conflict, charismatic churches have grown.

Bibliography. Burgess, Stanley, and Gary B, McGee, eds. *Dictionary of Pentecostal and Charismatic Movements* (Grand Rapids, MI: Zondervan, 1988); McDonnell, Kilian, ed., *Presence, Power, Praise: Documents on the Charismatic Renewal* 3 vols. (Collegeville, MN: Liturgical Press, 1980); Quebedeaux, Richard, *The Charismatics II* (San Francisco: Harper and Row, 1983).

Douglas Weaver

Chauncy, Charles. Born in 1705 in Boston, Charles Chauncy became one of the ministers of Boston's prestigious First Church (Old Brick) in 1727, remaining there until his death in 1787. Throughout his career he was at the center of religious and political controversy in New England.

The revivals of the 1730s and 1740s known as the Great Awakening* first brought Chauncy to public attention. He condemned the revivals for promoting excessive religious enthusiasm. He believed that the emotion-laden calls for conversion denigrated the role of reason in religious experience and caused the faithful to doubt their own salvation. He also criticized the practice of itinerant preaching because it interfered with the work of the clergy and raised questions about their integrity. In this controversy, Jonathan Edwards* was his major opponent.

In the 1750s Chauncy became embroiled in a theological controversy over the doctrine of original sin. When works by John Taylor and Samuel Webster appeared attacking original sin, Chauncy decided to write a defense of the doctrine. Instead, he wound up rejecting the idea because he found its implications, especially the eternal damnation of children because of original sin, repugnant to reason.

Chauncy followed his thought to its logical conclusions. In the late 1750s he wrote several treatises that were so controversial that he would not publish them for nearly thirty years. Called "the pudding," these works argued that a benevolent God could will only the eternal happiness of all creatures. Such happiness must include their salvation. Hence universal salvation was God's design. These universalist writings helped pave the way for nineteenth-century Unitarianism.

In the 1760s Chauncy attacked a proposal to have a Church of England bishop in the colonies. He reasoned from Scripture that congregational polity was superior to episcopal polity. He also feared that bishops, representatives of England's established church, would use the coercive power of the state to thwart religious liberty.

When the move for American independence erupted, Chauncy endorsed the colonial cause. Like Boston's mercantile elite, Chauncy claimed that British policy would bring economic slavery. Such an attack on political liberty defied reason and should be resisted. Chauncy left an enduring legacy in his rational approach to religious experience, his calls for religious and political liberty, and his reasoned approach to universal salvation.

Bibliography. Corrigan, J., *The Hidden Balance: Religion and the Social Theories of Charles Chauncy and Jonathan Mayhew* (New York: Cambridge University Press, 1987); Griffin, E. M., *Old Brick: Charles Chauncy of Boston, 1705–1787* (Minneapolis: University of Minnesota Press, 1980); Lippy, C. H., *Seasonable Revolutionary: The Mind of Charles Chauncy* (Chicago: Nelson-Hall, 1981).

Charles Lippy

Cherry, Frank S. Frank S. Cherry was the founder of the Church of God, also known as the Black Jews. According to Brotz, around 1915 a number of congregations calling themselves Black Jews appeared in various northern cities. Cherry's Philadelphia congregation was one of these. Known as the prophet, Cherry was from the Deep South, but his date of birth was unknown. As a youth he had traveled the world as a sailor. When Fauset visited the congregation, he described Cherry as an elderly dark brown man with mixed gray hair and a large mole on his chin. A self-educated person, Cherry was conversant in Hebrew and Yiddish. His primary teaching was that African Americans were descendants of the original Jews who are spoken of in the Bible.

An autocratic leader, Cherry personally was responsible for all matters pertaining to faith and practice. Membership was open only to blacks. Located on Nicholas Street in North Philadelphia, Cherry's congregation met in two renovated adjoining houses, with an auditorium holding three hundred people. Characters of the Hebrew alphabet were displayed across the walls. The men wore black skullcaps, and women wore blue and white capes and red and blue straw hats fringed with short tassels. In the place of a choir, an orchestra, consisting of tambourines, drums, castanets, rattles, and guitars, provided the music. The service was in a semi-Holiness worship style, but speaking in tongues was disallowed. Cherry himself played a huge drum. Christian hymns such as "Joy to the World" and "We Are Climbing Jacob's Ladder" were lined by Cherry. He also read a chapter of the English Bible and explained it. Likewise, his sermons lasted for an hour or more. Services were held on Sunday, Wednesday, and Friday evening and all day Saturday, the Sabbath Day. Baptism and Passover were observed, but Christmas and Easter were not. The Ten Commandments were strictly observed. Secular dancing was forbidden, but moderate drinking of intoxicants was accepted. Sins of fornication and adultery were taboo. Although the members studied Hebrew, one informant complained to Brotz that Cherry never had "Temple Worship," a service in Hebrew. For this reason, this member moved to New York, where congregations had such a service, for the New York Black Jews were in contact with white Jews whose Judaism also was based upon "the oral law and the community of Talmudic tradition. In other words, shabbos goyim, non-Jews who were employed by orthodox Jews, performed minor services on the Sabbath Day, such as turning off lights." Likewise, some worked as janitors in synagogues.

In his teachings, Cherry took an extremely controversial position against white Jews. He taught that his own congregation members were the true Israelites, and not white Jews who were guilty of denying Jesus as Christ. He taught that Jesus also was black and that Gentiles (whites) had taken blacks' culture, land, money, and names and had cursed them with the title Negro. He also contended that whites would not advance in the world until "black Hebrews" advanced. Cherry traced the genealogy of blacks to Noah, his three sons, Abraham and Lot, and Isaac and Jacob. He taught that portraits of a white Jesus, which were commonplace, were false. Likewise, he regularly used profanity in his sermons.

During the great black migration at the turn of the twentieth century, religious black nationalism became quite common. Blacks discovered that racism was a major part of life in the North as well. If there were any differences, they were minor ones. In addition to mainline Christian denominations, the stresses and strains of black northern urban life gave rise to black religious cults, including those like Cherry's congregation. As a precursor to such groups as the Nation of Islam,* Cherry's congregation taught a form of black racial pride and created a glorious historical past by claiming kinship to the ancient Hebrews. Cherry's worldview enabled his congregation to subtly protest the racial conditions under which they lived. Cherry died in 1965.

Bibliography. Brotz, H., *The Black Jews of Harlem* (New York: Schocken Books, 1964); Fauset, A. H., *Black Gods of the Metropolis* (Philadelphia: University of Pennsylvania Press, 1971); Murphy, L. ed., *Encyclopedia of African American Religions* (New York: Garland Publishing, 1993); Wilmore, G. S., *Black Religion and Black Radicalism*, 2nd rev. ed. (Maryknoll, NY: Orbis Books, 1983).

Lawrence H. Williams

Christian Coalition. The Christian Coalition, founded in 1989, is a creation and creature of Pat Robertson. He is president of the organization and one of its four national directors, the others being the Reverend Billy McCormick of Louisiana, Dick Weinhold of Texas, and Gordon Robertson, Pat's son. Ralph Reed is the executive director, but there is no doubt that Robertson is the boss. Reed attests to that himself. Critics of Robertson suggest that this new vehicle is a form of occlusion, seeking to distance his political agenda from the hundreds of extreme statements associated with him over the past twenty years. A column in the *Wall Street Journal* suggested that it was a case of "good cop/bad cop."

Reed is young, smiling, pleasant, and seemingly reasonable, but always consistent with Robertson's agenda; and even Reed, early in his tenure, told his followers that the coalition would be involved in "stealth" activities to take over school boards. He suggested that the opposition would not know what hit them. He made good on the promise to be devious, but had very little success in the elections.

In the election of 1994 the coalition played a major role in supporting the Republican Contract with America. Reed has been a constant consultant to that party's political leadership. When Reed announced in May 1996 that he was willing to negotiate a bit on the abortion* plank in the Republican platform, the press saw this as a major event in the party's campaign. When his associates in the religious right objected, Reed claimed to be misquoted by the *New York Times*. The troubling issue of abortion had become the single most divisive subject as Republicans moved to their national convention. No one denied that the coalition was a major player on that issue.

In 1995 the coalition claimed a membership of 1.7 million. If true, that would be an impressive accomplishment, and its very size would enhance the coalition's fund-raising and political clout. Americans United for Separation of Church and State was skeptical. The coalition sends its publication, *Christian America*, to anyone who contributes as little as fifteen dollars a year. The U.S. Postal Service must publish sales information for all second-class postage. Americans United asked for that data for *Christian America*, and according to the Postal Service 310,293 copies of the magazine were mailed in September 1995 by the coalition. If the 1.7 million figure were correct, then 1.3 million would not have paid their dues and did not receive the publication. Replying to that charge, the coalition claimed that the other 1.3 million were "supporters." They were people who signed nothing and contributed nothing but were known to be sympathetic.

Regardless of numbers, the coalition is a savvy political organization with a Christian fundamentalist platform. It is similar to dozens of other lobbies from the National Rifle Association to Common Cause. If one is to evaluate the coalition, it would be better to look at its platform and its membership, rather than to allow the lobbyist, Ralph Reed, to become the presumptive spokesperson for the Republican party. In 1996 there were indications that a goodly number of Republicans wanted their party back from the brink of fundamentalism.

As the 1996 party conventions neared, the Federal Election Commission brought suit against the coalition asserting that the group had acted illegally to promote several Republican candidates in 1990, 1992, and 1994. The commission claimed that the coalition channeled money illegally into several campaigns, endorsing particular candidates, including Newt Gingrich, Oliver North, and President George Bush.

Bibliography. Boston, Rob, *The Most Dangerous Man in America? Pat Robertson and the Rise of the Christian Coalition* (Amherst, NY: Prometheus Books, 1996); *Church and State* 48, no. 9 (October 1995): 4; 49, no. 7 (July/August 1996); *New York Times,*

July 31, 1996, 1; Robertson, M. G. "Pat," "Squeezing Religion out of the Public Square," *William and Mary Bill of Rights Journal* 4, no. 1 (1995): 223–76;"The 700 Club," various dates as broadcast on cable television, 1993–1996.

Robert S. Alley

Christian Reconstructionism. Christian Reconstructionism is a conservative evangelical movement that teaches that Christians should reconstruct society and government according to Old Testament law. From its inception in the 1960s with the teachings of Rousas J. Rushdoony*, Christian Reconstructionism, variously known as theonomy or dominion theology, began gaining adherents, especially in Reformed evangelical circles, but also in the broader evangelical community, most notably among charismatics. The ideology was popularized in the 1970s and 1980s by economist Gary North and theologian Greg Bahnsen, and it exhibited some influence on certain segments of the Christian right.

Christian Reconstructionism is based on three concepts that reveal the strong Calvinistic and covenantal orientation of its original proponents: theonomy, postmillennialism, and presuppositionalism. (1) "Theonomy," as understood by Reconstructionists, is the implementation of divine law—including Old Testament, Mosaic law—in every area of life (Rushdoony, for example, observes kosher dietary laws). (2) Reconstructionists view "postmillennialism" as the scriptural view of the end times, arguing that we are presently in the millennium and that the world will become increasingly Christianized ("reconstructed") until Christ returns after the millennium. In such a reconstructed society, Old Testament law will be legally enforced. (3) Reconstructionists teach a version of "presuppositionalism," the Reformed epistemology of the late Cornelius Van Til of Westminster Theological Seminary. Presuppositionalism contends that ultimate truth and reality can be known only through the presupposition of the triune God of the Bible; thus the possibility and necessity of empirical proof for the truth of Christianity are disavowed.

While some Reconstructionists argue that the reconstructed society may yet be hundreds or thousands of years from fruition, others argue that it might emerge soon. All Reconstructionists believe that reconstruction will be nonviolent and will only occur when the majority of the world's population have converted to Christianity. The reconstructed society will return to the law of the Old Testament, including capital punishment for such things as not only murder and rape, but also, for example, adultery and Sabbath breaking. The millennial society envisioned by the Reconstructionists will be marked by such features as a free market, the abolition of property taxes, and a return to the gold standard. Such a society will also forbid industrial pollution and abolish prisons, substituting for them a system of restitution and temporary slavery.

Christian Reconstructionism has been sharply controversial in the evangelical community at large, but it has caused the most contention in conservative Presbyterian and Reformed circles. The movement has drawn harsh criticism not only from Reformed thinkers, as is evidenced by the publication of *Theonomy:*

A Reformed Critique, an anti-Reconstructionist symposium of the faculty of Westminster Theological Seminary, but also from dispensational fundamentalists.

Bibliography. Barker, William S. and W. Robert Godfrey, eds., *Theonomy: A Reformed Critique* (Grand Rapids, MI: Zondervan Publishing House, 1990); Clapp, Rodney, *The Reconstructionists* (Downers Grove, IL: InterVarsity Press, 1990); House, H. Wayne, and Thomas Ice, *Dominion Theology: Blessing or Curse?* (Portland, OR: Multnomah Press, 1988); North, Gary, ed., *Theonomy: An Informed Response* (Tyler, TX: Institute for Christian Economics, 1991).

J. Matthew Pinson

Church Growth Movement. The church growth movement proposes a theory and system of evangelism that is based upon the principle that ''men like to become Christians without crossing racial, linguistic, or class barriers.'' This ''homogeneous unit principle'' dictates that evangelistic and mission efforts are most effective when they are directed at homogeneous groups within a society.

The church growth movement can be dated from the publication of Donald McGavran's *The Bridges of God: A Study in the Strategy of Missions* in 1955. McGavran, the primary leader in the church growth movement, went on to establish the School of World Mission and Institute of Church Growth at Fuller Theological Seminary in Pasadena, California. Another formative figure in the movement was C. Peter Wagner, author of *Our Kind of People: The Ethical Dimensions of Church Growth in America* (1979) and *Church Growth and the Whole Gospel: A Biblical Mandate* (1981).

McGavran grew up in India, the son and grandson of missionaries. His strategy and theory grew out of his missionary zeal and experience. He was also influenced by the Reconstructionist Movement, which was committed to ''Christianize'' entire societies.

Basic to the church growth movement is the understanding that growth is the very essence of the church. Therefore the church should search for the most efficient methods to expand church membership. It is not enough to have a ''search mentality,'' that is, ''seeking and sowing.'' Rather, the church must adopt a ''harvest mentality,'' that is ''finding and reaping.'' Supporters contend that in missions and evangelism the most successful methodology has proven to be the use of the ''natural bridges'' between people (family, friends, neighbors, and coworkers).

''Cultural free'' evangelism does not force potential converts to abandon their culture in order to become believers. It also avoids ''cultural proselytizing'' by evangelists and missionaries because they do not condemn the cultures of the nonbelievers. Indeed, it is characteristic of the church growth movement to be very accepting of human culture in general. This sentiment reflects the postmillennial optimism that characterizes the movement.

Cultural pluralism and not integration is God's plan for human society. Furthermore, God's plan for the church is reflected in the kind of denominational distinctions that exist in today's church and not in the model of the church universal that is proposed by the ecumenical movement. Each local church should be composed of persons from a very homogeneous cultural group.

The church growth advocates contend that it is important to distinguish between the discipling work of the evangelist and the perfecting work of the prophet. At the moment of discipling or conversion the new believer is called to a commitment to the person of Christ and not to any specific ethical system. Furthermore, the surest way to achieve the Christianizing of a society is through church growth.

Supporters of this movement usually defend it for its success in the most important work of the church, evangelism. Its critics fault it for its diminution of individual responsibility in the Christian life, for failing to take seriously the theological and ethical content of the Christian gospel from the very beginning of the Christian life, and for promoting cultural divisiveness within the Christian church .

Bibliography. Copeland, E. Luther, *World Mission, World Survival* (Nashville: Broadman Press, 1985); Costas, Orlando E., *Christ outside the Gate: Mission beyond Christendom* (Maryknoll, NY: Orbis Books, 1982); Crosby, David Eldon, "Church Government in the Church Growth Movement" (Ph.D. diss., Baylor University, 1989); Shenk, Wilbert R., ed., *Exploring Church Growth* (Grand Rapids, MI: Eerdmans, 1983); Smith, Ebbie C, *Balanced Church Growth* (Nashville: Broadman Press, 1984).

Daniel B. McGee

Churches of Christ. The Churches of Christ is a Christian communion, primarily in the United States, that arose out of the Stone-Campbell tradition of the 1800s. Barton W. Stone* was an evangelical Presbyterian whose observation of James McGready–led sacramental revivals (1799–1800) and whose own leadership of a similar event at Cane Ridge, Kentucky (1801), led him into an independent (Springfield) presbytery and subsequently (1804) into an independent New Light or Christian movement. This movement stressed revivalistic evangelism (practical Christian unity being a feature thereof), Christian experience, the work of the Spirit, the Bible, and gospel liberty. The 1804 *Last Will and Testament of the Springfield Presbytery* articulated these themes against the authority of the juridical and legislative structures, creeds, confessions, and clergy of Presbyterianism. An early, highly expectant consciousness among New Light Christians was blunted by defections to the United Society of Believers in Christ's Second Appearing (Shakers*), returns to the Presbyterians, and the passage of years. This and some genuinely shared values encouraged Stone and a core of followers into union with the Campbell movement in 1832.

The movement of Thomas and Alexander Campbell* had been launched with Thomas's 1809 *Declaration and Address of the Christian Association of Washington, Pennsylvania,* which called for the creation of an evangelical society for the promotion of a pure gospel ministry. Underlying it was a sense of providential calling to eschew Old World corruptions and divisions for a New World restoration of the "ancient order" of the New Testament as the platform for a Christian unity that would convert the world.

Alexander Campbell expounded the "ancient order" in his periodical the *Christian Baptist* (1823–1830). Its circulation, Campbell's debating, and the evangelism of associates (Walter Scott* and others) had reached as far as central Kentucky by the mid-1820s. Here "Campbellites" encountered the two-decades-old "Stoneites," with whom they shared commitments to Christian liberty, evangelism, the practical Christian life, and the authority of Scripture. A union was enacted in a series of meetings that culminated in Lexington, Kentucky in 1832.

There were differences between Stoneites and Campbellites, too. The Stone churches were less anticlerical; their ministers had continued to meet in associations. The Campbellites tended toward "fierce" congregationalism. The Stone churches were less emphatic on baptism by immersion and on weekly Communion. The revival-born Stoneites were far less suspicious of the emotions and the work of the Spirit than were the highly rationalist Campbellites.

C. Leonard Allen and Richard T. Hughes have argued that the Stoneites were pessimistic and premillennial in outlook and that the Campbellites were optimistic and postmillennial in point of view. This argument and geographic research by R. L. Roberts suggest that fissures remained in the movement along the lines of its two main communities of origin. As early as the 1840s two different mind-sets were perceptible on the issue of the legitimacy of missionary societies. Opposition to missionary societies, along with opposition to instrumental music in worship, emerged between the Civil War and 1906 as two hallmarks of the Churches of Christ.

Prior to the mid-twentieth century the origin of the Churches of Christ was internally seen as a split between a conservative (or "faithful") party and a more liberal (or "digressive") party (Christian Churches, Disciples of Christ). Daniel Sommer from Indianapolis, whose "Sand Creek Declaration" (1889) decried "innovations" such as missionary societies, choirs, and (professional) preachers, noted that those adopting such innovations could not be regarded as "brethren."

Most recently, David Edwin Harrell, Jr., has stressed the importance of the Civil War and Reconstruction in the origin of the Churches of Christ. They have been, overwhelmingly, a communion of the South whose stances on missionary societies and instrumental music in worship were congruent with the poverty of their region. Antirebellion "loyalty resolutions" adopted by sectional "rump" versions of the American Christian Missionary Society during the war were remembered by Southerners. David Lipscomb, Nashville church leader and long-time editor of the *Gospel Advocate*, was a Southerner who embodied both the theological and sectional origins of the Churches of Christ. In 1906, at his urging, the Churches of Christ were listed as a separate religious body by the U.S. Census Bureau.

The Churches of Christ have continued the Campbellian debating tradition into the twentieth century and, with it, a fragility of internal unity that has generated several "subcommunions" among them. These include One-cup churches (resisting the adoption of individual Communion cups since the 1920s), Non–Sunday school churches (regarding Sunday schools as unauthorized by the New Testament, since the 1930s), premillennial churches (centered in Louisville and the work of R. H. Boll, since the 1930s), noninstitutional churches (resisting the support of educational or benevolent institutions by churches, especially in the post–World War II era), and the Boston churches (a distinctive cluster of congregations rooted in the ministry of Kip McKean).

Bibliography. Allen, C. Leonard, " 'The Stone That the Builders Rejected': Barton W. Stone in the Memory of Churches of Christ," in *Cane Ridge in Context: Perspectives on Barton W. Stone and the Revival,* ed. Anthony L. Dunnavant (Nashville: Disciples of Christ Historical Society, 1992), 43–61; Harrell, David Edwin, Jr., *A Social History of the Disciples of Christ* (Nashville: Disciples of Christ Historical Society, 1966; 2 vols. Atlanta: Publishing Systems, 1973); Hooper, Robert E., *A Distinct People: A History of the Churches of Christ in the 20th Century* (West Monroe, LA: Howard, 1993); Hughes, Richard, "The Apocalyptic Origins of the Churches of Christ and the Triumph of Modernism," *Religion and American Culture* 2 (Summer 1992):181–214.

Anthony L. Dunnavant

Civil Religion. Jean-Jacques Rousseau argued in *The Social Contract* that an orderly society required a civil religion to maintain the loyalty and cohesion of its citizens. Rousseau went on to prescribe the sort of religion he believed would best support the social contract. Since Rousseau's time, a variety of commentators have noted the religious characteristics embedded in nation-states.

The question of the existence of a generic American religion perplexed various students of religion and culture at various historical moments, but the publication of Robert Bellah's article "Civil Religion in America" touched off a new and more lively debate in academic circles. Many found the proposition of a common American faith ludicrous, given the diversity of the population and the varieties of specific religious expression found among these peoples. Others not only found the proposition plausible, but rushed to nominate various American institutions for particular roles in inculcating and promulgating that common faith. Some argued for the presidency as the office of the "high priest" of the American religion. Some pointed to the shroud of mystery surrounding the Supreme Court and its deliberations as the defining cultus of America's religion. Still others regarded the public school system as the essential entry point, where America's children received their baptism into Americanism and catechesis in citizenship before gaining admittance to the ultimate American rite, the voting booth.

Religion was bound with the apparatus of the state early in the colonial history of the United States. Settlers in Virginia brought the Church of England with them. Settlers in Plymouth Plantation, Massachusetts Bay Colony, and Connecticut brought the ethos of the English Puritan movement with them. Even in William Penn's vision for Pennsylvania, the impetus for toleration of religious variety came from the theology of the Society of Friends. In each case the apparent uniqueness of America, its apparently boundless possibilities, fostered a sense that this "New World" had a providentially ordained destiny of greatness. Many colonists, not just the Puritans, took to heart John Winthrop's admonition to behave as though the eyes of the world looked on. America's destiny, it seemed, was nothing less than the redemption of the corrupted world order.

The revolutionary generation found the particularity of religious establishments uncomfortable. Part and parcel with the rebellion against George III was rebellion against the Church of England. The revolutionaries had no desire to replace the Church of England with some other ecclesial structure and left the matter to the states to decide. Yet themes and symbols from Protestant Christianity and other spiritual aspects of late-eighteenth-century life provided rallying points for those same revolutionaries when they moved from rebellion to governance. Finding common ground in such symbols as Liberty Trees, the Stars and Stripes, Lady Liberty, Brother Jonathan, and, later, Uncle Sam to embody the spirit of the nation proved a powerful force in the life of the young republic. The older colonial vision of the redemptive potential of America found its way into the emphatic proclamation that in the United States had begun *novus ordo seclorum,* "the new order for the ages."

Similarly, the heroes of the revolutionary era took on mythic qualities. Sometimes, as with the "apotheosis of George Washington," America's heroes attain a status approximately equivalent to that of biblical heroes. Sometimes seen as Moses the deliverer, other times as a demigod, Washington came to embody the optimism of the new nation. When the nation turned on itself during the Civil War, new images came to the fore. Abraham Lincoln came to be the embodiment of the possibilities of the nation. His melancholy, brooding countenance was the face of a nation hardened by the hardscrabble life on the frontier, but it was also the face of a people determined to form a "more perfect union." If Washington was the father of the country, Lincoln was its savior, purchasing reunion with his very blood.

The heroes sought to protect the destiny of the nation. They also sought to uphold its sacred texts. The Declaration of Independence and the Constitution often appear as providentially given statements of faith of the nation. Together they form the creed that Americans fight and die to protect. Other documents, such as Lincoln's Gettysburg Address, his Second Inaugural Address, the text of important Supreme Court cases, or significant acts of Congress, serve only to explain or define these sacred texts—they can never supersede them.

A difficulty with analyzing the civil religion in America, however, is its unevenness. At times, as during World War II, the bicentennial celebration, or the Reagan administration, the rhetoric of faith in America and all it embodies fills the air. It becomes a spur to Americans' inactivity or inattentiveness. At other times, sometimes at the same time, the civil religion seems divisive. When, for example, the Reverend Dr. Martin Luther King, Jr.,* called upon the nation to live up to the promise of its creed, a substantial segment of the nation failed to respond. When large numbers of Americans invoked the language of the Declaration of Independence to oppose the nation's involvement in the Vietnam War, the political guardians of the public faith responded slowly.

Quite apart from the question of the potential for division, there loom substantial questions of religious conscience. Is it appropriate for a Christian, or a Jew, or a Muslim, or a Buddhist to express religious devotion to the nation? What of those instances when religious devotion conflicts with the aims of the nation's leaders, who purport to speak as guardians of the tradition? Questions of that sort prompted Will Herberg to posit that faith in the "American Way of Life" amounted to idolatry on the part of those Protestants, Catholics, and Jews who placed allegiance to the nation on a par with their faith.

Finally, many raise the objection that the nation is too diverse and too large to nurture a common faith. Moreover, none of the candidates nominated for the role of promulgation of the civil religion does so in any consistent way. Although there are certainly themes of nationalism and patriotism available for the invocation of the politicians, they are only themes. These themes are insufficiently developed to attain religious status.

The debate goes on not unlike the civil religion itself, ebbing and flowing as the mood of the country seems fit. President George Bush invoked the theme of the "new world order" during the Gulf War, illustrating the durability of one of the grand themes of the revolutionary era. Although the continuity of American civil religion is difficult to demonstrate, its power to address appropriate occasions is difficult to deny.

Bibliography. Albanese, Catherine L., *Sons of the Fathers: The Civil Religion of the American Revolution* (Philadelphia: Temple University Press, 1976); Bellah, Robert N., *The Broken Covenant: American Civil Religion in Time of Trial* (New York: Seabury Press, 1975); Bellah, Robert N., and Phillip E. Hammond, *Varieties of Civil Religion* (San Francisco: Harper and Row, 1980); Herberg, Will, *Protestant, Catholic, Jew: An Essay in American Religious Sociology*, rev. ed. (Garden City, NY: Doubleday, 1960); Richey, Russell E., and Donald Jones, eds., *American Civil Religion* (San Francisco: Mellen Research University Press, 1990 [1974]); Wilson, John F., *Public Religion in American Culture* (Philadelphia: Temple University Press, 1979).

Russell Congleton

Civil Rights. The broad rubric of "civil rights" includes both general (e.g., due process) and particular (e.g., women, minorities, and black Americans) racial and ethnic issues; and religious controversy has attended all of them. For our purposes here, "civil rights" refers to the struggle of black Americans for full constitutional protection of the freedoms and rights that citizens of the United States may have. Although slavery existed in the United States for more than two hundred years prior to the Civil War (1861–1865), the modern form of racial segregation began in the late 1800s. "Jim Crow" laws, which required that whites and blacks use separate public facilities (including separate Bibles for swearing court witnesses), were first developed in a few northern states in the early 1800s; in the late 1800s these laws were adopted by many southern states. Among several supporting decisions by the U.S. Supreme Court, none was more influential than *Plessy v. Ferguson* (1896), which upheld the constitutionality of the separate-but-equal doctrine. Owing to protests and marches and sit-ins, this system of de jure racial segregation began to erode in the 1900s: in its 1954 *Brown v. Board of Education of Topeka* decision, the Supreme Court ruled against de jure segregation in public schools; in the mid-to-late 1960s Congress enacted civil rights legislation that ordered an end to racial discrimination in housing, employment, public accommodations, and voter registration; and in 1969 the Supreme Court ordered public school districts to desegregate "at once."

The philosophical and theological predicates that underwrite racial discrimination generally, and slavery in particular, are as old as Plato and the Bible. When slavery was no longer viable, the "proslavery moral argument" (that is, some human beings are inherently superior to others who are inherently inferior, and the latter are therefore appropriately subject to the former) became the ground for a "pro–racial-discrimination" argument. From the beginnings of organized Christianity and Judaism in the United States, racial segregation has left an indelible mark. Although Judaism from its inception was clearly committed to ethnic identity, and Roman Catholic congregations are frequently marked by national and ethnic grouping, religious controversies surrounding civil rights in the United States have had mainly to do with Protestant Christianity. Many, if not most, black Christian judicatories are the product of white Christian racism.* Moreover, all of the mainline Protestant churches were institutionally fragmented over the race issue in the mid-nineteenth century, and most of them remained so until the mid-twentieth century.

All of them toward the end of the twentieth century, conservative and liberal churches alike, repudiated racism as contrary to the gospel. The Southern Baptist Convention* "unwaveringly denounce[s] racism, in all its forms, as deplorable sin"; the Assemblies of God "support[s] certain universal rights for all people regardless of race, and condemn[s] prejudice toward any person because of race"; the Mennonite Church declares that "racism is a particular social reality of evil our Lord asks us to confront in becoming God's people"; and the Lutheran Church–Missouri Synod "urge[s] its members to repent of any attitude or practice of racism . . . [and] repudiate[s] all racism." The Disciples of Christ affirms "its commitment to affirmative action and Civil Rights"; American Baptists declare support for continuing efforts to oppose racial discrimination in housing, employment, education, and jury selection; the United Church of Christ "reaffirms its commitment to racial justice, equal opportunity, and calls upon its constituency at all levels to so commit"; and the Presbyterian Church USA resolves to "combat vigorously any expression of racism either in policies or the implementation of them.'' The United Methodist Church "recognize[s] racism as sin and affirm[s] the ultimate and temporal worth of all persons''; the Episcopal Church affirms that "our Baptismal Covenant calls us to 'promote justice and peace among people and respect the dignity of every human being' ''; and the Greek Orthodox Church states that it "is against racial segregation, and believes in the full equality of all races and peoples.'' The position of Roman Catholicism is that "racism is a sin; a sin that divides the human family, blots out the image of God among specific members of that family, and violates the fundamental human dignity of those called to be children of the same Father . . . [Racism] is a denial of the truth of the dignity of each human being revealed by the mystery of the Incarnation.''

It may be just as well that the doctrine of church-state separation in the United States emancipates religious institutions from government by civil legislation, because the struggle for civil rights is deeply rooted in beliefs and commitments that are functionally religious. That is why legislated civil rights may be formal guarantees not always materially operational. Beyond that, of course, the evidence is clear that eliminating ecclesial de jure warrants for racism does not always alter its de facto reality. Despite ecclesial legislation and resolutions, it is widely acknowledged that "11 o'clock on Sunday morning is the most segregated hour in American life.'' Gunnar Myrdal's epic study of American racism, *An American Dilemma* (1944), concluded that racism is a problem in America owing to discontinuity and disjunction between what he called "the American creed'' and "the American deed.'' Religions call that "hypocrisy''; and despite virtual unanimity of official institutional opinion, it continues to generate contention and dispute among rank-and-file church members.

Bibliography. Judicatory position statements are available from the respective church commissions or headquarters. Also see the following: Allport, Gordon, *The Nature of Prejudice* (Garden City, NY: Doubleday Anchor Books, 1958); King, Martin Luther, Jr., "Letter from Birmingham Jail'' and other essays in *A Testament of Hope: The Essential Writings of Martin Luther King, Jr.*, ed. James M. Washington (New York: Harper and Row, 1986); Myrdal, Gunnar, *An American Dilemma*, 2 vols. (New York: Harper and Bros., 1944); Reimers, David M., *White Protestantism and the Negro* (New York: Oxford University Press, 1965); Tilson, Everett, *Segregation and the Bible* (New York: Abingdon Press, 1958).

Harmon L. Smith

Clarke, William Newton. William Newton Clarke (1841–1912) was a Baptist exponent of the liberal movement in American Protestantism. His major work, *An Outline of Christian Theology*, went through more than twenty-nine printings and was revised by William Adams Brown as *Christian Theology in Outline*. The two volumes were the most popular textbooks on liberal theology and influenced theological reflection and ministerial training for decades.

Born in Cazenovia, New York, Clarke was educated at Madison College and Hamilton Theological Seminary. He served as a Baptist minister in Keene, New

Hampshire; Newton Centre, Massachusetts; Montreal, Canada; and Hamilton, New York, for the first half of his life. He then became professor of theology at Colgate University and devoted the last half of his career to lecturing and writing. After his death the Baptist theological seminary at Colgate merged with the Baptist seminary at Rochester University to become Colgate-Rochester Theological Seminary. Clarke and Walter Rauschenbusch are each installed in a stained-glass window of the chapel as representative, respectively, of the Colgate and Rochester traditions.

Clarke exerted a major influence on the phase of liberalism that came to be known as Evangelical Liberalism. Essentially conservative, the movement represented a middle way between fundamentalism on the right and the more radical modernism on the left, especially of the "Chicago School." Rejecting notions of inerrancy, Clarke concluded that "the Bible itself releases us from all obligation to maintain its complete inerrancy, in the sense of freedom from all inaccuracy and incorrectness of statement, and shows us a higher quality, in which is manifest a higher purpose than that of inerrancy" (*An Outline of Christian Theology*, 35).

Harry Emerson Fosdick,* a student at Colgate in his formative years, credited Clarke with saving him and countless others from the untenable orthodoxy of the day and for the Christian ministry. In Fosdick's view, Clarke made it possible to embrace reason and faith, an openness to truth, and a commitment to genuine piety.

Near the turn of the century, Clarke became involved in a group its members chose to call "The Brotherhood of the Kingdom." Begun by a few Baptist theologians and ministers, the group rapidly became ecumenical in spirit and membership. In summer conferences near the Hudson River, theologians such as Clarke, Rauschenbusch, Zane Batten, and George Dana Boardman developed what were to become the formative principles of the Social Gospel movement.*

Clarke traced his own theological pilgrimage from traditional orthodoxy to liberalism in an immensely readable volume, still useful today, entitled *Sixty Years with the Bible*. This, together with *An Outline of Christian Theology*, *The Use of the Scriptures in Theology*, and *What Shall We Think of Christianity?*, were his most influential writings. He was the recipient of honorary degrees from Colgate, Yale, Chicago, and Columbia in recognition of his contribution to liberal Christianity, the Social Gospel, and ecumenism. His death notice in the North Carolina Baptist news magazine, the *Biblical Recorder*, concluded that his only flaw was a "too liberal theology."

Bibliography. Cauthen, Kenneth, *The Impact of American Religious Liberalism* (New York: Harper and Row, 1962); Clarke, E. S., *William Newton Clarke* (New York: Charles Scribner's Sons, 1916); Clarke, W. N., *An Outline of Christian Theology* (New York: Charles Scribner's Sons, 1898); Cochran, B. H., "William Newton Clarke: Exponent of the New Theology" (Ph.D. diss., Duke University, 1962).

Bernard H. Cochran

Cleage, Albert B., Jr. (Agyeman, Jaramogi Abebe). Albert B. Cleage, Jr.,
is a black Christian nationalist and the founder and holy patriarch of the Pan
African Orthodox Christian Church. Unlike most African-American ministers
and theologians in the 1960s, Cleage did not adhere to Martin Luther King,
Jr.,'s* philosophy of nonviolence. Unlike some other black power advocates
who viewed Christianity as a white farce, Cleage argued that black power and
the gospel were compatible and were related to the struggle for black liberation.
With these ideas in mind, Cleage, a United Church of Christ minister, wrote
two books, *The Black Messiah* (1968) and *Black Christian Nationalism* (1972),
explaining the new black theology.* His books consisted primarily of a series
of sermons.

Born on June 13, 1911, in Indianapolis, Cleage received an A.B. degree from
Wayne State University in 1937 and a B.D. from Oberlin School of Theology.
A soft-spoken person, Cleage, along with three hundred members, formed St.
Mark Congregational Church. In 1954 the church changed its name to the Shrine
of the Black Madonna. In 1962 the church became extremely active in community affairs, and Cleage ran for governor on the Freedom Now ticket. Greatly
influenced by Malcolm X,* Cleage became deeply involved in Detroit's black
power movement. He also was able to recycle a large number of black power
advocates into his church. In 1966 Cleage unveiled the painting of the Black
Madonna and Child, argued that the historical Jesus was black, and started the
Black Christian Nationalism Movement. That same year, he was one of the black
ministers responsible for organizing the Interreligious Foundation of Community
Organization (IFCO), an interracial organization with an emphasis on black
community economic development. From its beginning in 1966, Cleage was a
member of the National Committee of Black Churchmen and participated in the
first theological discussion of militant black clergy the same year.

Cleage also may have been the first person to have coined the term "black
theology." He may have used it during the Detroit riot of 1967 or earlier.
Calling it a "Black schoolmen's theology . . . written for white acceptance,"
Cleage denounced the first attempts at writing a black theology by the National
Committee of Black Churchmen. He was developing a black theology based on
his own experiences of preaching every Sunday in the ghetto. Cleage's own
grassroots black theology was not based upon white acceptance, but was a "demand for white repentance and material reparation." He attempted to get at the
crux of historical Christianity by arguing that Jesus was the black messiah who
as a Zealot brought revolution and separatism to the nation of Israel in its attempt
at overthrowing Roman domination. Jesus' message of corporate and national
salvation was later corrupted by being filtered through the teachings of Paul,
who preached universal love and individual salvation. For this reason, Cleage
contended that only the Old Testament was canonical, and blacks were the
chosen people of God. Israel became black during the sojourn in Egypt and
Babylon; therefore, God is fighting on the side of blacks in the contemporary
ghetto of America. It was the place of the black church to build African Amer-

icans into a black nation and lead the revolution against white Gentile oppression.

In 1970 Cleage changed his name to Jaramogi Abebe Agyeman. By 1974 Shrines of the Black Madonna were in Atlanta, Kalamazoo, and Houston. In 1978 the Shrine of the Black Madonna became a denomination, and the name was changed to the Pan African Orthodox Christian Church. Cleage, who still holds affiliation in the United Church of Christ, became known as founder and holy patriarch.

Bibliography. Cleage, A. B., Jr., *Black Christian Nationalism* (New York: William Morrow and Company, 1972); Cleage, A. B., Jr., *The Black Messiah* (New York: Sheed and Ward, 1968); Lincoln, C. E., ed., *The Black Experience in Religion* (Garden City, NY: Anchor Books, 1974); Payne, W. J., ed., *Directory of African American Religious Bodies.* (Washington, DC: Research Center on Black Religious Bodies–Howard University School of Divinity, 1991); Wilmore, G. S. and J. H. Cone, eds., *Black Theology* (Maryknoll, NY: Orbis Books, 1979).

Lawrence H. Williams

Communalism. Characterized by face-to-face relationships, commitment to consensual agreement, and deliberate efforts on the part of members to distinguish themselves from outsiders, communal groups are intentional societies held together by experiences of communal fellowship and personal identification with the group, and by some combination of allegiances to charismatic leadership, religious tradition, and well-defined codes of belief and behavior. Communal groups in North America have sometimes been persecuted. Quakers were punished and banned in colonial New England; early-nineteenth-century Mormons were tarred, feathered, and forced to leave New York and Illinois; and Hutterites were beaten and jailed for their refusal to participate in World War I. Native American groups, the oldest communal societies in North America, were denied religious freedom and were treated as savages for centuries.

As well as being frequent objects of persecution, communal societies have also flourished in American society. Indeed, persecution has often functioned to heighten insider commitment to a communal group and to justify the contrast drawn by insiders between the group's special status and the violence and impurity of the outside world. Among the Mormons, for example, persecution justified the creation of a separate society with an elaborate set of beliefs and rituals hidden from the gentile world.

Communal groups have flourished especially in times of social stress and change. In the early nineteenth century many Americans responded with a communal impulse to the emergence of a national economy and political system that began to eclipse certain forms of economic self-sufficiency and local government. This communal impulse involved efforts to recapture traditional forms of group identity and face-to-face consensus while at the same time embracing the inventiveness, labor-saving technology, and relish for experimentation that characterized the new age. Thus Shakers,* Rappites,* Owenites, and perfectionists at the Oneida* Community all combined commitments to self-sufficiency, religious authority, and fellowship with entrepreneurial zest and social innovation.

The guarantee of religious freedom in the First Amendment to the U.S. Constitution has contributed to the abundance of communitarian experiments in America, and many religious minorities have sought protection by appealing to it. Although the implications of religious freedom were at first defined rather narrowly, the First Amendment contributed to the growth of religious pluralism in the United States and to the establishment of a climate of individual religious decision making that has been conducive to both religious experimentation and communalism.

Communalism has also been nurtured by the congregationalist form of religious organization that has come to define religious behavior in the United States. In colonial New England, a marked shift away from ecclesial hierarchy toward congregations as the locus of religious life and authority helped define American independence from England and create a religious culture based on individual experience and interpersonal relationships. In other regions, the congregation became a means of cultivating religious identity in a pluralistic and sometimes secular society. Thus Roman Catholics developed a distinctively American concern for congregational authority, even as they maintained ties to a universal church organization and hierarchy of priestly authority.

In sum, communalism in America has been nurtured by the constitutional guarantee of religious freedom and by the congregational model of church organization typical of American society, but also by the persecution of minority religious groups and intolerance of religious difference that have also characterized American society. The hostility of outsiders has often strengthened communal resolve, even as the pluralistic and congregational structures of American religious behavior have nurtured communal institutionalization.

Bibliography. Bender, Thomas, *Community and Social Change in America* (New Brunswick: Rutgers University Press, 1978); Hatch, Nathan O., *The Democratization of American Christianity* (New Haven: Yale University Press, 1989); Kephart, William M., *Extraordinary Groups: The Sociology of Unconventional Life-Styles* (New York: St. Martin's Press, 1976); Wind, James P., and James W. Lewis, eds., *American Congregations*, 2 vols. (Chicago: University of Chicago Press, 1994).

Amanda Porterfield

Communism. Communism has its roots in the work of Karl Marx, the German political economist and philosopher (1818–1883). As with many ideas of influential thinkers, the popular current conception of communism bears little resemblance to the idea as originally articulated by Marx. In its original form, Marxism represented an unprecedented attack on, and alternative to, existing religions and other explanations of the human condition.

According to Marx, the engine of the capitalist system would create the conditions for revolution. This would occur through the inherent injustice of a system in which the means of production were held by the few and led to their enrichment at the expense of an increasingly dehumanized labor force. The appeal of Marx's ideas came partly from his critique of European capitalism,* but it also came from the alternative that he presented. He foresaw the emergence of "socialism," in which the working class would take hold of established political structures, which would then be followed by an ideal state of "communism." Capitalism would actually lead in the direction of communism because of the tremendous wealth and technological advances it would create. Communism would be the first system based not on a division of labor, but on common ownership of the means of production. There would be enough wealth for all, and machines would perform, by themselves, most of the repetitive and alienating labor that had previously been done by humans under capitalism. This would free humans to pursue creative labor, such as art, philosophy, and music.

In this regard, then, communism represented an alternative of sorts to previous conceptions of religion and human nature. Communism offered the appealing and tantalizing prospect of a society in which pressing human needs could be met. The absence of such ideal conditions in mid-nineteenth-century Europe brought on the need for some justification for human existence. This for Marx was where religion fit in. Religion was intended to justify the extreme dehumanization of existing conditions. According to Marx, this process took place among the masses as a desperate attempt to come to terms with their plight, and among those benefiting from the system, as an "opiate" to keep the masses dormant. The need for religion would fall away as more and more distinctly human needs were met by his ideal communist system.

The history of Marxism and communism has been plagued by the difficulties often associated with attempts to apply theories to reality. Marx devoted volumes of attention to analyses of capitalism and the division of labor, but his vision of communism for an industrialized Europe was somewhat fragmentary. In one of history's great ironies, movements describing themselves as Marxist have been most successful in less industrialized and prosperous areas such as Russia and China. In the process, Marxism, as practiced by governments, took on an almost unrecognizable form. Lenin in Russia was so successful in applying (and some would say twisting) Marxism to Russia that it is probably appropriate to equate subsequent Communist revolutionary movements more with the work of Lenin than of Marx. Mao in China was equally effective in applying Marx to an even less industrialized nation. But neither Russia nor China had experienced capitalism to any meaningful degree when revolutionaries seized power. The measure of the failure of these Communists to offer a compelling system of rule and an alternative to religion is most evident in the survival and growth of religion in countries now emerging from the yoke of communism.

The question that surrounds recent events is whether the fall of communism in the former Soviet bloc fundamentally discredits the original ideas of Karl Marx. Regardless, Marx's ideal version of communism continues to hold appeal for those who are attempting to come to some nonreligious understanding of the human existence.

Bibliography. Aronson, Ronald, *After Marxism* (New York: Guilford Press, 1995); Tucker, Robert C., ed., *The Marx-Engels Reader* (New York: W. W. Norton, 1978); Tucker, Robert C., *The Marxian Revolutionary Idea* (New York: W. W. Norton, 1969).

Frederick M. Shepherd

Cone, James Hal. James Hal Cone was the pioneer and primary architect of the new black theology* movement, which started developing in the late 1960s and early 1970s. Black theology came to be the religious side of the extremely militant and controversial black power movement. A Union Theological Seminary* professor, Cone became the first African-American systematic theologian to take a position favoring black power. Earlier African-American theologians were more inclined to advocate the nonviolent passive resistance theology of Martin Luther King, Jr.* But Cone's black theology was indicative of a new changing paradigm, and the next generation of black theologians followed his lead.

Cone was born on August 5, 1933, in Fordyce, Arkansas, and received his B.A. from Philander Smith College in 1958, B.D. from Garrett Theological Seminary in 1961, and Ph.D. from Northwestern University in 1965. Against the backdrop of the Detroit riot in 1967, Cone wrote *Black Theology and Black Power* (1969). He wanted to know if God had anything to say about the contemporary urban crisis. American theology, he believed, had a long history of being abstract and culturally biased. It was, Cone asserted, based on the Greek classics and not upon the Bible. Historically, the Judeo-Christian faith was not abstract, but concrete, biblically based, and concerned about liberation in this life. Contemporarily, this concrete God, who is black, can be found in the ghettoes fighting on the side of the oppressed. In his second work, *A Black Theology of Liberation* (1970), Cone integrated his black theology, putting it into systematic theological form. He contended that white liberals had been doing theology in a vacuum, especially independent of black suffering. On the other hand, he argued that white Southerners had used theology in the justification of racism. In *The Spirituals and the Blues* (1972), following the lead of those critics who argued that a systematized black theology was still white theology, Cone used indigenous black folk material in the next stage of developing his theology. His contention was that spirituals were powerful elements in the struggle for black survival and were historically grounded. They were storytelling through song, African in origin, and were used as coded messages of slave resistance during slavery.

Likewise, the blues could be dated to the Hayes-Tilden Compromise of 1877, causing the withdrawal of federal troops from the South, and the separate-but-equal law that officially segregated the country in 1896. Both the Hayes-Tilden Compromise and the separate-but-equal law placed African Americans in a status of inferiority. They caused the rise of the blues as a music "depicting

[the] joy and sorrow . . . and the burden of being free in a racist society.'' Like the spirituals, the blues, as a secular music form, had to be interpreted in terms of black suffering. So both indigenous black musical forms were appropriate for use in the black power movement and in developing a black theology.

In *God of the Oppressed* (1975), Cone discussed the importance of his own autobiography in building his black theology. He stated that his theological position was conditioned by having grown up in Bearden, Arkansas, a small town sixty miles from Little Rock, and by the black church and white racism. Upon receiving his Ph.D. in 1965, he began teaching at Philander Smith College in Little Rock, where teaching black students theological discourse was a glaring contradiction. He attempted to reconcile the contradiction of teaching Karl Barth to black students from the South, who were not used to God as a theological abstraction. Instead, for them, God was "Savior and friend," the "lily of the valley, the bright and morning star." In 1966, when the cry of black power was raised across America, Cone knew that American and European theology was unable to address the black experience, so he took upon himself the task of developing a black theology addressing the void. In 1979 Cone expanded his thought to include the liberation of women and peoples of the Third World.

Bibliography. Cone, J. H., *Black Theology and Black Power* (New York: Seabury Press, 1969); Cone, J. H., *A Black Theology of Liberation* (Philadelphia: J. B. Lippincott, 1970); Cone, J. H., *God of the Oppressed* (New York: Seabury Press, 1975); Cone, J. H., *The Spirituals and the Blues* (New York: Seabury Press, 1972); Matney, W. C., ed., *Who's Who among Black Americans* (Northbrook, IL: Who's Who among Black Americans, 1978).

Lawrence H. Williams

Conscientious Objection. The question of the right of American citizens to object to military service on religious grounds arises whenever the nation seeks to raise armed forces by means of conscription. The discussion of the issues implicated by conscientious objection tends to repose in peacetime, only to leap back to the forefront when the question of conscription arises.

Historically the "peace churches," those denominations espousing pacifism as a tenet of the faith, championed the cause of conscientious objection. In the revolutionary era the defense of peace by members of the Society of Friends and Anabaptist groups drew the ire and suspicion of rebellious colonists. While attracting special criticism during the period when the British held Philadelphia, the Friends continued business without significant interruption. As a result, Friends faced the scorn of their fellow colonists, who often accused Friends of Toryism. The German Anabaptists of Pennsylvania generally maintained more distance from the Revolution than the Quakers, partly as a result of geography and partly because of greater emotional distance from the quarrel. Both groups faced intense pressure from zealous revolutionaries recruiting militias to combat George III. That pressure often manifested itself in the form of tarring and feathering, beatings, and other methods of physical intimidation.

During the War of 1812 and the Mexican War pacifist groups maintained their opposition to warfare in all its forms. That stance subjected these groups to public scorn and ridicule, but little formal attention was given to objectors. The Mexican War divided Americans to the extent that Quaker opposition to the war drew less ire than it would have had the nation been united behind the war aims.

In the Civil War the need for soldiers pressed more urgently, and as a consequence the pacifists received special attention. Friends North and South received the taunts of their neighbors, but they also received menacing threats and, in many cases, physical violence. The wartime governor of Indiana, Oliver P. Morton, brought the coercive power of the state to bear on those who refused military service, ordering the prosecution of draft resisters. In addition to the public stigma of such prosecutions, those convicted faced arduous jail sentences. Government officials in the states of the Confederacy applied similar pressures, especially in North Carolina.

Opposition to wars of acquisition against the native tribes of North America was inconsistent. Friends often led the rush of European settlers (as opposed to traders) into newly opened territories. They were, for example, among the earliest settlers of what became the state of Indiana. Thus, while Friends opposed the violence against the tribes, their presence in areas previously unsettled by Europeans contributed to government efforts to "pacify" the natives.

Only at the time of World War I did the traditional peace churches manage a more or less unified opposition to conscription. Under the leadership of Rufus Jones, the American Friends Service Committee was formed to propose alternatives to military service for draft-age Friends. Mennonite and Amish groups formed similar committees, and occasionally these service committees presented a united front to Secretary of War Newton D. Baker. Many in the peace churches, however, objected to the concept of alternative service on the grounds that such service still aided the war effort in ways antithetical to pacifist teachings.

Even when Secretary Baker approved alternative service plans, the pacifists often faced basic training with their conscripted peers. In such settings many switched from alternative service to regular military service as a result of the derisive taunts of the draftees. With that problem in mind, many objectors insisted on protection from any service requirement at all during World War II. Even those among the "peace churches" who did not object to alternative service were wary of any plan that called for shared basic training. As it had done during World War I, the government recognized opposition to warfare based on the tenets of an established religious tradition. Adherents to "new religions," such as Jehovah's Witnesses,* received a more skeptical scrutiny from the government. Many in the War Department believed that the door to conscientious objection should never be opened in the first place. They were convinced that conscientious objection shielded many who had no religious convictions.

Basing conscientious objection on religious convictions opened the door to a different line of inquiry that came to a head during the Vietnam conflict. The question was simple to state: could one who had moral scruples against war but who was otherwise an atheist or agnostic receive conscientious objector status? To the military such a position opened a proverbial Pandora's box of unnecessary troubles. Military experts believed that such a ruling had the potential of vitiating the draft. On the other hand, proponents of conscientious objection based on moral reservations argued that the Constitution prevented the government from granting conscientious objector status only to those holding membership in a religious organization. The Supreme Court ultimately resolved the matter, holding in *United States v. Seeger* that conscientious objection to military service could indeed be based on moral reservations apart from any specific religious institution.

The institution of the volunteer army during the Nixon administration temporarily resolved the conscientious objection issue. It is certain that any reinstitution of conscription will inaugurate a new round of discussions of conscientious objection.

Bibliography. American Friends Service Committee, *Speak Truth to Power* (Philadelphia: American Friends Service Committee, 1955); Keim, Albert and Grant Stoltzfus, *Conscientious Objection and the Peace Churches* (Philadelphia: Mennonite Publishing House, 1985); Mayer, Peter, ed., *The Pacifist Conscience* (New York: Holt, Rinehart, and Winston, 1966); Nelson, Jacquelyn S., *Indiana Quakers Confront the Civil War* (Indianapolis: Indiana Historical Society, 1991); Perry, Shawn, ed., *Words of Conscience: Religious Statements on Conscientious Objection*, 9th ed. (Washington, DC: National Interreligious Service Board for Conscientious Objectors, 1980).

Russell Congleton

Conservative Baptist Association of America. The Conservative Baptist Association of America (CBAA) is an association of some 1,200 Baptist churches in the United States that was founded in 1947 following a schism in the Northern Baptist Convention. The association includes at least two seminaries (Denver Conservative Baptist Seminary in Colorado, and Western Seminary in Portland, Oregon), a Bible college (Southwestern Bible College, Phoenix, Arizona), and domestic and international missionary-sending agencies. Its member churches, located primarily in the northern and western United States, refer to themselves as an association because of their loose organizational structure, which has no unified denominational budget.

Conservatives in the Northern Baptist Convention spent two decades in unsuccessful attempts to shift Northern Baptist missionary efforts in a more conservative direction. Their desire was to combat liberalism in the mission agencies and to reduce the bureaucracy of the denomination. Finally, in 1943, under the leadership of Frank M. Goodchild, J. C. Massee, Richard Beal, and Albert Johnson, conservative Northern Baptists formed the Conservative Baptist Foreign Mission Society. The Conservative Baptist Association of America was formed in 1947 when it became apparent that the Northern Baptist Convention would not allow two mission-sending agencies under the parent denomination.

The Conservative Baptist Association of America grew rapidly at first. In 1950 it formed both the Conservative Baptist Home Mission Society and the Conservative Baptist Theological Seminary in Denver. It was beset by a schism in the 1960s when at least 200 churches broke with the association because of their desire to avoid cooperation with other evangelical denominations and to advance a dispensationalist eschatology. These churches organized themselves into the World Conservative Baptist Mission.

In recent years the CBAA has found itself in the theological mainstream of the nation as evangelicalism has gained in popularity. The association has developed a strong institutional base of colleges and seminaries in which to educate its clergy and mission agencies from which to extend its worldwide influence. It now has over 300,000 members, with about 1,000 home and foreign missionaries.

Bibliography. McBeth, H. Leon, *The Baptist Heritage: Four Centuries of Baptist Witness* (Nashville, Broadman Press, 1987); Shelley, Bruce L., *A History of Conservative Baptists* (Wheaton, IL: Conservative Baptist Press, 1971).

Robert N. Nash, Jr.

Conservative Judaism. Conservative Judaism arose in Europe under the name Historical Judaism as a response to the emancipation of Jews during the nineteenth century. As Jews emerged from their centuries of relative isolation from gentile society, new forms of governance and modern values impacted Jewish life. Reform Judaism* had forsaken many of the ritualistic practices that had previously defined Jewish life. Conservative Judaism began as a reaction to many of the perceived excesses of Reform. The new movement, which emerged during the last quarter of the nineteenth century, set about both conserving traditional religious practice and embracing modernity.

To this day, Conservative Judaism stands between the two poles of Reform Judaism and Orthodox religious practice. Modern academic criticism is embraced, rejecting the traditional view that the entire written and oral Torah (divine teaching) was delivered by God to the Jewish people at Mount Sinai. But most of the traditional practices that have defined the Jewish people historically are still held to be holy. Conservative Judaism still maintains the predominant use of Hebrew in worship and the traditional practices of *kashrut* (dietary laws) and Sabbath and holy-day observance. Major innovations include mixed-gender seating during worship, the ability to drive on holy days if the purpose of the travel is to attend synagogue worship, the modification of the traditional marriage document to effectuate a religious divorce (if the husband is unwilling or uncooperative), and most recently the ordination of women.

Conservative Judaism remains a *halakhic* movement, meaning that it defines its positions solely on its interpretation of Jewish law. It distinguishes itself from Orthodoxy by its greater willingness to undergo change and adopt innovation as a movement within *halakha* to reflect the changes in Jewish life over time. Its major institutions today are the Jewish Theological Seminary in New York, the Rabbinical Assembly, and the United Synagogue of America.

Bibliography. Dorff, Elliot N., *Conservative Judaism: Our Ancestors to Our Descendants* (New York: Youth Commission, United Synagogue of America, 1977); Gillman, Neil, *Conservative Judaism: The New Century* (West Orange, NJ: Behrman House, 1993); Gordis, Robert, *Understanding Conservative Judaism*, ed. Max Gelb (New York: Rabbinical Assembly, 1978); Marcus Jacob Rader, Abraham J. Peck, and Jeffrey S. Gurock, eds., *The American Rabbinate: A Century of Continuity and Change, 1883–1983* (Hoboken, NJ: Ktav Publishing House, 1985); Rosenblum, Herbert, *Conservative Judaism: A Contemporary History* (New York: United Synagogue of America, 1983); Sklare, Marshall, *Conservative Judaism: An American Religious Movement*, new augmented ed. (New York: Schocken Books, 1972).

Jonathan Miller

Conversion. Issues of conversion and religious experience have created numerous controversies in American religious life. New England Puritans, like many of their British counterparts, were concerned about the nature and genuineness of individual conversion. As Calvinists, these Puritans believed that God was the sole agent of salvation. Totally depraved human beings had no free will to choose God's grace, a benefit given only to those elected by God's sovereign choice. Conversion—a turning from one way of life to another—was often a lengthy process that began as the individual became concerned about spiritual things, sought to live a holy life, failed, experienced spiritual torment and frustrations, and finally cast all on God. At some point, the truly elect individual would sense the imparting of divine grace and be able to testify to that experience within the community of faith. Indeed, most New England congregations required a confession of personal faith before persons could be admitted to church membership. Disputes arose, however, over several aspects of the conversion process. Some insisted that the desire to be saved and an interest in prayer and Scripture were "signs" of ultimate election. The heart was prepared before salvation occurred. Others said that any human effort was a false hope based on improper "works righteousness."

Although the children of church members were baptized as infants, they were still required to make the necessary confession of faith for full church membership. When many failed to do so, a controversy arose in seventeenth-century New England churches. When these baptized but unconverted individuals brought their own children for baptism, the churches confronted a dilemma. Did the covenant extend to the grandchildren of the elect? In response to this issue, a synod of New England churches approved the so-called Half-way Covenant* in 1662. It allowed the children of baptized but unregenerate adults to be baptized, but they were not allowed to receive Communion or vote in church meetings (hence half-way members) until and if they made the necessary profession of faith. The Half-way Covenant was a transitional aspect of ecclesiastical life in the New England churches. Some congregations utilized it, others rejected it, while still others modified it significantly. The latter instances were evident with Solomon Stoddard, sixty-year pastor at Northampton, Massachusetts, and the grandfather of Jonathan Edwards.* Stoddard permitted baptized but unconverted persons to receive Communion as a "converting ordinance" in hopes that it would draw them closer to regeneration.

When Jonathan Edwards succeeded his grandfather in the pulpit of the Northampton church in 1729, he attacked the covenant, calling on persons to receive salvation before they came to membership. By 1735 the Northampton community was experiencing a widespread awakening, with numerous persons claiming conversion. When the enthusiasm abated in the late 1730s, Edwards documented the events in a treatise entitled *A Faithful Narrative of the Surprising Work of God* in which he described the nature of the conversions and traced the process through certain case studies with participants. Ultimately, Edwards's insistence on conversion as a prerequisite for Communion led to a controversy in the church and his dismissal as pastor in 1750.

Issues of conversion characterized other conflicts relative to what is known as the Great Awakening.* In 1740 Presbyterian preacher Gilbert Tennent* (1703–1764) preached a sermon entitled "The Danger of an Unconverted Ministry," in which he insisted that true Christians should separate themselves from these "blind guides" who could or would not testify to a specific work of grace in their hearts. The sermon created an uproar among clergy and laity during the period and presaged divisions within Presbyterian and Congregational camps into "New Light" (prorevival) and "Old Light" (antirevival) factions.

Controversies over the nature of conversion were also evident during the early nineteenth century and the so-called Second Great Awakening* in New England and across the western frontier. Traditionalists criticized the emotional outbursts—shouting, falling, running, jerking—that often characterized revivalistic conversions as false, external manifestations that might not even be "of God." Further, the introduction of certain "new measures," particularly as linked to the ministry of evangelist Charles G. Finney* (1792–1875), also created heated disputes. These methods, aimed at reaching the unchurched, emphasized human participation in the salvific process, the ability of sinners to exercise free will, and the identification of sinners publicly by name in religious services. Finney stressed that God desired the salvation of all persons, and that conversion was less a lengthy process than an immediate cry to God for the redemption that God was ready to bestow. Finney also utilized the "anxious bench," a specific location in the meeting house where sinners under conviction of sin could come to be "prayed through" to salvation. Opponents, particularly Calvinists, charged that such a practice was the worst sign of human effort and a rejection of divine sovereignty. Other, more liturgically oriented clergy such as John Williamson Nevin* (1803–1886), in a volume entitled *The Anxious Bench* (1843), insisted that the practice cheapened the salvation process and undermined the sacraments of the church. His arguments against such practices were echoed by New Englander Horace Bushnell* (1802–1876), who, in a book titled *Christian Nurture* (1847), reaffirmed the nurturing, sacramental role of the church in leading persons to conversions through gradual instruction and growth in the faith.

On the American frontier debates on conversion flared among those who supported and those who opposed revival techniques, dividing Baptists,* for example, into Regular (antirevival method) and Separate (prorevivalist) Baptist camps. Most frontier Baptist churches required some statement of personal faith before administering immersion baptism or admitting persons to church membership. The Restorationists, particularly the followers of Alexander Campbell,* suggested that conversion was a simple intellectual confession that Jesus is the Messiah, without need for some elaborate emotional outbursts.

Nineteenth- and twentieth-century revivalism* had a profound effect on conversion processes and debates in American religious communities. Dwight L. Moody, Billy Sunday* and Billy Graham* developed various "plans of salvation" for bringing sinners to repentance. Many evangelists encouraged would-be converts to exercise their free will, pray a "sinner's prayer," and "accept Christ immediately." So powerful were these methods that even Roman Catholics developed preaching missions and revival-like gatherings that called persons to salvation within the sacramental context of the church. Debates over these measures and methods increased as many sinners repeatedly walked the aisle, sometimes receiving conversion over and over again, never really assured that they had prayed the right prayer or understood the meaning of salvation. Southern Baptists, for example, lowered the age of conversion to elementary and preschool years, creating generations of persons who were "saved and baptized" as children, but who then wanted to be "saved again" when they really "understood" what they were doing.

Twentieth-century American evangelicals promoted the need for conversion of all persons but differed as to the nature and process of conversion itself. Some criticized "plan salvation" (the presenting of a plan of salvation and praying a simple prayer) as "cheap grace" and "easy believism." California pastor John McArthur was a particularly outspoken opponent of this kind of conversion process. He and other Calvinist-oriented evangelicals reasserted the Reformed approach to salvation with emphasis on the divine action in conversion, election, and perseverance as a sign of genuine faith. Others such as Norman Vincent Peale* and Robert Schuller stressed salvation through "Positive" or "Possibility Thinking," emphasizing conversion as turning from a poor self-image—a doctrine that many evangelicals found wanting. While American Christians gave great emphasis to the need for and possibility of conversion, they frequently divided over its nature and the process for securing salvation.

Bibliography. Bushnell, Horace, *Christian Nurture* (New York: Charles Scribner's Sons, 1861); Leonard, Bill J., "Getting Saved in America: Conversion Event in a Pluralistic Culture," *Review and Expositor* (Winter 1985): 111–27; McLoughlin, William, *Modern*

Revivalism (New York: Ronald Press, 1959); Miller, Perry, *Errand into the Wilderness* (New York: Harper Torchbooks, 1956); Pettit, Norman, *The Heart Prepared* (New Haven: Yale University Press, 1966).

Bill J. Leonard

Cooperative Baptist Fellowship. The Cooperative Baptist Fellowship (CBF) is a national organization of moderate Southern Baptists founded in 1990 in Atlanta, Georgia, in response to fundamentalist domination of the Southern Baptist Convention.* The CBF was initially established as a central contribution center to which moderate Southern Baptists could send funds to bypass official denominational structures. It has since evolved into a missionary-sending agency and a resource center for moderate Southern Baptist causes.

The seeds of the organization were planted in July 1990 after the annual Southern Baptist Convention (SBC) meeting in New Orleans. Daniel Vestal, pastor of the Dunwoody Baptist Church in Atlanta, Georgia, and failed candidate for the office of SBC president, issued a call to moderate Southern Baptists to meet in August to discuss future options for Southern Baptists who felt disenfranchised from the SBC.

The three thousand delegates to that meeting approved an alternate funding program for Baptist causes that bypassed the Executive Committee of the Southern Baptist Convention. Local Baptist churches were encouraged to defund Baptist institutions under fundamentalist control by sending their money through this alternative funding program, called the Baptist Cooperative Missions Program, Inc. The name Cooperative Baptist Fellowship was adopted at the second annual meeting in Atlanta in 1991.

Governed by a coordinating council of laypersons and clergy, the Fellowship provides an option for Southern Baptist churches to fund theological education, mission endeavors, and other Baptist causes outside official denominational circles. The organization is now considering whether or not to become a denomination. Cecil Sherman was named the first executive director; Vestal succeeded him in 1997.

Bibliography. Fletcher, Jesse C., *The Southern Baptist Convention: A Sesquicentennial History* (Nashville: Broadman Press, 1994); Leonard, Bill J., ed., *Dictionary of Baptists in America* (Downers Grove, IL: InterVarsity Press, 1994).

Robert N. Nash, Jr.

Coughlin, Charles E. Born in Canada in 1891, Charles E. Coughlin became priest of the Shrine of the Little Flower in Royal Oak, Michigan (near Detroit), in 1926. A Catholic in an age when anti-Catholicism was strong, Coughlin transcended both region and religion when he took to the airwaves in 1929.

Coughlin was a mesmerizing speaker in person and on the radio. He attracted a following because he articulated the fears and hopes of a generation ravaged by the depression. Coughlin became a voice for many who needed a scapegoat. Although he claimed that his perspective was grounded in Catholic teaching, he was ultimately silenced by church authorities because of the controversy his demagoguery produced.

Never trained in economics, Coughlin gained early notoriety by trying to explain the stock-market crash in 1929. He drew on the abiding fear of communism in many of his broadcasts. Then in the 1932 presidential race he endorsed Franklin Roosevelt as heartily as he condemned Herbert Hoover.

When Roosevelt won, Coughlin expected to become a public power, proclaiming the New Deal to be ''Christ's Deal.'' When Roosevelt distanced himself, Coughlin turned critic. By late 1933 he had become outspokenly anti-Semitic, finding a Jewish conspiracy behind every global problem. He alienated many when he claimed that satanic forces had driven God out of school and government. Sensitive critics recognized that Coughlin's position was nearly identical to that of Hitler and the Nazis. Forced from network radio, Coughlin broadcast on his own, founded the paper *Social Justice* to trumpet his views, and established the National Union for Social Justice as a third party in national politics. Humiliated by Roosevelt's victory in 1936, Coughlin was becoming an embarrassment to Catholicism, criticized in the Vatican paper *L'Osservatore Romano* and denounced by popular Catholic social justice advocate Father John A. Ryan.

When World War II broke out, Coughlin espoused an isolationist position and found himself mired in even greater controversy. The church hierarchy banned him from radio in 1942, but Coughlin had his new pro-Nazi Christian Front organization and *Social Justice* to propagate his views for a time. Finally, the U.S. government prohibited publication of *Social Justice*, arguing that it promoted espionage. Coughlin remained at the Shrine of the Little Flower until his retirement in 1966. He died in 1979.

Bibliography. Bennett, D. H., *Demagogues in the Depression: American Radicals and the Union Party, 1932–1936* (New Brunswick, N.J.: Rutgers University Press, 1969); Coughlin, C. E., *The New Deal in Money* (Royal Oak, MI: Radio League of the Little Flower, 1933); Coughlin, C. E. *A Series of Lectures on Social Justice, 1935–1936* (Royal Oak, MI: Radio League of the Little Flower, 1936); Tull, C. J., *Father Coughlin and the New Deal* (Syracuse: Syracuse University Press, 1965); Ward, L. B., *Father Charles E. Coughlin: An Authorized Biography* (Detroit: Tower Publications, 1933).

Charles Lippy

Crapsey, Algernon Sidney. Penurious circumstances following Algeron Sidney Crapsey's birth in Fairmount, Ohio, on June 28, 1847, meant that he enjoyed little formal schooling. He was soon on his own, serving briefly in the Union army (1862) and working at various clerkships until 1869. At the age of twenty he joined the Episcopal Church and decided to enter the ministry, studying for two years at St. Stephen's Seminary (now Bard) and graduating from General Theological Seminary in 1872. He joined the staff of New York's Trinity Church and after ordination in 1873 became a popular priest at St. Paul's Chapel. In 1879 he was appointed rector of St. Andrew's Church in Rochester, New York, taking a modest parish and building it into one of the city's largest and most influential. Through eloquent preaching, transparent sincerity, and contagious missionary zeal he became widely known as a clergyman whose ideals and concerns had to be reckoned with.

One of these ideals related to the church's obligation to help people in modern industrial society. In that regard Crapsey embodied both liberal theology and the Social Gospel, elements that often went together. Urging adjustment to modern conditions, he said that churches should become more scientific, democratic, and socialistic. This elicited strong reactions from many in a denomination usually thought of as creedalistic, autocratic, and capitalist. Still, his social protests were tolerated and even admired in some circles, as were those of his fellow townsman, Walter Rauschenbusch, with whom Crapsey often cooperated in reform enterprises. But a series of Sunday-evening lectures proved to have more serious consequences. He was brought up on charges of heresy when his ideas were printed in 1905 as *Religion and Politics.*

The specific charge made against him was denial of the Virgin Birth of Jesus. This accusation derived more from extrapolation than from any direct statement that Crapsey had made. It was true, however, that he did refer to Jesus as "Son of Joseph, a carpenter in upper Galilee." In another place he emphasized the loving accessibility of Jesus' person by saying that he "no longer stands apart from the common destiny of man in life and death," but was "born as we are born, dying as we died." Specifics aside, the basic issue lay in the fact that most Episcopalians interpreted the Nicene Creed literally, affirming an unchanging body of facts, whereas Crapsey regarded the confession of faith loosely, as a metaphor that was open to different interpretations and relative to varying circumstances.

Bishop William Walker of the Diocese of Western New York convened a court of prelates and laymen to consider several charges that moved swiftly from the question of the Virgin Birth to implicit denials of the incarnation, the divinity of Jesus, the Trinity, and resurrection of the flesh. The court found Crapsey guilty; he refused to recant; the bishop deposed and dismissed him on December 4, 1906; he severed all relations with the denomination for the rest of his life. Thereafter he lectured widely and wrote a great deal, but his influence waned steadily. In 1907 he organized a short-lived Brotherhood for Social and Spiritual Work. In 1914 he secured a modicum of financial security by serving as a state parole officer. Finishing his life in virtual anonymity, he died on December 31, 1927, in Rochester.

Bibliography. Crapsey, Algernon S., *The Last of the Heretics* (New York: Alfred A. Knopf, 1924); Crapsey, Algernon S., *The Re-birth of Religion* (New York: John Lane Co., 1907); Crapsey, Algernon S., *Religion and Politics* (New York: Thomas Whittaker, 1905).

Henry Warner Bowden

Crawford, Tarlton Perry. Tarlton Perry Crawford (1821–1902) was a Southern Baptist missionary who sparked the "Gospel Mission" controversy. Born in Kentucky, Crawford graduated from Union (Baptist) University in Murfreesboro, Tennessee, in 1851, the same year he and his wife, Martha Foster, were appointed missionaries to China. Arriving in Shanghai in 1852 under the auspices of the Southern Baptist Foreign Mission Board, he established a school and began extensive evangelistic work. In 1863 the Crawfords moved to Tengchow in Shantung Province.

Crawford was among the earliest missionaries to be sent out by the Southern Baptist Convention* following its beginning in 1845. These years were marked by financial and organizational instability. To support his family, Crawford began speculation in Chinese real estate and became quite successful in his efforts. He also developed a lifestyle that mirrored significant elements of Chinese culture in dress, language, and relationships.

In China Crawford demonstrated increased sympathy for Landmark views and the belief that Baptist churches were the only true expression of the New Testament church. Landmark insistence on the autonomy of the local congregation led its adherents to reject any ecclesiastical "hierarchy" evident in a denominational system. Thus he denounced mission boards and the collective funding of mission endeavors as contrary to the teaching of the New Testament. He insisted that mission boards be abolished and that missionaries receive funding directly from specific local churches. He called on Baptist missionaries to reject money from mission boards and raise their own support from churches and their own labor. In 1892 Crawford published a tract entitled *Churches to the Front!* that set forth his Landmark and anti–mission-board sentiments. This produced a controversy known as the Gospel Mission movement, a debate over the best and most biblical method of organizing Christian missions. For many years Crawford continued to receive his salary from the Southern Baptist Foreign Mission Board even as he criticized such funding. Finally, the board removed him from its list of missionaries. The controversy was only one facet of a larger debate over Landmark views and the mission enterprise among Southern Baptists.

Crawford was a controversialist even on the mission field. He argued extensively with his missionary colleagues. He and Baptist missionary J. B. Hartwell disagreed over such issues as the use of church property, the distribution of mission funds, and the best way to conduct worship among the Chinese. Crawford even suspected that Hartwell was somehow involved in a Chinese plot to assassinate him. Although most Southern Baptists rejected Crawford's views on mission funding, his Gospel Mission movement reflected a significant dilemma for a denomination that sought to balance biblical precedent with organizational efficiency.

Bibliography. Allen, Catherine B., *The New Lottie Moon Story* (Nashville: Broadman Press 1980); Leonard, Bill J., *Dictionary of Baptists in America* (Downers Grove:

InterVarsity Press, 1995), 97–98; McBeth, H. L., *The Baptist Heritage* (Nashville: Broad-man Press, 1987).

Bill J. Leonard

Creation Science. Creation science is based on the assertion that the early chapters of Genesis present a scientifically accurate, verifiable account of the earth's origins and life upon it. It arose from the impulse felt by fundamentalists in the early twentieth century to refute the scientific theories, particularly evolution, that had become the accepted intellectual coin in American universities. The only effective argument seemed to be an equally scientific theory giving a reasonable account of the Genesis story of creation. The earliest expositors of this idea were two self-proclaimed scientists, Harry Rimmer and George McCready Price. Rimmer, after two semesters at a homeopathic medical school and other miscellaneous education, set up a one-man Research Science Bureau in Los Angeles. An effective debater, he denounced evolution before hundreds of groups.

Price had a soupçon of training in geology and an avid amateur's knack for reading without really understanding. His first publication, *Illogical Geology* (1906), started him on a teaching career at several small church colleges. His most systematic book, *The New Geology* (1923), propounded his "great law of conformable stratigraphic sequences," an assertion that anomalies in the fossil record prove the lack of any natural sequence to the fossil-bearing rocks. His explanation of these anomalies was that the strata were all laid down by the (global) Genesis flood. Price held to a strict six-day creation and thus a very young age for the earth. He was William Jennings Bryan's* main source in his antievolution campaign, a fact that Clarence Darrow* turned against Bryan during the Scopes trial* in 1925.

Price and other creationists formed several short-lived organizations over the years: the Religion and Science Association (1935), the Deluge Geology Society (1941), and the American Scientific Affiliation (1941). Creationists themselves, however, differed over how Genesis should be interpreted. Price denounced any, including his former students, who took the days as ages or diverged in any way from his literalist viewpoint. Garland Press has collected the hard-to-find publications of these early creationists in a ten-volume series, *Creationism in Twentieth-Century America*, edited by Ronald Numbers.

A younger generation of Christian scholars who actually had scientific training emerged in the late 1940s, typified by J. Laurence Kulp of Columbia University. They rejected Price's unscientific claims and sought more valid arguments for their positions. Overall, the movement gained little national stature in this period, concentrating instead on pressuring individual schools or school boards to eliminate evolution from their curricula.

In 1961 Henry Morris and John Whitcomb published *The Genesis Flood*, essentially an update of Price's *New Geology* with footnotes and the accoutrements of a genuinely scientific study. The interest that this book reawakened led to the foundation in 1963 of the Creation Research Society (CRS). The CRS limited full membership to Christians with a graduate degree in some scientific field who would sign a statement acknowledging biblical inerrancy, special creation, and a global flood. Within ten years it had 450 members, plus over 1,500 sustaining members (those without scientific credentials), and was sponsoring research programs and publishing a journal.

Laypersons could join the Bible-Science Association, founded in 1964 by Missouri Synod Lutheran pastor Walter Lang. Some of the material published in Lang's newsletter, however, came so close to crackpot science that it proved embarrassing to the movement's more serious proponents. In the late 1960s two association members sued the California Board of Education to have the creationist viewpoint taught in the state's schools; to everyone's surprise, they won. This victory led to the establishment of the Creation-Science Research Center (CSRC) at Christian Heritage College in San Diego, which aimed to publish creationist material suitable for school use. Henry Morris joined the organization, but in 1972 its founders left and took the CSRC with them to pursue their political objectives. Morris organized the Institute for Creation Research (ICR), with more strictly academic aims. In 1974 the ICR published a creation-science textbook.

The creationists' strategy over the past two decades has been to deemphasize the biblical foundation of their ideas and play up the scientific aspect to avoid running afoul of restrictions against teaching religion in public schools and to avoid encouraging non-Christian faiths to demand that their beliefs be given equal footing. Several polls have shown that at the end of the twentieth century a higher percentage of Americans believed in creationism than did so at the beginning of the century.

Bibliography. Eve, Raymond A., and Francis B. Harrold, *The Creationist Movement in Modern America* (Boston: Twayne, 1991); Hyers, Conrad, "The Fall and Rise of Creationism" *Christian Century* 102 (1985): 411–15; Numbers, Ronald, *The Creationists* (Berkeley: University of California Press, 1991); Wiebe, Donald, "An Unholy Alliance? The Creationists' Quest for Scientific Legitimation," *Toronto Journal of Theology* 4 (1988): 162–77.

Albert A. Bell, Jr.

Creedalism. Creedalism is a pejorative term suggesting an ideology that is bound to and by an authoritative statement of orthodox faith. Christian traditions in the United States with anticreedal dimensions would include, among others, the Universalists, the O'Kelly "Christians," the "New Light" Christians led by Barton W. Stone,* and the Disciples of Christ led by Thomas and Alexander Campbell.* Arising especially in the early national period, such anticreedal groups typically alleged a contrast between the Old World, corrupted, clerically established, humanly derived, speculative character of creeds and the New World, restored, freely available, and divinely inspired character of biblical faith. Slogans such as the "the Holy Bible . . . our only creed" or "no creed but

Christ'' expressed this notion in the late eighteenth and early nineteenth centuries among the aforementioned groups. Among the heirs of Stone and the Campbells, the more radical Churches of Christ wing of this movement has been especially vigilant in this form of anticreedalism.

Anticreedal sentiment also was sometimes a feature of late-nineteenth- and early-twentieth-century American Protestant liberalism. In this later setting, creeds were not so much set over against a claimed biblical faith as they were viewed as an unnecessary or untenable expression of a bankrupt, doctrinaire orthodoxy. Ironically, this liberal form of anticreedalism may be seen beneath the adoption of the Social Creed of the Churches by the Federal Council of Churches (1908), for this expressed the preference of member churches' leadership at this time for ethics over doctrine. The traumas of the later twentieth century and their relationship to a cultural disestablishment of Christianity in the United States have blunted concern over creedalism as a perceived problem and have even introduced ''confessional'' or procreed reforms in a number of American churches.

Bibliography. Hatch, Nathan O., *The Democratization of American Christianity* (New Haven: Yale University Press, 1989); B. J. Longfield, ''Liberalism/Modernism, Protestant (ca. 1870s–1930s),'' in *Dictionary of Christianity in America,* ed. Daniel G. Reid, Robert D. Linder, Bruce L. Shelley, and Harry S. Stout (Downer's Grove, IL: InterVarsity Press, 1990).

Anthony L. Dunnavant

Criswell, Wallie Amos. Born in Eldorado, Oklahoma, in 1909, Wallie Amos Criswell is still active as copastor of the largest Southern Baptist church in the United States, First Baptist Church in Dallas, Texas. Experiencing an early ''call'' to the Christian ministry, he received his education at Baylor University and at the Southern Baptist Theological Seminary* in Louisville, Kentucky, where he was awarded the doctor of philosophy degree in 1937.

Criswell's first pastorate was First Baptist Church of Chickasha, Oklahoma (1937–1941) and then he served another brief term at the First Baptist Church of Muskogee, Oklahoma (1941–1944). In 1944 he received an invitation from First Baptist Church, Dallas, Texas, to become its pastor. He succeeded the eminent George W. Truett and in 1995 still served that church, though in a copastor capacity. During these fifty years as pastor, Criswell placed a great emphasis on evangelism, and the church grew into one of the megachurches of the United States, with a membership on paper of over 29,000 persons.

During the last half of the century, Criswell emerged as the leading neofundamentalist minister in the Southern Baptist Convention* with his insistence on biblical inerrancy, best illustrated in his 1969 publication *Why I Preach That the Bible Is Literally True.* His two-year term as president of the Southern Baptist Convention (1968–1970) established his leadership of the neofundamentalist party in the SBC with its political ambition of taking over the convention at the expense of all who might disagree with its doctrine, politics, and moral commitments. Criswell's earlier (1950s) prosegregation stance, inerrancy commitment, and antifeminism (against ordination of women), along with his charismatic speaking ability, qualified him as the patron saint of the 1980s fundamentalist political takeover of the Southern Baptist Convention. He was the inspiration and often the leader of the successful move by these neofundamentalists to control all the agencies of the SBC through the appointive power of the president of the convention to the various controlling boards. By the early years of the 1990s this party had successfully accomplished its goal. One of Criswell's special interests was also achieved in the purging of all those he considered to be ''liberal'' from the denomination's six seminaries. In 1970 he had founded Criswell College as an adjunct institution of his church. This is a degree-granting Bible college and at the time of founding was meant to protest liberalism and teach conservative fundamentalist values and doctrines.

Though in name semiretired in the 1990s, Criswell continued as senior minister of the church, which had supposedly called another minister, Joel Gregory. After only twenty-one months, Gregory resigned when it became obvious that Criswell had not really retired. This resulted in Criswell's own internal controversy, culminating in Gregory's exposé *Too Great a Temptation: The Seductive Power of America's Super Church*. This book told a graphic story of the neofundamentalist takeover as well as revealing internal conflicts among the neofundamentalists themselves. In October 1994 W. A. Criswell achieved his desired fiftieth anniversary at First Baptist Church, Dallas, Texas.

Bibliography. Criswell, W. A., *Why I Preach That the Bible Is Literally True* (Nashville: Broadman Press, 1969); Gregory, Joel, *Too Great a Temptation* (Fort Worth: Summit Group, 1994); Keith, Billy, *W. A. Criswell: The Authorized Biography* (Old Tappan, NJ: Revell, 1973).

George H. Shriver

Crummell, Alexander. Alexander Crummell was born in New York to free parents who descended from a West African tribe in the region of Liberia. He was educated there and while in high school began a lifelong friendship with Henry Highland Garnet, an influential Presbyterian abolitionist. He and Garnet attended the Hayes Academy, a school founded by abolitionists in Canaan, New Hampshire. When the academy closed due to pressure from the white community, he attended the Oneida Institute. Denied entrance to the General Episcopal Theological Seminary, he studied privately and was eventually ordained to the Episcopal priesthood in 1844. While on a fund-raising trip to England, he entered Cambridge University, earning a B.A. degree. He spent much of his adult life as a missionary in West Africa. Late in his life he was rector of St. Luke's Episcopal Church in Washington, D.C.

Crummell strongly believed that African Americans with intellectual skills should assume leadership responsibilities within the community. He was less interested in political solutions to African-American problems than in self-help methods and vocational education. For Crummell, the gospel of Jesus taught people to develop their own skills and abilities in order to protect their interests and contribute to the well-being of others. His emphasis on self-love was a motivating force for developing African-American potential. This idea was directly related to his mission interest in Africa. He was often critical of his race's lack of commitment to and pride in its African heritage. For Crummell, God was always to be regarded in the context of history. Since evil could be transformed into good, African Americans had an obligation to Christianize Africa as well as to rebuild and regenerate it.

Crummell was a tenacious advocate for civil rights* in America. He was convinced that as long as there were limitations placed upon African Americans' intellectual, social, and political progress, white people would be prisoners equally in the system. Any injury to one citizen destroyed the fabric of society for all members of society. For Crummell, the democratic system of America offered the best opportunity for overcoming injustice and oppression experienced by African Americans.

Bibliography. Crummell, Alexander, *Africa and America* (Springfield, MA: Wiley and Company, 1891); Meier, August, *Negro Thought in America, 1880–1915* (Ann Arbor: University of Michigan Press, 1963); Moses, Wilson J., "Civilizing Missionary: A Study of Alexander Crummell," *Journal of Negro History* 60 (April 1975): 229–51; Wilmore, Gayraud S., *Black Religion and Black Radicalism*, 2nd rev. ed. (Maryknoll, NY: Orbis Books, 1983).

Coleman Markham

Cummins, George David. Born near Smyrna, Delaware, on December 11, 1822, George David Cummins was strongly influenced by his mother's Methodist inclinations. By the time he graduated from Dickinson College in 1841, he had joined that denomination and volunteered to preach regularly in circuits of the Baltimore Conference. But after a few years of this (1842–1845), his preference for more orderly worship and a settled residence led him to join the Episcopal Church. Within six months he became a deacon and served as assistant rector in Baltimore. The year 1847 brought ordination to the priesthood, and for the next two decades Cummins served a series of parishes located in Norfolk and Richmond, Virginia, Washington, D.C., Baltimore, Maryland, and Chicago, Illinois. His eloquence and zeal drew favorable comments from many, and his elevation to assistant bishop of Kentucky in 1866 was a popular one.

Considering his early nurture and clerical habits, it is understandable that Cummins was decidedly evangelical or "low church" in his ecclesiastical views. He stressed the importance of his firsthand religious experience over liturgical niceties and the superiority of biblical truths to tenets supported by mere human authority. With this perspective Cummins became increasingly restive as some American Episcopalians embraced aspects of the Anglo-Catholic or "high-church" movement. He sharply criticized all sentiment that yearned for a return to pre-Reformation doctrine. He deplored any reliance on sacraments rather than a vital spiritual life as the key to salvation. Moreover, he refused to acquiesce in the claim made by some of his fellow clergy that only the Episcopal ordination was a valid one. Several published sermons emphasized his insistence that people received Communion at the Lord's table, not an altar. He also argued that the biblical record and early church records gave no support to claims of a divinely instituted episcopacy. At first Cummins hoped to remain within his flawed denomination in order to rectify its errors through exhortation and example, but as years passed, he feared that his official activities misled some observers to assume that he endorsed what he actually considered misguided and dangerous.

Always open to cooperating with like-minded clergy from other denominations, Cummins welcomed formation of the pan-Protestant Evangelical Alliance. After attending one of its sessions in New York City in 1873, he helped conduct an ecumenical Communion service, an act that drew a public scolding from the local bishop, Henry C. Potter. Stung by such pretentiousness, Cummins withdrew from office, condemning again in his letter of resignation the "dangerous errors symbolized by the services customary in ritualistic churches." A few months later, after a "Call to Organization," he met with twenty-eight others to lay the foundation for a new denomination. By mid-1874 the Reformed Episcopal Church* had been formed, and Cummins was named its first bishop. The new group produced a revised prayer book, averred that the Bible was its sole basis for doctrine and practice, and retained the episcopacy as a form of institutional management, not a divinely sanctioned office. Many followers expected Cummins to make impressive gains for his church through succeeding decades, but these efforts were cut short when he died on June 26, 1876, at his residence in Lutherville, Maryland.

Bibliography. Cummins, Alexandrine M., *Memoir of George David Cummins, D.D., First Bishop of the Reformed Episcopal Church* (Philadelphia: E. Claxton and Co., 1878); Cummins, George D., *Sermons by Bishop Geo. D. Cummins, D.D.* (Philadelphia: Reformed Episcopal Publication Society, 1884); Guelzo, Allen, *For the Union of Evangelical Christendom: The Irony of the Reformed Episcopalians* (University Park: Pennsylvania State University Press, 1994).

Henry Warner Bowden

D

Daly, Mary. Perhaps the most vocal feminist critic of patriarchal theology, Mary Daly, born in 1928, has given voice, linguistic form, and revolutionary energy to the quest for the full equality of women in Christian church and tradition. Two of her works remain standard for understanding the contours of American feminist theology: *The Church and the Second Sex*, written in 1968, and *Beyond God the Father*, written in 1973 and reissued in 1986. The first work precipitated her firing by Boston College in 1968. A flurry of protests by her students occasioned her being rehired, indeed with a promotion and tenure. This brief triumph of justice has subsequently been overshadowed by the college's refusal to make her a full professor because of her outspoken criticism of the Catholic superstructure.

Pivotal to her own formation as a philosopher and theologian, Daly had the opportunity to observe Vatican Council II* (1963–1965). She carried more encompassing hopes for the church's revitalization and full inclusion of women than did her similarly well-educated brothers in faith. The updating of the church for which she yearned was of little concern to the male-dominated programmatic framework for presentation and publication of proceedings. She heard only one paper, by a woman religious, that offered any substantive critique of the church's treatment of women. She left the conciliar gathering with disappointment at the church's inattentiveness to the significant concerns of women; the closing messages of the Vatican Council focused once again on women's sexual state as daughter, wife, and mother, consigned by God's eternal plan to the private sphere of the home and family. The messages to the men, not surprisingly, addressed their wide-ranging contributions to church and society as a whole.

After this dismissive conclusion, Daly also left with determined resolve to bring renewal, even revolution, on behalf of her sisters.

Although Daly was once a faithful Roman Catholic, her disenchantment with Christianity has in the last decades propelled her toward a post-Christian faith commitment; nevertheless, her provocative work continues to shape and inform Christian as well as secular feminist theory and construction. She has been deemed a reformer, a radical critic, and a revolutionary. The future of women in the Roman Catholic church and also Protestant ecclesial communions will depend in some measure upon the searing critique Daly has voiced.

Daly perhaps is best known for her creative use of language. She has a penchant for remaking language after unmasking its patriarchal bias. (It is probably to her credit that the word "patriarchy" has such currency in contemporary feminist writing.) She has persuasively argued that patriarchal concepts cannot illumine or elucidate the experience of women. Her more recent writings have continued her constructive quest for a feminist philosophy unencumbered by being cast as the "second sex."

Bibliography. Daly, Mary, *Beyond God the Father* (Boston: Beacon Press, 1973); Daly, Mary, *The Church and the Second Sex* (New York: Harper Colophon Books, 1975); Daly, Mary, *Gyn/Ecology: The Metaethics of Radical Feminism* (Boston: Beacon Press, 1978).

Molly Marshall

Darrow, Clarence S. Clarence Darrow (1857–1938) was a prominent lawyer who defended civil liberties and labor causes and who fought the power of large business monopolies and corporations. Born in Kinsman, Ohio, in 1857, Darrow received education from Allegheny College and the University of Michigan. In 1878 he was admitted to the bar and based his legal activities in Chicago. He and his second wife had one son, Paul. Registered as an Independent Democrat, he served for a while in the Illinois legislature. He was defense attorney in a number of prominent cases revolving around the exercise of civil liberties, including defense of the Socialist party leader Eugene V. Debs in the Railroad Union conspiracy accusation and of young African-American men in the Scottsboro trial in Alabama. From a religious perspective, perhaps his most important case was the John T. Scopes trial* in Dayton, Tennessee, in 1925. Shortly after the state passed a law against the teaching of Darwinian evolution, Scopes, a high-school teacher and coach, responded to the solicitation of the American Civil Liberties Union to file a constitutional challenge to the new law. Scopes, breaking the law, argued for freedom in his science teaching. To a considerable extent, that trial became the great legal and social battle between fundamentalism, represented by prosecutor William Jennings Bryan,* thrice Democratic presidential candidate and former secretary of state, and Darrow, the brilliant lawyer and agnostic. Scopes lost both the Dayton trial and his appeal, with the law not being formally rescinded by Tennessee until 1967 and similar laws in other states being nullified by the U.S. Supreme Court in 1968. Yet Darrow succeeded in casting aspersions upon the fundamentalism* of Bryan, with the result that in many quarters fundamentalism was severely tarnished (though by no means extinguished) and the American South was successfully portrayed as intellectually backward. Darrow published a number of pieces illustrating his agnosticism and the freedom of the individual, including *The Prohibition Mania* and, coauthored with Wallace Rice, *Infidels and Heretics*.

Bibliography. Darrow, Clarence S., *The Story of My Life* (New York: Scribner's, 1960); Hill, Samuel, Jr., ed., *Encyclopedia of Religion in the South* (Macon: Mercer University Press, 1984), *Westminster Dictionary of Church History* (Philadelphia: Westminster Press, 1971); *Who Was Who in America*, vol. 1 (Chicago: Marquis, 1942).

Sandy Dwayne Martin

Davenport, James. The great-grandson of New Haven cofounder and minister John Davenport, James Davenport (1716–1757), the brilliant yet bizarre rising young star of the New Lights,* carried the Great Awakening* revivalism* to new extremes, leaving his clergy colleagues divided among themselves but united against him. The top student and the youngest member of his 1732 class at Yale, he interrupted his postgraduate divinity reading for several months because of a breakdown. Davenport was eventually ordained in 1738 at Southold, Long Island, where he once preached to his congregation for twenty-four hours straight, confining himself to his room afterward for several days.

Davenport briefly joined the New York and New Jersey entourage of George Whitefield, who reportedly said that "he never knew one keep so close a walk with God as Mr. Davenport." Davenport itinerated alone throughout southern New England in 1741, where he became known for singing in the streets at the top of his lungs, often preaching to exhausted crowds as late as two in the morning. Reports described Davenport marching through town "with a large mob at his heels, singing all the way," resembling "Bacchanalians after a mad Frolick." Fellow clergy censured his support of lay exhorters—including women, children, African Americans, and Native Americans—his lack of decorum, his unbiblical hymns, his spontaneous preaching, and his personal attacks on other ministers.

At each stop, Davenport asked the local pastor about his salvation. Those who did not measure up were castigated as "carnal Pharisees," "blind guides," or "Jehosaphats in Ahab's army." They were "going to Hell," Davenport proclaimed, "drawing Multitudes after them"; it would be "better to drink bowls of poison" than to follow such unconverted ministers.

After spending the winter with his own congregation in Southold, Davenport set out again in the spring of 1742, preaching and raising funds for the Shepherd's Tent, an unlicensed coeducational seminary established that spring in New London, Connecticut. In its first year the Shepherd's Tent attracted more new students (fourteen) than either Harvard (thirteen) or Yale (ten).

The Connecticut General Assembly responded to Davenport's disruptions by banning uninvited itinerant preachers and threatening violators with the loss of a year's pay. After two Stratford residents filed a complaint scarcely a month later, the General Assembly declared Davenport "under the influences of enthusiastical impressions and impulses, and thereby disturb'd in the rational faculties of his mind." The sheriff and two files of musketeers escorted Davenport out of town.

Persistent as ever, Davenport traveled to Boston three weeks later, but the Boston and Charlestown Clergy Association barred him from its pulpits. Davenport made his customary call at the house of Old Light pastor Charles Chauncy* to inquire "into the reason of the hope" that was in him. The offended Chauncy responded by preaching his famous sermon "Enthusiasm Describ'd and Caution'd Against," publishing it with a prefatory letter to Davenport. Resolute, Davenport preached in the fields; he was soon arrested, tried, found "non compos mentis," and deported.

The height—or the depth—of Davenport's career occurred in early March 1743, when Davenport traveled to New London to ordain Shepherd's Tent student John Curtis as minister of the town's newly organized separatist congregation. On Sunday, March 6, townspeople returning home from worship were drawn by a "great Noise and Outcry" to the wharf, where they found Davenport and his followers around a bonfire, symbolically purging themselves of heresy by burning books of theological luminaries said to include Bishop Beveridge, Benjamin Colman, Charles Chauncy, Matthew Henry, Increase Mather, and Richard Sibbes. The next day they built another bonfire "to attack Idolatry," stripping themselves of ornamental apparel such as wigs, coats, pants, jewelry, and Davenport's breeches. A modest female onlooker saved the breeches, and another spectator persuaded Davenport that "he was under the Influence of an evil spirit, and that God had left Him."

After the bonfire, separatist leaders left town and the Shepherd's Tent folded. James Davenport returned to Southold, where his congregation dismissed him. Charles Chauncy renewed his attacks, and Jonathan Edwards* and Gilbert Tennent* publicly repudiated Davenport. Deserted by friend and foe alike, Davenport published his *Confession and Retractions* in 1744, admitting that the Lord had shown him the errors of his ways. Rehabilitated, Davenport served Presbyterian congregations in New Jersey and New York and in 1754 served as moderator of the (New Side) Synod of New York. Even then, controversy pursued him: members of his church petitioned for his removal just before he died.

Davenport's career left clergy and congregations divided among traditional Old Lights,* moderate New Lights, and radical separatists. Separations occurred in one-third of the New England congregations, and independent Strict Congregationalist conventions were organized in Connecticut, Long Island, and New Jersey. Many of Davenport's New Light colleagues—including Isaac Backus, Shubal Stearns, and Daniel Marshall—left the Strict Congregationalist movement to lead the Separatist Baptist surge in the Northeast and the southern "back country." Long after Davenport's death, his legacy survived.

Bibliography. Bushman, Richard L, ed., *The Great Awakening* (New York: 1969); Davenport, James, *Confession and Retractions* (Boston: S. Kneeland, 1744); Goen, C. C., *Revivalism and Separatism in New England, 1740–1800* (Middletown, CT: Wesleyan University Press, 1987); Stout, Harry, and Peter Onuf, "James Davenport and the Great Awakening in New London," *Journal of American History* 70 (1983): 556–77; Tracy, Joseph, *The Great Awakening* (Boston: Tappan and Dennet, 1842); Warch, Richard, "The Shepherd's Tent," *American Quarterly* 30 (1978):177–98.

David B. McCarthy

Death of God. In the 1960s and 1970s theological systems and traditional theology were eroded by a variety of forces, one of which was the death-of-God theology movement. European theologians and philosophers laid the groundwork for this movement. Karl Barth said that God could not be known apart from Jesus. Rudolf Bultman said that Jesus could not be known at all. What is important is not to know what Jesus said and did (one can't), but how Christ comes to people now in existential encounters. Bultman joined Friedrich Schleiermacher and Paul Tillich in focusing on "inwardness" (experience) as the address of God and authority. What was left? The answer for death-of-God proponents was nothing. This uniquely American theology, with acknowledged debts to such Europeans as Friedrich Nietzsche, redefined Christianity without God. Traditional Christianity was irrelevant.

The death-of-God theology became fashionable in 1965 in the academic and popular press, especially with feature stories in *Time* magazine. The proponents of this theology, mostly disillusioned Barthians, were Thomas Altizer,* Paul Van Buren, William Hamilton, Gabriel Vahanian, and the Jewish religious scholar Richard Rubenstein.

Thomas Altizer, influenced by Hegel, claimed that God had once existed but that when he became incarnate in Jesus Christ he ceased to exist as a reality independent of the world. For Altizer, the death of God is a historical event; God has died in our time, in our history, in our existence.

Paul Van Buren approached the "problem of God" from the viewpoint of linguistic analysis. No talk of God can be empirically verified, and therefore it is meaningless. There is a collapse in the meaning of religious words since verification is not possible.

William Hamilton as well as Van Buren called the phrase "death of God" a metaphor for the loss of transcendence in today's world and the growth of secular modes of thought in Western culture. With culture as the "norm," God was no more. Because God is dead, modern Westerners are to view the human Jesus as the model of sacrificial love and ethics.

Gabriel Vahanian, as early as 1961, claimed that Western culture had lost its sense of the sacred, that Westerners found no sacramental significance to their lives and no purpose in their lives, and that the history of their societies was devoid of any undergirding providence. For Western secular culture, God had died. Vahanian refrained from stating that God did not really exist but argued for a cultural transformation and the creation of a postmodern culture if the reality of God were to become viable once again.

Richard Rubenstein claimed that the Jewish Holocaust in World War II made it impossible to believe that God exists or that God had made a covenant with Israel or that there is any purpose for individual or social existence. Indeed, the only meaning is that which we ourselves make.

Controversy surrounded the movement and its advocates. It fitted the mood of the post-Kennedy era, a mood that called for activism and social change. It satisfied a psychological need of many. Advocates claim that they have been driven to Christian atheism by the need to be "truly contemporary" and to fit in with the most recent trends in culture.

The death-of-God theology is not able to "prove" that God is dead. The evidence produced is subjective, unreliable, and too much influenced by contemporary cultural and psychological variables. Critics ask, "Does God die when we like to imagine that he has? Does his existence depend on a show of hands and voting as to whether we want to believe in him or not? Does the creator appear and vanish at the whim of the creature? Is the Gallup poll our latest theological guide?"

The question of authority is at the bottom of the controversy over the death of God and its various proponents and takes many forms. Specifically, critics said that advocates did not take the Bible and its claims seriously. Also, Jesus was detached from the New Testament and the totality of the biblical world and its history. Others questioned giving linguistic analysis (Van Buren) or the philosophy of Hegel and Buddhist thought (Altizer) center stage in determining the nature, address (inwardness), or death of God. Why give the emptiness and relativity of modern culture and its loss of transcendence (Hamilton, Van Buren) the power to claim that God is dead? Why should the atrocities of the Holocaust be proof of God's nonexistence rather than of man's sinfulness and rebellion? The absolutism of the death-of-God advocates in proclaiming God's demise and in claiming that any other theology was irrelevant was a major source of controversy.

The death-of-God movement itself was not of lasting significance except as a reminder of the poverty of modern theologians who had severed their roots in Christian theism. Born in 1961, the death-of-God theology died in 1968. The theology of hope waited in the delivery room for its entry into the world.

Bibliography. Altizer, T.J.J., *The Gospel of Christian Atheism* (Philadelphia: Westminster Press, 1966); Altizer, T.J.J., ed., *Toward a New Christianity: Readings in the Death of God Theology* (New York: Harcourt, Brace and World, 1967); Altizer, T.J.J., and W. Hamilton, *Radical Theology and the Death of God* (Indianapolis: Bobbs-Merrill, 1966); Hamilton, W., "The Shape of Radical Theology," *Christian Century*, October 6, 1965;

Ice, J. L., and J. J. Carey, eds., *The Death of God Debate* (Philadelphia: Westminster Press, 1967); Rubenstein, R. L., *After Auschwitz* (Indianapolis: Bobbs-Merrill, 1966); Vahanian, G., *The Death of God* (New York: Braziller, 1961).

Robert K. Gustafson

Deloria, Vine Victor, Jr. Vine Victor Deloria, Jr., political historian, American Indian activist, and religious philosopher, was born in Martin, South Dakota, on March 26, 1933, the son of Vine Victor and Barbara Eastburn Deloria. The great-grandson of a Yankton Sioux medicine man and the grandson of a Yankton chief who converted to Christianity in the 1860s, Deloria wrote passionately about the bifurcated culture inhabited by many twentieth-century Indians, in which tribal values of community and sacred place conflict with Western individualism and secular materialism. The son of an Episcopal missionary and a graduate of the Augustana Lutheran School of Theology (M.Th., 1963), he helped direct national attention to the religious virtues of tribal cultures and to the failures of Christian leaders and institutions in their relations with American Indians.

Deloria's first book, *Custer Died for Your Sins* (1969), directed attention to Indian ability to outlast Christian lawmakers, government agents, anthropologists, and missionaries and called for a new form of Christianity, led by Indians, that would embody Christian ideas more fully than Westerners had. *God Is Red* (1983) posed the Indian complaint more radically, arguing that Christianity and Indian tribal religions were inherently incompatible, with Christian ideas about individuality and the transcendent authority of God fostering alienation and environmental destruction, while Native American respect for land and community offered hope for the future. In *The Metaphysics of Modern Existence* (1979), Deloria took the further step of condemning numerous theories accepted by mainstream biological and social scientists and of linking various dissenting theories to a welcome return to the subjective orientation and poetic idealism characteristic of tribal worldviews.

As a lawyer and chairman of the Institute for the Development of Indian Law in Washington, D.C. (1970–1976), and as professor of political science at the University of Arizona at Tucson (1978–1990) and the University of Colorado at Boulder (1990–   ), Deloria has also been an advocate of Indian judicial activism and a historian of Indian legal history. Thus in *Behind the Trail of Broken Treaties* (1985), he described the history of political relations between American Indians and the U.S. government that led to the Indian takeover of the Bureau of Indian Affairs in 1972 and to the protesters' demand that treaty negotiations between Indian tribes and the United States be reestablished. While acknowledging the role played by the Civil Rights* and anti–Vietnam War movements in galvanizing some young Indians to take this action, Deloria argued for the distinctiveness of Indian demands and identified precedents for these demands in the long history of Indian efforts to defend tribal sovereignty against assimilation. In this and other arguments characteristic of his writings,

Deloria contributed importantly to popular critiques of Western hegemony and to the ascendance in the 1980s of American rhetoric that defined the social and intellectual landscape in terms of multicultural tribalism.

Bibliography. Deloria, Vine Victor, Jr., *Behind the Trail of Broken Treaties: An Indian Declaration of Independence* (Austin: University of Texas Press, 1985); Deloria, Vine Victor, Jr., *Custer Died for Your Sins: An Indian Manifesto* (New York: Macmillan, 1969); Deloria, Vine Victor, Jr., *God Is Red* (New York: Dell Publishing Company, 1983); Deloria, Vine Victor, Jr., *The Metaphysics of Modern Existence* (New York: Harper and Row, 1979); Deloria, Vine Victor, Jr., with Clifford M. Lytle, *American Indians, American Justice* (Austin: University of Texas Press, 1983).

Amanda Porterfield

Dexter Avenue Baptist Church. In 1867 African Americans in Montgomery, Alabama, left the white Baptist church to form the First Colored Baptist Church. In 1877 this church split again, and in the forefront were former house slaves, whose church became known as Second Colored Baptist Church. By January 1879 a lot and building on Dexter Avenue, only a stone's throw from the state capitol, were purchased for $250. The name of the congregation was changed to Dexter Avenue Baptist Church. From the beginning, the church was composed of the black elite, who founded Alabama State College in the church basement. Dexter Avenue also was a ''deacons' church,'' meaning that the lay officers were in complete authority and not the pastor. Usually the authority in a typical black Baptist church was held by an autocratic pastor, but this was not the case at Dexter Avenue, so in this respect, Dexter Avenue was atypical. Although Dexter Avenue had a long tradition of choosing well-trained ministers, it also had a rapid turnover of pastors. Within the church's first ten years there were nearly a dozen pastors.

Dexter Avenue was the church pastored by Martin Luther King, Jr.,* from 1954 to January 1960 and during the Montgomery bus boycott (1955–1956). Vernon Johns, King's immediate predecessor as pastor, was an intellectual who paved the way for King's Social Gospel ministerial style. But as an eccentric, Johns was later dismissed from the pastorate, and the chairman of the board of deacons became known as a ''preacher killer.'' For these reasons, Martin Luther King, Sr., encouraged his son not to accept the pastorate. Among black Baptist ministers the church had gained a reputation of being difficult to pastor and antipreacher.

In spite of this negative advice, King accepted the Dexter Avenue pastorate on April 14, 1954, and the church and King proved to be an excellent fit. The three-hundred-member church offered King a parsonage and a $4,200 yearly salary, making him the highest-paid African-American minister in Montgomery. However, for King, a major priority was increasing pastoral authority over the lay leaders and increasing community activities. King led the church in becoming a life member of the NAACP* and regularly held civil rights* and community meetings in the church. But in spite of his superior preaching, the sanctuary was never full on Sunday morning, and there was no "shouting." Instead, needing little pastoring, the members viewed Alabama State College as their social center.

Dexter Avenue also served as a platform for King's activities during the bus boycott and aided his rise to national prominence. Because of its central location, the church was frequently used for meetings of the Montgomery Improvement Association (MIA). The church supported King financially during the boycott and in wider civil rights activities. In 1957 King and his wife, Coretta, made a trip to several foreign countries, including India and Ghana, that was made possible by a $2,500 bonus from the church. Dexter Avenue also served as a meeting place for the voting rights march from Selma to Montgomery in 1965.

Because of mounting Southern Christian Leadership Conference* (SCLC) responsibility, King resigned from Dexter Avenue effective January 1960 to return to Atlanta. He was constantly under the threat of death and believed that he was no longer adequately serving the church as pastor. On several occasions he apologized for inadequate performance, but no member complained about his civil rights activities. Instead, the congregation encouraged him to stay and preach only once a month. Fearing that pressure would be placed on his congregation, many of whom were schoolteachers, King resigned, for a newly proposed MIA target was school integration. Also, King could better serve SCLC in Atlanta while serving as the copastor of his father's church, Ebenezer. For years his father had pressured him to move, believing that Montgomery was physically unsafe.

A red-brick structure, Dexter Avenue is now called the Dexter Avenue–King Memorial Baptist Church. In 1974 it was declared a national historic landmark. The church has a mural depicting scenes of the civil rights movement, and a library containing personal artifacts belonging to King and his family.

Bibliography. Baldwin, L., *To Make the Wounded Whole* (Minneapolis: Fortress Press, 1992); Branch, T., *Parting the Waters* (New York: Simon and Schuster, 1988); Garrow, D. J., *Bearing the Cross* (New York: Vintage Books, 1988); King, M. L., Jr., *Stride toward Freedom* (New York: Harper and Row, 1958).

Lawrence H. Williams

Dispensationalism. Dispensationalism is a method of interpreting the Bible marked by the expression (made famous by C. I. Scofield* and Clarence Larkin) "rightly dividing the Word of Truth." In its broadest terms, dispensationalism divides Scripture chronologically into past time, the present age, and the age to come. Dispensationalism further divides the Bible and human history into seven dispensations, each one marked by a crucial event, test, failure, and judgment. Charles Ryrie defined *dispensation* as "a distinguishable economy in the outworking of God's purpose"; a lesson in stewardship on the part of humanity, a demonstration of progressive revelation on the part of God. To C. I. Scofield, a dispensation was "a period of time during which man is tested in respect of obedience to some *specific* revelation of the will of God." The seven dispensations are as follows: (1) *Innocence*, from the creation of man to the Fall; (2) *Conscience*, from the Fall until the Flood; (3) *Human Government*, from the Flood until the call of Abraham; (4) *Promise*, from the call of Abraham to the giving of the Law on Mt. Sinai; (5) *Law*, from the giving of the Law on Mt. Sinai through most of the public ministry of Christ (most generally up to his death on Calvary); (6) *Grace*, from the latter days of Christ's earthly ministry (for most this is post-Calvary) until the Second Coming of Christ (often called the Church Age); and (7) *Kingdom*, the Millennium, the literal one-thousand-year reign of Christ on earth commencing with his Revelation after the great seven-year Tribulation. Each dispensation reveals more of God's plan for man, but in each case, even the Kingdom age, man fails God's test, and judgment must follow.

In opposition to what they perceived to be the growing threat of "spiritualizing" among liberal theologians, dispensationalists insisted on a *literal* interpretation of the Bible, especially in historical and prophetic passages. As a result of this literalism, they have rigorously maintained an emphatic distinction between *national Israel* (God's chosen earthly people) and the *Church* (his peculiar heavenly people). The two are never one, which means that all promises to Abraham and his descendants must be literally fulfilled in the actual nation of Israel, either in the past, the present, or the future. Old Testament prophecies apply only to the nation of Israel. The Church is unforeseen in the Old Testament; hence it is a "mystery," the "Great Parenthesis" (coming between the sixty-ninth and seventieth weeks of Daniel 9) that interrupts God's ultimate plan for Israel. This has led to such a strict reading of the Gospels that many dispensationalists consider the Lord's Prayer and the Sermon on the Mount as "Jewish" and belonging to the dispensation of Law, not Grace. Thus the "parenthetical" Church exists in what dispensationalists refer to as "the times of the Gentiles" (from the Cross of Christ to the Rapture of the Saints), an epoch occurring solely within the dispensation of Grace, after which, during the seven-year Great Tribulation (Daniel's Seventieth Week) and a literal one-thousand-year Millennium, God will complete his long-interrupted plan for Israel. The majority of Old Testament prophecies, as well as the statements of Christ concerning the future of Israel, will be fulfilled during the Tribulation and Millennium. First, the Church will be "taken away," after which will follow the revelation of the Anti-Christ, the restoration of the Roman Empire, the return of the Jews to Palestine (in unbelief), the conversion of some and persecution of all the Jews and, finally, the Revelation of Christ at his Second Coming (with the saints of the Church Age) to defeat the forces of Anti-Christ at the great Battle of Armageddon. After this, the Millennium will commence, with Christ (along with the glorified saints) ruling as King from David's throne in Jerusalem over a restored and converted Israel, reinstituting the original "dispensational" practices and requirements of Temple worship, the sacrificial system, and the Law. Both John the Baptist and Christ offered the Kingdom to Israel, but the Jews refused; their refusal, however, only postponed the Kingdom until the completion of the Church Age. The "kingdom of God" has existed from the beginning and includes the Church Age; the "kingdom of heaven," however, that kingdom Christ came initially to establish, is Jewish, messianic, and Davidic—referring to a chosen people in a promised land for a certain period of time. It was "at hand" in the Gospels, was postponed by the rejection of Israel, and will be resumed during the Tribulation period and completed in the Millennium. Thus the Millennium is necessary, not so much for the completion of the Church as for the fulfillment of prophecies concerning national Israel.

The first systematic developer of premillennial, pretribulation dispensationalism was John Nelson Darby (1800–1882), a prolific writer and founder of the Plymouth Brethren. His works exerted significant influence in England and America, especially with C. I. Scofield, whose *Reference Bible* (1909) popularized dispensationalism more than any other single work. The fundamentalist movement in America, especially Baptist fundamentalism after 1930, has held to this view almost without exception, as have many evangelicals and such schools as Moody Bible Institute, Biola, Trinity Evangelical, and Dallas Seminary. Dispensationalism as formulated by Darby, Scofield, and others is by necessity premillennial; but premillennialism does not, by its historic definition, have to be dispensational. Dispensationalism is always at odds, however, with amillennialism and postmillennialism, and to this day adherents of each party have engaged in an ongoing debate over various implications of dispensationalism for the Church and the Jews, with an ever-increasing number of scholars in recent years questioning the veracity of dispensationalism as a sound biblical hermeneutic.

Bibliography. Brookes, James H., *Maranatha, or The Lord Cometh* (London: Alfred Holmes, 1870); Darby, John Nelson, *Synopsis of the Books of the Bible*, 5 vols. (London: T.H. Gregg, 1857); Graves, James R., *The Work of Christ in the Covenant of Redemption: Developed in Seven Dispensations* (Memphis: Baptist Book House, 1883); Scofield, C. I., *The Scofield Reference Bible* (Oxford: Oxford University Press, 1909; rev. 1917 and 1967); Larkin, Clarence, *Rightly Dividing the Word* (Philadelphia: Clarence Larkin, 1920); Lindsell, Harold, *The Gathering Storm* (Wheaton IL: Tyndale House, 1980); Lindsey, Hal, *The Late Great Planet Earth* (Grand Rapids, MI: Zondervan, 1970); Ryrie, Charles, *Dispensationalism Today* (Chicago: Moody Press, 1965); Walvoord, John, *The Millennial Kingdom* (Findley, OH: Dunham, 1959). Useful critiques of dispensationalism: Allis, Oswald T., *Prophecy and the Church* (Phillipsburg, NJ: Presbyterian and Reformed Publishing Co., 1945); Boettner, Loraine, *The Millennium* (Phillipsburg, NJ: Presbyterian and Reformed Publishing Co., 1957; rev., 1984).

Timothy D. Whelan

Dissent/Dissenting Movement. The term "dissent" applies historically to those who do not conform to the religious practices of a society but in turn create their own. A term sometimes used interchangeably with dissent is nonconformity, although it did not come into play as a term of designation until the second half of the eighteenth century. The term "dissent" may also have a political connotation that may be negative or positive depending upon the time and situation in which it is used. In England, dissent meant divergence from the established Church of England. The term was typically applied to Presbyterians, Congregationalists, and Baptists. After the Glorious Revolution of 1688–1689, the term also denoted these same religious bodies as supporters of the Revolutionary Settlement.

In the British American colonies where the Church of England was established, that is, Maryland through Georgia and three counties of New York City, Presbyterians, Congregationalists, and Baptists were dissenters. But in New England, where Congregationalism was established, Church of England constituents were dissenters. This meant that in both regions dissenters were suspected of political as well as religious opposition to the status quo. After the Declaration of Independence, separation of church and state* occurred within the southern states. In New England, the last state to abandon this relationship was Massachusetts in 1833. Hence a major objective of early dissent was achieved. A later view of dissent is that it opposes any interference with religion by the state and champions religious freedom, although this was not always true, because at one time Presbyterians would have had the government enforce their religious views, and early Congregationalists acknowledged the authority of the magistrate to maintain religious orthodoxy. It was only with the passage of time and the accumulation of experience that dissent came to repudiate state interference in religion and demanded disestablishment of state churches and complete religious liberty.

In the United States, where consent and dissent have both contributed to make democracy possible, what is dissent at one point may be orthodoxy at another time. It is this shifting platform that makes it difficult to define dissent and dissenting movement. Since there is no national church, dissent today is likely to focus on social and/or economic issues. As a clearly evolving attitude, dissent has played a significant role in shaping religious and political institutions. Those who have led in such activity are generally respected for their devotion, discipline, and commitment to a cause. Although the terms "dissent" and "dissenting movement" in modern times have been applied to radical groups, the historical legacy these terms represent is a vital part of contemporary life.

Bibliography. Cole, C. R., and M. E. Moody, eds., *The Dissenting Tradition: Essays for Leland H. E. Carlson* (Athens: Ohio University Press, 1975); Gaustad, E. S., *Dissent in American Religion* (Chicago: University of Chicago Press, 1973); Mecklin, J. M., *The Story of American Dissent* (New York: Harcourt, Brace and Co., 1934); Munson, J., *The Nonconformists* (London: SPCK, 1991); Watts, M., *The Dissenters* (Oxford: Clarendon Press, 1978).

Frederick V. Mills, Sr.

Dow, Lorenzo. A circuit rider and evangelist in America and Britain, Lorenzo Dow (1777–1834) created controversy with his eccentric manner and the emotionalism evoked at his meetings. Born in Coventry, Connecticut, Dow was given to religious impressions early in life. These included dreams, experiences of melancholia, and struggles with sin. He was converted in 1791 through the preaching of Methodist evangelist Hope Hull. Three years later he declared himself called to ministry but was not recognized by the Methodists until 1798. Controversy was evident in his ministry almost from the beginning. While appointed to Methodist charges, Dow was frequently disciplined for failure to stay in one specific circuit or parish. He was a free spirit who felt compelled to respond to the call of God wherever and whenever it might lead him. Indeed, his most frequent disputes with Methodists involved his failure to stay put in one definite assignment.

Dow was in and out of the Methodist system, traveling widely in the United States, Canada, and Great Britain. He made his first trip abroad in 1799 when he journeyed to Ireland. His last official Methodist appointment came in 1801 after his return from Ireland.

Dow's state of mind was affected by depression and extreme melancholia. One of his journal entries notes: "Whilst I am preaching, I feel happy, but as soon as I have done I feel such horror (without guilt) by the buffetings of Satan, that I am ready to sink like a drowning man . . . and I can get rid of these horrible feelings only by retirement in earnest prayer and exertion of faith in God." His pulpit mannerisms and public attacks upon his enemies (even his Methodist critics) led to his being labeled "Crazy Dow." Dow gave himself the nickname "the eccentric cosmopolite," a designation that suggested his unique form of preaching and his calling to travel extensively as an instrument of the Divine. Frequent illness left him haggard and exhausted. His gaunt, unkempt appearance, with long hair, ragged clothes, and flowing beard, also contributed to his eccentricity. His use of irony and sarcasm in preaching was entertaining to his supporters and fuel for his critics. Likewise, his concern for mystical revelations and his prophetic pronouncements led many to believe that he was heretical in his theological positions. Opponents sometimes sought to break up his meetings and occasionally instituted physical attacks upon him.

Dow married Peggy Miller in 1802. Her journal, one of the few written by the spouse of a nineteenth-century evangelist, details their troubles at home and abroad, the criticisms visited upon them, and the death of several of their children. Peggy Dow herself died in childbirth. Accompanied by his wife, Dow arrived in England in December 1805 and began preaching with support from the Methodist New Connection, a revivalistic Wesleyan movement.

In England Dow also created controversy by his practice of predicting or prophesying particularly dire events that were to fall upon individuals in his audiences. At an 1806 meeting in Frodsham he reportedly approached a young woman in the congregation and warned her that she would be dead in less than a year. The young woman was converted and died a few months later. Such actions created fear in many of his listeners and criticism from those who warned that he was unstable. The fact that many of the participants in Dow's meetings also claimed direct revelation through visions and dreams contributed to the criticism of his methods and ideas.

Dow himself was a frequent critic of the Methodist system when it led to conflict between the local itinerants and the traveling revivalists. He represented the revivalist wing, which was often at odds with the settled, pastoral segment of the denomination. In spite of his disagreements with the Methodist leadership, Dow remained devoted to Methodist doctrine throughout his life. His behavior and mental condition, along with his inability to conform to the Methodist itinerant program, led to his controversies inside and outside the church. Dow's journal and theological writings were published in 1856 in a collection entitled *The Life, Travel, Labors, and Writings of Lorenzo Dow*.

Bibliography. Carwardine, R., *Transatlantic Revivalism* (Westport, CT: Greenwood Publishing, 1978); Reid, Daniel G., *Dictionary of Christianity in America* (Downers Grove: InterVarsity Press, 1990): 365; Sellers, C., *Lorenzo Dow: The Bearer of the Word* (New York: Minton Balch, Inc., 1928).

Bill J. Leonard

Drew, Timothy. Timothy Drew was the first person to introduce Islam to the African-American masses at the turn of the twentieth century. Born in rural North Carolina on January 8, 1886, he was named Timothy Drew at birth. In spite of being reared poor and uneducated, Drew traveled extensively as a youth. Upon visiting Islamic countries, he became extremely impressed by the limited amount of racial prejudice. He also concluded that African Americans were Moors, descendants of Moabites of Canaan, and originally from Morocco.

Returning to the United States, Drew founded the Moorish Science Temple* of Islam in 1913 in Newark, New Jersey. He changed his name to Noble Drew Ali, saying that he had received the name from Sultan Abdul Ali Saud while visiting Mecca. His organization spread to several northern cities, and he established headquarters in Chicago in 1925. In 1927 Ali published *The Holy Koran*, which is not to be confused with the sacred text of orthodox Islam. His book was sixty pages long, consisting of Moorish Science beliefs and using Levi Dowling's *The Aquarian Gospel of Jesus Christ* as a primary source. Several chapters were supposedly based on a Tibetan text published by the de Lawrence Company in 1923.

Ali believed that before the American Revolution blacks freely flew the bright red Moorish flag. It was this flag that George Washington really cut down, and not a cherry tree. He also believed that the Continental army destroyed blacks' nationality, forcing them into slavery. Over time, blacks forgot their true identity and the religion of Islam. In turn, blacks became Christians. Ali's real mission as the prophet of Allah was to teach blacks their true religion and identity. With this idea in mind, Ali requested that President Wilson return the Moorish flag, believing that it had been kept in Independence Hall since 1776.

Ali also taught his followers that Islam was the religion of Moors, black Africans who had earlier conquered a major portion of Europe. For this reason, Ali pondered how African Americans could be treated so horribly now, when they were historically related to such a glorious past. Thus he concluded that there was a connection between what people were called and how they were treated. So his followers were no longer to be called Negroes or Africans. Instead, they were to be known as Moorish Americans. Each Moor was given a new name and an identity card declaring his religion and political status. This was especially important in American society, in which Christian Negroes were generally held in low esteem. To join the temple, it was necessary to accept Moorish identity and give a one-dollar donation.

Ali's movement used Qur'an, fezzes, Muslim names, and the rejection of basic Christian beliefs. It was a blend of Christian and Muslim ideals and practices.

Ali died under mysterious circumstances in July 1929. Some reports believed that his death was related to a power struggle within the organization itself. By 1928 Ali had established seventeen temples in fifteen states, with a membership estimated at twenty to thirty thousand. According to at least one scholar, the alleged stranger from the East and founder of the Nation of Islam,* Wallace Fard, had earlier been a member of Ali's movement. Regardless, Ali's Moorish Science Temple of Islam was the antecedent of several black consciousness movements, including the Nation of Islam, that would soon follow.

Bibliography. Fauset, A., *Black Gods of the Metropolis* (Philadelphia: University of Pennsylvania Press, 1971); Melton, J. G., ed., *Religious Leaders of America* (Detroit: Gale Research 1991); Murphy, L., ed., *Encyclopedia of African American Religions* (New York: Garland Pub., 1993); Wilmore, G. S., ed., *African American Religious Studies* (Durham: Duke University Press, 1989).

Lawrence H. Williams

Dyer, Mary. Described by many of her contemporaries as "fair" and "comely," the youthful Mary Barrett was married to the Puritan William Dyer, a milliner in London's New Exchange, on October 27, 1633. Like so many other English Puritans of that day, they saw persecution ahead if they remained in England, and so sometime in late 1634 or early 1635 the Dyers emigrated to New England, receiving admission to the church at Boston on December 13, 1635. They quickly came under the influence of Anne Hutchinson,* whose "antinomian" belief that the Holy Spirit dwelt within a justified person, granting each believer assurance of salvation and immediate revelation from God, the Dyers found most comforting. During the Antinomian Crisis of 1636–1638 they sided with Anne Hutchinson and the Reverend John Wheelwright against the civil and ecclesiastical authorities of the day and consequently were disenfranchised from the colony in the civil trial that was held in November 1637 for Anne Hutchinson and her followers. Shortly before this trial, on October 17, Mary Dyer, enduring her fourth pregnancy in four years, experienced a horrendous premature birthing. Assisted by Anne Hutchinson as midwife, she delivered a fetuspositioned upside down with the buttocks, not the head, appearing first. The baby, eventually delivered stillborn, was so grotesque that Hutchinson, upon the advice of John Cotton, removed the baby (before Mary had recovered) and buried it, as was the custom of the day. In many later accounts, Mary Dyer would be known as the "woman who had the monster." John Winthrop described the baby (after ordering the body exhumed for inspection) as having "a face, but no head, and the ears stood upon the shoulders and were like an ape's; it had no forehead, but over the eyes four horns, hard, and sharp; . . . it had two mouths, and in each of them a piece of red flesh sticking out; it had arms and legs as other children; but, instead of toes, it had on each foot three claws, like a young fowl, with sharp talons" (*History*, 267). To the anti-Hutchinsonians, Dyer's "monster" was evidence of God's judgment upon her and her family for embracing the "monstrous errors," as Winthrop put it, of Anne Hutchinson. She had been disciplined, and the hideous fetus was to serve as a lesson to all. After Anne Hutchinson's excommunication in March 1638, Mary Dyer and her husband joined the Hutchinsons and several others who had been disenfranchised in emigrating to Rhode Island.

During a stay in England (1652–1657) Mary Dyer converted to Quakerism, whose doctrine of the "inner light" was not that far from Anne Hutchinson's emphasis upon the "indwelling Holy Spirit." Upon her return to New England she became a crusader for the Society of Friends in a most hostile environment. Throughout much of New England numerous laws had been passed against "the cursed sect of heretics . . . commonly called Quakers," and Dyer was bent on challenging them all. On October 19, 1658, Massachusetts passed a law banishing all Quakers "upon pain of death." Two Quakers were already in jail, and Dyer decided to join them in the summer of 1659. After she had spent some time with them, all three were banished from the colony. They soon returned, however, and on October 19, 1659, she and the other Friends were tried once again, only this time Governor John Endecott pronounced a sentence of death upon them. On October 27, 1659, Mary Dyer, along with William Robinson and Marmaduke Stephenson, were led through the streets of Boston to the gallows accompanied by beating drums so that "none might hear her speak all the way" (Bishop, 163). The two men were hanged, but Dyer, though bound and haltered, was given a last-minute reprieve. Her husband and children were not Quakers, and they tried to keep her out of Massachusetts, but she made it known that her chief desire was to repeal "the unrighteous and unjust law of banishment upon pain of death" (Bishop, 164). On May 31, 1660, she fulfilled that mission, receiving once again a sentence of death from John Endecott. This time the execution was carried out the next day. She was steadfast to the end, proclaiming to the Boston crowd, "I came to do the will of my Father, and in obedience to his will I stand even to the death" (Bishop, 164). As with Anne Hutchinson, her early mentor and fellow excommunicant, her stand for freedom of religion was eventually recognized by the erection of a statue in her honor on the grounds of the Massachusetts State House in Boston.

Bibliography. Barbour, Hugh, and Arthur O. Roberts, eds., *Early Quaker Writings, 1650–1700* (Grand Rapids, MI: Eerdmans, 1973), 136–40; Bishop, George, *New England*

Judged (London, 1661), in *Major Problems in American Colonial History*, ed. Karen Ordahl Kupperman (New York: Heath, 1993), 162–64; Hall, David D., *The Antinomian Controversy, 1636–38: A Documentary History*, 2nd ed. (Durham, NC: Duke University Press, 1990); Plimpton, Ruth Talbot, *Mary Dyer: Biography of a Rebel Quaker* (Boston: Branden, 1994); Winthrop, John, *History of New England, 1630–49*, vol. 1, ed. James Kendall Hosmer (New York: Barnes and Noble, 1959); Winthrop, John, *A Short Story of the Rise, Reign, and Ruine of the Antinomians, Familists, and Libertines* (London, 1644), in Hall, *The Antinomian Controversy*, 199–310.

Timothy D. Whelan

E

Ecumenism. Early American ecumenical efforts were usually individual initiatives, often directed at common missionary efforts. John Eliot (1604–1690) advocated a hybrid Presbyterian-Congregational polity and urged cooperation in his missions to Native Americans. Cotton Mather (1663–1728) proposed international and interdenominational missionary societies and outlined a fourteen-point plan for church union. Jonathan Edwards* (1703–1758) followed the Scottish design of an ecumenical "Concert" of prayer groups as a prelude to the ecumenical revivals of the Great Awakening.* Nicolaus Ludwig Zinzendorf (1700–1760) convened a series of Pennsylvania synods from 1742 to 1748, urging Lutherans, Reformed, Presbyterians, Episcopalians, Quakers, Mennonites, Brethren, Sabbatarians, Inspired, and Individual Separatists to cooperate through intercommunion, pulpit exchanges, shared devotional literature, and a common mission to Native Americans. None of these individual efforts succeeded in attracting widespread, sustained support.

Nineteenth-century ecumenists pursued a pragmatic efficiency in the establishment of numerous voluntary societies, many of which continue to thrive. Such missionary societies included the American Board of Commissioners for Foreign Missions (1810), the American Education Society (1815), the American Bible Society (1816), the American Sunday-School Union (1824), and the American Tract Society (1825). Reform societies encompassed the American Society for the Promotion of Temperance (1826), the American Peace Society (1828), and the American Antislavery Society (1833). Controversies arose over the relation of individual denominations to such voluntary societies, and many individuals spurned such ecumenical cooperation: Methodists sponsored their own missionary societies, while Baptists* and Disciples viewed any such societies as "unbiblical," and most Episcopalians declined to participate.

Many nineteenth-century plans for interdenominational cooperation were short-lived. The 1801 Plan of Union between Congregational and Presbyterian churches effectively ended with the Presbyterian 1837 Old School/New School* schism. In 1838 Samuel Simon Schmucker (1799–1873) published his *Fraternal Appeal to the American Churches, with a Plan for Catholic Union, on Apostolic Principles*, proposing a federation of autonomous denominations subscribing to a "United Confession" with shared ministry and intercommunion, but subsequent discussions proved fruitless. Philip Schaff* (1819–1893) helped establish the International Evangelical Alliance in 1846, but an American branch was not established until 1867, when slavery had been abolished. William Reed Huntington (1838–1918) proposed a union around the fourfold list of Anglican "essentials" that became known as the Chicago-Lambeth Quadrilateral, but others perceived his plan as a thinly veiled invitation to join a broadened Episcopalian denomination.

Recent ecumenical efforts have been most successful at the grassroots level. Ministerial alliances have been organized in various metropolitan areas, beginning with Rhode Island's Westerly Plan in 1870 and the Baltimore Ministerial Union in 1885. States began to organize church federations at the turn of the century, beginning with Maine and New York by the end of 1900 and Massachusetts, Rhode Island, and Ohio the following year. Cities began to follow suit as Oswego, New York, and Hartford, Connecticut, led the way in organized local interchurch councils. National ecumenical efforts have been more controversial, however.

National interchurch councils have come under fire for their perceived political leanings. The Federal Council of the Churches of Christ in America (FCC), founded in 1908, came under attack by conservatives for its political support of labor unions, and by liberals for its political ineffectiveness. The 1929 American Legion annual convention demanded that Congress investigate the "subversive" influences on the Federal Council, and other critics charged the council with "socialism," "internationalism," and "communism." Carl McIntire* founded the American Council of Christian Churches (ACCC) in 1941 to "challenge and offset" the Federal Council of Churches, and the National Association of Evangelicals was established in 1942 as a centrist alternative to the FCC and the ACCC. More recently, the National Council of the Churches of Christ in the USA (founded in 1950) and the World Council of Churches (established in 1948) have similarly been criticized for their social policies. Many denominations, including the Southern Baptist Convention,* the Lutheran Church–Missouri Synod, and many Pentecostal and Holiness churches, have remained aloof from such interchurch councils, while others, such as the Unitarian Universalist Association and the Metropolitan Community Churches, have not been welcomed.

Twentieth-century efforts at ecumenical organic union have been controversial and unsuccessful thus far. At the invitation of the Presbyterian Church, seventeen denominations met in Philadelphia on December 4, 1918, to formulate the unsuccessful Philadelphia Plan for organic union. In 1949 seven denominations sent representatives to the American Conference on Church Union meeting in Greenwich, Connecticut, to develop the equally ineffective Greenwich Plan. Decades after the groundwork for the Consultation on Church Union (COCU) was laid by Eugene Carson Blake in his December 4, 1960, sermon at San Francisco's Grace Episcopal Cathedral, nine denominations continued to study and refine the merger proposal.

After the failure of the Philadelphia Plan, Ad Interim Committee chairman Joseph A. Vance discerned several barriers to ecumenical cooperation. First, churches were reluctant to sacrifice their denominational identity for the sake of ecumenism. Second, theological liberals and conservatives persisted in mutual distrust. Finally, differences of ''religious temperament and intellectual attitude'' continued to cause strife among Christians. Eight decades later, his observations still ring true.

Bibliography. Cavert, Samuel McCrea, *Church Cooperation and Unity in America: A Historical Review: 1900–1970* (New York: Association Press, 1970); Macfarland, Charles S., *Across the Years* (New York: Macmillan, 1936); Rouse, Ruth, and Stephen Charles Neill, eds., *A History of the Ecumenical Movement, 1517–1948*, 2nd ed. (Philadelphia: Westminster Press, 1967); Roy, Ralph Lord, *Apostles of Discord: A Study of Organized Bigotry and Disruption on the Fringes of Protestantism* (Boston: Beacon Press, 1953); Sanderson, Ross W., *Church Cooperation in the United States: The Nationwide Backgrounds and Ecumenical Significance of State and Local Councils of Churches in Their Historical Perspective* (New York: Association of Council Secretaries, 1960).

David B. McCarthy

Eddy, Mary Baker. Committed to a radically idealistic form of Christian thought, Mary Baker Eddy (1821–1910) believed that Christ was Love, and that Love triumphed over evil, death, and the illusion of material reality. She argued that Jesus and others who knew this Truth about the ultimate nature of reality were Scientists able to dispel illusions about the existence of disease and the suffering these illusions caused.

Eddy dated her discovery of Christian Science to 1866, when she was forty-five years old and rose from her bed three days after a fall on the ice in Lynn, Massachusetts, believing herself to have been healed by the power of Christ. In Boston in 1881, she founded the Massachusetts Metaphysical College, which enrolled hundreds of students in courses on Eddy's theology and its application in treating disease without medicine and enabling painless childbirth. In an effort to consolidate her work, Eddy established the Church of Christ, Scientist, and laid the cornerstone for the First Church in Boston in 1884. As a religious organization, the church was geographically far-reaching, financially successful, and highly centralized. Eddy's authority was so firmly institutionalized that after her death in 1910, the church continued to flourish under the guidance of its Board of Directors, and no other leader emerged to assume or recast her mantle.

Eddy's *Science and Health, with Key to the Scriptures* (1906; first edition 1875) remains the centerpiece of Christian Science life, along with the New Testament. *Science and Health* defines Christian doctrine in symbolic terms and interprets the central elements of Christianity in terms of mental experience. Thus prayer is truthful desire, eucharist the meeting of individual mind with Christ, and marriage the companionship of masculine and feminine qualities. The text explains the apparent existence of material reality as a consequence of erroneous belief. The suffering caused by this erroneous belief epitomizes mortal life, and Christian Science treats that suffering.

Numerous controversies plagued Eddy and the church she founded. Belief in Eddy's authority as the modern incarnation of Jesus emerged in the 1880s and proved difficult to expunge; in 1991 the Church of Christ, Scientist, reversed its earlier decision not to publish Bliss Knapp's *Destiny of the Mother Church*, which presented Eddy as an ''incarnation of truth'' comparable to Jesus, after Knapp's wife and sister made a $50-million bequest contingent on the book's publication. During her own lifetime Eddy became embroiled in conflicts with many of her disciples, some of whom she accused of attempting to kill her through negative mental influence. Controversy also swirled around the question of Eddy's indebtedness to Phineas P. Quimby,* on whose work Eddy built in her own efforts to treat pain through mental influence.

Important similarities exist between Eddy's thought and New England transcendentalism.* Although transcendentalism was on the wane in America after the Civil War, Eddy persisted in carrying forward its commitments to the ultimate reality of Spirit and to the authority of Spirit's revelation to individual mind. While her idealistic interpretation of the New Testament left her completely unencumbered by the anxieties about scientific and literary criticism of the Bible that plagued many of her contemporaries, she rode with the tide of popular enthusiasms for science and health current in late-nineteenth-century America and anticipated later reforms in American health care, such as natural childbirth and mental strategies for achieving wellness and freedom from pain. But however farsighted Eddy was in her belief in the power of mental influence, her gender and lack of formal education excluded her from discussions with contemporaries who participated in the professionalization of science in late-nineteenth-century America. Her Divine Science developed outside the main currents of scholarly thought, sidestepped the intellectual challenges of both social Darwinism and secularization, and addressed a constituency that was overwhelmingly female.

Bibliography. Dakin, Edwin Franden, *Mrs. Eddy: The Biography of a Virginal Mind* (New York: Charles Scribner's Sons, 1929); Gottschalk, Stephen, *The Emergence of Christian Science in American Religious Life* (Berkeley: University of California Press, 1973); Knee, Stuart E., *Christian Science in the Age of Mary Baker Eddy* (Westport,

CT: Greenwood Press, 1994); Peel, Robert, *Christian Science: Its Encounter with American Culture* (New York: Henry Holt and Company, 1958).

Amanda Porterfield

Edwards, Jonathan. Jonathan Edwards (1703–1758) was a Congregational minister. He earned a B.A. in 1720 and an M.A. in 1722 at Yale and assisted and succeeded his grandfather, Solomon Stoddard, at Northampton, Massachusetts, in 1729. Dismissed by his congregation in 1749, he accepted a call to a Native American mission in Stockbridge, Massachusetts. In 1758 the College of New Jersey (now Princeton) called him as president, but he died of a smallpox inoculation shortly after moving to his new appointment.

Alarmed at the influence of Deism, Arminianism, and budding Enlightenment thought, Edwards articulated Calvinist and Reformed beliefs that were often controversial. Against the Deist notion of the unmoved mover, Edwards believed that God was everywhere active and was creating the world at every moment. Edwards considered the world to be a divine language, a divine light that sinful minds could not see unless they were converted by the Holy Spirit.

Against the Arminians, who stressed human ability and believed that sin was caused by ignorance or moral dissolution, and that salvation was only a life lived in reasonable accord with Jesus' ethical teachings, Edwards said that human sin was inherent enmity against God. Salvation meant a radical conversion of the heart and was based totally on God's sovereignty.

Edwards wrote four controversial treatises defending the Great Awakening* against Arminian critics who disparaged emotional fervor and Enthusiasts who allowed religious feelings to become disruptive. In *A Treatise Concerning Religious Affections* Edwards underscored the importance of "affections" or feelings in religion, believing that there could be no true religion without them. Among the distinguishing signs of "truly gracious and holy affections" was a "new inward perception, different from any former kind of sensation of the mind," a sort of special "taste" (Jonathan Edwards, *A Treatise Concerning Religious Affections,* 1746). For Edwards, Christian spiritual experience was analogous to sensory experience, and such spiritual experience provided authentic knowledge of divine reality. The chief objective ground of these "gracious affections" was the "excellent nature of divine things as they are themselves." This internal evidence of the gospel was the surest evidence of the truth of the gospel. So feelings were not necessarily a form of madness or hysteria, and revivals were surprising works of God. The "affections" reflected a divine and supernatural light at work in the community. The whole heart (intellect, will, emotion) was affected by conversion. True religious experience involved a new sense of the heart, transforming the individual from love of self to love of God.

For Edwards, the true mark of conversion was a holy life. True faith was deeply private and arose from a transformed heart, but it was not privatistic or devoid of active concern for society. He believed that religion directed mankind's deeper actions away from natural tendencies of self-love toward the divine and supernatural glory of God, and that changed hearts led to social effects. In 1741 he drew up a covenant for his congregation at Northampton binding its members to live their faith visibly. Edwards's congregation resisted the radical notion that faith must be visible, some thinking that prosperity was a sign of God's blessing and favor already.

The controversy in his congregation over requiring members to live their faith visibly came to a head in 1749 when Edwards stated specific qualifications for complete and full communion. In doing so, he repudiated the Half-way Covenant* in vogue since the ministry of Solomon Stoddard that allowed unregenerate children of regenerate parents to baptize their offspring, providing they led an upright life and agreed to adhere to church covenants before the assembled congregation. Edwards was dismissed in 1750. He accepted a call to a Native American mission in Stockbridge, where he expressed the controversial views that Indian girls should be able to attend school, that the Massachusetts Assembly should honor treaty obligations to the Housatonnuk Indians, and that New England had "debauched" the Indians with strong drink instead of seeking their spiritual welfare.

Edwards was something of an ecumenist, a stance not universally appreciated. In 1747 he wrote *An Humble Attempt to Promote Explicit and Visible Union of God's People* and boldly envisioned all American congregations joining in prayer and common times with Scottish congregations.

Edwards had an extensive theology of church and state, in advance of his times and certainly controversial. He stressed Christians' public duties, including the duty to work for the public good with non-Christians. He believed that churchgoers had an obligation to help the poor, that Christians had a responsibility to society beyond their church walls, and that Christians should not hesitate to join forces with non-Christians in the public square to work toward common moral goals. Christians should support their governments but be ready to criticize them publicly when the occasion demanded. Christians should remember that politics was comparatively unimportant in the long run and that Christians should beware of national pride. The most important thing Christians could do for their country was to pray for revival and spiritual transformations.

Bibliography. Gaustad, E. S., *The Great Awakening in New England* (New York: Harper and Row, 1957); Goen, C. C., ed., *The Works of Jonathan Edwards* (New Haven: Yale University Press, 1972) (these works include *A Faithful Narrative of the Surprising Work of God,* 1737; *The Distinguishing Marks of a Work of the Spirit of God,* 1741; *Some Thoughts Concerning the Present Revival of Religion in New England,* 1742; and *A Treatise Concerning Religious Affections,* 1746); McDermott, G., "What Jonathan Edwards Can Teach Us about Politics," *Christianity Today* 38, no. 8 (July 18, 1994) 32; Miller, P., *Jonathan Edwards* (New York: William Sloan Associates, 1949).

Robert K. Gustafson

Electronic Church. The "electronic church" usually refers to the television ministries that are a central element of contemporary evangelicalism. Religious broadcasters, including Aimee Semple Mcpherson* and Charles E. Fuller, were actually some of the earliest radio pioneers during the 1920s and 1930s. Mc-Pherson became the first nationally known Pentecostal, and Fuller's "Old Fashion Revival Hour" included the earliest religious talk show.

Conflict sometimes surrounded religious radio. Mainline denominations attempted to keep fundamentalist preachers off the major networks. The exploitative tactics of sensationalism and exposés were present from the start. Father Charles Coughlin* drew large audiences for his controversial economic and political diatribes during the 1930s.

In the 1950s television ministries began. Oral Roberts,* Rex Humbard, Billy Graham,* and Bishop Fulton J. Sheen* were pioneers. Roberts, for example, televised tent revival services until 1967, when he shifted to the variety-show format. Denominations like the Southern Baptist Convention* also engaged in television ministry as early as 1954.

Television ministries grew as they made use of independent UHF stations. With the advent of cable and satellite technology, religious programming and separate networks, like Pat Robertson's Christian Broadcasting Network and Paul Crouch's Trinity Broadcasting Network, multiplied at a furious rate.

The electronic church, as it developed in the 1980s, covered a gamut of issues. Fundamentalists like Jerry Falwell* and Charles Stanley offered traditional worship formats with evangelistic preaching. Falwell also entered the political arena with his Moral Majority* leadership. Pat Robertson mixed in social and political commentary on his influential talk show, the "700 Club." Charismatic religion has been central to the electronic church, being promoted by Robertson, Jim Bakker,* Benny Hinn, and others.

Controversy continuously engulfs the electronic church. Evangelists are charged with constantly gouging people for contributions. Financial and sex scandals rocked the ministries of prominent evangelists Jimmy Swaggart and Jim Bakker and others. Critics of the religious right complain that religious television is simply an arm of conservative politics. Critics also contend that television evangelism only reaches persons who are already Christian, and while it helps strengthen their faith, the electronic church too often confuses the gospel with American cultural values of success and materialism.

Bibliography. Horsfield, P. G. *Religious Television: The American Experience* (New York: Longman, 1984); Martin, William, "Mass Communications," in *Encyclopedia of the American Religious Experience*, ed. Charles Lippy and Peter Williams, 3 vols. (New York: Scribners, 1988): 1711–26; Schultze, Q. J., "The Mythos of the Electronic Church," *Critical Studies in Mass Communication* 4 (1987): 45–61.

Douglas Weaver

Elijah Muhammad. Elijah Poole was born in Sandersville, Georgia, on October 7, 1897. His impoverished childhood allowed him only a third-grade education before he had to leave school to go to work. In 1923 he moved to Detroit to work in the auto factories. In Detroit he joined Marcus Garvey's* organization and then met Wali Fard Muhammad, founder of what came to be known as the Nation of Islam.* Poole joined Fard's movement by 1931 and was renamed Elijah Muhammad. He soon became the chief minister to Fard and in 1932 was authorized to establish Temple No. 2 in Chicago's South Side. Fard mysteriously disappeared in 1934, and in the ensuing struggle for leadership Elijah withdrew to his base in Chicago. His was the only faction among Fard's heirs to survive the tumultuous period.

Elijah remained the leader of the Nation of Islam for over forty years. Under his leadership the movement became a stable institution that allowed it to withstand the rigors of the depression years and World War II, as well as the distractions of the postwar civil rights* movements (as a separatist organization, the Nation had little patience with advocates of integration). His primary contribution in doctrine was the new teaching that W. Fard Muhammad was actually Allah incarnate and that Elijah Muhammad was Allah's messenger and prophet. Allah, then, was a black man and not the spirit or ''spook'' of the white man's Christianity. But Fard was not a god complete in himself; all black persons were divine and in some sense participated in his divinity.

By the 1960s the Nation of Islam had attained unprecedented popularity and notoriety, largely due to Elijah's charismatic chief minister Malcolm X.* In the midst of his triumph, however, Elijah faced trying challenges. One was that his son Wallace, whom he was grooming for succession to the leadership, was pressing for changes in doctrine and ritual that would bring the Nation into conformity with the world community of Islam. The other was the so-called Elijah affair, the discovery by Malcolm X that Elijah had had children by several of his secretaries. Malcolm's refusal to condone the practice led to his being silenced by Elijah and to Malcolm's departure from the Nation. It is a striking testimony to Elijah's leadership skills that Malcolm's defection and murder, combined with the emergence of competing militant black activist groups in the last half of the decade, did not deal a serious blow to the Nation of Islam. Elijah died in February 1975 after having named his son Wallace to be his successor, despite knowing that the latter intended to make radical changes in the organization.

See also Louis Farrakhan.

Bibliography. Lincoln, C. E., *The Black Muslims in America* (Boston: Beacon Press, 1961; rev. ed., 1973); Marsh, C. E., *From Black Muslims to Muslims: The Transition from Separatism to Islam, 1930–1980* (Metuchen, NJ: Scarecrow Press, 1984); Munir, F. Z., ''Islam in America: An African American Pilgrimage toward Coherence'' (Ph.D. diss., Temple University, 1993).

Vernon Egger

Equal Rights Amendment. The Equal Rights Amendment (ERA) was a failed amendment to the U.S. Constitution that would have guaranteed equal rights to persons irrespective of sex. First introduced in Congress in 1923 by the National

Woman's party, ERA became part of GOP and Democratic party platforms in the 1940s, but then languished until 1963, when it was rejected by President Kennedy's Commission on the Status of Women. It was resurrected in 1967 by the National Organization for Women, was passed readily by both houses of Congress, and was sent to the states for ratification in March 1972. Although ERA initially attracted little attention, it aroused national furor in state legislatures. Even with the deadline for ratification extended, it fell three states short of the required number and officially died in June 1982.

The battle over ERA was a religious controversy in two ways: it sparked conflict in particular religious communities, and it assumed the tenor of a spiritual and moral crusade. While some denominations supported and others opposed it, ERA especially divided Roman Catholics and Mormons. Catholic opponents included the National Council of Catholic Women, the Knights of Columbus, Holy Name Societies, and the Catholic Daughters. They argued that ERA threatened the natural order of the sexes and would cause women to abandon home and family. Opponents seized on *Roe v. Wade*, the 1973 Supreme Court decision legalizing abortion, as evidence of the immorality that would result from ERA's ratification. Phyllis Schlafly, the founder of Stop ERA, with branches in forty-five states by 1978, said a rosary daily for ERA's demise.

However, many Catholics supported ERA, including the Saint Joan's Society, the Canon Law Society of America, the National Conference of Catholic Charities, Women Theologians United, the National Coalition of Nuns, and National Assembly of Women Religious. Supporters argued that ERA was a justice issue. In 1974 Catholic Women for the ERA nailed a bill of women's rights to the doors of Saint Patrick's Cathedral in New York. While U.S. bishops took no official stand, twenty-three issued a statement in 1982 urging ratification.

The Church of Jesus Christ of Latter-Day Saints was instrumental in defeating ERA in Utah, Florida, Nevada, Georgia, and Virginia. The Mormon hierarchy officially opposed it in 1976, arguing that it erased natural differences between women and men. Calling on the faithful to defeat this ''unisex amendment,'' the church distributed anti-ERA literature and organized letter and phone campaigns. Mormons lobbied legislators relentlessly, usually without identifying themselves. In states with small Mormon populations, they created the illusion of a spontaneous groundswell of opposition.

Mormons for ERA (MERA) was formed in 1978. MERA exposed the covert tactics used by the church in state antiratification campaigns and challenged the hierarchy in the media. The church retaliated: in 1979, MERA leader Sonia Johnson was excommunicated. In doing so, the church rejected feminism; despite the admission of black men to the priesthood, the status of Mormon women would remain unchanged.

Besides dividing Catholics and Mormons, the ERA struggle itself became a religious crusade in which each side saw itself as waging ''spiritual warfare.'' For opponents, ERA violated God-given gender hierarchy. Its results would be blasphemous: homosexual marriage and child rearing, unisex bathrooms, and women serving in military combat. Arguing from biblical literalism, opponents declared that woman was created to be subordinate and submissive to man, not become man. Supporters also used religious imagery, albeit less than opponents. They argued from Genesis 1 that women and men were both created in the image of God and from Galatians 3:28 that in Christ there was no male nor female. Woman's role as wife and mother would be enhanced by equality and mutuality with men. A matter of divine justice, ERA promised salvation from the sin of sexism.

The ERA holy war had several lasting effects. It stimulated debate on ordination of women,* inclusive language about humanity and deity, and feminist theology. Moreover, its defeat was an early triumph for the New Christian Right. The success for "family values"* fueled later movements to reestablish prayer in public schools and overturn abortion rights.

Bibliography. Iadarola, Antoinette, "The American Catholic Bishops and Women: From the Nineteenth Amendment to ERA," in *Women, Religion, and Social Change,* ed. Yvonne Y. Haddad and Ellison B. Findly (Albany: State University of New York Press, 1985), 457–76.; Kennelly, James, "A Question of Equality," in *American Catholic Women: A Historical Exploration,* ed. Karen Kennelly (New York: Macmillan, 1989), 125–51; Mathews, Donald G., " 'Spiritual Warfare': Cultural Fundamentalism and the Equal Rights Amendment," *Religion and American Culture* 3 (Summer 1993): 129–54; White, O. Kendall, Jr., "Mormonism and the Equal Rights Amendment," *Journal of Church and State* 31 (Spring 1989): 249–67.

Evelyn A. Kirkley

Ethnic Hostility in the Catholic Community. During the colonial period, within the Spanish, French, and English colonies, there was virtually no ethnic hostility in the respective Catholic communities due to the homogeneous nature of the European population. However, in both the Spanish and French colonies of North America, there was considerable tension between the European rulers and the Native Americans. Spanish efforts to colonize Florida in the early sixteenth century provoked determined resistance from the native population; in New Mexico the Pueblo Revolt of 1680 resulted in the death of some four hundred Spaniards. French attempts to evangelize the Iroquois in upstate New York in the seventeenth century produced equally determined resistance.

In colonial Maryland the Catholic population was largely of English ancestry with an admixture of Irish. The first real ethnic diversity among Catholics in English-speaking America occurred with the immigration of German Catholics to Pennsylvania in the late eighteenth century. In Philadelphia in 1789 they established Holy Trinity Church, the first national parish in the United States.

Between 1815 and 1850 massive emigration from Ireland and Germany led to an increase in the Catholic population to two million. In Philadelphia, Baltimore, New York, Buffalo, and elsewhere German-speaking congregations clashed with non-German bishops. Ethnic hostility was often connected with lay trusteeism,* a widespread phenomenon in the American Catholic Church at that time, whereby lay boards of trustees laid claim to control the administration of parishes. Conflict was not limited to German-Irish confrontation. In Charleston and Norfolk Irish lay trustees resisted the appointment of French pastors; in New York French-born Bishop John Dubois (1826–1842) encountered widespread resentment from his largely Irish flock.

In the two decades after the Civil War, German Catholic immigration outstripped that of the Irish. The German Catholic presence was especially noticeable in the Midwest, where Germans complained of domination by the largely Irish-American hierarchy (which they dubbed the "hibernarchy"). In 1887 Peter Abbelen, vicar general of the Archdiocese of Milwaukee, presented a memorial in Rome calling attention to alleged discrimination against German national parishes. In 1890, under the leadership of Peter Paul Cahensly, the Raphaelsverein, an international German Catholic immigrant aid society, issued the Lucerne memorial, calling for proportional representation of all ethnic groups in the American hierarchy. Archbishop John Ireland of St. Paul, the leading assimilationist in the American hierarchy, mendaciously accused Cahensly of being an agent of the German imperial government and launched a campaign against "Cahenslyism."

The 1890s witnessed the first large-scale immigration to the United States of Italians and Eastern Europeans. Italian anticlericalism, lack of financial support for the church, and their own emotional devotional practices meant that often they were poorly received in established American parishes. The Polish Catholic immigrants produced the one enduring schism in American Catholicism, the Polish National Catholic Church, founded around 1904 as a result of disagreements between Polish priests and Irish-American bishops, and also as a result of rivalries among the Polish American clergy themselves. Like the German Americans in the nineteenth century, Polish Americans complained of their lack of representation in the American hierarchy and in the 1920s even appealed for help to the newly established Polish government. Ironically, among their severest critics was Cardinal George Mundelein of Chicago, the first German-American cardinal. Among Slovak Catholics—the second-largest Slavic group to come to the United States—internal divisions often pitted pro-Hungarian ("Magyarone") and anti-Hungarian nationalistic Slovaks against one another.

Ukrainian and Ruthenian Catholic immigrants posed a special pastoral problem for the American Catholic Church, since both of these Slavic peoples belonged to the Byzantine-Slavonic rite of the Catholic Church. In Europe they had their own non-Latin liturgy, their own hierarchy, and a long tradition of a married clergy. In the United States the Catholic bishops refused to sanction the presence of married priests of this rite, with the result that some 225,000 of these Slavic immigrants joined the Russian Orthodox Church. In 1907 Rome appointed the first Byzantine-Slavonic bishop for the United States, Soter Ortynsky. Internal dissension led Rome in 1924 to establish separate hierarchies for the Ukrainians and Ruthenians in the United States.

In the late nineteenth century French Canadians emigrated in large numbers from Quebec to the mill towns of New England. In the twentieth century in Maine and Rhode Island French-Canadian desire for the *survivance* of their ethnic identity erupted in open conflict with Irish American bishops. In the twentieth century the single largest Catholic immigrant group has been the Hispanics, who now constitute perhaps as much as one-quarter of the Catholic population of the United States. Their presence is especially obvious in Florida, Texas, California, and the Southwest. Hispanic Catholics are themselves divided into several distinct ethnic groups—most notably Mexicans, Puerto Ricans, Cubans, Dominicans, and Central and South Americans—who do not always relate well with one another. Although no formal schisms have occurred, large numbers of Hispanic immigrants have left the Catholic Church for Protestant churches of the evangelical and Pentecostal traditions.

Bibliography. Barry, Colman J., *The Catholic Church and German Americans* (Milwaukee: Bruce, 1953); Deck, Allan Figueroa, *The Second Wave: Hispanic Ministry and the Evangelization of Cultures* (New York: Paulist Press, 1989); Fogarty, Gerald P., "The American Hierarchy and Oriental Rite Catholics, 1890–1970," *Records of the American Catholic Historical Society of Philadelphia* 85 (1974): 17–28; Galush, William, "The Polish National Catholic Church: A Survey of Its Origins, Development, and Missions," *Records of the American Catholic Historical Society of Philadelphia* 83 (September–December 1972): 131–49; McCaffrey, Lawrence J., *The Irish Diaspora in America* (Bloomington: Indiana University Press, 1976) .

Thomas J. Shelley

Evolution Controversy. Debate over the teaching of Charles Darwin's theory of the development of species first flared up in the 1920s; today the subject is subsumed under the broader heading of creation science.* Opposition to the teaching of evolution in American schools was not widespread before World War I. The fundamentalist movement, which took formal shape in the first two decades of the twentieth century, exercised itself over biblical criticism, which had spread from Germany to many American universities and divinity schools by 1900. Conservative Christians felt that the foundation of their faith, the inerrant Bible, was under attack. Evolution remained a side issue.

More than any other person, William Jennings Bryan* brought evolution to the forefront of the fundamentalist movement. Though a lifelong Christian, Bryan was never a church leader. Most of his church contacts before 1921 were with theological liberals such as Washington Gladden, and he served on the general committee of the radical Interchurch World Movement of North America. But at the same time he was coming to see evolution as the philosophical basis of Germany's militarism, and he was disturbed by studies reporting a decline in college students' assent to Christian belief. He began speaking against evolution before church groups in the spring of 1920 but attracted little attention until he addressed a crowd of about 4,500 at the University of Michigan in the fall of that year. Criticism of his speech prompted Bryan to have it published as "The Menace of Darwinism."

In the fall of 1921 controversy followed Bryan to other college campuses, and a real furor broke out early in 1922 when he spoke at the University of Wisconsin at Madison. The university's president, E. A. Birge, reacted so negatively to the speech that Bryan suggested that the taxpayers of the state might want to select new leadership for their school. The news media began to pay close attention to the controversy. Leading Christian liberals, such as Harry Emerson Fosdick,* emerged to challenge Bryan's claims about the evils of the teaching of evolution. In 1923 Bryan published an article called "The Fundamentals" in the *Forum* that linked his antievolution crusade inextricably with the fundamentalist movement.

For the fundamentalists, evolution was an easier target than the biblical criticism that should have been their primary concern. Scholarly reading of the Bible required knowledge of several languages and of the Scriptures' historical and cultural context that even the leaders of the fundamentalist movement did not possess. Darwin wrote in English, and passionate emotions could be aroused by pointing to links between apes and humans, a tactic as old as Archbishop Wilberforce's question to Thomas Huxley at Oxford in 1860: "Do you trace your descent from the apes through your grandfather or your grandmother?"

The controversy reached its apex in 1925 with the trial of Tennessee teacher John Scopes.* The American Civil Liberties Union offered Clarence Darrow's* services, and the World's Christian Fundamentals Association persuaded Bryan to assist the prosecution. The issue of Scopes's guilt or innocence became lost in the larger conflict. Darrow finally maneuvered Bryan into taking the stand and exposed his ignorance of most facets of theology and biblical scholarship. Bryan died a few days later, and the antievolution crusade went into a period of eclipse by the end of the decade. Several more southern states did pass laws against the teaching of the theory, but no groundswell of support ever materialized.

This lack of success, along with more newsworthy issues such as the depression and World War II, diverted the press's attention from the antievolution crusade. The movement changed tactics in the 1940s and began pressuring local school boards to ban the teaching of evolution or, more recently, to allow the teaching of what is now called "creation science," the Genesis account presented as an alternative to the evolutionary view.

Bibliography. Gatewood, Willard B., Jr., "From Scopes to Creation Science: The Decline and Revival of the Evolution Controversy," *South Atlantic Quarterly* 83 (1984): 363–83; Livingstone, David N., "B. B. Warfield, the Theory of Evolution, and Early Fundamentalism," *Evangelical Quarterly* 58 (1986): 69–83; Szasz, Ferenc M., "William Jennings Bryan, Evolution, and the Fundamentalist-Modernist Controversy," in *Fundamentalism and Evangelicalism*, ed. Martin Marty (New York: Saur, 1993), 98–117; Webb, George, *The Evolution Controversy in America* (Lexington: University Press of Kentucky, 1994).

Albert A. Bell, Jr.

Exorcism. Exorcism is the expelling of an evil spirit from a person, place, or thing by prayer and other sacred rituals. Belief that such spirits exist and can inhabit and control human beings especially is common to many religions; the ancient Jewish and Hellenistic cultures within which Jesus of Nazareth ministered were familiar with exorcism, and the practice formed a significant aspect of his ministry.

Early Christians, both lay and ordained, continued the work of casting out demons. A special clerical order of exorcists was established in the Western church by the middle of the third century, but eventually its functions were largely taken over by the priests. The *Rituale Romanum* (1614) included an elaborate ritual for exorcism, the use of which was restricted to priests with episcopal permission.

The sixteenth-century Protestant Reformers retained belief in demons, but their general simplification of ritual and discrediting of the supernatural powers attributed to the clergy largely undermined the practice of exorcism in Protestant traditions. In America the seventeenth-century Puritans sometimes reported cases of possession, most notably in the detailed account by the Reverend Samuel Willard (1640–1707) of his unsuccessful attempts to exorcise a house servant. But the reaction to the Salem witch hysteria of 1692 ultimately led to widespread cynicism over any further claims of satanic activity.

The emerging materialist assumptions of the Enlightenment and the modern scientific method in the eighteenth century sought alternative explanations for the aberrant behaviors long associated with demoniacs. In the nineteenth century the religious model of treating mental disorders largely gave way to other approaches. The medical model came to view "demonic" symptoms as manifestations of organic dysfunction, even when the precise cause was not known.

Modern psychological theories of the demonic have varied. Freud saw evil spirits as the projection of evil wishes that have been rejected and repressed; Jung considered demons to be symbols forged by the "shadow" archetype within the "collective unconscious" of humanity. Other theorists have concluded that possession cases represent the blocking of personal growth by social forces or a form of adaptive learned behavior.

The mixed clinical results of these approaches have prompted criticism that biomedical rationalism fails to take seriously both the role of cultural factors and the possibility that noncorporeal, nonhuman entities actually exist and influence human behavior. Frequently reported paranormal occurrences (such as levitation) associated with possession cases suggest that more than physiological or psychological disorders are involved. Consequently, even some medical professionals refer patients to religious exorcists after concluding that therapy is ineffective.

Meanwhile, even in the religious community the issue is hotly debated. Theologically liberal Catholics and Protestants tend to deny the existence of demons altogether and trust the cure of the "possessed" to psychiatry. More traditional Christians hold to the ancient belief in unclean spirits, though they may recognize that many disorders once thought demonic (e.g., epilepsy) are not, and that genuine cases of demon possession are rare in America. The Catholic

Church still trains and employs exorcists, and officials such as Pope Paul VI, Pope John Paul II, and Cardinal John O'Connor* of New York have in recent years publicly reaffirmed the church's traditional teaching.

The twentieth-century Pentecostal* and charismatic movements,* whose adherents testify to a transforming encounter with the Holy Spirit, have discovered a heightened awareness of unholy spirits as well. Pentecostals have argued vigorously over the causes of possession and the frequency of its occurrence, the proper methods of exorcism (''deliverance'' ministry), and the issue of whether even ''Spirit-filled Christians'' can ''have a demon.'' As charismatics have spurred lively conversations within mainline and evangelical churches about ''spiritual warfare'' with demons, American popular culture has made its own contributions to the controversy. Televised exorcisms, formerly possessed talk-show guests, nonfiction best-sellers about demonic experiences, and films such as *The Exorcist* assure that demon possession and its cures will remain a perennial topic of debate.

Bibliography. Crabtree, A., *Multiple Man: Explorations in Possession and Multiple Personality* (New York: Praeger, 1985); Linn, M., and D. Linn, eds., *Deliverance Prayer: Experiential, Psychological, and Theological Approaches* (New York: Paulist Press, 1981); Martin, M., *Hostage to the Devil: The Possession and Exorcism of Five Living Americans* (New York: Reader's Digest, 1976); Nauman, St. Elmo, Jr., ed., *Exorcism through the Ages* (New York: Philosophical Library, 1974); Rodewyk, A., *Possessed By Satan: The Church's Teaching on the Devil, Possession, and Exorcism*, trans. M. Ebon (Garden City, NY: Doubleday, 1975).

T. Paul Thigpen

F

Faith Healing. Also called divine healing, faith healing refers to a practice integral to the Holiness, Pentecostal,* and charismatic traditions. Praying for the miraculous healing of the sick has been reported sporadically throughout the history of Christianity (for example, St. Francis, Waldensians, Quakers), but the modern-day faith-healing movement finds its origins in the "Faith Cure" movement that was a part of the larger Holiness movement of the late nineteenth century. The most influential Holiness faith healer was Episcopalian Charles Cullis. He wrote *Faith Cures* (1879), emphasizing the prayer of faith (cf. James 5:14–15) as the key to healing. Cullis persuaded many others who would become major faith-healing advocates of the 1880s, such as William Boardman, A. J. Gordon, and A. B. Simpson.

Various issues arose in the developing faith-healing theology. A. B. Simpson, who founded the Christian and Missionary Alliance on a fourfold gospel that included divine healing, argued that if sickness was the result of the Fall, then it must be included in the atonement (cf. Isaiah 53:4) and thus be available to believers as a result of salvation. Other healing advocates disagreed; they contended that healing was one possible benefit of the atonement, but was not a scriptural promise. Preferences regarding the method of healing also differed. Some, including Simpson, preferred private prayer in "faith homes"; others had emotion-laden healing revivals with prayer lines for the sick. While the National Holiness Association, the major vehicle of Holiness teaching, did not permit faith healing at its meetings, the practice of faith healing pervaded most of the Holiness movement and was a radicalization of the perfectionist push in Holiness teachings (see Dayton, *Theological Roots of Pentecostalism*). Divine healing gradually diminished among Holiness believers who did not become Pentecostals.

Superseding in popularity and controversy all previous faith healers was the independent John Alexander Dowie. He founded a theocratic city, Zion, Illinois, that prohibited medical professionals, even veterinarians (only a few healing evangelists discouraged the use of medicine). Dowie insisted that healing was always instantaneous. Others had said that it might be gradual; the faithful believer should affirm that healing had occurred even if symptoms remained at first.

From the outset, divine healing has been integral to the Pentecostal movement. Many Holiness supporters of faith healing became the first Pentecostals. Holiness preacher Charles Parham,* the founder of Pentecostalism, had a healing ministry. The famous Azusa Street* revival that ignited Pentecostalism in 1906 reported numerous healings. Prominent healers in the early twentieth century included F. F. Bosworth and Sister Aimee Semple McPherson,* whose ''foursquare'' gospel highlighted divine healing.

In 1947 a healing revival erupted in Pentecostalism, led by William Branham and Oral Roberts.* Branham's ministry emphasized the ''word of knowledge'' as his way to diagnose diseases. He also often required faith in himself as ''God's prophet'' as the key to being healed. Both ideas were used by later faith healers. Roberts, the most skilled of the postwar revivalists, made extensive use of radio and pioneered in televangelism by showing healing crusades. Pentecostal denominational leaders gradually distanced themselves from the revivalists for their extravagant claims and lack of accountability. The revival helped spur the growth of Pentecostalism and was a precursor to the charismatic movement,* the primary vehicle of faith-healing ministries into mainline denominations and Catholicism since the 1960s. Popular ministries have included those of Kathryn Kuhlmann, Oral Roberts, and, in the 1990s, Benny Hinn and the Vineyard Fellowship of John Wimber.

Criticisms of the faith-healing movements have been numerous: perceived healings that do not last, healings that are never verified by medical professionals, the willingness to blame the lack of healing on the inadequate faith of the believer, which produces intense feelings of guilt, and the excessively high numbers of healings claimed. Many critics contend that the healings are psychosomatic at most; some healers have brought disrepute to the movement through fraudulent healings, lack of financial accountability, and highly publicized moral failures. The most controversial development in the faith-healing movement is the ''Faith'' teachers, led by Kenneth Hagin, who emphasize a health and wealth gospel in which persons with enough faith can claim (not just request) their healing from God.

Bibliography. Dayton, Donald, *Theological Roots of Pentecostalism* (Grand Rapids, MI: Francis Asbury Press, 1987); Harrell, D. E., *All Things Are Possible* (Bloomington:

Indiana University Press, 1975); Weaver, C. Douglas, *The Healer-Prophet, William Marrion Branham* (Macon: Mercer University Press, 1987).

Douglas Weaver

Falwell, Jerry. Without question one of the most controversial religious figures of the second half of the twentieth century, Jerry Falwell during the past forty years has built a religious empire many have found inspiring, others terrifying, an empire some hold as emblematic of the American spirit, while others see it as dangerously close to a cult. Always an excellent student (he graduated valedictorian of his high-school class in 1950) and a notorious prankster and rabble-rouser (he was denied his right to deliver the valedictory address because of his involvement in a scheme to defraud the school of lunch money by means of counterfeit tickets), Falwell experienced a radical conversion one Sunday in January 1952 while listening to a broadcast of Charles Fuller's "The Old Time Gospel Hour." He went to Park Avenue Baptist Church that night, saw his future wife Macel Pate at the piano, and surrendered his life to Christ. He left Lynchburg College for G. B. Vick's* newly established Baptist Bible College in Springfield, Missouri, in the fall of 1952, graduating in 1956. He returned to Lynchburg to find about 100 members of the Park Avenue Church ready to leave and begin a church of their own. Though only twenty-two, Falwell displayed the kind of "independence" he has exhibited ever since by accepting their call as founding pastor despite the warnings of the leaders of the Baptist Bible Fellowship (BBF) that if he accepted the position he would be essentially "excommunicated" from the fellowship for creating "schism" in the fold.

Determined to show his friends within the BBF that they were wrong about his decision, Falwell worked tirelessly for his new church, the Thomas Road Baptist Church, knocking on a hundred doors a day, launching a radio and television ministry within the first year, renovating an old bottling company building, and recording a first-anniversary attendance of over 850. Throughout the years he continued to add ministries to the church, including the Elim Home for Alcoholics in 1959, Lynchburg Christian Academy in 1967, Lynchburg Baptist College (now Liberty University) in 1971, a seminary in 1973, and a home for unwed mothers in the early 1980s, to name a few. During these years attendance at Thomas Road continued to grow, eventually reaching 22,000 members by the mid-1980s, resulting in several building programs and making it one of the largest churches in America, with a media ministry that for many years was one of the top three in America. As a televangelist Falwell reached his peak in the early 1980s, broadcasting at that time on more than 450 stations and generating an income of over $100 million a year. Liberty University became accredited in 1980 and now has an enrollment of approximately 5,000 students.

For the first two decades of his ministry Falwell was an avowed fundamental independent Baptist preacher, believing in the autonomous local church led by the pastor (not committees or ecclesiastical hierarchies), preaching tenaciously the fundamentals of the Baptist faith, and holding to a strict separatist attitude toward much of American culture, politics, and ecclesiastical liberalism and ecumenism, all the while preaching a message of old-fashioned piety much in line with the conservative politics of the 1960s and early 1970s. Galvanized by the *Roe v. Wade* decision in 1973, Falwell became increasingly political in his television messages. By 1976 he was ready to take to the road for a series of "I Love America" campaigns in over 140 American cities, an effort that created a groundswell of support for the conservative causes he would later make the foundation points of the Moral Majority* (founded in 1979). These included his opposition to abortion,* gay rights,* the Equal Rights Amendment,* and pornography, as well as his advocacy of voluntary prayer in schools, free enterprise, a balanced budget, a strong national defense, and support for the nation of Israel. Comprised of conservatives from the ranks of fundamental Baptists, Catholics, Mormons, Jews, charismatics, and even the nonchurched, the more than two million members of the Moral Majority became a powerful force in the general conservative shift that occurred with the election of Ronald Reagan in 1980. Falwell, as director of the Moral Majority, became a household name and media phenomenon during the 1980s. In late 1986, exhausted from his efforts and convinced that much of the work of the Moral Majority had been accomplished, Falwell decided to leave the political arena and return to the "basics" of his ministries at Thomas Road and Liberty University. He resigned from the Moral Majority shortly thereafter and disbanded the organization completely in 1989. Though he still appears at various Republican functions, Falwell is definitely not the political figure today that he was in 1980.

Falwell, however, would have been controversial had he never entered the political realm. The financial track record of his religious ministries alone would have done that for him. As a result of his decision to enter the realm of the "electronic church"* in 1971, Falwell was forced to raise money far in excess of the normal tithes and offerings of Thomas Road Church. Knowing that a nationwide broadcast cost millions of dollars each week, Falwell needed a rallying cry that practically any Christian could support and a ministry that would virtually never be completed, and he found them in the message of morality advocated by the Moral Majority and the hope for America's future already present in the student body at Liberty University. By tying his "Old Time Gospel Hour Broadcast" to the ongoing success of the school, he found a means of creating a huge pool of money of which he could dispose with little outside interference. Falwell also discovered the other secret to his success during these years: not only would people give to a school in hope of creating a glorious future, but they would also respond to a crisis over past failures. Nearly every year since 1971 Falwell has managed to create three or four major crises a year, always involving a staggering debt that had to be paid by a certain date, or doom would fall upon all the ministry (and America as well). Using a direct-mail technique second to none among televangelists, Falwell knew how to stir the heartstrings and provoke the kind of response he wanted from his target audience (an older, conservative audience at that time). His eloquent "going out of business'' letters were tremendously successful in bringing in upwards of $100 million a year by the early 1980s, but strangely ineffective in reducing the actual indebtedness of the ministry.

Not everyone has been pleased with his financial dealings. The Securities and Exchange Commission challenged his first major sale of bonds in the early 1970s as being "fraudulent and deceitful." Falwell was found not guilty in August 1973 of any "intentional" violation of the law, but his ministry was placed into the hands of a special finance committee for three years as a result of the decision. Unfortunately, Falwell seemed to learn little from the experience, continuing throughout the 1980s to build Liberty University and manipulate the finances of the various ministries. By the late 1980s, though, the well was beginning to run dry. His venture into cable TV with his own Liberty Broadcasting Network and his ill-fated takeover of PTL in 1987 never materialized as he thought and instead weakened his support base and drained his ministries of millions of needed dollars. During this decade, despite some generous gifts to the university, Falwell's ministries accumulated an indebtedness of over $72 million. He tried various consolidation efforts, but none worked. He was eventually forced to use nearly all his properties as collateral on more loans, even losing some properties to foreclosures. His university nearly lost accreditation in 1993 over insolvency, but Falwell worked out agreements in which some debts were forgiven and others are being paid back over time, all of this now occurring under the strict eye of the courts and various government agencies. Falwell hopes to have his ministries debt-free by 1999, but that remains to be seen. It is doubtful that he will ever again be allowed to engage in the kind of freewheeling borrowing and spending practices he found so effective in the 1970s and 1980s.

Falwell has been controversial among his own followers as well. With his decision to enter televangelism, he became not only the most visible fundamentalist in America, but also a direct competitor for the wallets and affection of countless church members across America, many of whom were desperately needed in their own local congregations. Much resentment developed over Falwell's pleas for support, and as he began to change his message (steadily politicizing it to reach a broad conservative audience, not necessarily a fundamentalist one) and his methods (employing a sophisticated direct-mail machinery and glitzy media image that few local churches could compete with), many fundamentalists became increasingly critical of Falwell. With his entrance into politics in the late 1970s the rift grew even greater, as many now saw him selling out his religious principles for political gain. They also saw his "compromising" efforts at accreditation for Liberty University as well as the ecumenicity of his PTL venture as indicative of his movement away from fundamentalism* toward "new evangelicalism." Even his own Baptist Bible Fellowship censured him in late 1987 for his involvement with PTL. Falwell was clearly attempting to change the face of fundamentalism as well as its definition. By means of the Moral Majority, Liberty University, his book *The*

Fundamentalist Phenomenon (1981), and later his publication the *Fundamentalist Journal* (1982–1989), Falwell attempted to redefine fundamentalism along more broadly evangelical lines, emphasizing primarily one's adherence to the historic "five fundamentals" of *The Fundamentals** and not one's position on separatism. In fact, all of Falwell's efforts during the past two decades reveal an attempt to change the face of fundamentalism by incorporating evangelical attitudes of cooperation, inclusivism, and tolerance at the same time that he preached the kind of cultural piety savored by fundamentalists since 1930. He has always insisted that he is a fundamentalist with a capital "F," and the media have generally accepted him as the movement's most eloquent spokesman, but to most fundamentalists he is no longer one of them.

Bibliography. D'Souza, Dinesh, *Falwell, before the Millennium: A Critical Biography* (Chicago: Regnery, 1984); Falwell, Jerry, *Strength for the Journey* (New York: Simon and Schuster, 1987); Fitzgerald, Frances, "Reporter at Large," *New Yorker*, May 18, 1981, 52–54+; Hadden, Jeffrey K., and Anson Shupe, *Prime Time Preachers: The Rising Power of Televangelism* (Reading, MA: Addison-Wesley, 1981); Hadden, Jeffrey K., *Televangelism, Power, and Politics on God's Frontier* (New York: Holt, 1988); Murphy, Mary, "The Next Billy Graham," *Esquire*, October 10, 1978, 25–30+; Whelan, Timothy D., "Falwell and Fundamentalism," *Christianity and Crisis* 47 (1987): 328–31.

Timothy D. Whelan

Family Values. Regardless of political or religious affiliation, many Americans rue the passing of the mid-twentieth-century family idealized in the Waltons and Cleavers of 1960s television: two parents—a male breadwinner and decision maker and a female homemaker—and several respectful, if sometimes mischievous, children, all in church on Sunday. Several decades later, for a variety of reasons, and to the dismay of many, a majority of American families do not look like that any more. Some would argue that they never did.

Challenge and change have come to the traditional family from black, feminist, and gay civil rights revolutions, shifting social roles for women, divorce rates rising toward 50 percent, chronic homelessness and welfare dependency, growing numbers of out-of-wedlock births, pregnant teens, latchkey children from two-income, parentless, and single-parent households, and gay marriages, parenting, and adoptions. In the 1980s and 1990s these new social realities have brought about a grassroots, essentially religious "profamily" movement dedicated to the restoration of the traditional family and its values—religious faith, hard work, and self-reliance in a patriarchal setting—values that, for those in the movement, are the panacea for the ills that beset American society.

Although the profamily movement dates from the early 1970s (Phyllis Schlafly's Eagle Forum), its momentum went critical in 1992 when then Vice President Dan Quayle decried the "poverty of values" (Quayle, 318) leading to the Los Angeles riots and criticized a popular television character, Murphy Brown, "for mocking the importance of fathers by bearing a child alone and calling it just another 'lifestyle choice' " (Quayle, 386). In the aftermath of

Quayle's remarks, a stand for "family values" took center stage in the 1992 presidential election campaign, with Democrats and Republicans defining "family" in significantly different ways.

With the backing of conservative Christian groups like Focus on the Family, the American Family Association, the Traditional Values Coalition, and the Christian Coalition,* various Republican candidates articulated the faith—as the traditional family goes, so goes the nation—as well as the fears of the profamily movement: increasing secularism in public institutions, especially schools; feminism, including the Equal Rights Amendment* to the Constitution; liberal social trends endorsing same-sex relationships, sex education, contraception, condom use, and legal abortion*; and governmental policies that, rather than ameliorating social ills, result in "discouraging family formation, breaking up intact families, and trapping people in poverty for generations" (Gingrich, 1995, 78). Reiterating traditional positions on the same issues, the Roman Catholic Church, through the pope and the U.S. Conference of Catholic Bishops, unequivocally condemned abortion, birth control, and homosexual marriages ("false and fictitious families composed of two men or two women").

Partly in response to the women's liberation movement, men's movements, with varying emphases, also arose. Patriarchal concern for family values inspired the formation of the all-male, Christian Promise Keepers, founded in 1991 by Coach Bill McCartney at the University of Colorado. Among the seven promises of its members are commitments to "building strong marriages and families through love, protection and biblical values"; "worship, prayer, and obedience to God's Word"; "spiritual, moral, ethical and sexual purity"; male bonding in Christian fellowship; nurturing the unity of the biblical community; and evangelism.

From the political left, candidate and later President Bill Clinton, banking on the support of a Rainbow Coalition of minorities, promised an end to welfare-dependent families, "a place at the table" for gays and lesbians, and limited abortion rights ("abortions should be rare, and legal"). After leading a failed effort at family-friendly health care reform, First Lady Hillary Rodham Clinton, drawing on her long-time association with the Children's Defense Fund, published *It Takes a Village* and launched a nationwide book tour to articulate her prescription for healing the American family. Challenging stereotypes about their threat to families and children, lesbians and gay men, actively supported by groups like PFLAG (Parents, Family, and Friends of Lesbians and Gays), have adopted family issues as their own, seeking respect and justice in courts, state legislatures, workplaces, schools, and churches (Henderson, 2). To an extraordinary degree, then, the domestic politics of the 1990s is a religiously inspired struggle to redefine the American family and its values.

Bibliography. Clinton, Hillary, *It Takes a Village* (New York: Simon and Schuster. 1996); D'Emilio, John, "Family Matters" (Policy Institute of the National Gay and Lesbian Task Force, January 25, 1996); Gillespie, Ed, and Bob Schellhas, eds., *Contract with America* (New York: Random House, 1994); Gingrich, Newt, *To Renew America*

(New York: HarperCollins, 1995); Henderson, Mitzi, "The Golden Rule," *PFLAGpole* (Washington, D.C.), March–April 1996; Quayle, Dan, *Standing Firm* (New York: HarperCollins, 1994).

Fred Richter

Farrakhan, Louis. Louis Eugene Walcott was born in the Bronx on May 11, 1933, but his family of West Indian immigrants moved to Boston three years later. In 1955, in the midst of a career as a popular calypso singer and violinist, a speech by Elijah Muhammad* persuaded him to join the Nation of Islam.* In accordance with the Nation's practice of having its members drop their "slave" names, he assumed the new name of Louis X. In 1957 he became the minister of the organization's Boston temple, but he became widely known among the members of the Nation during the period 1963–1965. In 1963 Louis X denounced Malcolm X* for having informed several of the Nation of Islam's leaders of Elijah Muhammad's sexual indiscretions, and in 1965 he wrote a caustic series of articles that condemned Malcolm for having withdrawn from the Nation in order to found a new, competing organization. After Malcolm's assassination in February 1965, Elijah Muhammad appointed Louis to two positions that had formerly been filled by Malcolm: minister of Temple No. 7 in Harlem and national spokesman for the Nation. He also changed Louis's name to Louis Farrakhan.

When Elijah Muhammad died in 1975, his son Wallace (Warith) Deen Muhammad assumed the leadership of the Nation of Islam. For over a decade Wallace had urged his father to bring the organization into line with orthodox Sunni Islam, and by 1976 he had not only revised the doctrines and rituals of the organization but had also changed its name to the World Community of al-Islam in the West. In November 1977 Farrakhan announced that he was breaking with Wallace and would reestablish the Nation of Islam. He denied that Elijah Muhammad had died and claimed that Elijah was the Messiah that the monotheistic religions had sought. He himself claimed to be Elijah's prophet, whose words came to him from God.

In 1984 Farrakhan moved from relative obscurity on the national scene when he played a highly visible role in supporting the presidential candidacy of Jesse Jackson.* To endorse a political candidate entailed a historic break with tradition, for the Nation of Islam had always eschewed political involvement and had prohibited its members from voting. The campaign also brought to public notice the anti-Semitic tendencies of the Nation of Islam, and the furor over the remarks by Farrakhan and his leading spokesmen only increased over the next decade. It seemed that his movement would remain peripheral to mainstream African-American society, but in October 1995 he called upon African-American men to demonstrate in Washington, D.C., for dignity, responsibility, and family values. Almost one million men responded. Whether Farrakhan could capitalize on the one-day event to enhance the image and size of his organization remained to be seen.

Bibliography. Gardell, M., *In the Name of Elijah Muhammad: Louis Farrakhan and the Nation of Islam* (Durham: Duke University Press, 1996); Magida, A. J., *Prophet of Rage: A Life of Louis Farrakhan and His Nation* (New York: Basic Books, 1996); Mamiya, L. H., "Minister Louis Farrakhan and the Final Call: Schism in the Muslim Movement," in *The Muslim Community in North America*, ed. E. H. Waugh, Abu-Laban Baha, and Raqula B. Quereshi. (Edmonton: University of Alberta Press, 1983).

Vernon Egger

Father Divine's Peace Mission Movement. Under five feet tall, Father Divine, the son of former slaves, lacked formal education and dressed conservatively. Yet he was called God by many followers; he provided economic security for thousands during the Great Depression; and he challenged racism* in a racist society. Born George Baker in Savannah, Georgia (Braden), or Rockville, Maryland, in 1879 (Watts), he was a gardener in Baltimore in 1899. Influenced by evangelist Samuel Morris (Father Jehovia), he launched a series of careers: street preacher, evangelist, head of a commune, and spiritual and organizational leader of a sprawling religious movement. With each he assumed a new identity: the Messenger, Major Jealous Divine, Father Divine.

The Messenger encountered trouble on evangelistic missions in Georgia. He served a hard-labor sentence in Savannah, apparently for breach of racial mores. Jailed in Valdosta in 1913, he was judged to be insane because he called himself God and was ordered out of the state. Shaking the dust of Dixie, he moved to Brooklyn, where he opened a communal house in 1913, aided by Peninniah, a follower who became the first of two "spiritual" wives.

In 1919 Major Divine bought a house in Sayville, Long Island, a middle-class, mostly white community. To it came more prosperous African Americans with dependable jobs for free meals and spirited but orderly worship services. Now called Father Divine by the faithful, the leader served coffee, preached sermons marked by biblical knowledge and syntactical obscurity, and published a newspaper. He began to attract affluent, educated white followers from whom he rejected financial support.

Success led to opposition because of too many African Americans congregating in a white neighborhood. A police raid led to publicity that fueled his popularity and made him a symbol of opposition to racial injustice. He was tried for being a public nuisance in 1932 under a racist judge, Lewis J. Smith, who fined him $500, sentenced him to a year in jail, and embellished divinity by dropping dead three days later at age fifty-six. Father Divine responded from his jail cell, "I hated to do it."

Transferred to Harlem, the movement grew rapidly. To the headquarters "kingdom" other units of varying size (kingdoms, extensions, and connections) were added, peaking at 178 in 1941 (Braden, 12). These included communal centers and businesses, especially well-kept but inexpensive hotels. Concentrated in New York, New Jersey, and Philadelphia, where Father Divine moved in 1942, they could be found throughout the United States and overseas. In the kingdoms, members lived together at minimal cost for rooms and food. He had a sharp eye for bargains in real estate and other businesses, but routine management was in the hands of local councils.

Economic security, profitable businesses, a haven from racism, employment services—Father Divine offered these before Social Security, economic opportunity programs, and the civil rights* movement. However, they were not free. For true followers there was no sex, marriage, or family. They followed his "International Modest Code": No Smoking, No Drinking, No Obscenity, No Vulgarity, No Profanity, No Undue Mixing of the Sexes, No Receiving of Gifts, Presents, Tips or Bribes (Kephart and Zellner, 207). It was an ascetic Protestant ethic that encouraged group cohesion and job productivity.

Father Divine challenged racism, even the concept of race. His following was integrated. He competed in the white economic system. He took on Mississippi's Senator Theodore Bilbo in a campaign to pass antilynching legislation. After "Mother Divine" Peninniah died in 1943, he married Sweet Angel, one of several secretaries who recorded his public utterances; originally Edna Rose Ritchings, she was one-third his age, white, and an able second Mother Divine.

This untidy bundle of business, religion, and politics was bonded by Holy Communion Banquets—bounteous feasts held regularly among the kingdoms and always attended by Father and Mother Divine. There was spirited singing led by the Rosebuds, a girls' choir that wed African-American musical styles to lyrics proclaiming the greatness of Father Divine. His sermons followed the familiar affirmation-response pattern of African-American evangelical preaching. Participants called out their love for him and asserted that he was God. The experience was dramatic and participatory, creating unity around the person of Father Divine.

However, the Peace Mission movement was more than an extension of its charismatic leader. He and the movement were products of their time. He was a microcosm of displaced, urbanized African Americans—detached from old cultural roots, constantly hearing the optimistic promises of the American Dream but beset by racism. He launched a revitalization movement—"an effort by a repressed or minority group to wrest from a rapidly changing and anomic situation not only a more orderly cultural structure but also higher status" (Wallace, 267). Revitalization combines attractive elements from the dominant culture with aspects of traditional culture, in this case economic success with evangelical fervor. The force driving this movement was racism, which created a black undercaste hungry for higher status.

The Peace Mission movement was in decline before Father Divine's death on September 12, 1965, partly because others were pursuing the struggle against racism with greater vigor and effectiveness. Shorn of divinity and charisma by his death, it ebbed more rapidly but survived under Mother Divine.

Bibliography. Braden, Charles S., *These Also Believe* (New York: Macmillan, 1949); Burnham, Kenneth E., *God Comes to America: Father Divine and the Peace Mission Movement* (Boston: Lambeth Press, 1979); Kephart, William M., and W. W. Zellner, *Extraordinary Groups*, 4th ed. (New York: St. Martin's Press, 1991); Wallace, Anthony F. C., "Revitalization Movement," *American Anthropologist* 58: 267 (1956); Watts, Jill, *God, Harlem U.S.A.* (Berkeley: University of California Press, 1992).

Roger G. Branch

Feminism. Feminism is a movement inspired by belief in the equality of women and men in all spheres of life. As a political movement it seeks justice for women, who have historically been disqualified in some manner because of gender. The forms of feminism are varied: liberal feminism has been concerned with civil rights* for women; Marxist feminism has been concerned with economic autonomy; and romantic feminism has celebrated the natural, emotional, and relational in contradistinction to the rational, the technical, and unrelated objectivity. Each form has argued that women are being disenfranchised from full participation in the economic, political, religious, and social spheres of human concourse.

The women's movement in America can be traced as far back as the colonial period. Women's conscience and industry argued for the colonies' self-sufficiency through their domestic skills, thereby abetting the boycotts of British goods. Early feminist consciousness grew alongside the vision of democracy with liberty and justice for all.

The period of the Second Great Awakening* (1797–1840) also contributed to the participation of women in society as they were integrated into full membership in the church. Their reforming efforts—often in opposition to men—heightened their own personal awareness of oppression.

The modern feminist movement is usually dated to the Seneca Falls convention in July 1848. Abolitionist and feminist concerns occupied the gathering, and a push for suffrage emerged, although women would not be permitted to vote until 1920. After this pivotal event, the feminist movement was all but dormant until 1960.

The publication of Betty Friedan's *The Feminine Mystique* in 1963 signaled a renewed critique and action on the part of women desiring to move beyond oppression. The Equal Rights Amendment* became the test case for the eradication of women's second-class status and, ultimately, was defeated due to being caricatured beyond recognition. It became the ideological symbol for women's liberation, which was thought too threatening to the traditional (patriarchal) order.

Currently, feminism remains an active voice in religious, political, and academic spheres as women (and concerned men) strive to consolidate the gains garnered by feminist advocacy. Gender equity has not yet been fully accomplished, and a backlash has been occurring in all the arenas where feminists seek to claim their rightful places; however, the vision and energy of this significant movement have not abated and will continue to move women and men toward full equality.

Bibliography. Davis, Angela, *Women, Race, and Class* (New York: Random House, 1981); Gilligan, Carol, *In a Different Voice: Psychological Theory and Women's Development* (Cambridge: Harvard University Press, 1982); Hawkesworth, M. E., *Beyond Oppression: Feminist Theory and Political Strategy* (New York: Continuum, 1990); Saxonhouse, Arlene, *Women in the History of Political Thought* (New York: Praeger, 1985).

Molly Marshall

Finney, Charles Grandison. An antebellum evangelist who revolutionized revivalism, Charles Grandison Finney was born on August 29, 1792, in Warren, Connecticut, into a family of farmers. In 1794 the family moved to the frontier of Oneida County, New York. Finney attended Hamilton Oneida Seminary and became a lawyer. Although skeptical of the church, he had a dramatic conversion experience in 1821. Declaring that he had a "retainer from the Lord Jesus Christ to plead his cause," he abandoned his law career and was ordained an evangelist by the Presbyterian Church in 1824.

In 1825 Finney began conducting revivals in central and western New York, which he dubbed a "burned-over district" for the flames of religious enthusiasm that had swept the area. His revivals nonetheless caught fire, and thousands swooned, screamed, and wept as the spirit of God engulfed them. Part of the Second Great Awakening,* his work quickly spread from Utica and Rochester to Philadelphia, Boston, and New York. He became pastor of New York's Second Free Presbyterian Church in 1832, but his independence led him to affiliate with the Congregationalists in 1836. In 1837 he went to Oberlin Institute in northeastern Ohio as professor of theology and later became its president. He married three times, and his wives, Lydia, Elizabeth, and Rebecca played active roles in his ministry. He died on August 16, 1875.

Finney gained national and international fame as a charismatic preacher. Tall, with piercing eyes and mesmerizing voice, he presented the gospel message with lawyerly persuasiveness. With logic, humor, and story, he made complicated theological doctrines easily understandable and emotionally powerful. More controversial than his preaching style were his revolutionary revival techniques, spelled out in his 1835 *Lectures on Revivals of Religion*. These "New Measures" included (1) advance publicity, the use of media advertising and prayer meetings to prepare for a revival (2) women's praying and testifying before mixed audiences, a radical departure from women's customary silence in church, because Finney believed that women were especial channels of divine grace (3) protracted meetings, services held on successive evenings over several weeks in which defenses were worn down; and (4) the "anxious bench," a pew in front of the pulpit for troubled or "anxious" souls who felt the spirit of God stirring inside them. From there the preacher exhorted them directly, urging them to repent of their sins and accept God's grace.

Finney's radical methods embroiled him in controversy as early as 1827, when a group of ministers convened but took no action against him. Most disturbing to orthodox Christians was Finney's claim that revivals were no miracle or divine intervention, but a matter of human engineering. If the correct techniques were applied, revival would inevitably result. Finney's New Measures were controversial but indisputably successful and widely imitated. Wealthy businessmen were attracted to his results-oriented approach, and women saw in his methods an expanded role for themselves. In stressing human agency to harness the Holy Spirit, Finney shifted the focus from God to humanity and demystified revivalism.* His methods have been adopted by evangelists from Dwight Moody to Billy Graham* and continue to be used today.

Bibliography. Finney, Charles G, *Lectures on Revivals of Religion* (originally published in 1835), ed. William G. McLoughlin. (Cambridge: Belknap Press of Harvard University Press, 1960); Finney, Charles G., *Memoirs of Rev. Charles G. Finney, Written by Himself* (New York: Barnes, 1876); Hardman, Keith J., *Charles Grandison Finney, 1792–1875: Revivalist and Reformer* (Syracuse: Syracuse University Press, 1987); Weddle, David L., *The Law as Gospel: Revival and Reform in the Theology of Charles G. Finney* (Metuchen, NJ: Scarecrow Press, 1985).

Evelyn A. Kirkley

Fitzgerald, Edward M. Born in Ireland in October 1833, Edward Fitzgerald came to America with his parents in 1849. The following year he entered a Catholic seminary and was ordained to the priesthood on August 22, 1857, by Archbishop John Purcell of Cincinnati. After nine years in Columbus, Ohio, Pope Pius IX offered him the bishopric of Little Rock, an Arkansas diocese that had not had a prelate since 1862. Fitzgerald initially rejected the position, so the pontiff responded with a *mandamus*, an order to assume it under holy obedience. By the time he received this command, Fitzgerald had decided to accept the Little Rock Diocese after all. On February 3, 1867, at his parish church, Fitzgerald was consecrated as Arkansas's second bishop. At thirty-three, he was the youngest Catholic prelate in the United States.

He arrived in Little Rock on St. Patrick's Day and quickly discovered that he was in a poor diocese still suffering the devastation of the Civil War. In 1869 he traveled to Rome to attend Vatican Council I.* There he distinguished himself by being one of only two bishops in the world to vote against the doctrine of papal infallibility, and the only English-speaking prelate in the world to take such a stand. His was the first negative vote after 491 votes in affirmation. After the roll call concluded, the large-framed Irish prelate from Arkansas knelt before Pius IX and submitted to the decision of the council. In a speech given a decade later, Fitzgerald stated that he voted against the doctrine not so much from unbelief as because he believed it would hurt Catholic evangelization efforts. His courageous vote did not damage his future ecclesiastical career. Pope Leo XIII, Pius IX's successor, offered him the Archdioceses of Cincinnati and New Orleans and four other dioceses also, but none could lure him from Arkansas.

Returning to Little Rock in 1870, Bishop Fitzgerald had an active career over the next thirty years. He opposed the establishment of Catholic schools at the Third Plenary Council in Baltimore in 1884; he also supported the rights of workingmen and the Knights of Labor. He tried to attract Catholic immigrants and convert blacks to Catholicism. He suffered a stroke in January 1900 and spent the last seven years of his life as an invalid in a Catholic hospital in Hot Springs. Upon his death on February 21, 1907, his remains were placed under the Cathedral of St. Andrew in Little Rock, the edifice he had constructed in 1881.

Bibliography. Fitzgerald's obituary is in the Little Rock *Arkansas Gazette*, February 22, 1907, 1; personal papers are found mainly in the Archives of the Diocese of Little Rock, St. John's Catholic Center, Little Rock, Arkansas. Hennesey, James J., *The First Council of the Vatican: The American Experience* (New York: Herder and Herder, 1963); Petersen, Svend, "The Little Rock against the Big Rock," *Arkansas Historical Quarterly* 2 (June 1943): 164–70; Woods, James M., *Mission and Memory: A History of the Catholic Church in Arkansas* (Little Rock, AR: August House Publishing Co., 1993).

James M. Woods

Fosdick, Harry Emerson. Harry Emerson Fosdick (1878–1969) is widely regarded as the most influential Protestant minister in the first half of the twentieth century. He was the best-known spokesman for liberal theology in America and was therefore the target of fundamentalist attacks throughout his career. His roots were Baptist, but his ministry became increasingly ecumenical.

His engaging autobiography, *The Living of These Days*, was given the title from the recurring refrain "Grant us wisdom, grant us courage for the living of these days" in his well-loved hymn "God of Grace and God of Glory." In it he recounted his theological pilgrimage from conservative Baptist beginnings in Buffalo, New York, to his education at Colgate and Union Theological Seminary* in New York. After serving as minister of the First Baptist Church in Montclair, New Jersey, he became the Jessup Professor of Practical Theology at Union Theological Seminary, his alma mater.

While at Colgate he took courses with William Newton Clarke,* whose advocacy of Evangelical Liberalism had a profound influence on his theological development. He called Clarke "one of the most inspiring teachers I ever sat under" (*The Living of These Days*, 65). Fosdick declared that but for Clarke's liberal influence as an alternative to the "bondage" of the sterile orthodoxy of his day, he would never have become a Christian minister.

The controversy that engaged Fosdick throughout his career began while he was serving as a guest minister at the First Presbyterian Church in New York. Fundamentalist reaction to his widely circulated 1922 sermon "Shall the Fundamentalists Win?" was instant and severe. While it was intended as irenic, its effect was the opposite. Many in the church concluded that it was bad enough that liberalism was being preached in a Presbyterian church but even worse that a Baptist—incapable of being held to the Westminster Confession—was doing it. Forced to resign, Fosdick accepted the pastorate of the Park Avenue Baptist Church, which moved, built a new structure, and became the Riverside Church, renowned as the leading Protestant pulpit in America.

Until his retirement as minister and professor in 1946, Fosdick's radio sermons and books influenced a generation of ministers and laypersons. He was a prolific writer; his most enduring works include *The Living of These Days*, *The Modern Use of the Bible*, *The Meaning of Faith*, and *Abiding Truths in Changing Categories*.

Bibliography. Cauthen, Kenneth, *The Impact of American Religious Liberalism* (New York: Harper and Row, 1962); Fosdick, H. E., *The Living of These Days* (New York: Harper and Row, 1956); Hutchison, William R., ed. *American Protestant Thought: The Liberal Era* (New York: Harper Torchbooks, 1968).

Bernard H. Cochran

Fosdick Controversy. The Fosdick controversy was a protracted struggle (1922–1925) in the Presbyterian Church in the USA concerning the orthodoxy of the preaching of the prominent liberal Baptist Harry Emerson Fosdick,* a minister at First Presbyterian Church in New York City. On May 21, 1922, Fosdick, disturbed by the increasing attacks of Baptist and Presbyterian fundamentalists on theological liberals, preached the sermon "Shall the Fundamentalists Win?" in the First Presbyterian Church of New York. The sermon, which was later printed and widely distributed across the country, claimed that liberals were devout evangelical Christians seeking to reconcile traditional faith and modern knowledge, contrasted liberal and fundamentalist theology (focusing especially on biblical inerrancy and the Virgin Birth* and the Second Coming of Christ), and argued that since liberals would not leave the churches, tolerance and doctrinal liberty should prevail for the sake of effective mission.

Traditionalist Presbyterians, taking the sermon as a frontal assault on orthodox Presbyterian doctrine, responded immediately. Led by Clarence Macartney, pastor of the Arch Street Presbyterian Church in Philadelphia, conservatives requested the General Assembly, the church's highest governing body, to direct the Presbytery of New York to require the preaching at First Presbyterian Church of New York to conform to the Westminster Confession of Faith, the church's doctrinal standard. The 1923 General Assembly, after hours of strident debate, reaffirmed a declaration of the "five fundamentals" of the assemblies of 1910 and 1916 that the inerrancy of Scripture and the Virgin Birth, substitutionary atonement, bodily resurrection, and the miracle-working power of Christ were "essential and necessary" doctrines of the church and instructed the Presbytery of New York to bring the preaching at First Presbyterian Church of New York in line with the church's doctrine.

In response, liberals in the church, led most visibly by Henry Sloane Coffin, pastor of the Madison Avenue Presbyterian Church in New York, developed the "Auburn Affirmation."* The affirmation, which opened by professing the orthodoxy of its signatories and accepting the doctrine of the Westminster Confession, stressed the historic commitment of the church to doctrinal diversity. It went on to argue that inasmuch as the doctrine of the church could only be determined by the joint approval of the General Assembly and the presbyteries, declarations such as the "five fundamentals" had no ultimate authority. Finally, the affirmation claimed that the assembly's action against Fosdick was unconstitutional and insisted that effective preaching of the gospel required doctrinal liberty in the church. The affirmation was published before the 1924 General Assembly with over one thousand signatories.

The 1924 General Assembly elected Clarence Macartney as its moderator but took no action against the signers of the Auburn Affirmation. Inasmuch as the New York Presbytery had essentially exonerated Fosdick of all charges, the question of Fosdick's status was again before the assembly on appeal. The assembly addressed the struggle as a matter of polity rather than theology and invited Fosdick to enter the Presbyterian ministry if he wanted to continue to serve a Presbyterian church. This would have entailed subscribing to the Westminster Confession of Faith, and Fosdick could not, in good conscience, assent to the doctrinal standards of the church.

Fosdick therefore tendered his resignation from First Presbyterian Church and preached his last sermon there in March 1925. Though Fosdick's resignation essentially concluded this controversy, the Auburn Affirmation played a major role in the ongoing conflict and the ultimate decision of the Presbyterian Church to tolerate liberals. Fosdick, upon his resignation from First Presbyterian Church, accepted a call to Park Avenue Baptist Church, which later moved to Morningside Heights as the Riverside Church.

Bibliography. Fosdick, Harry Emerson, *The Living of These Days* (New York: Harper and Row, 1956); Hutchison, William R., *The Modernist Impulse in American Protestantism* (Cambridge: Harvard University Press, 1976); Loetscher, Lefferts A., *The Broadening Church* (Philadelphia: University of Pennsylvania Press, 1954); Longfield, Bradley J., *The Presbyterian Controversy: Fundamentalists, Modernists, and Moderates* (New York: Oxford University Press, 1991); Miller, Robert Moats, *Harry Emerson Fosdick: Preacher, Pastor, Prophet* (New York: Oxford University Press, 1985).

Bradley J. Longfield

Franckean Synod. A small pietistic Lutheran synod located in New York State that became well known especially for its uncompromising abolitionism.* Breaking away from the Hartwick Synod in 1837, it was named for the early German Lutheran pietist leader August Hermann Francke. Among its pietistic traits were its emphasis on personal religious conviction, its promotion of revivals, its Sabbatarianism,* its distaste for creedal formulations (including the Lutheran confessions), and its insistence on moral reform in the life of the individual Christian and of the nation. Regarding the latter, it emphasized total abstinence from alcoholic beverages and the immediate abolition of slavery.

The synod was soon shunned as a pariah by most of its fellow Lutherans, both for its nonconfessional theology and for its "ultra" positions on temperance and abolition. In 1839, when it applied for membership in the General Synod of the Evangelical Lutheran Church, the only national organization for Lutherans at that time, it was summarily turned away. It was said that the synod was "introducing practices which we consider contrary to the Word of God, thereby causing disturbances and divisions in our churches." Further support for the critics came in 1844 when a judge in a lawsuit over church property ruled that the Franckeans were essentially non-Lutheran; they seemed to him much like "a new sect denominating itself 'The Church of God,' which sprung out of the German Reformed Church in Pennsylvania in 1830." While the Franckeans strongly protested the capability of a non-Lutheran jurist to make such a judgment in a secular court, there is no doubt that they were on the extreme left of Lutheranism* in America in the 1830s and 1840s.

The Franckean Synod persevered in its pietistic program throughout the antebellum period. Its revivals were intensely emotional, which made even its fellow Lutheran revivalists uneasy. It recommended that all of its members take the pledge of total abstinence and required its ministers to do so. It refused to admit any clergy who did not share its views on abolition, and it refused Communion to slaveholders or anyone who held proslavery views. In 1837 it ordained Daniel Payne, a free African American who had been educated at Gettysburg Seminary; Payne later became a bishop in the African Methodist Episcopal Church and president of Wilberforce University. In 1842 it issued a "Fraternal Appeal" to the other Lutheran synods, asking them to embrace the abolitionist cause. Most synods declined to act on the appeal, as they did a balancing act among various opinions in their own bodies, or tried to maintain unity with the southern synods, or even denied that such a topic was a proper one for church discussion. The few synods that did eventually make antislavery statements would probably never have done so had they not been prodded by the Franckean Synod.

Despite its ecclesiastical isolation, the synod claimed that it had a right to be considered Lutheran. In 1864, when its abolitionism had come to seem less radical, it applied again for admission to the General Synod. This application precipitated a crisis in that body, which had grown more conservative, in a confessional sense, since the 1839 application. The confessionalists argued strenuously against admission of the Franckeans, claiming that "the whole history of the Franckean Synod presents it as having no relation nor connection whatever with the Augsburg Confession." When the General Synod approved the application anyway, the confessionalists withdrew and founded the rival General Council. Even its friends in the General Synod had problems with the Franckean Synod's nonconfessional pietism;* however, they forced it to insert a confessional paragraph in its constitution as a condition of membership.

The later history of the Franckean Synod was one of gradual rapprochement with its Lutheran neighbors in New York, particularly those of a more pietistic bent. In 1908 it merged with the Hartwick Synod and the New York and New Jersey Synod into a new Synod of New York.

Bibliography. Kreider, Harry J., *History of the United Lutheran Synod of New York and New England*, vol. 1, *1786–1860* (Philadelphia: Muhlenberg Press, 1954); Kuenning, Paul P., *The Rise and Fall of American Lutheran Pietism: The Rejection of an Activist Heritage* (Macon, GA: Mercer University Press, 1988).

Donald L. Huber

Free Methodists. One of the movements that broke away from Methodism* in the nineteenth century was Free Methodism. The term ''Free'' connotes certain distinctives of this group, but more importantly, the group represents one of many heavily influenced by Holiness teachings. The movement originated in western New York in the 1850s under the leadership of Benjamin Titus Roberts. Joined by a number of like-minded Methodist ministers, Roberts's protests culminated in the formation of the Free Methodist Church in 1860.

Roberts's dissatisfaction with the Genesee Conference of the Methodist Episcopal Church, North, arose over a number of issues, but two assumed primary importance. Both of those implicate the idea of freedom. First, Roberts objected vehemently to the decision of the conference to institute the practice of pew rental. To Roberts the practice of renting pews ran against the grain of everything Methodism stood for. The practice created inappropriate economic distinctions in the body of Christ that would inevitably result in dissension.

Second, Roberts expressed dissatisfaction with the position of the church on slavery. Roberts detested the compromises made in the 1840s and the lukewarm antislavery positions formally taken by Methodist leadership. He insisted that the Christian witness compelled the church to stand firmly against slavery and foursquare for equality. Therefore, he despised compromise efforts by some in the Methodist Episcopal Church to reunite the church by taking a ''hands-off'' approach to the slavery question.

In addition to these matters of church governance and the relation of the church to the broader society, Roberts also critiqued the ways in which the Methodist Episcopal Church had departed from John Wesley's vision of holiness. Roberts argued that the church could not spread scriptural holiness through the land, as Wesley had envisioned, without insisting on holy living by clergy and laity alike. He viewed the Methodist Episcopal Church as a church drifting away from the teachings of Wesley and toward the shoals of worldliness. In this way Roberts aligned himself with proponents of the Holiness movement.

In short, Roberts insisted on an egalitarian faith, a faith without class distinctions as represented by pew rentals, and on accountability for living a holy life. Like Wesley's followers, the followers of Roberts eschewed jewelry and other worldly adornments. They dressed plainly and lived simply.

Although his troubles with the Genesee Conference dated from 1852, Roberts formally established the Free Methodist Church in Pekin, New York, in 1860. In the twentieth century the church founded by Roberts continues to see itself as a counter to more worldly expressions of Methodism, including the United Methodist Church, aligning instead with more conservative Protestant groups, most notably the National Association of Evangelicals. Nonetheless, many continue to hope for a reunion of Free Methodists with the United Methodist Church.

Bibliography. Chesbrough, Samuel K. J., *Defence of Rev. B. T. Roberts, A.M., before the Genesee Conference of the Methodist Episcopal Church* (Buffalo: Clapp, Matthews and Co., 1858); Hogue, Wilson J., ed., *A Symposium on Scriptural Holiness* (Chicago: Free Methodist Publishing House, 1896); Reinhard, James Arnold, *Personal and Sociological Factors in the Formation of the Free Methodist Church, 1852–1860* (Iowa City: University of Iowa Press, 1971); Roberts, Benjamin Titus, *Why Another Sect* (Rochester, NY: The "Earnest Christian" Publishing House, 1879); Roberts, Benson Howard, *Benjamin Titus Roberts: A Biography* (North Chili, NY: "Earnest Christian" Office, 1900).

Russell Congleton

Free Will Baptists. An Arminian Baptist denomination with origins in the seventeenth and eighteenth centuries, Free Will Baptists can be traced to two separate beginnings. Most present-day Free Will Baptists descend from the southern movement, which originated in what is now North Carolina under the leadership of English General Baptists Benjamin Laker (1680s) and Paul Palmer (1720s). The movement in the North arose spontaneously in New England in the 1780s when Benjamin Randall was expelled from a Calvinistic Baptist church for his Arminian views. After most churches in the General Conference of Free Baptists (originally "Freewill Baptists") in the North merged with the Northern Baptist Convention in 1911, those churches that remained Free Baptist organized the Co-operative General Association. The National Association of Free Will Baptists, formed in 1935, was a result of the merger of this group and its larger counterpart, the General Conference of Free Will Baptists of the South.

Controversy among Free Will Baptists has primarily resulted from doctrinal conflict. The first example of such conflict emerged in the 1750s when the Calvinistic Philadelphia Association of Baptists dispatched John Gano to the Carolinas. Gano and his associates set out to purge the General Baptists, labeling them unregenerate and condemning them for Arminian theology and loose living. The proselytizing efforts of the ministers from Philadelphia resulted in the loss of the majority of the General Baptist churches, though after the reorganization of these churches, few of the former members remained.

The General Baptists of the Carolinas, who came to be called Free Will Baptists, regrouped from this loss. Remarkable growth occurred until the late 1830s and early 1840s, when the Disciples of Christ succeeded in proselytizing a large number of Free Will Baptist congregants and churches. Debate raged in numerous Free Will Baptist churches and conferences over baptismal regeneration, which Free Will Baptists rejected, and the use of confessions of faith, which they accepted, to the consternation of the Disciples. As a result of this controversy, the Free Will Baptists lost over one-fourth of their communicant membership. After a recovery of these losses and a short period of growth, anti-Masonry* became a source of controversy in the late 1840s and early 1850s. A number of ministers wanted the General Conference to prohibit church members from maintaining membership in the Masons, Odd Fellows, or any secret society. After a long and bitter conflict, the conference decided that this matter should be settled in local congregations. This decision resulted in the loss of a number of anti-Masonic ministers and congregations.

The Northern Free Baptists remained relatively free of controversy until the late nineteenth and early twentieth centuries. Conflict arose over two issues that were interrelated: the union of Free Baptists with another denomination and the issue of theological liberalism* or modernism.* Most Free Baptist leaders favored a merger with the Northern Baptist convention. Some conservatives insisted that the leadership of the Northern Baptist Convention was more conservative than that of the Free Baptists and thus favored the merger. Others contended that a merger with the Northern Baptists would amount to a capitulation to modernism. While a majority of Free Baptist churches became Northern Baptist in 1911, a minority, especially in the midwestern states, remained Free Baptist.

In the 1920s the Pentecostal movement claimed a few thousand Free Will Baptists, particularly in the Carolinas, resulting in the establishment of the Pentecostal Free Will Baptist Church. After the founding of the National Association in 1935, the denomination remained free from controversy until the late 1950s, when disputes arose over denominational publishing and higher education. Controversy intensified as hostility grew between the leadership of the North Carolina State Convention and some Free Will Baptist ministers in the Carolinas who had been influenced by the fundamentalism* of such men as Bob Jones* and John R. Rice* and who subjected the State convention and its institutions to harsh criticism. The controversy came to a head when one such minister sued the executive committee of North Carolina's Western Conference over a church polity dispute. In the court proceedings, several leaders of the North Carolina State Convention signed an affidavit affirming that connectional church government was the historic practice of North Carolina Free Will Baptists. This action drew the attention of the National Association, whose executive committee eventually requested that the North Carolina State Convention disavow connectionalism, maintaining that congregationalism was historic Free Will Baptist practice. This dispute resulted in the withdrawal of the North Carolina State Convention in 1961.

Since the early 1960s the major conflicts in the National Association have been initiated by strict fundamentalists who founded a privately owned Bible college in 1982. This party, profoundly influenced by Independent Baptists, have been opposed to the denomination's mainstream evangelical character. Since the 1960s, however, no intradenominational conflicts have resulted in schism.

Bibliography. Cherry, F. B., *An Introduction to Original Free Will Baptists* (Ayden, NC: Free Will Baptist Press, 1989); Davidson, William F., *The Free Will Baptists in America, 1727–1984* (Nashville: Randall House Publications, 1985).

J. Matthew Pinson

Fuller, Margaret. Sarah Margaret Fuller (1810–1850) was born just outside Boston of Unitarian parents. Her father, Timothy, was a lawyer and decided to give her the kind of education he would have given to a firstborn son, for which he had hoped. Her father and his teaching, her books, and churchgoing dominated her early life. By the age of six she was reading Latin classics and a bit later had mastered other languages as well as being widely read in history and literature. From her early years she was socializing and conversing with great writers of the time and became the only woman to play a major role in transcendentalism.* She participated with the likes of Ralph Waldo Emerson, William Ellery Channing, and Theodore Parker* in the Transcendental Club in Cambridge and was the editor of the *Dial*, the major literary outlet for the transcendentalists. Ill health and financial problems caused her resignation as editor; in 1842 she was replaced by Emerson. Fuller's own place in American intellectual history was won by her *Woman in the Nineteenth Century* in 1845. It was the first major literary effort in the United States on feminism and sexual equality, always controversial topics. Her life was tragically cut short in 1850; she, her Italian husband, and their two-year-old son died in a shipwreck off Fire Island at the close of their transatlantic voyage.

In her own time as well as in the late twentieth century, many of Fuller's ideas, especially as expressed in her *Woman in the Nineteenth Century*, were and are controversial in religious circles. Most of the controversial issues touch on feminism and have implications in religious circles. Fuller, religious herself, thirsted for truth and good, as she expressed it, rather than committing herself to any particular religious sect or dogma. She hoped for the time when "Man and Woman may regard one another as brother and sister, the pillars of one porch, the priests of one worship" (Miller, *The American Transcendentalists*, 333). She dared to urge sex education for women, to expose the hypocrisy of much of American Christianity in relation to sexual equality, to oppose the double standard of morality, and to attack traditional marriage ideals, among other reforms. She urged in relation to vocation and calling that a woman could fill any office, which had numerous implications in relation to religious institutions. She described the highest form of marriage to be "religious"; by that she meant partnership and intellectual companionship as well as the female having her own vocation if she so chose. She was insistent that females should have absolute freedom in choosing from a wide range of vocations, whether married or not. She creatively urged: "I wish Woman to live, *first* for God's sake. Then she will not make an imperfect man her god and thus sink to idolatry'' (Miller, 335). Fuller wanted to arrive at her own full selfhood, hoped to help other women to arrive at that same insight, and wished, in all, to see justice for females. Almost poetically she looked with hope toward the future: "The Woman in me kneels and weeps in tender rapture; the Man in me rushes forth, but only to be baffled. Yet the time will come when, from the union of this tragic king and queen, shall be born a radiant sovereign self" (quoted in Allen, *The Achievement of Margaret Fuller,* 151). Even though she was controversial, Fuller labored long and diligently to bring great changes for women in ongoing history.

Bibliography. Allen, Margaret V., *The Achievement of Margaret Fuller* (University Park: Pennsylvania State University Press, 1979); Blanchard, Paula, *Margaret Fuller* (New York: Delacorte Press, 1978); Brown, Arthur W., *Margaret Fuller* (New York: Twayne Publishers, 1964); Fuller, Margaret, *Woman in the Nineteenth Century* (New York: Greeley and McElrath, 1845); Miller, Perry, ed., *The American Transcendentalists* (Garden City, NY: Doubleday and Co., 1957).

George H. Shriver

Fundamentalism. When Curtis Lee Laws, editor of the *Watchman Examiner,* described in 1920 those members of the Christian community who were fighting for the fundamentals of the faith as "fundamentalists," he was using a new term to describe a group that had been forming for several decades. As early as 1844 Robert Baird in his important work *Religion in America* had attempted to separate evangelicals from nonevangelicals by noting six defining characteristics of evangelicals: (1) the existence of a trinitarian God; (2) the depravity and condemnation of all mankind; (3) atonement by Christ, the divine Son of God; (4) regeneration by the Holy Spirit via faith and repentance; (5) the final judgment of all mankind; and (6) a literal heaven for the saved and hell for the lost. By the last quarter of the nineteenth century, however, these tenets would come under attack from many within the traditionally evangelical denominations as the predominantly German-based higher criticism gained ascendancy in many denominational seminaries and colleges. In an effort to combat this growing liberalism* (a mixture of both a skeptical higher criticism and an optimistic, Pelagian romantic theology), conservative evangelicals began meeting independently of their respective denominations at both regional and national Bible conferences. The most popular and influential of the conferences were the various prophetic summer conferences held in the Northeast and Midwest between 1876 and 1901, resulting in some decisive doctrinal affirmations that laid the groundwork for the fundamentalist creeds that would emerge in the first quarter of the twentieth century. Though dominated by eschatology (premillennialism ruled the day), the men and women who attended these conferences were convinced that the basic doctrines of the Bible were being ignored and even attacked by the liberal forces within the church. The "Affirmations" compiled for the 1886 conference in Chicago argued for the necessity of an "inerrant" Scripture and a return to the "true principles" of biblical interpretation in which "the

Word of God is to be interpreted in its plain literal and grammatical sense" (*Prophetic Studies*, 215).

By 1910 the wealthy Stewart brothers of California were convinced that church workers around the world needed to know just what constituted the foundational truths of Scripture from a "literal," not liberal, perspective. Over the next five years they bankrolled the publication of *The Fundamentals*,* a series of small books comprised of articles by leading evangelical scholars around the world on what they considered to be the key doctrinal issues facing the church at that time. From this project emerged "The Five Fundamentals," a set of doctrines considered essential to Christian belief: (1) the inerrancy of Scripture; (2) the Virgin Birth* of Christ; (2) Christ's substitutionary atonement; (4) Christ's bodily resurrection; and (5) the literal Second Coming of Christ. By 1919 these conservative evangelicals formed the World's Christian Fundamentals Association as their initial vehicle for promoting these cardinal doctrines throughout the church.

Between 1900 and 1930 this emerging group of "fundamentalists" waged war on the liberals (also termed "modernists") within nearly every major denomination in America, but most noticeably within the Northern Baptist Convention and the Presbyterian Church in the USA. By the 1920s, however, fundamentalists found themselves not only defending what they considered to be the "fundamentals" of the faith in opposition to a surging liberalism within the church, but also defending a biblical view of man and creation against the advocates of Darwinism and modern science, as well as nineteenth-century notions of cultural piety against the perplexing changes within postwar American society of the 1920s. The Scopes trial* in Dayton, Tennessee, came to be a defining moment in the history of fundamentalism, for in the battle between the fundamental traditionalist William Jennings Bryan* and the modern skeptic Clarence Darrow,* fundamentalism received a black eye from which it never recovered. In the next ten years fundamentalists lost virtually every denominational battle, forcing a remnant to break away into new, independent denominations and affiliations. Some fundamentalist Presbyterians, led by J. Gresham Machen* and Carl S. McIntire,* were actually forced out of the Presbyterian Church in the mid-1930s, leading to the formation of the Orthodox Presbyterian Church and the Bible Presbyterian Church. Many joined together in 1942 in establishing the interdenominational National Association of Evangelicals (NAE). Others, primarily Baptists, became completely "independent," vowing never again to come under any ecclesiastical hammer, not even that of the generally "fundamental" Southern Baptist Convention.* It was primarily this latter group that carried the banner of fundamentalism after the mid-1950s.

If fundamentalism between 1900 and 1930 was marked by its advocacy of premillennialism, revolt against modernism,* and opposition to evolution, between 1930 and 1975 fundamentalism was marked primarily by a separatist mentality, both ecclesiastically and culturally. Fundamentalists separated first from the mainline denominations (1920s and 1930s), then from other evangelicals (1950s and 1960s), and finally from each other (1970s and 1980s), along the way distancing themselves from innumerable cultural changes and forming a distinct subculture that clung desperately to the values and symbols of late-nineteenth-century American society. In the mid-1950s fundamentalists found themselves at odds with evangelicals not so much over doctrine as over attitudes toward American culture and religion in general. The evangelicals of the 1950s and 1960s were "fundamental," if we hold that term to mean a belief in the historic fundamental doctrines as established in *The Fundamentals*, but in their actions and attitudes they were more broadly evangelical, not fundamental. When Billy Graham,* whose spiritual birthright and initial support came from fundamentalism, opened his 1957 New York City campaign to the ministerial alliance that included liberals and fundamentalists, Catholics as well as Baptists, he forced the fundamentalists to either accept a new definition of fundamentalism or reject him. They chose the latter, convinced that the methods of what they called "new evangelicalism" were unscriptural because they were too inclusive and ecumenical; they were in essence a form of "compromise" with unbelief, and that the fundamentalists could not tolerate. Fundamentalists thus used the doctrine of "separation" (in this case "secondary separation"*) to refrain from any cooperative efforts at evangelism that involved Christian groups not distinctively fundamental in all areas of belief and action.

As evangelicals became intent on cultural relativism in the 1960s and 1970s, the rift between the two groups grew even greater, for during the turbulent 1960s fundamentalists became culturally barricaded as never before, unable to accept contemporary displays of music, dress, and behavior as anything but rebellion against God's ideal for society (something closely resembling late-nineteenth-century piety). By the mid-1970s both contemporary culture and various new evangelical attitudes had found their way into many fundamentalist churches, forcing pastors to rethink positions on such cherished fundamentalist "ideals" as rock music, women's dress, hairstyles, new Bible translations, and cooperation with and tolerance of evangelicals. Jerry Falwell,* through his television ministry, publications, college, and political organization (Moral Majority*); John R. Rice,* through his editorials in the *Sword of the Lord*; Jack Van Impe, through his citywide revival campaigns; and others began to issue calls for change within fundamentalism that would reflect a more tolerant, broad-based platform, one considerably less critical and separatist. Many ardent fundamentalists, however, vehemently rejected these calls. In 1980 Bob Jones, Jr.,* called Falwell the "most dangerous man in America" and issued a plea for fundamentalist pastors to be proud of their separatist heritage as a "silent minority." Others termed Falwell, Rice, Van Impe, and those who would join them (and there were many) as "compromisers" contaminating the ranks of fundamentalism with the evangelical doctrines of "cooperation" and "inclusivism"; essentially they had renounced their fundamentalist birthright and had become "pseudo-fundamentalists." When Falwell briefly took over Jim Bakker's* scandal-laden PTL in 1987, Baptist fundamentalists were convinced that Falwell had sold out to the evangelicals.

What Falwell and others did in the late 1970s and 1980s was to challenge the definition of fundamentalism that emerged from the conflict with new evangelicals in the 1950s and 1960s. The best definition of that school came from George Dollar's *A History of Fundamentalism in America* (1973), in which he argued that "historic fundamentalism is the literal exposition of all the affirmations and attitudes of the Bible and the militant exposure of all non-biblical attitudes" (vi). The key word here is not "affirmations" or "attitudes" but "all"—it leaves no room for compromise or disagreement. It assumes that one can and does know "all" biblical attitudes and affirmations and can also determine when someone else does not. But the definition also requires the "knowing" fundamentalist to militantly expose the "compromising" other (whether fundamentalist, evangelical, liberal, or whatever) and to separate himself from such corruption. Such attitudes drove fundamentalists into cultural seclusion in the 1950s, 1960s, and 1970s. While building huge churches and schools through energetic evangelistic efforts, they steadfastly denied any worthwhile connection on their part to the larger secular culture and ecclesiastical and political establishments. In the late 1980s the changes within fundamentalism wrought by the political, cultural, and ecclesiastical activism of Falwell and others brought the fundamentalist movement to its most significant crossroad since the 1920s: enter the mainstream of American life and thought and risk losing one's "separateness," or remain in cultural and intellectual isolation in an effort to avoid "compromise." Does true fundamentalism seek to proclaim and preserve the "essential" doctrines of Christianity, or does it profess to know all the "affirmations and attitudes" of the Bible and militantly "expose" all those that are not? That remains the defining question for fundamentalism today.

Bibliography. Ammerman, Nancy T., "North American Protestant Fundamentalism," in *Fundamentalisms Observed*, eds. Martin E. Marty and R. Scott Appleby (Chicago: University of Chicago Press, 1991); Cole, Stewart, *The History of Fundamentalism* (New York: Smith, 1931); Dollar, George, *A History of Fundamentalism in America* (Greenville, SC: Bob Jones University Press, 1973); Falwell, Jerry, with Ed Dobson and Ed Hindson, *The Fundamentalist Phenomenon* (Garden City, NY: Doubleday, 1981); Furniss, Norman, *The Fundamentalist Controversy, 1918–1931* (New Haven: Yale University Press, 1954); Marsden, George, *Fundamentalism and American Culture* (Oxford: Oxford University Press, 1980); *Prophetic Studies of the International Prophetic Conference* (New York: Revell, 1886); Sandeen, Ernest R., *The Roots of Fundamentalism* (Chicago: University of Chicago Press, 1970).

Timothy D. Whelan

The Fundamentals. In 1909 two brothers, Lyman and Milton Stewart, Christian laymen and millionairoe oil magnates with an ardent desire for improving the biblical knowledge of Christian workers around the world and strengthening them in the major tenets of orthodox Christianity, used a portion of their great wealth to finance the composition, publication, and distribution of over three million copies of a great work known as *The Fundamentals: A Testimony to Truth*. With A. C. Dixon as chief editor, later assisted by Reuben A. Torrey, Louis Meyer, and Elmore Harris, *The Fundamentals* was originally published as a series of twelve volumes between 1910 and 1915. The introduction noted that these volumes were to be sent free of charge to "every pastor, evangelist, missionary, theological student, Sunday School superintendent, Y.M.C.A. and Y.W.C.A. secretary in the English-speaking world" (the average mailing list numbered around 250,000 persons). Sixty-four scholars of varying denominations (primarily Anglican, Presbyterian, Methodist, and Baptist) contributed approximately one hundred articles defending the beliefs of orthodox Christianity against the onslaught of evolution, "higher criticism," and modernism* that had developed in the latter decades of the nineteenth century. Contributors included such notables as Canon Dyson Hague (185–1935) and W. H. Griffith Thomas (1861–1924) of Wycliffe College, Toronto; James Orr (1844–1913) of Glasgow, Scotland; James M. Gray (1851–1935) of Boston (later president of Moody Bible Institute); B. B. Warfield* (1851–1921) and Charles R. Erdman (1866–1960) of Princeton Seminary; R. A. Torrey (1856–1928), noted evangelist and dean of the Bible Institute of Los Angeles; Charles Bray Williams (1869–1952) of Southwestern Baptist Theological Seminary*; C. I. Scofield* (1843–1921), editor of *The Scofield Reference Bible*; H.C.G. Moule (1841–1920), chaplain to Queen Victoria; Bishop J. C. Ryle (1816–1900) of Liverpool, England; G. Campbell Morgan (1863–1945) of Westminster Chapel, London; George Frederick Wright (1838–1921) of Oberlin College; E. Y. Mullins (1860–1928) of the Southern Baptist Theological Seminary,* Louisville, Kentucky; and A. C. Dixon (1854–1925), pastor of Spurgeon's Metropolitan Tabernacle in London. To Lyman Stewart, these men represented "the best and most loyal Bible teachers in the world" (Sandeen, 199).

A substantial number of articles centered upon what would become known as the "Five Fundamentals": the inerrancy of Scripture (five articles alone dealt with this one topic), the Virgin Birth* and deity of Christ, his substitutionary atonement, his bodily resurrection, and his Second Coming. "Inerrancy" implied a belief in the verbal, plenary inspiration of the Bible, with the original autographs not only inspired but also free from all error in their descriptions and affirmations, whether concerning matters of theology, science, history, or any other subject. The deity of Christ was not only a historical fact but could also be verified by the personal experience of all believers, Warfield argued (*The Fundamentals*, 2:239–46). The "supernatural" Virgin Birth was the most absolute fact corroborating Christ's deity; it was not an option, as the modernists argued. Nor was the death of Christ a supreme moral example for man to emulate, but rather the only possible propitiation for man's sins before the bar of God's righteous judgment. Christ's resurrection was not "spiritual" only, as modernists were advocating, but "literal" as well, an essential historical fact and the very foundation for Christianity itself. That fact would be made known to all at the Second Coming of Christ, a literal, bodily event occurring as the culmination of human history. Other articles included studies of regeneration and sin, attacks on Romanism, the importance of foreign missions and prayer, and even one on the biblical use of money. As Ernest Sandeen noted, the overall tone of the articles "was predominantly practical, apologetic, and pastoral" (206). An obvious effort had been made by the editors to forge a kind of conservative alliance against the forces of liberalism*; the more divisive issues within the Keswick movement and the millenarian camp were kept well in check. The emphasis was not on politics and social reform, but on "soul-winning," personal holiness, and sound doctrine. The "fundamentals" were not only to be experienced as realities in a subjective manner, but could also be verified in a rational, scientific manner as well. The writers stressed a criticism of the Bible that they believed was truly "historical," based upon a common-sense appropriation of the "facts" themselves, not a "speculative" or "higher criticism" based upon a priori hypotheses hostile to miracles and the supernatural. In 1917 R. A. Torrey and the Bible Institute of Los Angeles published a four-volume edition that included ninety of the original articles. In 1958 an abridged one-volume edition, under the general editorship of Charles Feinberg of Talbot Seminary, appeared.

The Fundamentals was one of the earliest attempts in the twentieth century by the forces of orthodoxy to ward off what they perceived to be the "threat" of modernism and higher criticism, which they felt was growing ever stronger in all the major denominations and which they believed to be essentially "non-Christian." Though they did indeed leave behind a fitting "testimony" to the labors and beliefs of those holding to the orthodox tenets of the Christian faith, they did not succeed in stemming the tide of modernism in the mainline denominations during the first quarter of the twentieth century. Nor did the publication of The Fundamentals receive anything more than scant attention in the theological journals and the popular religious magazines of the day. These writers did not go by the name "fundamentalist" yet (that would arrive in the early 1920s), nor would all of those who lived on into the 1920s identify themselves with the fundamentalist movement. Many would, of course, and in 1919 a significant number of the original contributors, along with over six thousand delegates from America, Canada, and Europe, attended "The World Conference on Christian Fundamentals" held in Philadelphia. In its opposition to liberal theology and Darwinism, The Fundamentals served as a fitting forerunner for much of the fundamentalist controversies of the 1920s; however, in its scholarly, ecumenical approach to theological controversy, it stands apart from the narrow, separatist attitude of post-1930 fundamentalism.

Bibliography. The Fundamentals: A Testimony to Truth, ed. R. A. Torrey, A. C. Dixon, 4 vols. (Los Angeles: Bible Institute of Los Angeles, 1917); Furniss, Norman F., The Fundamentalist Controversy, 1918–1931 (New Haven: Yale University Press, 1954); Marsden, George, "The Fundamentals," in Fundamentalism and American Culture (Oxford: Oxford University Press, 1980); Sandeen, Ernest, *"The Fundamentals,"* in *The Roots of Fundamentalism: British and American Millenarianism, 1800–1930* (Chicago: University of Chicago Press, 1970).

Timothy D. Whelan

G

Garvey, Marcus. Black Christianity was part of the pan-African, black separatist world vision of Marcus Mosiah Garvey, Jr., but his movement was fundamentally political. Born in 1887 at St. Ann, Jamaica, he became a printer's apprentice at age fourteen. Four years later he was foreman of a printing establishment in Kingston, a position that he lost because of union activism. Employed by the government printery, he plunged into Kingston's political life.

In 1910–1911 Garvey visited Central America as worker, labor agitator, and literary gadfly. By 1912 he was in London, short of money but nourished by Hyde Park's Speakers' Corner, visits to the House of Commons, work for the pan-African journal *Africa Times and Orient Review*, and visits to other European countries. Returning to Jamaica in 1914, Garvey began the Universal Negro Improvement Association (UNIA).

Seeking financial support, he traveled to the United States in 1916 for a lecture tour. Relishing Harlem's intellectual and political ferment, he transferred UNIA headquarters there and founded the publication *Negro World* in 1918. After World War I he led efforts to have Germany's African colonies returned to black rule, seeking a homeland for a pan-African nation. He established a steamship line and factories. Failing to secure Germany's colonies, he negotiated with the president of Liberia to establish Pan-Africa there.

However, Garvey's radical attacks upon W.E.B. Du Bois and others who favored assimilation eroded his support. Strongly opposed to interracial marriage, he met with a Ku Klux Klan* leader in 1922, infuriating many African Americans. When he was convicted of mail fraud on suspect evidence in 1923, UNIA fractured. Deported in 1927, he moved to Jamaica and London, where he died in 1940. Now a national hero in Jamaica, Garvey contributed to the birth of such separatist groups as the Nation of Islam* in the United States. **Bibliography.** Cronon, E. David, *Black Moses* (Madison: University of Wisconsin Press, 1955); Hill, Robert A., ed., and Barbara Bair, assoc. ed., *Marcus Garvey: Life and Lessons* (Berkeley: University of California Press, 1987); Martin, Tony, *Race First* (Westport, CT: Greenwood Press, 1976); Vincent, Theodore G., *Black Power and the Garvey Movement* (Berkeley: Ramparts Press, 1971).

Roger G. Branch

Gay Rights. The modern history of the struggle for gay rights dates from the mid-nineteenth-century work of German lawyer Karl Heinrich Ulrichs, whose prolific writings established many fundamental ideas about homosexuality* and advocated civil rights* for what he called "Uranians." Prior to this time homosexuality was generally understood as a behavior rather than a condition. Ulrich was succeeded in Germany by another activist, physician Magnus Hirschfeld, whose research and activism led in 1929 to the revocation of the antihomosexual Paragraph 175 of the German Constitution, ironically just prior to the ascendancy of the National Socialists and their campaign, under the banner of a blonde, Aryan, Christian Superman, to eradicate "degenerates," including homosexuals, marked by their pink triangles, the only group to be left behind, as criminals, when the American-led Allies liberated the Nazi concentration camps.

Gay rights activism in America falls roughly into three periods. The early homophile movement, including Harry Gerber's Society for Human Rights (1924), Harry Hay's Mattachine Foundation/Society (1950), and Del Martin's and Phyllis Lyon's Daughters of Bilitis (1955), emphasized conformity and asserted that gays and lesbians should be accepted because they differed from the mainstream only in terms of choice of mate. Difficult and largely unsuccessful efforts at assimilation, however, took a dramatic turn on June 17, 1969, when a group of harassed gay and lesbian patrons of a New York City bar, the Stonewall Inn, rioted during a police raid, thus launching the gay liberation phase of the gay rights movement.

Post-Stonewall organizations were more confrontational. The Gay Liberation Front (GLF) touted "Gay Power" and established "coming out," the public revelation of one's sexuality, as a political act. Women from the GLF joined ranks with the National Organization for Women (NOW), aligning feminism and gay rights where once mutual animosity and suspicion had prevailed. Subsequent developments have moved gay rights off the streets and into the courts and statehouses with a new focus on legal activism, the third and current phase of the movement.

In 1977, with the rallying cry of "Save Our Children" (from presumed homosexual recruitment), former beauty queen and born-again Christian Anita Bryant, supported by many religious and political leaders in Florida, led a successful campaign to repeal a Dade County ordinance, passed by voters six months earlier, prohibiting discrimination against gay people. Thereafter, beginning with a stabbing death, associated with Bryant's campaign, of a gay San Franciscan, violence against gays and lesbians began to make headlines. In November 1978 Harvey Milk, one of the first openly gay people elected to a public office, along with the mayor who supported him, was assassinated by a deranged fellow city councilman in San Francisco. Similar "hate crimes" and incidents of "gay bashing" became more common and have led to efforts on the part of homophile political groups to effect legislation designed to record and punish such crimes.

Since the early 1980s evangelical Christians like Jerry Falwell,* speaking for the Moral Majority,* and, more recently, Pat Robertson,* founder of the Christian Coalition,* have led the crusade against what they perceive as "the gay agenda"—to normalize homosexuality in medical, legal, educational, and social contexts. Falwell, Robertson, and their followers see themselves as "fighting a holy war" (Fackre, 9) against homosexuals who would, unchecked, "pressure Congress into passing Satan's agenda instead of God's" (Miller, 410).

In the 1990s, opposing political strategies have been to seek local and state legislation either guaranteeing what gay partisans call basic civil rights or prohibiting what antigay partisans call "special rights." In its 6–3 ruling on *Romer v. Evans* in June 1996, the U.S. Supreme Court came down in favor of the former, declaring unconstitutional Colorado's Amendment 2, a briefly successful ballot initiative intended to outlaw community antidiscrimination laws.

The dominant issue of the gay rights movement in the mid-1990s has become the legal recognition of gay unions, the prospect of which in the state of Hawaii led religious and political conservatives to introduce the Defense of Marriage Act (DOMA) in both houses of Congress in the spring of 1996. But to those for whom separation of church and state* is paramount, "acknowledging and endorsing [gay unions] rather than rejecting and discouraging them would be a socially positive act" (Bawer, 264). "In church one may believe what one will and condemn what one will. But to attempt to place restrictions on individual liberty and the right of others to pursue happiness is, quite simply, unAmerican" (Bawer, 139).

Bibliography. Bawer, Bruce, *A Place at the Table* (New York: Poseidon Press, 1993); Blasius, Mark, *Gay and Lesbian Politics* (Philadelphia: Temple University Press, 1994); Fackre, Gabriel, *The Religious Right and Christian Faith* (Grand Rapids, MI: Eerdmans Publishing Company, 1982); Miller, Neil, *Out of the Past* (New York: Vintage Books, 1995); Murphy, John, *Homosexual Liberation* (New York: Praeger Publishers, 1971).

Fred Richter

General Association of Regular Baptist Churches. The General Association of Regular Baptist Churches is a conservative evangelical, Baptist denomination with origins in the fundamentalist-modernist controversy. As theological changes emerged in the Northern Baptist Convention (NBC) during the first two decades of the twentieth century, urban fundamentalists within the NBC began to establish supradenominational coalitions to promote conservative theology within the convention. One such group was the Fundamental Fellowship of the NBC, which held its first meeting at a 1920 preconvention rally in Buffalo, New York. The fellowship met each year prior to the annual convention of the NBC to consider ways to check the rise of theological liberalism* within the denomination. Though the organization generated much controversy, it experienced little success in spurring the NBC toward a more fundamentalist posture. Two factions coexisted in the Fundamental Fellowship: moderate conservatives who wished to reform the convention from within and separatists who contemplated schism from the NBC.

The more aggressive separatists founded the Baptist Bible Union (BBU) in 1923. Such outspoken and controversial fundamentalist ministers as William Bell Riley, John Roach Straton, and A. C. Dixon united in the BBU with non-NBC fundamentalists such as Canadian T. T. Shields and Texan J. Frank Norris.* The constituents of the BBU held that the NBC had been corrupted by modernism* and unitarianism and had departed from historic Baptist polity.

In 1932, having abandoned all hope of changing the course of the NBC from within, the members of the BBU voted to reconstitute the union into a separate denomination, the General Association of Regular Baptist Churches (GARBC); over the next year the BBU's affiliated churches ratified that action and thus established the GARBC. Rather than create denominationally owned institutions, the new denomination chose to operate through a network of approved independent organizations, including mission agencies, publishing houses, colleges, and seminaries.

The GARBC Articles of Faith are similar to the New Hampshire Confession of Faith, with the exception of a strong affirmation of premillennial eschatology. The denomination requires member churches to subscribe to the Articles of Faith. While the militant tone of earlier generations has moderated, the GARBC continues to be characterized by conservative evangelical theology, Baptistic ecclesiology, and premillennial eschatology—as well as a robust Calvinism. The GARBC has grown rapidly since its beginning, with around a quarter of a million members in its 1,582 (1990) affiliated churches.

Bibliography. McBeth, H. L., *The Baptist Heritage* (Nashville: Broadman Press, 1987); Stowell, J. M., *Background and History of the General Association of Regular Baptist Churches* (Hayward, CA: General Tracts Unlimited, 1949).

J. Matthew Pinson

Glossolalia. Commonly known as speaking in tongues, glossolalia is a practice usually associated with the Pentecostal* and charismatic movements* of the twentieth century. Advocates affirm that ''tongues'' is one of the spiritual gifts of the ''full gospel'' of the New Testament that still should be practiced since ''Jesus is the same yesterday, today, and forever'' (Hebrews 13:8). Glossolalia is especially important for Pentecostals since they generally (with exceptions) consider ''tongues'' to be the ''initial evidence'' of the baptism of the Holy

Spirit.* Most charismatics also practice "tongues," but some consider it just one of the manifestations of the Holy Spirit and not the only certifying sign. Pentecostal theology cites numerous biblical passages for tongues, particularly Acts 2, 10, and 19 and 1 Corinthians 12–14. Some advocates cite the spurious ending of Mark, 16:17–18, if not for biblical support, then for evidence of glossolalia in the early church era.

Pentecostal theology describes two types of speaking in tongues, glossolalia and xenolalia. Both have been regarded as "heavenly speech" in which the words uttered are not the speaker's. Glossolalia is recognized as a mode of unintelligible speech and, following the biblical model in 1 Corinthians 12:10, is sometimes followed by the gift of interpretation by another believer if done in public worship. Glossolalic prayer, called the "prayer language" (1 Corinthians 14:4), has been emphasized in recent years, especially among charismatics, and is desired for use in private devotion.

Glossolalia is differentiated from xenolalia, the miraculous speaking of a language previously unlearned. Citing Peter and the disciples at the festival of Pentecost in Acts 2, the earliest Pentecostals claimed that all their speaking in tongues was xenolalia, and thus they were being equipped to usher in a final worldwide revival before the imminent Second Coming of Christ. While xenolalia now is deemphasized, Pentecostal theology affirms its possibility. Most non-Pentecostal linguists, however, concur that "tongues" is not the speaking of any known language.

Glossolalia has been reported sporadically throughout Christian history. In the early church era Montanism included a type of ecstatic unintelligible speech. In more recent history the Carmisards of the seventeenth century reported "tongues." Major outbreaks of glossolalia were claimed in the nineteenth century among the followers of Edward Irving in England, the Shakers,* the Mormons* and some in the Holiness movement.

The practice of glossolalia rose dramatically in the twentieth century with the birth of Pentecostalism. The Holiness movement spoke of sanctification in terms of a cleansing of inbred sin or a Pentecostal enduement of power. Some Holiness groups called this enduement of power the baptism of the Holy Spirit. Charles Parham,* a Holiness advocate, became the "father of Pentecostalism" when in 1901 he argued that glossolalia, following the pattern in Acts 2, was the sign of the "Baptism of the Holy Spirit." This connection of glossolalia and Holy Spirit baptism became a Pentecostal distinctive as the movement spread throughout the world via the famous 1906 Azusa Street* revival, led by Parham's convert William Seymour. When the Pentecostal experience reached non-Pentecostals in the charismatic movement that began in the 1960s, the practice of glossolalia spread even further.

Speaking in tongues has been one of the most contentious religious activities in the practice of Christianity during the twentieth century. Many critics, following the influence of B. B. Warfield,* the prominent Princeton theologian of the late nineteenth century, argue that "tongues" was only intended as a miraculous manifestation during the birth and establishment of the church and thus ceased with the apostolic age. Fierce critics have said that at worst, speaking in tongues is the work of the Devil, and at best, is a psychological release for the emotionally maladjusted that possesses no real spiritual value. More sympathetic nonpractitioners would agree with the adage of A. B. Simpson, founder of the Christian Missionary Alliance, "seek not, forbid not."

Bibliography. Anderson, R. M., *Vision of the Disinherited* (New York: Oxford University Press, 1979); Brumback, Carl, *"What Meaneth This?"* (Springfield, MO: Gospel Publishing House, 1947); Bruner, Frederick D., *A Theology of the Holy Spirit* (Grand Rapids, MI: William B. Eerdmans, 1970); Horton, Harold, *Gifts of the Spirit* (Springfield, MO: Gospel Publishing House, 1975.)

Douglas Weaver

Gordon-Conwell Theological Seminary. Gordon-Conwell Theological Seminary was one of the primary beneficiaries of the neoevangelical movement that swept America in the 1960s and 1970s. The efforts of Howard Pew, Billy Graham,* and Harold Ockenga led to the merger of Conwell School of Theology and the Gordon Divinity School. The Reverend Russell Conwell founded Conwell in 1884 from the proceeds of his famous sermon "Acre of Diamonds." Shortly thereafter, the Reverend A. J. Gordon created the Boston Missionary Training School in 1889 to train the increasing number of Baptist missionaries abroad, particularly for the new work in the Congo. After Gordon's death the Boston Missionary Training School became two institutions: Gordon College and Gordon Divinity School, both named for the founder.

Gordon-Conwell's close tie with American neoevangelicalism contributed to the controversy over the theology of New Testament Professor J. Ramsey Michaels that led to his dismissal in the spring of 1983. The immediate cause of the debate was Michaels's *Servant and Son*, a study of the Gospels. In this volume Michaels used redaction criticism, a technique that stressed the way in which the four evangelists shaped the Jesus traditions that they received. Redaction criticism builds on the prior results of form criticism, a technique that attempts to trace the history of particular pericopes, or units of tradition. Michaels's application of this method led him to conclude that the Gospel of John's account of Jesus' baptism contained elements that were not historical.

Even before the publication of *Servant and Son*, some of Michaels's Gordon-Conwell colleagues had found his work controversial. Michaels and Roger Nicole had debated the issues involved in this style of biblical criticism for years and had published part of their debate in *Inerrancy and Common Sense* in 1980. Nicole believed that evangelicals needed to develop a "hermeneutics" of inerrancy that would determine how evangelicals might use modern biblical criticism. In 1982 the executive committee of the seminary, chaired by Harold Lindsell, asked President Robert Cooley to begin a process to examine Michaels's writings on the Bible and to recommend action. After an investigation, the board presented its information to the Faculty Senate, which decided by a

6–1 vote that Michaels's teaching violated the seminary's position on inerrancy. After further consultations with Michaels, the professor resigned on April 2, 1983.

A related controversy over the biblical interpretation of Robert H. Gundry of Westmont College may have intensified the debate over Michaels's work. Conservative scholars had debated Gundry's views for some years, but the publication of his *Matthew: A Commentary on His Literary and Theological Art* in 1982 signaled a more serious controversy. Led by Norman Geisler, angry conservatives demanded that the Evangelical Theological Society, a conservative theological society, oust Gundy from membership. The issue was essentially the same as in Michaels's case: the use of redaction criticism. After a vote, Gundry was officially asked to resign from the society on December 17, 1993.

The controversy over Michaels's *Servant and Son* and Gundry's *Matthew* was part of a larger battle among conservative evangelicals. Conservative scholars had shown increasing interest in historical criticism since the 1960s. Other conservatives feared that even moderate criticism would undercut the authority of Scripture. In 1976 Harold Lindsell published *The Battle for the Bible*. The volume detailed the retreat from a strict definition of inerrancy at some evangelical seminaries and demanded that the schools return to a stricter orthodoxy. Lindsell's book was part of a wider pattern of concern. The issue was joined by Jack Rogers and Donald McKim, whose book *The Authority of the Bible: A Historical Approach* (1979) argued what strict inerrancy was. Evangelical scholars were struggling with the question, and in 1982 the Chicago Statement on Biblical Inerrancy attempted to provide some guidelines on the evangelical use of biblical criticism.

Bibliography. Gundry, Robert H., *Matthew: A Commentary on His Literary and Theological Art* (Grand Rapids, MI: Eerdmans, 1982); "The Issue of Biblical Authority Brings Scholar's Resignation: After Twenty-five Years Ramsey Michaels Is Out at Gordon-Conwell Seminary," *Christianity Today* 27 (July 15, 1983): 35–36; Michaels, J. Ramsey, *Servant and Son: Jesus in Parable and Gospel* (Atlanta: John Knox Press, 1981); Nicole, Roger R., and J. Ramsey Michaels, eds. *Inerrancy and Common Sense* (Grand Rapids, MI: Baker Book House, 1980); Pierard, Richard, "The Politics of Inerrancy," *Reformed Journal* 34 (January 1984): 2–4; Rogers, Jack, and Donald McKim, *The Authority and Interpretation of the Bible: An Historical Approach* (San Francisco: Harper and Row, 1979).

Glenn Miller

Graham, William (Billy) Franklin. American evangelical evangelist William (Billy) Franklin Graham was born in 1918 near Charlotte, North Carolina, to parents William Franklin and Morrow Coffey Graham. Converted at age sixteen during a crusade led by the fiery evangelist Mordecai Ham, Graham attended Bob Jones College for a short time, but eventually graduated from Wheaton College in Wheaton, Illinois. Here he met Ruth Bell, whom he married in 1943. After brief stints as a pastor, Youth for Christ evangelist, and Bible college president, Graham became nationally prominent as an evangelist as a result of his 1949 evangelistic campaign in Los Angeles. As the Los Angeles crusade seemed to be coming to an end, William Randolph Hearst issued orders to "puff Graham," the result of which was Graham's immediate national fame.

Most of the controversy surrounding Graham's ministry has revolved around his employment of what is known as "cooperative evangelism." Contention began in 1955 when Graham decided to broaden his base of support by accepting nonevangelical cooperation and financial support for his upcoming (1957) New York crusade. This not only entailed support from liberal, mainline Protestants, but also necessitated that converts at the crusade would be recommended to attend conservative and nonconservative churches alike.

Until this time Graham enjoyed the blessing of the entire evangelical community, including separatist fundamentalists. However, Graham's adoption of cooperative evangelism resulted in the disaffection of many of his former fundamentalist allies. In 1956, after news spread of Graham's cooperative efforts with nonevangelicals, militant fundamentalists such as the Methodist Bob Jones,* the Baptist John R. Rice,* and the Presbyterian Carl McIntire* began ruthlessly to criticize Graham. The most prominent example of this disapproval came from Graham's long-time supporter John R. Rice, publisher of the separatist fundamentalist* periodical the *Sword of the Lord.* After Graham's criticisms of fundamentalism in *Christian Life* magazine (June 1956) and his statement of enthusiastic support for the Cooperative Program of the Southern Baptist Convention,* which was aimed at the then-forming Southern Baptist Fellowship, an independent organization spearheaded by ultraconservatives within the SBC, Rice privately asked Graham to reaffirm the separatist fundamentalist statement of faith of the *Sword of the Lord.* Graham refused and asked that his name be dropped from the cooperating board of this publication. This action signaled the break between Graham and separatist fundamentalism. Graham was castigated in the major fundamentalist periodicals, including Rice's *Sword* and Carl McIntire's *Christian Beacon.* Bob Jones University soon instituted a policy that prohibited Graham's organization from holding meetings on its campus. Despite such controversy over Graham's evangelistic ministry, he has preached to around a hundred million individuals in person and countless more through the media of radio, television, and literature.

Bibliography. Marsden, George M., *Reforming Fundamentalism: Fuller Seminary and the New Evangelicalism* (Grand Rapids, MI: Eerdmans, 1987); Martin, William, *A Prophet with Honor: The Billy Graham Story* (New York: William Morrow, 1991); McLoughlin, William G., Jr., *Billy Graham: Revivalist in a Secular Age* (New York: Ronald Press, 1960).

J. Matthew Pinson

Graves, James Robinson. A controversial leader of the Landmark movement in the Southern Baptist Convention* (SBC) during the nineteenth century, James Robinson Graves (1820–1893) was born into a Congregationalist family in Vermont. Though he received meager formal education, he was self-educated and began his short career as a schoolteacher in Kingsville, Ohio, where he taught from 1840 to 1842. While teaching school in Jessamine County, Kentucky (1842–1843), Graves was ordained into the Baptist ministry and preached in churches in Ohio until 1845, when he accepted a teaching position in Nashville, Tennessee, and began serving a church there. In 1848 he succeeded R.B.C. Howell as editor of the *Tennessee Baptist,* a post Graves held for almost forty-seven years. By 1859 this periodical, with 13,000 subscriptions, had achieved the largest circulation of any denominational paper in the South. Graves also formed a publishing company that was influential in SBC life into the late nineteenth century. From this influential base he disseminated Landmark views.

During the 1850s Graves became the dominant leader of the Landmark movement, causing considerable controversy in the SBC. A. C. Dayton, secretary of the SBC's Bible Board from 1854 to 1858, came under the influence of Graves, and in 1857 Graves and Dayton founded the Southern Baptist Sunday School Union (SBSSU). They established this organization largely to compete with the more mainstream Southern Baptist Publication Society, located in Charleston, South Carolina. The SBSSU circulated Landmarkism* throughout the SBC, particularly in the West and Southwest, but not without opposition. The only Baptist periodical that did not denounce the SBSSU was Graves's own paper, the *Tennessee Baptist.*

Conflict developed between Graves and his predecessor, R.B.C. Howell, who opposed the formation of the SBSSU because of its Landmark views and its perceived divisiveness. Howell, president of the SBC from 1851 to 1859, had returned to Nashville from Richmond in 1857 to serve as pastor of the First Baptist Church. Though Howell was Graves's pastor, Graves mounted an aggressive campaign against Howell that resulted in Graves's exclusion from First Baptist in October 1858. Despite his expulsion, Graves was exonerated by the Concord Association of Tennessee. Notwithstanding Graves's local popularity, Howell was reelected at the 1859 meeting of the SBC in Richmond.

Through the *Tennessee Baptist* and the SBSSU, Graves polarized Southern Baptists into Landmarkist and non-Landmarkist factions. In spite of fierce opposition to Graves and Landmarkism, however, Graves still managed to bring the Board of Sunday Schools (BSS), created by the SBC in 1863, under Landmark control. The BSS, an outgrowth of the Southern Baptist Theological Seminary,* then in Greenville, South Carolina, made an attempt to propel Southern Baptist publishing back into the mainstream of the SBC through the efforts of such leaders as Basil Manly, Jr., and John A. Broadus. In 1868, however, the SBC approved a merger of the BSS and Graves's SBSSU. This new Sunday school board was moved to Memphis, where it declined steadily until 1873, when the SBC abolished it.

Graves was one of the most influential leaders of the SBC in the latter half of the nineteenth century. His Landmark views, made famous in his popular *Old Landmarkism: What is It?* (1880), continue to influence Southern Baptist life, but they have an even greater impact on the practices of Independent Baptists and denominations such as the American Baptist Association* and the Baptist Missionary Association* of America.

Bibliography. Graves, J. R., *Old Landmarkism: What Is It?* (Texarkana: Baptist Sunday School Committee, 1928); McBeth, H. L., *The Baptist Heritage* (Nashville: Broadman Press, 1987); Tull, J. E., *Shapers of Baptist Thought* (Valley Forge, PA: Judson Press, 1972).

J. Matthew Pinson

Great Awakening. The term "Great Awakening" describes a series of eighteenth-century colonial revivals that peaked in the 1740s with the preaching of George Whitefield (1714–1770) and impacted almost all aspects of colonial life. Depending on one's point of view, the Great Awakening did as much to promote controversy as it did to stimulate revival.

Catastrophic conversions, semiascetic moral ideas, organized meetings to cultivate the devotional life, and developed lay leadership were demanded by Theodore J. Frelinghuysen (1691–1748), pastor of Dutch Reformed churches in New Brunswick, New Jersey, for whom Christianity had been perfunctory and served to perpetuate their Dutch nationality. He required a profession of faith as a condition for admission to the Lord's Supper, pronounced upon the spiritual state of others, and required individuals transferring church membership by certificate to show evidence of conversion. These and other demands met with resistance, and the Dutch Reformed Church experienced divisions between prorevivalists and traditionalists.

The Presbyterian Church was divided over issues raised by the revivals. The number of ministers in the revivalist Synod of New York increased, while the number of those in the antirevivalistic Synod of Philadelphia decreased. Matters were not helped by the publication of Gilbert Tennent's* (1703–1764) "The Danger of an Unconverted Ministry," a scathing and not-too-veiled denunciation of both the purely academic training of ministers and the activities of unconverted ministers who could not convert others. His urging churches to abandon "unconverted ministers" was not universally appreciated.

Jonathan Edwards* (1703–1758), alarmed at the Arminians on one side and the Enthusiasts on the other, in 1734 preached a series of sermons on justification by faith that led to more than three hundred being added to his Northampton, Massachusetts, church rolls. He deplored the bizarre behavior of Enthusiastic evangelists who mistook babbling for the work of the Spirit. He wrote four treatises defending the Great Awakening, among them *A Treatise Concerning Religious Affections,* in which he argued that the affections (feelings) were necessary in religion and that there could be no true religion without them.

The revivals remained local in character until the preaching of George Whitefield unified the several previous efforts into one Great Awakening. While Whitefield's itinerant preaching electrified those who heard him, his censoriousness in denouncing the spiritual deadness of churches and his accusations that the universities were spiritually dead earned him a written rebuke from Harvard that is considered one of the clearest criticisms of the Great Awakening. He was criticized for his "enthusiasm" (an Enthusiast is one who acts according to dreams, hidden impulses, and impressions on the mind and imagines them to be from the Holy Spirit), for being censorious, uncharitable, and slanderous, and for his handling of money given. His manner of extempore preaching was deemed to be superficial. His itinerant way of preaching disrupted churches and alienated ministers from their congregations.

The Great Awakening undercut the traditional Puritan conception of the world and the Puritan synthesis of church, society, and government. Puritan churches were divided into four groups—Moderate New Lights, Separatist New Lights, Old Lights,* and Old Calvinists—that differed on theology, revivals, the individual covenant of grace, and the social covenant. No longer was there one voice; there were many.

By emphasizing the direct knowledge of God in personal experience, revivalists, with the exception of Jonathan Edwards, disparaged theoretical, theological, or intellectual approaches to Christianity. During the period of the revivals the assumption was that "experience" was from the Holy Spirit working in an individual. In the future this assurance was not so certain when experience might mean any religious experience or any human experience.

Suspicions led often to separation and to the establishment of new churches. Mass revivals with huge audiences meeting without the direction of a local pastor were a matter of deep concern to both friends and foes of the revivals. A rhetoric developed whose object was to persuade or communicate on a large, impersonal level detached from any one church or community.

Whitefield redefined the social context in which public address took place by encouraging people to take direct control of their own religious lives. Leadership and qualifications for leadership were at issue. The educated clergy, supported by the establishment and public taxes, were now challenged by the common people and a new wave of popular speakers in public arenas. The accepted forms of social hierarchy and deference that had characterized the established Puritanism gradually gave way to the egalitarianism of the Great Awakening.

Bibliography. Gaustad, E. S., *The Great Awakening in New England* (Harper and Row, 1957); Miller, P., *Jonathan Edwards* (New York: William Sloane Associates, 1949); Smith, H. S., R. T. Handy, and L. A. Loetscher, *American Christianity: An Historical Interpretation with Representative Documents,* vol. 1, *1607–1829* (New York: Scribners, 1960).

Robert K. Gustafson

Grimké, Angelina Emily. Along with her older sister, Sarah, Angelina Grimké (1805–1879) spoke early and often on public issues in the nineteenth century. Born in Charleston, South Carolina, in 1805, she pressed for the recognition of women's rights and for the abolition of slavery with tremendous vigor throughout her life. With her sister, Sarah, Lucretia Mott, and others she founded the Philadelphia Female Anti-Slavery Society in 1833. A birthright Quaker, she insisted on her right to be heard on such public matters.

In the year 1837 her public notoriety reached its peak. She published a strident antislavery commentary in William Lloyd Garrison's *Liberator*. Later that year she spoke to the Woman's Anti-Slavery Convention in New York City (again working with fellow Friend Lucretia Mott). She rounded out the year by publishing two inflammatory pieces, "Appeal to the Christian Women of the South" and "Appeal to the Women of the Nominally Free States." In both pamphlets she appealed to women to exert all the influence they could bring to bear upon the nation's political leaders to abolish slavery. For her efforts in 1837 she received many accolades, but she also received severe chastisement from the Massachusetts Congregational Ministerial Association. The Massachusetts group castigated her "unwomanly" behavior and worried about her willingness to speak to "promiscuous" (mixed-gender) audiences.

Undaunted by these and other critics of her work, Grimké testified before the Massachusetts legislature in 1838, the first woman to do so, advocating antislavery petitions. She then published a series of letters in the *Liberator* asserting her right, indeed her obligation, to speak her mind on public issues. She married Theodore Dwight Weld,* the Presbyterian abolitionist from Ohio, in 1838 at a ceremony attended by Frederick Douglass and his family. Her critics railed against the "race mixing" at her wedding, but her work continued unabated. Two days after her marriage to Weld, she addressed the Philadelphia Anti-Slavery Convention in Pennsylvania Hall. Later the hall and the city's Shelter for Colored Orphans burned to the ground.

In 1839 she and Sarah coauthored two works attesting to their revulsion with slavery and further fanning the flames of abolitionism* in the North. The first, *American Slavery As It Is*, offered readers a grim portrait of chattel slavery in the United States. The Grimkés hoped to counter southern apologies for slavery that touted the benevolence of the institution. In the other work, *Testimony of a Thousand Witnesses*, they rehearsed evidence of the evils of slavery based on accounts provided by former slaves.

Angelina Grimké expressed her pleas for slavery in passionate terms. She advocated women's rights with equal fervor. Though poor health curtailed her activity after 1850, her advocacy on volatile issues placed her at the center of many controversies and in the sights of numerous critics.

Bibliography. Lerner, Gerda, *The Grimké Sisters from South Carolina: Rebels against Slavery* (Boston: Houghton Mifflin, 1967); Lumpkin, Katharine DuPre, *The Emancipation of Angelina Grimké* (Chapel Hill: University of North Carolina Press, 1974); Weld, Angelina Grimké, "Appeal to the Christian Women of the South" and "Letters to Catharine Beecher," in *The Feminist Papers*, ed. Alice Rossi (New York: Bantam, 1974), 296–305 and 319–322; Weld, Theodore Dwight, *In Memory, Angelina Grimké Weld* (Boston: Press of G. H. Ellis, 1880).

Russell Congleton

Grimké, Francis J. Francis J. Grimké (1850–1937) was one of the premier African-American clergy of his time. He helped found the American Negro Academy, worked with W.E.B. Du Bois to organize the NAACP,* and served as a trustee for Howard University for forty years. For most of his career, he was pastor of the Fifteenth Street Presbyterian Church in Washington, D.C., church home to many of the capital's African-American elite. In all of his endeavors, he sought to give voice to the ideals of Christianity as they related to race relations.

Born to a slaveholder and a slave, he was raised as a freeman in Charleston, South Carolina. His white half brother tried to enslave him after the father's death; Grimké worked as a servant for a short period of time until the end of the Civil War. He then attended Lincoln University of Pennsylvania and Princeton Seminary, supported by his two aunts, the Grimké sisters, Quakers involved in the abolitionist movement. From Princeton he went to Fifteenth Street Presbyterian, where he would spend his entire career except for a short pastorate in Florida.

From his pulpit and in his writings, Grimké worked against the growing segregationist impulses in American culture and in the Presbyterian Church. He spoke out against reunion between the northern Presbyterian Church and two of its southern counterparts because of accommodation by the North to the South's Jim Crow church polity—separating African-American congregations into their own denomination. His prophetic side appears most clearly in his statements concerning World War I.

Bibliography. Ferry, Henry Justin, "Francis James Grimké: Portrait of a Black Puritan" (Ph.D. diss., Yale University, 1970); Ferry, Henry Justin, "Patriotism and Prejudice: Francis James Grimké on World War I," *Journal of Religious Thought* 32 (Spring/ Summer 1975): 86–94; Ferry, Henry Justin, "Racism and Reunion: A Black Protest by Francis James Grimké," *Journal of Presbyterian History* 50 (Summer 1972): 77–88; Grimké, Francis J., *The Works of Francis J. Grimké*, ed. Carter G. Woodson, 4 vols. (Washington, DC: Associated Publishers, 1942); Weeks, Louis B., "Racism, World War I and the Christian Life: James J. Grimké in the Nation's Capital," in *Black Apostles: Afro-American Clergy Confront the Twentieth Century*, ed. Randall K. Burkett and Richard Newman (Boston: G. K. Hall, 1978), 57–75.

Thomas J. Davis

H

Half-way Covenant. The question of eligibility for baptism* had long been discussed by the Puritans in colonial New England. Their covenant or federal doctrine of the church implied that church membership included both covenanting adults and their children. Children, as "federally holy," were eligible to receive the seal of the covenant at birth, namely, baptism. Upon arriving at a mature age of discretion, however, such children were bound to make a statement or confession of faith in order to be a "full" member with Communion and voting privileges. Suppose, however, that these persons never made that statement. Would the children of these "half" members be eligible to receive baptism?

In the second and third generations of Puritans, this question became relevant, for numbers of these "federally holy" parents had never made an adult or mature confession of faith. Such persons were actually nicknamed "half-way covenanters." When they requested baptism for their children, the Puritan ministers faced a dilemma, for baptism had been generally refused to infants unless at least one of the parents was a full covenanting member. By the mid-seventeenth century, however, some of the ministers were baptizing infants if at least one of the grandparents was a full member. The famous Cambridge Synod of 1646–1648 took no final action on this issue. More liberal ministers from Massachusetts and Connecticut met in 1657 in Boston and agreed that infants of "half-way covenanters" should be baptized. Conservatives opposed this decision, and the controversy over church memberships became a heated one.

Interestingly, the debate was so intense and fractious that the General Court of the Bay Colony finally ordered the ministers to meet and solve the problem. In 1662 seventy delegates met in Boston to address the issue. Strong arguments were heard from both sides, but when the vote was taken, the liberal position won by a seven-to-one margin. The Half-way Covenant's official answer, then, was that the children of "half-way covenanters" were indeed to be baptized, but without an adult confession of regeneration they were not to receive Communion nor enjoy the privilege of a vote in church matters. In coming years, of course, this left the door open to more liberal developments as some ministers decided that the "half-way" members certainly could receive Communion as well as enjoy having a vote. Controversy on the question of full membership continued for many years. As late as 1750 Jonathan Edwards* was forced to resign as pastor of Northampton Church as a result of his taking a more conservative position in relation to full church membership. For one, he did not agree that Communion should be given to "half-way covenanters."

The Half-way Covenant was probably not a sign of declining piety. On the other hand, it was a serious effort to wrestle with a question that the first generation of Puritans never faced. The various answers given to the new question explored numerous ways to deal with the basic question of church membership and its meaning.

Bibliography. Ahlstrom, Sydney E., *A Religious History of the American People* (New Haven: Yale University Press, 1972); Hudson, Winthrop S., *Religion in America*, 3rd ed. (New York: Scribner's, 1981); Mulder, John M., and John F.Wilson, eds., *Religion in American History* (Englewood Cliffs, NJ: Prentice-Hall, 1978); Smith, H. Shelton, Robert Handy, and Lefferts Loetscher, *American Christianity*, vol. 1 (New York: Scribner's, 1960).

George H. Shriver

Ham, Mordecai Fowler. Perhaps best known in his lifetime for being the preacher at the revival service when Billy Graham was converted in 1934, Mordecai Fowler Ham (1877–1961) was famed in his own time for his thunderous attacks on designated special sins and select groups of enemies of God and godliness.

Born in Allen County, Kentucky, Ham attended college in nearby Bowling Green and briefly pursued a business career in Chicago. Ordained to the Baptist ministry in 1901, he was a stationed pastor from 1927 to 1929 in Oklahoma City and conducted an itinerant ministry in the cities of the South for his entire career, most often in tents and tabernacles.

Ham was a genuine fundamentalist during an era when there were few in the South. He insisted on correct doctrine, roundly condemned heresy, which he found near and far, and delivered scathing attacks on several evils that he judged damnably ungodly, personal immorality, and the "liquor interests" including bootleggers, among them. But they extended to systemically evil people, notably Jews, the Catholic Church, evolutionists ("anti-Christian educators"), and communists. Inside the church, he abhorred "social Christianity" and condemned its institutionalization into denominations, boards, and agencies.

If Ham's reputation can be summarized, it is that he carried out "confrontation evangelism." He wanted people to get right with God and to repent of their evil ways. So he preached for conversion, claiming to have made one million converts. But the specificity of his message had more to do with particular evils and designated abhorrent groups than with an appeal to trust a gracious God. He never hesitated to single out conspicuous sinners for public denunciation. The Catholic Church was more than heretical, it was an abomination to the Almighty. Jews had become stiffnecked, hopelessly disobedient to God, their leaders set to destroy the America the Lord intended. Communists were a threat, undermining everything a righteous God stands for. Not surprisingly, he entertained conspiratorial notions, the major one his conviction that white Protestant America was about to be overturned by various evil forces. Late in his life he used the medium of radio with telling effect. Unlike most figures in the history of American religious controversy, M. F. Ham himself, not a cause or following that was associated with him, was the whole story.

Bibliography. Baker, James T., "The Battle of Elizabeth City: Christ and Antichrist in North Carolina," *North Carolina Historical Review*, 54 (Autumn 1977): 393–408; Ham, E. E., *50 Years on the Battle Front with Christ: A Biography of Mordecai F. Ham* (n.p.: Old Kentucky Home Revivalist Press, 1950); Ham, E. E., ed., *Sermons That Brought Revival by M. F. Ham* (n.p.: Old Kentucky Home Revivalist Press, 1950).

Samuel S. Hill

Hargis, Billy James. Fundamentalist evangelist Billy James Hargis capitalized on the growing fear of communism* in post–World War II America to create a controversial religious empire that mixed virulent anti-Communism, conspiratorial politics, patriotism, moralism, and Christian fundamentalism.* Hargis was born on August 3, 1925, in Texarkana, Texas, and grew up in the "Dust Bowl" during the Great Depression of the 1930s. After a brief education at an unaccredited Bible college, Hargis pastored a series of small churches in Oklahoma, Missouri, and Arkansas. The young preacher was dismissed by his first church's elders after admonishing them not to attend movies and publicly exposing the school principal's love affair with a teacher.

Hargis soon decided that all of America needed to hear his religiopolitical message. In 1948 he left the pastorate and devoted all his energies to Christian Echoes National Ministry, a Tulsa-based nonprofit organization established to battle communism and its "godless allies." The Communist front organizations from which America needed to be rescued came to include, among others, the United Nations, the American Civil Liberties Union, the National Council of Churches,* the World Council of Churches, and the National Association for the Advancement of Colored People (NAACP*). In sermons, radio broadcasts, and books, Hargis roundly denounced these groups as part of a larger Communist conspiracy. During the 1960s Hargis added such prominent national figures as John and Robert Kennedy, Lyndon Johnson, Martin Luther King, Jr.,* and Walter Reuther to his list of Communist dupes. In the main, Hargis's darkly conspiratorial message appealed largely to the uneducated and fear-ridden rural populations of the South Central plains.

Hargis came to national attention in February 1960 when the media reported that a U.S. Air Force training manual for which Hargis had provided material included the allegation of Communist infiltration of the National Council of Churches. Although the secretary of defense quickly withdrew the manual, Hargis gained considerable notoriety from the scandal. Hargis was also a key player in the Supreme Court's 1967 affirmation of the Federal Communications Commission's Fairness Doctrine. The doctrine stipulated that stations airing programs containing a personal attack on individuals or organizations must notify the attacked party within seven days and offer time for a response. A 1964 Hargis broadcast in Pennsylvania had pointedly attacked author Fred J. Cook. Since Cook was unhappy with his options of either paying for response time or proving that he was unable to pay, he successfully appealed his case all the way to the Supreme Court.

Shortly after opening the conservative American Christian College in Tulsa in 1970, Hargis was forced to resign as president when he admitted to sexual indiscretions with young male students at the college. The school, whose avowed purpose was to teach "anti-Communist patriotic Americanism," did not survive the scandal and closed in 1977. With his reputation in shambles, Hargis managed to create two new ministries, the Billy James Hargis Evangelistic Association and the Good Samaritan Children's Foundation. He continues to preach over radio and television in the South Central states.

Bibliography. George, John, and Laird Wilcox, *Nazis, Communists, Klansmen, and Others on the Fringe: Political Extremism in America* (Buffalo: Prometheus Books, 1992); Hargis, Billy James, *Communist America—Must It Be?* (Tulsa: Christian Crusade, 1960); Harris, Billy James, *My Great Mistake* (Tulsa: Christian Crusade, 1986); Penabaz, Fernando, *Crusading Preacher from the West* (Tulsa: Christian Crusade, 1965); Redekop, John Harold, *The American Far Right: A Case Study of Billy James Hargis and Christian Crusade* (Grand Rapids, MI: Eerdmans, 1968).

Phillip Lucas

Harper, William Rainey. Born on July 24, 1856, in New Concord, Ohio, William Rainey Harper manifested a precocious ability to master languages. Graduation from college at age fourteen and an earned doctorate from Yale at eighteen confirmed it. His family had been Presbyterian for generations, but in 1876 Harper affiliated with the Baptists. After filling a few minor teaching posts, in 1879 he became instructor in Hebrew at Baptist Union Seminary in Morgan Park, Illinois. While at the seminary he displayed several traits that characterized his mature years: he cared little for theological disputes and avoided such debates whenever possible; he had a tremendous capacity for hard work and simultaneously held down a number of responsible tasks; his energy and enthusiasm for various projects were contagious. One such venture was creating a summer school on campus, but more important, this developed into a system of correspondence courses that soon enrolled more than three thousand students. In addition to writing study plans, manuals, and textbooks for use in these courses, Harper also launched two journals, *Hebrew Student* (later *Biblical World*) and *Hebraica* (later *American Journal of Semitic Languages and Literature*), and edited both for years. In 1885, he became active in the Chautauqua movement and for years directed its college of liberal arts. These activities brought wide recognition as an authority in Hebrew scholarship. Beginning in 1885, he filled a five-year term as professor of Semitic languages at Yale, but it was already clear that greater opportunities lay ahead.

By 1890 plans were well under way for John D. Rockefeller to fund an institution of higher learning and for Harper to build it. Instead of planning just another college, he insisted from the outset that the new school embody all the qualities of a true university. Under his initiative the University of Chicago began with classes every quarter of the year, a summer school, an extension service, the nucleus of an extensive library, a press, and its own publications staff. Even more innovative was the policy of faculty controlling campus athletics, but most striking of all was Harper's firm determination to make research and graduate study a major feature of the university's educational program. In all these areas he set trends for other schools to emulate; he also set research and publishing in motion by recruiting a stellar faculty and allowing colleagues to pursue lines of inquiry with complete intellectual freedom. Conservatives in churches often criticized writings of Chicago professors, but Harper's support of academic freedom* never wavered. He created on campus an atmosphere of open-ended search for truth and hoped that his colleagues could advance knowledge through honest, candid exchange. The desired effect occurred rarely, but the ideal remained of teaching people how to think rather than imposing ideas on them like a creedal straitjacket.

Harper disturbed conservatives of his day in an additional way by defending modern critical approaches to Bible study. Convinced that linguistics, archeology, and history were valuable analytic tools, he argued that one should be free to study the Scriptures as one did any other set of writings. He held that the Bible was no more than an ordinary book, "and very ordinary at that." His resistance to orthodox watchdogs when controversies threatened created a haven for intellectual freedom and gave impetus to untrammeled research in both the arts and the sciences. Far sooner than expected, Harper died on January 10, 1906, in Chicago.

Bibliography. Harper, William R., *A Critical and Exegetical Commentary on Amos and Hosea* (New York: C. Scribner's Sons, 1905); Harper, William R., *Religion and the Higher Life: Talks to Students* (Chicago: University of Chicago Press, 1904); Harper, William R., *The Trend in Higher Education* (Chicago: University of Chicago Press,

1905); Wind, James P., *The Bible and the University: The Messianic Vision of William Rainey Harper* (Atlanta: Scholars Press, 1987).

Henry Warner Bowden

Hecker, Isaac. The son of German immigrants, Issac Hecker was born on December 18, 1819, in New York City. Mainly self-educated, Hecker concluded by 1842 that God was calling him away from ordinary pursuits in life. He moved to Brook Farm in West Roxbury, Massachusetts, where he met with Ralph W. Emerson, Henry D. Thoreau, and other transcendentalists. He soon became disillusioned with their answers, and tried various forms of Protestantism before converting to Catholicism on August 2, 1844.

A year later he entered the Redemptorist order, going to Rome for study. Ordained in England on October 23, 1849, he returned to the United States two years later. In trying to reach Americans, he desired to align the church with the spirit of American liberty and freedom, believing that only Catholicism could satisfy a free people's natural longings. These ideas were outlined in two books, *Questions of the Soul* (1855) and *Aspirations of Nature* (1857). After a quarrel with his American superior, Pope Pius IX released Hecker from his Redemptorist vows and then suggested that the young priest start another community. In 1858 Hecker founded the Society of Missionary Priests of St. Paul the Apostle, or Paulist Fathers,* the first male religious society formed in the United States.

Determined to prove that Catholicism was not an enemy of liberty but its guardian, Hecker spoke across America preaching to non-Catholics, who were often impressed by his personality, sincerity, and manner. In April 1865 he founded *Catholic World*, a national magazine of literature and the arts, and tried unsuccessfully to start a Catholic daily. While failing health prevented him from achieving all his goals, he still edited his national magazine and directed the affairs of the Paulists. He published *The Church and the Age* (1887), in which he argued that Catholicism could be compatable with American political institutions.

A mildly controversial figure during his lifetime, Hecker became the center of a major dispute after his death in New York City on December 22, 1888. A fellow Paulist wrote a laudatory biography of their founder in 1891. This biography was translated into French, and certain conservatives rushed to condemn Hecker's views of liberty and the operation of the Holy Spirit. In early 1899 Pope Leo XIII condemned some of these views under the title ''Americanism.''* Cardinal James Gibbons of Baltimore quickly assured the pontiff that Hecker's views had been distorted. Reconciling American freedom and Roman Catholicism would have to wait a few more decades.

Bibliography. Elliott, Walter, *The Life of Father Hecker* (New York: Columbus Press, 1891); Holden, Vincent F., *The Yankee Paul: Isaac Thomas Hecker* (Milwaukee: Bruce

Publishing Company, 1958): McAvoy, Thomas T., *The Americanist Heresy in Roman Catholicism, 1895–1900* (Notre Dame: University of Notre Dame Press, 1963).

                                                                    James M. Woods

Hell. In Christian tradition, hell is the final, definitive state of tormented separation from God in the next life by those who have rejected God in this life. Jesus repeatedly warned of the possibility of damnation, and hell has been a constant element in Christian teaching ever since.

The Second Council of Constantinople (553) condemned as heresy the view of Origen (c. 185–c. 254) that the pain of hell is merely remedial so that in the end, all will be saved (universalism). Belief in eternal punishment remained the Western Christian norm for more than a millennium, affirmed by later councils and popes. Though Protestant reformers largely continued in this view, some Anabaptists were Universalists, while others taught that the wicked would finally be destroyed (annihilationism).

The vivid portrayals of everlasting torment in the celebrated sermons of Jonathan Edwards* (1703–1758) reflected the sober Calvinist view of hell prevalent among the Puritans who settled New England. But the new assumptions of the Enlightenment, ruling out the notion of eternal divine retribution as unreasonable, eventually took root there as well. When itinerant preacher John Murray (1741–1815) came spreading the Universalist message, he provoked a vehement defense from the traditionalists, most notably Samuel Hopkins* (1721–1803), a student of Edwards.

Even so, the American Universalist movement grew, finding allies among disenchanted Puritans and some German pietists—though not among the African slaves, who usually insisted that hell was real and filled with damned slaveholders. The emerging liberal party in New England found a Universalist champion in Charles Chauncy* (1705–1787), pastor of the First Church of Boston (1727–1787) and vocal critic of Edwards. Later, Chauncy's Unitarian and transcendentalist heirs, in particular Theodore Parker* (1810–1860), continued to scandalize the orthodox community with public attacks on the doctrine of hell.

Though Universalists agreed in denying eternal punishment, they disagreed over the possibility of limited punishment. The "Restorationist" party insisted that the wicked suffered in a remedial hell after death before being restored to God. The "Ultra-Universalists," however, led by Hosea Ballou (1771–1852), taught that sin was punished only in this life.

The more liberal American churches continued to develop Universalist assumptions, in part under the influence of the German romantic theologian Friedrich Schleiermacher (1768–1834), who insisted that every human being was "predestined" to salvation. The this-worldly focus of the Social Gospel movement* at the turn of the century further deflected attention away from eternal suffering to present suffering. By the latter twentieth century the demythologizing project of German New Testament scholar Rudolf Bultmann (1884–1976) had settled the issue of hell for many by relegating it to the status of a myth needing reinterpretation.

Several new and distinctively American religious groups also challenged traditional doctrines about eternal punishment. Christian Scientists taught that hell was simply the mental anguish caused by sin; Mormons preached that all would be saved, each one in his or her "own order." Both the Seventh-Day Adventists and Jehovah's Witnesses* concluded that the wicked would be annihilated.

Evangelical Protestants have typically maintained more traditional notions of hell, though a few evangelical theologians in recent years have stirred controversy by declaring themselves annihilationists. American Catholics as a whole have also held to the traditional teaching, buttressed by Vatican Council I's* anathema against those who claimed that "the punishments of the damned in hell will not last forever" (1870). But Vatican Council II (1962–1965) opened up new possibilities by recognizing that some non-Christians might be saved, and since then some Catholic theologians have declared that even though the real possibility of hell must be affirmed, Christians may yet hope that no one will go there.

Increasing American religious diversity promises to spur new debates between Christians and adherents of other religions, who might advocate Hindu notions of reincarnation, the seven-layered hell of Islam, or the 8.4 million hells of Jainism. Meanwhile, a 1990 Gallup poll showed that 60 percent of Americans believe in hell, though only 4 percent think themselves likely to end up there.

Bibliography. Crockett, W., ed., *Four Views on Hell* (Grand Rapids, MI: Zondervan, 1992); Sachs, J. R., "Current Eschatology: Universal Salvation and the Problem of Hell," *Theological Studies* 52 (1991): 227–54; Walker, D. P., *The Decline of Hell* (Chicago: University of Chicago Press, 1964).

T. Paul Thigpen

High Church–Low Church. In its broadest scope the high-church–low-church controversy can be found in many types of churches because it derives as much from varying psychological attitudes as from ecclesiology. Nevertheless, the debate has surfaced most often in the Anglican Communion, going all the way back to Elizabethan times and undoubtedly beyond them. The fundamental argument is over the nature of the church and its role in salvation. Products of this perennial tension include such famous entities as seventeenth-century Puritans who represented low-church convictions, the nineteenth-century Oxford movement, and Congregationalist-Episcopal contentions during the intervening decades.

These church parties are vitally concerned with identifying genuine Christian forms and values. In this context one view has a "high" estimate of bishops, priests, the sacraments, and formal rituals, according them central importance as channels of grace and essentials of salvation. Embracing the label "Catholic," it emphasizes apostolic succession as crucial to a proper ministry and shows marked preference for the liturgy and creeds of ancient and medieval Christianity. The opposing view proclaims its "low" esteem for such elements. Espousing the label "Protestant" for contrast, this point of view has usually placed little value on ministerial office and the trappings of ritual behavior. It champions the importance of Scripture over traditions perpetuated by human institutions, showing a preference for primitive Christianity over medieval accretions.

In the first half of the nineteenth century these attitudes were embodied in two stalwarts who articulated opinions that were held by a great many other colleagues on respective sides of the ongoing debate. On the high-church side John Henry Hobart, bishop of New York, supported the centrality of Episcopal forms to Christian propriety. Representing the other side was Charles Pettit McIlvaine, bishop of Ohio, who prized earnest prayer and evangelical sermons, eschewing wooden liturgical procedures.

Opposing views in this controversy assumed more tangible, institutional shape in the second half of the nineteenth century. In 1873 George David Cummins* had already served as assistant bishop of Kentucky for several years, but he was publicly scolded by several fellow prelates for attending interdenominational services and accepting, at least by implication, the legitimacy of other churches and their clergy. Stung by such criticism and galvanized to articulate deep convictions that he already held, Cummins emerged as the founder and organizer of the Reformed Episcopal Church.* This group provided a home for those who disagreed with the overbearing insistence on episcopal polity and sacramental theology that high-church officials represented. One of these was Charles Edward Cheney, a priest who had been censured and then deposed because of his low-church practices. Cummins, already a bishop, consecrated Cheney to episcopal office, and since he died shortly afterward, it was Cheney who nurtured Reformed Episcopal growth into the twentieth century.

Today the group that once held such symbolic significance has become merely another small denomination in a land where splinter groups abound. Still, it survives as a reminder that this controversy will never end as long as people differ over priorities whenever inner promptings vie with external rubrics. The danger of stressing privatism too much is the loss of a living tradition that supports and nurtures faith. The danger of overemphasis on outer forms is a narrowness that distrusts new information and expressions. As with most controversies, perhaps wisdom points to some position between the two extremes.

Bibliography. Guelzo, Allen C., *For the Union of Evangelical Christendom: The Irony of the Reformed Episcopalians* (University Park: Pennsylvania State University Press, 1994); Holmes, David L., *A Brief History of the Episcopal Church* (Valley Forge, PA: Trinity Press International, 1993).

Henry Warner Bowden

Hodge, Archibald Alexander. Archibald Alexander Hodge (1823–1886) was an avid defender of the Princeton School of conservative Calvinism exemplified by his father, Charles Hodge,* and his namesake, Archibald Alexander, both of whom taught at Princeton Seminary. The younger Hodge completed his education at both Princeton College (1841) and Princeton Seminary (1846). For a brief period the Hodge family served as missionaries in India, but ill health forced Hodge to return. Between 1851 and 1862 Hodge, a Presbyterian, pastored in Virginia, Maryland, and Pennsylvania. In 1864 he began his career as a professor of theology at Western Theological Seminary in Allegheny, Pennsylvania. In 1878 he departed for his alma mater, Princeton Seminary, where he spent the balance of his life as a professor of didactic and exegetical theology.

Three of Hodge's books, *Outlines of Theology* (1878), *Life of Charles Hodge* (1880), and the posthumously published *Popular Lectures on Theological Themes* (1887), illustrate his theological positions. In these and other writings and lectures, Hodge made it clear that he was a defender of the conservative brand of Calvinistic Presbyterianism that adhered strictly to the Westminster Confession of Faith without modification, stressed the inerrancy and infallibility of Scriptures with no clearly proven contradictions, insisted that since both nature and the Bible are God's handiworks, correct interpretations of both demonstrated their compatibility, believed that biblical theism, not secularistic naturalism, should remain the foundation of higher education, opposed the separation of church and state* but favored an amended American Constitution that proclaimed the lordship of Jesus Christ, and argued for a rejuvenation of Calvinism that included both deep personal piety and strict adherence to orthodox doctrines. His stances contributed greatly to the emerging rift between the fundamentalists and the modernists or liberals at the turn of the twentieth century.
Bibliography. Ahlstrom, Sydney E., *A Religious History of the American People* (New Haven: Yale University Press, 1971); *Dictionary of Christianity in America* (Downers Grove: InterVarsity Press, 1970).

Sandy Dwayne Martin

Hodge, Charles. Charles Hodge (1797–1878) was a Presbyterian, a Princeton Seminary professor for over fifty years, a follower of Archibald Alexander, and a staunch defender of strict Calvinism against the emergence of more liberal ideas influenced by Darwinian science, revivalism,* biblical criticism, and other modern developments. Born in Philadelphia, Pennsylvania, Hodge completed studies at the College of New Jersey or Princeton College (1815) and Princeton Seminary (1819). He interrupted his Princeton teaching career, begun in 1820, to study in Berlin, Paris, and Halle (1826–1828). While in Europe he studied with F.A.G. Tholuck, J.A.W. Neander, and E. W. Hengstenberg. He also was exposed to the pietist tradition, European revivalism, and the theology of Friedrich Schleiermacher. In 1828 he returned to Princeton Seminary, continuing as professor of oriental and biblical literature. From 1840 until 1878 his title was professor of exegetical and didactic theology. Originally representing moderation in denominational matters, Hodge after the Old School/New School* division in 1837 became a fervent advocate for Old School Calvinism, to the extent that he unsuccessfully opposed the 1869 reunion of the Northern Presbyterians.

Through various avenues he defended Calvinist orthodoxy: as editor of the *Princeton Review* (originally *Biblical Repertory*) (1825–1871), author of a number of commentaries on books in the New Testament, and author of *The Way of Life* (1841), *What Is Darwinism?* (1873), and *Systematic Theology* (3 volumes) (1872–1873). Hodge advocated balancing personal piety and doctrinal orthodoxy, favored a biblical fundamentalism that accepted the view of a Sacred Text that was plenarily and verbally inspired, stressed the significance of God's grace against threats he saw emanating from Unitarian and Arminian theologies, and defended the substitutionary theory of atonement. He took delight in the observation that no novel theological idea had arisen at Princeton Seminary. His conservative influence during his lifetime was great and to a considerable extent long survived him.

Bibliography. Ahlstrom, Sydney E., *A Religious History of the American People* (New Haven: Yale University Press, 1972); Bowden, Henry H., *Dictionary of American Religious Biography* (Westport: Greenwood Publishing, 1976); *Dictionary of Christianity in America* (Downers Grove: InterVarsity Press, 1990); Brauer, Jerald C., *The Westminster Dictionary of Church History* (1971).

Sandy Dwayne Martin

Holiness Pentecostal Movement. Historically marked by diversity and conflict, the many groups sharing the Pentecostal* umbrella are linked by a shared belief in baptism by the Holy Spirit affirmed by speaking in tongues (glossolalia*) and by their appeal to the impoverished and socially disinherited. The movement's first organizational foundation had an unpromising beginning at Barney Creek Meeting House in eastern Tennessee in 1886 when Richard G. Spurling, Sr., a restorationist Baptist preacher disenchanted by changes in his society and denomination, led eight others in the creation of a new organization, Christian Union. Headquartered in Cleveland, Tennessee, this movement grew slowly under the direction of Richard G. Spurling, Jr., after his father's death, taking on a Wesleyan ''holiness'' character during a revival in 1896, and was renamed the Church of God in 1907. Still staggering under post–Civil War economic distress, southern Appalachia was ripe for sectarian reaction to a hostile environment. It came in the form of Pentecostalism, brought into the Church of God by A. J. Tomlinson from Indiana, who joined the body in 1903, received the Pentecostal experience in 1908, and became the first general moderator of the fledgling denomination in 1911. Vitalized by Pentecostal enthusiasm, it grew rapidly among socially disinherited Southerners even as they migrated to urban places.

This infusion of Pentecostalism into Holiness and restorationist Protestantism flows from the experiences and preaching of Charles Parham* of Kansas, beginning in 1901. His doctrine spread slowly until 1906, when his follower William Seymour took the message to a warehouse on Azusa Street* in Los

Angeles. Massive revival followed. Among those who became involved were Southern Holiness preachers like G. B. Cashwell, who returned to spread the fire of Pentecostal hope among people for whom life held little promise. Among his "converts" was A. J. Tomlinson.

Organizations proliferated as the movement swept the country. Charged with mismanagement of funds, Tomlinson left the Church of God in 1923, provoking a schism that led to the Church of God of Prophecy. At his death that organization split again, the newest offshoot being the Church of God World Headquarters. The less southern, less rural Assemblies of God was organized in 1914 and became the largest Pentecostal group. African Americans were major figures in the Azusa Street meetings. Predictably, black Pentecostal groups were born as separate entities. Charles Harrison Mason, a leader of the mostly black Church of God in Christ, headquartered in Memphis, Tennessee, visited Azusa Street and came away a Pentecostal. The introduction of Pentecostalism divided the Church of God in Christ, with the majority adopting Pentecostalism and retaining the group's name under Mason's leadership. Several smaller Pentecostal groups were formed over time on the basis of doctrinal or leadership issues.

Pentecostals of all stripes often were unpopular. Sectarianism is exclusive by nature, and exclusiveness provokes tensions. Pentecostal insistence upon "tongues" and other "gifts of the Spirit" as necessary for salvation relegated all others to the status of incomplete Christians or worse. Setting themselves apart by dress, hairstyle, and other signs of rejection of society generated negative reactions from ridicule to harassment. Highly emotional expressiveness and other manifestations of possession by the Holy Spirit struck outsiders as bizarre. During World War II the Church of God adopted a strong pacifist stance, leading to instances of arrest, harassment, and persecution. For the first half of the twentieth century the "Holy Rollers" were seen by outsiders as the fanatic fringe of religion and society.

In spite of internal division and external rejection, the Pentecostal movement has grown more rapidly than any other segment of Protestantism in the United States, and this trend continues. Spread to all parts of the world by ardent missionaries, it is also the fastest-growing religious group in Latin America. Its promise of dignity and status before God holds out hope for people whose lives are otherwise hopeless.

Bibliography. Blumhofer, Edith L., "Pentecostalism," In *Encyclopedia of Southern Culture*, ed. Charles Reagan Wilson and William Ferris (Chapel Hill: University of North Carolina Press, 1989), 1196–97; Crews, Mickey, *The Church of God: A Social History* (Knoxville: University of Tennessee Press, 1990); Faupel, David, *The American Pentecostal Movement* (Wilmore, KY: B. L. Fisher Library, Asbury Theological Seminary, 1972); Hughes, Richard T., "Restorationist Christianity," in *Encyclopedia of Southern Culture*, eds. Charles Reagan Wilson and William Ferris (Chapel Hill: University of North Carolina Press, 1989), 1303–6; Menzies, William, *Anointed to Serve* (Springfield, MO: Gospel Publishing House, 1971).

Roger G. Branch

Homosexuality. Is homosexuality a sin or a special grace? The question would not have been taken seriously before the latter half of the twentieth century. Triggered by the Stonewall Riots in New York City in June 1969, the gay rights* movement gave critical impetus to European and American biblical scholarship that has challenged the predominantly negative stance maintained by the Christian church since the first century of the common era. Reexamination of Scripture and tradition has ushered in a sea change in religious thinking about human sexuality held sacrosanct for nearly two thousand years.

Homosexual acts, particularly of males, were considered evil in biblical times essentially because they wasted human seed, disgraced a fellow human being, or represented idolatrous pagan practices. Apparent scriptural condemnation of homosexuality is traced back to the story of Sodom in Genesis 19:4–11 and to the Holiness Code in Leviticus 18:22; New Testament censure is found primarily in the letters of Paul (1 Corinthians 6:9–10; 1 Timothy 1:9–10; Romans 1:26–27). Developments in Roman law from 342 (Constantius and Constans) to 544 C.E. (Justinian) and in the teaching of church fathers like John Chrysostom and Augustine, as well as numerous pronouncements of church councils and synods from Elvira in 305–306 to Naplouse in 1120 (at which the impenitent were burned), created a tradition of condemnation that, with the writings of Aquinas in the thirteenth century, was essentially complete (McNeill, 80). Two books by historian John Boswell question that tradition, documenting far more tolerance for homosexuality during the Middle Ages, including even same-sex liturgical rites, than has previously been perceived. Nonetheless, it is to these antihomosexual interpretations of both Scripture and tradition that contemporary doubters of homosexual integrity still appeal.

Twentieth-century discoveries about human sexuality have led to new interpretations of both Scripture and tradition. On lexical evidence, such as the likely meaning of the Hebrew word *yadha* in the critical passage in Genesis (''Bring them out to us, so that we may *know* them''), as well as the testimony of Jesus himself alluding to the Genesis passage (''on that day it will be more tolerable for Sodom than for that town'' that denies hospitality to you, he tells his disciples in Luke 10:10–13), numerous scholars have made the case that the sin of Sodom was not homosexuality, but inhospitality. Examining Paul's use of the phrase *para phusin*, usually translated as ''against nature,'' they conclude that what Paul saw and warned Christians against in the pagan cultures around him was not inversion, that is, what contemporary understanding takes to be the natural condition of the homosexual person, but perversion, homogenital acts committed by people he understood to be heterosexual. Those whom Paul was condemning, according to these scholars, were debauched individuals or male prostitutes involved in pagan temple practices. Nowhere in Scripture do these scholars discern any prohibition against same-sex love.

Few denominations have been left untouched by the late-twentieth-century debate, which some would call a religious war, over homosexuality. The conservative Christian Coalition* condemns it as a virulent threat to morality and family, supporting "ex-gay" ministries to save repentant homosexuals from their sin; moderates in mainstream churches, seeking "more light" in dialogue with their gay and lesbian neighbors, instead condemn homophobia as the sin to be repented, a violation of the commandment against bearing false witness (Exodus 20:16), and have moved on to debate issues like ordination and blessing the unions of gay and lesbian people. Liberal theologians, affirming the integrity of same-sex love, understand homosexual orientation to be a gift, a special ethical burden: a "divine dispensation," a "task to be wrestled with, indeed . . . a talent to be invested (Luke 19:13ff.)" (Helmut Thielicke, in Scanzoni and Mollenkott, 145).

Bibliography. Boswell, John, *Christianity, Social Tolerance, and Homosexuality* (Chicago: University of Chicago Press, 1980); Boswell, John, *Same-Sex Unions in Premodern Europe* (New York: Villard Books, 1994); McNeill, John J., *The Church and the Homosexual* (Kansas City: Sheed Andrews and McMeel, 1976); Scanzoni, Letha, and Virginia Mollenkott, *Is the Homosexual My Neighbor?* (San Francisco: Harper San Francisco, 1994); Spong, John Shelby, *Living in Sin?* (San Francisco: Harper and Row, 1988).

Fred Richter

Hopkins, Samuel. Samuel Hopkins (1721–1803) was student, friend, biographer, and editor of Jonathan Edwards.* In his work to propagate Edwards's legacy, he was one of the founders of the New Divinity movement. Focusing particularly on the problem of the will, Hopkins sought to give revivalism* a theological underpinning in his works.

During his career Hopkins served two pastorates. The first was in Housatonic (later Great Barrington), Massachusetts, located in an area destined to become a center of New Divinity. The second was in the seaport of Newport, Rhode Island, where Hopkins's efforts as a moral reformer became as controversial as his work as a theologian.

As a theologian, Hopkins attacked the idea of "preparation" for grace. The idea that one could, through availing oneself of the means of grace, prepare oneself for the reception of God's grace had become widely accepted as one interpretation of the Puritan covenant theology. In 1765 Hopkins published *Enquiry concerning the Promises of the Gospel*. In it he claimed that all actions performed in the unregenerate state were wicked and unacceptable to God. Moreover, the unregenerate who used the means of grace and yet remained in their unregenerate state were worse in the eyes of God than other unawakened sinners who did not attend to the means of grace. This assertion caused Jedidiah Mills in 1767 to refer to Hopkins's ideas as "new" divinity, something strange and unheard of. Yet the notion of an immediate regeneration, worked inside by the Holy Spirit, was central to revivalism, and it was as a support to the revivalistic interests of the New Divinity that Hopkins's camp understood the need for immediate—rather than mediated—regeneration.

Hopkins's most important contribution to the theology of the eighteenth century may have been his notion of disinterested benevolence. Though the notion was present in Edwards, Hopkins took the idea in a new direction, one that emphasized the ability of the will, after regeneration, to engage in disinterested acts of love. Indeed, for Hopkins, this was conversion: the exercise of the will, after regeneration, in acts of benevolence toward God and God's intelligent creatures. Such a view affected Hopkins's view of both God and human beings. In regard to God, the notion of disinterested benevolence was elevated to a principle within the Godhead, such that God became primarily a moral governor who was bound to act in the best interests of being in general. In this view, Hopkins thought that God used even sin itself as a means to the greater good.

In relation to humanity, the notion of disinterested benevolence found expression in Hopkins's formula that one must be willing to be damned if it meant the greater glory of God. Indeed, a faith based on selfish motives of personal salvation could never meet the moral demands of disinterested benevolence. Though this was perhaps the most controversial of all Hopkins's ideas, Hopkins himself saw a person's willingness to be so damned as proof of regeneration and conversion and thus as an assurance that one would not be damned.

In the social realm, Hopkins sought to embody the notion of disinterested benevolence. Though his protests against the slave trade were the most controversial way his theology underpinned social reform, that theology also served as the foundation for how he lived his personal life—the poverty in which he often found himself, for example, was for him a living out of his theology.

Bibliography. Breitenbach, William, "Unregenerate Doings: Selflessness and Selfishness in New Divinity Theology," *American Quarterly* 34 (Winter 1982): 479–502; Conforti, Joseph A., *Samuel Hopkins and the New Divinity Movement* (Grand Rapids, MI: Christian University Press, 1981); Conforti, Joseph A., "Samuel Hopkins and the New Divinity: Theology, Ethics, and Social Reform in Eighteenth-Century New England," *William and Mary Quarterly* 34 (1977): 572–89; Hopkins, Samuel, *System of Doctrines Contained in Divine Revelation, Explained and Defended*, 2 vols. (Boston: Isaiah Thomas and Ebenezer E. Andrews, 1793).

Thomas J. Davis

Hopkinsianism. Hopkinsianism, sometimes known as "consistent Calvinism," was one of the cornerstones of the New Divinity and derived from the work of Samuel Hopkins. In this school of thought, Hopkins and his followers sought to compile a complete and consistent system of Calvinism, systematic in the sense that all its tenets were made consistent with the overarching principle of God's absolute sovereignty. This theology engaged the Calvinism of Hopkins's teacher, Jonathan Edwards,* and developed it in new ways as it sought particularly to square both revivalism* and human moral accountability with the principle of God's sovereignty. Hopkins's most original and provocative contributions to New Divinity theology were (1) the notion that God permitted and used sin to achieve the greatest good; (2) the notion that all acts of the unregenerate, including using the means of grace to try to prepare for the reception of grace, were unacceptable in the sight of God; and (3) the idea of disinterested benevolence.

In 1759 Hopkins published *Sin, through Divine Intervention, an Advantage to the Universe*. The concern for a consistent Calvinism is apparent—if sin exists, and if God is sovereign, then God must will its existence; sin cannot be accidental in a realm characterized by sovereignty. In this work Hopkins argued that God used sin to achieve good. God, in fact, "willingly suffered" sin so that the greater good of the universe could be served.

In 1765 Hopkins published *Enquiry concerning the Promises of the Gospel*. This work brought forth charges that it contained a "new divinity" in the way it understood human activity. Here Hopkins rejected the interpretation of the Puritan covenant theology that claimed that the means of grace could fruitfully be used by the unregenerate in preparation for the reception of grace. People who used these means and remained unregenerate were, in Hopkins's opinion, more guilty in the eyes of God than the unregenerate who did not use them. Hopkins's view that regeneration came not through preparationism but through the immediate action of the Holy Spirit upon the heart undergirded his revivalistic outlook.

In 1773 Hopkins published *An Inquiry into the Nature of True Holiness*. Here Hopkins set forth his notion of disinterested benevolence. In it he attacked all notions of conversion that seemed self-serving and in the interest of self-love. No conversion was true, he thought, if it centered on selfish motives of reward and punishment for the individual. Instead, he thought that at the point of regeneration the Holy Spirit inclined the heart to holiness, which for Hopkins was an inclination toward acts of disinterested benevolence, always thinking first and foremost of the greater good. A sign, he thought, of conversion—which for Hopkins involved the will actively choosing works of disinterested benevolence after the Holy Spirit's act of regeneration—was a willingness to be damned for the greater glory of God. Such a willingness, however, exhibited the mark of true regeneration and conversion and as such served as an assurance that one would not be damned. Again, this theology served to square the notion of sovereignty (regeneration as completely the work of God) with the idea of moral accountability—conversion as the moral activity of the regenerate, its absence as a rejection of true holiness by the unregenerate. As such, it had two effects: disinterested benevolence became a category applied to God, such that God's rule was characterized by disinterested benevolence, making of God very much a moral governor bound by God's nature to seek the greatest good for being in general. The eternal decrees of God were thus founded in love. Moreover, the theological concept of disinterested benevolence served as a cornerstone to evangelical social action.

The textbook for Hopkinsianism was Hopkins's *System of Doctrines Contained in Divine Revelation*, published in 1793. In what has been called the first truly American system of Calvinist thought, the *System* provided a textbook for the growing number of Hopkinsian ministers.

In addition to a textbook, the movement also eventually created schools for the propagation of consistent Calvinism. Andover Seminary was founded in

1808 in part as a bastion of Hopkinsian thought. Moreover, after the founding of Yale Divinity School and the development of the New Haven Theology by Nathaniel W. Taylor (Yale College had early been a source of New Divinity ministers), Hartford Seminary was established as a Hopkinsian alternative.

In terms of ecclesiology, Hopkinsianism also had controversial effects. Because of its theology and its revivalistic orientation, the movement discarded the Half-way Covenant* that had become popular in New England, an ecclesiology based on the notion of making the means of grace available to the unregenerate in hopes that their ministrations would prepare one to eventually receive grace.

Bibliography. Breitenbach, William, "Unregenerate Doings: Selflessness and Selfishness in New Divinity Theology," *American Quarterly* 34 (Winter 1982): 479–502; Conforti, Joseph A., *Samuel Hopkins and the New Divinity Movement* (Grand Rapids, MI: Christian University Press, 1981); Conforti, Joseph A., "Samuel Hopkins and the New Divinity: Theology, Ethics, and Social Reform in Eighteenth-Century New England," *William and Mary Quarterly* 34 (1977): 572–89; Hopkins, Samuel, *System of Doctrines Contained in Divine Revelation, Explained and Defended*, 2 vols. (Boston: Isaiah Thomas and Ebenezer T. Andews, 1793).

Thomas J. Davis

Hutchinson, Anne. Anne Marbury Hutchinson was born in late 1590 or early 1591 (she was christened in June 1591), the daughter of Francis Marbury, curate and schoolmaster of Alford, in Lincolnshire, a self-styled church reformer who in 1578 was imprisoned for his "Puritan" position on the role of the clergy and who, at the time of Anne's birth, had lost his preaching credentials for criticizing church authorities. In 1612 Anne married William Hutchinson, a wealthy sheep farmer and textile merchant from Alford. At the same time the revered Puritan preacher John Cotton was just beginning his career at St. Botolph's in the port city of Boston, Lincolnshire, some twenty-four miles to the north. The Hutchinsons, though only occasional visitors, soon came under the spell of Cotton's teachings, which they saw as elevating the role of grace in the believer's life as opposed to the mere fulfilling of the law (legalism). As conditions deteriorated for the Puritans in England under Archbishop Laud, Cotton and other notable divines were forced to flee to New England in 1633. Anne and her family followed in September 1634.

Anne was not long in New England before she revealed herself to be her father's daughter. Just as Francis Marbury had faced ecclesiastical censure in England, so Anne would soon find herself at odds with both church and state authorities in New England. During her years in Alford Anne not only embraced the Covenant of Grace as taught by Cotton, but also took its implications much further than Cotton ever intended. Convinced that a sanctified life of good works (strict personal holiness and conformity to the law of God) was not the surest evidence of inward grace (as most Puritan divines contended), Anne believed that the "Witnesse of the Spirit itselfe" was the primary evidence for true grace and assurance of election. To Hutchinson, such "grace" included the actual indwelling of the Holy Spirit within each believer, forming a union that was not dependent upon any external evidence. Such a union offered the believer the ability to receive revelations directly from God himself. One such revelation had commanded her to follow Cotton to New England; once there, she began holding meetings twice weekly in her home as a means of reviewing Cotton's Sunday sermons as well as providing her own instruction in the finer points of the Covenant of Grace. As many as sixty to one hundred people, including several prominent laymen, regularly attended Anne's meetings.

The civil and ecclesiastical authorities quickly became suspicious and critical. They not only saw her as overstepping the bounds of her "sex" by teaching in matters of theology, but they also saw her teachings as approaching perilously close to familism and antinomianism. Her power was evident in the Boston community by 1636, both in the election that year and the subscription for the Pequot War (the Hutchinsonians generally opposed it). When two of her followers, Henry Vane and John Wheelwright, attained prominent positions that year, the former as governor, the latter as Cotton's assistant pastor in the Boston church, many leaders, especially John Winthrop, Rev. John Wilson of the Boston church, and Thomas Dudley, perceived both their positions of authority and the theological integrity of the Commonwealth to be in jeopardy. Based upon her criticism of the clergy of New England (except for Cotton) as not being "able ministers" of the gospel because they did not fully preach a Covenant of Grace (she considered them "legalists" in their adherence to the importance of "works" as evidence of salvation), coupled with a sermon by her brother-in-law Wheelwright that espoused much the same sentiments, the ministers of New England in March 1637 took matters into their own hands, declaring Wheelwright's sermon "seditious" and quickly ousting the antinomian Vane as governor in the May election.

At a called synod in September 1637, the rulers of both church and state declared an end to all antinomian teachings in the colony and the removal of any who remained loyal to its tenets. In November 1637 the General Court held a two-day trial to deal with the crisis at hand. Anne Hutchinson was charged with disturbing the public peace, casting disrepute upon the clergy, and promoting false doctrines in her meetings. She defended herself well, but the verdict was known from the start of the trial. She was found guilty and banished from the colony, but not until the next spring. During the winter she was held under house arrest (she was also pregnant for the sixteenth time), and some sought her reclamation, but others held that she was fomenting worse opinions than before, even the materialist heresy (in which the soul dies with the body). In March she was tried once again, this time before the church authorities only; she was found guilty of heresy and excommunicated. By the end of March 1638 Anne had joined her husband and family in Rhode Island, where she survived a dangerous miscarriage at the age of forty-seven. In 1642, after the death of her husband, she moved her family to the Pelham Bay region of New Amsterdam, where in August 1643 she and her children were killed in an Indian raid, save for the youngest daughter, who was carried away into captivity. Though Hutchinson was banished and excommunicated from Massachusetts for her beliefs, her statue now graces the grounds of the Massachusetts State Capitol, a monument to her stand for the primacy of individual conscience and freedom of religion for all people, including women.

Bibliography. Barker-Benfield, Ben, "Anne Hutchinson and the Puritan Attitude toward Woman," *Feminist Studies* 1 (1973): 65–96; Battis, Emory, *Saints and Sectaries: Anne Hutchinson and the Antinomian Controversy in the Massachusetts Bay Colony* (Chapel Hill: University of North Carolina Press, 1962); Gura, Philip F., *A Glimpse of Sion's Glory: Puritan Radicalism in New England, 1620–1660* (Middletown, CT: Wesleyan University Press, 1984); Hall, David D., *The Antinomian Controversy, 1636–1638: A Documentary History,* 2nd ed. (Durham, NC: Duke University Press, 1990); Maclear, James F., "Anne Hutchinson and the Mortalist Heresy," *New England Quarterly* 54 (1981): 74–103; Stoever, William K. B., *"A Faire and Easie Way to Heaven": Covenant Theology and Antinomianism in Early Massachusetts* (Middletown, CT: Wesleyan University Press, 1978); Williams, Selma R., *Divine Rebel: The Life of Anne Marbury Hutchinson* (New York: Holt, Rinehart and Winston 1981).

Timothy D. Whelan

Hyper-Calvinism. An extreme wing of historic Calvinism, hyper-Calvinism has surfaced primarily within the Calvinistic Baptist (most noticeably the Particular Baptists and the Primitive Baptists*) and Presbyterian churches in England and America. One of the earliest and most eloquent influences upon hyper-Calvinism was John Gill (1697–1771), whose works *The Cause of God and Truth* (1735–1738), *The Doctrine of Predestination Staged* (1752), and *Body of Divinity* (1769) "drove out Arminianism from the explanation of every verse in the Bible" (Harrell, 651). A supralapsarian double predestinationist, Gill contended that God has "in his eternal purpose, fixed upon the particular persons whom he will call, and the time when he will call them . . . and the place when they shall be called" (Lambert, 56). The unregenerate sinner can effect no spiritual work; he receives divine knowledge from God alone, apart from any human means (a position moderate Calvinists felt opened the door to "antinomianism" and "enthusiasm"). The antimissionist hyper-Calvinists of the first half of the nineteenth century, in their sermons and such periodicals as the *Signs of the Times* (1832–1835), and in the very structure and activities of their "meeting-places," relentlessly pursued the five points of Calvinism within a logical framework that some critics thought came perilously close to fatalism. Convinced that the world was turned against God and headed for an eventual Armageddon, they argued that there was little for the saints to do but proclaim the fate of the lost and the privilege of the elect. Since "eternal unconditional election" had taken place "before the foundations of the world," no human effort could alter it. Those who would be saved would be saved, and those who would not, would not. Hence "perseverance of the saints" was ensured by God's decree, not human effort, just as were the consequences of "total depravity'' upon the nonelect, for one fact could never be ignored: ''the absolute predestination of all things.''

Placing total reliance on grace and the work of the Holy Spirit in salvation and the imparting of divine truth to the believer, hyper-Calvinists found themselves at odds with the revivalist mentality of the Protestant churches (both Calvinist and Arminian) in the early decades of the nineteenth century, which placed a corresponding emphasis on the means of grace as well as the individual's role in the act of repentance and faith. The ''protracted meetings'' of the revivalists, they claimed, only stirred up man's baser ''feelings,'' not his spirit. The ''sawdust trails'' of the camp meetings, with their Finney-like invitational pleas and mourner's benches, were unscriptural instruments of human origin replacing the work of the Holy Spirit. Hyper-Calvinists were opposed to several other unscriptural and inexpedient ''modern inventions'' of the church, as they called them, that detracted from the work of the Spirit in favor of human effort. These included tract societies, Sunday school societies, Bible societies, and all missionary societies, as well as Bible colleges and theological seminaries. Such ''inventions'' presumed a deficiency in the wisdom of God, an inability on his part to perform his will and work upon the earth. They disseminated religious sentiments but not necessarily true conversion. Hyper-Calvinists were convinced that the work of the Spirit was to be conducted through the agency of the local church alone, not collective societies, for no such societies existed in the New Testament church. Since divine truth could be known only to the mind illumined by God himself, and since only God could call and prepare men to preach, theological schools were unnecessary and presumptuous. As the writers of the ''Address to the Particular Baptist Churches of the 'Old School' in the United States'' noted in 1832, the difference between these ''hard-shell'' hyper-Calvinists and their evangelical brethren (whether Arminian or Calvinist) was this: ''They declare the gospel to be a system of means; these means it appears they believe to be of human contrivance; and they act accordingly. But we believe the gospel dispensation to embrace a system of faith and *obedience*, and we would act according to our belief'' (Lambert, 371).

Hyper-Calvinism stands in extreme opposition to Pelagianism, which emphasizes man's innate divinity and consequently denigrates the need for supernatural ''saving grace'' from without, as well as Arminianism, which views man as fallen but with the God-given ability (free will) to choose spiritual life in a world in which divine purposes are fulfilled without predestination.* Hyper-Calvinism should also be distinguished from what many would consider ''true,'' ''historic,'' or ''evangelistic'' Calvinism, in which the spiritual passivity of man as a result of his ''total depravity'' is inextricably combined with the physical activity of man required by the ''means of grace'' in a world in which predestination and human response mysteriously cohabit. To the hyper-Calvinist, man's total depravity and God's foreordination make any human effort or means of grace in salvation unnecessary, even an affront to God, whether before, during, or after regeneration. Not even the preaching of the gospel is necessary for evangelism, for the salvation of the elect is made certain by God's predestining power. Hence mission societies become an intrusion into God's sovereignty (the Primitive Baptists also opposed them as being extrabiblical and ultraecclesiastical) and an unnecessary activity, for the "gospel seed" is not to be scattered indiscriminately but planted within the elect only. To many hyper-Calvinists, a portion of God's elect will be saved without ever knowingly exercising faith in Christ or even hearing the gospel; they will be regenerated without ever experiencing conversion. Evangelistic Calvinists, however, though staunch predestinationists, reject vehemently the antimission, antimeans position of the hyper-Calvinists, which virtually eliminates human responsibility. They do not believe that predestination precludes the obligation of the elect to preach the gospel to the world (the "external" call) or the necessity of the elect to respond to the gospel in true faith and repentance (the "internal" call). To evangelical Calvinists, both the elect and the means of election have been predestined, making evangelism the necessary fulfillment of God's sovereign plan. To hyper-Calvinists, any use of an indiscriminate "external" call to repentance and faith is essentially Arminian in nature, flies in the face of predestination, and belittles God's sovereignty. Salvation is only for the elect through the divine means of an "internal" call. The evangelical Calvinist believes that few are chosen, though many are called; the hyper-Calvinist insists that few are chosen because few are called.

The debate between Arminians, evangelical Calvinists, and hyper-Calvinists has persisted in England and America for over 150 years and is very much alive today, as witnessed by such recent works as Iain Murray's *Spurgeon v. Hyper-Calvinism: The Battle for Gospel Preaching* (1995); the *Founder's Journal,* a periodical begun in the 1990s by the evangelical Calvinists within the Southern Baptist Convention*; the publications of David Engelsma and others within the Protestant Reformed Churches (PRC); and the continuing presence of the Primitive Baptists in America.

Bibliography. Engelsma, David J., *Hyper-Calvinism and the Call of the Gospel* (Grand Rapids, MI: Reformed Free Publishing Association, 1980); Harrell, Elder Cushing B., *History of the Church of God* (Middletown, NY: Gilbert Beebe and Sons, 1886); Lambert, Byron Cecil, *The Rise of the Anti-Mission Baptists: Sources and Leaders, 1800–1840* (New York: Arno Press, 1980); Murray, Iain H., *Spurgeon v. Hyper-Calvinism: The Battle for Gospel Preaching* (Edinburgh: Banner of Truth Trust, 1995); Packer, J. I., *Evangelism and the Sovereignty of God* (Downers Grove, IL: InterVarsity Press, 1961).

Timothy D. Whelan

I

Independent Baptists. Although Baptists* have always exhibited a brand of independence not usually found in other denominations, they have at the same time created some of the strongest associations of any denomination. In the nineteenth century Baptists formed the Southern Baptist Convention,* the American Baptist Convention, the Northern Baptist Convention, and several other lesser groups as well. During the fundamentalist-modernist controversy of 1900–1930, however, these conventions experienced considerable strain from within as forces greatly opposed to one another struggled for control of their denomination's resources, schools, and, more importantly, doctrinal position. When many of these early "fundamentalists" became convinced that they could not return their conventions to what they considered a historic fundamental Baptist position, they were faced with a very important decision: should they remain within the denomination and "compromise" their beliefs, or should they withdraw completely in order to maintain doctrinal and ecclesiastical "purity"? Some conservative laymen, teachers, and pastors did remain within the conventions and continued to raise a voice of opposition to modernism* and liberalism* throughout their careers, but many did not. To the fundamentalist the watchword became "Come out from among them and be ye separate, saith the Lord, and touch not the unclean thing" (2 Corinthians 6:17). The "unclean thing" became the denominational conventions, and the admonition seemed perfectly clear to the fundamentalists. By embracing liberalism the conventions had, according to the fundamentalists, sullied their spiritual birthright and contaminated the congregations with the pollution of false doctrine and lax discipline. Since their

efforts to "restore" the conventions had failed, they could not in good conscience remain in the midst of such "pollution."

The formation of the Fundamental Baptist Fellowship in 1920 (still in existence today) encouraged other advocates of the "independent" movement between 1925 and 1950 to make their break with the various Baptist conventions,
often forming new and relatively loose "associations" of independent Baptist
churches bound together by a markedly fundamentalist doctrinal statement.
Among these leaders were fellow Texans and former Southern Baptists J. Frank
Norris* (1877–1952), who was instrumental in forming the Bible Baptist Union
in 1923 and later the World Baptist Fellowship (WBF), and John R. Rice*
(1895–1980), who began his periodical the *Sword of the Lord* in 1934 primarily
for the purpose of denouncing denominational liberalism and promoting the
independent Baptist movement. Other leaders included Robert T. Ketcham
(1889–1978) of Gary, Indiana, who in 1933 founded the General Association
of Regular Baptist Churches* (GARBC), the purpose of which, according to
Ketcham, was "to provide a haven of Fundamental Fellowship" for those "independent" churches that had pulled out of the Northern Baptist Convention
(Falwell, Dobson, and Hindson, 113); B. Myron Cedarholm, whose Conservative Baptist Association of America* (CBAA) was formed in 1947 as a reaction
to the theological inclusivism and growing ecumenism within the American
Baptist Convention; George Beauchamp Vick* (1901–1975), whose Baptist Bible Fellowship* (eventually the largest body of independent Baptist churches in
the world), though it split from Norris's World Baptist Fellowship in 1950,
nevertheless maintained Norris's antagonism to the growing presence of modernism within the mainline Baptist conventions; and Lee Roberson of Chattanooga, Tennessee, whose leadership was instrumental in the formation of the
Southwide Baptist Fellowship in 1956. Other independent Baptist groups formed
during this time include the American Baptist Association* (ABA) and the Baptist Missionary Association* (BMA) (both influenced by Landmarkism*), Free
Will Baptists,* and the New Testament Association of Independent Baptist
Churches (NTAIBC).

W. E. Dowell's description of Norris's WBF would hold for all these associations: "It was a loosely-knit group of independent Baptists who voluntarily
fellowshipped together in the furtherance of the gospel. No ecclesiastical system
governed this group; it was strictly a matter of fellowship and *voluntary* cooperation. Each local church was a sovereign, autonomous body subject only to
Christ" (10–11). Their avowed "autonomy" immediately forced them to found
schools that would also be "independent" of denominational control and true
to fundamental Baptist doctrine, and they did. Taking their cue from Bob Jones
University (founded in 1926 and fiercely independent, though not exclusively
Baptist), independent Baptist Bible schools and liberal arts colleges sprang up
across America, including Norris's Bible Baptist Seminary in Fort Worth, Texas
(1939), Tennessee Temple College and Seminary in Chattanooga, Tennessee

(1946), Baptist Bible College in Springfield, Missouri (1950), Pillsbury Baptist Bible College in Owatonna, Minnesota (1957), Maranatha Baptist Bible College in Watertown, Wisconsin (1968), Hyles-Anderson College in Hammond, Indiana (1971), Lynchburg Baptist College (now Liberty University) in Lynchburg, Virginia (1971), and Pensacola Christian College in Pensacola, Florida (1974), to name a few. At the same time independent Baptists were building a network of colleges and seminaries, they were building some of the largest churches in America as well. With Norris's First Baptist of Fort Worth, Texas, establishing the pattern, other "superchurches" soon followed, including G. B. Vick's Temple Baptist in Detroit, Dallas Billington's Akron Baptist Temple in Akron, Ohio, Lee Roberson's Highland Park Baptist in Chattanooga, Tennessee, John Rawling's Landmark Baptist in Cincinnati, Ohio, Jack Hyles's First Baptist of Hammond, Indiana, and Jerry Falwell's* Thomas Road Baptist Church in Lynchburg, Virginia. All of these churches grew to an average attendance between 5,000 and 10,000 per Sunday during the period 1935–1980. They also bore all the marks of the Independent Baptist Church movement: its aggressive "soul-winning" home-visitation programs, its militant opposition to denominational liberalism, its unswerving loyalty to dispensational premillennialism, and its conviction that the local church must not only be autonomous from denominational control but must also be ultimately obedient to the leadership of the pastor, not church committees and deacon boards. As influential as J. Frank Norris has been to twentieth-century fundamentalism* and the independent Baptist movement, his greatest legacy may well have been his autocratic style as pastor, a belief that the pastor leads by determining himself what the church will do and tolerating little or no opposition to his wishes.

While the Independents deserted the mainline denominations during the 1930s and 1940s over doctrinal differences and ecclesiastical alignments (most notably the liberal ecumenism of the World Council of Churches* [WCC], formed in 1948), many remained within the denominations that were in every sense "fundamental," but by the 1940s they were not identifying themselves any longer as "fundamentalists." Instead, they were now using the broader term "evangelical," and in 1942 they formed the National Association of Evangelicals (NAE) under the leadership of Harold John Ockenga, later President of Fuller Theological Seminary. Eventually this group would find fertile ground both within the denominations and outside them among many nondenominational churches and associations. By the 1950s this "new evangelicalism," as the movement came to be known, stood between the separatist fundamentalism of the Independent Baptists and the ecumenical liberalism of the WCC, a compromise position acceptable to many intellectuals sympathetic to a conservative interpretation of Scripture and the church. Though the new evangelicalism was for the most part tolerated in the 1940s and early 1950s by the fundamentalist Baptists, by the mid-1950s, when evangelicals began promoting a more distinct attitude of cultural relativism, denominational "infiltration" (to use Ockenga's term), and "cooperative" or "ecumenical evangelism" (espoused by Robert O. Ferm and adopted by Billy Graham* and the Southern Baptist Convention, among others), Independent Baptists became militantly opposed to the new evangelical attitude, finding it as unacceptable as modernism had been in the 1920s and choosing instead to remain true to the "separatism" of post-1925 fundamentalism.

In the 1960s and 1970s the Independent Baptists continued their war on the conventions and new evangelicalism, but now new enemies—primarily the charismatic movement and 1960s pop culture—emerged, calling out for compromise, cooperation, and change, three anathemas to the Independent Baptist. As Independent Baptists continued within their associations to fight these external evils, they soon found their own churches, fellowships, and schools infiltrated by these forces of change. Taking the doctrine of separation (withdrawing fellowship from religious groups that countenance apostasy and liberalism) to a further extreme, they instituted the practice of "secondary separation"* as a means of keeping themselves pure and independent, not from denominations now but from "compromisers" within their own ranks. If the history of Independent Baptists was marked by any one thing between 1965 and 1980, it was their ability to maintain distinctions and create dissension within their own ranks based upon one's degree of cultural and ecclesiastical purity. The legacy of the infighting among Independent Baptists throughout the 1970s and 1980s has led to an overall decline within the movement itself, as is evidenced by shrinking memberships in many churches and fellowships, as well as dwindling enrollments in many of the Independent Baptist colleges. Some, taking their cue from Jerry Falwell,* Jack Van Impe, and others, have lessened their emphasis on cultural and ecclesiastical separation, moving ironically more toward the direction of "infiltration" and cooperation within American mainstream culture and ecclesiastical institutions more typical of new evangelicalism than fundamentalism. Though Falwell is still fiercely independent in his desire to control his own enterprises, he has since 1980 aggressively enlarged his constituency for his university and television ministry by embracing Southern Baptists (who now comprise over 30 percent of the student body at Liberty University) and charismatics (as was evidenced by his willingness to take over PTL, a ministry the vast majority of Independent Baptists held in contempt). Even the idea of being an "Independent Baptist" has come full circle by 1996, as some even within the Southern Baptist Convention have expressed a desire to pull out and become "independent," not because of a dislike for denominationalism or modernism (as Norris and others contended in the 1920s), but rather because of a dislike now of "fundamentalist" control within the denomination.

Bibliography. Dollar, George W., *The Fight for Fundamentalism* (Sarasota, FL: Daniels Publishing, 1983); Dollar, George, *A History of Fundamentalism in America* (Greenville, SC: Bob Jones University Press, 1973); Dowell, W. E., *The Birthpangs of the Baptist Bible Fellowship* (Springfield, MO: Temple Press, 1977); Falwell, Jerry, with Ed Dobson and Ed Hindson, *The Fundamentalist Phenomenon* (Garden City, NY: 1981); Gaspar, Louis, *The Fundamentalist Movement* (The Hague: Mouton, 1963).

Timothy D. Whelan

Indian Missions. Evangelical outreach to Native Americans has been the occasion of frequent and long-lived controversies launched by many who have criticized the way missionary work was conducted and by a few who questioned whether missions should have been pursued in the first place. Since the first days of discovering the New World, most Europeans have rejected native cultures and religions as inferior to their own. Some tried to eradicate Indian lifestyles while others tried to improve them, but all condemned what they saw as different from themselves. Early Spaniards thought that Indians were beasts of burden who had no souls, precluding any notion of whether they were worth saving or not. Largely under the persistent arguments of Bartolomé de Las Casas, Indians were recognized as human, and the Spanish crown supported a great deal of missionary work in its territories. In later colonizing efforts many English also rejected missions, wondering aloud why anyone would concern himself with people who were as savage as the wild animals they hunted. By the nineteenth century this inertia acquired an additional rationalization. As America expanded across the continent, many regarded Indians as obstacles to progress, and they argued that missions simply impeded the march of civilization. One way or the other, those who scorned natives found ways to explain their opposition to evangelizing among them.

Another point of controversy between and among missionaries touched on attitudes regarding the sacraments. Protestants charged that Catholics were too superficial in their conversion practices, relying on the ritual of baptism* as a sufficient guarantor of eternal life. It was more important, they maintained, to confer baptism only after lengthy instruction and a verification of the candidate's determination to live by new standards of belief and behavior. Catholics did not deserve the reputation of being more concerned about quantity than quality because they were careful to nurture converts in thoroughgoing changes in lifestyle, but priests baptized enough natives who were just at the point of dying from diseases or wounds to keep the Protestant charge circulating for generations.

In the twentieth century there has been much more controversy related to Indian missions, this time concentrating on the aftermath of such efforts. Looking at the sorry remnants of once-vigorous native civilizations, many modern observers have charged Indian missions with a wide range of shortcomings. When these cultures were still strong, hardly anyone thought native patterns worth preserving. But now that these cultures are threadbare vestiges, today's critics lament the loss of native languages, art, and lifestyles and the squelching of precontact ideas, values, and rituals. Some point to missionaries as carriers of disease and go so far as to accuse them of genocide when virulent maladies swept through native villages. Others bemoan the fact that missionaries often acted as mediators between Indians and U.S. government agents, persuading natives to cede their land and relinquish their cultural autonomy. Still others regret the theological imperialism of Christian missions that destroyed so many native religious orientations, either quickly through forced repression or slowly through gentle persuasion. All these criticisms are accurate to some degree, and missionaries to Indians in modern times are trying to avoid the excesses of previous generations. But as long as different cultural priorities exist and as long as Christianity flourishes within cultural contexts, controversies will swirl around the how and the whether of evangelical activity.

Bibliography. Berkhofer, Robert F., *Salvation and the Savage* (Lexington: University of Kentucky Press, 1965); Bowden, Henry W., *American Indians and Christian Missions* (Chicago: University of Chicago Press, 1981).

Henry Warner Bowden

Inerrancy Controversy. Inerrancy controversies concern the belief that the Christian Scriptures are without error in all matters they address. This belief includes not only issues of doctrine, morality, and spirituality, but also matters of science, history, and all other areas of life and faith. Controversy over the nature and authority of the Scriptures is not unique to American Christianity. Differences over the use and interpretation of Holy Scripture have occurred throughout Christian history. However, the Enlightenment and the rise of new science raised significant questions about the inherent authority and inspiration of the biblical text.

In the minds of many church leaders, Charles Darwin's *On the Origin of Species*, published in 1859, challenged the veracity of creation stories in the book of Genesis as well as the benevolence of the divine creator. Many religious critics of Darwin believed that his work and that of other scientists undermined the authority of the entire biblical revelation. Likewise, the use of certain historical-critical methods for studying the text and context of the biblical materials led conservative Christians to support theories regarding the inerrancy and infallibility of the testaments. By the late nineteenth and early twentieth centuries conservative scholars in such schools as Princeton Seminary were supporting the idea that the Scriptures could be verified on the basis of certain rational propositions that existed alongside their revelatory quality. Princeton Theology, therefore, was an early source of support for the doctrine of biblical inerrancy.

The Scopes "monkey" trial,* held in Dayton, Tennessee, in 1925, was one of the most famous public confrontations between conservatives and liberals over the issue of evolution and biblical authority. Liberal Clarence Darrow* defended schoolteacher John Scopes* against the charge of violating a Tennessee state law that forbade the teaching of evolution. Conservative William Jennings Bryan* prosecuted the case. Although Scopes was convicted, Bryan's testimony as an "expert" on the Bible revealed the difficulty of translating biblical language into a literal, scientific framework.

The Scopes trial was a populist expression of the conflict between theological fundamentalism* and liberalism* in American religious life. One of the early tenets of fundamentalism was belief in a "literal Bible." By the mid-twentieth century the term "inerrancy" replaced the word "literal" among most conservative-evangelical adherents of the idea. Most agreed that inerrancy applied primarily to the original manuscripts (not known any longer to exist), but acknowledged that existing translations were not far from the earliest text.

The inerrancy controversy has seriously divided American Christians, particularly evangelicals. In numerous traditions inerrancy became a divisive issue. This was particularly true in two American denominations, the Missouri Synod Lutheran Church and the Southern Baptist Convention.*

The Missouri Synod controversy began in 1970 when Jacob A. O. Preus,* president of the denomination, instituted procedures for investigating the faculty of Concordia Theological Seminary, St. Louis, Missouri, the primary source of theological education in the church. Charges were brought against certain faculty for denying or undermining the doctrine of biblical inerrancy. In 1972 Preus released a so-called Blue Book that he had compiled, listing certain unnamed Concordia faculty members guilty of teaching false doctrine. The faculty, led by seminary president John Tietjen,* resisted the effort to charge them with heresy. In 1974 Tietjen was suspended as seminary president, and the faculty declared that it considered itself also suspended. Faculty and a substantial number of students left the school to form Concordia Seminary in Exile (Seminex*) in St. Louis. It remained in existence until 1983, when the remaining faculty moved to Chicago, Berkeley, and Austin, Texas. Dissident Missouri Synod Lutherans* left the church and formed the Association of Evangelical Lutheran Churches with five cooperating synods. This organization was instrumental in a broader Lutheran union that linked it with the American Lutheran Church and the Lutheran Church in America in the formation of the Evangelical Lutheran Church in America in 1986.

The Southern Baptist controversy over inerrancy began in 1979 through the efforts of a group of conservatives (sometimes known as fundamentalists) to gain control of convention agencies and boards in order to reshape them in more conservative directions. Their rallying cry centered in the doctrine of biblical inerrancy and the charge that it was no longer being taught appropriately at Southern Baptist schools, particularly denominational seminaries. Fundamentalists charged that particular professors and pastors had rejected inerrancy and were therefore challenging the authority of Holy Scripture. A group of moderates (sometimes known as liberals) responded by affirming biblical authority and charged that the conservatives were politicizing the convention and distracting it from its primary calling to carry out missions and evangelism. For more than a decade each side sought to elect convention presidents sympathetic to its specific positions. Conservatives insisted that the statement that Scripture contained "truth without mixture of error for its matter" found in the Baptist Faith and Message, the denomination's confession of faith, be understood to mean the full inerrancy of the biblical text. Ultimately, conservatives gained control of the denominational organization and set about establishing inerrancy as the basic theory of biblical interpretation affirmed and promoted by the Southern Baptist Convention. By the 1990s disagreements developed among conservatives as to which of several types of inerrancy were most orthodox for defining the nature of biblical inspiration.

One effort to define inerrancy is found in the "Chicago Statement on Inerrancy," drafted by a group of evangelicals in 1979. While it has frequently served as an unofficial guide for interpreting the meaning of the word, not all evangelicals agree on its definitions.

Bibliography. Leonard, B. J., *God's Last and Only Hope: The Fragmentation of the Southern Baptist Convention* (Grand Rapids: Eerdmans Publishing Company, 1990); Marsden, G., *Reforming Fundamentalism* (Grand Rapids: Eerdmans Publishing Company, 1987); Tietjen, John, *Memoirs in Exile* (Minneapolis: Fortress Press, 1990).

Bill J. Leonard

Infant Baptism. Infant baptism is the practice of baptizing children a few days or weeks after birth; it is also known as paedobaptism or pedobaptism (from the Greek *paidion*, a child). The debate over infant baptism in America has followed denominational lines laid down in Europe in the sixteenth century and reflects differences of opinion over whether the rite—indeed, whether baptism* itself—is symbolic or sacramental and over how one becomes a Christian and a church member. Both sides seek their warrant in the New Testament and in the practices of the early church. The *New Catholic Encyclopedia* declares bluntly that "from the very beginning the Church has administered the Sacrament of Baptism to infants."

Infant baptism is a complex subject because of its theological implications. In those communions where baptism is understood as washing away original sin, an affirmative answer to the question of whether to baptize infants is automatic. On the other end of the theological spectrum, where the evangelical churches think in terms of individuals hearing the gospel and responding by seeking baptism, a negative answer to the question is a foregone conclusion. It is in the middle of the continuum, especially in the Reformed and Calvinistic churches, that the most frequent debates flare up. The 1960s saw an intense debate over the issue in the exchange between Joachim Jeremias and Kurt Aland. Jeremias argued that evidence of infant baptism could be found as far back as New Testament times, while Aland could find no sure proof of the practice before the third century.

Ecumenical discussions have often faltered on the issue of infant baptism. In 1982 the Faith and Order Commission of the World Council of Churches issued a report on "Baptism, Eucharist, and Ministry," sometimes called the Lima Report, which marked a step toward the mutual recognition of the two forms of baptism. Representatives of all communions, from Catholics to Baptists, participated in the writing of the report.

Bibliography. Aland, Kurt, *Did the Early Church Baptize Infants?* (Philadelphia: Westminster Press, 1963); Bridge, Donald, and David Phypers, *The Water That Divides: The Baptism Debate* (Downers Grove, IL: InterVarsity Press, 1977); Hunt, J.T.P., "Colossians 2:11–12, the Circumcision/Baptism Analogy, and Infant Baptism," *Tyndale Bulletin* 41 (1990), 227–44; Jeremias, Joachim, *Infant Baptism in the First Four Centuries* (Philadelphia: Westminster Press, 1960); Jeremias, Joachim, *The Origins of Infant Baptism: A Further Study in Reply to Kurt Aland* (London: SCM Press, 1963); Jewett, Paul, *Infant Baptism and the Covenant of Grace* (Grand Rapids, MI: Eerdmans, 1978); Wright, David, "One Baptism or Two? Reflections on the History of Christian Baptism," *Vox Evangelica* 18 (1988): 7–23.

Albert A. Bell, Jr.

Ingersoll, Robert Green. Robert Green Ingersoll (1833–1899) was a nineteenth-century American Enlightenment thinker, orator, and agnostic who utilized his considerable rhetorical skills to attack the inconsistencies and superstitions that he believed existed in the Christian faith. His scathing lectures, delivered across the nation, dripped with sarcasm, humor, and pathos and provided a considerable challenge to institutionalized Christianity.

Born in Dresden, New York, on August 11, 1833, Ingersoll was raised in a strict religious household by a devout Congregational pastor-father. His father's strict allegiance to Calvinist doctrine caused Ingersoll to reject many of the basic tenets of Christianity, primarily the idea of hell.* He turned instead to the works of Edward Gibbon, William Cowper, and Thomas Paine and discovered his affinity for Enlightenment thought with its emphasis upon human reason.

Ingersoll fought on the Union side in the Civil War, even spending a brief stint as a prisoner of war after the Battle of Shiloh in 1862. Following a short career as a teacher, he opened a law practice with his brother. His nomination of James G. Blaine for the presidency at the Republican National Convention in 1876 launched his career as a lecturer.

His most famous lectures included "The Gods" (1872), "Ghosts" (1877), and "The Liberty of Man, Woman, and Child" (1877). Four themes dominated these speeches: individual liberty, separation of church and state,* religious toleration, and the American home. In Ingersoll's estimation, these principles had sealed America's greatness in the past. The church had consistently opposed these ideas and therefore had opposed rationalism and the search for truth. As each individual was liberated from the shackles of religious superstition, the nation's salvation would be assured. Conservative elements in Christianity denounced Ingersoll as the personification of evil; liberals praised him as a champion of religious reform and a testimony to the potential of human reason. He died on July 21, 1899.

Bibliography. Cramer, C. H., *Royal Bob: The Life of Robert G. Ingersoll* (Indianapolis: Bobbs-Merrill Company, 1952); Ingersoll, R. G., *Complete Lectures of Col. R. G. In-*

gersoll, ed. Eva Ingersoll Wakefield (Chicago: Regan Publishing Company, 1926); Larson, Orvin, *American Infidel: Robert G. Ingersoll* (New York: Citadel Press, 1962); May, Henry F., *The Enlightenment in America* (Oxford: Oxford University Press, 1978).

Robert N. Nash, Jr.

Ives, Leon Silliman. While much of America's religious tumult has been of its own origination, some arose elsewhere and later appeared here. That was the case in the career of Leon Silliman Ives (1797–1867), an Episcopal clergyman who converted to Roman Catholicism while he was an incumbent bishop. At the time of his widely repudiated transfer, he held the episcopal office in North Carolina. Had he been a parish priest only, such a change would have created far fewer ripples. What he did create was something of a storm; of course, winds and seas had been roiling for several years before the actual thunderclap struck.

Born in Connecticut and reared Presbyterian, Ives moved early to New York, where he became an Episcopalian and studied for the priesthood. He married the daughter of Bishop John Henry Hobart, whose high-church orientation and association with England's Tractarian (or Oxford) movement influenced him heavily. In 1831 he was elected the second bishop of North Carolina, largely a missionary diocese to which he brought a zeal for mission causes, one being the education of Negroes. After the closing of a school he had founded, he turned eyes and passions to the mountain West, where he planted a mission station. It was unique, a "Protestant" monasticlike foundation. In the school in that remote place he sought to promote high-church doctrines and to train priests who would serve the mountain people.

The school at Valle Crucis was not supported by the diocese, nor was Bishop Ives's experiment there widely known. Increasingly his views came to public knowledge, and his status and reputation became controversial. He favored more elaborate vestments, Gothic architecture, and many worship usages of the ancient and medieval church. In 1848 and 1849 he began promoting auricular (private) confession to a priest, a practice that conferred a higher role of authority on priests, specifically a "fallible but authorized duty to pronounce." Although Ives treated confession as voluntary on the part of members and as no more than permissible, he was coming to be seen as "popish."

Diocesan conventions became forums for debate, even confrontation. Ives wrote and spoke his piece, sometimes pulling back from more extreme stances earlier taken. Accused of being unstable, he was actually assertive, self-assured, and sometimes self-pitying.

Never thoroughly Roman Catholic in the years of his episcopacy, he was nevertheless tending that way, one of America's most exemplary Tractarians. While visiting Rome in 1852, he abjured Protestantism and became a Catholic. A stormy decade among North Carolina's Episcopalians had come to an end. Ives, being married, never was ordained to the priesthood of his new church and spent his later years in social ministries in New York, especially with children's charities.

Bibliography. Malone, Michael T., "Leon Silliman Ives: Priest, Bishop, Tractarian, and Roman Catholic Convert" (Ph. D. diss., Duke University, 1970). Rankin, Richard, *Ambivalent Churchmen and Evangelical Churchwomen* (Columbia: University of South Carolina Press, 1993); Stamm, Henry E., IV, "The Episcopal Church in Western North Carolina, 1842–1898" (M.A. thesis, Appalachian State University, 1989).

Samuel S. Hill

J

Jackson, Jesse Louis. A Baptist minister, civil rights* leader, and politician, Jesse Jackson has been the most influential African American since the assassination of Martin Luther King, Jr.* Born in Greenville, South Carolina, in 1941, he briefly attended the University of Illinois but soon transferred to North Carolina Agricultural and Technical University after he was not given a fair opportunity to participate in the athletic program. Further schooled at Chicago Theological Seminary, he was ordained to the ministry in 1968. While in college he became involved with the civil rights movement and became an associate of King in the Southern Christian Leadership Conference* (SCLC), marching from Selma to Montgomery in 1965 and the next year heading a program to procure minority jobs in Chicago called Operation Breadbasket. In April 1968 he accompanied King to Memphis, where his mentor was assassinated. Appearing the next day on a television interview wearing a shirt he claimed to be stained with King's blood, Jackson symbolically laid claim to King's mantle of leadership. Others had other ideas, sparking controversy over King's legacy. Though he participated in the 1968 Poor Peoples' Campaign, led by new SCLC president Ralph David Abernathy,* in 1971 Jackson parted with the older organization to form People United to Save Humanity (PUSH), which sought to pressure Chicago officials to grant jobs and economic opportunities to minorities.

By the late 1970s and early 1980s a conservative resurgence that landed Ronald Reagan in the Oval Office inspired Jackson to increased involvement in electoral politics. After four years of Reagan's reactionary policies, Jackson yielded to cries of "Run Jesse Run" and entered the presidential primary campaigns. Appearing at rallies in African-American churches, he electrified crowds who put their political contributions into church offering plates and often declared, "I haven't felt this proud since Joe Louis." Representing the left wing of the Democratic party, he established an organization called the Rainbow Coalition. Jackson's liberal stances were aimed at combining the political forces of "red, yellow, brown, black, and whites." Included also in Jackson's coalition were gays and lesbians, or as he described his constituency to the 1984 Democratic National Convention, "the damned, the disinherited, the disrespected, and the despised." In that speech Jackson also issued a veiled apology for his controversial comments referring to New York City as "Hymietown" and his associations with Nation of Islam* leader Louis Farrakhan.* In 1988 Jackson again ran for president, garnering some six million primary votes. That campaign also generated controversy over the role of ministers in presidential politics, as the Reverend Pat Robertson also ran for the Republican nomination. Since his second run for the White House, Jackson has toned down his controversial statements and has served as the host of a CNN political talk show called "Both Sides."

Bibliography. Frady, Marshall, *Jesse: The Life and Pilgrimage of Jesse Jackson* (New York: Random House, 1996); Hatch, Roger D., *Beyond Opportunity: Jesse Jackson's Vision for America* (Philadelphia: Fortress Press, 1988); Reed, Adoph L., Jr., *The Jesse Jackson Phenomenon: The Crisis of Purpose in Afro-American Politics* (New Haven: Yale University Press, 1986); Washington, James Melvin, "Jesse Jackson and the Symbolic Politics of Black Christendom," *Annals of the American Academy of Political and Social Science* 480 (July 1985): 89–105.

Andrew M. Manis

Jarratt, Devereux. Born in Kent County, Virginia, Devereux Jarratt (1733–1801) grew up with little thought of religion. An avid reader and schoolteacher, he received encouragement toward the Christian faith from his Presbyterian friends. Having grown up a nominal Anglican, he chose to seek ordination from the bishop of London. He was ordained deacon on December 25, 1762, and the bishop of Chester elevated him to priest on January 1, 1763. Upon his return to Virginia, he became rector of Bath parish, Dinwiddie County, a position he held until his death. Dedicated to his work, Jarratt left most of his affairs to the management of his wives Martha and later Georgiana.

Jarratt was an apostle of "vital religion" in an environment that was formal or indifferent about spiritual matters. His preaching stressed the need for repentance and new birth, the reality of sin and the necessity of regeneration, the existence of heaven and hell,* and the importance of good works. In this respect, he was a product of the Great Awakening* via his Presbyterian friends and George Whitefield's sermons, which he had read. He appealed directly to the hearts of his hearers and made them conscious of their sinful condition. Although his appeal was with warmth and zeal, he did not like the emotional element that was evident in some revival services. His activity extended into other parishes in Virginia and North Carolina. Primarily as a result of Jarratt's efforts, between 1764 and 1772 there was a widespread religious awakening in this area. But his irregular style of preaching, itinerancy, and variation from the order of church service brought him into conflict with the established church in Virginia.

When in 1773 the Methodist Robert Williams came to Virginia, Jarratt assisted him after being assured that the Methodists did not intend to leave the Church of England. He saw Methodism* as an instrument to revive religion in his own church. But when the Methodist Church was organized at the Christmas Conference (1784) in Baltimore, Maryland, Jarratt felt betrayed. His friendship with the Methodists had added to the tensions with his fellow Anglicans. In 1790 he did preach for the Methodist Conference in Petersburg and to the Episcopal Church convention at Richmond in 1792. As an advocate of religious revival, Devereux Jarratt was a controversial figure.

Bibliography. Holmes, D. L., "Devereux Jarratt: A Letter and a Reevaluation," *Historical Magazine of the Protestant Episcopal Church* 47 (1978): 37–49; Jarratt, Devereux, *The Life of the Reverend Devereux Jarratt* (New York: Arno Press, 1969); Jarratt, Devereux, *Sermons on Various and Important Subjects*, 3 vols. (Baltimore: Warner and Hana, 1806); Middleton, A. P., "The Colonial Virginia Parson," *William and Mary Quarterly* 3rd ser., 26 (1969): 425–40; Rabe, H. G., "The Reverend Devereux Jarratt and the Virginia Social Order," *Historical Magazine of the Protestant Episcopal Church* 33 (1964): 299–336.

Frederick V. Mills, Sr.

Jefferson, Thomas. While there were several occasions when religious controversy swirled about Thomas Jefferson (see "Separation of Church and State" in this volume), it was in his Act for Establishing Religious Freedom, adopted by the Virginia Assembly in 1786, that Jefferson espoused the principles that cast him in opposition to large numbers of Protestants in the postrevolutionary period. Jefferson saw the authorship of that act as one of his three most significant achievements.

As the colony of Virginia prepared to join with twelve others to bring forth the American Revolution, in 1777 Jefferson composed the act and offered it to his colleagues in the Virginia General Assembly as part of a revision of the code of the new state. The act had three parts. The first was a prologue of justification. The second was the bill itself. The third advised all future assemblies that to tamper with the act would be to violate natural rights. The act, number 82 in the revised code, received no action while Jefferson was in the legislature. After the Revolution, while Jefferson was serving as ambassador to France, James Madison brought the bill forth for action by the General Assembly in the fall of 1785.

Assembly members bridled at some of Jefferson's assertions in the first paragraph. While they had little quarrel with the principle set forth by Jefferson, they resisted his religious views as manifested in the language they deleted. In particular the Assembly removed "well aware that the opinions and belief of men depend not on their own will, but follow involuntarily the evidence proposed to their minds'' and Jefferson's contention that religion should be extended ''by its influence on reason alone.'' The editors of Madison's papers noted, ''By the deletion of some of the more sweeping statements about the supremacy of reason, the broad base upon which Jefferson founded the bill was somewhat diminished.'' Madison, eager to accomplish passage of the bill, allowed the changes and achieved adoption in 1786. When Jefferson received word of the Assembly action, he wrote to Madison that the Virginia legislature ''had the courage to declare that the reason of man may be trusted with the formation of his own opinions'' (Jefferson to Madison, December 16, 1786).

Jefferson's Deism became a cause of political strife and serious attacks on his character during his quest for the presidency. In 1800 Yale president Timothy Dwight warned that election of Jefferson would mean that ''our churches may become temples of reason.'' A Dutch Reformed minister urged defeat of Jefferson because he rejected biblical revelation. Presbyterians attacked him for his Deism. Jefferson was hurt by these attacks and was angered as well. He later wrote, ''If there had never been a priest, there would never have been an infidel.''

Privately, Jefferson composed his own edition of the New Testament. It consisted of selected portions of the Gospels, excluding those references he believed to be nonhistorical. Had that information become generally known, it is likely that he would have faced even more severe criticism for his views. Almost two hundred years prior to the ''Jesus Seminar'' Jefferson employed a critical analysis of the Bible that extracted the events in the life of Jesus that he believed to have been nonhistorical. Using his own scholarly scissors, he excised all references to the Virgin Birth of Jesus, all references to Jesus as divine, all the miracle stories, the empty tomb, the resurrection, and the ascension.

Jefferson was sensitive to criticism he encountered from religious figures. He was most frequently respected by Baptists for his position on religious freedom; however, other Protestants with roots in ecclesiastical establishments frequently opposed Jefferson's strong separationist views. In 1802 President Jefferson heeded the advice of his attorney general, Levi Lincoln, and deleted a portion of his letter to the Danbury Baptists that would have explained why he refused to make thanksgiving proclamations. Jefferson penned in the margin of his revised draft, ''This paragraph was omitted on the suggestion that it might give uneasiness to some of our republican friends in the eastern states where the proclamation of thanksgivings etc. by their Executive is an antient [*sic*] habit and is respected.'' However, it was in the same letter that Jefferson asserted that the First Amendment built ''a wall of separation between church and State.''

Bibliography. Adams, Dickinson W., ed., *Jefferson's Extracts from the Gospels* (Princeton: Princeton University Press, 1983); Alley, Robert S., ''Public Education and the Public Good,'' in *William and Mary Bill of Rights Journal* 4, no. 1 (Summer 1995): 277–350; Gaustad, Edwin S., *Sworn on the Altar of God* (Grand Rapids, MI: William B. Eerdmans, 1996); Peterson, Merrill, *The Jefferson Image in the American Mind* (New

York: Oxford University Press, 1960); Rutland, Robert, and William M. E. Rachal, eds, *The Papers of James Madison,* vol. 8 (Chicago: University of Chicago Press, 1973).

Robert S. Alley

Jehovah's Witnesses. In 1872 Charles Taze Russell guided a small Bible study group in the study of biblical passages concerned with the Second Coming of Christ. This small group of followers in New York soon became convinced that the end of the world, occasioned by a great battle between Satan and Jehovah, was imminent. By 1884 Russell had formed the Watch Tower Bible and Tract Society, complete with a regular publication entitled the *Watch Tower.* The movement experienced rapid growth and now numbers well into the millions of followers all over the world. Witnesses have maintained a keen concern for an apocalyptic view of the world throughout their history. An ingrained pessimism toward the world's future naturally accompanies this worldview, as does a very negative perception toward the designs and aspirations of governments and nations. Though Witnesses are generally law-abiding citizens and, in America, believe that income taxes, at least in principle, represent payment for services rendered, they have refused historically to vote, hold office, or enlist in military service. Their refusal to serve their nations in time of war has contributed to their experience of persecution throughout the world.

The persecution of Witnesses, however, has been far more extensive worldwide than can be attributed merely to their lack of participation in military campaigns. In fact, the entire history of Jehovah's Witnesses swirls with controversy. Much of it during the early years resulted from both the group's hostility to all organized religion (leaders refused to acknowledge the movement's own status as a ''religion'') and its aggressive tactics in evangelism. When Russell died in 1916, Judge Joseph F. Rutherford assumed leadership in the movement; his extremely negative views of other Christian groups and of non-Christian religions made the Witnesses the object of much religious hostility. Clergy, especially among Catholics, most often the focus of Rutherford's diatribes, tried every legal means to limit the activities of the movement. The evangelism of Witnesses faced all manner of new city and state ordinances dealing with licensing laws, antipeddling legislation, and restrictions curbing littering. Occasionally, some clergy even resorted to mob violence against them. Since the early 1960s the conflict between Witnesses and other religious groups has cooled considerably in most locations, though it remains heated in Islamic countries particularly.

The most spectacular controversy involving Witnesses in the United States arose in the late 1930s when increasing numbers of children in the movement came to the attention of authorities when they refused to salute the flag in their public schools. In a period when Hitler's power was on the rise, and when patriotism in the United States was rising with it, the nonconformist behavior of these children incited considerable public anger. Jehovah's Witnesses looked to the Supreme Court for help in overturning the mounting convictions in state courts. In 1940 the Court dealt with the issue in *Minersville School District v. Gobitis*. In a vote of 8–1, the justices sided with the public school systems. Many Protestant leaders, including Harry Emerson Fosdick* and Reinhold Niebuhr, and advocacy groups like the American Civil Liberties Union immediately registered disagreement with the decision. Most public response, however, used the Court's decision to justify further persecution of the movement. With two new members on the bench, and other justices rethinking the wisdom of the previous decision, the Supreme Court agreed to hear another case (*West Virginia State Board of Education v. Burnette*) dealing with the issue just three years later. In a very unusual reversal, using freedom of speech as the primary rationale, the Court decided 6–3 in favor of the Witnesses.

Though the Witnesses have amassed a tremendous record of success in Supreme Court cases, they have suffered some significant losses. Since these cases involve the welfare of children, they have been surrounded by controversy as well. In 1944, in a case involving a child distributing religious literature at night, the Supreme Court ruled against Witnesses, upholding state child labor laws (*Prince v. Massachusetts*). State courts later used this case as legal precedent for a proactive stance in ordering medical procedures for children of Witnesses. With the general spread of blood banks in the mid-to-late 1930s, leaders began to interpret biblical prohibitions concerning the eating of blood (e.g., Leviticus 17:10; Acts 15:29) to cover blood transfusions. After World War II the church proclaimed an official ban on blood transfusions. Lower courts have consistently ruled that children cannot be refused blood transfusions based upon the religious objections of their parents. The Supreme Court has supported these decisions by refusing to hear any appeals. Adult Witnesses in need of blood transfusions continue to raise controversial issues for the courts.

Bibliography. Davis, D. S. "Does 'No' Mean 'Yes'? The Continuing Problem of Jehovah's Witnesses and Refusal of Blood Products," *Second Opinion* 19 (January 1994): 35–43; Flowers, R. B., "Withholding Medical Care for Religious Reasons," *Journal of Religion and Health* 23 (Winter 1984): 268–82; Macklin, R., "The Inner Workings of an Ethics Committee: Latest Battle over Jehovah's Winesses," *Hastings Center Report* 18 (February/March 1988): 15–20; Penton, M. J., *Apocalypse Delayed: The Story of Jehovah's Witnesses* (Toronto: University of Toronto Press, 1985); Stevens, L.A, *Salute! The Case of the Bible vs. the Flag* (New York: Coward, McCann and Geoghegan, 1973).

Mark G. Toulouse

Jesus Movement. Initially organized and led by students, the Jesus movement emerged in and spread from Southern California in the 1960s as a protest and an affirmation. It protested the system of established social, cultural, and religious institutions, including the religious consciousness of the counterculture that emphasized Eastern mysticism, new forms of self-awareness, spiritual narcissism, psychedelic experiences, while opposing the formalism of established churches.

Adherents affirmed essentially a conservative to fundamentalist Christianity. God has a simple plan of salvation. The four steps to salvation are the following:

(1) God loves you and has a plan for your life; (2) sin separates you from God, and cuts you off from God's love and plan; (3) Jesus Christ died for your sins and is your only way to God, for through him you experience God's love; (4) you must ask Jesus into your life as Lord and Savior. After being saved, one must read the Bible, pray, tell others, join a Jesus movement, and avoid sinning (no drugs, no sex outside of marriage, no hassling, and no violence). Many affirmed the fundamentalist credo of belief in (1) the Virgin Birth; (2) the penal substitutionary theory of the cross; (3) the bodily resurrection; (4) the actual bodily return of Jesus to earth to establish an earthly kingdom; and (5) the absolute inerrancy of the Bible.

Repudiating middle-class values, many of the movement's adherents were identifiable as "Jesus hippies" in appearance replete with long hair, beards, and ragged jeans. Many lived in communes scattered throughout California and other states where they engaged in farming or small business practices such as workshops that produced posters and publications. One commune, the Solid Rock of Novata, California, prohibited drugs and premarital intercourse.

At least five characteristics distinguished the Jesus movement from other recent spiritual movements: (1) Initially it was almost wholly led and organized by students (aged fifteen to twenty-five). (2) They identified with Jesus, the rebel against the establishment of his day, and therefore of these days. (3) There was a strong emphasis on caring for members of the new community. (4) The Bible was considered the inerrant and authoritative living Word of God, to be believed in every respect. (5) The characteristic, enterprising experimentation in outreach ranged from a Jesus nightclub (Right On in Sunset Strip, Hollywood), Jesus festivals (one was held in Minneapolis in 1971), employing the kind of post-jazz music and musicians that appealed to youth (*Jesus Christ Superstar* and *Godspell* were two successful musicals from this period), the Jesus procession (one in Grant Park, Chicago, drew a crowd of one thousand), and the establishment of communes already noted to the proliferation of Christian underground-press publications, of which the *Hollywood Free Paper* and David Wilkerson's *The Cross and the Switchblade* are examples.

The movement, in decline since the 1970s, has had many origins and manifestations, five of which are (1) the "Jesus Freaks" or "Street Christians," some of whom affect a hippie style, while others give it up upon becoming Christian; (2) the "Straight People," who are active in interdenominational thought and campus movements, seem to be more ecumenical in outlook, and in appearance look like Middle Americans; (3) the "Catholic Pentecostals," who, while loyal to the Roman Catholic Church, have chafed at authoritarianism and have championed spontaneity in worship and charismatic emphasis; (4) the "Children of God," initially a quasi–military/monastic movement that has generated a great deal of controversy and has come under severe scrutiny from state and federal agencies; (5) the "Jesus People USA," an intentional community of the Evangelical Covenant Church in Chicago.

The Jesus movement caused controversy on many levels. It forced mainline churches to reexamine their ministry to youth, the place of emotions and feelings in services, the nature of discipleship demanded of Christians by the gospel, and the primacy of Jesus Christ. It aided and abetted the evangelical movement. In repudiating drugs and promiscuity, and in affirming love and community, the Jesus People endeavored to affirm higher values than those of the prevailing secular culture.

There are other areas of controversy. The preference for subjectivity (or experience) over history diluted the historical Christian faith. This tendency led to adopting what was appealing in Jesus while ignoring the rest of his teachings, such as his hard sayings like "If any man would follow me, let him take up his cross." The tendency to fellowship with Jesus in his joy ignored sharing in what Paul called "the fellowship of Christ's suffering." With biblicism both absolutist and simplistic, proof-texting apart from considerations of specific contexts proved to be escapist and less than helpful in addressing specific concerns.

Bibliography. Ellwood, R. S., Jr., *One Way: The Jesus Movement and Its Meaning* (Englewood Cliffs, NJ: Prentice-Hall, 1973); Enroth, R. M., and E. E. Erickson, Jr, *The Jesus People: Old-Time Religion in the Age of Aquarius* (Grand Rapids, MI: William B. Eerdmans Publishing Company, 1972); Pederson, D., *Jesus People* (Pasadena, CA: Compass Press, 1971); Plowman, E. E., *The Jesus Movement in America* (Elgin, IL: David C. Cook, 1971); Streiker, Lowell D., *The Jesus Trip Advent of the Jesus Freaks* (Nashville: Abingdon Press, 1971).

Robert K. Gustafson

Jews for Jesus. The phenomenon of "Jews for Jesus" can be traced to the late-nineteenth- and early-twentieth-century Hebrew-Christian movement, which consisted of Jews who believed in Jesus. Most of these Jews joined churches, while some attempted to emulate Jewish rituals and attach to these rituals Christian beliefs, as was done by early Christianity. For example, the sacrifice of the Paschal lamb becomes a symbol of the sacrifice of Jesus. The Passover seder becomes a reenactment of the Last Supper. The wine and bread, used by Jews to consecrate meals and holy times, now become symbolic of the body and blood of Jesus. With the rise of evangelical activity in the late 1960s and 1970s, efforts were made by Christian groups to target Jews for proselytization and bring them to the Christian faith. Many of the missionizing groups found that they were more successful in attracting Jews to Christianity if they maintained a semblance of Jewish practice. Religious gathering places are called synagogues, clergy call themselves rabbis, and worship takes place on the Jewish Sabbath instead of Sunday. But their theology is entirely Christian.

Among every branch of the Jewish community, there is a universal dismissal of the religion of Jews for Jesus as having a valid place among Jewish religious movements. No responsible and recognized leader or organization within the Jewish community accepts this effort to syncretize Jewish belief with Christian theology and belief. The claim of Jews for Jesus and similar groups that they are, through their belief in Jesus, now "fulfilled" in their faith is seen by those within the Jewish community as an expression of Christianity, not Judaism. Jewish groups also condemn the surreptitious and covert efforts of Jews for Jesus and similar groups to attract Jews on the margins of the Jewish community to bring them to Christian belief.

However, there is a debate among Jews as to whether or not these Christian believers of Jewish background are still members of the Jewish people. This debate has serious implications for the nature of Judaism. Jewish tradition teaches that a Jew, even when he or she sins, still remains a Jew. Jews for Jesus, even though they have committed apostasy by professing the Christian belief of God incarnate, cannot divest themselves of their Jewish covenantal relationship. There is a tendency among the more traditional branches of Judaism to view these Christian-believing Jews as still members of the Jewish people. They are thus still obligated to follow Jewish law and are subject to the penalties for their sin. Among the more progressive branches of Judaism, there is a tendency to view these Christian-believing Jews as members of the church. They then, by adopting another faith, have in essence divorced themselves from the covenant of the Jewish people.

Bibliography. *An Inside Look at Jews for Jesus* (San Francisco: Jews for Jesus/Hineni Ministries, 1983); Kamentsky, Ellen, *Hawking God: A Young Jewish Woman's Ordeal in Jews for Jesus* (Medford, MA.: Sapphire Press, 1992).

Jonathan Miller

Jones, Bob, and Family. The main members of the Bob Jones family are Robert R. "Bob" Jones, Sr. (1883–1968); Robert R. "Bob" Jones, Jr. (1911–   ); and Robert R. "Bob" Jones, III (1939–   ). Bob Jones University, the leading separatist fundamentalist institution of higher education in the United States, was founded by Bob Jones, Sr., in 1926. Bob Jones, Jr., served as acting president from 1932 to 1947 and president from 1947 to 1971. Bob Jones, III, has served as president since 1971.

Reared in a small Alabama church of the Methodist Episcopal Church, South, Bob Jones, Sr., was licensed to preach at age fifteen and later emerged as an acclaimed evangelist. Best known for his ardent stance against modernism,* he was a controversial figure during the fundamentalist-modernist controversy. Sensing the need for a fundamentalist institution of higher learning, he founded Bob Jones College in St. Andrews Bay, Florida, in 1926. Though this venture fell through, he reestablished the college in Cleveland, Tennessee, where it remained until 1947. Renamed Bob Jones University, the school moved to Greenville, South Carolina, in 1947, where it remains to the present. In 1947 Bob Jones, Jr., assumed the presidency of the institution. Bob Jones, Jr., sought to make Bob Jones University a center for the arts, and the university's baroque art collection has achieved international appreciation.

Bob Jones University has been controversial as the center of militant fundamentalism* in the United States. An example of such activity is the university's critique of the ministry of evangelist Billy Graham.* Though Graham attended the school for a while, Bob Jones University became one of Graham's most outspoken fundamentalist critics, castigating Graham for his involvement in cooperative evangelism—cooperating with nonevangelicals in evangelistic causes—and what was perceived as a general attitude of social and theological compromise. Such disapproval of Graham and other "new evangelicals" led to Bob Jones University's policy of not allowing Graham's organization to hold meetings on campus. This policy led to vehement attacks on the university by those in the mainstream evangelical community. Bob Jones University also broke ties with such evangelical organizations as the National Association of Evangelicals and Youth for Christ and was highly critical of the periodical *Christianity Today*.

Bob Jones University's theological separatism has led to a social separatism as well. Thus the institution has always had a policy of remaining aloof from the educational establishment, shunning accreditation and recognition from the mainstream academic community. Perhaps the most controversial event in the history of the school was the court battle over Bob Jones University's policy of not allowing interracial dating on campus. The case proceeded to the U.S. Supreme Court in 1983, where the court ruled against Bob Jones University. This ruling caused the university to lose its tax-exempt status. Despite these setbacks, Bob Jones University thrives as the largest separatist fundamentalist university, with over 300 faculty members and 5,000 undergraduate and graduate students.
Bibliography. Dollar, G. W., *A History of Fundamentalism in America* (Greenville, SC: Bob Jones University Press, 1973); Wright, Melton, *Fortress of Faith: The Story of Bob Jones University* (Greenville, SC: Bob Jones University Press, 1984).

J. Matthew Pinson

Jones, Jim. The charismatic evangelist Jim Jones (1931–1978) came to international attention on November 18, 1978, when he led 914 followers in an act of collective suicide in Jonestown, Guyana. The enormity of this disaster transfixed public attention throughout the late 1970s and early 1980s and led to an increasingly hostile public attitude toward new religious movements.

Jones grew up in a conservative, racist, and fundamentalist environment in rural Indiana. He moved to Indianapolis after high school and began the Peoples Temple Full Gospel Church in 1954. The Pentecostal* congregation was notable because of its integrated membership and network of social services to the poor. Jones developed a reputation as a healer and social activist and began attracting significant crowds to his faith-healing services. He would later contend that these theatrical healing performances were a means of drawing people to his controversial teachings of apostolic socialism and racial equality.

In the early 1960s Jones foresaw in a vision the nuclear destruction of the midwestern United States. He and some loyal followers relocated to Ukiah, California, an area Jones believed would be protected from the impending apocalyptic holocaust. The Peoples Temple grew during the early 1970s and began attracting African Americans from Los Angeles and San Francisco. Jones was honored by California politicians for his service work and even gained appointment to the San Francisco Housing Authority.

Following the defections of eight close aides and a series of critical newspaper articles in the mid-1970s, Jones began planning a move to the socialist-ruled nation of Guyana. For Jones, Guyana represented the "Promised Land" where his vision of apostolic socialism could finally be realized. Jones moved to Guyana in July 1977, shortly before a major magazine exposé appeared calling for a criminal investigation of the Peoples Temple for financial fraud and the mistreatment of members.

In 1978 California congressman Leo Ryan spearheaded a federal investigation of Jones's Peoples Temple Agricultural Project. Ryan and his staff visited the community on November 17 and talked with both supporters and detractors. Together with fourteen defectors, Ryan and his entourage were about to return home when they were murdered by Jones's security forces. The mass suicide occurred the following day, after which Jones and an aide shot themselves rather than face murder charges. Although commentators disagree as to the degree of coercion involved, evidence indicates that a majority willingly embraced suicide as a revolutionary act. Following these events, U.S. Senate hearings were held during which mainstream religious representatives called for tighter governmental controls over new religious movements.

Bibliography. Chidester, David S., *Salvation and Suicide: An Interpretation of Jim Jones, the Peoples Temple, and Jonestown* (Bloomington: Indiana University Press, 1988); Hall, John H, *Gone from the Promised Land: Jonestown in American Cultural History* (New Brunswick, NJ: Transaction, 1987); Richardson, James T., "Peoples Temple and Jonestown: A Corrective Comparison and Critique," *Journal for the Scientific Study of Religion* 1980 no. 3: 239–55.

Phillip Lucas

Jones, Samuel Porter. Samuel Porter Jones was prominent Methodist evangelist from the South during the latter half of the nineteenth century. Born in 1847, the native of Alabama moved to Cartersville, Georgia, in 1856. After serving in the Confederate army, he began practicing law in 1869 but fell into poverty and drunkenness. In 1872 he pledged to his dying father that he would give up alcohol and change his life. Jones was converted to Christianity and soon became a minister in the North Georgia Conference of the Methodist Episcopal Church, South. He served several Methodist pastorates from 1872 to 1880 and then was an agent of a Methodist orphanage for a dozen years.

Jones developed a reputation for being a powerful preacher and achieved much success on the revival circuit. In 1885 he preached at T. Dewitt Talmage's prominent Presbyterian Church in Brooklyn, New York, which catapulted him onto the national scene. Called the "Moody of the South," Jones preached in all of the major cities of America and spoke on the Chautauqua circuit during the next fifteen years. From 1900 until his death in 1906 he generally confined his revivals to the South.

Amidst the social transformations of the late nineteenth century, Jones offered an unambiguous message: no alcohol, profanity, or gambling. He emphasized personal moral reform more than conversion, telling his hearers to "quit your meanness." Jones's delivery was controversial. Critics considered his use of blunt language, slang, and folksy humor to be irreverent and crude. His followers, however, responded to his entertaining denunciation of hypocrisy and nominal Christianity.

Bibliography. Jones, Laura M., *The Life and Sayings of Sam P. Jones* (Atlanta: Franklin-Turner Co., 1906); Jones, Sam, *Sam Jones' Sermons*, 2 vols. (Chicago: Rhodes and McClure, 1886).

Douglas Weaver

Jordan, Clarence. Born in Talbotton, Georgia, in 1912, Jordan died in 1969 of a heart attack at the religious commune he had founded near Americus, Georgia, Koinonia Farm.* Graduating from the University of Georgia with a B.S. in agricultural science in 1933, he continued with his education at the Southern Baptist Theological Seminary,* earning the Th.M. in 1936 and the Th.D. in 1939. While at the seminary he distinguished himself by his knowledge of biblical Greek.

A genuine visionary, Jordan took the Sermon on the Mount seriously and not only tried to live by its principles but also expected other Christians to try to do so as well. Any such person is destined to controversy.

Early on in his religious experience in a large family (he was the seventh of ten children), he wondered if black children were just as precious in God's sight as white children, and, if so, why these children were ragged, dirty, and hungry.

Toward the end of his high-school education he decided that he would be a scientific farmer and help poor farmers in south Georgia. He completed his course of studies in agricultural science at the University of Georgia and was headed for a commission in the army. A "call" to Christian ministry resulted in his being licensed to preach and heading to Louisville, Kentucky, for his seminary education. While completing his graduate degree there, he became involved in an inner-city ministry and had a dream for a radical experiment in Christian community. In Louisville he worked in an interracial setting and developed a small group that described itself with the Greek word Koinonia, a word used to describe the fellowship of sharing among the earliest Christians. With this special group he shared his dream of founding a farm in the South of a fellowship of Christians committed to peace and brotherhood and sharing their possessions in a common life. In addition, the community would be interracial.

In 1941–1942, Jordan and his friend Martin England incorporated the dream as Koinonia Farm, Inc., and found their location in 440 acres of land eight miles southwest of Americus, Georgia, on Route 49. As the nation moved full swing into the war, Jordan and his friends started their experiment in reconciliation—an experiment both religious and interracial. Suspect from the start, after the Supreme Court decision of 1954 and entrance into the chaotic civil rights* era of southern history, Jordan's community paid a tremendous price of persecution. That the community survived was nothing short of a miracle. In the midst of these and other problems, Jordan commenced his Cotton Patch Version of the New Testament project. There was some opposition to his earthiness in these translations of New Testament writings into red-clay English, but he began to have speaking engagements across the country as a result of this project. Koinonia breathed new life and was restructured as Koinonia Partners with major thrusts in communication, instruction, and application. The last thrust involved partnership industries, farming, and housing. Habitat for Humanity was born in this unlikely setting with the help of Millard Fuller, a new friend and colleague. The community continued to flourish despite the sudden death of its founder of a massive heart attack in October 1969. A few months earlier Jordan had addressed the American Baptist Convention. Baptists in the South may have generally been offended by him and his lively experiment, but surely they could not deny the plea that he made on that late May day of 1969: "It's when the Word of God becomes powerful among us, when His Spirit becomes energizing in us, creating us into the image of his Son, it is then that the world is faced with the presence of God Almighty on this earth. God is not in his heaven and all's well on the earth. He is on this earth and all hell's broke loose!"

Bibliography. Barnette, Henlee H., *Clarence Jordan* (Macon: Smyth and Helwys, 1992); Jordan, Clarence, *The Cotton Patch Version of Paul's Epistles* (New York: Association Press, 1968); Jordan, Clarence, *The Substance of Faith* (New York: Association Press, 1972); Lee, Dallas, *The Cotton Patch Evidence* (New York: Harper and Row, 1971).

George H. Shriver

K

Kaplan, Mordecai M. Mordecai Kaplan (1881–1983) was a rabbi and the founder of the Reconstructionist movement. His 102 years enabled him to experience
firsthand the internal struggles and identity crises of Judaism in the modern
world, especially Judaism in America. Lithuanian born, Kaplan emigrated with
his family to the United States when he was nine. Trained in Orthodox Judaism,
he began to encounter less orthodox understandings while in secondary school.
After ordination through the Jewish Theological Seminary, Kaplan became the
rabbi at the Orthodox synagogue Kehillath Jeshurun in New York, having served
as "minister"—a designation required by traditional technicalities—prior to actual ordination. But his growing discomfort with many aspects of Orthodoxy
found him uncomfortable with this position in the affluent Eastern European
population residing in this American community.

In 1909 he became dean of Teachers' Institute of the Jewish Theological
Seminary (a Conservative Jewish institution) and later was one of the founders
of the New York Kehillah (a short-lived and controversial experiment blending
Zionist, reformist, and cultural concerns), organized the first synagogue-center,
the Jewish Center, and served as its rabbi from 1917 to 1922. Kaplan founded
the Society for the Advancement of Judaism and, in 1935, the *Reconstructionist*
magazine and the Jewish Reconstructionist Foundation.

As a scholar and an activist, Kaplan during his adult life was surrounded with
controversy. When his long-in-preparation *Judaism as a Civilization* was finally
published in 1934, he achieved the reputation as "the most controversial Jewish
thinker in America, vilified by the Orthodox, rejected by Reform and upbraided

by colleagues on the [Conservative] Jewish Theological Seminary faculty'' (Libowitz, 192).
At the heart of Kaplan's vision of what Judaism could and must become—in order not only to survive but to regain its identity and reclaim its vitality—were Jewish Centers. In Kaplan's vision, these Jewish Centers would permit Jews to live as Jews since that was an inseparable element of the Jewish religion. Jewishness preceded Judaism. This theme was elaborated in numerous writings and projects, seeking to demonstrate that Judaism was not a religious philosophy but a religious civilization, "a cultural and spiritual complex of language, literature, history, customs, social institutions, organized about a conception of God which has the most far-reaching social and spiritual implications for human life of all times'' (Kaplan, *A New Approach to the Problem of Judaism,* 20).
Bibliography. Goldsmith, Emanuel S., Mel Scult, and Robert M Seltzer, eds., *The American Judaism of Mordecai M. Kaplan* (New York: New York University Press, 1990); Kaplan, M. M., *Judaism as A Civilization* (New York: Macmillan, 1934); Kaplan, M. M., *A New Approach to the Problem of Judaism* (New York: Society for the Advancement of Judaism, 1924); Libowitz, Richard, *Mordecai M. Kaplan and the Development of Reconstructionism* (Lewiston, NY: Edwin Mellen Press, 1983); Scult, Mel, *Judaism Faces the Twentieth Century: A Biography of Mordecai M. Kaplan* (Detroit: Wayne State University Press, 1993).

Robert L. VanDale

King, Martin Luther, Jr. Martin Luther King, Jr. (1929–1968), was born on January 15, 1929, in Atlanta, Georgia. He was a third-generation Baptist minister. His father and grandfather had been pastors of the renowned Ebenezer Baptist Church in Atlanta. Upon graduation from Morehouse College in 1948, he matriculated at Crozer Theological Seminary (1948–1951), where he was valedictorian and president of the student body. In 1955 he received a Ph.D. from Boston University. In 1954 he assumed the pastorate of Dexter Avenue Baptist Church* in Montgomery, Alabama. A year later he led the Montgomery bus boycott, which signaled the start of the modern civil rights* movement.
In 1985 Congress made Martin Luther King, Jr.,'s birthday, January 15th, a national holiday, placing King in a league with George Washington and Abraham Lincoln. His name and image have become ubiquitous, with his memory perpetuated in streets, buildings, and schools. However, most people are memorializing an early King without considering the major transition in his thought. For there was an early King who was an integrationist and assimilationist, but there also was a later King who leaned toward socialism and even Marxism.
There was a transition in King's thought after the March on Washington on August 28, 1963. Scholars like David J. Garrow have argued that at this time King moved "from reformer to revolutionary.'' He moved from the position of nonviolence and integration to Marxism, contending that society required a rad-

ical redistribution of economic and political power. King came to believe that the impending black revolution was forcing America to face its flaws of racism,* poverty, materialism, and militarism. In a similar manner, James H. Cone* has argued "that King has been earlier presented as one dimensional. He has been presented as an American hero who was attempting to reform whites." Instead, "King [has been] more a radical threat than a reassuring reformer." Likewise, J. Edgar Hoover and the Federal Bureau of Investigation saw this truth more so than did others. The bureau trailed King as he traveled the country, wiretapped his telephones, and planted information about his political and moral misconduct.

As an inexperienced black Baptist minister, obviously King needed professional help following the Montgomery bus boycott in 1956. So in organizing the Southern Christian Leadership Conference* in 1957, he surrounded himself with a group of northern advisors, including Stanley Levison, Bayard Rustin, and Jack O'Dell, who earlier had ties to the American Communist party. For this primary reason, they provided the impetus for Hoover to believe that the civil rights movement was Communist infiltrated. Ideologically, King continued to present himself as a somewhat naïve Baptist preacher, refusing to openly use the term "socialism" because it carried a negative meaning. According to Garrow, undoubtedly King also came to believe that President Kennedy and the Justice Department either would not or could not make integration work.

James H. Cone has argued that after Malcolm X's* assassination in 1965, King began to make a radical turn from his vision of the American dream. Instead, he saw the horrors of Malcolm X's "American nightmare." King's position was based upon the failure of whites to truly support integration. Likewise, the Vietnam War caused King to see America as one of the most violent nations in the world. In the light of Vietnam and the Watts Riot in Los Angeles, also in 1965, King realized that the problems in the United States were deeper than race; they were based upon class. So King called for democratic socialism as practiced in Scandinavia. He also saw white liberals as unwilling to eliminate poverty and redistribute wealth.

In King's transition, Cone also saw him moving toward Malcolm X. Each had experienced a transition bringing them closer to one another in thought. King moved in the direction of black nationalism, and Malcolm X in that of integration. But Michael Friedly has contended that although the FBI kept King and Malcolm X under surveillance, King was a greater national threat. He possessed a larger following and more mass support. As an activist, he caused more trouble in the South than Malcolm X ever caused in the North. Viewing King as the paramount threat to national security, the FBI only saw Malcolm X as someone to be studied.

Bibliography. Cone, J. H., *Martin and Malcolm and America* (Maryknoll, NY: Orbis Books, 1991); Fairclough, A., *Martin Luther King, Jr* (Athens: University of Georgia Press, 1995); Friedly, Michael, *Malcolm X: The Assassination* (New York: Carroll and

Graf, 1992); Garrow, D. J., *The FBI and Martin Luther King, Jr* (New York: Penguin, 1985).

Lawrence H. Williams

King James Only. In contrast to the traditional view of evangelicals and fundamentalists concerning the doctrines of inspiration and inerrancy of Scripture—that the Bible is verbally inspired throughout and is wholly without error in the original autographs—advocates of the King James Only position believe in the doctrine of "divine preservation"—that God has providentially preserved the very words of those "autographs" through copies, primarily the Masoretic Text for the Old Testament and the Textus Receptus for the New Testament. Since the 1611 King James Bible is the only version based solely on these two texts, it achieves, even through translation, the status of an inspired work. As one advocate put it, "The Textus Receptus is the verbally and plenarily *Inspired* Word of God and the King James Bible is the *Preserved* Word of God." All other translations since then, especially the Revised Version, the American Standard Version, and the New International Version, to name a few, rely on the Westcott-Hort text, a most "corrupt" text according to the King James Only proponents, the result of a "conspiracy" by an "Alexandrine Cult" of scholars opposed to inerrancy. (One King James Only group, the Dean Burgon Society, was formed in 1978 and took its name from the nineteenth-century Anglican dean who so vigorously opposed the Westcott-Hort text.) King James Only proponents argue that if the Bible is inspired and inerrant only "in the originals," then, since the originals are lost, the inspired, infallible Word no longer exists. However, the Psalmist says, "For ever, O LORD, Thy word is settled in heaven" (Psalms 119:89), and the Apostle Peter remarks that "the word of the Lord endureth for ever" (1 Peter 1:25). Thus, according to King James Only reasoning, God's very "words" must exist somewhere for man to read, even through copies and translations, and since the most "correct" copies are those associated with the Textus Receptus, then the King James Bible becomes the very inspired Word of God as well, for God's "words" (not just the meaning of his words) must reside somewhere, or else God is a liar. David Otis Fuller praises the King James Bible as the only translation without error, composed by the most godly and scholarly group of translators ever, based on the most accurate and authoritative texts, and occupying a position as the "lonestar of literature" for centuries.

King James Only advocates attach the doctrine of the verbal plenary inspiration of Scripture to the King James Bible itself, even to the italicized words inserted into the text by translators. According to Peter Ruckman, in many respects the "father" of the post-1970 King James Only movement, the English translation of the Authorized Version of 1611 *corrects* the original Greek and Hebrew. Any apparent discrepancies or errors in the King James Bible are merely the result of human ignorance on the part of scholars; such errors simply do not exist in the King James Bible. Ruckman and his followers (often called "Ruckmanites") are convinced that traditional views of inspiration are flawed when they hold that inspiration is essentially bound to the writer and his autograph, not the words of his text. If inspiration is with the original writer, then inspiration dies with him and his text. If it is tied to the words of the text, then inspiration lives as long as the words live. Thus they contend that God not only moved the original writers but has also continued to direct, or "inspire," the continued copying of the original texts and the subsequent translations, culminating in the King James Bible. The King James Only movement, though representing a minority within American fundamentalism,* has been a most vocal and divisive voice, with several associations, periodicals, and schools identifying exclusively with this doctrine.

Bibliography. Cimino, Dick, *The Book* (Harlingen, TX: Wonderful Word, 1975); Fuller, David Otis, "A Position Paper on the Versions of the Bible," *Flaming Torch*, June 1988, 1+; Fuller, David Otis, *True or False? The Westcott-Hort Textual Theory Examined* (Grand Rapids, MI: Grand Rapids International Publications, 1973); Fuller, David Otis, ed., *Which Bible?* (Grand Rapids, MI: Grand Rapids, International Publications, 1970); Hills, Edward F., *The King James Version Defended! A Christian View of the New Testament Manuscripts* (Des Moines, IA: Christian Research Press, 1956); Ruckman, Peter S., *The Christian's Handbook of Manuscript Evidence* (Pensacola, FL: Pensacola Bible Press, 1970).

Timothy D. Whelan

Know-Nothing Party. The Know-Nothing party was a political party that arose during the 1850s and was dedicated to restricting foreign immigration and discriminating against Roman Catholics, native-born or not. The heavy influx of Irish and German immigrants between 1830 and 1860, many of whom were Catholic, was the real basis for this party's growth. Also, since 1815 anti-Catholic sentiment had been growing in the United States. Thousands of books and tracts were published denouncing the dreaded influence of Romanism; some writers even viewed the whole immigrant influx as nothing more than a papal-directed attempt to undermine Protestantism and American liberty. By the 1840s there were scores of national anti-Catholic newspapers in circulation and a national organization, the American Protestant Society, formed in 1843, to alarm citizens to the Catholic menace. Controversies over Bible reading in the newly created public schools kept nativism* and anti-Catholicism alive during this era. During 1844, in two "Bible" riots in Philadelphia, directed mainly against the Catholic Irish, thirteen people were killed, more than fifty were wounded, and several Catholic churches were destroyed before peace was restored. Despite such hostilities, the number of foreigners entering the United States between 1845 and 1855 equaled roughly 10 percent of the existing population, the largest percentage of immigrants ever to enter this country. By 1850, when the U.S. census first asked citizens their religious affiliation, Catholics emerged as the nation's largest Christian denomination, due largely to foreign immigration.

Nativism first entered politics during the 1840s in local elections in Louisiana, New York, and Massachusetts, but these earlier efforts soon faded or voters moved into the national Whig party. The Know-Nothing party had its origins within a secret organization known as the Order of the Star Spangled Banner, founded by Charles B. Allen in 1849. The actual proceedings of this new order were hidden and members were sworn to secrecy, turning away all inquiries with the comment "I know nothing." This comment earned them their nickname, the "Know-Nothings." The order first entered politics indirectly in 1852 under its new leader, James W. Barker, who had its members vote against Catholics or foreigners for public office. By 1854 the group became a full-fledged political organization known as the American party, attacking both Catholics and immigrants. The historian of this movement maintains that the Know-Nothing party, as its enemies called it, was really more anti-Roman than nativistic, as it accepted certain Protestant immigrants into its ranks. "Only one force held members of the Know Nothing party together, and that was their hatred for the Catholic church."

During elections in 1854 and 1855 the new party made startling gains in various states. It won the governorships in Massachusetts and Delaware and control of the legislatures in Massachusetts, Connecticut, New Hampshire, Rhode Island, Maryland, Kentucky, and California. It also made strong showings in Louisiana, Virginia, and Tennessee. The party elected five U.S. senators and forty-three members of the U.S. House of Representatives. The gains for the American party in the South emerged after the Whig party died as members of that group sought another political vehicle to oppose their enemy, the Democrats. In the North, Know-Nothings did best where there were large pockets of Catholic immigrants, more in the Northeast than in the Midwest. In the Northwest, the newly created Republican party made greater gains with opposition to slave expansion in the West.

The American party eventually divided over the issue of slavery, failing to agree on the issue after 1855. It did run a presidential candidate, ex-President Millard Fillmore, a former Whig, together with Andrew Jackson Donelson, Old Hickory's nephew, as its vice-presidential candidate. (Ironically, Fillmore learned of his nomination after he had sought and obtained an audience with the pope during a European tour.) Fillmore gained about 22 percent of the popular vote in a three-way race for president and carried only Maryland in the electoral college. The party failed to accomplish any of its main objectives of restricting immigration and divesting Catholics of their civil and political rights. After its poor showing in the 1856 presidential election, the party quickly faded in power, but sentiment against Roman Catholics remained within a significant part of the American population well into the twentieth century.

Bibliography. Anbinder, Tyler, *Nativism and Slavery: The Northern Know Nothings and the Politics of the 1850s* (New York: Oxford University Press, 1992); Billington, Ray A., *The Protestant Crusade, 1800–1860: A Study of the Origins of American Nativism*

(New York: Macmillan, 1938); Overdyke, William D., *The Know-Nothing Party in the South* (Baton Rouge: Louisiana State University Press, 1950).

James M. Woods

Koinonia Farm. While a student at Southern Baptist Theological Seminary,* Clarence Jordan* had a dream of founding a farm in the South that would involve a fellowship of Christians committed to peace and brotherhood and to sharing their possessions in a common life. In the summer of 1942 he and his wife, Florence, joined their friends Mable and Martin England to found such a religious commune. The dream was incorporated as Koinonia Farm and was located on 440 acres of land eight miles southwest of Americus, Georgia, on Route 49. As the nation moved full swing into the war, Jordan and his friends started their experiment in reconciliation. From the start, the community was religious and interracial.

Opposition to their project was fairly immediate when it was learned that long-standing southern traditions were being broken, such as blacks and whites eating at the same table. Klu Klux Klan* (KKK) visits of intimidation began as well as the community being under the watchful eye of all who drove by. Soon, during the war years, the community also made less threatening contributions to the neighborhood such as improved egg production and peanut harvesting as well as a "cow library" loan system. During these years the Jordans and Englands were accepted members of the nearby Rehoboth Baptist Church.

By the close of the war Koinonia had grown in numbers as well as acreage, to 1,100 acres and then to 1,500. It was also at this time, however, that what the community was about received greater visibility. As a result, trouble with the surrounding community began to increase. The Supreme Court decision of 1954 in relation to school segregation also resulted in bitter southern feelings. In 1950 the Jordans and several other Koinonia members were dismissed from the membership of Rehoboth Baptist Church. At this time and for a decade, Koinonia paid a heavy price of persecution— physical, mental, psychological, social, and economic. In short, members were shot at, their buildings were burned, their lifestyle was ostracized, and economically they were boycotted. Night riders of the KKK made open war on the community. That it survived this kind of sustained attack is nothing short of miraculous. After several years the violence subsided and the community set itself to the task of internal development. During the boycott period Koinonia established a mail-order business for fruitcakes and certain pecan products in order to sustain itself economically.

In 1956 Koinonia numbered sixty persons (fifteen were African Americans), but within ten years the number had dwindled to two families. Jordan thought that the community might be facing the end of its road. It was at this time that another of his gifts surfaced in his Cotton Patch Version of the New Testament Scripture project. These "red-clay" English translations brought visibility and needed economics into the community. Koinonia was humming with life again.

In 1968 Jordan and the millionaire Millard Fuller reincorporated Koinonia Farm into Koinonia Partners with major thrusts in communication, instruction, and application. The last thrust involved partnership industries, farming, and housing. Despite the sudden death of Clarence Jordan in 1969, the community has flourished. Its low-cost, interest-free building program (as of now, more than 185 houses) brought new life to Koinonia. By the 1970s there were over thirty-six members and numerous visitors. In 1976 Millard Fuller and his wife left the community in order to found Habitat for Humanity International, now with extensive national and international visibility. Thousands of houses around the world have been built for the poor by Habitat.

Koinonia itself has survived and now flourishes with farming, food-processing industry, low-cost housing, a child-development center, and an outreach program providing paralegal assistance, counseling, care of foster children, and visitation of prisons. Any surplus funds that come into Koinonia go directly into a fund to meet other human needs. Surviving controversy and criticism, Koinonia has continued to speak a prophetic word with courage and to minister to a needy world.

Bibliography. Barnette, Henlee H., *Clarence Jordan* (Macon: Smyth and Helwys, 1992); Jordan, Clarence, *The Cotton Patch Version of Paul's Epistles* (New York: Association Press, 1968); Lee, Dallas, *The Cotton Patch Evidence* (New York: Harper and Row, 1971).

George H. Shriver

Ku Klux Klan. The Ku Klux Klan (KKK) was founded in 1866 in the South as an organization of terror to affirm white supremacy, stop black voting, and curtail Republican political power. After waning in influence, it was revitalized as a fraternal lodge in 1915 by a former Methodist minister, William J. Simmons. Anti-Semitism and anti-Catholicism joined white supremacy as central tenets of the movement.

The KKK found adherents throughout the United States, but its strength was in the Midwest and the South. While it declined in the 1930s and 1940s, the KKK received much publicity for its bombing of Jewish synagogues and African-American churches in the civil rights* era. As the organization developed, the KKK fragmented. While still holding to anti-Semitism and white supremacy, some KKK groups now include Catholics as well as Protestants.

Originally portrayed as a militant defender of an Anglo-Saxon national Protestantism, the KKK supported traditional values of school prayer,* prohibition, law and order, and patriotism through the use of vigilante violence. A fraternal order known for the secrecy of the masked hood, the KKK uses religious symbols, including the Bible (for its white supremacy stance) and a flaming cross that symbolizes "Christ as the Light of the World."

Historians regard the KKK as a part of a larger American nativism* that feared foreigners (immigrants) and nonwhites. The American public has reputed the KKK as a group of white-hooded cross-burning men that represents a violent expression of racism and unhealthy religion.

Bibliography. Chalmers, David, *Hooded Americanism* (Garden City, NY: Doubleday, 1968); Horn, S. F., *Invisible Empire: The Story of the Ku Klux Klan* (Boston: Houghton Mifflin Company, 1939); Lester, John C., *Ku Klux Klan, Its Origin, Growth, and Disbandment* (St. Clair Shores, MI: Scholarly Press, 1972).

Douglas Weaver

L

Landmarkism. A movement that traced Baptist origins to the first century and the claim that Baptists* represented the only true church, Old Landmarkism, as it was originally known, created controversy among Baptist groups, particularly in the South. The name was taken from Proverbs 22:28, ''Remove not the ancient landmark which thy fathers have set.'' While the movement began in the 1840s, it gained momentum in 1854 with a question raised by J. M. Pendleton (1811–1891), pastor of First Baptist Church, Bowling Green, Kentucky. Pendleton authored a brief treatise that asked whether Baptists could permit pedobaptists (infant baptizers) to preach in Baptist churches. The treatise was published by J. R. Graves (1820–1893), editor of the *Tennessee Baptist*, under the title *An Old Landmark Re-set*. Graves, Pendleton, and Mississippi layman and former Presbyterian A. C. Dayton were the most prominent leaders of the early Landmark movement.

The Landmarkers believed that Baptist churches alone could trace their lineage through a succession of dissenting churches all the way back to Jesus' own baptism by John the Baptist. They insisted that only Baptist congregations retained the marks of the true church. These included the following: (1) Baptist churches are the only true churches. All other groups are simply ''societies'' of Christians. (2) The true church is found only in local congregations. The New Testament knew no idea of the universal church. (3) Local churches are synonymous with the kingdom of God. (4) Non-Baptist ministers should not be permitted to participate in ''pulpit-affiliation'' with Baptists. (5) Only an organized church can perform the actions of the church. Since Baptists have the only true baptism, all other baptisms were invalid. Landmarks rejected infant baptism* and even refused to accept "alien immersion,"* immersion baptism by any group other than Baptists. Likewise, the Lord's Supper was a "close (or closed) Communion" given only to members of the specific congregation in which it was observed. (6) Baptist churches represent an unbroken succession from apostolic times to the present. Many Landmark adherents pointed to various dissenting sects, including Anabaptists, Cathari, Waldensians, Paulicians, Donatists, and Montanists, as "Baptist in everything but name" throughout the history of the church. Texas preacher J. M. Carroll published a tract entitled *The Trail of Blood* that detailed the Baptist legacy through persecuted sects in Christian history.

Controversy developed as Landmark supporters sought to impose their doctrines on Baptist churches throughout the South, with particular intensity from 1857 to 1859. The movement endures in certain independent fundamentalist Baptist churches and fellowships. Landmark questions continue to influence baptismal and membership policies in Southern Baptist churches.

Bibliography. Graves, J. R., *Old Landmarkism: What Is It?* (Memphis: Baptist Book House, 1880); McBeth, H. L., *The Baptist Heritage* (Nashville: Broadman Press, 1987); Patterson, W. M., *Baptist Successionism: A Critical View* (Valley Forge, PA: Judson Press, 1969); Pendleton, J. M., *An Old Landmark Re-set* (Nashville: Southwestern Publishing House, 1857); Tull, J. E., "A Study of Southern Baptist Landmarkism in the Light of Historical Baptist Ecclesiology" (Ph.D. diss., Columbia University, 1960).

Bill J. Leonard

Lane Seminary. When Presbyterians founded Lane Seminary in 1830 in Cincinnati, the enterprise looked almost hopeless. Despite a significant gift of real estate, the school lacked such amenities as buildings, books, and faculty. The trustees were desperate to find a way to finance their nascent institution. This caused them to look to the prosperous East for support. The trustees' eastern strategy had three separate, but related, goals. First, they wanted to attract a strong student body. The trustees believed that Theodore Weld,* a student at the Oneida Manual Labor Institute and already an important antislavery leader, would attract others. Second, they wanted to gain the support of Arthur and Lewis Tappan. The Tappans were wealthy New York businessmen who passionately believed in social reform and evangelism. They were among Charles Finney's* strongest supporters, and they already knew Weld's work as an antislavery activist. When Weld agreed to attend Lane, the Tappans paid his expenses along with the expenses of the other Oneida students who transferred to the new school. Third, the trustees, led by their agent Franklin Vail, wanted to attract a minister with an already-established reputation to the school. After much consultation, Vail recommended Lyman Beecher.* Beecher was then at the height of his powers. In addition to the pastorate of the influential (and wealthy) Hanover Street Church in Boston, he was noted for his support of missions, voluntary societies, and Christian education. Beecher agreed to become president of the school as soon as he could put his Boston affairs in order.

He also planned to spend some time before moving west establishing a network of wealthy supporters. Interestingly enough, Beecher also accepted the pastorate of Cincinnati's Second Presbyterian Church. Both church and school expected him to serve concurrently. When the trustees attained these three goals, Lane's future as a center of education, social reform, and Christian education seemed secure.

The great promise of the school was never to be realized. Almost from the moment its dynamic president arrived in the Queen City, the school was deep in a series of controversies. Theodore Weld was absolutely committed to anti-slavery, and Cincinnati's location on the Kentucky border was an ideal base for an attack on the enemy. Further, Weld believed that immediate abolition was an issue of conscience. For the fiery young abolitionist, slavery was a sin. Hence Christian institutions were called to renounce slavery just as they were called to renounce other evils.

Lyman Beecher was also concerned with the slavery issue. He was a long-time supporter of the American Colonization Society and believed that the United States needed to wean itself gradually from the slave system. Like other northern evangelists, Beecher saw the revivals of his day as the beginning of the end of many national evils. In time the impact of the revival would end slavery just as it would end drunkenness, prostitution, and ignorance.

In 1834 Weld and his student allies asked Beecher for a public debate on the issue of abolition. Although Beecher had some reservations about the time of the debate, he accepted the students' invitation. For some eighteen days the two sides debated the issue. When the discussion had ended, few positions had changed. Beecher was still supporting gradual emancipation; the students were still for immediate abolition.

The whole affair might have ended there, but the students established an active ministry among the city's free black population that included evening reading classes and three Sunday schools. They also had elaborate plans for an African American ''Female School'' and a circulating library. This attracted much hostile attention. Cincinnati was a deeply prejudiced, even racist, city. Earlier the city had tried to ban African Americans from residence. Failing in that, many residents were committed to a strict policy of racial segregation. Perhaps many in the city and on the Board of Trustees might have accepted the schools for African Americans, but the insistence of the students on visiting African Americans in their homes was one step beyond their tolerance. Although the students apparently were not as socially liberal as many believed, the common report was that they often walked with young African American women and that they frequently called on such young ladies by sending their personal cards. As often happened in antebellum America, the combination of race and sexuality led many ''gentlemen of property and standing'' to talk loudly about a violent attack on the seminary. Mobs could act where individuals and courts could not.

Beecher did not understand the potentially dangerous situation in the city. In the midst of the debate over the African-American mission, Beecher went east for the meetings of the missionary societies and to raise money for his school. He believed that the situation was in hand. During his absence the Board of Trustees ordered the students to end their ministry. When the president returned, the battle was joined. The students sent a note to the president and faculty demanding an explanation of the trustees' action. When the explanation did not satisfy them, the majority of the students withdrew. Only five out of forty students remained in the theology department and only five of sixty in the preparatory department. Apparently, many prospective students decided not to apply. The Tappans, who supported the students in this battle, agreed to finance Charles Finney's move to Oberlin College as professor of Theology, and they agreed to support the students at that school. In 1837 the Tappans discontinued all support of Lane, despite the fact that they had guaranteed Beecher's salary as president.

In addition, there was a battle over Beecher's own theology. Lyman Beecher was a convinced supporter of the revival who earnestly believed that Protestant activism would transform the United States into something like the Kingdom of God. Although he had some interest in theology, Beecher was not a contemplative or deep thinker. For Beecher, it was more important to overcome evil than to determine its exact nature. Beecher's concern with the needs of society led him close to a de facto secularization.

Conservative Presbyterians had a clear majority among the Ohio River Valley churches, although not in the city of Cincinnati itself. These later Old School leaders were suspicious of Beecher from the beginning. Beecher was from New England and was a Congregationalist. He became a Presbyterian through the Plan of Union, an 1801 agreement between Connecticut Congregationalists and the Presbyterian Church that allowed western ministers to be called from either denomination and that granted them standing in both denominations. Perhaps foolishly, Beecher did not present himself initially to the Presbytery of Cincinnati. Instead, he made his formal entry into the Presbyterian Church through the Third Presbytery of New York City, a body already suspect to the conservatives. The enmity of the surrounding ministers eventually led to formal charges of heresy in 1835. Although the Cincinnati Presbyterians acquitted Beecher, his accusers appealed to the General Assembly. In 1836, however, the revival party still had a clear majority. The charges were withdrawn, although the accusers were far from satisfied.

The effects on Lane were nonetheless devastating. Beecher's school had lost standing with the local churches. When the Presbyterians divided into Old and New School denominations in 1837–1838, Lane became a New School enclave in the midst of what was almost solidly Old School territory. Further, the split of the denomination did not end the dispute. Lane's identification with the New School was a continuing source of controversy. The Kemper family who had donated the original land for the school belonged to the Old School, and they wanted their investment returned. From 1842 to 1848 the Kempers repeatedly brought suit either to have the funds returned to them or the present faculty expelled from the premises. Since the Ohio laws concerning trusts established the trustees as sole owners, the Kempers lost their suits, but the legal actions drained the resources and energies of the school. Although Lane continued to attract some able faculty, the school never completely recovered from its early history.

Bibliography. Fraser, James, *Pedagogue for God's Kingdom: Lyman Beecher and the Second Great Awakening* (Boston: University Press of America, 1985); Henry, Stuart, *Unvanquished Puritan: A Portrait of Lyman Beecher* (Grand Rapids, MI: Eerdmans, 1973); Snyder, Stephen, *Lyman Beecher and His Children: The Transformation of a Religious Tradition* (Brooklyn: Carlson Publishing Company, 1991).

Glenn Miller

The Last Temptation of Christ. On August 12, 1988, Universal Pictures released Martin Scorsese's *The Last Temptation of Christ.* Never before had a film opened in the face of such controversy. Christians across the denominational spectrum joined in denouncing the film. Bill Bright of Campus Crusade offered to pay for the movie if the studio would turn the film over to him.

These protests should have surprised no one. The film was based on a 1955 book by Nikos Kazantzakis that was also subject to attack—vilification by the Greek Orthodox Church; a place on the Catholic Index of Forbidden Books; censorship efforts by conservative Christians in the United States. Most critics of the book and the movie echoed the same complaint: *The Last Temptation* was blasphemous, distorting the Gospels and the Jesus they portray.

Yet neither the book nor the movie claim to be an accurate historical reconstruction of Jesus of Nazareth. In the preface to the book, with which the movie begins, Kazantzakis explained the point of the work: to use the symbol of Jesus, within the context of fiction, to explore the conflict of spirit and flesh. The movie is an effective exploration: it lays bare what a real struggle between spirit and flesh looks like.

The real achievement of the movie is, in fact, its "look." Christians tend to make up a Jesus that looks like them. If one runs the gamut of American-made films about Jesus, one quickly recognizes this truth—Jeffrey Hunter's Jesus in *King of Kings,* for example, both looks and acts the way Americans expect.

Willem Dafoe as Jesus in *The Last Temptation* is not the generally recognizable American Jesus. His image is a dark one: he struggles with God's call and fights against his destiny. He is scared of the prospect of what the future holds. That he might be God's son comes to him slowly, and he fights the idea. He is so wracked by his inward struggle that the look of ambiguity is practically stamped on his face. If the face of Jesus painted by Warner Sallman (*Head of Christ,* 1941) is the most beloved picture of Jesus in America, a face of complete serenity and calm power, no wonder the look of Jesus in *The Last Temptation* stirred such controversy. It is an unfamiliar face.

The most controversial part of the film has to do with the last temptation of Christ: the temptation to come down from the cross and lead a normal, happy life. In this sequence Satan, disguised as a young girl who claims to be Jesus' guardian angel, convinces Jesus that he is not the Messiah, that he does not have to suffer and die, and that God is found in the happy routines of everyday life. Jesus marries Mary Magdalene, who dies. He next marries Mary of Bethsaida, but also fathers children with her sister Martha. He works at carpentry, plays with his children, and laughs. At the end of Jesus' life, Judas—his friend and confidante throughout the film—reveals Satan's subterfuge and convinces Jesus to return to the cross. Jesus accepts his messiahship, takes on death, and fulfills his destiny. The last temptation—to lead a happy life rather than die for God's cause—is overcome.

Though a few scenes constituted the core of criticism of the film—Jesus' sexual relations, for example—the entire film is, in fact, a protest against both what Americans value most for themselves and the predominantly held image of Jesus that sanctions what Americans value. *The Last Temptation of Christ* attacks the American cult of happiness, a cult comfortable with the easy capitulation of the spirit to the concerns of the flesh. *The Last Temptation* has a "hard" look for any who would like to see Christianity conform to that cult.

Moreover, *The Last Temptation* presents an image of Jesus that reckons with human nature in its full ambiguity. A 1986 Gallup Poll book, *Who Do Americans Say That I Am?*, discovered that Americans see Jesus most strongly in images that reflect traditional notions of divinity. The most profound implication of the religious controversy surrounding this film may be the way it confronts traditional Christianity with an affirmation of Christ's full humanity—to see in Christ not just a God who smiles benignly on American life but also a man who struggles with temptation and who, as a man, ultimately chooses the side of spirit over flesh, responsibility over happiness, suffering over the good life. In other words, the film's most controversial aspect is its look of indictment, using Christianity's central symbol to focus that powerful—and uncomfortable—look.

Bibliography. Babington, Bruce, "From Main Street to Mean Streets: Martin Scorsese's The Last Temptation of Christ (1988)," in *Biblical Epics: Sacred Narrative in the Hollywood Cinema* (New York: St. Martin's Press, 1993); Bien, Peter, "Scorsese's Spiritual Jesus," *New York Times*, August 11, 1988; Keyser, Lester J., "The Last Temptation of Christ (1988)," in *Martin Scorsese* (New York: Twayne, 1992).

Thomas J. Davis

Leland, John. John Leland (1754–1841) was a fiercely independent thinker among Baptists* during the founding period of American history. Some of the controversies in which he played a part involved matters of Baptist ecclesiology—the "laying on of hands" during ordination, associational cooperation and centralization, the union of Regular and Separate Baptists,* his reluctance to observe the Lord's Supper, and his negative views regarding missionary funding. The controversial issue that most engaged his best efforts, however, was the struggle for religious liberty* and disestablishment in Virginia and New England.

Largely self-educated, Leland served a number of churches in Virginia from 1776 until his departure in 1791, a period that marked the shift from religious persecution to the passage of Jefferson's Act for Establishing Religious Freedom in 1786. The Baptists in Virginia were the first to send petitions to the House of Burgesses regarding religious liberty, and Leland emerged as their most insistent spokesman. Contending that religious liberty is a "right and not a favor," he further asserted that "Government has no more to do with the religious opinions of men than it has to do with the principles of mathematicks" ("The Rights of Conscience Inalienable," in *The Writings of the Late Elder John Leland*, 13).

Convinced that the new federal Constitution did not make sufficient provision for the guarantee of religious liberty, Leland and the Virginia Baptists determined to oppose its passage. Whether by effective communication of his concerns to James Madison or an actual meeting, as alleged, Madison's intention to offer a "bill of rights" to be added later led to Leland's support and Virginia's and the nation's ratification of the Constitution. Contained in Madison's papers in the Library of Congress is a document entitled "Leland's Objections to the Constitution."

Just before leaving Virginia in 1791, Leland obtained passage by Virginia Baptists of a resolution denouncing slavery as a "violent deprivation of the rights of nature" and urged the removal of this "horrid evil from the land" (Greene, "Further Sketches," in *The Writings of the Late John Leland*, 51). Leland spent the remainder of his life in New England involved in the disestablishment of the Congregational Church in Connecticut and Massachusetts.

A mammoth, 1,235-pound cheese was presented to the newly elected president, Thomas Jefferson, by Leland, a gift from his Cheshire, Massachusetts, congregation. A lifelong Jeffersonian Democrat, Leland held views on church-state neutrality that were principled and consistent. He opposed the payment of military chaplains with government funds as "unconstitutional, inconsistent with religious liberty, and unnecessary" ("The Virginia Chronicle," in *The Writings of the Late John Leland*, 119). He also rejected legal enforcement of the Sabbath and temperance legislation and maintained that mail delivery on Sunday should be allowed since its prohibition on Saturday could be equally argued on religious grounds.

Leland is sometimes confused with the English John Leland, noted for a two-volume work on Deism. Leland's collected writings contain mostly sermons and tracts on liberty of conscience. As his requested epitaph states, he is most remembered for his efforts "to promote piety and vindicate the civil and religious rights of all men'' (*Some Events in the Life of John Leland, Written by Himself,* in *The Writings of the Late Elder John Leland,* 38). **Bibliography.** Butterfield, L. H., *Elder John Leland, Jeffersonian Itinerant* (Worcester, MA: Davis Press, 1953); Cochran, Bernard H. ''An Examination of the Influence of John Leland (1754–1841) on Baptist Life and Thought'' (Th.M. thesis, Southeastern Baptist Theological Seminary, 1957); Dawson, J. M., *Baptists and the American Republic* (Nashville: Broadman Press, 1956); Gewehr, Wesley M., *The Great Awakening in Virginia, 1740–1790* (Durham: Duke University Press, 1930); Leland, John, *The Writings of the Late Elder John Leland,* ed. Miss L. F. Greene. (New York: G.W. Wood, 1845).

Bernard H. Cochran

Liberalism. Liberalism was a movement that began in late-nineteenth-century American Protestant theology and lasted until the mid-twentieth century, when it was superseded by Neo-Orthodoxy.* It was influenced by parallel movements in Britain and on the Continent and, while there were liberal tendencies that emerged in American Catholicism, was essentially a Protestant phenomenon.

While a beginning date is difficult to pinpoint with exact precision, 1881 seems accurate enough. Unquestionably the chief precursor of the liberal movement was Horace Bushnell,* though his early response to Darwinian evolution was an alarmed and negative one. One of the earliest statements regarding an emerging self-conscious liberal theological movement came from Lewis French Stearns. In 1881 in his inaugural address as professor of theology at Bangor Theological Seminary, entitled ''Reconstruction in Theology,'' he declared:

> I believe that a new theology is coming, better and fuller of truth than the old, certainly better adapted to our times. But the truth which it will express will be the unchanging truth of the ages, the truth of the Bible, the truth of Jesus Christ. . . . We want to rescue that grand old word, liberality . . . and restore it in its true meaning to the theology of our age. (*New Englander* 41, [January 1882], 101)

A primary concern of the earliest liberal theologians was to make clear that the ''New Theology'' had not abandoned all that was central in the old; it was merely recasting it in a new mold. Newman Smyth, observing a burned-out church being rebuilt, discovered in the image of workmen stripping away the charred, weakened timbers of the old structure and building on the solid remaining foundation an analogy for the intention of liberalism. The title of his work, *Old Faiths in New Light,* clearly described the liberal agenda. For this reason the early phase of liberalism was called at various times ''Progressive Orthodoxy,'' ''the New Orthodoxy,'' ''Modern Orthodoxy,'' ''Real Theology,'' ''the New Theology,'' ''Liberal Evangelicalism,'' ''Evangelical Liberalism,'' and ''Modern Liberalism.''

An important distinction must be made between the more moderate Evangelical Liberals and the more radical Modernistic Liberals. Evangelical Liberalism included theologians such as the ''Andover Liberals,'' William Newton

Clarke,* Walter Rauschenbusch,* Lewis French Stearns, Harry Emerson Fosdick,* Charles A. Briggs,* William Adams Brown, and others. Modernistic Liberalism included the "Chicago School" and representatives such as Shailer Mathews, D. C. Macintosh, and Henry Nelson Wieman. Whatever its form, liberalism represented an attempt to reexamine and restate the Christian faith in response to the new scientific, historical, and biblical truth that could not be denied. It was the resistance of fundamentalism* to such assumed accommodation and acculturation that led to its bitter and unrelenting opposition. Charges of heresy and, in some denominations, actual heresy trials were not uncommon.

The regnant theological perspective in the late nineteenth century that liberalism attempted to modify has been generically termed Traditional Orthodoxy, the view of most mainline Protestant traditions. It was characterized by biblical literalism, an emphasis on the transcendence of God, an acceptance of the traditional view of original sin ("In Adam's fall, we sinned all"), an individualistic view of the nature of sin, and an "otherworldly" understanding of the church's mission.

The forces that shaped liberal theology came from a variety of directions. Continental theology, especially the influence of Friedrich Schleiermacher and Albrecht Ritschl, was pivotal. The emergence of biblical criticism significantly altered the traditional understanding of biblical revelation. Finally, the inescapability of Darwinian evolution challenged prior notions of creation based on a literal understanding of the Genesis account.

The central emphases of liberalism included the following: (1) the acceptance of the historical-critical method of biblical interpretation, which resulted in a view of Scripture as both a divine and human creation; (2) the acceptance of evolutionary thought, which led to an emphasis on the immanence of God in nature and in human personality; (3) a Christocentric emphasis that affirmed that God is like Christ and that all theological statements are to be judged by the highest revelation, namely, Jesus; (4) the repudiation of the doctrine of original sin, especially imputed guilt, since the historicity of the Genesis account of creation was called into question; (5) the development of a naïve optimism in much liberal thinking regarding human personality and its potential for God-likeness; (6) a shift in attitudes toward non-Christian religions from militant opposition to an acceptance of shared truths, with Christianity seen as perhaps the highest "evolved" religion; and (7) the emergence of the Social Gospel under the leadership of Rauschenbusch and others that resulted from the liberal understanding that God's kingdom is to come "on earth as it is in heaven."

Opposition to liberalism was twofold. The extreme reaction took the name fundamentalism from its reduction of the irreducible, nonnegotiable essence of the Christian faith to its five "fundamentals." The resultant conflict split most mainline Protestant denominations into warring camps; fundamentalists, with the exception of Southern Baptists a generation later, came off second best. Neo-Orthodoxy represented an attempt to counter perceived liberal extremes, especially its optimistic view of human nature and its shallow view of sin. While liberalism may be said to have expired by the mid-twentieth century, many of its emphases have been significant and enduring.

Bibliography. Cauthen, Kenneth, *The Impact of American Religious Liberalism* (New York: Harper and Row, 1962); Dillenberger, John and Claude Welch, *Protestant Christianity* (New York: Macmillan, 1988); Hutchinson, William R., ed., *American Protestant Thought: The Liberal Era* (New York: Harper Torchbooks, 1968); Williams, D. D., *The Andover Liberals* (New York: King's Crown Press, 1941).

Bernard H. Cochran

Liberation Theology. Liberation theology, a discrete branch of contemporary constructive theology, grew from the initial proposals of theologians in the 1960s and, despite severe warnings by Pope John Paul II, remains a significant voice as the century comes to a close. Its context of origin was (and remains) the crushing poverty and experience of marginalization experienced by countless millions of people. Hence it is a systematic interpretation of Christian faith out of the experience of the poor. Fostered initially in Latin America among Roman Catholic Christians, both clergy and lay, liberation theology has become an umbrella term for any contextual theology that seeks advocacy for those oppressed by racial, economic, political, sexual, or ecclesiastical structures. Thus black theology,* feminist/womanist/mujerista theology, Native American theology, and Third World theologies could all be considered forms or accents of liberation theology.

The signal text charting the direction of liberation theology is usually considered to be Gustavo Gutierrez's *A Theology of Liberation* (1973). Other influential texts that have helped shape the methodology of liberation theology are Paulo Freire's *Pedagogy of the Oppressed* (1970), Mary Daly's* *Beyond God the Father: Toward a Philosophy of Women's Liberation* (1973), and Gayraud Wilmore and James Cone's* *Black Theology: A Documentary History, 1966–1979* (1979).

Although the concerns of the groups being addressed differ, there are some commonalities in the methodological approach of liberation theologians. Each attempts to construct theology as an interpretation of Christian self-understanding out of suffering, struggle, and hope; each offers a critique of society and the ideologies sustaining it; and each contributes a critique of the activity of the church and of Christians from the angle of the marginated constituency for which the theologian advocates.

Two sources in particular provide critical coordinates for liberation theology: the Bible, especially as it is read by the poor; and Marxism, as critically engaged by Latin American theologians. The Bible as taught and learned within basic Christian communities is a relevant and revolutionary document as their hermeneutical engagement evokes the Bible's profound liberating tradition. Central themes suffuse liberation theology: the Exodus, where God attends to the cry of the people and acts in their behalf; the ministry of Jesus, "bringing glad tidings to the poor . . . and liberty to the captives"; and the stories of the early church in which Christian communities shared their goods and no one was poor. The prophets' denouncement of corrupt religion that ignores the poverty-stricken also receives significant attention. The reality of suffering as predicted by Jesus and endured by the early Christian communities resonates with the contemporary experience of those in the liberation movement.

American and European critics have attempted to dismiss the significance of liberation theology because of its conversation with Marxism. Indeed, it would be very hard to construct theology in the Latin American context without some measure of engagement because the culture is rife with its influence. Liberation theologians have attended to the questions posed by the Marxist analysis and program for social change without appropriating the whole ideology. The level of engagement differs with respect to geographical distinctions and theological perspectives. Important to note is the caution with which these theologians assess the Marxist contribution to the groaning need of marginated and oppressed persons.

The most systematic attack on liberation theology, beginning around 1972, has come from within the Catholic Church. Theologians have been silenced by the Roman curia; their constructive methods have been condemned as being too concerned with the transformation of the present concrete situation of the poor rather than seeking their spiritual salvation. The resistance of the church's hierarchy points to a high level of discomfort at having the plight of oppressed people as the starting point for theological praxis.

Key manifestations of the approach of liberation theology are the Christian base communities (a new model of church), a movement from experience to theology, and a critical vision of human rights. The durability of these concerns suggests that the agenda of liberation theology will continue as a significant force in constructive theology.

Bibliography. Berryman, Phillip, *Liberation Theology* (Bloomington, IN: Meyer/Stone Books, 1987); Boff, Leonardo, *When Theology Listens to the Poor* (San Francisco: Harper and Row, 1988); Sobrino, Jon, *The True Church and the Poor* (Maryknoll, NY: Orbis Books, 1984).

Molly Marshall

Lubavitch. Lubavitch is the designation given to the community (''court'') within Hasidic Judaism tracing its immediate roots to the town of Lubavitch (Lyubavichi) in Belorussia in the early nineteenth century. The name preferred by adherents of this court of Hasidic Judaism is Habad (Chabad), an acronym derived from *Hokhmah, Binah, Da'at*—wisdom, understanding, and knowledge—by the first Chabad-Lubavitcher Rebbe, Rabbi Shneur Zalman of Ladi (1745–1813). In 1940 the sixth Lubavitcher Rebbe, Rabbi Joseph Isaac (Yosef Yitzchak) Schneersohn (1880–1950), moved to the United States, and the Crown Heights section of Brooklyn became the center for the court's worldwide efforts. The very nature of Habad or Lubavitcher Hasidism means that the story of the Habad court in the United States is henceforth intertwined with stories of their sixth Rebbe and his son-in-law, Rabbi Menachem Mendel Schneerson (1902–1994), who became the seventh Lubavitcher Rebbe in 1950.

Controversy has surrounded the Lubavitch court from its beginning. To understand the nature and the implications of these controversies, one should study the history of controversy surrounding the Hasidic movements overall—a task beyond the scope of this entry. The foci of the controversy, however, are theological, liturgical, and practical.

Theologically, Habad's mystical approach, reflecting the Kabbala, challenged much of Orthodox Judaism from the outset. The emphasis on God as the only reality flew in the face of the major views within Judaism. The Jewish (especially the Orthodox) traditions relating to mysticism and daily observance of the commandments of Torah vis-à-vis Habad are perhaps best captured in this summary statement by a recent student of the Hasidic movements in the United States:

> Despite their metaphysical bent, Lubavitch programs stress the application of what is commonplace for all Orthodox Jews: to observe the Shabbes [Sabbath], eat only kosher food, put on tifillin daily, educate their children in Jewish law and custom, pray daily, attach a mezuzah to their doorpost, keep a charity coin box, bring prayer books into their homes, and so on through the 613 mitzvot, commandments of the Torah. Underlying Chabad actions is the view that wholesale return by the Jewish community to their religious roots is a necessary requirement for the arrival of the Messiah and the redemption of the Jews. (Mintz, 50)

Some of the key issues separating the Lubavitch court from other Hasidic courts are the degree and form of support for the nation of Israel; openness to Jews (and even non-Jews) outside of their own court while engaging in efforts to reclaim other Jews; remaining distinct from non-Jewish ways while being open to some aspects of contemporary styles of dress; and a variety of behavior codes, especially vis-à-vis the Satmar and M'lochim courts. Another source of tension within Judaism surrounds the Lubavitch community's style of being Hasidic centers in the "campaigns" initiated under the seventh Rebbe. These campaigns, especially as they involve the "Army of God" (*Tzivos HaShem*), seek to "reclaim" (many observers describe this as proselytizing, which Judaism in general tends to reject) non-Hasidic Jews (and even, at times, other Hasidic Jews). The goal of these campaigns is to get Jews worldwide to observe the 613 mitzvot by introducing one mitzvah at a time. The campaigns are a practical expression of the Habad messianic vision, whereby doing the mitzvot will bring the Messiah and usher in the "Kingdom of G-d" (*sic*; this way of writing The Name preserves the sense of awe, the realization that G-d is "above and beyond all words"). At the heart of the campaigns is the effort to give expression to the mitzvah "Love your fellow as yourself," with the primary focus on love for fellow Jews by bringing them into the joy of observing the mitzvot.

Controversy has also been present within the Habad community, especially with regard to the selection of the successor to the seventh Rebbe. That controversy found expression through U.S. courts in a case surrounding the library of earlier Rebbes.

Bibliography. In addition to helpful introductory articles in *New Encyclopaedia of Religion* (Macmillan) and *Encyclopaedia Judaica* (Jerusalem, NY: Macmillan, 1971–72), recent helpful works include the following: Jacobson, Simon, *Toward a Meaningful Life: The Wisdom of the Rebbe* (New York: William Morrow and Co., 1995); Mintz, Jerome R., *Hasidic People: A Place in the New World* (Cambridge: Harvard University Press, 1992).

Robert L. VanDale

Lundy, Mary Ann Weese. A native of West Virginia and an ordained elder in the Presbyterian Church (USA), Mary Ann Lundy was born in 1932 and graduated from West Virginia University (1954) and New York's Union Theological Seminary* (1957). Lundy has served as a public school teacher (1958– 1966) and a campus minister (1972–1980) and in various executive positions for the Presbytery of the Twin Cities (1981–1982), the National Student YWCA (1982–1987), the national offices of the Presbyterian Church (USA) (1987– 1994), and the World Council of Churches (1995–). She twice appeared at the center of national controversies, once as a supporter of the Sanctuary movement in 1986, and later as a key organizer of the 1993 Re-Imagining Conference.

Lundy became involved in the Sanctuary movement soon after her husband was installed as pastor of St. Luke's Presbyterian Church in affluent Wayzata, Minnesota, in 1980. On March 24, 1982, the second anniversary of Archbishop Oscar Romero's assassination in El Salvador, the Reverend John Fife announced that his Southside Presbyterian Church and several other congregations around the country had declared themselves "sanctuaries" for Central American refugees. Fife cited United Nations policy, U.S. and international law, and Jesus' own example to support this open challenge to the asylum policy of the Immigration and Naturalization Service. Fife addressed Lundy's church in May, and by the end of 1982 St. Luke's became one of fifteen self-declared sanctuary churches nationwide when it harbored refugee René Hurtado.

When Lundy became director of the National Student YWCA in New York City that September, she took her concern for the Sanctuary movement with her. She quickly established a regional coalition on sanctuary and became co-chair of the Sanctuary Committee at New York City's Riverside Church, the city's only sanctuary church. Lundy was among more than sixty unindicted coconspirators cited in the Tucson trial of Fife and several of his coworkers, and she and two other American religious leaders were summoned to testify for the prosecution as hostile witnesses. All three religious activists appeared before the court on February 18, 1986, and refused to testify. When Lundy told the court, "I choose not to testify on the basis of my First Amendment right to freedom of religion and invoke my privilege as a Presbyterian Elder not to speak against my community of faith," the courtroom rose in sympathetic silent protest. Judge Earl Carroll placed all three leaders under house arrest, and Lundy was confined to her Wayzata home until the trial ended on March 15. She received over four hundred letters of support, including a blocklong scroll of personal prayers signed by members of Riverside Church.

In 1987 Lundy became director of the Women's Ministry Unit of the Presbyterian Church (USA). After her unit submitted several suggestions for a churchwide capital campaign, the General Assembly Council approved its proposal for a women's theological colloquium in conjunction with the World Council of Churches' Ecumenical Decade: Churches in Solidarity with Women (1988–1998). Lundy approached the Reverend Sally L. Hill, a former associate pastor of St. Luke's, who agreed to spearhead the conference planning in her new capacity as director of the ecumenical Twin Cities Metropolitan Churches Commission. To underwrite the estimated $390,000 cost, funding was secured from several denominations, ecumenical agencies, and philanthropic foundations. As the conference convened in Minneapolis on November 4, 1993, almost 2,200 participants (including 83 men) represented forty-nine states and twenty-seven countries. More than 400 Presbyterians attended, including 20 members of the national staff. The four-day conference included numerous workshops and plenary presentations, an innovative milk-and-honey liturgy, demonstrations of lesbian solidarity, and explorations of the biblical concept of Wisdom, or Sophia. After the conference the Twin Cities Presbytery commended Lundy and Hill for their leadership roles, but others were not as complimentary.

Although the conference speeches represented a variety of viewpoints, conservative caucuses charged conference organizers with heresy, lesbianism, and "goddess-worship." When the *Presbyterian Layman* criticized financial and staff support of the Re-Imagining Conference, church officials were caught off guard. Denominational leaders hastily circulated churchwide letters, which mollified neither the critics nor the defenders of the conference. Not only had Lundy not been censured or fired, but she became associate director of the General Assembly Council for Churchwide Planning in 1994 when a budget-tightening reorganization eliminated her Ministry Unit. Under pressure, the Executive Committee of the General Assembly Council released a statement alleging Lundy's judgment lapses, but the full council voted 32–31 to take no action on its recommendation to review her job performance. Despite private assurances of support, Lundy was terminated on May 19. A few weeks later the 1994 General Assembly tried to end the resulting furor as it overwhelmingly approved a conciliatory report, acknowledging mistakes on both sides and affirming that "theology matters." When several commissioners rose to ask the assembly to express its thanks to Lundy for her eight years of service, the moderator ruled them out of order.

Many continued to applaud Lundy for her work. Union Theological Seminary accorded her its Distinguished Alumni-ae Award, and Hartford Seminary named her visiting scholar and adjunct faculty member. In 1995 she began a four-year term as deputy general secretary of the World Council of Churches.

Bibliography. Berneking, Nancy J., and Pamela Carter Joern, eds., *Re-Membering and Re-Imagining* (Cleveland: Pilgrim Press, 1995); Crittenden, Ann, *Sanctuary: A Story of*

American Conscience and the Law in Collision (New York: Weidenfeld and Nicolson, 1988); General Assembly of the Presbyterian Church (USA), "Resolution on the Re-imagining Conference Controversy," *Church and Society* 84, no. 6 (July–August 1994), 7–14; "Meet Mary Ann Lundy, WMU Director," *Women's Voice* 4 (June 1992): 1, 4.

David B. McCarthy

Lutheranism. Lutheranism in America has been characterized by several significant controversies. In its earliest years the division between pietism* and Scholastic orthodoxy that was characteristic of European Lutheranism was carried also to America. Pietism was ascendant in early American Lutheranism, as was exemplified in the work of its patriarch, Henry Melchior Muhlenberg (1711–1787). In 1748 Muhlenberg did not even invite nonpietists to the first sessions of the Ministerium of North America, forerunner of all subsequent Lutheran synodical organizations in North America. On the other hand, classical Lutheran orthodoxy was not without its outspoken advocates; in 1749 William C. Berkenmeyer (c. 1682–1751) of New York publicly attacked a fellow clergyman as a "crypto-Herrnhutter" (secret Moravian) because he had departed from the teachings embodied in the *Book of Concord* (1580) and the writings of the seventeenth-century orthodox theologians. For his part, Muhlenberg was fond of saying that the trouble with pastors like Berkenmeyer was that they tried to adhere to the unaltered Augsburg Confession with unaltered hearts. The tension between pietist and orthodoxist perspectives continued in the nineteenth and twentieth centuries, although many later Lutheran leaders combined elements of both in their theology and practice.

Closely related to pietist-orthodoxist tensions was the controversy over confessional subscription that occurred beginning in the 1820s. Many of those of pietist persuasion had by then become enamored of the revivalism* and moralism of the Second Great Awakening.* Under the leadership of Samuel S. Schmucker (1799–1873), they gave only a conditional allegiance to historic Lutheran doctrines and practices as they emphasized their essential oneness with other evangelical Protestants. These "American Lutherans" were opposed both by newer immigrants such as Carl F. W. Walther (1811–1887) and by native Americans such as Charles Porterfield Krauth (1823–1883), who were dubbed "Old Lutherans" because they advocated a return to the orthodoxy of the sixteenth and seventeenth centuries. The result was several decades of theological warfare that contributed greatly to the organizational fragmentation of Lutheranism in North America.

Even within the confessional movement there was considerable controversy. Confessionalists argued beginning in the 1860s about the propriety of pulpit and altar (Communion) fellowship with non-Lutherans, and even with some fellow Lutherans. This controversy resulted in the birth of rival confessional organizations—the General Council (1866) and the Synodical Conference (1872). Another bitter controversy among the confessionalists was over the doctrine of predestination,* beginning in the 1870s. Walther and others taught a doctrine that seemed much like that of Calvinism to their opponents, who were led by

Friedrich A. Schmidt (1837–1928) and Matthias Loy (1828–1915). Schmidt and Loy favored a position that Walther in turn called synergistic or semi-Pelagian. This bitter controversy resulted in the movement of pastors and congregations from one synod to another, and to significant realignment of intersynodical relationships.

In the twentieth century controversy focused most often on the nature and authority of the Bible, especially the concept of inerrancy that is found in the writings of the Scholastic theologians. Lutherans were drawn into the fundamentalist-modernist clash early in the century, although not all synods experienced open controversy. While most synods gradually moved to a neo-orthodox position that emphasized the authority of Scripture while not insisting on its inerrancy, some—most notably the Lutheran Church–Missouri Synod—insisted on the older scholastic understanding, which was similar to that of fundamentalism.* When this understanding was challenged from within the Missouri Synod, a major controversy erupted in the 1960s and 1970s that culminated in the dismissal of John Tietjen,* president of Concordia Seminary (St. Louis), the formation of the independent Concordia Seminary in Exile (Christ Seminary–Seminex*), and the organization of the Association of Evangelical Lutheran Churches.

In addition to the major controversies outlined here, American Lutheranism has experienced numerous lesser ones of a local or more limited nature. This is hardly surprising in a church body that drew its initial membership from the ranks of immigrants from several European countries, who often seemed to have little more in common than the name ''Lutheran.'' Much of the energy of Lutheran leaders over the past 250 years has been devoted to various controversies and the attempts to resolve them. Additionally, Lutheranism as a non-British immigrant church had important issues of acculturation to deal with as late as the 1920s and 1930s; these often led to controversies within congregations and synods (for example, on the use of the English language in worship) that had an important impact on the development of the denomination.

Bibliography. Nelson, E. Clifford, ed., *The Lutherans in North America* (Philadelphia: Fortress Press, 1975).

Donald L. Huber

M

Machen, John Gresham. Militant conservative Presbyterian clergyman and New Testament scholar John Gresham Machen (1881–1937) was raised in Baltimore, Maryland, in the Old School Southern Presbyterian tradition. He was educated at Johns Hopkins, Princeton Theological Seminary, Princeton University, Marburg, and Göttingen. While studying in Germany, Machen was attracted by the liberal theology of Wilhelm Herrmann and endured a profound religious crisis. Nevertheless, he returned to Princeton Seminary in 1906 as an instructor in New Testament and eventually became a staunch adherent of the conservative Princeton Theology. In 1914 he was ordained in the Presbyterian Church in the USA and in 1915 was promoted to assistant professor of New Testament. In the course of his career he published two significant studies in the New Testament: *The Origin of Paul's Religion* (1921) and *The Virgin Birth of Christ* (1930).

Machen was at the center of much of the fundamentalist-modernist controversy that wracked the Northern Presbyterian Church in the 1920s and 1930s. Concerned about the advances of liberal Christianity in the years after World War I, Machen published *Christianity and Liberalism* in 1923, in which he argued that liberalism was a completely different religion from Christianity and that liberals ought to withdraw from Christian churches.

As controversy between conservative and liberal Presbyterians grew in the 1920s, Machen gained prominence as a leader of the fundamentalist party in the church. He strongly opposed efforts of liberals to win tolerance from the church and labored to buttress the militant conservative cause. When the administration of Princeton Theological Seminary was reorganized in 1929 to allow a broader theological stance, Machen and some other conservative faculty members founded Westminster Theological Seminary in Philadelphia to preserve the tradition of the "Old Princeton."

In 1933 Machen, convinced that the church tolerated liberal missionaries, founded an Independent Board for Presbyterian Foreign Missions. The 1934 General Assembly of the church ordered all clergy to sever their connection with the independent board or face discipline, but Machen refused and was suspended from the ministry. In response, he led in founding the Presbyterian Church of America (later the Orthodox Presbyterian Church) in 1936. Machen died on January 1, 1937, in Bismarck, North Dakota, while traveling to raise support for the new denomination.

Bibliography. Hart, D. G., *Defending the Faith: J. Gresham Machen and the Crisis of Conservative Protestantism in Modern America* (Baltimore: Johns Hopkins University Press, 1994); Longfield, Bradley J., *The Presbyterian Controversy: Fundamentalists, Modernists, and Moderates* (New York: Oxford University Press, 1991); Stonehouse, Ned B., *J. Gresham Machen: A Biographical Memoir* (Grand Rapids, MI: William B. Eerdmans, 1954).

Bradley J. Longfield

Madison, James. One of Madison's greatest legacies was his authorship of *A Memorial and Remonstrance* in 1785. Its roots lay in a fundamental confrontation between Madison and the Virginia-established Anglican Church in 1773–1774. Returning to his home in Montpelier after three years (1769–1772), at the College of New Jersey, the young scholar engaged in a serious correspondence with classmate and friend William Bradford of Philadelphia. In January of 1773 Madison described his frustration and outrage over the imprisonment of citizens for preaching their convictions as Christians. He told of his incessant opposition to such treatment that was being meted out by local authorities and members of the Anglican clergy. He described it as ". . . that diabolical Hell conceived principle of persecution." He added, "To their eternal Infamy the Clergy can furnish their Quota of Imps for such business." He was, he wrote, at the end of his common patience and was praying for liberty of conscience "to revive among us."

The chosen target of Madison's outrage was the idea of an established religion and its resulting infringement of the rights of conscience. When he was elected to the 1776 Virginia Revolutionary Convention, Madison was selected to serve on the committee "to prepare a declaration of rights" for the new state. When the chairman, George Mason, offered his version of the article concerning religion he employed the phrase "all men should enjoy the fullest Toleration in the Exercise of Religion." Madison rejected the concept of toleration and suggested substitute language, "all men are equally entitled to the free exercise of religion, according to the dictates of conscience." That wording was adopted with Mason's support.

As the Revolution became a reality the Virginia General Assembly was confronted with two bills of importance for this discussion, both of which were held over until the end of the war. One dealt with replacing the Anglican Church as the established religion of Virginia. The other mandated paying tax funds to Protestant churches to employ teachers of religion, later known as the General Assessment Bill.

After the Revolution Madison was elected to the Virginia House of Delegates in 1784. The two bills were still on the agenda and in the Fall of 1784 both were introduced for a vote. Madison vigorously opposed any religious establishment, but he saw the ultimate danger in the Assessment Bill that would have created a plural establishment. Madison knew he could not defeat both bills and he was convinced that establishing the Episcopal Church would be far less dangerous than passage of the Assessment Bill. He predicted that an Episcopal establishment would be abolished within a decade as Baptists and Presbyterians demanded it. In fact the Episcopal Incorporation Act was repealed in 1787. Madison had seen it as the lesser of two evils and, as he wrote to his father, its passage parried ''for the moment'' the Assessment Bill, which otherwise would have been ''saddled upon us.''

Madison accomplished that delay by asking for time to circulate the Assessment Bill among the voters. This was done and thousands of signatures on scores of petitions flooded the Assembly members by the Fall of 1785. The most effective petition was written by Madison, who listed fifteen reasons to oppose the Assessment Bill. Madison prevailed and the Assessment Bill was never voted upon. He seized that opportunity to introduce the Jefferson Act for Establishing Religious Freedom in Virginia, which was duly passed (see ''Thomas Jefferson'' in this volume).

On the national scene Madison successfully convinced the first Congress to adopt the religion clauses of the First Amendment. They reflected Madison's full commitment to religious freedom and, as he phrased it in an 1819 letter, the ''total separation of the Church from the State.'' (See ''Separation of Church and State'' in this volume).

Bibliography. Alley, Robert S., ''On Behalf of Religious Liberty: James Madison's *Memorial and Remonstrance*,'' *This Constitution* 27 (Fall 1986): 26–33; Padover, Saul K., *The Complete Madison: His Basic Works* (New York: Harper and Brothers, 1953); Rutland, Robert A., *James Madison and the American Nation 1751–1836: An Encyclopedia* (New York: Simon and Schuster, 1994); Rutland, Robert and William M. E. Rachal, eds., *The Papers of James Madison*, 2 vols. (Chicago: The University of Chicago Press, 1962, 1973).

Robert S. Alley

Malcolm X. Malcolm Little was born on May 19, 1925, in Omaha, Nebraska, but grew up in Lansing, Michigan. He was a bright child, but the death of his father was soon followed by the commitment of his mother to a mental institution, and his family was broken up. In 1941 he went to live with his elder half sister in Boston and almost immediately became involved in hustling, pimping, and robbery in Boston and New York. He was jailed in 1946 for robbery and served over six years of a ten-year prison sentence. While in prison he read widely and converted to the Nation of Islam.*

Upon his release from prison in 1952, Malcolm dropped his "slave" name and became Malcolm X. Over the next decade he became the central figure in the explosive growth of the Nation of Islam, which grew from a few hundred activists to a membership numbered in the tens of thousands. Operating from his position as minister of Temple No. 7 in Harlem, he was instrumental in establishing temples in numerous other cities. An electrifying speaker, he became the most visible representative of the Nation, eclipsing Elijah Muhammad,* whose ill health forced him to make fewer and fewer public appearances. By 1963 Malcolm was the second most requested speaker on the college circuit after Barry Goldwater.

In late 1962 a rift developed between Malcolm and Elijah Muhammad when Malcolm learned that Elijah had fathered several children by his secretaries. In November 1963 Elijah used an extemporaneous remark by Malcolm regarding the assassination of John Kennedy as a pretext for prohibiting him from making any more public statements. In March 1964 Malcolm resigned from the Nation, and he embarked on a pilgrimage to Mecca in April. In widely distributed letters that he wrote during his pilgrimage, he announced that he had learned from meeting Muslims from all over the world that not all whites were "devils," contrary to the doctrine of the Nation. Upon his return he began trying to replace the doctrine that whites are racists by virtue of their biology with a theory that American society nourishes racism. He abandoned the Nation's policy of noninvolvement in political affairs (including the civil rights* movement) in favor of supporting mass-based attempts to address the day-to-day problems afflicting African Americans "by any means necessary." In 1965 he created the Organization of Afro-American Unity, which sought to promote the unity of all blacks, regardless of religious affiliation, in the fight for justice in a white-dominated society. He was addressing a meeting of the OAAU when he was assassinated on February 21, 1965. Because of his charismatic personality and his ambiguous teachings, which were in flux at the time of his death, his memory has been revered by individuals and groups with quite divergent agendas.

Bibliography. Breitman, G., *Malcolm X: The Man and His Ideas* (New York: Pathfinder Press, 1969); Decaro, L. A., Jr., "Malcolm X and the Nation of Islam: Two Moments in His Religious Sojourn" (Ph.D. diss., New York University, 1994); Goldman, P., *The Death and Life of Malcolm X*, 2nd ed. (Urbana: University of Illinois Press, 1979); Malcolm X, with A. Haley, *The Autobiography of Malcolm X* (New York: Grove Press, 1965); Wood, J., ed., *Malcolm X: In Our Own Image* (New York: St. Martin's Press, 1992).

Vernon Egger

Marian Devotion. Marian devotion refers to Christian, especially Catholic and Eastern Orthodox, forms of spirituality explicitly connected to Mary, the mother of Jesus. Recognizing Mary's unique role in salvation history, Marian forms of piety, with accompanying theological controversies, date to ancient times. But the lush medieval proliferation of popular devotional practices in the West—the rosary and other forms of Marian prayer, the scapular, pilgrimages to Marian shrines—seemed especially objectionable to sixteenth-century Protestant Reformers, who viewed them as superstition or idolatry. Their theological heirs in America have thus tended to denounce the Marian devotions of their Catholic neighbors.

In the nineteenth century Marian piety intensified around the globe. Several events in Europe stirred excitement among American Catholics and prompted condemnations from American Protestants: the issuing of the Miraculous Medal with Mary's image (1832); the apparitions of Mary at Lourdes, France (1858), and other locations; and the definition of the dogma of the Immaculate Conception (that Mary was conceived without original sin) by Pope Pius IX (1854), eight years after the American bishops had declared the Immaculate Conception the patronal feast of the United States. American Marian religious magazines such as *Ave Maria* publicized these events, ran testimonies of Marian miracles, and sponsored Marian devotional organizations.

Marian fervor continued into the early twentieth century with apparitions at Fatima, Portugal (1917), and elsewhere. The Vatican offered further encouragements, such as Pius XII's consecration of the world to the Immaculate Heart of Mary (1942), proclamation of a Marian Year (1954) with observance of the new feast of the Queenship of Mary (May 31), and, above all, the definition of the Assumption of Mary (1950). This last act in particular—proclaiming as official Catholic dogma the doctrine that Mary's body was taken to heaven at the end of her earthly life—was censured by many American Protestants as a new and formidable barrier to closer ecumenical relations.

The years immediately following Vatican Council II* (1962–1965) saw a lull in Marian piety, but a revival was clearly under way by the 1980s, fueled by the Catholic charismatic movement, Pope John Paul II's highly visible devotion to Mary, and a number of new apparitions, most notably the one at Medjugorje in what was then Yugoslavia (beginning in 1981). Protestant critics remained vocal in their suspicions.

Yet Marian controversy has not been confined to Protestant-Catholic disputes. American Catholics have themselves debated the authenticity of reported Marian apparitions in Necedah, Wisconsin; Conyers, Georgia; Bayside, New York; and Lookout Mountain, Colorado. Visionaries' claims at these sites have attracted both excited worshippers and bishops' warnings that some of the "private revelations" are heterodox.

Marian devotion has also been criticized in recent years by Catholic feminists. Mary's exaltation, some insist, has been employed by a celibate male church hierarchy to subjugate women, who can only feel sinful and inadequate next to the impossible ideal of Mary's purity and power. Since Mary's chief qualification for glory was her maternity, she embodies the sexist assumption that "biology is destiny."

Other Catholic feminists, however, counter that Mary's high station actually reflects popular efforts to validate women's power and importance and has perennially challenged official teachings about feminine inferiority. Mary's virginity and the Virgin Birth are signs that she was free from sexual subjugation to men and that her relationship to God was not mediated through a male, either husband or priest. Marian devotion has actually preserved an awareness of the divine maternity that corrects and complements male images of the deity.

Pressing for an even higher place for Mary, some traditionalists are calling on Rome to define her position as Co-Redemptrix and Co-Mediatrix alongside Christ, and at least one theologian has spoken of "the hypostatic union" of Mary and the Holy Spirit. The current diversity of perspectives guarantees that Mary will remain a catalyst for controversy.

Bibliography. Graef, H., *Mary: A History of Doctrine and Devotion*, 2 vols. (New York: Sheed and Ward, 1965); Greeley, A. M., *The Mary Myth: On the Femininity of God* (New York: Seabury, 1977); Warner, M., *Alone of All Her Sex: The Myth and the Cult of the Virgin Mary* (New York: Knopf, 1976); Zimdars-Swartz, S. L., *Encountering Mary: From La Salette to Medjugorje* (Princeton: Princeton University Press, 1991).

T. Paul Thigpen

Marshall, Molly Truman. Born in Muskogee, Oklahoma, on December 30, 1949, Molly Marshall was baptized in the First Baptist Church on April 8, 1956. She graduated with a B.A. degree from Oklahoma Baptist University in 1972. In 1975 she received the master's of divinity degree from the Southern Baptist Theological Seminary,* where she also received a Ph.D. in 1983. Her doctoral dissertation was titled "'No Salvation outside the Church? A Critical Inquiry.'" Additional educational experiences, including sabbatical study, were in Cambridge University (1980), Tantur Ecumenical Institute, Jersusalem, Israel (1980), and Princeton Theological Seminary (1990–1991). She married Dr. Douglas Green on May 30, 1981.

Marshall's early focus was ministry in the local church, with special interest in youth. From 1969 to 1978 she served the following churches: Valley Baptist Church in Lutherville, Maryland; First Baptist Church, Cushing, Oklahoma; First Baptist Church, Comanche, Texas; Pulaski Heights Baptist Church, Little Rock, Arkansas. She also served as the associate campus minister for Jefferson Community College in Louisville, Kentucky (1972–1975) and spent 1974 as a summer missionary doing student work in Jerusalem, Israel. In 1983 she became the pastor of Jordan Baptist Church in Eagle Station, Kentucky, where she served for two years before serving as the interim pastor of Deer Park Baptist Church in Louisville, Kentucky, in 1985. She is a regular pulpit supply and frequent Bible study leader in the local church.

Marshall began her teaching career at the Southern Baptist Theological Seminary in 1984, where she served as assistant professor of Christian theology (1984–1988), associate dean in the School of Theology (1988–1990), and associate professor of Christian theology (1988–1994). Under pressure, she was forced to resign from her teaching post in 1994 after repeated attacks from conservative elements within the Southern Baptist Convention.* Her theological views on salvation as well as her position on the role of women in the church were scrutinized and were found not in agreement with the fundamentalist agenda of the seminary and convention leadership. Presently Marshall is the visiting professor of theology, worship, and spiritual formation at Central Baptist Theological Seminary in Kansas City, Kansas.

Along with her teaching responsibilities, Marshall is a well-known lecturer and published author. She has been the Staley Lecturer in many colleges, religious emphasis speaker for various campuses, and lecturer at many pastors' schools and ministerial conferences. She has served on the editorial boards of the National Association of Baptist Professors of Religion, Smyth and Helwys Publishing, and the *Review and Expositor*. She belongs to the Society of Biblical Literature, the American Academy of Religion, the Society for the Scientific Study of Religion, Baptist Women in Ministry, the Whitsitt Society, the American Association of University Professors, the American Association of University Women, the Coalition for the Homeless, and the National Organization for Women.

When asked what she would like to be published for future readers to remember about her life and vocation, Marshall replied, "I want to be remembered as a person who put the interests of her students above 'proving a point' theologically; hence, I did not go through the firing process because of six doctoral students. I would want to be remembered for unapologetically standing for justice for women in the life of the church. I would want to be remembered for sustained reflection on 'theologia crucis' as the pivot of Christian life and thought."

Bibliography. Some of Marshall's publications include the following: "A Ministry of Dissent," *Baptists Today* May 4, 1995, 4–5; *No Salvation outside the Church? A Critical Inquiry*, NABPR Dissertation Series, no. 9 (Lewiston, NY: Edwin Mellen Press, 1993); *What It Means to Be Human* (Macon: Smyth and Helwys, 1995).

Linda McKinnish Bridges

McCall, Duke Kimbrough. Duke Kimbrough McCall was president of the Southern Baptist Theological Seminary,* Louisville, Kentucky, from 1951 to 1982. A native of Mississippi, born in 1914, McCall earned degrees from Furman University and Southern Baptist Theological Seminary. Before becoming president of the seminary, McCall was president of Baptist Bible Institute (later New Orleans Baptist Theological Seminary) from 1943 to 1946 and executive secretary of the Southern Baptist Convention's* Executive Committee from

1946 to 1951. In 1980 McCall was elected to serve a five-year term as president of the Baptist World Alliance.

Early in McCall's presidency the seminary experienced an internal controversy that resulted in the firing of thirteen professors by the Seminary's Board of Trustees. Known as the "1958 Crisis," the controversy developed over several years as the relationship between McCall and the faculty of the School of Theology gradually deteriorated.

From McCall's perspective, three factors became intertwined to form a juggernaut. First, there had been significant changes in the nature of theological education. To the School of Theology had been added a School of Church Music and a School of Religious Education. Practical theological education had entered the curriculum alongside the traditional academic theological education. Second, the rapid growth in the student body and the faculty necessitated a restructuring of administration. New levels of bureaucracy created more distance between the president and the faculty. Third, up until McCall, the president had functioned as chairman of the faculty, a status of first among peers. Under McCall (and his predecessor, Ellis Fuller) the office of president became solely administrative. Given this context, the "1958 Crisis" can be understood as the institution struggling to assimilate these changes.

The perspective of the faculty on the crisis was quite different. They held that through several specific situations, the integrity of the president was unavoidably called into question. It was not the role of the president within the institution but the abuse of the role of president with which the faculty was outraged. Finally, the overall relationship between the president and the faculty had created a situation of such extremely low morale that on two occasions the faculty of the School of Theology passed votes of "no confidence" in the president.

The crisis climaxed in the spring of 1958. The faculty was convinced that the president intended to remove two or three professors who had been most vocal. A power bloc of thirteen faculty members was formed. The intent was to communicate with the president and the Board of Trustees as a bloc in order to gain protection and leverage. At this point, there seem to have been two tragic misjudgments. First, the bloc of faculty thought that the trustees would not take the drastic step of terminating almost half the faculty. Second, the Board of Trustees thought that the shock of termination would bring the thirteen faculty members to their senses and lead to reconciliation and reinstatement. Both were wrong. There were no winners: the entire bloc was fired (though one did accept the offer for reinstatement), the effectiveness of the president was diminished, the reputation of the seminary was tarnished, and, most important, relationships within the denomination were bruised and broken.

The situation prompted the American Association of Theological Schools, the accrediting agency for the seminary, to investigate. No formal probation was applied, but significant changes were suggested and implemented regarding the internal workings of the institution and the responsibilities, salaries, and benefits of professors.

It is difficult to chronicle the events of the controversy because of the lack of sources. McCall had all seminary documents relating to the situation, including the Board of Trustees' Minutes, sealed for at least fifty years. None of the terminated professors has yet published an account of the "1958 Crisis."

A similar though less devastating situation occurred late in McCall's tenure. Tension between the faculty and the president was again present. Low faculty morale was attributed to administrative style and philosophy and a lack of faculty involvement in decision-making processes. A significant faculty member left the seminary. Through this time of crisis, the president worked with two faculty-appointed committees to resolve problems and bring the situation to a satisfactory conclusion.

Bibliography. *Encyclopedia of Southern Baptists*, vols. 3 and 4 (Nashville: Broadman Press, 1971, 1982).

Andrew Pratt

McCune, William Clement. On December 18, 1876, W. C. McCune was charged with disloyalty to the Presbyterian church. Thomas H. Skinner, on behalf of the Committee of Prosecution, presented the charges to the Presbytery of Cincinnati. The trial began on Monday, March 5, and continued until Tuesday, March 27, 1877. The general offense was supported by two charges: that McCune's opinions constituted disloyalty, and that his actions did likewise. The bulk of the prosecution's evidence derived from McCune's work for the Christian Union movement, an ecumenical movement that sought to clear barriers from among evangelical denominations. McCune's involvement in such a movement, the prosecution claimed, was a direct threat to the distinctive beliefs and practices of the Presbyterian Church.

The reunion of Old School and New School Presbyterians in 1869 had its doctrinal basis in the Westminster Confession as the standard of the church's faith and practice. Skinner claimed that McCune violated that basis—for which McCune himself had voted—by holding Christian Union views and participating in the work of the movement, especially by his accepting a pastorate at a church in a Cincinnati suburb based on Christian Union principles. The most damning of his opinions, as the prosecution read the evidence, was that McCune held denominations to be essentially sinful, with no scriptural right to exist.

McCune's defense centered around a clarification: the general situation of broken church Communion was sinful, not the particular evangelical denominations themselves. Furthermore, he claimed that denominations had a right to their peculiar beliefs; what he questioned was the right of enforcement to the exclusion of evangelical Christians. As for himself, he held to the Westminster Confession of Faith, but with a proviso provided by the confession itself: that only God is Lord of the conscience. Thus he claimed for himself the right of private judgment and liberty in how he interpreted both Scripture and the confession.

The presbytery acquitted McCune while disagreeing with his Christian Union opinions and with his irregular actions in taking a pastorate without following proper procedure. The prosecution appealed to the General Assembly, which in 1878 stated that the Presbytery of Cincinnati had erred in not reprimanding McCune. It did not matter; McCune had transferred, with proper Presbyterian dismissal, to the Congregational Church. Though the broader church in Mc-Cune's immediate times did not wish to grant him the liberty he desired, the action of the presbytery pointed to the future, when such right of private judgment would become standard in the church.

Bibliography. Loetscher, Lefferts A., *The Broadening Church: A Study of Theological Issues in the Presbyterian Church since 1869* (Philadelphia: University of Pennsylvania Press, 1954), especially 15–17; *Minutes of the Presbytery of Cincinnati* (Presbytery of Cincinnati Microfilm Records); Nutt, Rick, *Contending for the Faith: The First Two Centuries of the Presbyterian Church in the Cincinnati Area* (Cincinnati: Presbytery of Cincinnati, 1991), especially 71–73; *The Process, Testimony, and Opening Argument of the Prosecution, Vote and Final Minute, in the Judicial Trial of Rev. W. C. McCune* (Cincinnati: Robert Clark and Co., Printers, 1877).

Thomas J. Davis

McGiffert, Arthur Cushman. A. C. McGiffert (1861–1933) created a storm of protest in 1897 when, as a professor of theology at Union Theological Seminary* in New York, he published *A History of Christianity in the Apostolic Age*. Having been a doctoral student of Adolf von Harnack, McGiffert insisted on freedom to pursue questions such as the authorship and accuracy of the biblical writings, Jesus' intentions in celebrating the Last Supper, and the views of early Christians about the atonement.

In his book McGiffert speculated in a footnote whether Jesus intended the Last Supper to be repeated as a perpetual rite. Another idea, questioned by critics, was his implication that Christ was mistaken in some of his views. Some were disturbed when he argued that early Christians did not hold substitutionary views of the atonement like those popular among many Presbyterians. But the deepest offense came to those who believed that McGiffert had undermined the authority of Scripture by questioning traditional authorship of some books, redefining what inspiration meant, and noting what he believed were contradictory teachings in the New Testament. He was accused of heresy before the General Assembly of 1898 by the Presbytery of Pittsburgh, and the General Assembly urged McGiffert to reconsider his views or withdraw from the Presbyterian ministry. McGiffert made it clear that he would do neither.

At the next year's General Assembly ten presbyteries called attention to McGiffert's unchanged views and urged action against him. The issue was referred to the New York Presbytery, which expressed the opinion that while the majority did not agree with McGiffert's views, he should not be charged with heresy. This failure to act was unacceptable to Dr. George W. F. Birch (who had earlier chaired the committee that had prosecuted C. A. Briggs* for heresy).

Birch prepared a lengthy diatribe detailing McGiffert's supposed errors for the General Assembly of 1900. Fearing formal action against him that would destroy the unity of the Presbyterian Church, McGiffert quietly withdrew from the Presbyterian ministry and joined the Congregational Church. He retained his position at Union, however, found that his prestige as a teacher and scholar was enhanced by the experience, and eventually became president of that institution.

Bibliography. Bowden, Henry Warner, "Liberal Theology and the Problem of Continuity in Church History: A. C. McGiffert as a Case Study," *Union Seminary Quarterly Review* 27 (Winter 1972): 67–79; Loetscher, Lefferts A., *The Broadening Church: A Study of Theological Issues in the Presbyterian Church since 1869* (Philadelphia; University of Pennsylvania Press, 1954).

Stephen R. Graham

McIntire, Carl. Carl McIntire (1906–1992) represented zealous fundamentalism* for his entire adult life. He firmly believed that he followed faithfully in the footsteps of his mentor and hero, J. Gresham Machen.* McIntire devoted his life to the exposing and eradication of heresy in the church. He drew tight boundaries for the faith and insisted fervently that to cross these boundaries amounted to a departure from true Christianity. He called for a twentieth-century reformation to recapture true Christianity from the clutches of liberalism* in all its forms.

After completing his education at Machen's Westminster Theological Seminary in Philadelphia, McIntire set up his operation in Collingswood, New Jersey. Crafting a complex operation that eventually included radio and television broadcasting facilities, a Bible college (Faith Theological Seminary), a weekly news publication (*Christian Beacon*), and a publishing house (Christian Beacon Press), as well as a church (Bible Presbyterian Church), McIntire spoke in strident tones on all the major issues of his day, but reserved his most virulent attacks for communism and its surreptitious friends, especially the Federal Council of Churches and its successor, the National Council of Churches.*

A persistent and outspoken critic of the Federal and then the National Council of Churches, McIntire founded the American Council of Churches of Christ in 1941 to counter what he viewed as the apostasy of the older body. McIntire also sharply criticized the National Association of Evangelicals after its formation in 1942, complaining that the organization coddled liberals.

After World War II McIntire aligned himself against all things Communist, and as he looked around him in the United States, he found nearly all things Communist. He openly accused the National Council of Churches of Communist leanings, directing some of his most vitriolic rhetoric at Methodist bishop G. Bromley Oxnam. He permitted himself an inadvertent form of ecumenism by supporting a Roman Catholic, Senator Joseph McCarthy, in his quest against Communist infiltration of the American government.

McIntire did not fire all of his salvos against the theological and political left, however; he also found the energy to castigate such theological conservatives as Billy Graham* and Carl F. H. Henry. The unwillingness of Graham, Henry, and other "neoevangelicals" to disown completely the National Council of Churches tainted them in McIntire's eyes. He called for a "second degree" of separation. Not only must the faithful separate themselves from evil (read theological liberals), the faithful must also assiduously avoid contact with those in contact with the apostate. McIntire thus wedded himself to a concept of the church as a tiny righteous remnant with rigorous requirements for admission and continual monitoring of adherence to these requirements for sustaining membership.

McIntire preached a combination of Americanism, antiliberalism, and fundamentalism, vociferously attacking any and all who stepped outside the bounds of the orthodoxy he found in his study of Scripture. His call for a twentieth-century reformation centered on his argument that the church desperately needed to recapture those essential beliefs that theological liberalism had undercut earlier in the twentieth century. McIntire died in 1992, one of the most controversial figures among American Protestants in the twentieth century.

Bibliography. Marsden, George M., *Reforming Fundamentalism* (Grand Rapids, MI: Eerdmans Publishing Co., 1987); McIntire, Carl, *The Death of a Church* (Collingswood, NJ: Christian Beacon Press, 1967); McIntire, Carl, *Modern Tower of Babel* (Collingswood, NJ: Christian Beacon Press, 1949); McIntire, Carl, *The Rise of the Tyrant: Controlled Economy vs. Private Enterprise* (Collingswood, NJ: Christian Beacon Press, 1945); McIntire, Carl, *Twentieth Century Reformation* (Collingswood, NJ: Christian Beacon Press, 1946).

Russell Congleton

McPherson, Aimee Semple. Controversy that befitted her Hollywood location swirled around the life and ministry of Aimee Semple McPherson (1890–1944). She was born in Ontario; one of the greatest influences on young Aimee was the ministry of her mother, Mildred, within the Salvation Army.* At age nineteen Aimee married Pentecostal* evangelist Robert Semple, and the couple soon left for China as missionaries. After only three months Robert died, and the next month Aimee gave birth to a daughter, Roberta.

Soon after returning to the United States, Aimee married Harold McPherson, but the marriage was not a happy one. Aimee sensed a call to preach and chafed under the constraints of home and family. In 1915 she left her husband and became an itinerant evangelist. Later joined by Harold, Aimee led healing and evangelistic meetings, gradually developing her flamboyant and controversial style. Harold became dissatisfied with his role in the background, and the marriage deteriorated, finally ending in divorce in 1921. McPherson's third marriage lasted only four years (1931–1935), also ending in divorce. Unlike many Pentecostal evangelists, McPherson was able to weather the disgrace that surrounded divorce in these circles and maintain her ministry.

Controversy also surrounded her relationship with her mother and her daughter, who were coworkers in her ministry for many years, especially after Aimee founded the Angelus Temple in 1923. Mildred served as business manager, but eventually relations between mother and daughter soured and they went their separate ways. Aimee's daughter Roberta had been viewed by many as Aimee's eventual successor, but their relationship also broke down, and Roberta left her work at Angelus Temple in 1936.

Many criticized McPherson for her flamboyant ministry style. She borrowed liberally from the Salvation Army practice of dramatic illustrated sermons and also from Hollywood pageantry. Often dressed in flowing white robes to preach, McPherson used drama, elaborate scenery, and numerous players to convey the message of the gospel to her rapidly growing audiences.

The most controversial event in her fascinating career, however, was her "kidnapping" in 1926. McPherson had gone to the beach with her secretary, Emma Schaffer, and, according to Schaffer, had gone into the water for a swim, but had never returned. For the next five weeks authorities searched and followers prayed for McPherson's safe return. Finally, a memorial service was held on June 20, but just three days later McPherson reappeared in an Arizona hospital reporting that she had been kidnapped. She claimed she that had been taken to Mexico and locked in a hut, but had escaped and had wandered through the desert of northern Mexico until she reached Arizona.

The whole event took on spectacular proportions as skeptics accused McPherson of having taken a romantic vacation with her former radio engineer, Kenneth Ormiston. The case received nationwide publicity, but neither side of the story was ever proved conclusively. McPherson's followers believed her version, and her critics held to their explanation.

Finally, as befitted a controversial life, McPherson's death raised questions. She died in 1944 of an overdose of sleeping pills. While the medical examiner ruled the death accidental, speculation remained about whether McPherson had taken her own life. More than fifty thousand mourners filed past her body in Angelus Temple, and thousands more around the country wept over the death of this remarkable and controversial woman.

Bibliography. Blumhofer, Edith L., *Aimee Semple McPherson: Everybody's Sister* (Grand Rapids, MI: Eerdmans, 1993); Epstein, Daniel Mark, *Sister Aimee: The Life of Aimee Semple McPherson* (New York: Harcourt Brace Jovanovich, 1993).

Stephen R. Graham

Mennonites. Mennonites originate from the Anabaptist movement, which began in Switzerland in 1525 as a radical expression of the Protestant Reformation. They share the core commitment of Anabaptism to the restitution of the New Testament church and became known by the name taken from their Dutch leader, Menno Simons (c. 1496–1561). At the heart of the Mennonite faith is the conviction that the Christian church is a voluntary community of believers who are marked by uniquely Christlike features that distinguish them from the world. This emphasis on the life of faith led them to value orthopraxy (correct behavior) over orthodoxy (correct belief) and to insist that salvation is more than substitutionary atonement.

The emphasis on voluntarism identifies the Mennonites with the Arminian tradition and is reflected in their practice of believers' baptism and in their belief in the priesthood of all believers. This priestly relationship to God is not individualistic, as in some Protestant traditions. Rather, the effort to understand and fulfill God's will is a communal experience.

The Mennonite vision is of a community that shares the features of Christ's ministry. Their lifestyle is typically simple in both manner and dress. This simplicity is not an end in itself but is to free the believers from the pursuit of worldly pleasures so that they can live a life of service. Mennonites have always been at the forefront of social service ministries.

Probably the most widely recognized feature of the Mennonite tradition is its peace witness. Christ's followers are called to turn the other cheek and thereby achieve reconciliation with those who oppose and persecute. In a world where conflict and violence are the norm, "turning the other cheek" becomes the defining mission of the church. The Mennonites have specialized in risky and innovative efforts to bring warring parties together. This commitment to peace has been a costly enterprise. Suffering is a certain feature of the Christian life and explains why throughout Mennonite history a central document for their community has been the *Martyrs' Mirror*, a 1660 collection of stories about those who had suffered in the faith.

With Protestantism, Mennonites share an emphasis on the authority of the Bible. However, unlike some Protestants, the writings of Paul and the Gospel of John are not the primary sources of their theology. Rather, the synoptic Gospels, and especially the teachings of Jesus in the Sermon on the Mount, are the standard by which the rest of the Bible and all theology are tested.

The congregational form of government prevails among Mennonites. The local congregations cooperate with each other through worldwide conference organizations. Most of the approximately one million Mennonites today are found in the following conferences: the Mennonite Church, the General Conference of the Mennonite Church, the Evangelical Mennonite Church, the Mennonite Brethren Church, and the Brethern in Christ. Most Mennonites have fellowship through the Mennonite World Conference. The Mennonite Central Committee is the worldwide service agency through which most Mennonites cooperate in relief services.

Bibliography. Dyck, Cornelius J., ed., *An Introduction to Mennonite History*, rev. ed. (Scottdale, PA: Herald Press, 1981); Estep, William R., *The Anabaptist Story*, rev. ed. (Grand Rapids, MI,: Eerdmans, 1975); Klaassen, Walter, ed. *Anabaptism in Outline: Selected Primary Sources* (Scottdale, PA: Herald Press, 1981); *The Mennonite Encyclopedia*, 5 vols. (Scottdale, PA: Herald Press, 1989); Wenger, John C., *What Mennonites Believe*, rev. ed. (Scottdale, PA: Herald, 1990).

Daniel B. McGee

Mercersburg Theology. Presently, Mercersburg is a quaint Pennsylvania village in the foothills of the Appalachian Mountains. In the mid-nineteenth century, however, it was the site and center of religious turmoil within the German Reformed Church—turmoil that would influence numerous other denominations in the themes upon which it touched. The college (Marshall) and seminary of this small denomination had been located here since the 1830s, and two men on these faculties would give these institutions and this sleepy village greater visibility and distinction than they had ever known before or after. John Williamson Nevin* (1803–1886), the theologian, and Philip Schaff* (1819–1893), the historian, created there what soon became known as the Mercersburg Theology. Heresy trials and extended debate over their ideas continued even into the twentieth century.

Nevin had experienced a twisting and turning pilgrimage in his religious outlook, for he had grown up in Puritanism and at Mercersburg reacted against many features of it or what might more correctly be called "low evangelicalism." After a brilliant student career at Princeton under the famous Charles Hodge,* Nevin taught for a decade at Western Theological Seminary in Pittsburgh. In 1840 he arrived in Mercersburg to teach in the seminary and moved on to theological positions that would become hallmarks of the Mercersburg Theology.

In 1843 Nevin published *The Anxious Bench*, which attacked this kind of evangelism as sheer quackery and more contrived than essential. Nevin urged the "system of the catechism" as opposed to the "system of the bench" and undue emotionalism as the legitimate church approach of Christian nurture. Expanding what he considered to be correct Reformation themes a few years later, he published a far deeper work, *The Mystical Presence: A Vindication of the Reformed or Calvinistic Doctrine of the Holy Eucharist* (1846). In this important work he charged that virtually all the Calvinistic churches in America had departed from the authentic sixteenth-century Reformed position on the Eucharist. He urged that "deteriorated Zwinglianism" be replaced by a restored genuinely Reformed faith. His salvos were aimed in many directions, including his former mentor at Princeton, Charles Hodge. Nevin's *The History and Genius of the Heidelberg Catechism* in 1847 called Reformed communions to a proper and correct historical and doctrinal awareness of their long and rich Reformation heritage. Here began the lengthy and heated eucharistic and liturgical controversy within the German Reformed Church, with reverberations in many other denominations.

In 1844 Philip Schaff, Swiss-German and a recent graduate of the University of Berlin, joined Nevin on the seminary faculty. In their views of history, the church, the sacraments, and liturgy, these two men essentially were in agreement. Within two years of his arrival Schaff had undergone two heresy trials because of his ideas about historical development as well as "the middle state." In a context of anti-Catholicism, Schaff had argued in *The Principle of Prot-*

estantism (1845) that the Protestant Reformation had evolved quite naturally out of the best in medieval Catholicism. There had been no "break" in history and no "trail of blood" of true believers outside of Catholicism, as so many Protestants in the United States believed. Cleared of heresy, Schaff continued to teach and write with academic freedom* for the rest of his career at Mercersburg. His trials cleared the air in this denomination about the nature of education and academic freedom.

Together, Nevin and Schaff founded one of the truly great theological journals of the nineteenth century, *The Mercersburg Review* (1849). Dozens of scholarly and semischolarly articles filled the early volumes of the *Review*, illustrating and setting forth the major themes of Mercersburg Theology. Some articles drew more fire than others. The most oft-heard criticism was that of "Romanism" as these scholars expanded their idea of historical development. Attacking "low evangelicalism," both writers called for a greater historical awareness and consciousness in their own denomination as well as in the entire American religious scene. Liturgical reform was urged and nurtured in their articles. Ecumenism was another subject that crisscrossed their articles. Schaff and Nevin called for Christian unity during a time of denominational competition. In this respect they both became bridge builders between the United States and Europe. Schaff especially acquainted Europe with religion in America as well as introducing American scholars to the latest theological science in Europe.

In 1851 Nevin left the seminary and for one year served as president of Marshall College. Due to sickness he then became relatively inactive. Schaff continued at the seminary and during his second decade there became truly an international figure in church history through his numerous and excellent volumes. By 1862 Schaff was essentially absent from Mercersburg and in 1864 was living in New York City, where he eventually joined the faculty of the Union Theological Seminary* and became the most famous prophet of the modern ecumenical movement.

The creative period of Mercersburg Theology thus lasted for two decades, but the major themes of the then-controversial movement have penetrated American religious history in a variety of ways. The Mercersburg heritage is difficult to assess, but it definitely extended far beyond the more localized controversies within the German Reformed Church. In many matters the movement became a paradigm of what would happen generally to the Reformed tradition by the turn of the century. Since the 1940s the specific issues pushed by Schaff and Nevin have come to the denominational forefront. Indeed, as James H. Nichols has correctly observed: "The agenda of the twentieth-century ecumenical movement . . . read like the heads of the Mercersburg controversy" (*Romanticism in American Theology*, 310). On all the present themes of ecumenism, the Mercersburg Theology speaks with amazing penetration and sensitivity. American religious history is far richer due to the fact that the Mercersburg scholars and movement rode out the storm of controversy they caused to make their own lasting and creative contributions.

Bibliography. Binkley, Luther J., *The Mercersburg Theology* (Manheim, PA: Sentinel Printing House, 1953); Klein, H.M.J., *A Century of Education at Mercersburg, 1836–1936* (Lancaster, PA: Eastern Synod, 1936); Nichols, James H., ed., *The Mercersburg Theology* (New York: Oxford University Press, 1966); Nichols, James H., *Romanticism in American Theology* (Chicago: University of Chicago Press, 1961); Richards, George W., *History of the Theological Seminary of the Evangelical and Reformed Church at Lancaster* (Lancaster, PA: Theological Seminary, 1952); Schaff, Philip, *America* (New York: Scribner's, 1855; Reprint. Cambridge: Harvard University Press, 1961); Schaff, Phillip, *Germany* (New York: Sheldon, Blakeman and Co., 1857); Schaff, Phillip, *History of the Apostolic Church* (New York: Scribner's, 1854); *What Is Church History?* (Philadelphia: J.B. Lippincott and Co., 1846; Reprint. Philadelphia: J. B. Lippincott 1972); Shriver, George H., *American Religious Heretics* (Nashville: Abingdon Press, 1966).

George H. Shriver

Merton, Thomas. Born of artist parents in Prades, France, in 1915, Thomas Merton was educated at Cambridge University and Columbia University. While a graduate student at Columbia, he converted to Catholicism and entered the monastic Order of Cistercians of the Strict Observance (OCSO)—familiarly known as Trappists—at the Abbey of Gethsemani in Kentucky on December 10, 1941, three days after the bombing of Pearl Harbor. While a student at Cambridge, he had been active in war resistance and in 1934 signed the Oxford Peace Pledge.

In 1948 Merton's autobiography, *The Seven Storey Mountain*, became a publishing sensation. The book chronicled his childhood and youth, his conversion experience, and the call to a monastic vocation. By the early 1960s, Merton's public image would radically change from the persona of the secluded, contemplative monk who had little or no contact with the world to that of the outspoken and controversial social-critic monk who insisted that he risked being a "guilty bystander" if he did not voice his protest against violence and war as a means of settling international disputes or against racism as social injustice.

While Merton had described himself to his New York draft board in early 1941 as a "partial Conscientious Objector, asking for noncombatant service" during World War II (Mott, 169), his entry into the monastery later that year rendered moot the question of his draft status. (He was granted a deferment as a religious.) In the early 1960s he published a poem, "Chant to Be Used in Processions around a Site with Furnaces," as an ethical protest of the Auschwitz concentration camp. This was followed in 1962 by the trenchant prose-poem *Original Child Bomb*, a satiric condemnation of atomic warfare and of the U.S. decision to use the bombs in 1945, forcing Japan into unconditional surrender. While he easily published such poetry, in 1961 the Cistercian censors objected to Merton's prose essays on peacemaking. They accused Merton of being an activist and insisted that his contemplative vocation precluded writing as a social critic of war. He published a censored version of the essay "Peace: A Religious Responsibility" in a September 1962 volume he edited, *Breakthrough to Peace: Twelve Views on the Threat of Thermonuclear Extermination.* In May 1962 his book typescript *Peace in the Post-Christian Era* was embargoed by a directive from the Cistercian abbot general ordering him to publish no more on war and peace.

Merton continued his revisionist studies of the just-war theory in a nuclear age while submitting to his religious superiors. He hoped that the upcoming Vatican Council II* would deal openly with the issues of peacemaking in the modern world. In 1961–1962, for just over a year before the Cuban missile crisis, Merton circumvented the censors by mimeographing and circulating hundreds of copies of his letters to friends from around the world on war and peacemaking: he held that this collection, "The Cold War Letters," did not constitute publication and did not require censors' permission. With the publication of Pope John XXIII's encyclical letter on war and peacemaking, *Pacem in Terris,* in 1963, Merton felt vindicated. Close contacts with Dorothy Day led to publication of several of his controversial essays on war and racism in the *Catholic Worker* newspaper. His 1964 book *Seeds of Destruction* included the heart of his *Peace in the Post-Christian Era* work, along with his own commentary on *Pacem in Terris* and an essay on Gandhi's nonviolent spirituality. The book also included "Letters to a White Liberal," in which Merton criticized the spiritual authenticity of white participation in the civil rights* movement; this position was complemented by his essays in *Faith and Violence* analyzing racism* in the United States in the late 1960s, including his appreciation of Malcolm X.*

In November 1964 Merton hosted a retreat entitled "Spiritual Roots of Protest" sponsored by the Fellowship of Reconciliation. Participants included Daniel and Philip Berrigan,* A. J. Muste, Jim Forest, and J. H. Yoder. Merton's open opposition to the Vietnam War was articulated as a "theology of resistance" in *Faith and Violence.* He was accidentally electrocuted on December 10, 1968, in Bangkok, Thailand, while at a conference on East-West monastic dialogue. He had traveled to Southeast Asia to converse with the Dalai Lama and to show solidarity with the peoples suffering from U.S. war policy.

Bibliography. Forest, Jim, *Living with Wisdom: A Life of Thomas Merton* (Maryknoll, NY: Orbis, 1991); Kilcourse, George, *Ace of Freedoms: Thomas Merton's Christ* (Notre Dame: University of Notre Dame Press, 1993); Merton, Thomas, *Faith and Violence* (Notre Dame: University of Notre Dame Press, 1968); Mott, Michael, *The Seven Mountains of Thomas Merton* (Boston: Houghton Mifflin, 1984); Shannon, William, ed., *Passion for Peace: The Social Essays* [of Thomas Merton] (New York: Crossroad, 1995).

George Kilcourse

The Message of Genesis. *The Message of Genesis* was a book by Ralph H. Elliott published by Broadman Press in 1961 that interpreted the creation story in Genesis symbolically and that unleashed a firestorm of protest among conservative Southern Baptists. Elliott, then professor of Old Testament at Midwestern Baptist Theological Seminary in Kansas City, Missouri, intended for the book to bridge the gap between conservative biblical scholarship and emerging scientific critiques of the Genesis account. Instead, he found himself under attack from conservatives across the Southern Baptist Convention* who failed to appreciate his intellectual effort at melding the Bible with science.

The conservative protest was led by K. Owen White, a pastor in Houston, Texas, who wrote an article condemning Elliott's views. The article was published in most state Baptist papers across the Southern Baptist Convention. At first Elliott garnered significant support from trustees of Midwestern Baptist Theological Seminary and the Sunday School Board of the Southern Baptist convention. The issue was extensively debated during a divisive annual Southern Baptist Convention meeting in San Francisco in 1962. While the convention did not ban the book, it did reassert its allegiance to the Bible as the infallible Word of God.

After the convention both trustee boards became less supportive. Elliott was asked to promise that the book would not be republished. When he refused to grant this request, he was dismissed for insubordination. The Sunday School Board, though it could have republished the book, never did so. The controversy resulted in the adoption of a confession of faith at the 1963 Southern Baptist Convention in Kansas City.

Bibliography. Fletcher, Jesse C., *The Southern Baptist Convention: A Sesquicentennial History* (Nashville: Broadman and Holman, 1994); Shurden, Walter B., *Not a Silent People: Controversies That Have Shaped Southern Baptists* (Nashville: Broadman Press, 1972).

Robert N. Nash, Jr.

Methodism. Methodism is a name that identifies the doctrine, polity, and discipline of several Protestant denominations tracing their heritage to an eighteenth-century revival in Great Britain under John and Charles Wesley, and their sometime associate George Whitefield. As students at Oxford around 1725, while diligently preparing for holy orders, they stressed "inward religion, the religion of the heart" and as a result organized the Holy Club. Due to the regularity of their lifestyle and work they were called Methodists. The two Wesleys accompanied General James Oglethorpe to Georgia in 1735 as missionaries of the Society for the Propagation of the Gospel in Foreign Parts. On the journey they became favorably impressed with a group of Moravian colonists. It was the Moravian doctrine of the assurance of justifying faith and their belief in instantaneous conversion that became central to Methodism.

Returning to England, John Wesley had his heart "strangely warmed" on May 24, 1738. Thereafter he preached salvation by faith. Forming societies to supplement the Church of England, he invited all who desired "to flee from the wrath to come." In 1743 he prepared *Nature, Design, and Rules* for his societies, and introduced lay preachers. He held a conference on doctrine and organization in 1744, and at subsequent conferences between 1744 and 1747, the major tenets of Methodist preaching were articulated. These were salvation by grace through faith, evidenced by good works; the personal witness of the Holy Spirit; the doctrine of Christian perfection or being made perfect in love; and the absence of a guaranteed spiritual status. In John Wesley's first four volumes of *Sermons* (1744–1760) and *Explanatory Notes upon the New Testament* (1755), these doctrines were elaborated.

The network of societies was a connection, and in 1747 and 1751 Ireland and Scotland, respectively, were added to England and Wales. British immigrants, initially the Irish, brought Methodism to America. In 1769, 1771, 1773, and 1774 John Wesley sent pairs of preachers to America, of whom Francis Asbury became the most influential. Staying during the War of Independence, Asbury helped the Americans to organize an independent church within Methodism at the Christmas Conference in 1784. Although John Wesley had previously opposed separating from the Church of England, this did happen in the United States and in Great Britain after his death in 1791.

In the United States, Methodism expanded and divided more rapidly than in Great Britain. The African Methodist Episcopal Church (1816), the African Methodist Episcopal Zion Church (1820), the Methodist Protestant Church (1830), the Methodist Episcopal Churches, North and South (1844), and the Christian Methodist Episcopal Church (1870) were some of the bodies that formed. Others, such as the Wesleyan Methodist Connection (1843), the Free Methodist Church (1860), and the Church of the Nazarene (1908), stress the need for biblical holiness.

The early catholicity of Wesley's societies was evident in the 1881 Ecumenical Methodist Conference and the World Methodist Council. In 1939 the Methodist Episcopal Churches, North and South, along with the Methodist Protestant Church, reunited to form the Methodist Church. The Evangelical United Brethren and the Methodist Church merged in 1968 to form the United Methodist Church. Discussions continue among other Methodist bodies to harmonize the many branches of Methodism.

Bibliography. Baker, F., *John Wesley and the Church of England* (London: Epworth Press, 1970); Davies, R. E., and E. G. Rupp, eds., *A History of the Methodist Church in Great Britain*, 4 vols. (London: Epworth Press, 1965); Harmon, N. B., gen. ed., *The Encyclopedia of World Methodism*, 2 vols. (Nashville: United Methodist Publishing House, 1974); Norwood, F. A, *The Story of American Methodism* (Nashville: Abingdon Press, 1974); Outler, A. C., ed., *John Wesley* (New York: Oxford University Press, 1964.

Frederick V. Mills, Sr.

Millennialism. Although the millennium is mentioned only once in the New Testament (Revelation 20:4–6), the word "millennialism" draws its life from the commonly held Christian expectation of a one-thousand-year earthly reign of Christ at the end of time. Most often, movements categorized under this term emphasize an expectation of an imminent end time, like the Millerites or the Branch Davidians,* and thus may also be described by terms such as "apocalyptic," "chiliastic," "adventist," or "millenarian." But because of this term's focus on the radical, transforming, earthly rule of God (or some other good), some scholars have also described as millennialist utopian groups such as the Oneida* Community, a nineteenth-century contemporary of the Millerites, or even secular philosophies like Marxism or the "religion" of science and technology. Moreover, others argue that the millennialist vision in one form or another has been one of the driving forces in American religion. The popular American form of millennialism has most often espoused a democratic vision of hope for all, born out of commonsense rationality (not mystical experience), that challenges or even breaks with all established religious authorities. For many, the American Revolution and all that has grown out of it constitute an apocalyptic upheaval that has had profound religious as well as political significance.

Although millennialists may be radically different in their eschatology and other beliefs, theorists argue that all movements motivated by this kind of vision long for dramatic social change in times of extreme cultural stress. Given the social climate in which such groups thrive and the often extremist ideologies developed in the context of stress, it is not surprising that millennialist movements have been the source of great controversy, not only in American religious life but throughout Christian history and in the history of other religions as well. Theories about the life cycle of millennialist movements, developed largely by anthropologists, suggest that a radical vision of future hope, whether it be of the Parousia or of a more earthly social utopia, serves as a kind of survival mechanism while groups construct new ways of explaining and dealing with social stress and change. Ultimately, according to theory, if such movements survive at all, their eschatological expectations become less urgent and/or their radical demands diminish as adherents develop new worldviews (or mazeways). Often the satisfaction derived from strong community bonds developed in the face of their shared vision becomes a proleptic experience of the eschaton and thus a substitute for more extremist and even antisocial views, as, for example, in the case of early Mormonism or the Jehovah's Witnesses.*

Though not always associated with extremist movements, American Protestant evangelicalism developed a variety of views on the biblical millennium, and this diversity has contributed to theological controversy. Postmillennialism was very popular in the early history of America, especially in the Northeast among notables like Jonathan Edwards.* This viewpoint assumed that Jesus would return to claim his already-established kingdom after the millennium had been accomplished through the power of God working in the faithful; this contributed to a very positive view of social progress among many believers. During the second half of the nineteenth century, pessimism, brought on in part by the Civil War and a diminishing faith among postmillennialists in the bodily return of Jesus, led to the virtual demise of postmillennialism by the turn of the century.

According to many interpreters, the practical impact of this perspective was eventually subsumed in the Social Gospel or more secular reform movements. Eventually, religious liberals influenced by postmillennialism would identify themselves as amillennialists, persons who do not think that the millennium literally represents a specific historical period.

Having had a following even in the eighteenth-century South, premillennialism, which contends that Jesus will return bodily before the millennium, began its rise to national prominence with early-nineteenth-century Adventists in the Northeast, whose message offended postmillennial revivalists like Charles G. Finney* but helped adherents make sense of a variety of troubling natural disasters and social crises. Although Adventist movements lost widespread influence before the middle of the nineteenth century, premillennialism, bolstered by pessimism in the latter half of the century, became an incentive for evangelism and a distinctive mark in the fundamentalist and Pentecostal* movements of the twentieth century. Premillennialism is inclined toward a more literal interpretation of Scripture and is generally less hopeful concerning worldly progress than postmillennialism. Though these differences should not be overstated, the inclinations associated with each eschatology have at times been quite divisive. This is especially true of the radical tenets of dispensational premillennialism, which was made popular among fundamentalists by *The Scofield Reference Bible*. This belief identified seven distinct ages through which God works out his preordained plan for the world's salvation. Updated biblical versions of this eschatology, along with Hal Lindsey's *Late Great Planet Earth* (1970), the most popular book of the decade of the 1970s, have continued to make premillennialism a source of controversy and the spark for new movements in the second half of the twentieth century.

Bibliography. Albanese, Catherine, *America: Religions and Religion*, 2nd. ed (Belmont, CA: Wadsworth Publishing Co, 1992); Barkun, Michael, *Crucible of the Millennium: The Burned-over District of New York in the 1840s* (Syracuse: Syracuse University Press, 1986); Hatch, Nathan O., ''Millennialism and Popular Religion,'' in *The Evangelical Tradition in America*, ed. Leonard I. Sweet (Macon: Mercer University Press, 1984); Moorehead, James H., ''The Erosion of Postmillennialism in American Religious Thought, 1865–1925,'' *Church History* 53 (March 1984): 61–67; Weber, Timothy P., *Living in the Shadow of the Second Coming: American Premillennialism (1875–1982)* (Grand Rapids, MI: Academic Books, 1983).

Helen Lee Turner

Miller, William. Though he was not happy with the title himself, William Miller (1782–1849) is known as the founder of the Adventist movement, the largest premillennialist movement of the nineteenth century. While he spent most of his later life as a lay Adventist preacher (1831–1847), Miller's early career, apart from a few years in the military, was that of a farmer in Vermont and New York. A radical Jeffersonian and outspoken advocate of Deism before his conversion in a local revival in 1816, he became convinced after carefully studying the King James Version of the Bible and the chronology developed by Archbishop James Ussher that the Second Coming of Christ would occur around 1843. This declaration was not based on mystical or visionary experience but was arrived at by applying what he believed was rational, mathematical science to scriptural prophecy. Like many founders of new movements, William Miller did not intend to divide the churches. He considered himself a Baptist all his life. Instead, he was convinced that his insights would return the church to its original faith and thus eliminate the divisive accretions that had inhibited unity for centuries.

In the beginning Miller, a rather colorless individual who lacked any real charisma, was very cautious in his presentation of his millennialist vision, preaching only in his home area in traditional pulpits to which he was invited. He did not even publish his ideas on the Second Coming until 1835. But when Joshua V. Himes began directing Miller's efforts in 1840, and as the sense of urgency grew with the passage of time, Miller's cause grew into a competitive movement engaged in open controversy. In the first year of his leadership, Himes began a newspaper in Boston titled *Signs of the Times*, and shortly thereafter he began a similar paper in New York entitled *Midnight Cry*. These became vehicles for the organization of a vocal movement, which began in rural areas but soon spread to urban populations through camp-meeting-style revivals held both in a famous mammoth tent and in town halls across the Northeast. For many hearers, Miller's message about the eschaton provided a way of understanding the series of natural disasters (floods, epidemics, and crop failures) and social crises (economic collapse and disruptions in family life) that occurred in the Northeast in the first half of the century.

Official organization of the Millerites came with a conference in 1840 in which officers were elected and committees established. After several conference meetings, Adventist identity was becoming fixed, and in late 1841, at the request of Miller, limited standards for lecturers (not ministers) were set. However, splits within the ranks came in this process as well. There was decided disagreement over the exact date of the Parousia, whether or not the millennium would be temporal, and whether or not the Jews would return to Jerusalem. There was a splintering of the cause as some in leadership left the movement.

In 1842 the Second Advent Association began holding regular Sunday-afternoon meetings in several major northeastern cities, and though they carefully avoided conflict with the established churches' time slot, there was clearly a new pull on adherents' loyalty because of the organization's growing demands for gifts of money and energy in service to the Adventist cause. This more public campaign led to caricatures and other forms of criticism in the popular press, and some sources went so far as to say that Millerism was associated with insanity and was a public danger greater than yellow fever or cholera. The reactions were severe: church doors were frequently closed to Adventists, they were excommunicated from congregations, and ministers identified with the movement were dismissed. In many cases, Millerites regarded this treatment as a badge of honor, especially after Miller himself was excluded from his church in 1844. Consequently, significant growth eventually was to be found only in the rural counties of western New York.

Miller's excommunication came, of course, after the disappointments of 1843 and 1844 when Christ did not return. But for the most loyal this failure only increased their faith that the end was, nevertheless, near at hand. As their enthusiasm grew, especially after the initial failure of 1843, so did tensions with the churches. Several well-known Millerite lecturers began to advocate separation from the churches on practical grounds, some even arguing that denominations were trying to hold on to Adventists in order to keep their influence and money. Other Millerites went so far as to call all non-Adventists "Babylon" or the "anti-Christ." From this perspective, "coming out" of the churches had become a necessity. But "coming out" did not bring unity to the Adventists. There were fierce disagreements about hell,* the state of the dead, and the nature of the millennium, to name a few issues. Within a decade the movement that once threatened the traditional churches was divided by internal controversy.

Bibliography. Arthur, David T., "Millerism," in *The Rise of Adventism*, ed. Edwin Gaustad, (New York: Harper and Row, 1974); Miller, William, *Dissertation on the True Inheritance of the Saints* (Boston, 1842); Miller, William, *Evidence from Scripture and History of the Second Coming of Christ* (Troy, NY: Kemble and Hooper, 1836, and many subsequent editions); Numbers, Ronald L., and Jonathan M. Butler, eds., *The Disappointed: Millerism and Millenarianism in the Nineteenth Century* (Bloomington,: Indiana University Press, 1987); Rowe, David L., *Thunder and Trumpets: Millerites and Dissenting Religion in Upstate New York, 1800–1850* (Chico, CA: Scholars Press, 1985).

Helen Lee Turner

Missouri Synod Lutherans. On April 26, 1847, the German Evangelical Lutheran Synods of Missouri, Ohio, and other states were organized into a confessional, Lutheran synod in Chicago, Illinois. The Missouri Synod came into being at a time when Lutheran immigration was beginning to surge. Although the Lutheran Church arrived in the 1600s, by the early 1800s small groups were looking for fellowship and theological consistency. Martin Stephan, one of the early leaders, moved his congregation from Germany to Missouri in 1836, searching for religious liberty.* Wilhelm Loehe had been supporting the work by training German leaders to come to America. With his focus on theological education, Loehe was an important leader in the early development of the Missouri Synod. He helped establish theological schools in Fort Wayne, Indiana, and Springfield, Missouri.

The first constitution of the synod was developed after ten meetings of discussion and close scrutiny. The reasons for the organization of the synod were as follows: (1) the example of the apostolic church; (2) the conservation and continuance of the unity of the true faith and a united effort to resist every form of schism and sectarianism; (3) the protection of the pastor and congregation in the fulfillment of their duties and the maintenance of their rights; (4) the endeavor to bring about the greatest possible uniformity in church practice, church customs, and, in general, congregational affairs.

The first controversy of the Missouri Synod was with another group called the Buffalo Synod, founded in Buffalo, New York, and southern Wisconsin. The controversy lasted until 1866 and concerned the doctrines of the church, the responsibilities of ministry, and the office of the keys. The Buffalo Synod taught that the Church visible is not a group of scattered believers but those who gather around the Word and Sacrament without doctrinal error. On the other hand, the Missouri Synod maintained that the Church invisible included those Christians who were in churches that tolerated false doctrine, as long as they did not deny the Word of God outright. Buffalo charged that the keys of the kingdom were not given just to any believer but only to pastors. The Missouri Synod said that the keys were given to the whole church.

By 1872 the Missouri Synod had 415 pastors serving 20 states with 543 congregations. In 1875 the seminary began in Springfield, Illinois. In 1897 the synod had 1,986 congregations with 1,564 pastors and professors. In 1917 the Board of Directors was created in order to administer the work of three seminaries in St. Louis, Fort Wayne, and Springfield and several normal schools, along with missionaries in every state, and, by 1922, 3,508 pastors and 5,240 congregations. Involved in missions, publishing, and young people's work, the denomination entered the twentieth century strong and vital.

In the 1960s, however, battle raged between the traditionalists and progressives in the Synod. The center of the controversy was in Concordia Seminary in St. Louis, Missouri. The doctrinal controversy concerned the authority and interpretation of Scripture. Interviews were conducted with each faculty member to determine if he or she was guilty of teaching false doctrine. On February 17, 1974, faculty members whose positions were declared intolerable by the church received documents of dismissal from Concordia Seminary. Teaching, however, was to continue. Students, faculty, and executive staff formed Concordia Seminary in Exile (Seminex*). The exiled seminary kept its commitment to the teachings of the Lutheran Church–Missouri Synod and prepared students to serve within the church, stating that ''the synodical administration and seminary Board of Control are silencing the Word of God, stifling the biblical Gospel.'' Classes were held in student and faculty homes, churches, Eden Seminary, and St. Louis University. Over 100,000 members left the church during this crisis.

In the 1990s the Missouri Synod is the second-largest Lutheran body in the United States with 2,609,000 members and 5,369 churches (the Evangelical Lutheran Church in America is the largest). Today the synod operates 16 colleges and seminaries and 1,500 secondary schools, with mission work in thirty foreign countries.

Bibliography. Baepler, Walter A., *A Century of Grace: Missouri Synod, 1847–1947* (Saint Louis: Concordia Publishing House, 1947); Bohlmann, Ralph A., ''American Lutheranism,'' *Lutheran Forum* 30 (February 1996): 12–19; Danker, Frederick W., *No Room in the Brotherhood: The Preus-Otten Purge of Missouri* (St. Louis: Clayton Publishing House, 1977); Mead, Frank, revised by Samuel Hill, *Handbook of Denominations in the United States*, 10th ed. (Nashville: Abingdon, 1995).

Linda McKinnish Bridges

Modernism. Modernism was a theological movement in Protestant churches from around the 1870s to the 1930s that sought to conserve the influence of Christianity by accommodating the traditional faith to modern culture. In the late nineteenth century intellectual, social, and cultural changes challenged traditional Protestantism. The rise of evolutionary thought with Charles Darwin's *On the Origin of Species* (1859), the advent of higher criticism of the Bible, and developments in the fields of psychology, sociology, and anthropology combined to threaten traditional understandings of the Bible, God's providence, and the finality of the Christian revelation. Rapid urbanization, immigration, and industrialization in American society contributed to the strains on Victorian orthodoxy.

Theological modernism or liberalism* in the United States emerged by the 1880s as a distinct, self-conscious movement in response to these trends. Though challenged by conservatives, the strength of liberalism grew so that by the 1920s liberals held sway at perhaps half of the country's Protestant seminaries and filled a third of Protestant pulpits.

Borrowing from such European thinkers as Immanuel Kant, Friedrich Schleiermacher, and Albrecht Ritschl, and from the native work of Unitarians, transcendentalists, and Horace Bushnell,* modernists stressed the immanence of God, the goodness of humanity, the role of religious experience, the historical relativity of the Scriptures, and the priority of ethics over doctrine in the Christian faith. Borrowing from Darwinian evolutionary thought, they understood God to work in and through the progress of history and culture rather than through supernatural intervention. Likewise, the Scriptures were understood to be the record of the progressive religious experience of humanity, and doctrines were perceived to need periodic reformulation to adjust to humanity's increasing knowledge. Some liberals, such as Washington Gladden and Walter Rauschenbusch, concerned about the social problems occasioned by the urbanization and industrialization of America, subscribed to a Social Gospel* that called for the application of Christian ethics to the economic and political realms as well as to individuals.

In the 1920s modernists were condemned by both fundamentalists and scientific humanists for their failure to make a clean decision between traditional Christianity and humanism. In many mainline churches fundamentalists and modernists engaged in protracted battles, but by the late 1920s the modernist appeal for freedom and tolerance had won the day, and liberals were guaranteed a place in these communions.

With the rise of totalitarianism in Europe, the Great Depression, and the advent of Neo-Orthodoxy, many modernists abandoned their sanguine view of history and humanity but maintained other aspects of their faith. Though chastened, liberals continued, in the coming years, to play a major role in mainline denominations.

Bibliography. Averill, Lloyd J., *American Theology in the Liberal Tradition* (Philadelphia: Westminster Press, 1967); Hutchison, William R., ed., *American Protestant Thought in the Liberal Era* (Lanham, MD: University Press of America, 1968); Hutchison, William R., *The Modernist Impulse in American Protestantism* (Cambridge: Harvard University Press, 1976).

Bradley J. Longfield

Monk, Maria. Maria Monk was the subject and alleged author of the scandalous *Awful Disclosures of the Hotel Dieu Nunnery of Montreal* (1836), a prurient and fabricated tale whose numerous reprintings and wide circulation made it perhaps the most influential volume of nineteenth-century anti-Catholic propaganda in America. In *Awful Disclosures* and several sequels, Monk claimed that she had been raised Protestant, but after entering the Hotel Dieu Convent in Montreal to be educated, she became Catholic and decided to become a nun.

Soon after she took her vows, Monk insisted, she was initiated into the "crimes" of cloistered life, being told by the Mother Superior that the sisters must submit to the priests' sexual advances. Children born as a result were immediately baptized and strangled. Nuns who refused to have intercourse with the clergy were executed and buried alongside the babies in a hole in the convent basement. After becoming pregnant herself, Monk escaped from the cloister, attempted suicide twice, and finally sought refuge in a charity hospital. A Protestant clergyman she met there asked her to expose the horrors of popery by writing an autobiography for publication.

The story of Monk's life as told by her mother was quite different. Her daughter, she testified, had been a wild girl, continually in trouble, and had finally been confined in a Catholic Magdalene Asylum for wayward girls in Montreal. Even there she had gotten into trouble; a former lover—the real father of the child born in New York—helped her escape. Never had Maria been in the Hotel Dieu Convent; the entire sordid tale was the product of a brain injury in infancy. Other testimonies and later events suggested that the mother's account was substantially correct.

A storm of debate raged after the publication of *Awful Disclosures*; the anti-Catholic press hailed the volume as a bold and truthful exposé of nunneries, and even Protestant religious papers eventually joined the chorus of praise. Indignant Catholics responded in their own papers and with a book-length rebuttal. Continued charges and countercharges led to tracts and public debates nationwide between priests and preachers.

As the controversy intensified, representatives from both sides resolved to settle the matter by an examination of the inside of the Hotel Dieu Convent. Two impartial Protestant clergymen were finally allowed to inspect the facilities; afterward they reported that all of Monk's accusations were false. Her backers accused the ministers of being Jesuits in disguise and insisted that the convent buildings had been altered.

Soon another fugitive "nun" appeared in New York City, claiming to corroborate Monk's story. Her story was also exposed as a fabrication. A second inspection of the convent was made by the respected Protestant editor of a commercial newspaper in New York; after he confirmed the report of the earlier investigators, many Protestant publishers finally denounced Monk.

She disappeared briefly and then reappeared, claiming to have been kidnapped by Catholic priests. Next came a sequel, *Further Disclosures by Maria Monk* (1837), but plans for a lecture tour in a nun's habit never materialized. She was cheated out of her profits by the Protestant clergymen who had backed her and lost several lawsuits that failed to substantiate her stories.

In 1838 Monk gave birth to a second child. After this further scandal the public lost interest quickly. She married, but her new husband left her because she quickly consumed his earnings in drink and riotous living. In 1849 she was jailed for picking the pockets of her current lover in a Five Points brothel, and she died in prison soon after.

Though its author was publicly discredited, *Awful Disclosures* sold 300,000 copies before the Civil War. The "Uncle Tom's Cabin of Know-Nothingism," Monk's sensational tale provided inspiration for further anti-Catholic propaganda and continues to be circulated even today.

Bibliography. Billington, R. A., "Maria Monk and Her Influence," *Catholic Historical Review* 22 (October 1936): 283–96; Billington, R. A., *The Protestant Crusade, 1800–1860* (Gloucester, MA: Peter Smith, 1963); Monk, Maria, *Awful Disclosures of the Hotel Dieu Nunnery of Montreal* (New York: Howe and Bates, 1836).

T. Paul Thigpen

Moon, Rev. Sun Myung. No religious figure of the last third of the twentieth century surpasses Rev. Sun Myung Moon for vigorous reaction, surely most of it negative. Moon is the founder of the Unification Church,* whose proper title is the Holy Spirit Association for the Unification of World Christianity; its members are usually referred to as "Moonies."

Rev. Sun Myung Moon, or "Father," was born in 1920 in Korea to parents who converted to the Presbyterian faith when he was ten. Always deeply religious, he prayed often, and in 1936 experienced an appearance of Jesus. During the next few years, spent mostly in Japan, he engaged in study of religions and of electrical engineering. He also became politically active, participating in the Korean independence movement, for which the Japanese imprisoned him. Back in Korea in 1945, Moon continued both his spiritual quest and his political involvement. The latter activity landed him in Communist prisons several times, the period 1948–1950 being especially harsh and oppressive. Growing out of this experience was a profound opposition to communism as both political system and economic theory, a dedication that has endured and has informed his life and the church's agenda.

A second predominant value, commitment to marriage and family, defines the movement. Moon himself married in 1960, no ordinary turning point. He and Mrs. Moon are True Parents, a term and role to be understood as theological. Family is a, perhaps the, central metaphor and practice in Unification life. The extraordinary, in fact sensational, nature of the event and meaning of marriage is probably what the public associates most readily with "Moonies." In the end, mates are selected by Father, and, typically, the wedding of each pair is conducted as part of a mass ceremony in which several hundred or a few thousand couples experience "the Blessing."

Moon has been sent into the world to complete the unfinished mission of Jesus. Accordingly, he is the Lord of the Second Advent. The movement founded by Moon in 1954 was the source of great consternation in the America of the 1970s when it seemed that the children of privileged families were being converted in great numbers. Actually, the total membership in the United States never exceeded ten thousand. But Moon continues as one of the most conspicuous and least appreciated and understood religious leaders of the late twentieth century.

Bibliography. Chryssides, George D., *The Advent of Sun Myung Moon* (New York: St. Martin's Press, 1991); Fichter, Joseph H., *The Holy Family of Father Moon* (Kansas City, MO: Leaven Press, 1985); Sontag, Frederick, *Sun Myung Moon and the Unification Church* (Nashville: Abingdon Press, 1977).

Samuel S. Hill

Moorish Science Temple. The Moorish Science Temple began as a movement that combined black nationalist aspirations with religious rituals and ethical injunctions. As such, it served as a complement to Marcus Garvey's* secular Universal Negro Improvement Association. At the peak of its influence in the late 1920s the group claimed 100,000 members, although there is reason to believe that the actual membership may have been half that figure. The majority of its members were in the industrial cities of the Northeast and Midwest, but a scattering of temples were found in small towns across the South.

The movement was founded by Timothy Drew,* who was born in North Carolina in 1886. Almost nothing is known about his youth, but he appears to have had only a rudimentary formal education. Nevertheless, he managed to acquire some knowledge regarding Islam and Eastern philosophies and was highly successful in communicating his ideas and influencing people. In 1913 he established the Moorish National and Divine Movement, but soon changed the name to Moorish Science Temple of America. Drew himself took the name Noble Drew Ali.

Over the next sixteen years the Moorish Science Temple became a dynamic part of the various attempts by African Americans to redefine themselves in American society in the face of discrimination and economic hardship. It appears to have been the first African-American group to utilize Islamic symbols and doctrine in the effort to forge a new identity for blacks. Some of the actual doctrines and rituals are carefully guarded secrets and are not divulged to non-initiates. In general, however, it is clear that Noble Drew Ali taught that African Americans are descendants of "Asiatics" whom he identified as Canaanites, Moabites, and Ethiopians, who migrated from Asia across Africa and into Morocco. Islam, not Christianity, was their religion. Likewise, salvation for African Americans can come only if they discard the identities forced upon them by the dominant white race in America and begin living as what he variously called Asiatics, Moors, or Moorish Americans.

Drew Ali published a small book that he called *The Holy Koran of the Moorish Science Temple of America*, but that does not presume to be the Qur'an of Islam. It and smaller pamphlets contain teachings that resemble those of Islam, but there are also echoes of the ideas of Christianity and of Eastern philosophies. Jesus figures prominently in *The Holy Koran*, and Eastern religions are said to be vehicles through which Allah is revealing himself. The book claims that Noble Drew Ali is a prophet whose task is to carry the message of Islam to the people of African descent in America. Noble Drew Ali enjoined his followers to withdraw from the white man in order to escape the destructive effects that contact with whites had brought over the centuries, but he simultaneously taught obedience and loyalty to the government of the United States. The movement was thus not separatist in the sense that the later Nation of Islam* was, but it was exclusionary. Among themselves "Moorish Americans" should practice the five principles of love, truth, peace, freedom, and justice. A spartan life was enjoined upon the members of the community. Polygamy was strictly forbidden, and most frivolous entertainments were banned, as was the use of cosmetics, alcohol, and tobacco. Noble Drew Ali realized that the plight of African Americans would not change appreciably until they were able to benefit from economic development. With his encouragement members set up businesses, and an organization-owned manufacturing company was in place by 1928.

By the late 1920s the movement had become so large that Noble Drew Ali felt compelled to share the leadership with better-educated members who, he felt, were qualified to manage the business affairs of the organization. Unfortunately, several of them were unscrupulous and began selling charms and potions to the membership. Bitter controversies broke out, and Noble Drew Ali himself was challenged for the leadership. In 1929 he died mysteriously, and his organization splintered. One group believed that he had been reincarnated in the form of a self-appointed leader, while others rejected the reincarnation doctrine. Both groups still exist, but are not as visible as other African-American Islamic groups.

See also Black Muslims.

Bibliography. Bontemps, A., and J. Conroy, *They Seek a City* (Garden City, NY: Doubleday, Doran and Company, 1945); Fauset, A. H., *Black Gods of the Metropolis* (Philadelphia: University of Pennsylvania Press, 1944); Haddad, Y. Y. and J. I. Smith, *Mission to America: Five Islamic Sectarian Communities in North America* (Gainesville: University Press of Florida, 1993); Lincoln, C. E., *The Black Muslims in America* (Boston: Beacon Press, 1961. rev. ed. 1973).

Vernon Egger

Moral Majority. The movement that has come to be known as the religious right had its beginnings in the 1970s. As President Jimmy Carter prepared for his second campaign, a group of extremely conservative men, who advocated alterations to the First Amendment religion clauses, were vigorously opposed to the *Roe v. Wade* decision of 1973, and were strongly committed to free-market economic theory cast about for ways to harness the newly minted right-wing evangelical fervor exemplified in a new breed of television ministers such as Jerry Falwell.* These New Right leaders sensed an untapped political force and began to work with Robert Billings, an ordained preacher who was urging Christians to form private schools to escape the secular humanism of the public alternative. Richard Viguerie, direct-mail mogul, Paul Weyrich, head of a conservative think tank, and Howard Phillips, formerly with the Nixon administration, joined together to harness what they perceived as a major political force.

As the host of "The Old Time Gospel Hour," broadcast from Lynchburg, Virginia, Falwell became energized to engage in political action. He and other television preachers like James Robison, James Bakker* and Pat Robertson were making news with their strong condemnation of the Supreme Court and its decisions on abortion and school prayer.

In 1979 Weyrich and Phillips went to Lynchburg to pitch to Falwell the idea of an organization of religious fundamentalists. Falwell had been suggested to them by Ed McAteer, head of the Religious Roundtable, organized in 1979. Weyrich coined the phrase "Moral Majority" and Falwell agreed to form it (*New York Times*, August 18, 1980, sec. B, p. 7). It held its first meeting in June 1979. Commenting upon their plans, Pat Robertson remarked in December 1979 that the Moral Majority was intended as a political force. "It'll be a gradual process. It will take three or four years to say we've made some progress" (*National Journal*, December 22, 1979, 2142). Soon its legislative scope included opposition to the SALT II treaty.

In the fall of 1980 Falwell's new organization was well focused and financed. In September Ronald Reagan visited Falwell's Liberty College and was greeted by a host of religious broadcasters sporting bumper stickers proclaiming "Christians for Reagan." The movement brought new voters to the polls in several states, and that may well have affected the outcome of a number of Senate races. By that time Pat Robertson had left the Falwell bandwagon and, as we now know, began to craft his political alternative through his television "700 Club." However, in 1980 he told *Newsweek* that "active partisan politics" was the wrong path for true evangelicals. "There's a better way," he said: "Fasting and praying . . . appealing, in essence, to a higher power" (*Newsweek*, September 15, 1980, 28).

Falwell was the most visible religious presence in the Reagan White House, while Billings became the President's in-house religion advisor. The long tradition of mainline Protestant denominations having the ear of the president came abruptly to an end, and only in 1993 did that situation change with President Bill Clinton. The irony is that the chief villains in the eyes of the Moral Majority have been Carter and Clinton, both Southern Baptists, representing a progressive posture that in the past fifteen years has disappeared from the denomination's leadership and educational institutions.

Public attention and press hyping gave the Moral Majority far more clout in the public arena than it ever had at the polls. By 1985 Falwell had his most controversial round of publicity, appearing on the cover of *Time* with a related story about his attack on Bishop Desmond Tutu as a phony ("An Unholy Uproar," *Time*, September 2, 1985, 51). The decision of Pat Robertson to shed his ordination and contend for the Republican presidential nomination in 1988, was the death knell, not completely obvious at the time, for the Moral Majority even though Falwell had supported George Bush. Even as free media exposure had been the wellspring for Falwell's influence in the halls of political power, its decline cost him dearly. By 1989, with Liberty University and his television ministry in considerable financial difficulty, Falwell closed the book on the Moral Majority and by 1995 was reduced to hawking a videotape on the "Old Time Gospel Hour" accusing President Clinton of complicity in murders that occurred in Arkansas.

Bibliography. Boston, Robert, "A Short History of the Religious Right," in *Why the Religious Right is Wrong about Separation of Church and State* (Buffalo: Prometheus Books, 1995), 231–35; Mayer, Allan J., "A Tide of Born-Again Politics," *Newsweek*, September 15, 1980, 28ff.

Robert S. Alley

Muhlenberg, William Augustus. William A. Muhlenberg (1796–1877) was a pioneer Episcopal urban minister whose efforts to improve the spiritual quality of his ministry and to extend it to people of all social classes involved him in ecclesiastical controversy. An able and innovative pastor and administrator, Muhlenberg founded a private preparatory school for boys on Long Island in 1828 and St. Paul's College in 1838. In 1846 he became rector of the Church of the Holy Communion in New York City and organized the first Protestant sisterhood in America to carry on the parish's charitable work. Muhlenberg later established St. Luke's Hospital to serve the city's poor people, and from 1858 until his death he served as its superintendent and pastor. In 1868 he created St. Johnland, a community that included an orphanage, an old men's home, and inexpensive cottages for working-class families.

Because he believed that enhancing the aesthetic and devotional quality of worship services could improve the spiritual lives of his parishioners and patients, Muhlenberg used various "high" liturgical practices (antiphonal singing by boys' choirs in vestments, weekly Eucharist, daily hours of prayer) throughout his ministry. He also composed hymns and liturgical music that helped awaken liturgical reform throughout the church.

Muhlenberg saw evangelistic outreach and the liturgical tradition of the church as complementary tools for ministry, and from 1851 to 1853 he published a journal called the *Evangelical Catholic*, in which he promoted the most useful elements of both high- and low-church traditions. In an Episcopal Church that was sharply divided between a Tractarian-influenced Anglo-Catholic party and an anti-Roman Evangelical party, Muhlenberg's "evangelical Catholic" position seemed an attractive *via media* that included the best features of both movements. Muhlenberg, who declared his distaste for civil as well as ecclesiastical politics, denied that he intended to mediate between the two parties; he was simply advocating practical solutions to pastoral problems.

Toward the same practical ends, Muhlenberg drafted a memorial to the House of Bishops in 1853 that called for the bishops to ordain competent ministers of other denominations and to allow them to continue following their own customs of worship and preaching in all areas that the Book of Common Prayer deemed nonessential. This change, he argued, would increase the church's ability to reach unchurched Americans with the gospel and offset its elitist reputation. Muhlenberg's memorial did not win the bishops' approval, but it engendered widespread discussion in the church and helped refocus the church's attention on its mission in American society. It also boosted Muhlenberg to prominence in the ecumenical movement in America.

Bibliography. Ayres, Anne, *The Life and Work of William Augustus Muhlenberg* (New York: Harper and Brothers, 1880); Muhlenberg, William A., *Evangelical Catholic Papers* (New York: T. Whittaker, 1875); Skardon, Alvin Wilson, *Church Leader in the Cities: William Augustus Muhlenberg* (Philadelphia: University of Pennsylvania Press, 1971).

John P. Rossing

N

NAACP. The National Association for the Advancement of Colored People (NAACP) was founded in January 1909 as one of the early African-American secular organizations. A very important fact is that it was founded and supported with the help of the black church. As a matter of fact, black church membership and that of the NAACP overlapped. The founding of the NAACP was a way for more progressive black church leaders to deal with "more complex and pluralistic environments." Nor did the founding of the NAACP require a complete separation of church and state. Lincoln and Mamiya contend that, unlike most social scientific views of religion in modern society, which differentiate between spheres of polity and economy, the NAACP created no similar divisions. Nor was the black church at the turn of the century a case of "privatized religion." Instead, the lines between black organizations such as the NAACP and the black church were blurred.

Some of the leading urban black clergy realized the need for a civil rights* organization with a broad secular base such as the NAACP. From the beginning, such organizations found their major support in the black church and black clergy. This relationship meant that NAACP meetings followed worship services in many black congregations.

Along with W.E.B. Du Bois, progressive-minded black clergy like Reverdy Ransom of the African Methodist Episcopal Church had been members of the 1905 Niagara Movement, which had been founded as a reaction to Booker T. Washington's "racial gradualism." They also supported the founding of the NAACP as an interracial organization protesting for black rights in the political area. As an organization, the NAACP was in the tradition of the earlier Baptist mutual-aid societies. These quasi-church organizations were the first social institutions created by African Americans. According to Lincoln and Mamiya, "They often existed in symbiotic relationship" and spread rapidly in areas where there were large numbers of free blacks. In function and purpose, they were forerunners of the NAACP and the National Urban League.

Over the years, the powerful white influence in the early NAACP, with which black churches were allied, caused the NAACP to assume a mainstream, comfortable middle-class position that has lasted until today. For this reason, according to Wilmore, even during the King era of the modern civil rights movement (1950s and 1960s), a number of conservative black pastors and their members preferred "the NAACP style of reformist activities through the courts."

In recent years two executive directors of the NAACP have been black clergy, Benjamin L. Hooks and Benjamin F. Chavis. In 1977 Hooks, a Baptist minister, replaced Roy Wilkins as executive director, serving in that capacity for fifteen years. In 1993 Chavis, former executive director of the Commission for Racial Justice of the United Church of Christ, replaced Hooks. Chavis unjustly spent four and one-half years in a North Carolina prison as a member of the Wilmington Ten during the 1970s, but the case was overturned by a U.S. court of appeals. Embracing such black leaders as Louis Farrakhan,* leader of the Nation of Islam,* Chavis worked to bring the work of the NAACP closer in line with the needs of the black masses. Encountering the wrath of the organization's board in relation to a sexual harassment suit, Chavis was forced to resign in 1994.

Bibliography. Lincoln, C. E., and L. H. Mamiya, *The Black Church in the African-American Experience* (Durham: Duke University Press, 1990); Luker, R. E., *The Social Gospel in Black and White: American Racial Reform, 1885–1991* (Chapel Hill: University of North Carolina Press, 1991); McPherson, J. M., *The Abolitionist Legacy: From Reconstruction to the NAACP* (Princeton: Princeton University Press, 1975); Wilmore, G. S., *Black Religion and Black Radicalism*, 2nd rev. ed. (Maryknoll, NY: Orbis Books, 1983).

Lawrence H. Williams

Nation, Carry. Born in Kentucky on November 25, 1846, Carry Amelia Nation grew through a creative and somewhat boisterous childhood to a stature of nearly six feet tall. A mental picture forms easily when one attaches a weight of some 175 pounds to that tall frame of a body, imagines a hatchet in her right hand, and places a stern look of dogged determination on the rugged features of her face. She struck fear into many a Kansas bartender's heart. Her raids on the drinking "joints" of her day were daring and brutal. Controversy met Carry Nation at every turn for precisely this reason. Never before had Americans witnessed a woman capable of expressing the force of her convictions with such persuasive and intimidating prowess.

The failure of Carry Nation's two marriages (though she never divorced her second husband) contributed in significant ways to her career as a reformer opposed to liquor, tobacco, and the Masonic Lodge, among other things. Though she had great love for her first husband, Dr. Charles Gloyd, she lived with him only a very brief time. An alcoholic who spent most of his evenings getting drunk at the Masonic Lodge, Gloyd neglected his young wife, who was already with child. She left him early in the first year of their marriage. His alcoholism killed him about six months after their daughter Charlien was born. Her second husband, David Nation, some nineteen years older, proved himself a deceptive man who never truly loved her. Carry Nation often grieved her lack of a loving home environment, but concluded in her autobiography, "The very thing that I was denied caused me to have a desire to secure it to others." Since alcohol often led to broken homes, she directed her passion to rid the world of its curse.

Elected president of the Barber County chapter of the Woman's Christian Temperance Union* (WCTU) in 1888 in Medicine Lodge, Kansas, Carry Nation began her physical crusade against saloons only after she had exhausted her written appeals to political authorities in the state to shut down the illegal drinking establishments. After receiving a call from God through prayer early in the summer of 1900, she trashed three saloons in Kiowa. When she traveled to Wichita and used an iron rod and a brass cuspidor to wreak havoc on the beautiful Hotel Carry bar, she found the publicity that would make her famous. She was arrested, but released, and the story of her activities brought invitations from throughout Kansas. She preferred hatchets the next year (1901), when she smashed her way through some twenty or more saloon raids.

Her hatchet brought her the fame reserved mostly for highly controversial figures. The mainstream of the WCTU leadership and membership rejected her methods. Her home church, the local congregation of the Disciples of Christ, openly questioned the soundness of her faith. Though she often spoke before large crowds on the lecture circuit in 1901 and in later years, raising enough money to buy two homes for "Drunkards' Wives and Children," she had fervent support among only a few fanatics wherever she went. Her untimely condemnation of President McKinley shortly after he was shot increased the volume of controversy surrounding her. Nation loved attention of any kind and hoped for a martyrdom she never experienced. She challenged every stereotype women of her generation faced and, though controversial, gave heart to the emerging women's movement both in America and in Europe.

Bibliography. Holbrook, S. H., ed., *Dreamers of the American Dream* (Garden City, NY: Doubleday and Company, 1957); Nation, C. A, *The Use and Need of the Life of Carry A. Nation* (Topeka: F. M. Steves and Sons, 1904); Taylor, R. L., *Vessel of Wrath: The Life and Times of Carry Nation* (New York: New American Library, 1966).

Mark G. Toulouse

Nation of Islam. The Nation of Islam was begun in Detroit in 1930 by the enigmatic Wali Fard Muhammad (also known as Wallace Delaney Fard and Master Wali Farrad, among other names). Many of his followers regarded him as the reincarnation of Noble Drew Ali (Timothy Drew*), founder of the Moorish Science Temple* movement. Fard taught that the "so-called Negroes" were actually the Asiatic black people, who were Allah's first creation. Some six thousand years ago Yakub, a black scientist in rebellion against Allah, sought to challenge Allah by creating the white race. These "blue-eyed devils" subsequently came to dominate and exploit the other peoples of the earth, and the only way to gain freedom from them was through economic independence. Echoing the black nationalist rhetoric of the period, Fard demanded a separate territory for African Americans. Unlike Marcus Garvey's* plan to emigrate to Africa, Fard demanded that the government of the United States allocate one or more states for the purposes of the Asiatic black people, where they could govern themselves and develop a separate black economy.

Fard disappeared in 1934, and after a struggle for power his chosen successor, Elijah Muhammad,* assumed leadership of the group. Elijah remained the leader of the organization from 1934 until his death in 1975. Under him the Nation developed its distinctive identity as a separatist religious group in America. It developed a strict discipline. Members were enjoined to pray five times a day and to abstain from alcohol and tobacco. They were to eat but once a day and to dress modestly. Despite its Islamic attributes, significant departures from Islam caused Muslims across the world to question its authenticity: it had temples instead of mosques and ministers instead of imams and the month of fasting was December instead of Ramadan. The doctrine that was patently blasphemous from an orthodox Sunni perspective was Elijah's declaration that Fard was Allah.

Doctrine, however, was never the main attraction for the Nation's adherents. Its inculcation of discipline, self-respect, and morality were far more important, as were the many economic enterprises that Elijah encouraged, which had the aim of developing economic independence from the white-dominated economy. The Nation was a small movement, perhaps not exceeding one thousand members, until the early 1950s, when Malcolm X* became Elijah Muhammad's chief minister. With this charismatic representative, thousands of young African Americans joined the movement, impatient with the slow progress of the civil rights* movement. The period of the Nation's greatest growth was 1959–1965. In 1959 Mike Wallace of the CBS network broadcast a show entitled "The Hate That Hate Produced," catapulting the Nation into the national spotlight, with Malcolm X as chief spokesman for Elijah Muhammad's movement. After Malcolm's assassination the Nation's growth appears to have slowed, both because of the apparent complicity of the Nation in the assassination and because of the rise of other black activist organizations.

Elijah Muhammad died in 1975 and was succeeded by his son Wallace Deen Muhammad. For over a decade he had urged his father to bring the organization into conformity with orthodox Sunni Islam. Now he changed his name to Warith Deen Muhammad, renounced the goal of racial separation, and began to make doctrines and rituals consistent with Islam. In 1976 he renamed the organization the World Community of Islam, and in 1980 he changed its name once again to the American Muslim Mission. In 1986 he disbanded it so that nothing would distinguish his followers from the rest of the world Muslim community. In 1977 Louis Farrakhan* seceded from Muhammad's group and claimed to carry on the true legacy of Elijah Muhammad. He revived the name and the apparatus of the Nation of Islam.

Bibliography. Lincoln, C. E., *The Black Muslims in America* (Boston: Beacon Press, 1961; rev. ed., 1973); Mamiya, L. H., "From Black Muslim to Bilalian. The Evolution of a Movement," *Journal for the Scientific Study of Religion* 21, no. 2 (June 1982): 138–52; Marsh, C. E., *From Black Muslims to Muslims: The Transition from Separatism to Islam, 1930–1980* (Metuchen, NJ: Scarecrow Press, 1984); Munir, F. Z., "Islam in America: An African American Pilgrimage toward Coherence" (Ph.D. diss. Temple University, 1993).

Vernon Egger

National Council of Churches. Formed in 1950, the National Council of Churches of Christ in America (NCC) carried on the social and ecumenical tradition of its parent body, the Federal Council of Churches of Christ in America, organized in 1908. Though mostly mainline Protestant in membership, the denominations within the NCC are still quite diverse. Like its predecessor, the NCC has included within its central mission the examination of critical social and public issues the world over. In its earlier years the council, through its various program units, generally researched social problems and produced educational resources for member denominations, over thirty in number. During the early 1960s, stirred by the civil rights* movement, the council took on a much more activist role in working toward social change.

The diversity of the NCC sometimes provides the occasion for internal controversy. Church leadership in the larger African-American denominations has tended to be more socially and theologically conservative than the other Protestant churches in the council. Eastern Orthodox member churches, as well, have expressed dissatisfaction with council pronouncements on human sexuality, abortion,* women and the church, and other issues important to the more progressive Protestants in the ecumenical body. Internal controversy is as old as the NCC itself. In its early years the council's desire to increase lay participation led to the formation of the National Lay Committee, chaired by J. Howard Pew. Well known for his very conservative views, Pew stacked the committee's membership, hoping to redirect the NCC's activities toward more evangelistic directions. In the mid-1950s, when the efforts of the National Lay Committee began to affect the stability of the council itself, leadership had no choice but to discontinue its activities. Pew redirected his efforts by funding a new periodical, *Christianity Today*, which throughout its history has been a severe critic of the NCC.

The most divisive issue internally these days involves gay civil rights and the place of homosexual Christians within the church itself. In 1975 the Governing Board of the NCC, by a vote of 86–17, indicated support for persons deprived of their civil rights "because of their affectional or sexual preference." In 1982 the Universal Fellowship of Metropolitan Community Churches (UFMCC) requested membership in the NCC. The denomination, numbering over 30,000 members, was formed in 1968 to serve homosexual Christians as a worshipping community. The request has stirred considerable debate within the council, along with threats from some denominations to abandon membership if the request is granted. The council has been unable to find the agreement necessary even to grant the UFMCC "observer" status, an honorary designation carrying no rights of membership.

The council's active engagement with political and social issues has created external controversy with some regularity. Within a decade after Mao Tse-tung's success in China in 1949, the council urged normalization of diplomatic relations with the People's Republic of China. NCC leaders consistently recommended seating a Communist Chinese delegate on the Security Council of the United Nations in the seat occupied by the Republic of China on Taiwan. In 1952 the NCC published the Revised Standard Version (RSV) of the Bible, which immediately came under attack by conservatives as Scriptures tainted by sympathy for communism. An official U.S. Air Force training manual warned that thirty church leaders associated with the NCC and working on the RSV project had Communist affiliations. The source utilized by the author of the training manual turned out to be fundamentalist preacher Billy James Hargis.* The manual was withdrawn in 1960 after the NCC filed an official protest.

The council was an early advocate of racial justice and ardent defender of desegregation. Its leadership became increasingly critical of the Vietnam War throughout the early 1960s. In later years NCC leaders added other issues of importance to their activist agenda, including the fights to secure rights for American Indians, the poor in urban areas, migrant workers, and gays. Council stances on these issues have caused their share of controversy. More recently, the NCC has supported mission endeavors in Third World locations where anti-American sentiment runs high. Especially during President Ronald Reagan's administration, the council's open criticism of both American foreign policy and the excesses of American capitalism, combined with its advocacy for liberation movements in Africa, Nicaragua, and other locations in the world, led to new rounds of controversial charges surrounding its activities.

The Institute on Religion and Democracy (IRD), an organization composed of sophisticated conservative Christian thinkers who oppose the progressive theological and political drift of mainline Protestant trends in the last few decades, made an early career of attacking the NCC. IRD leadership has charged the council with funding Marxist organizations and antidemocratic forces across the world. These charges captured public attention in January 1983 when the popular CBS television program "60 Minutes" devoted an entire program segment to an uncritical airing entitled "The Gospel According to Whom?" The January *Reader's Digest* attacked the World Council of Churches in an article entitled "Do You Know Where Your Church Offerings Go?" IRD leadership had connections to both media events. Though the NCC has survived these controversial years, its financial base of support among member denominations has diminished considerably. The administrative bureaucracy of the NCC, though necessary for its work, does not easily lend itself to the loyalty of the average congregation in America.

Bibliography. Findlay, J. F., *Church People in the Struggle: The National Council of Churches and the Black Freedom Movement, 1950–1970* (New York: Oxford University Press, 1993); Lyles, J. C., "Not to Decide . . . ," *Christian Century* 100 (November 30, 1983): 1099–1100; Pratt, H. J., *The Liberalization of American Protestantism: A Case Study in Complex Organizations* (Detroit: Wayne State University Press, 1972).

Mark G. Toulouse

Native American Church. The Native American Church, a legally constituted religious organization, is one of the more visible components of peyotism. As such, it has often been the focal point of wide-ranging criticisms and antipeyote campaigns.

Peyote is a cactus native to northern Mexico and southern Texas. Its fruit, known as a "mescal bean" or "button," produces hallucinations when ingested, and Indians have used this plant ritually for thousands of years. Customarily confined to the Rio Grande area, peyotism began diffusing northward through the central plains during the nineteenth century. People use the plant because it offers physical curing and spiritual visions. Though local variations are manifold, using peyote in worship exhibits some common features, including ceremonies that last all night (usually Saturdays) where participants sing, witness, and pray while arranged in a circle around a sacred fire and a crescent-shaped mound altar that holds peyote buttons for distribution. The event ends with a communal breakfast, after which many leave to attend Sunday services at other Christian churches.

By the 1890s there was evidence of vigorous opposition to peyotism. This antagonism presumed that the effects of peyote were intoxicating, and opponents proceeded to curtail its use through laws that outlawed liquor on Indian reservations. By 1916 a national prohibition bill had passed the House of Representatives, but it failed in the Senate. The possible success of such widespread restriction led representatives from several tribes to seek incorporation and thus secure the protection enjoyed by other American religious institutions. In August 1918 they met in El Reno, Oklahoma, to establish a formal organization, elect officers, and adopt a body of rules. On October 10 of that year they received legal sanction through a state charter, using the name Native American Church (NAC). Since any group's charter is legitimate unless a state specifically voids it, peyotism burgeoned under the NAC's aegis. The Oklahoma institution functioned as a mother church, furnishing supplies and counsel that strengthened growth among affiliate societies. Expansion occasioned name changes, and in

1950 the NAC of North America referred to some 225,000 coreligionists found in at least 50 tribes, residing in 18 states and 2 Canadian provinces.

Controversies have swirled around practices in the NAC. They center on using peyote, a substance unknown to most tribes before 1800. Because of that, native traditionalists have resisted the new element, regarding it as either an intrusion on accepted standards or a distraction from loyalty to them. Within the NAC, whose members are a minority in every tribe where they are found, adherents believe peyote to be a sacrament. Even though additional features include Jesus, the Bible, and an ethic of sobriety, many Christian traditionalists denounce the NAC as stemming from pagan roots. This spectrum of differing criticism— Indian purists finding danger in nontribal traditions and white Christian purists finding danger in unbiblical elements—plainly underscores the syncretistic dynamics of this religious perspective.

Most of the controversies, however, have been fueled by questions about the nature of peyote itself, its chemical properties, and the effects produced. Law officials, reservation agents, and missionaries first tried to control peyote through local liquor laws, then the Volstead Act, interstate commerce regulations, and finally through drug-abuse legislation. Only three states originally refused to acknowledge the NAC's original charter, but antagonism increased through the 1950s, and the number of hostile states grew to a dozen. Municipal, county, and state legislation has proved largely futile, and since all efforts to secure a national ban have failed, harassment of church members has lessened considerably in recent decades. Peyotists have sustained their legal rights, and in 1978 the American Indian Religious Freedom Act specifically stated that use of peyote in an NAC ceremony is protected by law. Widespread misunderstanding and suspicion still exist, however, and many peyote churches have adopted a policy of secrecy. Ignorance on one side and protective silence on the other do little to lower the wall separating the two perspectives or to mitigate controversies that grow in its shadow.

Alongside debates between the NAC and outsiders, internal difficulties also emerged among participants. In 1956 the church's annual convention elected Frank Takes Gun as president. This energetic and ambitious Crow tribesman incorporated churches for greater protection in various states and enlisted the American Civil Liberties Union to defend Indians in peyote cases. Driven by the strength of his convictions, Takes Gun chafed under the restrictions of democratic procedures. His grasp for power and unconstitutional tactics alienated many long-time members, and splinter groups emerged as marks of protest. Other separations have occurred due to different preferences in polity and liturgy. The NAC of North America may justifiably be designated an outstanding example of pan-Indian collaboration in the twentieth century, but subgroups such as the NAC of Navajoland, the NAC of the Four Corners, the NAC of Jesus Christ at Porcupine, and the Ancient NAC of South Dakota show that the familiar phenomenon of denominationalism is appearing here as it has in most American religious institutions.

Bibliography. Stewart, Omer C., *Peyote Religion: A History* (Norman: University of Oklahoma Press, 1987).

Henry Warner Bowden

Nativism. Used in the American context, the term "nativism" usually refers to Protestant anti-immigrant and/or anti-Catholic bias. It is natural for people in every culture and time frame to harbor a sense of esteem for themselves and correspondingly negative attitudes regarding those of different ethnic or religious identities. When Protestant-Catholic antagonisms reached extremes in the late sixteenth century, they became deeply rooted in English life and were thus transferred to New World colonies in subsequent decades. Protestants dominated affairs in every colony except one, Maryland, whose first proprietors were Catholics who launched America's first experiment in religious freedom. This magnanimous act of 1649 was soon reversed by Protestant settlers who took both political power and religious liberty from their Catholic neighbors. Succeeding generations of indigenized or "native" Americans in almost every colony demanded that later immigrants conform to prevalent standards or suffer retaliation against their "foreign" ways.

Most American colonists retained their anti-Catholic bias while accepting immigration as essential to social and economic stability. In the nation-building years after the Revolution, however, nativist outbursts became more violent. By the 1830s Irish immigrants received the brunt of increased fear and anger directed toward foreigners and their alien practices. After a spate of anti-Catholic diatribes from Boston pulpits, notably that of Lyman Beecher,* a mob descended on an Ursuline convent in Charlestown, Massachusetts, and in August 1834 burned it to the ground. Such actions were echoed in Philadelphia (1844) and Louisville (1855), where riots caused deaths among both desecrators and defenders of local Catholic churches. Throughout these decades hostile presses poured forth salacious "true accounts" of Catholic life, and newspapers gave lengthy coverage to debates between detractors and advocates of the faith. Finally reaching the level of political action, nativism was the driving force behind the Know-Nothing party* which succeeded in electing representatives to a few northern legislatures and some even to the nation's Congress. The party's platform for safeguarding the country from outsiders was soon eclipsed by issues that led to secession and civil war.

In the 1880s nativism once again developed a widespread public virulence. Finding supporters more in midwestern towns than in eastern cities, the American Protective Association fanned the flames of anti-immigrant and anti-Catholic resentment. Economic slumps made it easy to blame cheap labor just off the boat for hard times. The Catholic Church was still seen as a foreign power, and many found it easy to believe that there was a papal plot to overthrow the American government and slaughter Protestants in their beds. Such charges and accusations circulated among those who needed someone to blame for their difficulties. As with a fever, nativist passions gradually subsided by the mid-1890s.

The twentieth century has also witnessed forms of this constant in American culture, including enthusiasm in the 1920s for laws restricting immigration and Ku Klux Klan* denunciations of all who deviated from the white, Anglo-Saxon, Protestant ideal. This sentiment was a large factor in the 1928 defeat of Catholic presidential candidate Alfred E. Smith. It surfaced in several ways throughout later decades, but the presidential campaign of 1960 helped dampen nativist ardor. John F. Kennedy proved many anti-Catholic fears to be groundless, and in recent decades they have been more latent than overt. But since nativism has existed in America from its beginnings, it will probably continue to exist in one form or another, and it will find new ways of expressing itself in future decades of national life.

Bibliography. Billington, Ray A., *The Protestant Crusade, 1800–1860: A Study of the Origins of American Nativism* (New York: Macmillan, 1938, 1952); Higham, John, *Strangers in the Land: Patterns of American Nativism, 1860–1925* (New Brunswick, NJ: Rutgers University Press, 1988).

Henry Warner Bowden

Neo-Orthodoxy. Within Protestantism (there have been ''neo-orthodox'' movements within Roman Catholicism as well as within Judaism), the Neo-Orthodoxy designation is given to a movement and several key theologians with its primary origins in Europe in the early twentieth century, but with a global influence. The movement has been marked by internal diversity as well as by mixed external perceptions. Two other designations are often used for this movement: Crisis Theology and Dialectical Theology. Most followers as well as observers appear to accept the implications of the designation ''neo-orthodox'' as itself a reasonable way to understand the main characteristics of the movement from a historical perspective, with ''dialectical'' as an appropriate designation for the theological method employed and a recognition that the term ''crisis'' carries the meaning of ''significant time'' and ''decision.''

The ''orthodox'' dimension of the movement is what clearly marked it off from the then-dominant (at least within Protestantism) liberal view of religion in general, and of Christianity in particular. Key themes in this quasi-return to Reformation Protestant orthodoxy were suspicion of human nature after the Fall, especially of human reason as a means of knowing God and the divine will; and a calling into question of human experience as the foundation on which to base religious beliefs or as a reliable guide to religious practice. The seriousness of human sin and the need for divine grace in human salvation were central affirmations. This return to Protestant orthodoxy found adherents stressing the qualitative distance between God and fallen humanity, and the concomitant reliance on the grace of God to bridge this gap.

The "new" helps to identify what distinguishes this form of Protestant orthodoxy from the former (essentially Protestant) "orthodoxy" of the seventeenth and eighteenth centuries. Central to this newness was the attitude toward and appropriation of historical-critical methods on the part of those within the movement in working with the Bible, and a parallel freedom to reinterpret the major themes of (again, essentially Protestant) theology.

Neo-orthodox writers took the Bible very seriously and subscribed to the Reformation maxim of "sola scriptura," but they were not fundamentalists. They also took seriously the enduring central Reformation theological themes—sin, justification, redemption, and even predestination*; but what they did with these themes was not always acceptable to other "orthodox" Christians of their day. They understood, as had Protestant liberalism before them, the need to represent the timeless truth of the Scriptures and of the doctrines of the church in ways that impacted on the realities of their own day. They sought to be true to the threefold meaning of the "Word of God": the life, death, and resurrection of Jesus the Christ as "the Word made flesh"; the Bible as the normative witness to Jesus Christ; and the faithful proclamation of this Word of God in the preaching of the church. But the neo-orthodox emphasis on the Christ of faith vis-à-vis the Jesus of history is one area where the "new" was unacceptable to traditional Christian orthodoxy.

The resulting blend of "orthodox" and "new" is seen perhaps most clearly in the writings of the generally acknowledged founder of the movement, Karl Barth, as well as in the works of Gustaf Aulen. But the variety of ways in which this blending could move can also be seen in Emil Brunner and his "debates" with Barth, especially regarding "natural revelation."

In the United States, two other names often associated with this movement were Paul Tillich and the brothers Niebuhr, Reinhold and H. Richard. But these latter three, perhaps because of their American context, were often seen as more "new" and less "orthodox." Whereas earlier neo-orthodox theologians tended to stress the role of theology in differentiating between "church" and "world" (an extension of the underlying distance between God and fallen humanity apart from saving grace), these theologians tended to present theology as performing an important mediating function between church and world. A recurring theme of these theologians was their identification of the continuing presence of grace within the fallen creation.

Bibliography. *Encyclopedia of Religion*, 16 vols., NY: Macmillan 1987; *New Catholic Encyclopedia* (New York: McGraw-Hill, 1967). In addition to consulting works by and about the theologians mentioned in this entry, see the following works: Hordern, William, *The Case for a New Reformation Theology* (Philadelphia: Westminster Press, 1959); Robinson, James M., ed. *The Beginnings of Dialectic Theology* (Richmond: John Knox Press, 1968).

Robert L. VanDale

Nevin, John Williamson. Mercersburg theologian John Williamson Nevin (1803–1886), who with his colleague Philip Schaff* created a distinctive type of theology in America, found himself embroiled in controversy throughout his career. Nevin came to Mercersburg in 1840 and two years later found himself at odds with the parishioners of the Mercersburg Village Church when they extended a call to a minister who had adopted the revival measures of Charles G. Finney,* including the altar call. The controversy broadened when Nevin published *The Anxious Bench* (1843), in which he blasted the excesses of revivalism and advocated the ''system of the catechism'' against the ''system of the bench.'' Many in the German Reformed Church who had been influenced by Finney's ''New Measures'' revivalism* took umbrage at their seminary's new theological professor.

Controversy broke out again when Nevin was joined by young, Swiss-born, German-educated Philip Schaff, who came to Mercersburg in 1844. Schaff's inaugural address, later published as *The Principle of Protestantism* (1845), created a storm of protest because of its author's suspected Romanistic tendencies. Nevin plunged into the fray and strongly defended his colleague and himself. Schaff was exonerated, but in the years to come Nevin would take on all comers with vigor and incisive logic. Both Nevin and Schaff expressed appreciation for the catholic tradition of the church and held a high view of the sacraments.

Nevin's *The Mystical Presence* (1846) challenged Reformed Christians in America to recapture the concept of sacramental presence advocated by John Calvin. Most American Christians, Nevin argued, had become thoroughly Zwinglian in their understanding of the Lord's Supper.

Ongoing attacks on Roman Catholicism by German Reformed leaders prompted Nevin to intensive study of early Christianity. Against American sectarianism and individualism Nevin argued for catholic unity and the organic character of the historical church. Despite obvious corruptions, Nevin always insisted that the historical church was the true church. Indeed, the ''church question'' engrossed Nevin throughout his career.

Later, when Nevin contemplated joining the Catholic Church and corresponded with noted convert Orestes Brownson,* many saw that step as the natural result of his flirtations with Rome. So distressed was Nevin about the lack of unity and theological authority in so much of American Christianity that he contemplated moving toward the objective authority of the Roman Church. Eventually, Nevin found himself again firmly rooted within the Protestant tradition, but controversy continued to follow him because of those who could not accept even the most measured appreciation of the catholic tradition.

Finally, Nevin became involved in the controversial effort to revise the liturgy within the German Reformed tradition. Conservatives strongly opposed revision efforts as attempts to destroy the theological heritage of the church, while Nevin and others insisted that the liturgy must be revised to recognize theological and ecclesiastical developments. Nevin unstintingly blasted American individualism, revivalism, and sectarianism, calling for American Christians to appreciate the Christian past and to learn from it.

Bibliography. Appel, Theodore, *The Life and Work of John Williamson Nevin* (Philadelphia: Reformed Church Publication House, 1889); Conser, Walter H., Jr., *Church* *and Confession: Conservative Theologians in Germany, England, and America, 1815–1866* (Macon: Mercer University Press, 1984); Hamstra, Sam, Jr., and Arie J. Griffioen, eds., *Reformed Confessionalism in Nineteenth-Century America: Essays on the Thought of John Williamson Nevin* (Lanham, MD: Scarecrow Press, 1995).

Stephen R. Graham

New Age Movement. The relatively recent all-encompassing term "New Age movement" refers to a movement that has existed for a long time, not to a single organization. It is a mixture of secularism, Eastern religion, humanistic psychology, ancient and medieval witchcraft, pagan pantheism, science, and pseudoscience. It has mainstreamed its way into culture in music, education, motivational training, television, movies, books, and products in every market. Roughly 30 million Americans believe in reincarnation, a key belief of the New Age. Two-thirds report having psychic experiences such as ESP. The New Age is ultimately a vision of a world transformed, a heaven on earth, a society in which problems of today are overcome and a new existence emerges. Advocates claim that the New Age is a millennial movement that deals with efforts to improve, if not perfect, human behavior and human life, that it is a very old view that attempts to create spiritual values in a material world and that lends itself to individual private events that end up transforming society.

There are at least two expressions of this movement: (1) the occult expression, which involves reincarnation, crystal power, channeling, spirit guides, UFOs, and extraterrestrials; and (2) the humanistic expression, which is intent on developing unlimited human potential. Both versions see themselves as offering "salvation" to humankind through a hoped-for imminent, evolutionary transformation that will propel humanity into deification.

The following New Age premises are points of controversy with traditional Christian thought: (1) God is impersonal and not separate or distinct from creation, the aggregate consciousness of all living things, expanding through human evolution. (2) Jesus is not the supreme and final revelation of God but is a spiritually attuned or evolved being who serves as an example for spiritual discovery and evolutionary development, having tapped into the power that is available to anyone. (3) Humanity shares the essential being of God and is therefore divine since what is termed God is within one's being. (4) Humanity's crises come not from sin or evil but from ignorance of divinity and one's awareness—indeed, arrival at perfection, omnipotence, and immortality comes through an awakening, a transformation. (5) A new way of thinking about old problems (a "paradigm shift") is needed in which dualistic perceptions of reality (Creator-created) are replaced by holistic ones. The old paradigm divides and separates; the new paradigm makes room for the unity between reality and the divine. Each person can actualize his or her divine nature and achieve the ultimate unifying principles by utilizing psychotechnologies such as induced sensory isolation or sensory overload, biofeedback, chanting, psychodrama, meditation, use of crystals, channeling, and pyramidology. (6) The sequel to expanded personal awareness is planetary transformation characterized by mass enlightenment and social evolution. "Earth Day" celebrations are examples. The focus of controversy between traditional Christian theology and New Age thinking is evident in the summary of New Age thinking: All is One; God is All; and All is God. Humanity is deified; death is denied; and ignorance, not evil or sin, is the enemy.

Bibliography. Chandler, Russell, *Understanding the New Age* (Grand Rapids, MI: Zondervan, 1993); Ferguson, Marilyn, *The Aquarian Conspiracy: Personal and Social Transformations in the 1980's* (Los Angeles: J. P. Tarcher, 1980); Lochhaas, Philip H., *How to Respond to the New Age Movement* (St. Louis: Concordia, 1988); Streiker, Lowell D., *New Age Comes to Main Street* (Nashville: Abingdon Press, 1990).

Robert K. Gustafson

New Divinity Men. In 1765 Samuel Hopkins* published *Enquiry concerning the Promises of the Gospel*. In a 1767 response Jedidiah Mills charged that the divinity in Hopkins's work was "new." Hence the term "New Divinity" became a label for Hopkins and the school of thought he represented.

The New Divinity men were theological heirs of Jonathan Edwards.* They propagated Edwards's work while at the same time innovatively adding to Edwards's legacy. Their theological work—centered particularly around a defense of the Calvinistic doctrine of God's sovereignty as it related to human moral agency—progressed alongside and in support of their views of revivalism,* church membership, and social concerns.

Samuel Hopkins provided much of the writing that undergirds the New Divinity. He was representative of New Divinity thought in his teaching: (1) sinners could not prepare for grace; rather, it was an immediate action of the Holy Spirit upon the heart; (2) God willingly permitted sin to achieve the greater good; and (3) disinterested benevolence served as the substance and proof of holiness. His claim that one must be willing to be damned for the greater glory of God was understood by him to signal that one's heart was truly holy, for it sought selflessly after the greater good rather than selfishly after its own salvation. In the New Divinity scheme, God was a moral governor who ruled from the perspective of disinterested benevolence. Hopkins's 1793 work, *System of Doctrines Contained in Divine Revelation* became the textbook for the New Divinity.

Joseph Bellamy was, in many ways, the teacher of the movement. In his parsonage he taught many young men attracted to the New Divinity movement. Taking the view that God was primarily a moral governor, he developed a theory of the atonement that emphasized that Christ's death was not a payment for a debt owed to an angry father; rather, Christ's death was a moral necessity, needed to show the importance of upholding God's law and moral justice. As such, the atonement was not limited, as taught in some classic expressions of Calvinism; it was a general atonement that set the moral universe aright.

Nathanael Emmons, Jonathan Edwards, Jr., and Stephen West were other well-known New Divinity men. They were active, along with Hopkins and Bellamy, in establishing New Divinity tenets in western Massachusetts and Connecticut. Indeed, Litchfield County, Connecticut, and Berkshire County, Massachusetts, served as the original strongholds of the New Divinity men, from which the movement spread.

The New Divinity men were greatly influenced by the Great Awakening.* Edwards sought to explore the theological meaning of the Great Awakening; his followers also carried this concern. Between the time of the Great Awakening in the early 1740s, during which time the young Hopkins experienced regeneration, and the start of the Second Great Awakening* in the early nineteenth century, the New Divinity men labored at a theological scheme that made the experience of grace understandable. Many of the older New Divinity men saw the beginning of the Second Great Awakening as a vindication of their labors.

Yale College served as fertile ground for the recruitment of New Divinity men. Young men from Yale found the intellectual rigor of the movement, combined with its concern for the affective side of religion, appealing. In the first decades of the movement, graduates who sought ministerial positions studied with New Divinity ministers in "schools of the prophets," where they learned both the intricacies of New Divinity theology and the practical work of preaching. Because of cultural changes, these schools eventually gave way to seminary education. Andover Seminary was established in 1808 as a professional school that trained New Divinity ministers (in cooperation with moderate Calvinists in reaction to liberal Harvard).

It has been noted that the New Divinity was the first truly American school of theology. But, like all schools, it eventually split. The issue was one at the heart of the New Divinity—human moral agency. The conservative wing of New Divinity followed Hopkins (Hopkinsians, or consistent Calvinists) in his understanding of the will. Hopkins taught that humanity was responsible for its acts of sin because the intellect was not depraved—it could naturally recognize the good. Yet the unregenerated heart did not do the good because, morally, it was inclined to evil and had a "taste" for selfishness. This moral depravity was such that the "will not" of the will effectively became a "could not." Nathaniel William Taylor, who assumed a position at Yale Divinity School in 1822, accepted much of New Divinity teaching—such as God as a moral governor—but thought the teaching on moral agency was confusing. In 1828, his sermon *Concio ad Clerum* claimed that for humanity to be truly responsible for sin, human beings must have real choices, and a real choice involved having a real "power to the contrary"; that is, if an act of sin is to truly be held against a person, that person, in his or her choice, had to have the power to act otherwise than he or she did. Elsewise, it is not a real choice, and only real choices carry real accountability. Taylor was charged by the consistent Calvinists with Arminianism,* but his emphasis on true freedom in choice served as the theological rationale for some of the emerging evangelists, such as Charles G. Finney* and Lyman Beecher.*

Bibliography. Breitenbach, William, "Unregenerate Doings: Selflessness and Selfishness in New Divinity Theology," *American Quarterly* 34 (Winter 1982): 479–502; Conforti, Joseph A., *Samuel Hopkins and the New Divinity Movement* (Grand Rapids, MI: Christian University Press, 1981); Endy, Melvin B., Jr., "Theology and Learning in Early America," in *Schools of Thought in the Christian Tradition*, ed. Patrick Henry (Philadelphia: Fortress Press, 1984); Kling, David W., *A Field of Divine Wonders: The New Divinity and Village Revivals in Northwestern Connecticut, 1792–1822* (University Park: Pennsylvania State University Press, 1993); Kuklick, Bruce, "The New Divinity," in *Churchmen and Philosophers* (New Haven: Yale University Press, 1985).

Thomas J. Davis

New England Theology. In 1852, Edwards A. Park published "The New England Theology" in *Bibliotheca Sacra*. In this work Park sought to give a new name to the New Divinity, particularly in its Hopkinsian expression. Park, by family and education a Hopkinsian, argued that the consistent Calvinism of Samuel Hopkins* and his followers constituted *the* New England Theology. Park, a leading scholar of Jonathan Edwards* and his followers, sought to establish consistent Calvinism as the true tradition of New England theology, steering between Nathaniel William Taylor's New Haven theology and the Princetonian orthodoxy, which centered around the Westminster Confession of Faith.

The term in its original usage, however, admitted—at least in theory—a broader interpretation. Indeed, the very phrase New England Theology represented a compromise term as Old Calvinists and Hopkinsians worked out a creed acceptable to both parties in the founding of Andover Seminary. Neither side, however, made much use of the term. It was left to Park to revive its usage, giving to it a Hopkinsian twist.

In a broader sense, however, the term can designate the efforts of particularly (though not solely) New England Congregationalists to come to grips with the thought of Jonathan Edwards. The theological knot of God's sovereignty and how it relates to human moral agency—particularly how one is to understand the interconnections of sin, responsibility, the will, and grace—occupied the minds of theologians for well over a century.

Viewed from this perspective, the New Divinity—in its Hopkinsian or consistent Calvinism form—represented the first, but not the only, stage of New England Theology. Frank Hugh Foster, a student of Park, authored one of the first comprehensive treatments of the New England Theology, *A Genetic History of the New England Theology*. Therein, moving beyond his teacher's agenda, he understood the New England Theology to include not just Hopkinsianism* but also the work of Taylor and the New Haven theology, Horace Bushnell,* New School Presbyterianism as represented in Henry Boynton Smith, and Charles Grandison Finney.* He also placed Park and his work within the context of the New England Theology, seeing in him its ripest expression just before the collapse of this school of thought.

The concerns of the New England Theology dominated the intellectual work of New England Congregationalists (and to a lesser extent Presbyterians) for well over a century. Bruce Kuklick has noted that it constitutes the longest intellectual tradition in American culture. Moreover, it was a theological tradition tied to Protestant evangelicalism, social concern, and revival. Thus, more than just an intellectual tradition studied by professional theologians, it was a school of thought that found embodiment in several aspects of church life and culture unique to American life.

Bibliography Conforti, Joseph A., *Jonathan Edwards, Religious Tradition, and American Culture* (Chapel Hill: University of North Carolina Press, 1995); Foster, Frank Hugh, *A Genetic History of the New England Theology* (Chicago: University of Chicago Press, 1907); Haroutunian, Joseph, *Piety versus Moralism: The Passing of the New England Theology* (New York: Henry Holt, 1932); Kuklick, Bruce, *Churchmen and Philosophers* (New Haven: Yale University Press, 1985); Whittemore, Robert C., *The Transformation of the New England Theology* (New York: Peter Lang, 1987).

Thomas J. Davis

New Lights. New Lights is a term used to describe a group of Christians, primarily clergy, who emphasized the doctrine of the "new birth" believed to have been obscured by formalism in religion. It grew out of the Great Awakening,* traceable to Dutch Reformed churches in New Jersey around 1726. Prominent proponents of this position were the Tennents and George Whitefield, but others more intellectually inclined were Samuel Davies of Virginia and Jonathan Edwards* of Massachusetts. All were exponents of revivalism, stressing the importance of a crisis religious experience, critical self-examination, and individual responsibility to society.

The style and substance of the "New Lights" and their opponents, "Old Lights,"* were different. To the former, preaching was dramatic, enthusiastic, informal, and directed toward the heart; for the latter, it was directed more to the mind, careful in expression, calm in delivery, and intended to produce understanding. Both sides claimed to be orthodox. The "Old Side" held that understanding was of a higher order than the affections. "Rebirth" was the result of a gradual process wherein God worked by rational persuasion. Outward behavior was the basis for pastoral examination rather than an interrogation of the inner self. The "Old Sides" believed that persons needed encouragement and comfort rather than judgment in their journey of faith.

At the height of the Great Awakening, 1739–1742, and in subsequent decades, the differences between New and Old Lights were evident in several denominations. Among Presbyterian and Congregational bodies, comparable terms were "New Side" and "Old Side"; Baptists divided into Regular and Separatists. Similar differences were discernible among Lutherans and pietistic groups. When Methodism* became a factor in America's religious life, it was clearly "New Light." Among Anglicans, those who sided with the revivalists were few, but Devereux Jarratt* of Bath parish, Virginia, was one. While "Old

Lights'' charged that revivals were mere wildfire and enthusiasm, preying upon the terrors of judgment and exploiting emotions, ''New Lights'' affirmed the awakening as the work of God to convince and convert the careless and errant. Some ''New Lights'' did acknowledge that excesses and disorders had occurred, but claimed that adjustments and refinements had been made. The one who came closest to intellectually reconciling the respective positions was Jonathan Edwards, who in his *A Treatise Concerning Religious Affections* (1746) defended the revivalists' position. Affections, he argued, are the springs of human action, including a rebirth and a vital awareness of what is beautiful and excellent in religious matters.

Bibliography. Bumsted, J. M., ed. *The Great Awakening* (Waltham, MA: Blaisdell Publishing Co., 1970); Gaustad, E. S., *The Great Awakening in New England* (New York: Harper and Row, 1957); Goen, C. C., *Revivalism and Separatism in New England, 1740–1800* (Middletown, CT: Wesleyan University Press, 1987); Heimert, A., and P. Miller, eds. *The Great Awakening* (Indianapolis: Bobbs-Merrill Co., 1967); Lambert, F., *Pedlar in Divinity* (Princeton: Princeton University Press, 1994).

Frederick V. Mills, Sr.

New Morality. New morality is the theory that moral action is best guided not by moral laws or rules but by the context within which a person acts and/or the inner self of the person. This position emerged in the mid-twentieth century as a reaction against what its proponents viewed as the rigid legalism that dominated much of both Catholic and Protestant moral thought. It was closely associated with, and for some indistinguishable from, ''situation ethics'' and ''contextual ethics.'' The best-known proponents of the new morality were John A. T. Robinson in *Honest to God* (1963) and *Christian Morals Today* (1964) and Joseph Fletcher in *Situation Ethics* (1966).

There are several features that characterize this movement. First, ethics is a practical and not a theoretical undertaking. Proponents reject deductive reasoning, in which conclusions about right action are derived from universal principles. Rather, inductive reasoning is used to allow moral obligations to emerge from the person's encounter with historical circumstances. This inductive approach grows out of the conviction that the human experience is very complex and changing. Furthermore, the will of God is complex and beyond easy or simple elaboration. Therefore, responsible living requires flexibility and spontaneity in order to be true to God and relevant to life.

These features of the new morality led to an ethical system that rejected the deontological tradition for a teleological or casuistic approach. No set of rules or laws can be adequate to contain the will of God or to cover the variables of human experience. Supporting this approach is the assumption that persons have the wisdom and moral competency to discern the best course of action. Morally responsible action is marked not by blind obedience to a predetermined pattern of behavior but by intellectual and moral struggle with concrete realities.

The new moralists denied being antinomian. A typical approach was Fletcher's emphasis on the primacy of love in guiding moral decisions. He argued that other guidelines might shed some light on a given situation, but none of them ever took precedence over compassionate love. In general, this movement proposed the overall welfare of persons as the standard by which all action is measured.

Most evaluations of the new morality recognize that it successfully demonstrated the inadequacies of a thoroughgoing legalism. A more nuanced and analytical approach to ethics was fostered. Also some elements of the new morality, especially what some called "contextual ethics," contributed to the development of the contemporary virtue or character-ethics movement.

Critics of the new morality offer several criticisms. It seems to be built around both an optimistic and individualistic view of humanity. It presumes that humans have the moral and intellectual capacity to find their way through life's complexities with little assistance. There is little felt need in the moral life for either time-proven rules or a guiding or supportive community. The critics conclude that while the warning about excessive legalism is well taken, there is a need for some rules to provide structure to the moral enterprise.

Bibliography. Cox, Harvey G., ed., *The Situation Ethics Debate* (Philadelphia: Westminster Press, 1968); Cunningham, Robert L., ed., *Situationism and the New Morality* (New York: Appleton-Century-Crofts, 1970); Lunn, Arnold, and Garth Lean, *The New Morality* (London: Blandford, 1964); Outka, Gene H., and Paul Ramsey, eds., *Norm and Context in Christian Ethics* (New York: Scribner, 1968).

Daniel B. McGee

New Orleans Baptist Theological Seminary. The Southern Baptist Convention (SBC)* met in New Orleans in 1917 and authorized the establishment of a theological school in that city. In 1918, the Baptist Bible Institute began holding classes. In 1925, the SBC began to elect the trustees of the seminary. In 1946, the name of the school was changed to New Orleans Baptist Theological Seminary.

The seminary experienced no controversy under its first three presidents, B. H. DeMent (1917–1928), W. W. Hamilton (1928–1942), and Duke K. McCall* (1943–1946). Of the four succeeding presidents, Roland Q. Leavell (1946–1958), H. Leo Eddleman (1959–1970), Grady Cothen (1970–1974), and Landrum P. Leavell (1975–1995), only Dr. Cothen was not called upon to deal with theological controversy.

In 1945 Helen E. Falls came as dean of women, and in 1946 she began teaching missions, one of the first women in America to teach in a graduate school of theology. In 1951, along with the other Southern Baptist seminaries, New Orleans began to admit black students; the impetus to do so came from the students and faculty more than from administrators and trustees. Either or both of these events may have contributed to a growing sense of tension in the seminary.

In 1956, four doctoral students persuaded President Leavell that Dr. Frank Stagg, professor of New Testament, was teaching things about the Bible that were imcompatible with the seminary's "Articles of Religious Belief." In his commentary, *The Book of Acts: The Early Struggle for an Unhindered Gospel,* published in 1955, Dr. Stagg had drawn parallels between the reluctance of early Jewish Christian leaders such as Peter to accept Gentiles as equals in the church, and the reluctance of many white American churches to accept black members. The full Board of Trustees of the seminary met with Dr. Stagg for two days, away from the campus, and exonerated him of theological error. He remained on the seminary faculty until 1964, when he went to teach at the Southern Baptist Theological Seminary in Louisville.

In 1960, the Board of Trustees dismissed Dr. Ted Clark, professor of theology. In his book, *Saved by His Life* (1959), Clark had called for less emphasis on the blood of Christ and the death of Christ and for more emphasis on the resurrection of Christ and on the Holy Spirit and the church. Clark, who was described by one of his former students as "one of the greatest Christians I've ever known," apparently was surprised when his book, which he thought of as a meditation, became controversial. It seems likely that, more than anything else, it was Clark's disapproval of the theology of some of the traditional hymns about the cross of Christ that created a sense of alarm. In dismissing Clark, the trustees alleged that Clark's communication skills were not acceptable, although *Saved by His Life* is a lucid book. Like Dr. Stagg, Dr. Clark taught that racial segregation was wrong.

Also during the presidency of Leo Eddleman, the seminary's three professors of theology resigned in the space of a single semester. In 1969, Robert Soileau left to study sociology and to engage in social work in Baton Rouge, Louisiana; Clark Pinnock went to teach at Trinity Divinity School in Chicago; and Samuel J. Mikolaski left New Orleans to teach at an American Baptist seminary in South Dakota. None of these men was officially dismissed, but President Eddleman was known to have disagreed with the theology of Dr. Soileau and to have been displeased about the controversies generated by Dr. Pinnock as the latter issued dramatic warnings to Southern Baptists about the imminent dangers of liberal theology.

In 1979 the SBC began to experience a theological controversy that has resulted in new leadership in the convention. Faculty members at New Orleans, like the faculty at the other Southern Baptist seminaries, were accused of not teaching in accordance with the beliefs of the majority of Southern Baptists. The seminary's journal, *The Theological Educator,* published two special issues dealing with the controversy, one in 1985 and one in 1988. Also in 1988, Dr. Paige Patterson, the President of the Criswell College in Dallas and a graduate of New Orleans Baptist Theological Seminary, publicly debated the doctrine of the atonement with Dr. Fisher Humphreys of the seminary faculty, at Humphrey's request. Apart from informal pressure, the seminary in New Orleans has

been spared many of the effects of the convention's controversy and has been less affected by that controversy than the other Southern Baptist seminaries.
Bibliography. Howe, Claude L., Jr., *Seventy-Five Years of Providence and Prayer: An Illustrated History of New Orleans Baptist Theological Seminary* (New Orleans: New Orleans Baptist Theological Seminary, 1993); Mueller, William A., *The School of Providence and Prayer: A History of the New Orleans Baptist Theological Seminary* (New Orleans: New Orleans Baptist Theological Seminary, 1969); *The Theological Educator*, vols. 30 and 37 (New Orleans: New Orleans Baptist Theological Seminary, 1985, 1988).

Fisher Humphreys

Norris, J. Frank. Probably the most controversial preacher of the first half of the twentieth century, J. Frank Norris was an innovative pastor, dynamic pulpiteer, ardent fundamentalist, autocratic ruler, and master of promotion—a man capable of inspiring great affection and deep hatred. Dubbed the "Texas Tornado" in the early 1920s, the premillennial "independent" Norris became a thorn in the flesh to both the Northern and Southern Baptist Conventions. His power was legendary among his followers, his methods were copied by fundamentalist preachers across America, and his influence over the form and content of Independent Baptist fundamentalism* was second to none. The 3,500 churches associated with the Baptist Bible Fellowship,* the World Baptist Fellowship, and its splinter group, the Independent Baptist Fellowship International, along with their corresponding schools—Baptist Bible College, Arlington Baptist College, and the Norris Bible Baptist Institute—all owe their origins, in one way or another, to Norris. Even the Southern Baptist Convention* is still not beyond his reach, as many editors in the 1980s referred to the upsurge in fundamentalist activity within the convention as a return to "Norrisism."

Born in 1877 in Alabama, Norris moved to Hubbard, Texas, as a child, experienced conversion under the ministry of "Cat" Smith, and later entered Baylor University, receiving a B.A. in 1903. After completing a Th.M. at Southern Baptist Theological Seminary in Louisville, Kentucky, he returned to Texas as pastor of the McKinney Avenue Baptist Church of Dallas, during which time he gained some prominence in the Texas State convention, editing the *Baptist Standard*, leading the war against racetrack gambling, and helping B. H. Carroll and others establish Southwestern Baptist Theological Seminary* in Fort Worth. In 1909 he accepted the call to First Baptist of Fort Worth and remained there until his death in 1952, transforming the "Church of the Cattle Kings" into the largest and most controversial Baptist church in America.

The achievements of Norris are staggering, as are his many controversies. His pulpit style was unorthodox, yet spellbinding. He became, next to Billy Sunday,* the most famous "preacher" of his day, combining his inimitable charisma with a keen sense of audience expectations, so much so that some preachers later accused him of holding an almost cultic power over his listeners. He was a believer in the power of the printed word, spreading his fiery brand of fundamentalism from 1917 onward through the voice of his own publications, first the *Fence Rail* (1917–1921), then the *Searchlight* (1921–1927), and finally the *Fundamentalist* (1927–1952), with a circulation at its peak of more than 70,000. After being voted out of the Tarrant County Baptist Association in 1922 (no official action was ever taken by the Southern Baptist Convention on Norris), Norris ceased his support of all convention programs and became an independent, devoting much of his time, sermons, and pen to attacking convention preachers, programs, and schools. Besides his support for the World's Christian Fundamentals Association, in 1923 he joined with T. T. Shields of Toronto and W. B. Riley of Minneapolis in founding the Bible Baptist Union (BBU), an "independent" fellowship of pastors dissatisfied with the drift toward modernism,* primarily within the Northern Baptist Convention. When the BBU fell apart in 1932, Norris began his own organization with the residue of the BBU, calling his group the World Fundamental Baptist Missionary Fellowship (WFBMF). All the while his church, with the assistance of Louis Entzminger, Norris's gifted Sunday school administrator and teacher, continued to grow, adding a radio station in 1926 and reaching an average attendance of 5,000 that year. In 1934 he held a series of meetings in Detroit and soon found himself pastor of Temple Baptist Church, leading its members out of the Northern Baptist Convention and commencing a thirteen-year odyssey as pastor of the two largest Baptist churches (both independent) in America. By 1948 the two churches had a combined membership of over 25,000 and an average attendance of over 7,000. When the churches were combined with the 300 ministerial students at Bible Baptist Seminary and the several hundred pastors affiliated with the WFBMF, Norris stood at the head of the most prolific empire of fundamentalist activity the twentieth century would produce.

His controversies, however, are probably better known than his achievements, and they began early in his career. Suspicious fires involving his church and parsonage in 1912 brought charges of arson, but he was acquitted each time. He was always at war with the "liquor crowd" and the powers of the Catholic Church. It was this latter hatred that led to the most damaging controversy of his life. Norris was convinced that Fort Worth mayor and department-store owner H. C. Meacham had allowed the Catholic Church to profit unduly from a land sale to the city, a sale for which Norris held Meacham personally responsible. Norris charged Meacham accordingly in the *Searchlight,* and Meacham responded by firing all employees of his store who were members of First Baptist. One of Meacham's supporters, D. E. Chipps, threatened Norris in his office on July 17, 1926. When he returned again in a similar rage, Norris was convinced that Chipps was about to shoot him, and so he fired first, killing Chipps. Norris was acquitted of murder on the basis of self-defense, but his reputation as the "gun totin'" preacher would follow him the rest of his life, costing him many friends within the fundamentalist movement itself. His greatest battles, however, were against what he and many others perceived to be the forces of modernism seeping within the church through its organizations and schools. His attack on the teaching of evolution at Baylor in 1919 eventually led to his rejection of the Southern Baptist Convention (for allowing liberalism*) and its rejection of him (for noncooperation). Norris carried his vendetta against the SBC the rest of his life, holding "rump" conventions of his own during the regular SBC meetings and maintaining a feud throughout the 1940s against then SBC President Louie Newton, calling him a "Modern Jehoshaphat" in 1947 because of his somewhat favorable remarks concerning Russian communism.

Norris generated conflict not only within the convention, but among his own followers as well, most notably at the annual meeting of the WFBMF in 1950. For two years George Beauchamp Vick,* Norris's copastor at Temple Baptist in Detroit, had been acting president at Norris's Bible Baptist Seminary in Fort Worth. An able administrator, Vick reorganized the seminary and put his own distinctive mark upon its ministry. His growing power became intolerable to the egocentric Norris, and as a result, he took measures in May 1950 to return control of the seminary to himself and the Fort Worth church. By now, however, Vick had developed a loyal following himself. At a meeting on May 23, Norris attacked Vick ruthlessly for over an hour, after which Vick responded, exposing Norris as a ruthless conspirator and autocratic dictator. Many in the audience, all of whom viewed Norris as their spiritual "father," saw Vick as the more credible leader. The battle-scarred Norris, the man "who [had] never lost a fight in his life," as his secretary would later write, lost this one. The majority of the pastors present at that meeting left Norris (most were never reconciled to him) and formed the Baptist Bible Fellowship, of which Vick was the titular head for the next twenty-five years. Norris was voted out (by a count of 3,000 to 7) as copastor in Detroit, and his power base in Fort Worth was clearly shattered. Some pastors remained with Norris, forming the World Baptist Fellowship and later Arlington Baptist College (formerly Bible Baptist Seminary). Norris remained as pastor at First Baptist until his death two years later, but his reign as the most powerful leader of the Baptist fundamentalists in America was over.

Bibliography. Entzminger, Louis, *The J. Frank Norris I Have Known for 34 Years* (Fort Worth, TX: New Testament Ministries, n.d. [originally published 1947]); Haldeman-Julius, Marcet, *A Report of the Rev. J. Frank Norris' Trial* (Girard, KS: Haldeman-Julius Publications, 1927); *Inside History of First Baptist Church, Fort Worth, and Temple Baptist Church, Detroit: Life Story of Dr. J. Frank Norris* (New York: Garland, 1988); Kemp, Roy A., *Norris Extravaganza! A Biography of J. Frank Norris* (Fort Worth, TX: Calvary Publications, 1988); Ritchie, Homer G., *The Life and Legend of J. Frank Norris* (Fort Worth, TX: Homer G. Ritchie, 1991); Tatum, E. Ray, *Conquest or Failure?: A Biography of J. Frank Norris* (Dallas, TX: Baptist Historical Foundation, 1966).

Timothy D. Whelan

Noyes, John Humphrey. Born in Vermont in 1811, John Humphrey Noyes abandoned preparation for a legal career and entered Yale to study for the ministry after he was converted in a revival led by Charles Grandison Finney.* At Yale Noyes became absorbed with Perfectionist thinking, which also intrigued Finney and numerous preachers and theologians of the day. Noyes combined his conviction that believers could have lives of perfect holiness with an idiosyncratic millennialism. He asserted that the Second Coming of Christ had occurred in A.D. 70, making it possible for humans to live now the way Scripture described heavenly existence. This controversial perspective led to Yale's forcing Noyes to withdraw.

In 1836 Noyes gathered a group of followers in Putney, Vermont, where they launched an attempt at communal living. Claims that the group engaged in immoral behavior quickly appeared, for Noyes instituted the practice of complex marriage in which all men were the spouses of all of the women and vice versa. Critics called this adultery and charged that Noyes adopted the practice because he became attracted to a married woman in the community after his wife had difficulties with childbearing. Noyes insisted that his views were grounded in Scripture, which declared that there was no marriage in heaven.

The Putney group migrated to Oneida, New York, in 1848, where Noyes implemented his views on a grander scale. He developed a form of socialism called Bible communism where the community held all property and possessions in common, following the practice of early New Testament Christianity. Noyes exerted strong control over his followers. Although an elected committee theoretically guided the enterprise, Noyes was a near dictator. He imparted his views to members through ''home talks'' given each evening in lieu of traditional worship.

When the community became economically stable, Noyes instituted a procedure where selected couples were given permission to have children, but without having an exclusive marriage. When it became clear that Noyes fathered more children than any other, criticism within the community against his leadership style joined with external criticism of the community's sexual practices to force Noyes to flee to Canada. He then called on his followers to abandon complex marriage. Noyes died in 1886 without ever returning to Oneida,* which disbanded in 1881.

Bibliography. Klaw, S., *Without Sin: The Life and Death of the Oneida Community* (New York: Viking Penguin, 1993); Noyes, J. H., *The Religious Experience of John Humphrey Noyes* (Reprint. Manchester, NH: Ayer, 1977); Parker, R. A, *A Yankee Saint: John Humphrey Noyes and the Oneida Community* (Reprint. Hamden, CT: Archon Books, 1973).

Timothy D. Whelan

O

O'Connor, John J. Archbishop of New York since 1984, John Joseph Cardinal O'Connor is a vigorous defender of Roman Catholic orthodoxy and the Vatican's positions on social issues. While his critics object to his conservative views on abortion* and gay rights,* he is also admired as a warm humanitarian, an advocate for the poor, and a compassionate pastor.

Born in 1920 and ordained a priest in 1945, O'Connor worked with mentally handicapped children until he entered the navy during the Korean War. He rose through the ranks to become a rear admiral and chief of navy chaplains, earning graduate degrees in ethics, psychology, and political science along the way. In the 1960s he defended U.S. military policy in Vietnam (a position he later reconsidered) but decried the suffering and destruction of war.

On his retirement from the navy in 1979, he was consecrated auxiliary bishop in charge of Catholic military chaplains. He became bishop of Scranton, Pennsylvania, in 1983 and archbishop of New York the following year. In 1985 he was created cardinal.

His adherence to the church's moral and doctrinal positions has repeatedly embroiled him in public disputes. In 1984 he attacked vice-presidential candidate Geraldine Ferraro's views on abortion, and in 1990 he suggested that bishops have the authority to excommunicate Roman Catholic politicians who disregard the church's prolife teaching. He has angered gay rights and women's health activists by his opposition to sex education and AIDS education in New York's parochial schools and to the use of condoms to prevent the spread of AIDS. In 1984 he rejected a New York executive order banning discrimination against homosexuals in social service agencies with municipal contracts.

In contrast to his conservative moral and doctrinal views, O'Connor is outspokenly progressive on other social issues. He supports labor unions and housing programs for the poor and has pledged the church's financial resources to fight the effects of poverty in New York.

In January 1987 he traveled to Israel and met with Israeli leaders against the wishes of the Vatican. He drew criticism from American Jews when he called for both Palestinian and Jewish homelands in the Middle East and when he applied a Christian theology of redemptive suffering to the Holocaust. O'Connor has stated that his conservative views of sexual morality and his liberal socioeconomic views share a common foundation in his commitment to the sacred worth of every human being (including the unborn) and to the immutability of God's natural law.

Bibliography. Hentoff, Nat, *John Cardinal O'Connor: At the Storm Center of a Changing American Catholic Church* (New York: Scribner, 1988); O'Connor, John J., *A Chaplain Looks at Vietnam* (Cleveland, OH: World Publishing Co., 1968); O'Connor, John J., *In Defense of Life* (Boston: St. Paul Editions, 1981); O'Connor, John J., and Edward I. Koch, *His Eminence and Hizzoner: A Candid Exchange* (New York: William Morrow, 1989).

John P. Rossing

O'Hair, Madalyn Murray. In 1963 the Supreme Court handed down its decision in *School District of Abington Township v. Schempp*. The decision also rendered an opinion in *Murray v. Curlett*, a Maryland case brought by Madalyn Murray on behalf of her son, William, who was enrolled in the public Woodbourne Junior High School in Baltimore.

A 1905 rule passed by the Baltimore Board of School Commissioners provided for the holding in the city schools of opening exercises consisting primarily of the ''reading, without comment, of a chapter in the Holy Bible and/or the use of the Lord's Prayer.'' Murray asked that the rule be rescinded, and the school officials refused. The suit was brought to compel its ''rescission and cancellation.'' Murray testified that it was ''the practice under the rule to have a reading on each school morning from the King James version of the Bible; that at petitioners' insistence the rule was amended to permit children to be excused from the exercise on request of the parent and that William had been excused pursuant thereto; that nevertheless the rule as amended was in violation of the petitioners' rights 'to freedom of religion under the First and Fourteenth Amendments' and in violation of 'the principle of separation between church and state.'''

Madalyn Murray affirmed that she and her son were atheists and that the 1905 rule violated their rights, ''in that it threatens their religious liberty by placing a premium on belief as against non-belief and subjects their freedom of conscience to the rule of the majority; it pronounces belief in God as the source of all moral and spiritual values, equating these values with religious values, and thereby renders sinister, alien and suspect the beliefs and ideals of your Petitioners, promoting doubt and question of their morality, good citizenship and good faith.'' The lower courts upheld the school practices, leading to the *Murray v. Curlett* case of 1963 that found on behalf of Murray.

The fact that Madalyn Murray and her son were atheists is significant. Few church-state cases have involved atheists. Most have cast citizens of a minority religious tradition against a majority of citizens professing a different faith. That was the case with Ellory Schempp, a Unitarian. Many American citizens have appeared willing to condemn atheists who contended for their rights, while being more understanding of the same stance taken by Unitarians, Jews, Amish, Baptists,* and Lutherans with similar claims. Opponents of the Supreme Court rulings on matters of religious establishment have unabashedly employed the Murray family to claim, falsely, that suits involving religious establishment are and have been antigod and irreligious. That is patently false. Most suits have been brought by persons of faith who were at odds with the local de facto establishment. Further, none of the suits have been about religious belief, but rather about the Constitution's prohibition against state establishment of any religion, majority or minority. The 1963 decision actually affirmed religion as an appropriate academic subject in high school.

Madalyn Murray (O'Hair) has spent her life as an outspoken advocate of atheism, creating American Atheists, Inc., in 1977. In the late 1970s William began to turn away from atheism and rejected his mother's beliefs. Around 1980 he became a Christian fundamentalist. With his new faith he became a ''poster boy'' for fundamentalist attacks on the public schools. He is, they argue, proof of the dangers of public schools without religion. More plausible is the conclusion that the unremitting attacks by ''religious'' people disrupted the Murray family and drove them from Baltimore. The persecution of the Murrays created a living hell for a young boy as religious fanatics sought to marginalize his mother. That Jerry Falwell* can parade him as a means to demonize his mother does no credit to either.

Madalyn Murray O'Hair has been in the news frequently since 1963. She was the first guest when Phil Donahue began a new audience-participation television show in 1967. In 1975 she was accused, falsely, of seeking from the Federal Communication Commission (FCC) a ban on religious broadcasts. By 1978 the FCC had received 8 million chain-letter protests against this imagined effort. By 1996 that figure reached 25 million, and the FCC was begging people to stop. The disappearance of O'Hair, with her son Jon and her granddaughter Robin, both active in the atheist organization, added mystery to her long battle against religion in American culture.

Bibliography. Wilson, John F., and Donald L. Drakeman, eds., *Church and State in American History*, 2nd ed. (Boston: Beacon Press, 1965). For relevant court cases see Wilson John F., and Donald L. Drakeman, eds., *Church and State in American History*, 2nd. ed. (Boston: Beacon Press, 1965). See also newspaper reports, including *New York Times*, May 14, 1975, 29; *New York Times*, December 16, 1988, 10; *Washington Post*, October 22, 1995, sec. A, 3.

Robert S. Alley

O'Kelly, James. James O'Kelly (died 1826) was a first-generation American Methodist leader and later founder of the Republican Methodists who became the "Christian Churches in the South." O'Kelly was apparently born and reared in Ireland before emigrating to the United States either just prior to or during the American Revolution. O'Kelly's wife, Elizabeth Meeks, had embraced Methodist principles, and James seems to have followed her lead after their son, William, was converted through the influence of Methodist preachers. O'Kelly himself became active as a leader in Methodist circles in Virginia and North Carolina by the late 1770s. He was also an ardent "Whig," or proponent of the American Revolution, who later recalled having served a tour of duty with the American "patriots" and having been detained by the British and ill treated for his refusal to collaborate with them. W. E. MacClenny, a sympathetic early-twentieth-century biographer, suggested that O'Kelly's "Whig" sentiments are relevant to the interpretation of his conflict with Francis Asbury, who might be classified (at least passively) as a "Tory."

The conflict between Asbury and O'Kelly was fundamentally a conflict over church polity. Asbury became the advocate of a strong episcopal structure for Methodism,* while O'Kelly championed a more collegial and presbyterial approach. The conflict over polity was related to American Methodism's emergence, notably at the Christmas Conference of 1784, as a church separate from the Church of England and no longer a renewal movement within it. Francis Asbury had been appointed by John Wesley to be, along with Thomas Coke, one of the "superintendents" for the American Methodists. Asbury, however, had been in North America since 1771, and his longer and more continuous American experience put him in a position to become the most influential leader of American Methodism.

Between 1784 and 1792 Coke traveled several times between England and the United States and in 1791 even approached the new Protestant Episcopal Church about union with the Methodists. Meanwhile, Asbury's focus remained firmly on America's Methodist Episcopal Church, and he worked tirelessly to give a strongly episcopal form to it under his own strict guidance. Asbury had briefly championed a "council" structure as against a "general conference" of Methodist elders (preachers).

When the general conference was called for 1792, it became the setting for James O'Kelly's suggestion that preachers should have the right to appeal their appointment (by the superintendent or bishop to their "circuit") to the conference and, if the conference sustained their appeal, to be reassigned elsewhere. O'Kelly's motion to this effect was defeated, and thereafter he and several colleagues withdrew from association with the Methodist Episcopal Church to form the Republican Methodists in 1793. Centered in Virginia and North Carolina, this body numbered about four thousand at (or shortly after) its emergence. In 1794, at the particular urging of Rice Haggard, this group took "the name Christian to the exclusion of all party and sectarian names" and affirmed alongside it the sole Lordship of Christ in the church, the Bible as the only creed, Christian character as the test of fellowship, and liberty of conscience.

Some of the Christian Churches in the South united briefly with the "Christians" of New England led by Elias Smith and Abner Jones. Some leaders, notably Rice Haggard, became associated with Barton W. Stone's* "New Light"* Christians. Haggard is generally credited with helping to bring to the Stoneite group their strong emphasis on the name "Christian." These associations, and the Stoneites' eventual union with the "Disciples" led by Alexander Campbell,* occasioned the false attribution to O'Kelly or his followers of views such as Arianism, "low Christology," or Unitarianism (those typically ascribed to the New England Christians) on the one hand or "Campbellism" on the other (typically referring to understanding baptism* as the immersion of penitent adult believers for the remission of sins). Neither of these accusations were justified, since O'Kelly's dispute with Asbury and, eventually, with the Methodists in general conference was on the matter of polity and the issue of ecclesiastical liberty as O'Kelly understood it, not on Christology or sacramental theology. O'Kelly set forth his views in an *Apology for Protesting against the Methodist Episcopal Government* (1798) and *A Vindication of the Author's Apology with Reflections on the Reply* (1801), which were answered by Nicholas Snethen, in support of Asbury, in *A Reply* (1800) and *An Answer to James O'Kelly's Vindication of His Apology* (1802).

Bibliography. MacClenny, W. E., *The Life of James O'Kelly and the Early History of the Christian Church in the South* (Suffolk, VA: n.p., 1910. Reprint. Indianapolis: Religious Book Service, 1950); Norwood, Frederick A., *The Story of American Methodism* (Nashville: Abingdon Press, 1974).

Anthony L. Dunnavant

Old Lights. The revivals of New England's First Great Awakening* were eagerly embraced by many of the clergy, who hoped that such revivals would rekindle their own congregations. Consensus soon gave way to controversy, however, as clergy divided among "Old Light" antirevival traditionalists, moderate "New Light" revivalists, and radical "Strict" or "Separate" Congregationalists. During his 1740 preaching tour of New England, itinerant evangelist George Whitefield preached and taught as the guest of Charles Chauncy* in Boston's First Church, yet only a few years later Chauncy championed the antirevivalist cause of the Old Lights.

Whitefield quickly alienated many of his New England clergy supporters when his published journals attacked them as "unconverted ministers" preaching "an unknown and unfelt Christ." New England congregations were dead, Whitefield warned, "because they had dead men preaching to them." The city of Boston, he charged, "has the form of religion kept up, but has lost much of its power." The *Boston Gazette* published a spirited defense of New England's established clergy, and Whitefield's conciliatory response was published almost a year later.

Jonathan Edwards* and Charles Chauncy took up the New Light and Old Light causes, respectively, in two well-known sermons. Jonathan Edwards defended the revivalist cause as a "Work of God" in his famous 1741 sermon *The Distinguishing Marks of a Work of the Spirit of God*, preached in New Haven, Connecticut, on the day following Yale's commencement. Edwards's task was complicated by the extremes of Separatist itinerants such as Andrew Croswell and James Davenport,* whose antics undermined the established authority of New England's resident, settled clergy. After James Davenport called on Charles Chauncy to inquire "into the reason of the hope" that was in him, the offended Chauncy preached his renowned sermon "Enthusiasm Describ'd and Caution'd Against," later published with a prefatory letter to Davenport. Chauncy distrusted the "confusion" that marked revival phenomena as a form of mental illness—the self-delusions of religious "enthusiasm." Such "enthusiasm," Chauncy warned, was a "mischief" and a "genuine force of infinite evil" that had been "a pest to the church in all ages, as great an enemy to real and solid religion as perhaps the greatest infidelity."

The debate heightened as Edwards and Chauncy each revised their sermons into books. Edwards expanded and revised his New Haven sermon and published it as the 1742 treatise *Some Thoughts Concerning the Present Revival of Religion in New England*, urging ministers to "do their utmost to encourage and promote" the work of the awakenings, even as he distanced himself from the excesses of Davenport, Croswell, and others. To prepare a point-by-point refutation of Edwards, Chauncy undertook a three-hundred-mile tour of New England to document revivalist excesses and failures, which he summarized in his 424-page *Seasonable Thoughts on the State of Religion in New England*. Chauncy described the debate in terms of the seventeenth-century Antinomian Crisis* that had erupted at his own First Church in Boston. His analysis aligned the New Light enthusiasts with Anne Hutchinson* and the antinomians and cast himself and the Old Light establishment as defenders of orthodoxy.

Chauncy and the Old Lights were social and theological conservatives who opposed the subversive disruptions of the revivals on several grounds. First, they objected to itinerant preachers, who neglected their own parishes for the sake of "intrusions" into the established territories of others, thus undermining the authority of the local clergy. Second, they protested disorderly worship services that offered impassioned, extemporaneous exhortations instead of reasoned, well-crafted sermons and sometimes featured as many as five or ten lay exhorters, who were unordained, were often uneducated, and sometimes included women, children, African Americans, and Native Americans. Third, they decried the revivalists' "censoriousness," their personal denunciations of the established clergy and their church members as "unconverted." Fourth, they lamented the church divisions and schisms that occurred in over one-third of the New England congregations in the wake of the revivals. Finally, they deplored the New Light doctrinal errors, including their antinomian appeal to the "heat and fervor of their passions" at the neglect of "reason and judgment."

The New England clergy soon reached an uneasy truce. James Davenport published his *Confession and Retractions* in 1744, and when George Whitefield returned to New England later that fall, he found the clergy and universities closing ranks against him. Long after the debate between Edwards and Chauncy had ceased, the tensions persisted, eventually leading to permanent schism among Separatist Baptists, Unitarians, and Congregationalists.

Bibliography. Chauncy, Charles, *Seasonable Thoughts on the State of Religion in New England* (Boston: Rogers and Fowle, 1743); Gaustad, Edwin Scott, *The Great Awakening in New England* (New York: Harper and Row, 1957); Schmidt, Leigh Eric, " 'A Second and Glorious Reformation': The New Light Extremism of Andrew Croswell," *William and Mary Quarterly*, 3rd ser. 43 (April 1986): 214–44; Tracy, Joseph, *The Great Awakening* (Boston: Tappan and Dennet, 1842).

David B. McCarthy

Old School/New School. The 1837 Old School/New School division in the Presbyterian Church reprised many of the themes of the Old Side/New Side schism of 1741–1758. Once again, theological conservatives defended the doctrinal purity of the Presbyterian Church against the perceived theological laxness of revivalists. These theological tensions were complicated by issues of extradenominational alliances and slavery.

Since 1801 Presbyterians and Congregationalists had collaborated in frontier missionary efforts under a Plan of Union that allowed ministers and congregations of either church to switch their denominational affiliations at will. As a result, many Congregational ministers became de facto Presbyterians without subscribing to the Westminster Confession, and Congregational laymen became voting delegates at Presbyterian meetings. Theological conservatives charged that the Plan of Union had opened the Presbyterian Church to a broader confessionalism, a relaxed polity, non-Presbyterian voluntary societies, revivalist excesses, and New Divinity theology. As the New School's abolitionism* grew stronger, southern traditionalists joined in the Old School cause and tipped the balance against the New School.

Albert Barnes became a focal point of the theological controversy. A graduate of Hamilton College and Princeton Theological Seminary, Barnes served as pastor of the Presbyterian Church in Morristown, New Jersey. In his 1829 revival sermon "The Way of Salvation," he appeared to attenuate the Calvinist doctrine of original sin, provoking conservative charges that he held to the "Pelagian" New Haven theology of Nathaniel W. Taylor. When Barnes was called as pastor of the First Presbyterian Church in the heart of the Old Side/Old School bastion of Philadelphia, *Christian Advocate* editor Ashbel Green fought to prevent his installation. The Synod of Philadelphia ordered a thorough investigation, and the Philadelphia Presbytery subsequently condemned his sermon. When both sides appealed the decision, the 1831 General Assembly acquitted Barnes with only a mild rebuke. After Old School conservatives once again charged Barnes with heresy, the 1836 General Assembly not only exonerated Barnes, but defended his theology. That same year, the General Assembly established Union Theological Seminary* in New York as a New School alternative to Princeton and violated its previous neutrality by debating the volatile issue of abolitionism.

In 1837 a coalition of theological conservatives and social traditionalists gained the upper hand at that year's General Assembly and unilaterally abrogated the 1801 Plan of Union, declaring it unconstitutional and repudiating any previous General Assembly actions taken under its provisions. The Old School thus exscinded the four New School synods of Western Reserve, Utica, Geneva, and Genesee that had been organized under the Plan of Union, effectively excommunicating 509 ministers and 60,000 members in 28 presbyteries in Ohio and western New York. Solidifying the Old School victory, the General Assembly broke ties with the American Home Missionary Society and the American Education Society and defended its actions in a circular letter to other denominations.

Later that year the New School party met in Auburn, New York, where it declared the General Assembly actions null and void and issued the Auburn Declaration in its defense. When the 1838 General Assembly convened at the Seventh Presbyterian Church in Philadelphia, the Old School moderator refused to seat the exscinded delegates, who seized the floor to elect their own officers and adjourn their meeting to Philadelphia's First Presbyterian Church, taking 47 sympathetic Old School delegates with them. Each party then declared itself the "General Assembly of the Presbyterian Church in the United States of America." After congregations and ministers chose sides in the dispute, the Old School claimed the allegiance of 1,221 ministers and 126,585 members in 1,763 congregations in 96 presbyteries. New School Stated Clerk Edwin F. Hatfield reported an estimated 106,736 members and 1,093 ministers in 1,260 churches and 75 presbyteries; the New School dominated New York, Ohio, Michigan, Illinois, and eastern Tennessee, evenly split the presbyteries in New Jersey and Indiana, and divided countless congregations and presbyteries across the country.

In 1857 the New School church divided into northern and southern factions over the issue of slavery, while the Old School church split soon after the onset of the Civil War. The southern Old and New Schools merged in 1864, and the northern parties put aside their differences in 1869. Nevertheless, questions of doctrinal purity and ecclesiastical tolerance persisted, erupting once again during the fundamentalist-modernist controversy of the early twentieth century.

Bibliography. Balmer, Randall, and John R. Fitzmier, *The Presbyterians*, Denominations in America no. 5 (Westport, CT: Greenwood Press, 1993); Hatfield, Edwin F., "Statistics of the Church (New School Branch) since 1837," in *Presbyterian Reunion: A Memorial Volume, 1837–1871* (New York: De-Witt C. Lent and Company, 1870) Marsden, George M., *The Evangelical Mind and the New School Presbyterian Experience: A Case Study of Thought and Theology in Nineteenth-Century America* (New Haven: Yale University Press, 1970); Parker, Harold M., Jr., *The United Synod of the South:*

The Southern New School Presbyterian Church (Westport, CT: Greenwood Press, 1988); Thompson, Ernest Trice, *Presbyterians in the South*, 3 vols. (Richmond: John Knox Press, 1963–1973).

David B. McCarthy

Oneida. In 1848 the Perfectionist preacher John Humphrey Noyes* came with a group of followers to Oneida, New York, from Putney, Vermont, where they had already established communal living arrangements. Controversy surrounded Oneida from then until it disbanded in 1881.

Noyes was drawn to Perfectionist thinking while a theological student at Yale in the 1830s. While interest in Perfectionism was not uncommon at that time, Noyes developed his thinking in a unique fashion. Believing that the Second Coming of Christ had occurred in A.D. 70, Noyes was convinced that if the faithful replicated practices of New Testament Christianity and what Scripture taught about heavenly existence, they could achieve perfection here and now. Perfection for Noyes had to do with intent more than action. It did not mean that one would not make mistakes, but that actions of those intent on following God's will would be devoid of a sinful nature or quality.

Controversy ensued more when it came to implementing this ideology of perfection. To outsiders, the most questionable practice concerned relations between men and women. Because Noyes believed that there would be no marriage in heaven, he insisted that every adult male in the community would be the husband of every woman, and every woman the wife of every man. Oneidans expressed this "complex marriage" sexually, although the community was hardly the bastion of "free love" that religious and social critics presumed.

Noyes insisted that the members practice a form of birth control dubbed "male continence" or *coitus reservatus*. The male would enter the female, but cease sexual activity before orgasm. Nor were individuals free to have such sexual relations with anyone they chose. Men had to approach women through a third party. In theory, women had to consent to having sex with a male member of the community.

Critics also condemned the community's practice of "Bible communism," or holding all property and possessions in common. Noyes referred to this practice as a form of socialism, but believed that there was biblical mandate in the New Testament statement that the early church held all things in common.

Besides the structures surrounding sexual activity, other controversial mechanisms developed to maintain order within the community. Eschewing traditional forms of worship, the community gathered nightly for "home talks" frequently given by Noyes expounding his understanding of perfection and Bible communism. Many of these were published.

More controversial was the practice of "mutual criticism" in which members would regularly submit to a process in which other members of the community would note ways their conduct and attitude could be improved. For Oneidans, mutual criticism was an aid to achieving perfection of intent; to others it smacked of tyrannical control over individual initiative.

The greatest controversy came when the community had achieved a secure economic base and decided to permit selected couples to have children. Noyes called this practice "stirpiculture." In effect, it was an unscientific effort at genetic control, for a committee would determine which couples were worthy of becoming parents. Such couples were not expected to develop an exclusive relationship, nor could they raise their children as they wished.

Ultimately, the stirpiculture experiment and Noyes's near-dictatorial leadership proved the community's undoing. Under the stirpiculture experiment, Noyes fathered more children than any other man in the community. Critics who believed that his female partners had not always consented attempted to bring charges of rape against him. A younger generation of followers resented Noyes's leadership style. With criticism mounting internally and externally, Noyes fled to Canada in 1879, never to return to Oneida.

Noyes then urged his followers to abandon complex marriage. As many entered into traditional legal marriages and developed exclusive relationships, they were unwilling to accept communal control of property. In 1881 the community formally dissolved and reorganized as a joint-stock company. Among the many business ventures of the company, which at one time included the manufacture of steel animal traps and the sale of preserved fruit, the most well known was the manufacture of good-quality silver plate.

The Oneida community was one of many American experiments in utopian living; it was also one of many expressions of the pursuit of millennial ideals in American religion. But the controversy that surrounded its practice of complex marriage, Bible communism, mutual criticism, and stirpiculture eventually shattered its Perfectionist vision. At its peak, the Oneida Perfectionists numbered around three hundred, with communities in Oneida, New York, and Wallingford, Connecticut.

Bibliography. DeMaria, R., *Communal Love at Oneida: A Perfectionist Vision of Authority* (New York: Edwin Mellen Press, 1983); Fogarty, R. S., ed., *Special Love/Special Sex: An Oneida Community Diary* (Syracuse: Syracuse University Press, 1994); Foster, L., *Women, Family, and Utopia: Communal Experiments of the Shakers, the Oneida Community, and the Mormons* (Syracuse: Syracuse University Press, 1991); Kern, L. J., *An Ordered Love: Sex Roles and Sexuality in Victorian Utopias* (Chapel Hill: University of North Carolina Press, 1981); Noyes, J. H., *Mutual Criticism* (Reprint. Syracuse: Syracuse University Press, 1975); Robertson, C. N., *Oneida Community: An Autobiography, 1851–1876* (Syracuse: Syracuse University Press, 1981).

Charles Lippy

"Oneness" or "Jesus Only" Pentecostals. One of the most divisive arguments in the early Pentecostal* movement revolved around what was called the "new issue." It involved rejection of the doctrine of the Trinity and alteration of the centuries-old Christian formula for baptism.*

Searching through the Book of Acts, a number of Pentecostals discovered that baptisms by the apostles were "in" or "into" the "name of Jesus" and not according to the trinitarian formula of Matthew 28:19 (in the name of the Father, and of the Son, and of the Holy Ghost). When a "revelation" came to Pentecostal preacher John G. Scheppe after an all-night prayer vigil during a Pentecostal camp meeting in 1913, a number of ministers rebaptized one another according to the new formula. Soon they had spread the message throughout the Pentecostal movement, sparking opposition from traditional trinitarian Pentecostals.

The fledgling Assemblies of God was torn apart by the "new issue" when more than 25 percent of the ministers left the denomination after the 1916 General Council passed a "Statement of Fundamental Truths" that mandated use of the trinitarian formula for baptisms. The statement also dealt with the related issue of the nature of God and mandated affirmation of a trinitarian view of God in opposition to those who rejected the doctrine of the Trinity along with the trinitarian formula for baptism.

Calling themselves "Oneness" because of their uncompromising affirmation of the one God, the anti-Trinitarians argued that since the word "trinity" is not found in the Bible, it is not appropriate as a description for God. Their developing theology emphasized the second person of the Trinity, prompting some to call them "Jesus only." This label was rejected by those in the movement since they affirmed God as Father in the Old Testament, God as the Son, Jesus, in the Gospels, and God as the Holy Spirit in the apostolic and post-apostolic periods. Neither is it appropriate to label the movement "unitarian," since unlike the Unitarian tradition in America, Oneness Pentecostals insist on the full divinity of Jesus.

Oneness Pentecostals accused Trinitarians of being tritheists since the commonsense meaning of the language of three "persons" in the Godhead used in the traditional creeds implied the existence of three separate distinct beings. Given a general lack of sophistication on either side within Pentecostalism concerning classical Greek philosophical categories, and a belief that salvation itself hangs on correct theology, especially the correct formula for baptism, conflict was inevitable. Often disputes broke out over the issue of rebaptism of converts. Oneness Pentecostals fought trinitarian Pentecostals over converts, some being subjected to numerous rebaptisms.

Another key distinctive of some Oneness Pentecostals is their belief that Peter's sermon in Acts 2 delivered to the church a "plan of salvation." In verse 38 Peter commanded those who asked "What must we do to be saved?" to "repent and be baptized every one of you in the name of Jesus Christ and ye shall receive the gift of the Holy Ghost" (King James Version). Many Oneness Pentecostals insist that without the three steps of repentance, baptism (by immersion with the correct formula "in the name of Jesus Christ"), and reception of the baptism of the Holy Ghost (always signified by speaking in tongues), a person is not saved. Thus their urgency to bring people to "proper" baptism and the experience of speaking in tongues is ultimate.

Conflict and debate have continued through the years as Oneness Pentecostals seek to convince other Christians of the truth of their beliefs and some trinitarian Christians accuse Oneness believers of heresy or label them as a cult. The two largest Oneness Pentecostal denominations in the United States are the United Pentecostal Church, International, and the Pentecostal Assemblies of the World.

Bibliography. Boyd, Gregory A., *Oneness Pentecostals and the Trinity* (Grand Rapids, MI: Baker Book House, 1992); Reed, David, "Aspects of the Origins of Oneness Pentecostalism," in *Aspects of Pentecostal-Charismatic Origins*, ed. Vinson Synan (Plainfield, NJ: Logos International, 1975).

Stephen R. Graham

Open Membership. For at least three decades a controversial question has been posed for Baptist churches that has caused many of these churches to do some serious thinking about the nature of the church and its sacraments as well as about the nature of Baptist history, both past and present. That important question has to do with "open membership." To non-Baptists the phrase probably means very little and/or is misleading. It involves a number of issues at the heart of Baptist practice as well as this tradition entering the ecumenical age.

A vast majority of Baptist churches (especially those associated with the Southern Baptist Convention*) require that members of other Protestant (as well as Catholic and Orthodox) denominations who wish to transfer their membership to one of these Baptist churches be rebaptized by immersion before being admitted if that baptism* has not been believer's adult baptism by immersion. Some hyperconservative Baptist churches even require the latter to be rebaptized by a Baptist minister. The term "closed membership" is used to describe this strict position. On a linear construct moving left from this far-right position, there are several options. The first option is as just stated—acceptance of believer's adult baptism by immersion in a tradition other than Baptist. However, there are several other options that have been considered and followed by a minority of Baptist churches in relation to their doctrine and policy. The first other option is acceptance of believer's adult baptism without requiring that the mode be by immersion. The second is acceptance of "meaningful baptism," which may not necessarily be believer's adult or by immersion. Either of these practices would describe the practice of "open membership." It must be pointed out, however, that this issue only involves transfer of membership from another denomination. In relation to new converts, all Baptist churches practice believer's adult baptism by immersion. Baptist churches that adopt the last two options for transferring members as their rule of church order are referred to as "open membership" churches, however.

The "open membership" position among some Baptist churches continues to emphasize normative baptism as being believers' adult baptism by immersion, but in their denominations they become an advance guard in relation to the ecumenical movement and in recognizing baptism as one of God's sacraments instead of only the denomination's. These churches illustrate the motif of pilgrimage and being "en route." Conservative Baptist positions oppose this view and judge it to be an unacceptable compromise; moderate and liberal Baptists accept it as giving deeper susbstance and witness of Jesus' prayer that "all may be one; . . . that the world may believe."

Bibliography. Brackney, William Henry, *The Baptists* (Westport, CT: Greenwood Press, 1988); Brooks, Hays, and John E. Steely, *The Baptist Way of Life* (Macon: Mercer University Press, 1981); Shriver, George H., "Open Membership: An End to Rebaptism?" *Journal of Ecumenical Studies*, 1969, 423–429; Torbet, Robert G., *A History of the Baptists*, 2nd ed. (Valley Forge, PA: Judson Press, 1963).

George H. Shriver

Ordination of Women. In the second half of the twentieth century ordination of women has been among the most hotly contested issues confronting American churches, particularly Protestantism, sometimes leading more conservative members to form separate denominations and raising obstacles to ecumenism, especially between Anglicans and Catholics. Women played crucial roles in the New Testament churches and the nonbiblical ancient churches, acting as prophetesses, deacons, and, some scholars suggest, priests and bishops. The New Testament contains passages used both to support and oppose women's ordination. Early church councils gradually restricted the roles of priesthood, the diaconate, and the episcopacy to men, although the practice of ordaining women as deaconesses, an office designed specifically for women, continued in some sections. The exclusion of women from the priesthood fundamentally went unchallenged during and after the Reformation era.

This situation changed, however, during the 1800s with the push for women's suffrage and the latter half of the 1900s with greater challenges to patriarchy. The Quakers' insistence that everyone is equal before God greatly encouraged the quest for gender equity in churches and society. Methodism's* practice since the days of John Wesley of employing women as local preachers also provided an avenue for women preaching. While both Congregationalist Antoinette Brown Blackwell* (1853) and AME Zion Mary Jane Small (1898) were among the earliest American women ordained as "pastoral" ministers, many of the Holiness and Pentecostal* denominations, first forming in the second half of the nineteenth and the early part of the twentieth centuries, were the most consistent in ordaining women. In addition to those already named and others, the Presbyterians, Episcopalians, and the United Church of Christ have been in the forefront of ordaining women. Conversely, the Roman Catholic Church, Eastern Orthodoxy, Mormons, and Southern Baptists have been among those most adamantly opposed.

Opponents to women's ordination point to the Bible, including Christ's non-appointment of women among the Twelve, portions of the Pauline Corpus forbidding women's leadership over males, and passages, for example, Genesis 3, highlighting wives' subordination to husbands. Second, opponents observe that Christian practice overwhelmingly rejects women's ordination. Catholics and Orthodox argue that the priest (like the male Christ), representing the people before God, should be male, reflecting the gender of Christ and avoiding issues of cleanliness reflected in Old Testament Levitical laws. Sometimes opponents have advanced cultural arguments, for example, people's rejection of female leadership, the need for masculine stamina, and conflict with performing domestic duties, but these have not been the main points of opposition.

Proponents also point to the Bible: while women were not among the Twelve, they did play crucial roles in support of Christ's ministry; women exercised religious leadership over both males and females in certain Old and New Testament passages; and Paul states the principle (in Galatians 3:27–28) that salvation in Christ supersedes gender distinctions. Furthermore, church tradition has not been unanimously negative regarding women's ministry, as is illustrated by specific literary and artistic portrayals in the earliest Christian centuries. Regarding Christ's maleness, proponents argue on the basis of Genesis 1 that both genders are created in God's image and thus both may be represented in the priesthood. Protestant supporters generally emphasize the priesthood of all believers and, thus, often employ a different understanding of the ministry than Catholics and Orthodox. The cultural arguments advanced by the opponents have been met with counterarguments, including the embrace of gender equity in and outside the home and the specific examples of women ministers.

Bibliography. Keller, Rosemary Skinner, and Rosemary Radford Ruether, eds., *In Our Own Voices: Four Centuries of Women's Religious Writing* (San Francisco: Harper San Francisco, 1995); Reid, Daniel G., ed., *Dictionary of Christianity in America* (Downers Grove: InterVarsity, 1990).

Sandy Dwayne Martin

P

Palmer, Phoebe. Phoebe Palmer (1807–1874) first came to prominence through her Tuesday Meetings for the Promotion of Holiness. At these meetings and in her later writings she developed her theology of "entire sanctification," which would be a source of theological controversy, particularly within the Methodist Church.

Between 1851 and 1856 at various times controversy rose and fell concerning Palmer's views about sanctification as critics and champions battled. In particular, critics rejected Palmer's view that there was a "shorter way" to sanctification, in contrast to the lifelong strenuous efforts advocated by some. Her views, they claimed, had created division and strife within the Methodist movement.

Palmer advocated an "altar theology" that insisted that when one was willing symbolically to place everything "on the altar of sacrifice" to God, one would be entirely sanctified. The altar theology described a three-step process. First, one must consecrate oneself entirely to God. Second, one must believe that God keeps God's promise to sanctify that which has been consecrated to God. Third, one must bear witness to what God has done. Though a number of Holiness denominations adopted versions of Palmer's theology, many writers wrote bitter denunciations of her ideas.

While the charges ranged from Palmer's alleged disrespect for ministers to theological deviations, the gist of the matter seems to have been disagreement over the nature and process of sanctification. Palmer believed that she was only being true to the views of the founder of Methodism,* John Wesley, while her opponents rejected that assertion. While there is some substance to theological charges against Palmer, much of the opposition seems to have been due to the fact that she was a layperson, a woman, and very popular.

Palmer also anticipated the emergence of the Pentecostal* movement by advocating Spirit baptism that was available to every believer. She instructed her followers to wait for the "promise of the Father" that would purify, empower, and revive them, but unlike the later Pentecostals, she never associated the baptism with speaking in tongues.

Palmer was also controversial as a woman in ministry and a feminist who influenced many who would lead the feminist movement in the decades to come, including Catherine Booth and Frances Willard. She published one of the earliest defenses of the public ministry of women in 1859, *The Promise of the Father.*
Bibliography. Oden, Thomas C., ed., *Phoebe Palmer: Selected Writings* (New York: Paulist Press, 1988); Raser, Harold E., *Phoebe Palmer: Her Life and Thought* (Lewiston, NY: Edwin Mellen Press, 1987); White, Charles Edward, *The Beauty of Holiness: Phoebe Palmer as Theologian, Revivalist, Feminist, and Humanitarian* (Grand Rapids, MI: Zondervan, 1986).

Stephen R. Graham

Papal Infallibility. Papal infallibility holds that the bishop of Rome, when teaching *ex cathedra,* in his capacity as head of the church, on matters of faith and morals, as the successor to the supreme Apostle, Peter, teaches without error, whether he is teaching in harmony with the other bishops or acting alone. Promulgated officially by Vatican Council I* (1869–1870) of the Roman Catholic Church but long believed by many Catholics, papal infallibility is a logical extension of the centuries-old belief in papal supremacy, that the bishop of Rome is the authoritative head of all Christians. Popes have employed this power on two occasions: pronouncing in 1854 that the Virgin Mary was conceived immaculately (without original sin) and in 1950 that Mary's body upon death did not experience corruption but was assumed bodily into heaven. In the mid-1990s John Paul II came exceedingly close to invoking infallibility in making a categorical statement against the ordination of women.

A number of nonbiblical factors contributed to the emergence of papal supremacy: the association of Peter with Rome, the location of the papacy in the imperial capital, the fact that popes in the early doctrinal debates were usually on the winning side and thus established a record for orthodoxy of beliefs, the relative isolation of Rome from other major Christian metropolitan areas, the strong leadership of the bishop of Rome in the face of "barbarian" invasions of the Roman Empire, and the need to have an authoritative voice in the face of the multiplication of churches during the Reformation and the modern rise of scientific and cultural issues, such as Darwinism, that challenged the traditional understanding of the Christian faith.

Biblically speaking, Pope Leo I (reigning 440–461) was one of the first popes to claim leadership over the entire Christian church based upon his interpretation of Peter's confession in Matthew 16, a confession to which Jesus announced that he would build his church upon that "rock." Traditional supporters of papal supremacy have interpreted this passage as giving supreme apostolic authority to Peter. Through Peter's association with Rome, along with the principle of apostolic succession (authority passing from the apostles to those whom they ordained to succeed them), the bishop of Rome, accordingly, becomes the supreme head of the church. Other Christians differ sharply with this interpretation. Eastern Orthodox churches have always emphasized the equality of all apostles, pointing out that elsewhere in the Bible Christ gave the "keys" to the kingdom to all apostles, though Orthodoxy does acknowledge the Roman bishop's first place in honor and prestige. Protestants dispute the Catholic interpretation of Matthew 16, insisting that it was the confession of Peter, not Peter himself, a person known for personal weaknesses and shortcomings, upon which Christ established the church. In addition, Protestants are fiercely opposed to giving to any person or group the authority that most of them say belongs only to the Bible.

Vatican Council II* (1962–1965) perhaps signaled a step away from papal infallibility with emphasis upon episcopal collegiality. Indeed, a number of Catholic theologians, such as Hans Kung, have challenged the church to reject infallibility and substitute indefectibility, that is, the church occasionally errs but can be trusted to preach correctly on vital matters regarding salvation. Such arguments have not been received very warmly by most Catholic officials, and papal infallibility constitutes one of the major obstacles to reunion between Catholics and other Christians.

Bibliography. Brauer, Jerald C., *The Westminster Dictionary of Church History* (1971); *Dictionary of Christianity in America* (Downers Grove: InterVarsity Press, 1990); Urban, Linwood, *A Short History of Christian Thought* (New York: Oxford University Press: 1986).

Sandy Dwayne Martin

Parham, Charles Fox. Called by many the "father of the Pentecostal movement," Charles F. Parham (1873–1929) was at the same time one of the most controversial and most influential leaders in the early Pentecostal* movement. His newspaper, the *Apostolic Faith*, was one of the most important vehicles for the spread of the Pentecostal message, and he helped shape some of the key doctrines of the Pentecostal movement.

Parham's early ministry was within the Methodist Episcopal Church, but Methodist authorities suspected him of doctrinal aberrations and questioned his involvement in the Holiness and healing movements. Chafing under the hierarchical authority structure of Methodism,* he left that denomination in 1895 for an independent evangelistic ministry emphasizing divine healing and holiness. Later, when he became a leader in the emerging Pentecostal movement, he alienated many in the Holiness and healing movements. The greatest storms of controversy, however, erupted from within the Pentecostal movement itself.

Parham became troubled by what he viewed as excesses in early Pentecostalism, particularly among those labeled "holy rollers." Parham insisted that the Pentecostal movement was dignified, not crude and overly emotional as some experienced it. Stung by criticisms of the movement, he in turn blasted the leaders of the Azusa Street* revival (1906–1909), including his former pupil William J. Seymour, for allowing inordinate emotional displays and careless mixing of races and genders.

His precipitous decline from the leadership of the movement, though, resulted from rumors about his sexual behavior. Early in 1907 rumors began to circulate that Parham had been caught in a homosexual act with a young man in Texas. Parham was arrested, and headlines in the *San Antonio Light* announced that the evangelist had been taken into custody and charged with sodomy. Even though no formal indictment was ever filed and solid evidence was scarce, irreparable damage was done. Most Texas Pentecostals officially disfellowshipped Parham, and as others around the country learned of the charges through the ubiquitous religious newspapers and word of mouth, Parham lost most of his remaining influence in the Pentecostal movement. Parham's most recent biographer concluded that finally, Parham's behavior remains a mystery. Though virtually unknown by second-generation Pentecostals at the time of his death, Parham remains one of the most important leaders of early Pentecostalism.

Bibliography. Goff, James R., Jr., *Fields White unto Harvest: Charles F. Parham and the Missionary Origins of Pentecostalism* (Fayetteville: University of Arkansas Press, 1988); Parham, Sarah E., *The Life of Charles F. Parham* (Joplin, MO: Tri-State Printing Co., 1930).

Stephen R. Graham

Parker, Daniel. Daniel Parker was born in Virginia and reared in Georgia in a context of severe poverty and complete absence of formal education. Baptized as a Baptist in 1802 in Franklin, Georgia, he was soon licensed to preach by his local church. In 1803 he moved to Tennessee and was ordained in 1806. Soon his pilgrimage led him to Illinois, where at one point he entered politics and served a term as a state senator, 1826–1827. In 1834 he moved to Texas and was founder and pastor of the Pilgrim Church of Predestinarian Regular Baptists. Nine other affiliated churches were soon founded in east Texas. Entering the political arena again, he was a member of the Council of the Texas Provisional Government and was later elected to serve in the First Congress of the Republic of Texas. He never served in this post because the Texas Constitution forbade ministers to fill such a position.

His life as a religionist embodied two important controversial emphases—antimissionism (which included attacks on seminaries and benevolent and Bible societies) and his doctrine of "two seeds." Baptists* in the United States had only recently begun missionary efforts. As early as 1815, due to his hyper-Calvinism,* Parker began to oppose bitterly all missionary activities.

The basis for his hyperopposition to missions was his doctrine of "two seeds," which eventually resulted in the Baptist sect Two-Seed-in-the-Spirit Predestinarian Baptists. The "two seeds" concept came from the doctrine that Eve had a good seed and a bad seed within her and that all those whom God had foreordained to be saved were descended from the good seed. On the other hand, the descendants of the bad seed were bound for hell,* and any effort to evangelize these persons was doomed. Besides, such effort was also considered to be an interference with God's divine plan. It is also apparent that Parker resented eastern interference on the frontier in relation to education, mission gifts, and boards not sanctioned by the Bible. He often labeled mission promoters as estate builders, religious publications as attempts to supersede the Bible, and theological seminaries as attempts to manufacture preachers from graceless and lazy young men. He had a strong appeal on the uneducated frontier with its inbuilt resistance to "eastern ways."

Parker was small in size, often coarse in conduct, and of limited formal education. He was also an outstanding debater, with powerful oratorical skills. Doubtless he spoke the populist language of the frontier and in this context made a strong impact. During the time of Baptist expansion on the frontier, he was a major player in the whirlwind of controversy, dissension, and opposition.

See also Antimissions.

Bibliography. Bowden, Henry, *Dictionary of American Religious Biography* (Westport, CT: Greenwood Press, 1977); Carroll, B. H., *The Genesis of American Anti-Missionism* (Louisville: Baptist Book Co., 1902); Elliott, L. E., *Centennial Story of Texas Baptists* (Dallas: Baptist General Convention, 1936); Torbet, R. G., *A History of the Baptists*, 2nd ed. (Valley Forge, PA: Judson Press, 1963).

George H. Shriver

Parker, Theodore. Ralph Waldo Emerson called Theodore Parker (1810–1860) the Savonarola of transcendentalism for his aggressive attacks on church authority and orthodoxy. Possessor of a prodigious intellect, Parker learned to read twenty languages and mastered the scholarly literature in most of them, including the new radical German biblical criticism. He graduated from Harvard Divinity School in 1836.

In 1841 Parker issued a daring challenge to conservative Unitarianism in a sermon on "The Transient and the Permanent in Christianity," in which he rejected the historical manifestations of religion in favor of its permanent essence. The historical accretions, he asserted, included christological formulations and notions of the authority of Scripture. Parker valued Jesus' teachings but considered his nature irrelevant, and he believed that the validity of the Bible's message was independent of any alleged divine origin. The permanent essence of Christianity, he declared, is belief in the existence of God, love of humanity, and moral action from the highest motives.

In 1846 Parker assumed leadership of the Twenty-eighth Congregational Society in Boston and spent the rest of his life speaking and writing on the critical theological and social issues of the day. His enthusiasm for radical views earned him the censure of the more conservative Unitarian clergy, who ostracized him after the mid-1840s. In 1859, when Parker lay on his deathbed, the Harvard Divinity School alumni voted down a resolution of sympathy.

Because Parker believed that love and moral action lay at the center of true Christianity, he used his pulpit and his pen to advance various social and humanitarian reforms. He advocated women's rights, prison reform, peace, and temperance and was one of New England's leading abolitionists. He denounced the Fugitive Slave Law and sanctioned civil disobedience in assisting escaped slaves. He raised funds for John Brown's antislavery campaign in Kansas, and shortly before his death he defended Brown's raid on Harper's Ferry. Unlike many of his contemporary reformers, who portrayed social problems as simple matters of moral choice, Parker developed an insightful analysis of the economic, religious, and political forces that shape communities and called for a thorough reform of American society.

Bibliography. Commager, Henry S., *Theodore Parker: Yankee Crusader* (Boston: Little, Brown, and Co., 1936); Miller, Perry, ed., *The American Transcendentalists: Their Prose and Poetry*, Anchor Books ed. (Garden City, NY: Doubleday and Co., 1957); Parker, Theodore, *Theodore Parker: American Transcendentalist: A Critical Essay and a Collection of His Writings*, ed. Robert E. Collins (Metuchen, NJ: Scarecrow Press, 1973).

John P. Rossing

Parks, Rosa Louise McCauley. (1913–), the "Mother of the Civil Rights Movement," refused on December 1, 1955, to surrender a bus seat to a white man, endured arrest and a fine of fourteen dollars, and thereby sparked a series of protests, beginning with the Montgomery bus boycott of 1955–1956, that eventually led to the dismantling of racial segregation and discrimination practices across the country. Born in Tuskegee, Alabama, she spent much of her childhood in Montgomery in search of greater educational opportunities. There she attended a church-supported private high school and Alabama State College. She and Raymond Parks, a barber, married in 1932, a union that lasted until his death in 1977. During her life she worked as a file clerk, seamstress, insurance saleswoman, and during 1969–1988 on the congressional staff of John Conyers of Michigan.

Parks's own writings and closer examination of both Parks's civil rights* activities prior to and during the boycott suggest that the bus incident might have been a part of an orchestrated plan to challenge legal segregation. She was actively associated with the Montgomery NAACP,* the Brotherhood of Sleeping Car Porters, the Montgomery Voting League, the Highlander Folk School in Tennessee, the Montgomery Improvement Association, and, later, the Southern Christian Leadership Conference.* In 1957 she and her husband relocated to Detroit, Michigan, after a brief stay in Hampton, Virginia. In recent decades more attention has been paid to her pivotal role in civil rights activities with her speaking tours and her receipt of honors, including the renaming of Detroit's

Twelfth Street, the Martin Luther King, Jr., Nonviolent Peace Award by the MLK Center for Nonviolent Social Change, the NAACP's Spingarn Medal, and *Ebony* magazine's recognition of her as the African-American woman making the greatest contribution toward racial freedom. In 1987 she established the Rosa and Raymond Parks Institute for Self-Development in Detroit to advance career preparation for youth.

Bibliography. *Encyclopedia of African-American Culture and History*, vol. 4 (New York: Macmillan Library Reference, 1996); Hine, Darlene Clark, *Black Women in America: An Historical Encyclopedia*, vol. 2 (Thousand Oaks, CA: Sage Publications, 1993); King, Martin Luther, Jr., *Stride toward Freedom* (New York: Harper, 1958); Parks, Rosa, *Rosa Parks: My Story* (New York: Dial Books, 1992).

Sandy Dwayne Martin

Paulist Fathers. Paulist Fathers is the popular name of the Congregation of the Missionary Society of St. Paul the Apostle, an association of Catholic priests and seminarians. Its founder, Isaac Thomas Hecker* (1819–1888), was a convert from a German-American family of Lutheran and Methodist backgrounds.

In 1845 Hecker joined the Congregation of the Most Holy Redeemer (the Redemptorists) and was ordained a priest. In 1849, with three other Redemptorist converts, he devoted himself successfully to preaching, especially among German immigrants. In 1857 a conflict arose between the four missionaries and Redemptorist leaders; the general of the order expelled Hecker from the congregation.

After lengthy deliberation, the Vatican dispensed all the members of Hecker's missionary band from their vows as Redemptorists. In 1858, with the approval of Pope Pius IX, they established a new congregation with the explicit goal of American missions. Hecker began publishing *Catholic World* (now the *New Catholic World*) in 1865, and the next year he established the Catholic Publication Society, now known as the Paulist Press.

After Hecker died in 1888, the congregation continued to grow throughout the United States and Canada, becoming famous for the appealing and intelligent apologetic literature it produced. Within a few years, however, the Paulists were drawn into the Americanist* controversy, a complex ecclesiastical crisis that divided American Catholics over the question of how far the church should accommodate itself to American culture. The conflict was reflected in a number of interconnected issues, with disagreements over organized labor, Catholic schools, the German congregations, temperance, ecumenical relations, and the Catholic University of America.

In all these battles the opposing sides demonstrated somewhat consistent profiles. The Americanists, like many of their Protestant counterparts, enthusiastically promoted America's special messianic status in the modern world. They called for quickly integrating immigrant Catholics into American society and adapting Catholicism to the contours of the American "character." The conservative party, on the other hand, viewed Catholicism and the American way of life as fundamentally at odds. For them, American society was a largely hostile environment against which Catholics should be protected.

The Paulists were caught up in the argument because many of the ideas Hecker had expounded in his written works—"Heckerism," they came to be called—supported the Americanist position. Concerned to make Catholic converts in America, Hecker had promoted Catholicism as a fulfillment and guarantee of the ideals of American democracy. The American arrangement of freedom, religious voluntaryism,* and church-state separation, he had insisted, was a favorable environment for the growth of the church. In the enthusiasm of his pro-American stance, Hecker had celebrated "Anglo-Saxon virtues" and spoken disparagingly of "the Latin race," raising fears in Europe as well as the United States that his ideas were both nationalist and racist.

Hecker's emphasis on active rather than passive virtues appeared to press for doctrinal revisions in traditional Catholic ethics. In addition, his teachings on the Holy Spirit seemed to some a depreciation of the institutional church. The Paulists were in fact nicknamed "the Protestant Catholics" because of their association with these doctrines.

All these distinctive views were championed in Father Walter Elliott's *Life of Father Hecker* (1891), a book that soon provoked controversy on both sides of the Atlantic. In 1898, amid rumors that Elliott's biography would soon appear on the Vatican's Index of Forbidden Books, Pope Leo XIII reserved the question of "Americanism" to himself. On January 22, 1899, Leo published *Testem Benevolentiae,* an apostolic letter addressed to Cardinal James Gibbons, the Americanist archbishop of Baltimore. The letter referred to the French translation of Hecker's biography and pronounced certain doctrines to be in error, yet without explicitly claiming that Hecker himself or any other Americans had taught these doctrines. The encyclical condemned Americanism, which it said was based on the false idea that Catholicism's adaptation to the modern world required adjustments in doctrine as well as discipline. In imitation of recent developments in certain secular states (especially America), Leo claimed, a false liberty was being introduced into the church, with dangerous consequences involving the Catholic understanding of two important issues on which Hecker had focused: the role of the Holy Spirit in Christian life and the nature of Christian virtue. Archbishop Gibbons's reply, not published until 1944, insisted that no Catholic leader in the United States had ever held such views. That question has remained a matter of debate, as has the larger question of Catholic accommodation to American culture.

Bibliography. Elliott, Walter, *The Life of Father Hecker* (New York: Columbus Press, 1891); Farina, J., ed., *Hecker Studies: Essays on the Thought of Isaac Hecker* (New York: Paulist Press, 1983); O'Brien, D., *Isaac Hecker: An American Catholic* (New York: Paulist Press, 1992).

T. Paul Thigpen

Peace Movement. The concept of a peace movement emerged when citizens began to perceive that they could influence government policies related to war* and national security. As such, it is closely linked to the advent of democracy in nations. Peace movements in the United States have usually been based at least partly in Christian teachings. The role of religion in peace movements in the United States has traditionally been associated with New Testament teachings against violence under any circumstances. But peace movements have also been based on more specific nonreligious considerations related to perceptions that certain wars are not justified, especially if they involve significant loss of life for a vaguely defined goal.

The phenomenon of the peace movement is often seen as relatively recent in the United States, linked most closely to protests over U.S. policy in Southeast Asia. A close reading shows that there is an enduring history of peace movements in the United States. Nevertheless, potential peace movements lay dormant after World War II. The historical lesson known as the "Münich analogy" worked against potential peace movements by drawing attention to the dangers of military weakness and appeasement of aggressors. This lesson was quickly reapplied to the worldwide "Communist menace." This setting gave U.S. policymakers a great deal of leeway in pursuing foreign policy aims, whether through "proxy wars" in remote areas of the globe or through the threatened use of a powerful nuclear arsenal.

What is now known as the peace movement emerged in the mid-1960s in response to excesses associated with these global strategies. It drew much of its energy and focus from opposition to U.S. policy in Vietnam. U.S. intervention in Vietnam actually had widespread popular support in the United States until roughly 1965. But as the scale of intervention increased and as the war dragged on without visible political and military success, opposition to the war mushroomed. This opposition took place for two reasons: a moral outrage at the kind of punishment being inflicted by an extremely violent U.S. war machine, and a more practical opposition felt by those questioning the drafting of their family members, or themselves, for a war of doubtful relation to U.S. national security. By 1968 the movement opposing the Vietnam War had a nationwide following and was extremely active on college campuses, but it never was able to translate its popularity into presidential politics, as Richard Nixon was twice elected despite heated opposition from the peace movement.

The peace movement was able to last well beyond the end of U.S. participation in the Vietnam War in 1973. Vietnam had brought on profound mistrust between the American populace and the government in matters of foreign and military policy. Thus, for example, groups formerly mobilized over Vietnam policy were successful in opposing aggressive, anti-Communist Reagan administration policy in Central America. The antinuclear movement gained considerable momentum in the 1970s and 1980s. This branch of the peace movement was successful in pushing nuclear weapons treaties in the 1970s and opposing the Reagan administration's Strategic Defense Initiative (also known as "Star

Wars'') in the 1980s. Pressure from the peace movement was also instrumental in pushing for the rapid reductions in nuclear weaponry taking place in the post–Cold War atmosphere of the late 1980s and 1990s.

Religious groups were central to the peace movement. Matters of military policy had an immediacy lacking in many other issues. The general sense of betrayal that accompanied revelations about policies in Vietnam and elsewhere brought an additional moral element to the peace movement. For example, Father Philip Berrigan* was one of the most visible early Vietnam protesters, actively encouraging young Americans to avoid the draft. Various denominations, from Unitarians to Catholics, played an active role in a sanctuary movement that supported refugees fleeing U.S.-supported violence in Central America. Most enduring, perhaps, was institutional support, especially among the Catholic hierarchy, for reductions in nuclear weaponry.

Bibliography. Gitlin, Todd, *The Sixties: Years of Hope, Days of Rage* (New York: Bantam Books, 1987); United States Catholic Conference, *The Challenge of Peace: God's Promise and Our Response* (Washington DC: United States Catholic Conference, 1983); Walzer, Michael, *Just and Unjust Wars* (New York: Basic Books, 1977); Wicker, B., *Nuclear Deterrence: What Does the Church Teach?* (London: Catholic Truth Society, 1985).

Frederick M. Shepherd

Peale, Norman Vincent. The eldest of three children, Norman Vincent Peale was born on May 31, 1898 to his mother, Anna, and father, Clifford, an evangelical Methodist minister in Bowersville, Ohio. This pious and close-knit Christian home formed a character of strict moral fibre concerned with the development of an individual spirituality that tended to define Peale's entire ministry. His upbringing also helped to shape conservative political leanings, a healthy dose of skepticism toward ministerial hierarchy, and a committed evangelical outlook.

During the Cold War period of the 1950s a revival of "religion in general" emerged as a last-gasp tribute to a homogeneous Protestantism attempting to hold its ground in a culture increasingly threatened by a visible religious, and often nonreligious, pluralism. Norman Vincent Peale (along with Billy Graham*) became a household name during these years through his reputation as a respected and popular religious innovator helping Christians weather the storms of anxious times. His ministry quickly became controversial as he attempted to mix mainstream religion with the positive-thinking tradition of metaphysical spirituality associated with Anton Mesmer, Mary Baker Eddy,* and Phineas Quimby.*

Peale's emphasis on practical Christianity quickly transformed the power of positive thinking into a tool of Christian spiritual renewal, hoping to challenge the impoverished theological liberalism* of the mainline establishment with a form of Christian faith able to meet the popular needs of everyday Christians in crisis. Since Peale was himself identified with the Protestant establishment, his efforts to champion this cause became especially controversial in the circles of mainstream Protestantism. Two particular controversies, with long-lasting results, showered negative criticism all over the world on Peale's positive thinking.

With the publication of *The Power of Positive Thinking* in 1952, Norman Vincent Peale became both a celebrity and the focal point of swirling controversy. His book found immediate popular acceptance as a best-seller. Though Peale was not without his cultural critics, he grieved most over the theological criticism leveled at his work. Reinhold Niebuhr and other leading theological figures described Peale's New Thought practical Christianity as abandonment of the transcendence of God, of the Christian emphasis on sinful human nature, and of the theme of sacrificial service associated with the incarnation of Christ. Religious critics also attacked the individualistic orientation of positive thinking and its heavy emphasis on achieving worldly success and cultural status.

Peale's association with the National Association of Evangelicals led to the second major controversy of his career. In early September 1960 evangelicals met in Washington to discuss the politics of the Roman Catholic Church and express Protestant concern about the candidacy of John F. Kennedy for president. Peale presided at the meeting and met with the press afterward. Public response to the pronouncements of this evangelical group was swift, widespread, and critical. Critics rather convincingly exposed the church-state concerns of this group as anti-Catholic bigotry and political partisanship. This controversial encounter sobered Peale some, and thereafter he tried to moderate his involvement in politics. Yet his close friendship with Richard Nixon, and later with Ronald Reagan, guaranteed a political presence well into the future.

Perhaps the controversy between critics and supporters of Peale over the past four decades represents better than any other the power of religious populism to outperform the ability of scholarly religious leaders to reach the common Christian with concerns for the theological themes of Christian faith. Peale's ministry served also as a constant reminder to the mainstream of its inability to reach individuals well at the point of their needs.

Bibliography. George, C.V.R., *God's Salesman: Norman Vincent Peale and The Power of Positive Thinking* (New York: Oxford University Press, 1993); Gordon, A., *Norman Vincent Peale: Minister to Millions* (Englewood Cliffs, NJ: Prentice-Hall, 1958); Meyer, D. B., *The Positive Thinkers: Popular Religious Psychology from Mary Baker Eddy to Norman Vincent Peale and Ronald Reagan* (Middletown, CT.: Wesleyan University Press, 1988); Williams, P., *Popular Religion in America* (Urbana: University of Illinois Press, 1989).

Mark G. Toulouse

Pentecostal. The Pentecostal movement has been viewed by many as fraught with controversy since its beginnings. Despite the widely shared opinion that Pentecostals are unconcerned about doctrine, they have had within their history some bitter doctrinal controversies.

Even the commonly accepted distinctive of Pentecostalism, speaking in tongues, was the source of disputes in the early years of the movement, ranging from whether tongues were intended primarily for missionary purposes to disagreement about whether speaking in tongues was the exclusive sign of receiving the baptism of the Holy Spirit,* or whether there were different kinds of tongues.

Since the early Pentecostals came out of varying theological backgrounds, many of their assumptions differed despite their common affirmation of particular Pentecostal beliefs, such as speaking in tongues or an emphasis on divine healing. For example, Pentecostals who came out of a Methodist-Holiness background usually accepted that tradition's emphasis on an experience of sanctification subsequent to conversion, a second work of grace prior to the baptism with the Holy Spirit. Thus they could speak of being "saved, sanctified, and filled with the Holy Ghost" as three distinguishable experiences of God's grace.

Pentecostals from other backgrounds, however, such as Baptist or Presbyterian traditions, had never identified sanctification as a separate work of grace and therefore emphasized only two works of grace, salvation and baptism with the Holy Spirit. A controversy broke out in the decades following the Azusa Street* revival (1906–1909) over what was called the "finished work" doctrine, the doctrine of those who believed in only two works of grace and said that sanctification began with regeneration and not with a second distinctive experience of grace. The Assemblies of God, destined to become the largest predominantly white Pentecostal denomination, was founded by "finished work" advocates, while the Church of God in Christ (the largest African-American Pentecostal body) and the Pentecostal Holiness Church continued to teach three works of grace.

A third controversy that tore the new movement apart had to do with the doctrine of the Trinity and the practice of baptism.* Some early Pentecostals had been considering the idea that the doctrine of the Trinity was not scriptural, among other reasons because the word "Trinity" was not found in the Bible. They emphasized the absolute oneness of God and insisted that God's single name was "Jesus." They were joined by Pentecostals who, having searched the Scriptures for the true New Testament baptismal formula, came to the conclusion that the early Christians had baptized converts exclusively "in" or "into" the name of Jesus. At a Pentecostal camp meeting in Arroyo Seco (near Los Angeles), California, in 1913, some ministers believed that they had received a revelation from the Holy Spirit about Jesus' name baptism. Eventually, many were rebaptized and began to advocate the formula "in the name of Jesus Christ" as the scriptural baptismal formula rather than the traditional formula from Matthew 28:19, "in the name of the Father and the Son and the Holy Spirit." The movement was split by the controversy a few years later when the Assemblies of God rejected the new ideas and nearly 25 percent of its ministers left the denomination rather than submit to the newly adopted confession of faith.

Another controversy within the Pentecostal movement has been the question of the proper role of women. In the early years a number of women played central roles in the development and spread of the movement, and some, most notably Aimee Semple Mcpherson,* founded denominations. As Pentecostals were influenced by fundamentalism* in the 1910s and 1920s and became more institutionalized, however, some began to argue that women's proper place was in the home, not the pulpit. Today, some Pentecostal denominations ordain women, while many do not.

In recent years the Pentecostal movement has been shaken by doctrinal irregularities by leaders teaching the so-called prosperity gospel and extremes by some in the signs and wonders movement. In addition, scandals among some of the most notable Pentecostal evangelists, especially some of those with large television audiences, have caused controversy within the movement. The independent, entrepreneurial spirit of many leaders in the movement, combined with reliance on inspirations by the Holy Spirit and resistance to institutional or confessional checks on individual opinion, has led to much diversity within Pentecostalism and considerable controversy throughout its history.

Bibliography. Anderson, Robert Mapes, *Vision of the Disinherited: The Making of American Pentecostalism* (New York: Oxford University Press, 1979); Burgess, Stanley, and Gary B. McGee, eds., Patrick H., Alexander, assoc. ed., *Dictionary of Pentecostal and Charismatic Movements* (Grand Rapids, MI: Zondervan, 1988); Dayton, Donald W., *Theological Roots of Pentecostalism* (Grand Rapids, MI: Francis Asbury Press, 1987).

Stephen R. Graham

Pietism. Pietism was an international and interconfessional Protestant movement of the seventeenth and eighteenth centuries, with continuing impact in the nineteenth and twentieth, that aimed at nothing less than a ''Second Reformation'' of the church. Disturbed by doctrinal aridity and moral laxness among Protestants, adherents of pietism emphasized the personal nature of faith and the purity of the church; these emphases led to the requirement of visible manifestations of new birth for individuals, to the necessity of demonstrable personal holiness, to the importance of articulating a biblical norm for faith and ethics, and to the imperative of actively pursuing church reform. Inspiration for the movement came from the evangelical witness of the great reformers (especially Luther and Calvin), the moral earnestness of the Reformed tradition (especially Puritanism), the continuation of certain mystical traditions within Protestantism (for example, in the devotional writings of Johann Arndt), and the countercultural vision of the Anabaptists. Important pietist leaders included Philip Jacob Spener (1635–1705), August Herman Francke (1663–1727), Nicholas Ludwig, Count von Zinzendorf (1700–1760), and John Wesley (1703–1791). Pietism was controversial from the beginning; confessional opponents disliked the pietists' tendency to ignore the finer points of doctrine, church officials feared their disdain of church structure and historic patterns of worship, and secular authorities found their conventicles and disregard for political boundaries to be at least potentially subversive.

Pietism early divided into two main streams. Churchly pietists remained (or tried to remain) within the established territorial churches in Europe or within their denominational equivalents in America. They understood themselves as a reforming movement within the churches, aiming to bring to fruition the thwarted promise of the original Reformation. Radical pietists separated from the established denominations, either to create small utopian communities or to form new denominations. Among the better-known pietist utopias in America were the German Seventh Day Baptists (Ephrata Community), the Harmony Society (Rappites*), and the Community of True Inspiration (Amana Colony). Denominations of a radical bent included the Unity of Brethren (Moravians) and the United Brethren in Christ. As these examples show, radical pietism in America was heavily German in origin. Some churchly groups had radical tendencies, the best-known example being early Methodism.*

Pietism made important contributions of both style and substance to the American churches. It was largely responsible for the growth of the Sunday school movement, it developed new methods of theological education, it inspired many moral reforms, and it gave birth to the tradition of revivalism* that has been so prominent in American Protestantism. Protestant missionary efforts in the nineteenth and twentieth centuries, both European and American, were rooted in pietism. Its perfectionistic emphasis gave the American churches a strongly moralistic (its critics said legalistic) flavor, which carried over into secular life as well.

Pietists were regularly involved in controversy. Several denominations developed pietist and orthodoxist parties in the eighteenth and nineteenth centuries. Whether it was ''American Lutherans'' versus ''Old Lutherans,'' ''New School'' Presbyterians versus the ''Old School,'' or ''Evangelical'' versus ''High Church'' Episcopalians, the issues were much the same. The pietists called for a reform of individuals, the church, and the broader society along lines that their opponents found offensive from the point of view of traditional theology and church practice. In the Reformed tradition, the theological issues centered on the understanding of human ability in the process of salvation, with most pietists jettisoning Calvin's views in favor of those of Arminius. In Lutheranism,* controversies tended to focus on the sacraments and the nature of the new birth. Among Episcopalians, liturgical and ecclesiological questions were central. By the early nineteenth century a major reaction against pietism had set in, as the proponents of resurgent churchly traditions challenged the pietists' subjectivity, excessive moralism, narrow biblicism, casual interdenominationalism, and reliance on revivalistic techniques. The opponents of pietism were often themselves profoundly affected by the movement, however, as they selectively adopted pietist perspectives and practices.

Pietist influence remains strong in several historic American denominations, but is most obviously manifest today in the traditionally pietist denominations, Holiness and Pentecostal* groups, and in many nondenominational congregations and ministries. The parachurch movement is also deeply indebted to pietism.

Bibliography. Brown, Dale W., *Understanding Pietism* (Grand Rapids, MI: Eerdmans, 1978); Stoeffler, F. Ernest, ed., *Continental Pietism and Early American Christianity*, (Grand Rapids, MI: Eerdmans, 1976); Stoeffler, F. Ernest, *The Rise of Evangelical Pietism* (Leiden: E. J. Brill, 1965).

Donald L. Huber

Pike, Bishop James A. Episcopal churchman James Pike (1913–1969) became a lightning rod for theological and ecclesiastical controversy during his period of national preeminence between 1954 and 1968. While respecting the doctrines of traditional Christianity, he seemed compelled by inner doubts and by a strong social conscience to question and challenge what he considered to be outmoded ideas and attitudes in the church. Pike's personal spiritual quest mirrored the religious ferment that thrust much of mainstream Christianity into turmoil during the late 1950s and 1960s.

Pike intended to enter the Roman Catholic priesthood when he enrolled at Santa Clara University after high school. Soon, however, he began to have serious doubts about such Catholic teachings as papal infallibility* and birth control.* After leaving school and the church, Pike became a lawyer and worked as a government attorney in Washington, D.C., during the early 1940s. Following a divorce, he decided to become an Episcopal priest. He completed a theology degree at Union Theological Seminary* and refashioned the Department of Religion at Columbia University.

During the 1950s Pike became a national figure as dean of New York City's Saint John the Divine Cathedral. He took controversial stands in favor of civil rights* and birth control and against capital punishment.* His eloquence helped establish him as one of the preeminent political and social liberals of his time. As host of two national religious television shows during the 1950s, Pike pioneered both debate and interview formats that allowed frank discussion of disputed issues in theology and society.

Following his election as bishop of California in 1959, Pike worked tirelessly to refashion his church so that it spoke to the challenges of the modern world. In his writings he questioned the doctrines of the Trinity and the Virgin Birth and warned his peers against limiting God with traditional theological concepts. At Grace Cathedral in San Francisco he commissioned stained-glass windows that featured Albert Einstein and Thurgood Marshall, and he invited Martin Luther King, Jr.,* to preach in his pulpit. Pike was an early advocate of women's equality and broke with tradition by ordaining the first Episcopalian woman minister.

The bishop's views aroused strong opposition among his conservative peers, who charged him with heresy. Bishop Pike responded to these charges in three substantial theological works, *A Time for Christian Candor* (1964), *What Is This Treasure?* (1966), and *If This Be Heresy* (1967). Following a struggle with alcoholism, a scandalous love affair, and his son's suicide during the mid-1960s, Pike endured professional censure by the House of Bishops and a ban on priestly functioning. He died from exposure during a research trip in the Judean desert in 1969.

Bibliography. Pike, James A. and Diane Kennedy, *Search: The Personal Story of a Wilderness Journey* (Garden City, NY: Doubleday, 1970); Pike, James A., with Norman Pittinger, *The Faith of the Church*, vol. 3 of *The Church's Teaching* (Greenwich: Seabury, 1953); Stringfellow, William, and Anthony Towne, *The Bishop Pike Affair: Scandals of Conscience and Heresy, Relevance and Solemnity in the Contemporary Church* (New York: Harper and Row, 1967).

Phillip Lucas

Political Correctness. Political correctness is a term that arose in the mid-1980s in response to several intellectual and cultural trends. It is a term used with some irony (and often put into quotes) by its supporters and is taken extremely seriously by its detractors. It gained much of its relevance through the somewhat superficial analysis of the popular press.

In the wake of the political upheavals of the 1960s and early 1970s, new political, intellectual, and cultural approaches emerged, based on a questioning of traditional values and ways of thinking. Just as college and university campuses were the focus of protest in these decades, so they became the location for much of what has been branded political correctness in the 1980s. Students looking to rebel against what they saw as a sterile and conservative ''real world'' began to don the somewhat bohemian, countercultural garb of political correctness, attaching to this appearance a significant political statement. There was an element of celebrating non-Western cultures and religions in this approach, reflecting both rejection of precollege authority figures and recent exposure to nontraditional curricula. It represented a relatively easy and superficial attack on authority. This group often attached itself to more explicitly political campus protest movements. These movements, 1980s versions of the civil rights* and antiwar protests, practiced a more coherent and principled version of ''political correctness.'' This distinction was lost on the popular press.

Related to this cultural development were far more coherent and sophisticated intellectual developments, primarily among faculty on many of the same campuses. While these trends no doubt encouraged student ''political correctness,'' they were part of a more sophisticated critique of U.S. society and in this way were closer in spirit to the political struggles of the 1960s. Specific manifestations of intellectual ''political correctness'' were ''revisionist'' history, neo-Marxist political science and sociology, postmodern literary criticism, and a general infusion of non-Western appreciation into religious studies and the fine arts. This approach was energized by the introduction of new voices into traditional scholarship.

This intellectual approach was loosely allied with radical religious groups. For instance, liberation theology* and the radical, revolutionary path it advocated in Latin America and other regions fit into the larger "politically correct" mind-set. But on a more general level, the antitraditionalist focus of political correctness put it into direct conflict with much of established Christianity. It tended to celebrate non-Western and "New Age" religions. It also advocated alternative lifestyles, such as sex outside of marriage and homosexuality,* and it pushed a political agenda well to the left of all but the most radical church groups. More generally, the thoughtful practitioners of political correctness advocated an approach that questioned dominant institutions and mind-sets, including Christianity and the existence of a deity. Traditional denominations, especially those associated with the Christian right, saw these developments as something to be actively opposed. These denominations, as well as the rest of society, came to assign practitioners of political correctness far more influence than they actually had.

Bibliography. Berube, Michael, and Cary Nelson, eds., *Higher Education under Fire: Politics, Economics, and the Crisis of the Humanities* (New York: Routledge, 1994); Friedman, Marilyn, and Jan Narveson, *Political Correctness: For and Against* (Lanham, MD: Rowman and Littlefield, 1995); Wilson, John K., *The Myth of Political Correctness* (Durham: Duke University Press, 1995).

Frederick M. Shepherd

Portland Deliverance. The Portland Deliverance was a declaration of the 1892 General Assembly of the Presbyterian Church in the USA, meeting in Portland, Oregon, requiring all clergy in the church to subscribe to the inerrancy of Scripture. In 1881 Archibald A. Hodge,* a professor at Princeton Seminary, and Benjamin B. Warfield,* a professor at Western Seminary in Allegheny, Pennsylvania, responded to historical-critical views of the Scriptures by arguing that "all the affirmations of Scripture of all kinds . . . are without any error when the ipsissima verba of the original autographs are ascertained and interpreted in their natural and intended sense." In 1891 Charles A. Briggs,* a Presbyterian clergyman and prominent biblical scholar, challenged such views upon his inauguration into the chair of biblical theology at Union Theological Seminary* in New York. In his inaugural address Briggs insisted that the Scriptures did contain errors and denied the Mosaic authorship of the Pentateuch and the unitary authorship of Isaiah.

Conservatives quickly challenged Briggs's views as a violation of Presbyterian doctrine, while Henry Preserved Smith,* professor at Lane Theological Seminary,* came to Briggs's defense, asserting that he also denied biblical inerrancy. In response, the 1892 General Assembly adopted the Portland Deliverance, which declared that "the inspired Word, as it came from God, is without error" and enjoined all Presbyterian clergy to adhere to this doctrine. The assembly thereby endorsed the Princeton view of Scripture propounded by Hodge and Warfield.

The Portland Deliverance played a major role in the suspension of Briggs and Smith from the Presbyterian ministry in the following two years and set the precedent for future assemblies of the church to define fundamental doctrines of the church. Accordingly, the General Assembly of 1899 determined four "fundamental doctrines" of the church, including scriptural inerrancy, leading to the resignation of Arthur Cushman McGiffert,* professor of church history at Union Seminary, from the Presbyterian ministry. Additionally, the General Assemblies of 1910, 1916, and 1923, concerned about the doctrinal soundness of liberal ministerial candidates, declared five doctrines, including the inerrancy of Scripture, to be "essential and necessary" doctrines of the church. Finally, in 1927, after years of fighting between liberals and conservatives, the General Assembly decided that the assembly by itself could not declare an article of faith essential and necessary and thereby rejected the doctrine of scriptural inerrancy as binding on the church.

Bibliography. Loetscher, Lefferts A., *The Broadening Church* (Philadelphia: University of Pennsylvania Press, 1954); Massa, Mark S., *Charles Augustus Briggs and the Crisis of Historical Criticism* (Minneapolis: Fortress Press, 1990); Noll, Mark A., ed., *The Princeton Theology, 1812–1921* (Grand Rapids, MI: Baker Book House, 1983).

Bradley J. Longfield

Powell, Adam Clayton, Jr. Adam Clayton Powell, Jr., was born on November 29, 1908, in New Haven, Connecticut. He was educated at Colgate University, where he received an A.B. in 1930, and Columbia University, where he received an M.A. in 1932. The vanguard of a new type of black clergyman-politician, Powell replaced his father as pastor of Abyssinian Baptist Church in Harlem in 1939. Building on his father's Social Gospel ministry, Powell led the extremely large congregation in the fight for welfare rights, and the fight against job discrimination. Likewise, Powell was one of the first African-American clergy to use "radical strategies" such as boycotts and pickets to secure civil rights.*

In 1941 Powell launched his political career. That year he was able to defeat Tammany Hall with the help of the larger Harlem community, becoming the first black to be elected to the New York City Council. In 1944 Powell was elected to the U.S. Congress, with 89 percent of the black vote, and served eleven consecutive terms. Powell also served as chairperson of the House Committee on Education and Labor, becoming the most powerful black politician in history. His legislative contributions made a major impact in the area of civil rights and paved the way for the rise of the modern civil rights movement.

Flamboyant and extremely controversial, Powell was a spellbinding orator. During his tenure in Congress, Abyssinian was the largest black church in the nation, with 20,000 members. Although the church was Baptist, it was not affiliated with any of the national Baptist conventions. In 1943 Powell divorced his first wife, Isabel Washington, an actress, and married Hazel Scott, a concert and jazz pianist. In 1954 *Ebony* magazine named him one of the ten best black preachers in the nation. In 1960 Powell divorced Scott and married Yvette Marjorie Flores Diago. Quite arrogant, he openly lived the lifestyle of a playboy.

In 1963 Powell began to attack the NAACP* and Martin Luther King, Jr.,* accusing them of being "co-opt[ed] by the white liberal establishment." That same year, he began to link his Harlem ministry to that of Malcolm X.*

But his political decline began in 1960 when a Harlem woman won a libel suit against him. Refusing to acknowledge the case and the financial judgment against him, Powell took up residence on Bimini, an isle in the Bahamas, only coming to New York to preach on Sundays. As a result, in 1966 he was convicted of criminal contempt, and in 1967 he was removed from Congress on ethics charges relating to the misuse of public funds. In a special election later that year, his black Harlem constituency returned him to the House. In 1969 the Supreme Court ruled his unseating unconstitutional. Upon settling the libel suit, Powell was returned to Congress, after being stripped of his seniority. However, in 1970 he was defeated at the polls by Charles Rangel. He returned to Bimini and died two years later, on April 4, 1972, in Miami.

Bibliography. Haygood, W., *King of the Cats: The Life and Times of Adam Clayton Powell, Jr.* (Boston: Houghton Mifflin, 1993); Lincoln, C. E. and L. H. Mamiya, *The Black Church In the African-American Experience* (Durham: Duke University Press, 1990); Melton, J. G., ed., *Religious Leaders of America* (Detroit: Gale Research, 1991); Murphy, L. G., ed., *Encyclopedia of African American Religions* (New York: Garland Publishing, 1993); Wilmore, G. S., *Black Religion and Black Radicalism*, 2nd rev. ed. (Maryknoll, NY: Orbis Books, 1983).

Lawrence H. Williams

Predestination. One of the most vexing philosophical questions throughout church history, the doctrine of predestination and its relation to free will and human responsibility have occupied some of the finest minds within Christianity. Augustine, Gottschalk, Aquinas, Erasmus, Luther, Calvin, Arminius, Jonathan Edwards,* Wesley, Charles Hodge,* Charles Finney,* C. H. Spurgeon, A. W. Pink, and Karl Barth all have presented powerful cases either for or against predestination. Falling under the heading of the sovereignty of God, predestination (and its analogous terms, foreordination and election) is the belief that God from eternity in his sovereign wisdom and power has foreordained all things that are to come to pass, including the destinies of the good and bad. How he does this (if indeed he does) without imposing upon man's personal will and destroying human responsibility has made the doctrine of predestination one of the most controversial and divisive subjects within Christendom.

Proponents of predestination find their greatest biblical support in the Old Testament motif of the national election of Israel as God's "chosen people," as well as the New Testament Pauline theology of sovereign grace and individual election of the saints. The primary passages concerning predestination, foreordination, and election include Psalms 139:16; Acts 2:23, 4:27–28, 13:48; Romans 8:29–30, 9:23; 1 Corinthians 2:7; and Ephesians 1:5, 1:11, 2:10. Though largely ignored by the patristic writers, the doctrine was revived by Augustine during his confrontation with Pelagius, elaborated upon by Aquinas in the thirteenth century, and given a central place in Reformed theology by Martin Luther's *Bondage of the Will* (1525), John Calvin's *Romans* (1540) and the *Institutes of the Christian Religion* (especially the final version of 1559), and the Westminster Confession (1647). All three placed a preeminence upon the salvation of the elect as God's predestined work alone, denying Erasmus's assertion of human cooperation. Luther, however, urged caution in drawing a similar conclusion concerning the nonelect, but Calvin did not. In the *Institutes* he defined what would become known as "double predestination": "We call predestination God's eternal decree, by which he compacted with himself what he willed to become of each man. For all are not created in equal condition; rather, eternal life is foreordained for some, eternal damnation for others. Therefore, as any man has been created to one or other of these ends, we speak of him as predestined to life or to death" (1.21.7).

Calvin and the Calvinist Reformers who followed him were convinced that the essence of Reformed theology depended upon this doctrine, and accordingly volumes were written in its defense, especially against the charges brought by both Catholic theologians and other Reformers (especially Arminius) that such a doctrine denied to mankind free will and responsibility, while burdening God with arbitrary choice and the creation of evil. The Westminster Confession was clear in its position concerning predestination: "God from all eternity did, by the most wise and holy counsel of his own will, freely and unchangeably ordained whatsoever comes to pass: yet so as thereby neither is God the author of sin, nor is violence offered to the will of the creatures, nor is the liberty or contingency of second causes taken away, but rather established. . . . By the decree of God, for the manifestation of his glory, some men and angels are predestinated unto everlasting life, and others foreordained to everlasting death" (3:1, 3). Thus to the Calvinist Reformers election and reprobation were not the result of any human effort or inherent worth, but instead were wrought by the mere pleasure of God for his glory alone. In the eighteenth century Jonathan Edwards championed the cause of predestination against the Arminianism* of the Wesleyan movement, as did Charles Hodge of Princeton in the first half of the nineteenth century against the Arminian revivalist theology of Charles Finney. The works of A. W. Pink, Loraine Boettner, and J. I. Packer, among others, have continued this unbroken line of Calvinistic predestinarians into the twentieth century.

At least three distinct attitudes toward the doctrine of predestination have emerged within the church since the Reformation. One is an extreme view (often associated with hyper-Calvinism*) that holds that predestination does indeed preclude all human endeavor. Since God's predestining power ensures that "what will be will be" in a world devoid of free will, all responses to the events of human history are irrelevant, freeing man of any responsibility within the realm of secondary causes, even that of leading a holy life.

Calvin himself argued against this view in the *Institutes* (3.23.6–14). Such an extreme, almost fatalistic, view opened the door to antinomianism and arrogance. Like Augustine, Calvin and the Reformers argued for a "compatibilist" position, in which God's predestining power and foreknowledge do not destroy man's ability to choose nor his responsibility for his choices. God's foreknowledge and predestining power are one and the same. Hence man does not possess "free will," for nothing of man can be free of God's foreknowledge; nor does man, as spiritually dead due to his total depravity, have the ability to choose spiritual good. Yet within the foreknowledge of God and the "bondage of human will," to use Luther's words, exists the "voluntary necessity" of human actions. As a result, human actions are not deeds of compulsion to Calvin, but rather voluntary choices for which each individual is responsible, made within a world in which God has foreknown (predestinated) these very choices from "before the foundations of the world." Boettner provided a useful summary of the Augustinian-Reformed view in these words: "An act is not free if determined from without; but it is free if rationally determined from within, and this is precisely what God's foreordination effects. The comprehensive decree provides that each man shall be a free agent, possessing a certain character, surrounded by a certain environment, subject to certain external influences, internally moved by certain affections, desires, habits, etc., and that in view of all these he shall freely and rationally make a choice. That the choice will be one thing and not another, is certain; and God, who knows and controls the exact causes of each influence, knows what that choice will be, and in a real sense determines it" (251).

A third view, held by many Catholic theologians, Arminians, and liberal theology in general, is that of "synergism," in which God's predestining grace cooperates with man's will in effecting salvation for the elect. Arminius argued that God predestined to save those whom he foreknew would believe. Man's nature was not so fallen that no vestige of faith remained. When man activated that spark of faith by means of his will, election was ensured. Calvin saw such a use of predestination as illogical, for "what consistency is there in saying that the things derived from election [give] cause to election?" (*Institutes*, 3.22.3). Wesley, Finney, and a host of nineteenth- and twentieth-century evangelicals, however, found this doctrine more amenable to human experience than Calvinism, and it became the dominant view in the twentieth century.

Bibliography. Boettner, Loraine, *The Reformed Doctrine of Predestination* (Phillipsburg, NJ: Presbyterian and Reformed Publishing Co., 1932); Calvin, John, *Institutes of the Christian Religion*, ed. John T. McNeill, 2 vols. (Philadelphia: Westminster Press, 1960); Farrelly, M. John, *Predestination, Grace, and Free Will* (Westminster, MD: Newman Press, 1964); Pink, A.W., *The Sovereignty of God* (Swengel, PA: Bible Truth Depot, 1918); Wallace, Dewey D. J., Jr., *Puritans and Predestination* (Chapel Hill: University of North Carolina Press, 1982).

Timothy D. Whelan

Preus, Jacob A. O., Jr. Jacob A. O. Preus, Jr. (1920–1994), was president (1969–1981) of the Lutheran Church–Missouri Synod during the height of its theological controversies in the 1960s and 1970s. Born in St. Paul, Minnesota, on January 8, 1920, Preus was the son of J.A.O. Preus, cofounder of the Lutheran Brotherhood Insurance Company (1917) and governor of Minnesota (1921–1925). Numerous ancestors and other relatives were prominent in Norwegian-American Lutheran church affairs. Preus attended Luther College, Luther Seminary, and the University of Minnesota (Ph.D., 1951). From 1946 to 1958 he taught at Bethany College of the Evangelical Lutheran Synod, a small conservative church body with ties to the Missouri Synod. He also served two pastorates during this period. In 1958 he became professor of Greek, Latin, and New Testament at Concordia Seminary, Springfield, Illinois. In 1962 he became president of that seminary and played an increasingly active role in the theological controversies that were rocking the synod. Preus was a staunch conservative who believed that those clergy and theological professors who had been influenced by newer theological trends, especially the Neo-Orthodoxy that had become popular in American Lutheranism,* were being unfaithful to the biblical and confessional standards of historic Lutheranism. He became the acknowledged leader of the party that sought to reverse recent theological trends in the synod and in its St. Louis seminary. Elected president of the synod in 1969, a post he held until his retirement in 1981, he saw his major task as replacing the leadership of Concordia Seminary, St. Louis (as well as many leaders in the synod's national offices and colleges), with more conservative persons; to that end, he engineered the removal of John Tietjen* as seminary president, an action that led to the founding of Concordia Seminary in Exile (Christ Seminary–Seminex*) and eventually to the establishment of the Association of Evangelical Lutheran Churches, a small body composed of his ''moderate'' opponents. He continued scholarly pursuits throughout his career; his publications included a translation of Martin Chemnitz's *The Two Natures of Christ* (1970) and a biography of Chemnitz, *The Second Martin* (1994). He was married to Delpha Mae Holleque in 1943; they were the parents of eight children. He died on August 13, 1994.

Bibliography. Adams, James E., *Preus of Missouri and the Great Lutheran Civil War* (New York: Harper and Row, 1977).

Donald L. Huber

Primitive Baptists. Primitive Baptists are groups of Baptists* that derive their separate existence from the antimissions* conflict of the nineteenth century. The missionary impulse dominated Baptist life in the early 1800s. The Triennial convention and other missionary societies were created, and agents like Luther Rice began traveling throughout the country to raise funds to support missionaries. Educational institutions were advocated to train ministers and missionaries.

In reaction to the perceived dangers of this developing denominational bureaucracy, an antimissions movement erupted among Baptists. In 1826 the Kehukee Association in North Carolina preferred a rigid biblicism and attacked missionary societies and theological seminaries as man-made inventions that encouraged nonpredestinarian (too much room for human effort) theology. Antimissions advocates on the frontier also disliked the attempt by missionary supporters to take their money through mission offerings and then consolidate power in societies they controlled back east. Kehukeeism became synonymous for antimissions, and soon other associations followed suit. Splits occurred and new groups of Baptists were formed. Supporters of missions often referred to themselves as "missionary Baptists."

Primitive Baptists generally hold to the following beliefs: (1) a strict "five-point" Calvinism: the total depravity of humankind, unconditional election by God of those chosen for salvation, limited atonement in which the benefits of the cross are reserved for the elect, God's irresistible grace for the elect, and the perseverance of the saints. This Calvinism, which Primitives affirm as biblical, emphasizes the total sovereignty of God and a rigid double predestination* of the elect to heaven and the nonelect to hell. (2) Primitive Baptists affirm older Particular Baptist confessions of faith and claim to be the true ancestors of these earlier Baptists. (3) The ordinances include believer's baptism* by immersion in a Primitive Baptist church and the Lord's Supper, served with red wine and unleavened bread. Closed Communion of the Lord's Supper is practiced (persons who are not members of the association cannot participate). Many Primitives practice footwashing; some make it a test of fellowship. (4) Worship services usually occur one weekend a month since churches are often scattered in rural and mountain areas and ministers serve more than one congregation. Worship is reserved emotionally and usually does not include musical instruments. "Lined" singing is practiced. (5) Ministers are bivocational and are not often given salaries for God's work (in the antimissions conflict paid ministers were called "hirelings"). Ministerial education is not encouraged since God "calls" pastors. Education can be affirmed if it was received before the divine calling. (6) Churches follow congregational church government and emphasize the autonomy of the local church. They usually belong to associations for the purpose of fellowship but condemn state and national bodies as a centralization of power. Some Primitives will do missions, but only through the local church. Mission boards and other auxiliaries like Sunday schools, Bible tract societies, and theological seminaries are rejected as extrabiblical and too "human effort" oriented (Jonah did not need a mission board to send him to Ninevah).

Several types of Primitive Baptists have developed since the antimissions conflict, primarily in the rural sections of the South, East, and Midwest. Old Liners affirm predestination but make believers responsible for obedience in Christian living. The Absoluters contend that every detail of life is predestined. The Progressive Primitive Baptists are the least predestinarian; they have Sunday schools, salaried ministers, and a college. Black Primitive Baptists formed the National Primitive Baptist Convention of the USA.

Bibliography. Dorgan, Howard, *Giving Glory to God in Appalachia* (Knoxville: University of Tennessee Press, 1987); McBeth, H. Leon, *The Baptist Heritage* (Nashville:

Broadman Press, 1987); Sweet, W. W., *Religion on the American Frontier: The Baptists, 1783–1830* (Chicago: University of Chicago Press, 1931).

Douglas Weaver

Purgatory. In Catholic theology, purgatory is the interim state after death in which the souls of those who die in the state of grace, but are not yet free of all imperfection, are purified before they enter heaven. In this process, the dead may be benefited by the living through the latter's prayers and charitable works. Christians spoke of purgation from the earliest generations of church history, and prayer for the dead was a practice inherited from Judaism. But the doctrine of purgatory as a specific place on the "map" of the afterlife emerged with clarity only in the twelfth century.

Later the official Catholic dogma developed in response to doctrinal differences with the Eastern churches (Second Council of Lyons, 1274; Council of Florence, 1439) and the Protestant Reformers (Council of Trent, 1563). While the Eastern tradition understood the interim state of those bound for heaven as a place of maturation, the Western tradition saw it more as a penal or judicial process of expiation. The Protestant Reformers asserted that the doctrine of purgatory failed to take seriously Christ's redemptive work, and they could find no basis for it in the Bible (though Catholics cited such passages as Matthew 12:31–32, 1 Corinthians 3:11–15, and 2 Maccabees 12:41–46). Prayers, masses, and alms for the sake of the dead were thus fruitless, and indulgences were simply a papal scheme for accumulating wealth. Many of the controverted issues of Reformation debate in fact clustered around the doctrine of purgatory: the authority of Scripture and tradition, the value of faith and works, the role of the pope, and the relation of human free will to divine sovereignty.

These heated controversies continued in America; Protestant books, tracts, and newspapers repeatedly condemned "the pope's purgatory." In perhaps the most famous of a number of public Catholic-Protestant debates, Alexander Campbell* (1788–1866), founder of the Disciples of Christ denomination, raised this issue and others with Archbishop John Purcell (1800–1883) of Cincinnati in 1837. Campbell's claim was typical of those made by Protestant opponents: The doctrine of purgatory "was the philosopher's stone . . . which has brought more gold to Rome, than the discovery of America itself." In response to similar challenges throughout the nineteenth century, Purcell and other Catholic leaders such as Bishop John England (1786–1842) of Charleston and James Cardinal Gibbons (1834–1921), archbishop of Baltimore, presented vigorous defenses of the teaching in print, pulpit, and podium.

Some American Protestants developed controversial purgatorial doctrines of their own. Since ancient times certain forms of Christian universalism (the belief that all people will ultimately be saved) have assumed that the wicked must undergo a painful cleansing after death. Such was the belief of the Restorationist wing of the American Universalist movement; one of its leaders, Elhanan Winchester (1751–1797), taught that 50,000 years after the end of the world would be required for all people to be fully purged. Mormons, also operating on universalist assumptions, practice baptism* for their dead loved ones to assist them in their preparation for heaven.

In recent years many Catholic theologians have moved away from the medieval notion of purgatory as a place and have viewed it instead simply as a state. Since official church teaching is restrained, saying nothing about the location or duration of purgatory and little about its nature, considerable room is left for speculation and differences of opinion. A few contemporary theologians situate the process of purging within the experience of death itself. What purges is not some externally applied divine chastisement but rather the individual's burning desire to be fully united with God and the encounter with God's own loving, cleansing holiness. Much like the Eastern view, this notion of purgatory involves the maturation of an individual's decisive "yes" to God as it is integrated fully into every aspect of the person's being. Because the process includes dealing with the consequences of a lifetime of choices that have often hurt both the self and others, it inescapably involves suffering, but it ultimately leads to joy.

Bibliography. Fenn, R. K., *The Persistence of Purgatory* (Cambridge: Cambridge University Press, 1995); Hayes, Z., "The Purgatorial View," in *Four Views on Hell*, ed. W. Crockett (Grand Rapids, MI: Zondervan, 1992); Le Goeff, J., *The Birth of Purgatory*, trans. A. Goldhammer (Chicago: University of Chicago Press, 1984); Schreiter, R., "Purgatory: In Quest of an Image," *Chicago Studies* 24 no. 2 (1985): 167.

T. Paul Thigpen

Q

_____

A Question in Baptist History. *A Question in Baptist History* was a book published in 1896 by William Heth Whitsitt, president of the Southern Baptist Theological Seminary* in Louisville, Kentucky, in which Whitsitt argued that the Baptist denomination was born out of the English Separatist movement of the sixteenth century. This view was at variance with the prevailing belief (called Landmarkism*) that Baptists could trace their history in unbroken succession back to the first century. Whitsitt was subsequently fired as the seminary's president, though his theory of Baptist origins is now widely accepted.

Religious competition for converts on the American frontier created a context in which Baptists,* Methodists, the Church of Christ, and other denominations gained converts by depicting their denomination as the only "true church." Baptist pastors watched helplessly as scores of their members joined Alexander Campbell's* Church of Christ, a new denomination that asserted that only those baptized into its membership rolls were truly Christian. In response, Baptist leaders like J. R. Graves* and A. C. Dayton of Nashville, Tennessee, and J. M. Pendleton of Bowling Green, Kentucky, promoted the idea that it was actually the Baptist denomination that was most like the early church in doctrine and practice.

Their movement was called Landmarkism, a name taken from Proverbs 22: 28: "Remove not the ancient landmark which thy fathers have set." Its basic tenets included the idea that Baptist doctrine alone was supported by the Bible, that the local congregation was the supreme authority for the believer, and that Baptist beliefs, including adult immersion, had existed throughout the history of the church among various groups.

In 1893 Whitsitt published an article in *Johnson's Universal Cyclopedia* that argued that the immersion of adult believers was "invented" by English Baptists in 1641, *A Question in Baptist History*, published in 1896, further clarified his belief that Baptists emerged out of the English Separatist movement of the sixteenth century. Whitsitt's carefully researched conclusion deeply offended Baptists in the South who strongly held to the Landmark position.

T. T. Eaton, pastor of the Walnut Street Baptist Church of Louisville, Kentucky, and editor of the Kentucky Baptist paper, immediately called for Whitsitt's resignation from the presidency of Southern Baptist Theological Seminary. Whitsitt resigned in 1899 from both the presidency and his teaching position in church history. He taught at Richmond College in Richmond, Virginia, until his death in 1911.

Bibliography. Leonard, Bill J., ed, *Dictionary of Baptists in America* (Downers Grove, IL: InterVarsity Press, 1994); Meigs, J. T., "The Whitsitt Controversy," *Quarterly Review* 31 (1971); Mueller, W. A., *A History of Southern Baptist Theological Seminary* (Nashville: Broadman Press, 1959); Shurden,W. B., *Not a Silent People: Controversies That Have Shaped Southern Baptists* (Nashville: Broadman Press, 1972).

Robert N. Nash, Jr.

Quimby, Phineas Parkhurst. One of the most important figures in the New Thought movement, Phineas P. Quimby (1802–1866) constructed a philosophy that influenced Warren Felt Evans and Julius and Anneta Dresser, as well as the founder of Christian Science, Mary Baker Eddy.* Although his students were relatively few in number and his writings were not published until more than fifty years after his death, Quimby's understanding of the power of mental influence and its relationship to both science and Christianity played an important role in the history of American religious psychology.

Born in Lebanon, New Hampshire, in 1802, and raised in Belfast, Maine, Quimby had little formal education. In 1838, while working in Belfast as a watch and clock maker, daguerreotypist, and inventor, he was inspired by the lectures and demonstrations of the traveling mesmerist and Frenchman Charles Poyen, who attributed his ability to control the behavior of his subjects to a magnetic fluid believed to pass between persons. Poyen's ideas derived from the work of the eighteenth-century Austrian physician Franz Anton Mesmer, who studied mental influence between one person and another, which he believed was passed through an invisible magnetic fluid. Historians have credited Mesmer with the modern discovery of hypnotic influence and with pioneering efforts to understand that phenomenon in scientific terms.

Building on the "electrical psychology" of mesmerism, Quimby employed a young clairvoyant, Lucius Burkmar, as an aid in his own experiments and public demonstrations. Called upon by physicians to help treat persistent disease, Quimby discovered that Burkmar's suggestions had a therapeutic power of their own, quite apart from the medicines he prescribed. This led Quimby to the conclusion that the illnesses Burkmar diagnosed were caused by his patients' beliefs, and that he should treat these beliefs directly, rather than the illnesses they caused. Dispensing with Burkmar's services, Quimby established a medical practice based on the principle of spiritual healing. Although he continued to use the mesmerist technique of scalp manipulation because his patients were not satisfied without it, he no longer believed that he was actually transmitting electrical fluid during his sessions, but rather that scalp manipulation contributed to his patients' belief in the effectiveness of his treatments. In 1859, eager to expand his work, Quimby moved to Portland, Maine, and remained there until his death in 1866.

Quimby linked the science of mental healing to Christianity and often used biblical references to describe the healing operations of mental influence. He was disdainful of clerical authority and skeptical of many forms of Christian belief popular in his day, but he believed fervently in the power of Christ, which he equated with the mind's influence over material reality.

Quimby's most famous patient and student, Mary Baker Eddy, was even more saturated in the language of the New Testament and eventually devoted herself to building a church based on the principles she learned from Quimby. Eddy dated her discovery of Christian Science to her recovery from a fall on the ice in Lynn, Massachusetts, while meditating on the New Testament stories of Jesus' healings, sixteen days after Quimby's death. The question of Eddy's indebtedness to Quimby precipitated much controversy, especially among her critics, who claimed that she plagiarized Quimby's writings in her own publications. During Quimby's lifetime Eddy revered him, but later distanced herself from him. In response to complaints about her failure to acknowledge her indebtedness, Eddy maintained that Quimby had borrowed from her. Hoping to minimize this controversy, Quimby's son George kept his father's writings closely guarded. Only when they were finally published in 1921 did evidence of Quimby's influence on Eddy become public.

Bibliography. Dresser, Horatio W., ed., *The Quimby Manuscripts* (1921. Reprint, Secaucus, NJ: Citadel Press, 1969); Fuller, Robert C., *Mesmerism and the American Cure of Souls* (Philadelphia: University of Pennsylvania Press, 1982); Parker, Gail Thain, *Mind Cure in New England: From the Civil War to World War I* (Hanover, NH: University Press of New England, 1973); Quimby, Phineas Parkhurst, *The Complete Writings*, ed. Ervin Seale, 3 vols. (Marina del Rey, CA: DeVorss, 1988).

Amanda Porterfield

R

Racism. Racism is the doctrine that the different qualities and capacities of humans are determined by inherited biological and physical characteristics that constitute different racial groups. These "racial" differences are the basis for the institutionalization of unequal treatment of the different racial groups.

In the ancient world the concepts of race and blood were used to distinguish among different human groups, but racism as a doctrine with its attendant dominant-subordinate social system is a modern phenomenon. Modern racism emerged in the fifteenth and sixteenth centuries as Europeans began their overseas conquests. The racist ideology was constructed to justify these conquests and the resulting colonial systems of slavery and segregation. These ideologies were composed of a mixture of religious, philosophical, and scientific arguments designed to prove that the unequal treatment was justified by ontological differences among human beings of different races. This doctrine of racism was created to counter criticisms that were being leveled at the cruel treatment inherent in these discriminatory practices.

The arguments of Count Joseph Arthur de Gobineau (1816–1888), a French orientalist and diplomat, were decisive in the development of racism. His studies of the archeological and anthropological evidence regarding the contributions of the different races to the building of civilizations were translated into English as *The Moral and Intellectual Diversity of Races* (1856) and *The Inequality of Races* (1915). These ideas were popularized on the American scene by Madison Grant in *The Passing of the Great Race* (1916), Lothrop Stoddard, and Henry Fairfield Osborn. His ideas had also been developed by the English writer Houston Stewart Chamberlain and had been widely publicized in Germany. Adolf

Hitler's *Mein Kampf* (1925–1927) was greatly dependent upon Chamberlain's arguments.

Among the examples of modern racist systems, three of great historical significance have been found in the United States, Germany, and South Africa. In the United States the legal isolation of Native Americans on reservations and the enslavement and later segregation of the African slaves and their descendants have been defining features of American society and history. In Germany the belief in the superiority of the Aryan race and the resulting institutionalizing and global expansion of that idea became a dominant factor in shaping twentieth-century history. In South Africa the establishment and more recently the disestablishment of apartheid stand as prime examples of the role of racism in colonial Africa and of a heroic effort to extricate a nation from the machinations of such a social system.

The challenge to racism has come from the growing social, economic, and political power of the people of color around the world and from a series of ideas that tend to deny the truth of racism. The kind of racial distinctions within the human community proposed by racism is not supported by recent biological and genetic studies. Furthermore, the Christian claim that all humanity both is created in the image of God and is the object of a nondiscriminating and reconciling love belies any effort to make the kind of distinctions that have characterized racism.

Bibliography. Barzun, Jacques, *Race: A Study in Superstition*, rev. ed. (New York: Harper and Row, 1965); Goldberg, David. ed., *Anatomy of Racism* (Minneapolis: University of Minnesota Press, 1990); Kelsey, George D., *Racism and the Christian Understanding of Man* (New York: Charles Scribner's Sons, 1965); Montagu, Ashley, *Man's Most Dangerous Myth: The Fallacy of Race*, 4th ed. (Cleveland: World Publishing, 1964); West, Cornel, *Race Matters* (Boston: Beacon Press, 1993).

Daniel B. McGee

Rappites. The Rappites were followers of George Rapp (1757–1847), who formed the Harmony Society in 1805 at Harmony, Pennsylvania. Rapp, a weaver by trade, was a radical pietist who separated from the Lutheran Church of Württemberg in 1785, declaring that in that church he was ''weakened rather than strengthened.'' In 1798 Rapp said that he was simply attempting to restore ''the ancient Christian religion of the first Christians . . . after its well-known decay.'' This primitive Christianity, he declared, must always allow for the freedom ''to speak as the Spirit convinces us.'' In line with many other radical pietists, Rappites denied the efficacy of infant baptism, combined the Lord's Supper with an agape meal, refused to send their children to the local school, denied the usefulness of confirmation, refused to swear oaths, and refused to serve in the military. These practices kept them continuously in trouble with the authorities. When Rapp began to proclaim millennial doctrines in 1799, relationships with his neighbors worsened, for his followers now declared themselves to be those who would rule with Christ for a thousand years. In 1803 the government declared its intentions to severely punish further Rappite breaches of civil law, although it continued to allow separatist meetings for purely religious purposes. Rapp, however, was already in America looking for an alternative location for his movement, which numbered over 200.

On May 1, 1804, the first group of Rappites left for America. They were by this time functioning as a communal society, with their treasury in the hands of Rapp's adopted son, Frederick. Arriving in Butler County, Pennsylvania, early in 1805, they founded the town of Harmony and incorporated themselves as the Harmony Society. In spite of occasional dissension and defections to other groups, the Harmony Society under "Father Rapp" soon became one of the most successful of American utopias.

Dissatisfied with their economic prospects and tiring of their unsympathetic neighbors, the Rappites left Harmony in 1814 to found a new settlement at New Harmony, Indiana. There they built a model German village in the midst of the American frontier. By this time they had become even more "peculiar" in the minds of outsiders. Among other things, Rapp encouraged them to practice celibacy, either by remaining single or by refraining from sexual intercourse in marriage; it was considered a mark of increasing spirituality when the number of children born in the community began to decline. The number of Harmonists nonetheless increased as new members arrived from Germany.

The years at New Harmony, 1814 to 1824, were the high point of the Harmony Society, which prospered spiritually and materially; New Harmony stood in stark contrast to the impoverished Yankee settlements nearby (in one of which lived the young Abraham Lincoln). Occasional defections continued; one who left explained that he had had his fill of "error, superstition, and religious mania" directed by "this concentrated monk." On the other hand, many testified to the contentment that they found in the society.

In 1824, concerned that life had become too easy and believing that another move would fulfill biblical prophecy, Rapp sold New Harmony to Robert Owen, the Scottish industrialist and social theorist. The Rappites moved back to western Pennsylvania, founding the town of Economy. Although the move from their comfortable village severely tried the faith of some of Rapp's followers, most of the 615 Harmonists made the transition successfully. From 1824 until Rapp's death in 1847, the community functioned much as it always had, with Rapp becoming increasingly dictatorial in his old age. Among the defections at this time was a group that organized a communitarian "Society of United Germans" along secular lines; although their attempts to acquire a portion of the financial assets of Economy failed, this was the beginning of a series of challenges to the absolute authority of Rapp and his successors.

Throughout its history the Rappite movement attracted attention and controversy. Rapp's religious ideas were considered speculative and even heretical by many, and his one-man rule was criticized as antidemocratic. The financial success of the movement, coupled with the absolute control exercised by Rapp and his successor trustees, caused numerous problems. The later years of the society

were ignominious, as the original religious zeal waned and various individuals and factions struggled for control of its wealth; it was dissolved in 1905.
Bibliography. Arndt, Karl J. R., *George Rapp's Harmony Society, 1785–1847*, rev ed. (Rutherford, NJ: Fairleigh Dickinson University Press, 1972); Arndt, Karl J. R., *George Rapp's Successors and Material Heirs, 1847–1916* (Rutherford, NJ: Fairleigh Dickinson University Press, 1971).

Donald L. Huber

Rastafarians. The Rastafarians (also Ras Tafarians) are a movement that began in Jamaica in the 1930s and has continued to have its primary influence in that country. Its appearance in the United States began among Jamaican expatriates, but an increasing number of African Americans in the United States appear to be attracted to the movement. Historically, the controversies surrounding the movement have been both internal and external. General research on the Rastafarians in the United States has been minimal; this calls for an exercise in extrapolation in commenting on potential as well as actual controversy in the United States.

The messianic and millenarian movement derives its name from the prethrone name of Emperor Haile Selassie of Ethiopia (crowned 1930, dethroned 1974, murdered 1975), Ras (''prince'') Tafari. The international coverage given to Haile Selassie's coronation and to his appeals to the League of Nations and the regularly cited biblical verse Psalms 68:31, ''Princes come out of Egypt; Ethiopia shall soon stretch out her hands unto God,'' provided the popular and biblical impetus to the earliest followers. There were several earlier Afro-Caribbean movements upon which the Rastafarians built their identity, especially Marcus Garvey's* Universal Negro Improvement Association.

A central feature of the movement, in its many forms, is black identity. Most of the early forms and many of the continuing expressions of the movement have been associated, in the minds of observers, with the ''liberation theology''* genre because of the political, economic, social, and theological implications of—as well as the reactions against—the movements from within the dominant Jamaican culture. Internal ''controversy'' has also been present along these same lines. (Since there is no generally acknowledged center of authority among the Rastafarian groups, there has been a tendency within the movement to ''live and let live'' among these groups—hence the quotation marks.)

One observer has contended that the following conceptual commonalities were present among most of the groups prior to the death of Haile Selassie (which death is not accepted by all present groups): (1) former transgressions of the black people resulted in their being exiled to the West Indies; (2) black people are superior to white people; (3) the situation of the black people in Jamaica is hopeless; (4) Ethiopia is the promised land, or even heaven; (5) Haile Selassie is the living God, or at least the Messiah; (6) Haile Selassie will enable African expatriates to return to the ''homeland'' (especially Ethiopia itself, but also elsewhere in Africa); and (7) white people will eventually be required to serve black people as punishment for the way whites have treated blacks (Simpson, 126).

The dominant culture (in Jamaica as well as in England and the United States) has been fascinated by the Rastafarians' unique language (e.g., "I 'n I"), dreadlocks (expressive of their focus on "return to nature" vis-à-vis the unnatural sins of the so-called civilized industrial nations, especially England, the United States, and the dominant Jamaican class—all of which, along with the institutional church at times, are classified as "Babylon"), and music; but these characteristics, along with the tendency of the Rastafarians to keep to themselves, have also contributed to the suspicions that accompany the externally positioned controversies—especially the use of ganja. The movement gained additional international recognition when Bob Marley's versions of reggae drew a large following.

Bibliography. A brief overview can be found in *The Encyclopedia of Religion*, vol. 3 (NY: Macmillan, 1987), under "Caribbean Religions: Afro-Caribbean religions." Barrett, Leonard E, *The Rastafarians: Sounds of Cultural Dissonance* (Boston: Beacon Press, 1977); Chevannes, Barry, *Rastafari: Roots and Ideology* (Syracuse: Syracuse University Press, 1994); Johnson-Hill, Jack A, *I-Sight: The World of Rastafari: An Interpretive Sociological Account of Rastafarian Ethics* (Metuchen, NJ: Scarecrow Press, 1995); Owens, Joseph, *Dread* (Kingston: Sangster's Book Stores, 1976); Simpson, George E., *Black Religion in the New World* (New York: Columbia University Press, 1978); Witvliet, Theo, *Place in the Sun: An Introduction to Liberation Theology in the Third World* (Maryknoll, NY: Orbis Books, 1985).

Robert L. VanDale

Reconstructionism. Reconstructionist Judaism is a distinctly American phenomenon with no European antecedents. Its founder, Rabbi Mordecai Menahem Kaplan* (1881–1983), came to the United States at the age of nine. He was ordained from the Conservative movement's Jewish Theological Seminary in New York, where he served as the first principal of the Teachers' Institute and later its dean. Kaplan had tremendous influence on several generations of American-trained rabbis. He founded the Society for the Advancement of Judaism and edited the periodical *Reconstructionist.*

Kaplan's seminal work *Judaism as a Civilization* was published in 1934. It drew heavily upon the emerging fields of sociology and anthropology. Kaplan was the boldest rationalist philosopher of the twentieth century. For many Jews, Kaplan redefined Judaism. Instead of Judaism being the religion of a people in covenant with God, who chose them, redeemed them, and then revealed his commandments for the people to follow, Judaism was redefined as a civilization. God lost all of its supernatural being and became the idea generated from within the people that helped the people persevere through history. Practices and theology were viewed not as reflecting fundamental truths of a commanding God, but rather as an emanation of the unique Jewish genius to derive meaning and purpose from their existence. Deleted from Kaplan's prayerbook were all references to the Jewish people as being chosen and concepts of messianic redemption.

Kaplan was an ardent Zionist who later in life emigrated to Israel. Since he viewed Judaism as a civilization, unlike other Zionist thinkers who viewed the Jewish people as a polity, he endorsed Jewish life in both Israel and the Diaspora. He was a supporter of all aspects of Jewish culture and social activity and re-created the synagogue to serve as a center to meet all the needs of the people. Kaplan also supported equal participation by women in Jewish life. In 1922 Kaplan's daughter was the first reported bat mitzvah in America.

Organizationally, Reconstructionist Judaism has not had overwhelming success in America. In 1968 the Reconstructionist Rabbinical College was established in Philadelphia. Rabbinical students are also expected to earn a graduate degree in religious studies or some associated field in conjunction with their rabbinical studies. But Reconstructionism has had a major impact on the American Jewish community's self-definition as it has had to cope theologically and programmatically with the challenges of the twentieth century.

Bibliography. Eisenstein, Ira, *Reconstructing Judaism: An Autobiography* (New York: Reconstructionist Press, 1986); Kaplan, Mordecai, *The Future of the American Jew* (New York: Macmillan, 1948); Kaplan, Mordecai, *Judaism as a Civilization* (New York: Reconstructionist Press, 1957. Reprint, Philadelphia: Jewish Publication Society, 1981); Kaplan, Mordecai, *Judaism without Supernaturalism: The Only Alternative to Orthodoxy and Secularism* (New York: Reconstructionist Press, 1958); Kaplan, Mordecai, *The Meaning of God in Modern Jewish Religion* (New York: Reconstructionist Press, 1962); Marcus, Jacob Rader, Abraham J. Peck, and Jeffrey S. Gurock, eds., *The American Rabbinate: A Century of Continuity and Change, 1883–1983* (Hoboken, NJ: Ktav Publishing House, 1985).

Jonathan Miller

Reform Judaism. Reform Judaism's intellectual roots were planted in nineteenth-century Germany, but the movement flourished in America. Its leaders began to bring what were then considered to be innovations to centuries-old Jewish practice. The innovations were modest at first, but soon became a movement to reform Judaism. The vernacular was used in worship. Musical accompaniment was welcome. Men and women sat together in worship. Traditional liturgy and practice were abbreviated and modified to express the rationalist theology and critical textual scholarship prevalent in nineteenth-century academic circles.

Intellectually, Reform Judaism made a distinction between the ritual and ethical mandates of Judaism. Jewish rituals were understood to be determined by the particular time and place within which Jews lived. They were not seen, in the details of their execution, to be commanded by God. Ethics, on the other hand, were viewed as permanent and unchanging commandments. Singular among Reform Judaism's principles is the belief in the autonomy of the individual concerning the ritual practices to be followed.

Early in its development in America, Reform Judaism eschewed many of the practices that set Jews apart from non-Jews. Dietary laws, Jewish dress, Hebrew, and much ritual and nonrational beliefs were not widely observed by Reform Jews. Reform Jewish synagogues resembled Protestant churches, and some even ceased to hold Sabbath services on Saturday, preferring to worship on Sunday, America's day of worship.

Today, Reform Judaism has turned back and embraced many of the ritual practices and beliefs once rejected by its forebears. Many Reform Jews have sought a spiritual connection to God in nonrational ritual practices. Reform Judaism has also brought about many innovations that have proved to be controversial, but later have become more widely accepted in some circles. The ordination and full participation of women in religious life, patrilineal descent (the acceptance as Jews of those born of either Jewish parent, providing the child is raised as a Jew), outreach to the unaffiliated, and an emphasis on social justice are all innovations of Reform Judaism.

Reform Judaism's institutions in America were started in the previous century by its organizational architect, Rabbi Isaac M. Wise. These include the seminary, Hebrew Union College–Jewish Institute of Religion; the congregational organization, the Union of American Hebrew Congregations; and the rabbinic association, the Central Conference of American Rabbis.

Bibliography. Fein, Leonard J., *Reform Is a Verb: Notes on Reform and Reforming Jews* (New York: Long Range Planning Committee, Union of American Hebrew Congregations, 1972); Maslin, Simon J., *What We Believe—What We Do: A Pocket Guide for Reform Jews* (New York: UAHC Press, 1993); Marcus, Jacob Rader, Abraham J. Peck, and Jeffrey S. Gurock, eds., *The American Rabbinate: A Century of Continuity and Change, 1883–1983* (Hoboken, NJ: Ktav Publishing House, 1985); Meyer, Michael A., *Response to Modernity: A History of the Reform Movement in Judaism* (New York: Oxford University Press, 1988); Plaut, W. Gunther, *The Growth of Reform Judaism: American and European Sources until 1948* (New York: World Union for Progressive Judaism, 1965); Plaut, W. Gunther, *The Rise of Reform Judaism: A Sourcebook of Its European Origins* (New York: World Union for Progressive Judaism, 1963).

Jonathan Miller

Reformed Episcopal Church. The Episcopal Church in America, true to its Anglican heritage, has been committed to unity and continuity, but these ideals have sometimes foundered on treacherous shoals. The first occurrence of dissent generating disunity that led to schism reached its climax in the formation of the Reformed Episcopal Church in 1873. The events that symbolized that formation centered in the determination of the assistant bishop of Kentucky, George David Cummins,* to assert classical (Reformation) Protestant teachings in a communion that had been registering impact from the Tractarian (or Oxford) movement within the Church of England from the 1830s until about 1850. Deeply convinced that the Episcopal Church had become overweighted on the Catholic side of its *via media* course, Cummins steadily enlarged both his critique of Catholic influences and doctrines and his advocacy of the church's Protestant legacy.

He and his colleagues repudiated transubstantiation* as the faithful interpretation of what occurs at the Eucharist; also moral regeneration as the nature of God's work in baptism*; and finally the exclusive validity of the episcopal government of Christ's church, that is, by those properly ordained by bishops in apostolic succession. These heresies into which the Tractarian-inspired church had fallen bespoke Romanizing and ritualizing tendencies to these reformers. Cummins especially condemned assumptions about the "real presence" in the consecrated elements of the Communion, and "baptismal regeneration" as the effect of that sacrament. Instead, he upheld more symbolic views of the divine action in both. In a similar vein he denied that anything sacerdotal took place in ordination.

On the affirmative side, he championed ecumenism. He found like-minded Christians in many denominations, especially those evangelically inclined. Particularly upsetting to his Episcopal Church was his taking part in Communion services with the Evangelical Alliance, a world outreach society that had association with evangelist Dwight L. Moody and the Moody Church in Chicago. That evangelistic agency also participated in Hudson Taylor's call for a thousand missionaries to go out to China, of which Cummins approved. Further identifying the Alliance was its rootage in Scandinavian evangelical groups, pietist, that were critical of the formalism of the state church in those northern European countries.

Cummins also affirmed moral holiness, this too in an evangelical way. Accordingly, he took vigorous exception to ordinations conducted by the bishop of Pennsylvania, Henry U. Onderdonck, who had become addicted to brandy, a usage he had originally developed in response to a chronic disorder. Thus both in Cummins's sense of the church's mission, to be evangelistically missionary, and of the ethical requirements incumbent upon all Christians, to be personally pure and righteous, he found himself at odds with his beloved Episcopal Church's "Sacerdotalism and Ritualism."

"Beloved" is an accurate portrayal of his relation to the body in whose ministry he was priested in 1847 and elevated in 1866. Schism was not what he had in mind, but rather, helping open the church's eyes to its departure from its Reformation heritage and its being engulfed by corrupt medieval practices. He loved the Book of Common Prayer and sought to live his ministry in its setting. He contended for a more critical and expansive liberty with respect to the text of the Prayer Book. In so doing, he was "Protestant" both as to the Prayer Book's meaning and in a freedom-in-the-Spirit approach to interpreting it.

During the first seven years of his episcopacy, he propagated his positions in other dioceses as well as his own. The crisis erupted after he debated on the floor of the 1871 General Convention of the church. In 1873 the church censured him and he resigned, sadly but with full conviction. The Reformed Episcopal Church was organized on December 2, 1873, when 6 clergy and 20 laymen took formal action. Soon the new body numbered 5,000 members, a figure that doubled to its high point about 1900. The church lives to the present, reporting some 6,000 members. Its particular textual authorities are a slightly amended Book of Common Prayer and Constitutions and Canons. Its holy orders are respected by the Episcopal Church, and it receives members from other Protestant communions on the strength of their baptism in them.

Bibliography. Carter, Paul A., "The Reformed Episcopal Schism of 1873: An Ecumenical Perspective," in *Historical Magazine of the Protestant Episcopal Church* 33 (September 1964); Cheney, Charles Edward, *What Reformed Episcopalians Believe* (N.p.: Christian Education Committee, Reformed Episcopal Church, 1961); Guelzo, Allen C., *The First Thirty Years: A Historical Handbook for the Founding of the Reformed Episcopal Church, 1873–1903* (Philadelphia: The Reformed Episcopal Publication Society, 1984); Guelzo, Allen C., "A Sufficiently Republican Church: George David Cummins and Reformed Episcopalians in 1873," *Filson Club History Quarterly* 69 (April 1995): 115–39.

Samuel S. Hill

Reincarnation. Historically, reincarnation has been a major doctrine only in certain Asian religions, but within the last century its appeal has spread to the West, bringing with it growing controversy in the areas of philosophy, morality, and religion. Philosophically, many question the justice of karma. If individual memory is obliterated after death, then the reincarnated soul is really a different person, laden with someone else's karma, yet without the knowledge of why he or she is being punished. Thus the original suffering increases through its karma, burdening future generations with accumulated punishment. This view is alien to those schooled to watch for the coming of the Kingdom of God on earth. Believers, on the other hand, maintain that an Oversoul, or core spiritual identity, survives and benefits from the experiences of successive lives.

Morally, the Western mind sees an opportunity within reincarnation for political opportunism. It allows the rich and powerful to claim a right to their privilege, while giving them a karmic justification for maintaining the ill fortune of the underprivileged. Eastern religions, because of their belief in the value of a person's karmic suffering, tend to foster an attitude of indifference toward the condition of others, while the Christian is commanded to help the sufferer in the name of Christ. Yet in traditional reincarnationist thought, this help interferes with the other person's karma and dooms him to even greater suffering in his next life. Western reincarnationist thinking tends to moderate this view, teaching that the alleviation of suffering is a karmic advantage to all concerned.

Religiously, many who accept the belief in reincarnation come from the Christian tradition, although the church has opposed this kind of theological eclecticism. Robert Morey, commenting on surveys that indicate that a majority of Americans believe in reincarnation, concluded, "The Christian Church has miserably failed to indoctrinate its membership in the biblical view of life after death" (*Reincarnation and Christianity*, 1980, 9) illustrating the common view that reincarnation and Christian theology are mutually exclusive.

Some argue that the Jews, Essenes, and the early church believed in reincarnation. They point to Origen, who taught the preexistence of the soul and regarded the circumstances of birth as rewards and punishments for virtue and sin in the soul's previous existence. However, Christian theologians stress that an accurate reading of Origen indicates that he believed that these previous existences were spiritual rather than mortal.

Still, many Christian reincarnationists believe that the theory was accepted within Christianity until 553, when the Second Council of Constantinople rejected the belief by a narrow majority. These people state that reincarnation was taught by the Gnostic movement and that certain references in the New Testament (i.e., Matthew 11:14, where Jesus states that John the Baptist is Elijah, and John 9:2, where karma seems to apply to a man born blind) seem to teach reincarnation.

But the church, denying that the council in 553 did anything other than reaffirm its traditional stand against the belief, points out that Gnosticism has always been considered a heresy and refers to John 9:2 as a metaphor, while stressing that Jesus healed the blind man, thereby destroying the value of any personal karma and changing the focus to that of Christian grace and forgiveness.

The final argument for Christians is the resurrection, the central dogma of the faith. They believe that Christ paid in full the debt for sin and, stated on the cross, ''It is finished.'' That means that believers are purged from sin and that there is no need for karma or for future lives through which to balance that karma. A belief in reincarnation would obviate the cross and the resurrection, thus destroying the faith.

The increasing popularity of reincarnation in the West, especially among young people, will force the church to come to terms with the concept. It must admit that many of its responses have been shallow and doctrinaire, and that it will risk losing future generations if it does not make some kind of theological accommodation.

Bibliography. Albrecht, Mark, *Reincarnation, A Christian Appraisal* (Downers Grove, IL: InterVarsity Press, 1982); Beecher, Edward, *Conflict of the Ages* (Boston: Phillips, 1953); Ducasse, Curt John, *A Critical Examination of the Belief in a Life after Death* (Springfield, IL: Charles C. Thomas, 1961); Head, Joseph, and S. L. Cranston, *Reincarnation: The Phoenix Fire Mystery* (New York: Warner Books, 1977); Morey, Robert A., *Reincarnation and Christianity* (Minneapolis: Bethany House Publishers, 1980).

John W. Sloat

Religion and Education, Public and Private. The Reformation and post-Reformation religious controversies in Europe linked religion and education. Important theological issues divided Europe into Catholic and Protestant camps. Certainly, the leaders of both religions relied on governments to establish their churches. But the leaders of both camps believed that the best way to establish their faith in the hearts and minds of the people was through education. Both

Catholics and Protestants wrote new catechisms for children and adults. A catechism was a series of questions and answers drawn from the church's creeds and central Scriptures that children memorized. Ideally, the parents were the principal teachers, but pastors and priests often shared responsibility.

The Reformation led to the reform of older schools and the creation of new schools. Protestants and Catholics adopted different educational strategies. Protestants stressed the establishment of common schools and worked toward the spread of literacy. Melanchthon's activities in reforming German education were so extensive that he was popularly known as the Preceptor of Germany. John Knox, the principal reformer in Scotland, followed a common pattern when he included the creation of schools in the documents that created the new church. The various religious wars with their immense cost in people and materials slowed the Protestant educational advance, but by 1700 its effects were obvious. Many Protestant countries had attained literacy rates of more than 90 percent.

The Catholic approach to education was different. Led by the Jesuits, Catholics established many elite schools across Europe. These schools helped create loyalty to the church when Catholic armies captured territories, such as Poland, that had earlier embraced Protestantism.

The establishment of European rule over the Americas coincided with the Reformation and the great wars of religion. Even in the New World the purpose of religious instruction in the schools was not only to inspire piety; sound instruction also bound a person to his or her particular party and its cause.

In New Spain the church followed a twofold educational strategy. As in Spain itself, religious orders established excellent schools, ranging from elementary schools to universities. These primarily served the colonists. The religious and secular education of the Native Americans, many of whom converted to Catholicism, was a more complex matter. Initially, the Spanish settlers enslaved the indigenous people. When Spanish law ended that practice, the settlers replaced it with peonage. In this context, the missionaries gathered their charges into communities where they taught the Native Americans religion, agriculture, and other arts. The fathers tried to identify the most able children among their charges and to prepare them for further study. Nonetheless, the education received by indigenous peoples was customarily far inferior to that received by settlers. France never settled its vast American empire with a sufficient density of population to support as many schools or as varied kinds of schools as Spain. Yet French religious orders also established schools for French colonists and provided some education, usually very elementary, for the Native American subjects and allies.

The controversy between Protestants and Catholics also shaped Puritan education in New England. The New England settlers shared the general Protestant confidence in education. Soon after they arrived, the Puritans took up the task of transmitting literacy to their children. Although Scripture was the foundation of Puritan education, they interpreted the Bible in a distinctly Protestant fashion. It was not long before New England's Puritans had reproduced and extended the full English educational order: the so-called Old Deceiver Law (1647) required every town to teach writing. In addition, laws required the larger to maintain grammar (Latin) schools as well. Harvard College, founded in 1636, and Yale College, founded in 1701, topped the educational order.

Protestantism lacked the institutional coherence of Catholicism. In the relatively free situation of North America, Protestants early began to drift into competing and often antagonistic religious denominations. By the eighteenth century these tensions were reflected in the establishment of schools and colleges that reflected the teachings of this or that church. Awakeners established the College of New Jersey, later Princeton, to support their cause. A band of Connecticut divines, deeply upset by Yale's unwillingness to reinstate David Brainerd, whom the school had expelled for excessive religious zeal, spearheaded the drive for a new school. They joined revivalist Presbyterians in a petition to the governor of New Jersey for a charter allowing them to grant degrees. Baptists felt deeply their exclusion from the New England Puritan establishment. In 1764 they founded the College of Rhode Island to provide an alternative to the religious atmosphere at the two older schools. Anglicans later founded King's College, later Columbia, giving them a strong educational presence in the Middle Colonies.

From the beginning, sectarian colleges faced countervailing forces. The Baptists who established Brown, for instance, lacked the political power to secure a charter from the colony's powerful legislature. While they controlled the presidency, the charter forced them to share power on the board with Anglicans, Congregationalists, and Quakers. The need to recruit students forced the Presbyterian school at Princeton to turn to the South for students and to find ways to make the sons of planters sit peacefully with the children of dissent.

The early denominational colleges point to a pattern in the way that American higher education has dealt with religious issues. Often, religious passion—whether for a denomination, a doctrine, or a movement—has generated the passion to establish a school to educate the faithful and to win new, younger allies. However, the voracious financial demands of higher education, even in the antebellum period, made educational exclusivity almost an impossible dream. Few groups have had sufficient funds to go it alone. Sooner or later, poverty has forced the group to recruit students, money, and educational talent beyond its borders. The cost of these overtures is the partial abandonment of the original passions that established the institutions.

While finances were the primary force that encouraged colleges to abandon controversial stances, money rarely stood apart from other influences. The Enlightenment was the most important intellectual factor. In the late seventeenth century European philosophers and scientists began to claim a larger place for human reason and science than either traditional Catholic or Protestant thought had allowed. Although often personally devout, such scientists as Isaac Newton demonstrated their basic conclusions without direct reference to God or religious doctrine. As time passed, scholars dropped even indirect religious language from most serious scholarly and scientific publications. By 1850, although most institutions of higher learning retained chapels and had some religious instruction, most of the curriculum was secular. If a college had a pious atmosphere, the instructors' personal faith created it, not the subject matter. The nature of scholarly inquiry had ruled most religious controversies out of court. Although Andrew D. White,* an influential college president, wrote *A History of the Warfare of Science with Theology in Christendom* (1896) to detail the ways in which religion had impeded human progress, the battle was not fought in college classrooms. With a few exceptions, the most important disputes about academic freedom* were over political rather than religious issues. Darwin's theory of evolution, a major issue in elementary and high schools, did not seriously interrupt this development. Few seriously objected to its dissemination in state-sponsored colleges and universities. The situation was the same in denominationally influenced schools. If a denomination's membership balked at the new teaching, they were more likely to lose their college than have the school restrict its classrooms.

New forms of higher education also protected the colleges and universities from religious controversy. The original purpose of the colonial colleges was to educate leaders for church and state. In the early nineteenth century alternative educational structures permitted colleges to redefine their missions. One such new creation was the state university. Thomas Jefferson, whose memories of Anglican William and Mary were negative, designed the University of Virginia to serve as a center of arts and sciences for the whole state of Virginia. He hoped that the school would stand above religious controversy. Later state-owned schools followed a similar formula. Such presidents as Lewis Tappan of the University of Michigan had to struggle to put this new idea into place. In Tappan's state the various Protestant denominations took turns demanding that their teachers be appointed to the school and requesting other favors. But despite these battles, the ideal of a comprehensive, government-controlled university captured the imagination. In 1862 the Morrill Land Grant Act provided endowments for state institutions.

The churches made it easier for colleges and universities to so redefine themselves. In 1808 Andover Seminary opened on the campus of Philips Academy in Andover. While the new seminary wanted its students to be college graduates, it assumed the task of teaching prospective ministers religious and theological subjects. Other denominations quickly followed suit. Many of the controversies that might have enveloped colleges and universities, had they remained the primary educator of ministers, whirled around the seminaries instead.

The private college was another American type of institution that enabled some schools to avoid religious controversy. In its simplest terms, a private college was one governed by a self-perpetuating board of trustees and was primarily responsible to its own graduates and financial supporters. The Dartmouth College case (1819), brilliantly argued by Daniel Webster, allowed such schools to be formed. In time, the former colonial colleges availed themselves of the opportunity to sever their connections with their state governments and become independent "private" colleges. Other schools became private colleges by separating themselves from their original religious affiliations.

The relative independence of colleges and universities did not extend to elementary and secondary education. In part, the popular mind believed that the supposed greater vulnerability of children required greater vigilance on the part of society. Controversy was also a natural result of the history of American schooling. During the early nineteenth century a devoted band of American reformers called the Friends of Education mounted an increasingly successful drive for free, universal elementary education for white children. They believed that schools were the best way to teach republican virtue and the skills needed for success in an industrializing society. The Friends of Education wanted schools that did not teach the tenets of any particular church, but they wanted schools to teach values and patriotism. Hence the schools often had a religious and moralistic tone. William Holmes McGuffey, a leader of the Friends, expressed their philosophy in his six *Eclectic Readers*. In addition to Bible readings, the books contained moral lessons that reflected Protestant values. The readers exhorted children to work hard, avoid strong drink, and keep the Sabbath. McGuffey sold more than 122 million copies of the popular textbooks.

The nonsectarian religion of McGuffey and the other Friends of Education was not as inoffensive as its sponsors believed. American Roman Catholics, deeply conscious of anti-Catholic and anti-immigrant feelings, saw the public schools as promoting Protestantism. New York Archbishop John Joseph Hughes was so vocal in his protest that the state adopted a law secularizing the city's schools in 1842. Other Catholic prelates kept up pressure against the more Protestant elements in the schools. The Cincinnati "Bible War" of 1869 and the Edgerton, Wisconsin, case of 1886 ended the use of the King James Bible in these school systems. Perhaps because Protestant nonsectarianism had moved so close to secularization, these cases indicated that the Protestant majority was willing to adjust the public schools to meet the objections of other religious people.

American Catholic leaders were not initially as concerned with educational issues as their European counterparts. The First Provincial Council, held in Baltimore in 1829, mentioned schools as part of the church's mission. Catholic convictions about the need for such schools increased in the turbulent 1830s and 1840s. During these decades a virulent anti-Catholicism was prominent in American public life. Acts of violence like the burning of Boston's Ursuline convent in 1834 and armed attacks on Catholic churches in New York and Philadelphia reflected popular distrust of Catholics and immigrants. At the same time, such semipornographic works as Rebecca Reed's *Six Months in a Convent* (1835) and Maria Monk's* *Awful Disclosures of the Hotel Dieu Nunnery in Montreal* (1836) further inflamed anti-Catholic passions. Nativists formed the American party, also known as the Know-Nothing party,* to combat Catholic influence in America and to limit, if possible, immigration. Although the party vanished as the issue of slavery came to dominate the politics of the 1850s, many continued to hold nativist and anti-Catholic views. The First Plenary Council, held in 1852, urged that Catholics construct schools in every diocese. This action was the foundation of the 1884 Third Plenary Council's call for a Catholic education for every child. The council believed that the best way to attain this goal was to establish a school in every parish and charged local priests with this establishment.

The Catholic system of schools occasioned one of America's longest and most bitter controversies about the role of religion in education. Some opponents believed that Catholic education should be discouraged. The Bennett Law (1889) in Wisconsin required the use of English in all schools, and Oregon passed a law requiring attendance in the public schools in 1922. The Supreme Court struck down this latter law in *Pierce v. the Society of Sisters* in 1925.

The most common controversies, however, have been about whether Catholic schools should receive public support. The costs of education have risen steadily since 1800. Without the donation by members of religious orders of their labor, Catholics would not have been able to maintain their institutions. Even with that help, the price of Catholic education was almost debilitating. (As an aside, when the membership of religious orders fell following Vatican Council II,* finances forced many schools to close when they could not afford lay instructors.) On the one hand, Catholics believed that the government ought to bear at least part of the cost for their schools. After all, the schools provided students (and the society) with the same benefits as the public schools. In contrast, advocates of the public schools believed that the common school was an important element in the creation of a common American identity. Although not all opponents of aid to Catholic schools harbored anti-Catholic views, many did. Unfortunately, some of their writings reflected this bias.

Advocates of complete public support of Catholic schools have won few victories. Both the Lowell Plan in Massachusetts (1831–1852) and the Pough-keepsie Plan in New York (1873–1898) were unable to maintain themselves. St. Paul Archbishop John Ireland's 1891 attempt to place Catholic schools under public control in exchange for funding failed to win the support of the prelate's fellow American Catholics or Roman officials. In the twentieth century the controversy has usually posed the question of aid in terms of specific programs. In *Cochran v. the Board of Education* (1930) the Supreme Court ruled that the real purpose of a Louisiana law purchasing textbooks for all students was to aid the child and not the church. The Court upheld this line of reasoning in a later case, *Everson v. Board of Education*, in 1947. Since then the courts have tried to find ways to set appropriate limits to this practice.

Most private day schools are Catholic, but conservative Protestants have developed a substantial interest in private schools since the 1960s. Like Catholic parochial schools, conservative Protestant schools stress the importance of personal discipline, moral and religious education, and basic educational skills. Their advocates have maintained that these schools are primarily designed to offer an alternative to the increasingly secularized public schools. Although the courts had earlier struck down provisions for religious activities in public education, Protestant conservatives were deeply disturbed by Supreme Court decisions ending prayer in public schools (*Engel v. Vitale*, 1962) and Scripture readings (*School District of Abington Township v. Schempp*, 1963). These decisions helped create a politically conscious religious right that kept prayer in the public schools at the center of the American debate in the 1980s and 1990s. Further, new tendencies in public education alarmed conservatives. In particular, collateral reading that seemed to call into question traditional values, such as J. D. Salinger's *Catcher in the Rye*, attracted the attention of concerned parents. The popular movement toward multiculturalism in textbooks also raised controversy.

Some conservative Christians have provided home schooling for their children. Home schooling was traditional among missionaries and others serving abroad. As concern with public education mounted, these curricula were further developed and marketed for use at home. Despite some debates over the practice in state boards of education, home schooling has become an important option, especially for conservatives who live in areas where Christian schools are either nonexistent or inadequate.

Like their Catholic counterparts, conservative Protestants have found the costs of private education to be staggering. As a result, conservative Protestants and Catholics have formed a coalition to advocate new forms of aid to private education. Advocates have tended to favor a tuition voucher that a student can spend at the school of his or her choice, although tuition tax credits are also a popular idea. In addition, advocates often present this proposal as a way to help inner-city schoolchildren, some of whom presently attend public schools of dubious quality. *Mueller v. Allen,* a 1983 case involving tuition tax credits in Minnesota, indicates that the courts may allow more federal and state aid to private schools. In 1996 a Cleveland plan to provide vouchers for public schools won tentative approval by the lower courts, while public pressure defeated a similar proposal in New York City. Such aid will be the focus of intense controversy over the next decade and possibly beyond.

The place of the teaching of evolution in public schools has been a major issue since the 1920s. The movement to prohibit the teaching of evolution had such important leaders as three-time Democratic presidential candidate William Jennings Bryan* and a number of conservative religious leaders. Since conditions in each state varied, the reasons for the defeat of specific proposals varied. In North Carolina, for instance, the strong opposition of Davidson College (Presbyterian) and Wake Forest College (Baptist) presidents swayed influential alumni in the legislature. Yet the most important event in the controversy was the Scopes trial* in 1925. The Tennessee legislature passed an antievolution law early in 1925. John T. Scopes,* then a high-school teacher in Dayton, broke the law with the support of the American Civil Liberties Union. The trial that followed took place in the midst of all the hubbub of the times. Reporters noted all the peculiarities of the people attending the trial, and their descriptions helped to identify antievolutionary views with the more retrograde parts of rural America. The case climaxed when defense attorney Clarence Darrow,* a sophisticated Chicago attorney and agnostic, questioned Bryan, a "guest" prosecutor. Bryan had claimed to be an expert on the Bible, but Darrow's questions indicated that he actually knew little about the text. Although Bryan won the case, he was a defeated man.

Antievolutionary sentiments did not decline after the Scopes trial, although the crusade to prohibit the teaching of evolution in the public schools subsided. Conservatives continued to pressure textbook publishers. This pressure had some effect. The leading biology books from the 1930s to the 1950s paid far less attention to the theory than contemporary biology warranted. Many high-school teachers and high-school textbooks avoided controversy by avoiding evolution altogether. These accommodations, however, became suspect after the National Science Foundation gave a grant to the Biological Sciences Curriculum Committee to make recommendations for a new curriculum. The committee's recommendations, while carefully drawn, featured evolution as a primary framework for interpreting contemporary biological theory. Shortly thereafter, religious conservatives renewed their struggle against Darwinism in earnest.

The new antievolutionary campaign was far more sophisticated than the old. Some opponents noted the Supreme Court's apparent willingness to prohibit religious teaching in the schools and claimed that Darwinism had significant religious overtones and implications. To teach it, consequently, was to inculcate these teachings in the minds of the young. In contrast, the creation-science* movement argued that the scientific evidence for evolution is far weaker than is ordinarily supposed. The argument for a comparatively recent creation, they maintain, has as good or better evidence behind it. Many arguments by people involved in creation science, in fact, do not mention the Bible or theology. In 1981 the state legislatures of Louisiana and Arkansas adopted laws that provided that public schools had to give equal time to both evolutionist and creationist perspectives. One year later, Judge William Overton ruled in *McLean v. Arkansas* that the law was unconstitutional. The judge also disposed of the argument that evolution was as much a religious doctrine as creation. If that were so (and he did not think that it was), the appropriate act would be to ban the teaching of evolution, not to provide a balanced discussion in class.

Judge Overton's decision, however, marked a turning point in the public debate. Both scientists and the popular press began to examine the issue more closely and countered the assertions of creation scientists with their own arguments. In 1985 a Louisiana state court reached a similar decision in a challenge to the Louisiana law that the creationists subsequently appealed to the Supreme Court. The high court decided in *Edwards v. Aguillard* (1987) that the Louisiana law violated the First Amendment. Evolutionists also won significant battles in California and Texas textbook disputes. These state and federal actions, however, may have simply shifted the battle to local school boards. Often the religious right has had more power on the local than the national level because fewer people participate in local elections.

Many contemporary disputes over religion and education involve issues of style as well as substance. The debate over prayer in public schools, for instance, is often only part of a larger debate. While the two sides are not exclusive, those who advocate prayer in public schools tend to believe that the primary purpose of education is to incorporate children into the community and its values. Adherents believe that school prayer, like the pledge of allegiance, is a symbol that the schools still honor this understanding of education. Such persons are apt also to want textbooks that are morally conservative and that mention religion in a favorable way. In contrast, those who oppose prayer in public schools tend to see schools in terms of the nation's need for educated people. Many such advocates also believe that schools should promote diversity and tolerance. The clash between these two points of view will probably continue at center stage for some years.

Bibliography. Alley, Robert S., *School Prayer: The Court, the Congress, and the First Amendment* (Buffalo, NY: Prometheus Books, 1994); Boles, Daniel E., *The Bible, Religion, and the Public Schools* (Ames: Iowa State University Press, 1961); Buchanan, Jim, *Government Regulation of Private Schools: A Bibliography* (Monticello, IL: Vance Bibliographies, 1985); Mawdsley, Ralph D., *Legal Problems of Religious and Private Schools* (Topeka, KS: National Organization on Legal Problems of Education, 1983); Numbers, Ronald, *The Creationists* (New York: Alfred A. Knopf, 1992); Perko, F. Michael, *A Time to Favor Zion: The Ecology of Religion and School Development on the Urban Frontier, Cincinnati, 1830-1870* (Chicago: Educational Studies Press; Ames: Distributed by the Iowa State University Research Foundation, 1988); Power, Edward J., *Religion and the Public Schools in Nineteenth-Century America: The Contribution of Orestes A. Brownson* (New York: Paulist Press, 1996); Webb, George Ernest, *The Evolution Controversy in America* (Lexington: University Press of Kentucky, 1994); Whitehead, John W., *The Rights of Religious Persons in Public Education* (Wheaton, IL: Crossway Books, 1991).

Glenn Miller

Religion and Politics. The emergence of a "religious right" in the 1980s created a stir of unease in many Americans who felt that religion and politics should not mix in the United States. In fact, the two rarely venture far from one another in the American system. As observers such as Crèvecoeur and Tocqueville noted early in the life of the United States, religion played a paramount role in the political life of the United States in the nineteenth century. More recently, Garry Wills noted that politicians in the late twentieth century who disregard the influence of religion in American politics do so at their peril (*Under God: Religion and American Politics*).

Despite the pervasive role of religion in American politics, Christian political parties have managed only temporary successes in the United States. The American party of the 1840s and 1850s put forward a presidential candidate in 1856 (former President Millard Fillmore) and held a few seats in Congress, but faded as the sectional crisis deepened. Moreover, the American party left an unsavory legacy of nativism* to those who dreamed of a Christian party in the United States.

After the demise of the American party, Christian efforts to organize into a political entity tended to revolve around a single issue of great import, such as prohibition. In fact, a Prohibition party regularly ran candidates for office, including the presidency, throughout the latter third of the nineteenth century and into the twentieth century, but religious influences have centered more on attempts to persuade candidates and officeholders to take certain stances on particular issues or for particular causes.

The formation of the Moral Majority* by the Reverend Jerry Falwell* in 1979 portended not an attempt to create a party, but an attempt to create a pressure group. Falwell's group hoped to persuade politicians to enact laws to overturn Supreme Court rulings on abortion* and prayer in public schools and to permit tax credits for parents sending children to private, church-based schools. Though Falwell claimed to have ensured Ronald Reagan's election in 1980, most commentators point to other causes outside Falwell's reach. It cannot be doubted, however, that the high visibility of Falwell and his appeals at grassroots levels contributed to Reagan's victory.

The study of political activism by religious leaders in the United States during the twentieth century usually centers on efforts of traditional Christians to reverse what they view as negative trends in society. Pleas to protect the environment, for example, are couched in terms of morality: it is immoral to kill baby seals, or pollute bodies of water, or spew industrial waste into the atmosphere. While the moral and religious overtones of the civil rights* movement appear clear to commentators, appeals by women, gays, lesbians, and native tribes, to name but a few, are similar moral appeals to politicians and the electorate.

The impression of an increasingly secular United States through the twentieth century led many to proclaim the final divorce of Christianity and politics in the United States (see, for example, Harvey Cox's *The Secular City*). Other commentators find that turn of events nothing to celebrate (see Richard John Neuhaus, *The Naked Public Square*). Wills argued, however, that rumors of the death of the role of religion in American politics were greatly exaggerated and in *Under God* noted many examples of its persistence, including the Gary Hart affair and Mario Cuomo's difficulties with the abortion issue. The ''Murphy Brown'' debate involving Vice President Dan Quayle during the 1992 presidential campaign signaled the continuing strength of moralistic, religion-based appeals to the American electorate, as did nagging questions of President Bill Clinton's alleged extramarital relationships. Though many complain of the irrelevance of religion in American political debate, the moralistic tone of the rhetoric persists.

Bibliography. Cox, Harvey, *The Secular City* (New York: Scribner's, 1965); Marty, Martin E., and R. Scott Appleby, *Fundamentalism and the State: Remaking Politics,*

Economics, and Militance (Chicago: University of Chicago Press, 1993); Neuhaus, Richard John, *The Naked Public Square* (New York: Oxford University Press, 1984); Noll, Mark A., ed., *Religion and American Politics* (New York: Oxford University Press, 1990); Wills, Garry, *Under God: Religion and American Politics* (New York: Simon and Schuster, 1991).

Russell Congleton

Religious Liberty. It is fair to argue that religious liberty as espoused by the U.S. Constitution is a native American idea. When the American English colonies were established, Great Britain had a state church and no real place for dissent. Under James I those who rejected the Anglican way could easily find themselves in prison or worse.

Contrary to popular conceptions, neither the Puritans of Massachusetts nor the Anglicans in Virginia intended to alter that pattern of an established Christian church that they brought to the colonies. In one form or another all the colonies except Rhode Island were founded with an establishment, some mild, some harsh. Roger Williams* sincerely believed in separation of government from religion, and he had high regard for the role of each. For him the principle of separation led to humane and equal treatment of all forms of conscience.

After 1681 and the death of Roger Williams, Rhode Island fell into a mild establishment. Williams' legacy lay dormant. With numerous forms of establishment functioning in the following century, a kind of religious "tolerance" took shape by the time of the Revolution.

Madison rejected toleration, a concept that Tom Paine would later describe as despotism. In 1776 Madison, while drafting the Virginia Declaration of Rights, offered his famous alternative to George Mason's words that assured "fullest Toleration in the Exercise of Religion." Madison's proposal to eliminate the toleration language and replace it with "free exercise of religion, according to the dictates of conscience" was adopted. In 1786 Madison piloted Jefferson's religious freedom bill through the Virginia legislature. Jefferson wrote from Paris, "It is honorable for us to have produced the first legislature who has had the courage to declare that the reason of man may be trusted with the formation of his own opinions."

The theory of a free conscience in a free state took center stage in New York at the meeting of the first Congress in 1879. Through the work of Madison the phrase "free exercise" became a part of the Bill of Rights. Originally, the First Amendment applied only to acts of Congress. In the nineteenth century only one significant case arose for Supreme Court action, *Reynolds v. United States* (1879). The justices were dealing with the territory of Utah, under the direct control of Congress, which had outlawed bigamy in Utah. While admitting that the law overrode free exercise, the Court invoked a test of compelling state interest and supported the legislation.

After passage of the Fourteenth Amendment in 1868, the Court began to apply the Bill of Rights to state legislation. Under what is known as the incorporation doctrine, it made all state and local laws subject to Court review in matters of constitutionality. One of the first cases under the new doctrine was the *Gobitis* case of 1940. The Court allowed Pennsylvania to override the consciences of Jehovah's Witnesses* in a law requiring all children in public schools to pledge allegiance to the flag. Once again, perceived state interest overrode free exercise. Three years later a Court with new appointments by President Franklin Roosevelt overturned the *Gobitis* decision in the *Barnette* case. Justice Robert Jackson affirmed, "If there is any fixed star in our constitutional constellation, it is that no official, high or petty, can prescribe what shall be orthodox in politics, nationalism, religion, or other matters of opinion or force citizens to confess by word or act their faith therein." This was a compass that has guided most decisions since. Yet it is important to understand that free exercise is not absolute and that while the Court has generally sought, where possible, to give precedence to the free exercise of conscience, some decisions have found a compelling reason to deny specific acts such as involving children in snake handling.

In a strange departure from this long tradition of highest scrutiny for free-exercise cases, in 1990 five justices of the Court in *Oregon v. Smith* found that a law that unintentionally restricts free exercise need not receive the highest level of scrutiny by federal courts and that the decision can be reached without invoking the test of compelling state interest. Essentially that would reduce the Bill of Rights to the level of local ordinances. This caused a storm of protest from all segments of the religious community, from liberal to conservative in persuasion. The result was the Religious Freedom Restoration Act, which requires that all laws that affect in any way institutions funded with federal monies must carry a proviso allowing judicial testing of that law in light of compelling interest. It was signed into law by President Clinton in 1994.

Bibliography. Alley, Robert S., "Public Education and the Public Good," *William and Mary Bill of Rights Journal* 4, no. 1 (Summer 1995): 277–350; Banning, Lance, *The Sacred Fire of Liberty: James Madison and the Founding of the Federal Republic* (Ithaca: Cornell University Press, 1995); Ivers, Gregg, *Redefining the First Freedom* (New Brunswick, NJ: Transaction Publishers, 1993); Strossen, Nadine, "How Much God in the Schools?" *William and Mary Bill of Rights Journal* vol. 4, no. 2 (Winter 1995): 607–38.

Robert S. Alley

Reorganized Church of Jesus Christ of Latter-Day Saints. The Reorganized Church of Jesus Christ of Latter-Day Saints (RLDS) is the second-largest of several Mormon churches, sects, and denominations tracing their origins to founding prophet Joseph Smith, Jr.,* and accepting the Book of Mormon as Scripture, with headquarters in Independence, Missouri, and a membership of around 300,000. (The largest is the Church of Jesus Christ of Latter-day Saints with headquarters in Salt Lake City, Utah, and a membership of around 9 million.)

The name "reorganized" has its origins in the controversies surrounding the questions of who should succeed Joseph Smith, Jr., after his murder by a mob in Carthage, Illinois, on June 27, 1844. At the time the most successful among numerous claimants to succession was Brigham Young, who, as president of the Quorum of the Twelve Apostles, was able to persuade a sizable contingent of Mormons to follow him to the Rocky Mountains (settling primarily in what is now the state of Utah). However, many others regarded Young as a usurper, and a significant number of these, including Smith's wife Emma, argued that Joseph's son Joseph Smith III had been personally called by his father to succeed him. Those who rejected Young also rejected many of the radical innovations implemented in Nauvoo, Illinois, especially polygamy and the theocratic kingdom, arguing that these practices were concocted by Young, either behind Smith's back or after his death, with a false ex post facto imprimatur. Waiting until "young Joseph" had come of age, these followers "reorganized" the church, which they claimed had fallen into disarray, in 1860, installing Joseph III as prophet and successor to his father and establishing a precedent for succession by bloodline through Joseph and Emma Smith that was followed until 1996, when an apostle not related to the Smith family was elevated to lead the church. Many members settled in Iowa, around the community of Lamoni, where a church school, Graceland College, was established in 1897. Headquarters of the church were moved to Independence, Missouri, revealed by Joseph Smith as the center of Zion, where a temple was to be built in preparation for the Second Coming of Christ. Because Utah Mormons likewise accept this belief, ownership of the temple site has been a matter of contention, with the Reorganized Church owning substantially more of the property than the Utah church and erecting a modern temple in the 1980s. Other sources of controversy, especially polygamy and the theocratic kingdom, as well as denial of the lay priesthood to black males—all at one time principles of the Utah church—have lessened since Utah Mormons have abandoned these beliefs and practices, though in recent years another area of friction has arisen because the Reorganized Church has opened the priesthood to women, a practice vigorously opposed by the Utah church, as well as by conservatives within the Reorganized Church, some of whom have launched a breakaway movement. However, until well into the twentieth century, the Reorganized Church experienced much less controversy with its neighbors than its Utah "cousins," not being tainted by polygamy, and having been until recently socially and culturally very much in harmony with conservative Protestantism. Ironically, as the contemporary leadership of the RLDS church is pushing for liberalization, it is distancing itself both from its conservative members and its Protestant counterparts, even as the conservatism of the Utah church increasingly facilitates harmony with culturally conservative Protestants.

Bibliography. Davis, Inez Smith, *The Story of the Church*, 9th rev. ed. (Independence, MO: Herald House, 1977); Edwards, Paul M., *Our Legacy of Faith: A Brief History of the Reorganized Church of Jesus Christ of Latter-Day Saints* (Independence, MO: Herald House, 1991); Launius, Roger D., *Joseph Smith III: Pragmatic Prophet* (Urbana and Chicago: University of Illinois Press, 1988); Quinn, D. Michael, *The Mormon Hierarchy:*

Origins of Power (Salt Lake City: Signature Books, 1994); Smith, Joseph, III, Heman C. Smith, and F. Henry Edwards, eds., *The History of the Reorganized Church of Jesus Christ of Latter-Day Saints*, 6 vols. (Independence MO: Herald House, 1951–1970).

Klaus J. Hansen

Restorationism. Restorationism, or Christian primitivism, is an ideology that identifies early Christianity (variously defined) as the timeless norm for Christian doctrine and practice. Restorationism's adherents seek to replicate this normative "early Christianity" in their own times.

The restoration idea has appeared many times in various forms in the history of Christianity. The emergence of Christian monasticism, for example, and certainly the renewal movements within that tradition contain primitivist elements. What eventually influenced the history of religion in the United States more powerfully, however, was a nearly continuous restorationist motif that is identifiable from late medieval Christian humanism through the continental Reformed tradition, British Reformed and Puritan groups and movements rooted in the Reformed and Puritan traditions to more distinctively American restorationist movements.

Late medieval Christian humanism's characteristic enterprise of seeking to return to the ancient sources of Western civilization, both classical and Christian, was taken up with particular force in Reformed Protestantism's approach to the Bible. Both continental Zwinglian/Calvinist and Anabaptist forms of restorationism were brought to the United States by churches with three European roots.

Broadly, the British Reformed and Puritan-related churches include Presbyterians, Congregationalists, Baptists,* and to a degree, evangelical Anglicans and, later, Methodists. Their differing characteristic polities and sacramental practices were frequently rooted in their distinctive restorationist readings of the Bible. The Wesleyan tradition in the United States has also extolled primitive Christianity, though its restorationist emphasis was more skewed to piety than to polity.

Primitivism's preference for the "roots" over against the "branches" of the church sets up a critical tension with the historic and contemporary church. Restorationism's Protestant forms have traditionally been anti–Roman Catholic. From the sixteenth through the nineteenth centuries, especially, this often took the form of a schema of history in which the "pure" early church was seen to have "apostatized" through the formation of Roman Catholic institutions. The apostasy was viewed as reversed, or to be reversed, by the restoration.

Ironically, the presence of primitivism in Protestant traditions creates an inherent fragility within. That is, as these traditions develop in history, they themselves become suspect because of their inevitably growing historical distance from their own "pure," restored foundations. In the United States, Presbyterianism, Wesleyanism and Methodism* (including the Holiness traditions and, on the same trajectory, Pentecostalism), and the Baptist churches (especially in the

Landmark schism) have all debated and divided, in part, because of this divisive dynamic within the restoration motif.

The same fragility has also been apparent in the indigenous restorationist communities that have arisen in the United States. The New World setting and the eighteenth- and nineteenth-century contexts (with their political, literary, and artistic neoclassicism and Romantic Arcanianism) made the United States fertile ground for the development of its own religious restorationist movements. The Stone-Campbell traditions (Churches of Christ, independent Christian Churches, and the Christian Church [Disciples of Christ]) began with a providential and eschatological commitment to restoring the New Testament's faith and order as the basis for a unity that should prove evangelistically triumphant. Yet even the internal unity of this movement proved impossible to sustain in America's volatile context amidst conflict about what ''restoring the New Testament's faith and order'' should be.

The Church of Jesus Christ of Latter-Day Saints (Mormons) also made restorationist claims and also divided during its transition to a second generation. The Mormons' restorationist self-understanding was partially based on the early-nineteenth-century discovery of a set of founding texts for which an ''ancient-source'' character was claimed. This points to another aspect of the fundamental irony of American restorationism—the inherent tension between the modernity of its own historical setting and sensibility over against its internally claimed preference and striving for the ancient.

Restorationism-related controversies may be found in the particular histories of each of the aforementioned broad denominational ''families.'' Most of the controversies will be found to relate to the basic tension inherent in restorationism—that it is a historically modern mind-set that is ideologically antimodern (proancient) and antihistorical (preferring the stasis of the sought-for ancient norm to the dynamism of historical change). Some of the controversial questions that have related to this tension have been the following: What is the authoritative source for the ancient norm? (The Bible? The Book of Mormon? The experience of the baptism of the Holy Spirit?*) What are the essential practices derived from this source? (A particular form of polity? Immersion baptism? Holiness of life? Glossolalia?*) What is to be our (the restorers') relationship to those outside our community? (Conversionist zeal? Chialiastic alarm? Aloofness?) What is to be our relationship to those within our community who read the source or identify the essential practices differently than we do? (Tolerance? Schism?) Differing responses to these restorationist questions have provided considerable grist for American religious controversies.

Bibliography. Hughes, Richard T., ed., *The American Quest for the Primitive Church* (Urbana: University of Illinois Press, 1988); Hughes, Richard T., and C. Leonard Allen, *Illusions of Innocence: Protestant Primitivism in America, 1630–1875* (Chicago: University of Chicago Press, 1988).

Anthony L. Dunnavant

Revivalism. Revivalism within Christianity in the United States is associated with the evangelical awakenings of the 1700s, the frontier sacramental revivals of the early 1800s, the "domesticated" denominational revivals of the middle 1800s, the urban revivalism of the late nineteenth and early twentieth centuries, and the evangelistic crusades and "televangelism" of the middle and late twentieth century. Key figures in the first Great Awakening* (late 1720s to the 1760s) included Jonathan Edwards,* Theodore Frelinghuysen, the Tennents (Gilbert,* William, and John), the Wesleys, and George Whitefield; the latter trio illustrates the transatlantic character of these events. James McGready was a primary leader of the Second Great Awakening* (late 1780s to 1810s) whose influence flowered in its western phase (the Great Revival in the West).

Although important to subsequent American developments, the Great Revival in the West, the apogee of which was the Cane Ridge revival in Kentucky (1801), rested on a centuries-old tradition of ecstatic Communion gatherings in Scots-Irish Presbyterianism. Americans gave these roots distinctive growth by routinizing and "domesticating" revivals into regular camp meetings and intermittent evangelistic meetings in local congregations. The Baptists* and Methodists were at the forefront of "denominational" revivalism by the middle of the 1800s.

Among the Methodists the emergence of a distinctive Holiness tradition in the two generations surrounding the Civil War spawned new schisms alongside new growth. It was out of the Holiness matrix that twentieth-century Pentecostalism arose, most prominently as the Azusa Street* revival in Los Angeles, California (1906).

The urban revivalism of the late nineteenth and early twentieth centuries was, again, a transatlantic phenomenon, especially in the ministry of Dwight L. Moody. This wave of revivalism was accompanied by a lay-led, broad evangelical-mainline Sunday school movement. Early in the twentieth century revival leader Billy Sunday* brought his rustic and flamboyant style of preaching to itinerant evangelism. This style has, in part, been continued in the increasingly television-oriented evangelistic ministries of figures such as Billy Graham,* Oral Roberts,* Jimmy Swaggart, and Pat Robertson.

Some controversial aspects of revivalism have remained similar over the past two and one-half centuries. The primary question surrounding the revivals themselves has been whether they have been authentic "awakenings," works of the Holy Spirit and genuine renewals of the church, or merely manifestations of "enthusiasm," or emotionalism unleashed and manipulated. Were the ecstatic exercises associated with revivals manifestations of real conversion to Christianity and deepening of personal faith or simply the symptoms of a temporary hysteria that would soon subside? The implicit and sometimes explicit accusations by revivalists and their advocates that the church had become cold, had fallen asleep, or even that its ministry was "unconverted" (as in Gilbert Tennent's famous 1740 sermon) have often stood over against the suspicion on the part of the institutional churches and their leaders that revivalists could be theologically unschooled or unorthodox, ecclesiologically undisciplined or "irregular," or even immoral or psychologically unbalanced (as in the case of James Davenport* [1740]).

Revivalism, therefore, has often been accompanied by alienation and schism in the history of American (and closely related English) Christianity. "Arminiam" John Wesley and Calvinist George Whitefield parted company. "New Light" Congregationalist Jonathan Edwards was hounded from his Northampton, Massachusetts, pulpit. The Presbyterians experienced a temporary New Side/Old Side schism in the first Awakening and more permanent New Light (Stoneite) and Cumberland Presbyterian splinters from the western phase of the second Awakening. Revivalistic New Light "Christians" themselves divided when some joined with the Campbell movement in 1832—a group perhaps more suspicious of "enthusiasm" than the Presbyterians. Mid-nineteenth-century Holiness Revival Methodists divided from their parent tradition to form a number of new denominations, and from Holiness, Pentecostalism became a separate family of denominations as well.

Theologically, revivalism is strongly associated with the "Arminianization," "Methodistizing," or "Pelagianizing" of American Christianity. First Awakening New England revivalism was, to Jonathan Edwards, a "surprising work of God," but Charles G. Finney's* "New Measures" (1820s and thereafter) for evangelism seemed to leave far less room for God's "surprises." Ecclesiologically, revivalism has been linked to the "triumph of the laity" and "democratization of American Christianity." Politically, different forms of revivalism have contributed to both reform and polarization in the public arena.

In the late twentieth century the long-traditional concern on the part of denominational or church-based theologians and pastors over the dangers of charlatanism among virtually autonomous revival leaders has been profoundly deepened by the unprecedented power of mass media (television, especially) and the scandals that have touched several televangelists. Though prominently associated with mass media in the recent past, revival has also appeared in other contexts such as at Asbury College in Kentucky in 1970.

Bibliography. Blumhofer, Edith L., and Randall Balmer, eds., *Modern Christian Revivals* (Urbana: University of Illinois Press, 1993); Hatch, Nathan O., *The Democratization of American Christianity* (New Haven: Yale University Press, 1989); McLoughlin, William G., *Revivals, Awakenings, and Reform* (Chicago: University of Chicago Press, 1978); Schmidt, Leigh Eric, *Holy Fairs: Scottish Communions and American Revivals in the Early Modern Period* (Princeton: Princeton University Press, 1989); Westerkamp, Marilyn J., *Triumph of the Laity: Scots-Irish Piety and the Great Awakening, 1625–1760* (New York: Oxford University Press, 1988).

Anthony L. Dunnavant

Rice, John R. Born and raised near the west Texas towns of Gainesville and Dundee, the son of a journeyman farmer-preacher, John R. Rice (1895–1980) was converted at the age of nine and early on demonstrated an interest in church work and spiritual concerns. After a brief stint as a teacher in a nearby one-room country schoolhouse, Rice enrolled in 1916 at Decatur Baptist College in Decatur, Texas. Despite a short interruption by army duty in World War I, Rice eventually graduated from Baylor University with a B.A. degree in 1920, excelling in debate, oratory, and literature. He left a teaching position at Wayland Baptist College in Plainview, Texas, in the spring of 1921 to attend the University of Chicago, pursuing a graduate degree in education. While in Chicago, however, he answered the call to preach, abandoned his studies, returned immediately to Texas, and married Lloys Cooke, a former classmate at Decatur College and Baylor. They both enrolled for the fall term at Southwestern Baptist Theological Seminary* in Fort Worth. After two years he left Southwestern without a degree, pastored for a while, and then returned to Fort Worth in 1926, working as a full-time evangelist in the shadow of J. Frank "Two-Guns" Norris,* a controversial pastor of First Baptist Church and self-styled titular head of the fundamentalist movement in America. Both Rice and Norris had been attacking modernism* for some time. As the controversy grew over Norris's charges of modernism within the Southern Baptist Convention* and at Baylor University, many in the convention warned Rice to distance himself from Norris and to remove his radio program from Norris's KFQB in Fort Worth. Though Rice disagreed with many of Norris's methods, he agreed with Norris about modernism and, like Norris, refused to be coerced by the powers of the convention, adopting instead a Norris-like "independent" attitude toward his ministry that he would never relinquish. He began holding independent citywide revival campaigns across Texas and Oklahoma that lasted from ten to twelve weeks at a time. At the end of each revival he would organize a new "independent" Baptist church. In 1932, after a revival in Dallas, he founded the Fundamentalist Baptist Church (later the Galilean Baptist Church) and remained as its pastor for over seven years. While at the church he founded what would become the most influential periodical within the fundamentalist movement, the *Sword of the Lord.* He resigned that pastorate in 1940 and moved his family and ministry to Wheaton, Illinois, to devote his energies solely to the *Sword* and his revival campaigns.

Before he left Texas, however, Rice experienced a major controversy with Norris, only this time Norris was the problem, not modernism. In December 1935 Rice objected publicly to Norris's treatment of another famous evangelist, Sam Morris. Never one to take criticism kindly, Norris retaliated against Rice by attempting to sabotage his January 1936 revival in Binghamton, New York, by notifying the host pastor that Rice had become a Pentecostal* "holy roller." Rice promptly received a wire stating that the meeting had been canceled, but he went nevertheless, defending himself in letters to the ministers against the charges then appearing in Norris's newspaper, the *Fundamentalist.* Norris had boasted to Rice once that "no man will get anywhere in the cause of fundamentalism in the north, east, or outside of Texas if he fails to have the love and confidence of [Norris's] the First Baptist church" (Sumner, 104). Norris was wrong. Rice survived the attack on his ministry and never again sought the "confidence" of J. Frank Norris.

Throughout the 1940s Rice patterned his citywide revival campaigns after the example of Wilbur Chapman and Billy Sunday,* in which as many as one hundred fundamental churches of various persuasions (Baptist, Presbyterian, Methodist, Christian and Missionary Alliance, and Nazarene, to name a few) would band together nightly for upwards of four to five weeks in a large, rented downtown auditorium or a massive outdoor tent. Built on evangelistic singing, hard preaching, and lengthy altar calls, Rice's revivals were the most successful of any evangelist's during the 1940s. By the early 1950s, however, with the emergence of Billy Graham* as a national revivalist, Rice began to cut back on his citywide campaigns and focus more time and energy on his periodical the *Sword of the Lord,* a paper whose stated objective epitomized midcentury fundamentalism*: "An Independent Religious Weekly, Standing for the Verbal Inspiration of the Bible, the Deity of Christ, His Blood Atonement, Salvation by Faith, New Testament Soul Winning and the Premillennial Return of Christ. Opposes Sin, Modernism and Denominational Overlordship" (Sumner, 129). Circulation began at 5,000 and reached its apex in the mid-1970s, averaging over 250,000 copies worldwide. Virtually every fundamentalist minister in America between 1940 and 1980 at some point in his career came under the influence of John R. Rice, either through his meetings, the *Sword,* or his numerous publications. A prolific author, Rice penned over 200 books and pamphlets during his career. His most famous tract, "What Must I Do to Be Saved?" would exceed 48 million copies by the time of his death in 1980. Other popular titles include *What's Wrong with the Movies?* (1938); *What's Wrong with the Dance?* (1939); *Tobacco: Is Its Use Sin?* (1940); *Bobbed Hair, Bossy Wives, and Women Preachers* (1941); *Prayer: Asking and Receiving* (1942); *Lodges, Examined by the Bible* (1943); *The Backslider* (1943); *The Home: Courtship, Marriage, and Children* (1945); and his most controversial pamphlet within the ranks of fundamentalists, *Storehouse Tithing—Does the Bible Teach It?* (1954). In 1963 he moved the Sword of the Lord Foundation to Murfreesboro, Tennessee, where it remains to this day. Though the paper's circulation numbers have receded significantly since the 1970s, it still enjoys considerable influence within fundamentalism.

As a fundamentalist Rice fought tirelessly against all its enemies—the ecumenism of the National Council of Churches* and the World Council of Churches, denominational apostasy, new visions of the Bible, cultural taboos (such as dancing, drinking, Hollywood movies, and so on), and new evangelicalism. The latter produced two of the sharpest controversies of his career, involving two of the leading religious figures of the last half of the twentieth century—Billy Graham and Jerry Falwell.* In 1957 Rice (and eventually nearly all fundamentalists) reluctantly broke with his young friend and protégé Graham over the latter's decision to implement the new evangelical policies of inclusivism and ecumenism during his New York City crusade that spring. He remained

Graham's friend, but as a "separatist" (fundamentalism's most distinguishing characteristic between 1940 and 1980) he could not condone or cooperate with Graham's evangelistic activities any more. Subscriptions to the *Sword* were cut in half by the controversy. The *Sword* recovered by 1970, and during that decade it enjoyed its greatest circulation, only to experience more controversy near the end of the decade. This time, however, the controversy was between Rice and his fellow fundamentalists, not new evangelicals and liberals, and it concerned one of fundamentalism's most controversial figures, Jerry Falwell. Through his television ministry, his various publications, his "I Love America" campaigns, and his college, Falwell appeared to many strict fundamentalists to be replaying Graham's error of adopting new evangelical inclusivism at the expense of fundamentalism's historic "separatist" position. Unlike the Graham episode of 1957, however, this time Rice defended Falwell against the charges of "pseudofundamentalism" being hurled at him by fundamentalists who Rice believed were unfairly applying the doctrine of secondary separation* against Falwell. Because of his position on Falwell, however, many "militant" fundamentalists ended their subscriptions to the *Sword*, thereby separating themselves from the man who, as much as any figure in the twentieth century, had represented the separatist mentality of modern fundamentalism.

Bibliography. McClellan, Ruth, "Interview with Mrs. John R. Rice," *Fundamentalist Journal*, December 1982, 26–29+; Sumner, Robert L., "John R. Rice: A Man Sent from God!" *Fundamentalist Journal*, December 1982, 24–25+; Sumner, Robert L., *Man Sent from God: A Biography of Dr. John R. Rice* (Murfreesboro, TN: Sword of the Lord, 1959); Walden, Viola, *John R. Rice, "The Captain of Our Team"* (Murfreesboro, TN: Sword of the Lord, 1990).

Timothy D. Whelan

Roberts, Granville Oral. Prominent healing evangelist, Oklahoma native Oral Roberts was born in 1918. Roberts was converted at the age of seventeen and became a Pentecostal* Holiness minister like his father after claiming a divine healing from tuberculosis and stuttering. Ordained in 1936, Roberts achieved recognition in his denomination for four successful pastorates in the next eleven years.

In 1947 a healing revival erupted in the ministry of William Branham to Pentecostals. That same year Roberts began a healing ministry. He and Branham were the giants of the revival, which lasted until the mid-1950s. Headquartered in Tulsa, Roberts ministered in large tent crusades and on radio. Beginning in 1954, he pioneered in television evangelism with a weekly show that gave increased publicity to divine healing outside Pentecostalism. For over thirty years Roberts had the number-one-rated syndicated television religious program. Roberts also was influential in the rapid growth of the Full Gospel Business Men's Fellowship International.

As the healing revival waned in the late 1950s, Roberts proved adaptable to the developing charismatic movement in the mainline denominations and was its major leader. He opened Oral Roberts University in 1965, which became the preeminent charismatic university in America, and joined the United Methodist Church in 1968. In 1969 he switched from televising healing crusades to having prime-time religious variety-type shows. Many supporters consider Roberts's hospital, the City of Faith Medical and Research Center in Tulsa, which opened in 1981, to be his crowning achievement. In the late 1970s, however, he began reaffirming his older Pentecostal identity and became less ecumenical.

Because of Roberts's healing evangelism, his message had always been controversial to mainstream America. In his later ministry he was harshly criticized for opening the hospital, with its financial demands. Critics disliked his monetary requests that depended on visions from God, including one in which Roberts said that God would kill him if the needed funds were not raised. Roberts has also been criticized for his support of the controversial "Faith" teachers and their health and wealth gospel that flourishes on the radical fringe of Pentecostalism.

Bibliography. Harrell, David Edwin, Jr., *Oral Roberts: An American Life* (Bloomington: Indiana University Press, 1985).

Douglas Weaver

Robertson, Pat. Marion Gordon Robertson was born in 1930, two years prior to the election of his father, A. Willis Robertson, to the U.S. House of Representatives. He was later elected to the Senate, where he served until 1966. His father was a Democrat, but an extremely conservative politician, completely loyal to his patron, Senator Harry F. Byrd. Pat graduated from Washington and Lee University where he majored in history. After service in Korea with the Marines, he entered Yale Law School in 1952. After graduation, unable to pass the bar exam, he went into business in New York. Failure in those ventures led to severe depression.

Robertson's mother, Gladys, was an intensely religious person who left the Baptist church in Lexington, Virginia, where the family lived, to join a charismatic group. In 1956 she introduced her son to some of her charismatic friends and he subsequently enrolled in New York Theological Seminary where he graduated in 1959. He moved to Virginia Beach and was ordained as a Southern Baptist minister although his beliefs in speaking in tongues, faith healing, and spiritual gifts were at odds with that denomination. He became a minister of a church.

In 1960 Robertson purchased a struggling UHF television station in Portsmouth for the sum of $37,000 and got a charter for his Christian Broadcasting Network (CBN). With financial assistance from friends he went on the air. In 1963 he asked seven hundred viewers to pledge $10 per month to defray expenses at the station. The givers became known as the 700 Club. At that time Robertson believed that tidewater Virginia was "rife with Satan's power."

In 1965 Robertson hired Jim and Tammy Bakker and their 1966 on-air flood-gate of tears brought large contributions to the station. This resulted in the launching of a nightly program emceed by Jim Bakker. The audience, small at first, grew quickly with the expansion of cable television. During this phase Robertson became a popular faith healer. In one appearance in Philadelphia he "healed" hemorrhoids, teeth, gums, tumors, and other assorted disorders. It was at this time in his activities that he began to predict that the end of the world would occur prior to the year 2000, a concept that infected the Reagan administration.

As right-wing conservative political operatives Paul Weyrich and Howard Phillips began searching for support for Ronald Reagan's bid for the presidency, they saw the potential in harnessing the growing number of on-air preachers for political ends. Originally Robertson was involved but following the creation of the Moral Majority and selection of Jerry Falwell as its leader, Robertson backed away from his peers and struck out on his own. In 1981 he formed his first political group, the Freedom Council, designed to encourage people to become involved in politics. CBN, by then quite wealthy, put some $5 million into the Council, sparking an IRS inquiry. After Reagan's inauguration, appearances by many of the highest officials in the President's administration made frequent appearances on the 700 Club. Robertson used the program to push his political agenda which more and more seemed focused on his own ambitions. He called for an amendment to repeal *Roe v. Wade*, he demanded an amendment to authorize public school prayer, and he urged support for funding of private religious schools. Particularly harsh were his attacks on the public schools, which he felt should be abandoned. When it came to foreign policy, Robertson used his peculiar brand of biblical inerrancy to predict events in the Near East. In one broadcast he asserted that a passage in Ezekiel was "the only time the United States is mentioned in the Bible" (Videotape of 700 Club). The public took particular notice of him when he claimed to have convinced God to divert a hurricane from the Virginia coast so that it might strike Massachusetts.

Robertson, abandoning his ordination and refusing the press access to CBN tapes, ran for President in 1988. This failed campaign caused him to reevaluate his strategy, leading to the founding of the Christian Coalition. Using his constant access to the public on television he continued to perform faith healing, to attack President Clinton, and to encourage laws to "correct" the Bill of Rights. He gave active support, including funds, to Oliver North's unsuccessful run for the Senate in 1994. Today Robertson is extremely wealthy. He presides over Regent University and recently purchased the television production company MTM.

Bibliography. Boston, Rob, *The Most Dangerous Man in America?* (Buffalo: Prometheus Books, 1996); Robertson, Pat, *Shout It from the Housetops* (Virginia Beach: The Christian Broadcasting Network, 1986).

Robert S. Alley

Ruether, Rosemary Radford. Theologian, author, teacher, and activist, Rosemary Radford Ruether has offered her considerable academic gifts to the struggle for women's liberation in the latter half of the twentieth century. She has served for many years as the Georgia Harkness Professor of Applied Theology at Garrett-Evangelical Seminary in Evanston, Illinois. Prodigious in her scholarship, Ruether has served as a key analyst of Western culture's oppression of women and of all the feminist theologians has addressed the most wide-ranging cultural and theological concerns. Her topics include Jewish-Christian relations, politics and religion in America, ecological theology, and feminist theory and strategy. Specifically, she has offered a percipient critique of the misogyny of the Christian tradition's systemic exclusion and diminution of women.

Along with that of Mary Daly,* Ruether's contribution has been catalytic to the academic community, as they were instrumental in the formation of the women's caucus in the American Academy of Religion in 1971. Ruether's essays, articles, monographs, and edited collections are numerous and evince a distillation of perceptive theological and social analysis. Her analytic capacity for interpreting overarching themes and movements is unparalleled in contemporary feminist theology.

Remaining a part of the Roman Catholic tradition has not been easy for Ruether, yet her efforts at reform have required that she stay in close communion and conversation with this formative matrix. Her own relationship to the institutional church is not without ambivalence, and she is sharply critical of the ways in which it suppresses its daughters' gifts, causing them to suffer, in her words, "liturgical deprivation" and "eucharistic famine."

Ruether has resisted the trajectory toward post-Christian moorings, believing that the "prophetic-liberating tradition" within the Bible provides a sufficiently subversive and deconstructive approach to oppressive texts. Although access to the priesthood has been denied and liturgy remains exclusivistic, Ruether nevertheless believes that these myopic renderings of Christian tradition can be ameliorated. In the meanwhile she advocates communities of nurture in which women can participate until these institutional forms can be remediated. She has devoted considerable energy to writing liturgical materials addressing those areas of women's lives that have been historically ignored in traditional ecclesial worship.

Ruether continues her remarkable contribution to theological analysis and construction. Her effort in mentoring women and men as theological educators and social activists remains a vital part of her work.

Bibliography. Ruether, Rosemary Radford, *Religion and Sexism: Images of Women in the Jewish and Christian Traditions* (New York: Simon and Schuster, 1974); Ruether, Rosemary Radford, *Sexism and God-Talk: Towards a Feminist Theology* (Boston: Beacon Press, 1988); Ruether, R. R., and R. S. Keller, eds., *Women and Religion in America*, 3 vols. (San Francisco: Harper and Row, 1981).

Molly Marshall

Rushdoony, Rousas John. Rousas John Rushdoony is the foremost leader of the Christian Reconstructionists, a group made up primarily of conservative Calvinists who believe that it is the Christian's duty to reconstruct society and government according to biblical law. Born on April 25, 1916, to parents of Armenian descent, Y. K. Rushdoony, a minister, and Rose G. Rushdoony, he married Dorothy Barbara Ross, and together they reared six children. Rushdoony was ordained to the Presbyterian ministry in 1944 after a four-year ministry to Chinese Americans in San Francisco, California (1940–1944). After his ordination he and his family moved to Owyhee, Nevada, where they served as missionaries to the Paiute and Shoshone Indians for eight years. After a ten-year stint as a Presbyterian pastor in Santa Cruz, California, Rushdoony worked a few years in two private educational foundations, the William Volker Fund and the Center for American Studies in Burlingame, California. Rushdoony was educated at the University of California, Berkeley, where he earned a B.A. in English and an M.A. in education, and then at Pacific School of Religion, where he earned the B.D.

In 1965 Rushdoony spearheaded the Christian Reconstruction movement with the establishment of the Chalcedon Foundation. This foundation was founded, said Rushdoony, "to further Christian reconstruction in every area of life and thought." Further, the Chalcedon Foundation is "hostile to the pietistic retreat from life which has long marked much of orthodox and evangelical Christianity" and seeks "to relate biblical faith to every area of life and thought." This foundation, the basic vehicle for the growth of the Christian Reconstruction movement in its infancy, has sponsored numerous symposia, books, periodicals, and lecture series. Such subsequent leaders of the movement as Gary North were affiliated with Chalcedon early on.

Rushdoony's views have been expressed in numerous lectures as well as over thirty full-length books. Most notable among his works are his *Messianic Character of American Education* (1963) and his two-volume magnum opus, *Institutes of Biblical Law,* which served more than any other book to extend his views to conservatives outside Presbyterian circles.

A card-carrying Reconstructionist, Rushdoony has distinguished himself from many others in the Reconstruction movement by advancing such controversial practices as the maintenance of Old Testament (kosher) dietary codes. This practice arises not only from his view of the place of Old Testament law in present-day life, but also from his Armenian heritage.

Bibliography. *Contemporary Authors,* vols. 93–96 (Detroit: Gale Research Company 1980); North, Gary, ed. *Foundations of Christian Scholarship* (Vallecito, CA: Ross House Press, 1976).

J. Matthew Pinson

S

Sabbatarianism. Two different controversial movements in American Christianity both advocated the strict observance of the Christian holy day. The first movement encouraged Americans to observe Sunday as a day of rest and worship and promoted legislation to guard the Sunday Sabbath against secularization; the second invited Christians to observe Saturday as their sacred day in keeping with the Sabbath commandment in the Decalogue.

Strict observance of the Sunday Sabbath was an important feature of the Bible-centered, practical, and moralistic Protestantism that British colonists transplanted to America. Sabbath keeping served as a test of religious orthodoxy and social morality as well as a means of promoting discipline and decorum on the frontier. All thirteen colonies passed strict Sunday laws, and the uniformity of legal Sabbath sanctions was often cited as evidence of a national religious culture and of the new republic's covenant with God.

Alarmed at the threat that disestablishment posed to the national religious identity, evangelical Christians campaigned to preserve the legal status of Sunday rest. The General Union for Promoting the Observance of the Christian Sabbath petitioned Congress in 1829 to stop Sunday mail delivery. Congress rejected their petitions, and Richard Johnson of Kentucky wrote two eloquent committee reports in defense of religious liberty.*

After the postal petition campaign failed, Sabbatarians struggled to find a compelling argument for a national day of rest. Justin Edwards, leader of the American and Foreign Sabbath Union in the 1840s, argued that the Sabbath was a necessary symbol of a national moral tradition. Responding to waves of immigration and growing religious pluralism, several national Sabbath conventions and societies in the 1850s claimed the Sabbath as part of America's cultural heritage that even non-Christians should respect.

During the Civil War the National Reform Association launched a campaign to amend the Constitution to declare the United States a Christian nation. Sabbatarians generally supported the Christian amendment movement, since the amendment would have removed the constitutional obstacle to a national Sabbath law.

Once the crisis of the war passed, however, popular support for the Christian amendment dissolved. Moreover, national recreational habits were changing, and many people used their Sundays for leisure and sports rather than for religious reflection. Proponents of a national Sabbath institution, therefore, increased their use of civic and humanitarian arguments and toned down their religious rhetoric. Wilbur Crafts, organizer of the American Sabbath Union in the 1880s, made Sunday laws a labor issue, arguing that every worker was entitled to one day of rest each week. He also identified respect for the traditional Christian Sabbath with patriotism; all citizens, regardless of their religious beliefs, should observe the Sunday Sabbath for the same reasons that they observed Independence Day and Washington's Birthday.

It was the humanitarian argument that preserved Sunday as a legal day of rest into the twentieth century. Sunday laws no longer enforced the religious Sabbath, but instead protected people's right to a day off from work. After refusing for nearly a century to bow to religious pressure, the post office discontinued Sunday service in 1912 as a cost-saving measure after new labor laws reduced the work week. Even state Sunday laws, which generally imposed limits on Sunday commerce well into the twentieth century, based these limits increasingly on the rights of workers and the competitive needs of small businesses.

A second form of Sabbatarian belief, the seventh-day movement, also stirred controversy in the United States in the nineteenth century. A Seventh Day Baptist congregation began meeting in Newport, Rhode Island, as early as 1671. The seventh-day practice appealed to millennialists who read the Bible literally and in minute detail for evidence of the Second Coming and who considered the correct interpretation of biblical dates and times especially important. Thus many of the Adventist followers of William Miller* in the 1840s and 1850s embraced the Saturday Sabbath and organized the Seventh-Day Adventist Church.

Both Seventh Day Baptists and Seventh-Day Adventists ardently opposed Sunday laws in America and conducted campaigns of their own in response to the efforts of the Sunday moralists. Abram Herbert Lewis, a Baptist, and John N. Andrews, an Adventist, both wrote tracts and books on their Sabbath doctrine and on the need for religious liberty in America, and W. H. Littlejohn fought a running battle in the editorial column of the *Advent Review* against the advocates of the Christian amendment to the constitution in the 1870s. In the late twentieth century, however, Saturday and Sunday Sabbatarians have found common cause in their efforts to protect the right of all workers to observe their own holy day. **Bibliography.** Crafts, Wilbur F., *The Sabbath for Man*, 9th ed. (Washington, DC: Author's Union, 1894); Lewis, A. H., *A Critical History of Sunday Legislation from 321 to 1888 A.D.* (New York: D. Appleton and Company, 1888); Littlejohn, W. H., *The Constitutional Amendment: or, The Sunday, the Sabbath, the Change, and Restitution* (Battle Creek, MI: Steam Press of the Seventh Day Adventist Publishing Association, 1873).

John P. Rossing

Salvation Army. Started by William and Catherine Booth in London in 1865, the Salvation Army (which was called the Christian Mission until 1878) officially landed in the United States in 1880. The beliefs and praxis of the Army drew on several religious traditions popular in mid-to-late-nineteenth-century England—including Methodism,* Wesleyan revivalism, the Society of Friends, and the Holiness movement. From Methodism came a belief in structure culminating in Booth's adoption of a military hierarchy that Protestant critics disparagingly compared to the Roman Catholic Church. From the Wesleyan and the Holiness movements the Booths borrowed the doctrine of sanctification and its corollary—that the second blessing* set the believer apart from worldly pursuits. Echoing the Quakers, William Booth advocated simple living, lay ministry, and, after 1883, forgoing the sacraments. Also influential on the Army's development were American revivalists James Caughey, Charles Finney,* Phoebe Palmer,* and Hannah and Robert Pearsall Smith. From these teachers the Booths adopted an activist, postmillennial theology, new techniques to encourage conversion, Holiness doctrines, and support for women's ministry.

"General" William Booth aimed to convert the unchurched masses. Following his order to "Attract Attention," Salvationists frequently borrowed the idioms and instruments of popular culture to share their message. In their early days in America, Salvationists passed out P. T. Barnum–like handbills, promoted female preachers, and paraded loudly through the streets. Their brass bands played familiar tunes to attract listeners to indoor meetings where lusty singing and enthusiastic testimonies reminded some spectators of a "variety show." Such behavior shocked contemporaries. Religious and secular journals reported that the Army's sensationalism, absolutism, and irreverence alienated conventional churchgoers. Critics wondered whether the Army's ends justified its means.

Yet in cities where the poor embodied middle-class fears of alcoholism, crime, and indolence, the Army's initiatives could not be completely discounted by citizens whose own churches distanced themselves from the slums. Even critics admitted that the Army reached a population whom others ignored. But advances came to a halt in 1884 when a dispute erupted between William Booth and his American commander, Major Thomas Moore. Moore wanted to incorporate the

Army under the laws of New York State since the alternative, placing Army holdings in his name as Booth's agent, left him personally liable for all the American property. Booth, convinced that incorporation would limit the authority of International Headquarters, refused permission. When Moore continued to move forward, the General relieved him of his commission. Moore, backed by his officers, incorporated and registered all Army insignia under state laws. Although his actions were, on the surface, the result of a disagreement over incorporation, issues of national loyalty fueled the split. American Salvationists felt slighted by Booth's decision not to attend their fourth-anniversary celebration in 1884. Moreover, the majority of new recruits knew little and cared less about the movement's British origins. Moore initially swore fidelity to the General, but when Major Frank Smith was sent to take command of the American army, Moore renamed his organization the Salvation Army of America and declared himself General in 1885. Starting strong, with a majority of officers and assets, Moore's army soon faltered. In January 1889 Moore's own officers relieved him of command. They rejoined Booth's Army in October.

Ten years after the Moore schism, the American army faced another rift. Maud and Ballington Booth, William Booth's son and daughter-in-law, had taken over the American troops in 1887 and soon won widespread public support. Among their strategies was synthesizing American culture with the Army—promoting American officers, displaying the American flag, and placing an eagle atop the crest of the Army newspaper. Despite their success, Maud and Ballington angered General Booth, who perceived their activities as "Americanizing" the Army. In January 1896 Maud and Ballington received notification that they would be transferred to a new post. Surprised, they asked International Headquarters to reconsider, explaining that the American work needed continuity. When their request was refused, Maud and Ballington announced that they would retire from the Army rather than transfer. English emissaries sent to mediate only inflamed the situation, which quickly commanded headlines condemning British tyranny. Although many officers and wealthy supporters urged Maud and Ballington to declare an independent American Army, they refused to split the ranks. Instead, they left the movement and started the Volunteers of America, a religious organization similar to the Army.

In the early 1900s the Army, which had added a large array of social services to its evangelical mission, came under attack by secular philanthropists, sociologists, and several ex-officers. These critics accused the Army of commingling funds for its spiritual and social service work and of instituting programs that "pauperized" recipients by fostering dependence and indolence. The Army rebutted the accusations and, since its celebrated work with American soldiers on the German front during World War I, has rarely been the object of controversy and critical attacks.

Bibliography. Lamb, Edwin G., "The Social Work of the Salvation Army" (Ph.D. diss., Columbia University, 1909); Marts, Nora, *Facts about the Salvation Army* (Chicago: Rand and McNally, 1889); McKinley, Edward H., *Marching to Glory: The History of* *the Salvation Army in the United States, 1880–1980* (San Francisco: Harper and Row, 1980); Murdoch, Norman H., *Origins of the Salvation Army* (Knoxville: University of Tennessee Press, 1994)); Winston, Diane, "Boozers, Brass Bands, and Hallelujah Lassies" (Ph.D. diss., Princeton University, 1996).

Diane Winston

Saved by His Life. This phrase by the Apostle Paul (Romans 5:10) was also the title of a book published late in 1959 by Theodore R. Clark, then associate professor at New Orleans Theological Seminary.

On February 18, 1960, the Board of Trustees of the seminary announced that they had voted unanimously to dismiss Clark from the faculty. The Board released a press statement that said:

> In the light of problems which the board has dealt with over a period of several years, it accepted unanimously the recommendation of a special committee that Theodore R. Clark be relieved of his status as associate professor, and his teaching responsibilities as of March 12, 1960. His salary will be continued for twelve months, and the possible renewal of his relationship to the institution may be revealed on or before the expiration of a five-year period. His recently-published book is one of several instances in which the board has been confronted with questions as to limitations in the area of communication with students and hearers as well as content of lecture materials.

In reply, Clark said that he was "confused and grieved in heart over the controversy that has arisen over my book." He pointed out that "Jesus himself had difficulty communicating his ideas to certain people." He said that he thought that objections to his book concerned his doctrine of hell, his teaching on missions, and his view of the atonement. He wrote a letter of protest to the board in which he said: "I for one am convinced that rigid doctrinal tests and authoritarian control of life and thoughts are, and always will be, inimical to our true Baptist heritage."

In *Saved by His Life,* Clark mentioned in passing his belief that the immortality of human beings is conditional. The thesis of the book is that the church has emphasized the death of Christ more than the New Testament did and that, in order to be true to the New Testament, the church should begin to place more emphasis on the life of Christ. Clark stated that the excessive emphasis on Christ's death is apparent especially in hymns, and he offered some hymns of his own as illustrations of the way in which a greater emphasis could be placed on the life and ministry of Christ.

After Clark left New Orleans, he accepted a position at Pan American College in Edinburg, Texas, where he remained until his retirement.

Bibliography. *The Baptist Message,* February 25, 1960; Clark, Theodore R., *Saved by His Life: A Study of the New Testament Doctrine of Reconcilition and Salvation* (New York: Macmillan Company, 1959); Richards, W. Wiley, *Winds of Doctrines* (Lanham,

Maryland, University Press of America, 1991); *The Times–Picayune* (New Orleans), February 19, 1960.

Fisher Humphreys

Schaff, Philip. Called to teach in rural Pennsylvania in 1844, young Philip Schaff could not have foreseen the storm of controversy that would soon swirl around him. In his inaugural address as professor at the German Reformed Mercersburg Theological Seminary, Schaff expressed his appreciation for all periods of church history, including the Middle Ages. Some of his hearers were alarmed by his concessions to the pre-Reformation church and what they viewed as "popery," and eventually the Philadelphia Classis brought Schaff up on charges of heresy before the Synod of York in 1845. The address, published as *The Principle of Protestantism* (1845), clearly articulated a strong Protestant position, but the reflex of some in the German Reformed Church caused them to condemn the whole volume because of Schaff's expressed admiration for much that was good in every period of the history of the church. Though he was exonerated by the synod, Schaff and his colleague at Mercersburg, John Williamson Nevin, remained under suspicion for their theology, which stressed a high view of the sacraments, appreciated the catholic traditions of the church, and critiqued the revivalism* that was taking American Christianity by storm.

The heresy hunters launched another attack on Schaff the next year, questioning his views about the state of the soul after death. Charges were leveled against Schaff's first published work, *Die Sünde wider den Heiligen Geist*, a treatise in which he speculated on a number of theological questions in common German fashion. An American minister translated and published excerpts from the book, raising a storm of controversy, especially among some of the more conservative Dutch Reformed ministers, whose denomination had been contemplating union with the German Reformed Church.

Schaff had engaged in speculations about those who had not heard the gospel, pondering whether they would have a chance to respond to Christ after their physical death. Such theories were commonly pondered by German theologians, but American Christians for the most part believed that ideas of that type were better left unexpressed. Brought before the Synod of 1846, Schaff defended himself by saying that some of his views had changed since he wrote about those issues as a student. He had always maintained a high Christology, he said, but some of the charges dealt with issues that were at best obscure in Scripture.

Though he was cleared formally by the synod, controversy continued to surround Schaff and his colleague at Mercersburg, John Williamson Nevin. Particularly, ministers and professors from the Dutch Reformed Church (some of whom had joined that Communion after failing to rid the German Reformed Church of professors like Schaff) continued to accuse Schaff and Nevin of capitulating to Roman Catholicism. The most vitriolic diatribe came from the pen of Rev. J. J. Janeway, who published an *Antidote to the Poison of Popery in the Publications of Professor Schaff* (1854).

Schaff moved beyond the controversies of the Mercersburg Theology* when he moved to New York City in 1863, and in 1870 he became a professor at Union Theological Seminary.* For the most part, Schaff's career at Union was without the turbulence he had encountered at Mercersburg. Yet the Presbyterian Church, USA, and Union faced some years of controversy that necessarily affected Schaff. Closest to him was the heresy trial of his junior colleague Charles A. Briggs,* whose right to academic freedom* Schaff supported wholeheartedly. It is one of the great ironies of American religious history that this most irenic and ecumenical man should have borne the weight of so much controversy throughout his career.

Bibliography. Graham, Stephen R., *"Cosmos in the Chaos": Philip Schaff's Interpretation of Nineteenth-Century American Religion* (Grand Rapids, MI: Eerdmans, 1995); Shriver, George H., ed., *American Religious Heretics: Formal and Informal Trials* (Nashville: Abingdon Press, 1966).

Stephen R. Graham

School Prayer. Since the Supreme Court decision in *Engel v. Vitale* (1962), "school prayer" has been a phrase almost exclusively employed to describe various forms of prayer in public schools. The *Engel* opinion declared unconstitutional all forms of organized classroom prayer. The Court never inhibited then, nor has it since, individual acts of devotion initiated by a student so long as they are not disruptive of good order. In 1963 in *School District of Abington Township v. Schempp* the Court forbade teachers from reading the Bible or reciting the Lord's Prayer in class. These two cases brought forth a storm of protest from politicians and led to some nine years (1962–1971) of strife in the Congress over dozens of unsuccessful efforts to overturn the Court rulings by some type of constitutional amendment. The search for acceptable language for such an amendment dominated the debate. Some in Congress urged support for prayer in public schools, while others suggested restricting adjectives such as nonsectarian, nondenominational, or voluntary. The intent appeared to be to make prayer as inoffensive as possible in order to gain maximum support. Some leaders would have been satisfied with the term "meditation." All efforts at constitutional amendments failed, in large measure because of the strong opposition by the National Council of Churches,* individual Protestant denominational leaders, including Presbyterian and Southern Baptist spokespersons, and various representatives of Jewish groups.

With the election of President Ronald Reagan in 1980 "school prayer" became a part of the Republican agenda both in Congress and in court appointments. Throughout the decade of the 1980s several serious efforts were mounted in the Senate to produce a constitutional amendment on school prayer. Some made a move to authorize a moment of silence as a ruse by which to bring sectarian prayer into the school systems of numerous states. In *Wallace v. Jaffree* (1985) the Supreme Court recognized this ploy in an act by the Alabama legislature to mandate a moment of silence in public schools. The Court found that the legislative intent of the law was to support prayer and therefore ruled it unconstitutional. In the final year of President George Bush's term the administration directed Solicitor General Kenneth Starr to defend a Providence, Rhode Island, public school that had invited a rabbi to pray at a middle-school graduation. Starr's tactic was to admit at last that while *Engel* and *Schempp* were properly decided, graduation was different since it did not involve compulsory attendance and was not in the classroom. In a somewhat shocking turn of events two recent Republican appointees to the Supreme Court voted with the majority to declare the graduation prayer unconstitutional in the 5–4 *Lee v. Weisman* (1992) decision. It was a crushing blow to the president.

By 1993 a vigorous movement led by religious fundamentalists began to press for what was described as "student-initiated prayer" at ceremonies like graduation. In 1997 the Supreme Court has still rendered no decision on that subject, and circuit courts have been divided.

In the spring of 1996 two new constitutional amendments were floated by Republican sponsors. One by Representative Ernest Istook stated that nothing in the Constitution shall prohibit "student-sponsored prayer in public schools." The other amendment, offered by Represenative Henry Hyde and Senator Orrin Hatch, abandoned the school-prayer issue and endorsed rather the agenda of the Christian Coalition* to seek vouchers for religious schools. That amendment read in part that no law "shall deny benefits to or otherwise discriminate against any private person or group on account of religious expression, belief or identity." The word "benefits" was intended to establish religious schools through state funding.

From the beginning of the debate opposition to Court decisions was based on the assumption that the United States is a religious nation, probably Christian, that must instill religious doctrine in children to make them morally upright. The problem is that the First Amendment forbids all such state aid as an establishment of religion. The fundamentalist majoritarianism inherent in every effort, no matter how innocuous, to put prayer in the public schools would run roughshod over the rights of minorities. Federal courts have consistently struck down such efforts as forbidden by the First Amendment. Religious fundamentalists, intent upon some form of government-mandated religious activity in public schools and/or government funding of religious schools, continued to press both strategies in the form of constitutional amendments in the 1996 Congress. The Christian Coalition, which has pressed this agenda, remains antagonistic to separation of church and state* as espoused by James Madison, father of the Bill of Rights religion clauses, whose view was best articulated in an 1819 letter to Robert Walsh, "The Civil Government though bereft of everything like an associated hierarchy possesses the requisite stability and performs its functions with complete success."

Bibliography. Alley, Robert S., *School Prayer* (Buffalo: Prometheus Books, 1994); Alley, Robert S., *Without a Prayer* (Amherst, NY: Prometheus Books, 1996); Dreisbach, Daniel L., *Real Threat and Mere Shadow* (Westchester, IL.: Crossway Books, 1987);

Ivers, Gregg, *To Build a Wall* (Charlottesville: University Press of Virginia, 1995); Kramnick, Isaac, and R. Laurence Moore, *The Godless Constitution* (New York: W. W. Norton, 1996); Levy, Leonard, *The Establishment Clause* (New York: Macmillan, 1986).

Robert S. Alley

Scofield, Cyrus Ingerson (C. I.). Cyrus Ingerson Scofield was born in 1843 in Lenawee County, Michigan, 1921 and died in Douglaston, New York. His career included a stint in the Confederate army (1861–1865), service as an attorney in Kansas and Missouri (1869–1882), the pastorate of First Congregational Church, Dallas, Texas (1882–1895 and 1902–1907), and the pastorate of Trinitarian Congregational Church in East Northfield, Massachusetts (1895–1902). The Dallas church's withdrawal from its denomination in 1908 and Scofield's time in the pulpit at East Northfield, Dwight Moody's home church, foreshadowed the controversies he would influence, those between fundamentalists and mainstream groups. Although Scofield's own direct involvement in these divisive controversies was minimal, a work produced during his retirement, *The Scofield Reference Bible,* has had a profound influence. This book, which since its first publication in 1909 has sold well over ten million copies, is the primary vehicle for the popularizing of the millennialist theology developed by John Nelson Darby known as dispensationalism.* This theology, which Scofield learned through the Niagara Bible Conferences beginning in 1887, has in many ways set the tone for militant fundamentalism.*

Scofield was not converted until 1879 after a divorce and a bout with alcoholism, but his early career as an attorney may have enabled him to produce a reference Bible that for many laypeople and little-educated pastors was a simple, compact, and authoritative key to the mysteries of Scripture. But it is the theoretical underpinning of dispensationalism even more than the work's clarity that is most crucial. Dispensationalism's identification of seven distinct ages through which God works out his plan for the world's salvation has a kind of scientific and historical quality that was and is widely appealing. This element of dispensationalism, which Scofield's commentary so ably captures, has convinced many of the validity of a literal reading of the Bible. Moreover, the emphasis on the end of time provides a kind of urgency that has given and continues to give energy to fundamentalist movements.

It was Scofield's own belief that ignorance of dispensationalism led to confusion in approaching the biblical text and that only with this understanding could one "rightly divide the word of truth" (2 Timothy 2:15), a phrase that had been used in the title of his first significant work, published in 1888. Over the years many ministers and Bible schools have found *The Scofield Reference Bible* to be a powerful weapon. Originally written to provide guidance to laymen who had been enlisted to help meet the clergy shortage of the early twentieth century, the interpretive system Scofield presents explicates even complex texts so that they can be used to defend the faith. Along with the commentary are detailed cross-references, which are intended to confirm not only basic Christian doctrines but also a divine master plan. Survey data gathered in the last ten years confirm the continuing influence of this Bible on the thinking and theology of fundamentalist ministers active in contemporary controversies.

Bibliography. Be Vier, William A., "A Biographical Sketch of C. I. Scofield" (Master's thesis, Southern Methodist University, 1960); Crutchfield, Larry V., "C. I. Scofield," in *Twentieth-Century Shapers of American Popular Religion,* ed. C. H. Lippy (New York: Greenwood Press, 1984); Scofield, C. I., *The New Scofield Reference Bible,* ed. E. Schuyler English 1967; Scofield, C. I, *Rightly Dividing the Word of Truth,* rev. ed. (Fincastle, VA: Scripture Truth Book Co., n.d. [first published in 1888]); Scofield, C. I., *The Scofield Reference Bible* (New York: Oxford University Press, 1909; revised, 1917); Trumbull, C. G., *The Life Story of C. I. Scofield* (New York: Oxford University Press, 1920).

Helen Lee Turner

Scopes, John T. John T. Scopes was a Tennessee teacher who stood trial for violating the state's law against the teaching of evolution in 1925. Scopes was born in Paducah, Kentucky, in 1900. His father encouraged his son and four daughters to think for themselves. The elder Scopes left the Presbyterian church in Paducah, and his son walked out of a Sunday school class there as well. When Scopes was a teenager the family moved to Salem, Illinois, birthplace of William Jennings Bryan.* Scopes heard Bryan speak on several occasions, including his high-school graduation.

Scopes graduated from the University of Kentucky in 1924 with a major in law and a minor in geology and accepted a job in Dayton, Tennessee, as a mathematics and physics teacher and coach. In March 1925 the Tennessee legislature passed a bill forbidding anyone to teach "any theory that denies the story of the Divine Creation of a man as taught in the Bible, and to teach instead that man has descended from a lower order of animals." Scopes had substituted for the regular biology teacher during an illness. Only after the trial did he confide to a reporter that he was not certain he had taught the theory. The textbook covered it, but because he was running behind schedule, he did not remember talking about it in class.

In May 1925, however, Scopes agreed to let himself be charged in order to test the law. The American Civil Liberties Union (ACLU) had offered to defend any teacher who would let him or herself be tried. The course of the trial, and its dramatic confrontation between Clarence Darrow* and Bryan, is part of American folklore. Scopes himself did not speak at the trial except for a brief statement before the judge assessed the $100 fine, for Scopes was found guilty. The decision was overturned by the Tennessee Supreme Court in 1927 because the fine had been imposed by the judge, not by the jury.

Scopes never returned to teaching. The expert witnesses at his trial arranged for a scholarship for him, and he enrolled in the fall of 1925 at the University of Chicago. Two years later he took a job as a geologist for an oil company, a field he worked in for the rest of his life. Scopes died in 1970.

Bibliography. de Camp, L. Sprague, *The Great Monkey Trial* (Garden City, NY: Doubleday, 1968); Ginger, Ray, *Six Days or Forever: Tennessee v. John Scopes* (Boston: Beacon Press, 1958); Scopes, John T., and James Presley, *Center of the Storm: Memoirs of John T. Scopes* (New York: Holt, Rinehart and Winston, 1967).

Albert A. Bell, Jr.

Scopes Trial. The famous 1925 trial in Dayton, Tennessee, of John T. Scopes,* a high-school biology teacher, who was accused of violating the state's statute prohibiting the teaching of biological evolution of humans in the public schools, became emblematic of fundamentalist opposition to the teaching of evolution. Soon after Charles Darwin published *On the Origin of Species* in 1859, American Protestants began to address the theory of biological evolution and its implications for the Christian faith. While some theological conservatives, such as Charles Hodge,* found evolution utterly incompatible with the biblical record and the doctrine of divine providence, others, such as Benjamin Warfield,* came to allow for some form of evolutionary development. Theological liberals, such as Lyman Abbott and Henry Ward Beecher,* enthusiastically embraced evolution as God's way of working in the world.

In the aftermath of World War I many theological conservatives, most notably Presbyterian layman and three-time presidential candidate William Jennings Bryan,* became convinced that a Darwinist "might-makes-right" philosophy provided the basis for Germany's military aggression and threatened to undermine the foundations of American Christian civilization. Fundamentalists, led by Bryan, went to work to encourage states to pass laws forbidding the teaching of human evolution in public schools.

These efforts climaxed in the trial of Scopes in Dayton, Tennessee. Scopes, encouraged by the American Civil Liberties Union (ACLU), decided to test the recently passed state law forbidding the teaching of human evolution in Tennessee public schools. The renowned agnostic lawyer Clarence Darrow* signed on as counsel for the defense, and Bryan volunteered to serve as counsel for the prosecution. The trial rapidly escalated into a major media event, with over a hundred reporters descending on the town to wire news of the trial across the country. The small hamlet took on the atmosphere of a carnival as vendors and preachers filled the streets.

At the climax of the trial, Darrow, who had been denied the right to call expert witnesses, called Bryan to the stand as a witness for the defense. Bryan, a better orator than debater, could hardly refuse the invitation. The result was an unmitigated disaster for the fundamentalist cause. Under Darrow's relentless questioning, Bryan revealed his ill preparation in matters of religion and science, confirming the stereotypes of fundamentalists as unthinking and uneducated.

Scopes was convicted, but the ruling was later overturned on a technicality. The spectacle of the trial, however, left the indelible impression that fundamentalism* was a rural, anti-intellectual movement that would pass away with the advance of an educated, urban culture. Though in the years immediately following the trial antievolution efforts were confined mostly to the South, by the 1960s the rise of creation science* returned antievolutionary protests to the spotlight.

Bibliography. Levine, Lawrence, *Defender of the Faith: William Jennings Bryan, the Last Decade, 1915–1925* (New York: Oxford University Press, 1965); Marsden, George M., *Fundamentalism and American Culture: The Shaping of Twentieth-Century Evangelicalism, 1870–1925* (New York: Oxford University Press, 1980); Numbers, Ronald L., *The Creationists: The Evolution of Scientific Creationism* (New York: Alfred A. Knopf, 1992); Szasz, Ferenc M., *The Divided Mind of Protestant America, 1880–1930* (University: University of Alabama Press, 1982).

Bradley J. Longfield

Scott, Walter. Walter Scott (1796–1860) was an evangelist in the Stone-Campbell movement. His success in evangelizing in association with the movement of Thomas and Alexander Campbell* in the Ohio Valley beginning in the late 1820s led to his becoming regarded, along with the Campbells and Barton W. Stone,* as one of the "four founders" of the Stone-Campbell traditions.

Scott was born in Moffatt, Scotland, and his early religious training was in the Church of Scotland. Scott attended the University of Edinburgh (c. 1812–1818) before emigrating to the United States and teaching at the Union Academy in Long Island. In 1819 Scott moved to Pittsburgh and befriended George Forrester, who led a congregation and academy there of the Haldane Christian primitivist movement. When Forrester was drowned in 1820, Scott assumed his mantle. Studying for his new responsibilities, Scott discovered works by "Scots Baptists," particularly Henry Errett. Errett's *On Baptism* and his lectures that Scott attended became formative for Scott's thought, which came to focus on the divine Sonship and Messiahship of Jesus. Scott called these truths the "Golden Oracle," and around them he organized his subsequent life.

Becoming a tutor in the home of Robert Richardson in the winter of 1821–1822, Scott met Alexander Campbell. This was during the period (c. 1815–1830) of the Campbellites' affiliation with Baptist associations. The Campbells and their followers had joined the Redstone (Pennsylvania) Baptist Association without surrendering the distinctive vision of Campbell's *Declaration and Address* (1809). Tensions soon arose around the Campbellites, or Reformers, who withdrew from the Redstone into the Mahoning (Ohio) Baptist Association, which Reformers dominated (1824–1830).

Scott had moved with his wife Sarah Whitsette to Ohio and became the itinerant evangelist for the Mahoning Association in 1827. Scott's evangelism called for faith in the "Golden Oracle," repentance, and submission to immersion baptism. God could be trusted to grant remission of sins, the gift of the

Spirit, and eternal life. Scott's "orderly" arrangement of the gospel, or plan of salvation, was sometimes presented as a "five-finger exercise" by arranging the elements on the fingers (combining the gifts of the Spirit and eternal life).

Scott's "five-finger exercise" evangelism met with enormous success between 1827 and the dissolution of the Mahoning Association in 1830. Many thousands were eventually brought into the Stone-Campbell movement by the preaching of Scott and scores of imitators. The "five-finger exercise" also fixes Scott's place in the history of religious controversies.

Scott's anti-Calvinistic evangelism stood over against the practices of Congregationalists, Presbyterians, many Baptists,* and other Reformed traditions. Scott denied the Spirit's direct, regenerative action on individuals in conversion. Rather, the Spirit had inspired the Scriptures through which one came to faith. Once faith was embraced and baptism* submitted to, the Spirit would be given to the new member of the Body of Christ.

Scott's understanding of conversion and his association with Alexander Campbell (champion of immersion of believers for the remission of sins) left him vulnerable to the accusation of being a "water regenerationist." To Calvinists (and even Wesleyans), Scott's "five-finger exercise" could appear to be basically Pelagianism or "works righteousness" because it emphasized persons' actions of believing, repenting, and submitting to baptism.

Scott became controversial within the Stone-Campbell movement by identifying the restoration of the gospel with his own actions in conjunction with the conversion of William Amend (1827). Alexander Campbell found Scott's claims offensive (personally and philosophically).

Scott is associated to a lesser degree with controversies within the movement as to the legitimacy of extracongregational structures and on the proper understanding of Christian eschatology. On these issues Scott appears to have made some reversals during his long career. He either led or acquiesced to the dissolution of the Mahoning Baptist Association in 1830, only to emerge decades later as a national leader in the movement's extracongregational American Christian Missionary Society. Scott's eschatology changed from premillennialism in the 1830s and 1840s to postmillennialism in the 1850s. Scott was also a moderate emancipationist who engaged in a minor print controversy against abolitionist Nathaniel Field, with Scott opposing Field's advocacy of making slavery a "test of fellowship" in the churches.

Bibliography. Gerrard, William A., III, *A Biographical Study of Walter Scott: American Frontier Evangelist,* (Joplin, MO: College Press, 1992); Stevenson, Dwight E., *Walter Scott, Voice of the Golden Oracle: A Biography* (St. Louis: Christian Board of Publication, 1946).

Anthony L. Dunnavant

Seabury, Samuel. Born in New London, Connecticut, Samuel Seabury (1729–1796) received a B.A. from Yale College in 1748, served as a catechist at Huntington, Long Island, and studied medicine at Edinburgh (1752–1753). Ordained deacon and priest on December 21 and 23, respectively, in 1753, he was licensed by the bishop of London and assigned by the Society for the Propagation of the Gospel (SPG) to New Brunswick, New Jersey, where he served from 1754 to 1757. On October 12, 1756, he married Mary Hicks of Staten Island. From 1757 to 1766 he was rector of Grace Church, Jamaica, New York. Here he espoused the cause of fellow Anglicans seeking to control the proposed King's College and became second only to the Reverend Thomas B. Chandler as a champion of the Church of England in America. He moved to St. Peter's Church, Westchester, in 1766, where he remained until 1776.

As tension mounted between Great Britain and its colonies, Seabury wrote a series of pamphlets supporting Loyalists signed "A. W. Farmer." These were answered by Alexander Hamilton in "A Full Vindication of Measures of Congress." In 1766–1767, Seabury served as secretary to a convention of Anglican clergy seeking the appointment of a colonial bishop. This activity provoked William Livingston to write a newspaper series entitled "The American Whig" in opposition. These publications were countered by "A Whip for the American Whig" penned by Chandler, Seabury, and Charles Inglis.

Seabury's efforts in the Loyalists' cause led to imprisonment in November 1775. Upon release in December, he resided in New York City for the duration of the War of Independence. Here he served as chaplain to a provisional hospital and to a British man-of-war. He was awarded a D.D. by Oxford University, and the SPG assigned him to Staten Island, where he became chaplain to the King's American Regiment.

Returning to Connecticut after the war, he was the alternative choice of the Anglican clergy, Jeremiah Leaming having declined, to go to England and seek episcopal consecration. Departing on June 7, 1783, he failed to win his cause in England, but on November 14, 1784, he was consecrated bishop in Scotland by nonjuring bishops. On June 20, 1785 he was back in the United States. He became rector of St. James' Church, New London, Connecticut, and presided as the Episcopal bishop in Connecticut and Rhode Island until his death. Although he was unsympathetic to the liberalizing ideas of his American brethren, he did participate in the creation of the Protestant Episcopal Church in the United States of America at Philadelphia, Pennsylvania, September 30–October 16, 1789.

Bibliography. Beardsley, E. E., *Life and Correspondence of the Right Reverend Samuel Seabury* (Boston: Houghton, Mifflin and Co., 1881); Cameron, K. W., *Seabury Traditions: The Reconstructed Journal of Connecticut's First Diocesan*, 2 vols. (Hartford: Transcendental Books, 1983); Mills, Frederick V., *Bishops by Ballot: An Eighteenth-Century Ecclesiastical Revolution* (New York: Oxford University Press, 1978); Steiner, B., *Samuel Seabury, 1729–1796: A Study in the High Church Tradition* (Columbus: Ohio University Press, 1971); Thoms, H., *Samuel Seabury, Priest and Physician: Bishop of Connecticut* (Hamden, CT: Shoe String Press, 1963).

Frederick V. Mills, Sr.

Second Blessing. Common to the Wesleyan/Holiness tradition, the term "second blessing" designates a distinct religious experience subsequent to conversion that is variously called Christian perfection, entire sanctification, or holiness. In the late eighteenth century John Wesley asserted that persons, having been converted, should grow in holiness and could attain to Christian perfection. While this was not a sinless perfection since sin resulted from mistakes and ignorance, the believer might be entirely sanctified so as to live by perfect love, a purity of motives, and an absence of intentional sin. According to Wesley, the second blessing was a gift from God received by faith and could be experienced as part of the larger process of growth in grace and as an instantaneous event.

Wesley's belief in a second blessing traveled to America via Methodism.* In the middle of the nineteenth century a renewed focus on sanctification occurred that cut across denominational lines. The revivals of Charles Finney* emphasized conversion and sanctification. His counterpart at Oberlin College, Asa Mahan, wrote *Christian Perfection* (1839), in which he emphasized the purification of the will of the believer. This Oberlin theology lent itself to moral and social reform movements.

Fearful of a drifting away from Wesley's emphasis in Methodism, Methodist evangelists like Phoebe Palmer* were at the forefront of the Holiness movement. In a manner akin to the shortening of conversion from a gradual process to a transactional event in frontier revivalism,* Palmer taught that the second blessing of sanctification could be immediately received. The gift, she preached, could be received by "only believing," laying one's all on the altar.

In the latter half of the nineteenth century Methodism was rocked by controversy over the doctrine of the second blessing. Several denominations emerged that declared a belief in a second blessing of entire sanctification (for example, the Pentecostal Holiness Church, the Church of the Nazarene, and the Christian and Missionary Alliance).

Leaders in the Holiness movement, including Palmer and Mahan, gradually adopted the Pentecostal imagery of Acts to describe the second blessing, characterizing sanctification as the baptism of the Holy Spirit (Wesley had used Christocentric language, "having the mind of Christ in you," to describe the second blessing). An alternate view of holiness developed, however, in the Keswick movement of England, which influenced Americans like Reuben Torrey and Dwight L. Moody. Keswick teachers rejected the traditional Wesleyan view of sanctification as an instantaneous second blessing in favor of describing holiness as progressive throughout the believer's life. The baptism of the Holy Spirit, moreover, was redefined as an "enduement of power," the power to evangelize the world in the last days.

Both of these views of the second blessing were passed on to Pentecostalism, which was birthed in the ministry of Holiness (Keswick-styled) preacher Charles Parham.* Keswick Pentecostals (Assemblies of God) affirm the baptism of the Holy Spirit* as a second blessing, with speaking in tongues as the "initial evidence" of its reception. Wesleyan Pentecostals (Church of God, Church of

God in Christ) affirm three blessings: conversion, sanctification for cleansing of inbred sin, and the baptism of the Holy Spirit for power.

During the nineteenth century Methodist critics of the second blessing argued that a focus on the second blessing led to spiritual pride and an actual lack of focus on the blessing of conversion. Holiness believers were also attacked for identifying possession of the second blessing with externals like whether a woman wore makeup or had cut her hair. Conflicts arose between different Holiness believers and between Holiness and Pentecostal adherents over the true definition of the second blessing. Non-Holiness believers and non-Pentecostals argued that there was not a separate second blessing.

Bibliography. Dayton, Donald, *Theological Roots of Pentecostalism* (Grand Rapids, MI: Francis Asbury Press, 1987); Peters, John L., *Christian Perfection and American Methodism* (Nashville: Abingdon Press, 1956); Synan, Vinson, *The Holiness-Pentecostal Movement in the United States* (Grand Rapids, MI: William B. Eerdmans, 1971).

Douglas Weaver

Second Great Awakening. The term "Second Great Awakening" refers to a diverse series of revivals that took place in the latter years of the eighteenth century in the East and on the frontier after the excitement and effects of the Great Awakening* had deteriorated into apathy and indifference. While the exact beginnings of the new revivalism* are difficult to pinpoint, an early outbreak of religious fervor can be traced to revivals in Sydney College and Washington College in Virginia in 1787. Revivals spread to Maine, Massachusetts, Connecticut, and central and western New York. Because of the preaching of Timothy Dwight, who became president of Yale College in 1795, more than a third of the student body was converted, including Lyman Beecher,* who embraced the new revivalism. Lawyer-turned-evangelist Charles G. Finney* converted in 1821. Believing that a revival of religion was not miraculous in any way, but rather was the proper application of humanly contrived means, he forged a unique style of evangelistic techniques, including the use of advance teams to pray for and publicize meetings and the "anxious bench" for people close to conversion but not yet converted.

The revival on the frontier was driven by a theology that replaced the Calvinist doctrine of predestination* with an Arminian theology promising salvation to all who sought it. Baptist and Methodist frontier preachers were successful, and church roles increased, but while Presbyterians participated in leadership roles in phases of frontier revivals, many were disenchanted with the strange emotional aspects of the movement.

In 1800 Presbyterian ministers James McGready, William Hodges and John Rankin led the first frontier camp meeting. In 1801 Barton Stone* led a revival at Cane Ridge, Kentucky, that lasted a week and involved as many as twenty-five thousand participants, many of whom experienced strange physical manifestations. Some fell to the ground, "slain in the spirit"; others experienced violent shakings known as the jerks.

The Second Great Awakening had positive results in the East and on the frontier. Converts were numerous, church membership increased, and new revival techniques proved successful. Schools and colleges in the South and East experienced the positive results of the revival. Princeton Seminary and Yale Divinity School and Union Theological Seminary in Virginia as well as Andover had their roots in this revival. The effect of the revival upon religious literature was astounding. Pamphlets, tracts, devotional books, and volumes of sermons were published.

There were points of controversy. Many were appalled at the evangelistic tactics, the excessive emotionalism, and the pressure for decisions while emotionally stirred. Many believed that emotionalism encouraged immorality, and the charge was heard that ''more souls were made than saved'' at camp revivals.

The Presbyterian Church divided into the New Lights,* revivalists, and the Old Lights,* antirevivalists. The Cumberland Presbyterian Church in Kentucky came into existence as a result of the schisms within Presbyterianism during the Second Great Awakening.

One of the elements of the Kentucky revival, the Stonites, took their name from the Reverend Barton W. Stone,* who with Richard M'Nemar and others led their groups into the millennial Shaker sect. Millennialists took their doctrine of the immediate return of Christ so seriously that family life was forbidden, separate dormitories were maintained for women and men, and procreation was forbidden. It was but a step into Shakerism for the Stonites, to whom the chief gains of the revival were bodily agitations and an overemphasis on the immediate return of Christ.

Presbyterians were concerned that conversions would be accompanied by great excitement that would decrease the sense of family responsibility and the covenant responsibilities as they related to baptized children. Another point of controversy was the belief that the only way a person could become a Christian was through a conversion experience that had to occur at a revival. The importance and place of traditional theology and any kind of Christian nurture was minimized in favor of the ''conversion experience.''

Bibliography. Johnson, C. A., *The Frontier Camp Meeting* (Dallas: Southern Methodist University Press, 1950); Lacy, B. R., Jr, *Revivals in the Midst of the Years* (Richmond: John Knox Press, 1943); McLoughlin, W. G., Jr., *Modern Revivalism: Charles Grandison Finney to Billy Graham* (New York: Ronald Press Company, 1959); Smith, H. S., R. T. Handy, and Lefferts Loetscher, *American Christianity: An Historical Interpretation with Representative Documents*, vol. 1, *1607–1820* (New York: Charles Scribner's Sons, 1960).

Robert K. Gustafson

Secondary Separation. By the 1940s fundamentalism* had already established itself as a distinct entity within American religion and culture. As the movement grew, however, tensions developed within it, resulting in a split by the late 1940s and early 1950s between the more moderate evangelicals and the more militant fundamentalists. At the center of this split was the ministry of Billy Graham,* who in the mid-1950s moved away from his fundamentalist heritage by joining with evangelicals in what became known as "cooperative evangelism." The most noticeable instance of Graham's interdenominational evangelical outreach occurred in the 1957 New York City crusade, in which the liberal Henry Van Dusen, president of Union Theological Seminary,* was asked to participate, along with representatives of the New York Roman Catholic Diocese, as well as fundamental Baptist leaders from the New York City area. The fundamentalists involved in the crusade begged Graham to reconsider or lose their support, but he would not, and so a break occurred between Graham and the fundamentalist movement that has never been healed.

This split between Graham and fundamentalists was an early yet most fitting example of the doctrine of second-degree or "secondary" separation. Ernest Pickering has defined a secondary separatist as one who refuses to cooperate with (1) apostates (this would refer to all unbelievers, but especially liberals and modernists), (2) evangelicals who "aid and abet" apostates by maintaining some form of organizational or cooperative alignment with them (this would refer to such cooperative efforts in evangelism as those practiced by the Billy Graham Association and the Southern Baptist Convention*), and even (3) fundamentalists who maintain any form of fellowship with those in the two previous categories (such as John R. Rice,* J. Vernon McGee, Jerry Falwell,* and others). Secondary separationists take as their texts three key passages—Romans 16:17–20 ("Mark them which cause divisions and offences contrary to the doctrine which ye have learned, and avoid them"); 2 Corinthians 6:14–7:1 ("Be ye not unequally yoked with unbelievers. . . . Wherefore come out from among them, and be ye separate, saith the Lord"); and 2 John 7–11 ("If there come any unto you, and bring not this doctrine, receive him not into your house, neither bid him God speed: For he that biddeth him God speed is partaker of his evil deeds")—deriving from these verses a compelling responsibility to identify any person, organization, or church that has turned from biblical truth to apostasy and to avoid them in all respects. The question was no longer whether Christians should separate from unbelievers, but whether Christians should separate from other Christians, and even more pointedly, whether fundamentalists should separate from other fundamentalists. The pressing issues were not only doctrinal and ecclesiastical but cultural as well, involving matters of personal dress and grooming, alcohol and tobacco use, contemporary music (both secular and sacred), and Hollywood movies. Fundamentalists used the doctrine of secondary separation to separate not only from those who did not "believe" correctly, but also from any who did not "look" and "act" the way a good fundamentalist should look and act.

It was this "militant" aspect of secondary separation that became most distinctive within fundamentalism in the 1960s and 1970s, leading eventually to a position of ecclesiastical and cultural isolation for many groups within the movement. The more militant fundamentalists used the doctrine like a sledgehammer against any evangelical or fundamentalist who violated its principles. Charles

Woodbridge, a former professor at Fuller Theological Seminary, was convinced by 1969 that "new evangelicals," with their revived doctrine of "infiltration from within," were "following the downward path of *accommodation* to error, *cooperation* with error, *contamination* by error, and ultimate *capitulation* to error," and accordingly fundamentalists should separate from them (15). If they did not, then those fundamentalists were to be separated from as well. If refusal to separate from "unbelief" identified one as a "compromising believer," then "obedient" believers had no choice, if they were to maintain their purity (and identity), but to separate from such sullied believers. Even the great fundamentalist John R. Rice, editor of the *Sword of the Lord*, came under attack by Bob Jones* and others for his "friendly" stance toward such Southern Baptist leaders as W. A. Criswell* and R. G. Lee and in the late 1970s for his defense of Jerry Falwell. Rice argued that his position was the one taken by Bob Jones, Sr., and the historic fundamentalists, in which separation referred primarily to apostasy and unbelievers, not believers. Christian fellowship was dependent primarily upon doctrinal agreement (the five fundamentals), not secondary issues. Organizations considered to be infected with unbelief were to be separated from, but not fundamental believers within those organizations. Thus the Independent Baptist Rice remained friends with the Southern Baptist W. A. Criswell at the same time that he could not support the Southern Baptist Convention and its Cooperative Program. To Rice, secondary separation was neither biblical nor a part of the historic fundamentalism of Dwight Moody, Torrey, J. Frank Norris,* and W. B. Riley. To the militant fundamentalists, however, this was capitulation and compromise. By the late 1970s such fundamentalists as Rice, Jack Van Impe, and especially Jerry Falwell, all of whom continued to violate the doctrine of secondary separation, both in their associations with evangelicals and in their actions and attitudes toward popular culture, were now being labeled "pseudofundamentalists" by the militant fundamentalists. With his short-lived takeover of PTL in 1987 Falwell, despite his claims to be a fundamentalist with a capital "F," found himself virtually cut off from nearly all his original fundamentalist associations, a direct result of his violation of the doctrine of secondary separation.

Bibliography. Ashbrook, William E., *Evangelicalism: The New Neutralism* (Columbus, OH: Calvary Baptist Church, 1963); Cohen, Gary G., *Biblical Separation Defended* (Philadelphia: Presbyterian and Reformed Press, 1966); Dollar, George W., *The Fight for Fundamentalism* (Sarasota, FL: Daniels Publishing, 1983), 128–39; Pickering, Ernest, *Biblical Separation: The Struggle for a Pure Church* (Schaumburg, IL: Regular Baptist Press, 1979); Rice, John R., *Come Out or Stay In* (Nashville: Thomas Nelson, 1974); Sumner, Robert L., *Fundamentalist Foibles* (Ingleside, TX: Biblical Evangelism Press, 1987); Woodbridge, Charles, *The New Evangelicalism* (Greenville, SC: Bob Jones University Press, 1969).

Timothy D. Whelan

Seminex. Seminex is an acronym for Seminary in Exile, the name adopted by faculty and students of Concordia Seminary of St. Louis when they left the school in February 1974 rather than accept the suspension of President John H. Tietjen* by its Board of Control. The controversy became the centerpiece of a movement that led to the founding of the Evangelical Lutheran Church in America in 1988.

The controversy began brewing in 1969 when Jacob Preus* was elected president of the Lutheran Church–Missouri Synod (LCMS), the culmination of a conservative movement in the denomination that had been gaining strength for several years. Preus announced as one of his primary objectives the removal of Tietjen from his position at Concordia. It was not until the church's biennial convention in New Orleans in July 1973 that Preus was able to get the church to vote to condemn the theological positions of Tietjen and forty-five of the seminary's fifty faculty members. The convention also appointed a new Board of Control for the seminary, with a six-to-five majority supporting Preus. Several factors delayed the board's action, but on January 20, 1974, it suspended Tietjen on grounds of doctrinal heresy and administrative malfeasance. The next morning some 80 percent of the seven hundred students began a boycott of classes, demanding that either Tietjen and the faculty be tried for heresy or the charges be dropped. The forty-five faculty members joined in the moratorium.

Preus believed that the "revolt" would collapse and took no immediate action beyond naming a loyal faculty member, Martin Scharlemann, acting president of the seminary and appointing his own brother, Robert Preus, as vice president of the faculty, a powerful position analogous to a provost or chancellor. On February 17 the Board of Control voted 6–5 to require all professors to give written notice by noon of the next day that they would return to classes. In response, faculty and students moved to the campuses of St. Louis University and Eden Theological Seminary to resume classes. Costs were high for all involved. Faculty were fired and evicted from their offices and many from seminary housing. Students lost housing, loans, and campus jobs and could not be certain whether LCMS churches would issue calls to them upon graduation.

Seminex functioned for almost a decade. Its graduates at first received degrees granted by the Lutheran School of Theology in Chicago until Seminex obtained its own accreditation. In August 1975 it moved into its own facilities. Moderates within the LCMS, described as "trauma victims of the New Orleans convention," had organized the Evangelical Lutherans in Mission (ELIM) in August 1973 as a protest against the dominance of Preus's faction. By 1977 ELIM was joined by other concerned Lutherans, split from the LCMS, and became the Association of Evangelical Lutheran Churches (AELC), with about 100,000 members. AELC supplied about a third of Seminex's financial support, with the rest coming from individuals. In the fall of 1977 Seminex changed its name to Christ Seminary–Seminex.

The new seminary soon faced problems. Student enrollment declined after a few years as new entering students opted for the original Concordia Seminary, which had struggled to keep its doors open with a handful of faculty and a few score students. Reduction of the size of the faculty at Seminex became necessary in 1977; discussion of that issue proved acrimonious. The question was how an institution could operate on an anti-institutional philosophy. As AELC moved toward union with the American Lutheran Church and the Lutheran Church in America, Seminex prepared to join with theological schools from these denominations. Agreement was reached in 1982 to share Seminex faculty and resources with other Lutheran schools. Seminex held its final commencement in 1983, although the organizational structure was not formally dissolved until 1987.

Bibliography. Adams, James E., *Preus of Missouri and the Great Lutheran Civil War* (New York: Harper and Row, 1977); Jewett, Robert, "The Gospel as Heresy: Concordia Seminary in Exile," *Christian Century* 91 (1974); 336–40); Leuking, F. Dean, "Trial by Fire at Concordia," *Christian Century* 91 (1974): 116–17; Tietjen, John H., *Memoirs in Exile: Confessional Hope and Institutional Conflict* (Minneapolis: Fortress Press, 1990).

Albert A. Bell, Jr.

Separate Baptists. The Separate Baptists were a Baptist group that originated in the revivalist-antirevivalist controversy among Baptists and the Old Light–New Light controversy among the Congregationalists in the middle of the eighteenth century. During the Great Awakening* many Baptist churches divided into revivalistic (Separate) and antirevivalistic (Regular) factions. The first Separate Baptist church arose from a split that occurred in the First Baptist Church of Boston in 1743. After the revivalistic preaching of George Whitefield had influenced a contingent within the church, seven members withdrew to form the Second Baptist Church (Separate) of Boston. Many such schisms occurred in Baptist churches in the Northeast.

Numerous Separate Baptist congregations began as a result of controversy among Congregationalists. The most notable example of this phenomenon is the Separate Baptist church of which Isaac Backus was pastor. This congregation, which had begun as a New Light Congregational church in Middleborough, Massachusetts, in 1748, began to practice believer's baptism and eventually broke from the Congregationalists, becoming a Baptist church in 1756. Nearly half of the New Light Congregationalist churches eventually became Separate Baptists.

Separate Baptists differed from Regular Baptists in their passionate evangelism, mild Calvinism, and anticonfessionalism. The Separates, who allowed women to preach and resisted a learned and paid ministry, prefigured the Second Great Awakening* with their camp meetings and evangelistic invitations at the conclusion of worship services.

While the disparity between Separates and Regulars was stark in the middle of the eighteenth century, it subsided near the end of the century, when Separate Baptists strengthened their Calvinism (perhaps in reaction to the Arminianism* of the New England Freewill Baptists) and entered Regular Baptist associations. Most Separate Baptists in the South followed patterns similar to their northern counterparts, and Separate ministers such as Richard Furman became influential in Southern Baptist life. Others, having moved to open Communion and Arminian views, became Free Will Baptists.*

Some churches, however, retained their Separate Baptist identity and remained in distinct associations, especially in Kentucky, Tennessee, Indiana, and Illinois. These bodies merged in 1912 to form the General Association of Separate Baptist Churches and in 1975 united with the Christian Unity Association of North Carolina and Virginia. The present denomination is characterized by such original Separate traits as moderate Calvinism, footwashing, and anticonfessionalism. In 1982 the General Association comprised 100 churches with 8,984 members.

Bibliography. McBeth, H. L., *The Baptist Heritage* (Nashville: Broadman Press, 1987); Mead, F. S., and S. S. Hill, *Handbook of Denominations in the United States*, 8th ed. (Nashville: Abingdon Press, 1985); Torbet, R. G., *A History of the Baptists*, 3rd ed. (Valley Forge PA: Judson Press, 1973).

J. Matthew Pinson

Separation of Church and State. The phrase "separation of church and state" is a popularized version of a statement by Thomas Jefferson in a letter to three leaders of the Danbury Connecticut Baptist Association. In that 1802 letter President Jefferson described the first sixteen words of the First Amendment as "building a wall of separation between church and state." It is true that Roger Williams espoused and practiced church-state separation in seventeenth-century Rhode Island, but it was Jefferson's phrase that found an enduring place in American history.

The story began on October 7, 1801, when the three Baptists wrote an extremely cordial and admiring letter to Jefferson. He received it on December 30, 1801. It affirmed, "Our Sentiments are uniformly on the side of Religious Liberty—That Religion is at all times and places a matter between God and individuals . . . —That the legitimate Power of civil government extends no further than to punish the man who *works ill to his neighbor*." Sadly, they noted that in Connecticut "religion is considered as the first object of legislation; and therefore what religious privileges we enjoy (as a minor part of the State) we enjoy as favors granted and not as inalienable rights."

Moved by the letter's sentiments, the president drafted a response with a desire to offer his views on the subject raised by the Baptists. He sent it to Attorney General Levi Lincoln, requesting that "he examine the answer and suggest any alteration which might prevent an ill effect, or promote a good one, among the people." Lincoln replied on the same date, making several suggestions that Jefferson heeded when he composed the final draft that was sent to the Danbury Baptists on January 1, 1802.

Jefferson wrote, "The affectionate sentiments of esteem and approbation you are so good as to express towards me, on behalf of the Danbury Baptist Association, give me the highest satisfaction." Jefferson then turned to the association's concerns, stating, "Believing with you that religion is a matter which lies solely between man and his God, that he owes account to none other for his faith or his worship, that the legislative powers of government reach actions only, and not opinions, I contemplate with sovereign reverence that act of the whole American people which declared that their legislature should 'make no law respecting an establishment of religion, or prohibiting the free exercise thereof,' thus building a wall of separation between church and state.''

In 1879 Jefferson's phrase was employed by the Supreme Court in *Reynolds v. United States* to facilitate the admission of Utah to the union. Judicially, there was then a lull until several Court rulings from 1943 to 1952 (*Barnette, Everson, McCollum, Zorach*) in which Jefferson's description was freely employed to buttress significant church-state decisions. This triggered a civilized scholarly debate over the validity of such use of Jefferson's words.

However, when Justice Hugo Black cited Jefferson's phrase in the *Engel* prayer decision of 1962, many opponents of Black's opinion found fault with his use of the metaphor. Concurrent with this growing debate, many opponents of the Court's direction of thinking on church-state issues made a concerted effort either to discredit Jefferson or to rewrite history. Frequently both strategies were employed simultaneously.

Justice William Rehnquist in his dissent in *Wallace v. Jaffree* (1985) claimed that the metaphor was bad history and should be abandoned. He made much of the fact that Jefferson was in Paris when the religion clauses were adopted by Congress in 1789. Rehnquist conveniently ignored the fact that there were thirty-six letters exchanged between Jefferson and James Madison from 1787 to 1789. Further, much of that correspondence focused on whether there should be a Bill of Rights, with Jefferson seeking to convince Madison of the necessity of such a document. Finally, passage of Jefferson's Virginia Statute on Religious Freedom was accomplished by Madison in 1786. When Jefferson critics argue that the ''separation'' phrase was in some way unique to the sage of Monticello, they ignore a lifetime of Madison's writing that affirms exactly the same sentiment, most dramatically in a letter to Robert Walsh in 1819: ''Whilst the number, the industry, and the morality of the Priesthood, and the devotion of the people have been manifestly increased by the total separation of the Church from the State.''

Bibliography. Alley, Robert S., ''Public Education and the Public Good,'' *William and Mary Bill of Rights Journal*, 4, no. 1 (Summer 1995) 277–350; Hunt, Gaillard, *The Writings of James Madison*, vol. 8 (New York. G. P. Putnam, 1910); Jefferson Papers, Library of Congress, reel 25, document 20592; Levy, Leonard, *The Establishment Clause: Religion and the First Amendment* (New York: Macmillan, 1986); Petersen, Merrill, ed., *Thomas Jefferson: Writings* (New York: Library of America, 1984).

Robert S. Alley

Serpent Handling. The contemporary practice of serpent handling began around 1910 in southeastern Tennessee. Its most well-known early advocate was a charismatic preacher, George Went Hensley, who for a time was associated with the Pentecostal*-oriented Church of God. The practice spread rather quickly in parts of Tennessee, Alabama, Georgia, the Carolinas, Kentucky, and West Virginia, largely through the itinerant preaching of Hensley. Today many who handle serpents in the context of worship are second- and third-generation practitioners.

Serpent handlers base their practice in part on a literal interpretation of Mark 16:17–18, which indicates that five signs follow believers: casting out devils, speaking in tongues, faith healing, taking up serpents, and drinking deadly substances. Serpent handling became associated with glossolalia,* ingestion of strychnine, fire handling, and healing.

Hensley and his associates argued that Scripture demanded that believers appropriate God's power in visible ways. Not all persons who attend congregations where serpent handling occurs engage in the practice; nor do those who handle serpents do so every time serpents are present. Some adherents insist that spiritual anointing must create an ethos conducive to affirming faith before serpents are handled. Others handle by faith alone.

Controversy surrounded the practice from the first. Some who shared the Pentecostal style believed that the practice represented a misappropriation of spiritual gifts because it seemed to glorify individuals rather than promote the welfare of all. Others claimed that the practice tempted Christ with human arrogance. Some supporters have seen the ability to handle serpents as a sign to unbelievers of the necessity to repent.

From the beginning, many critics expressed concern when practitioners were bitten. Most practitioners refuse medical treatment for such bites. While many reported that no harm came from the venom, several died; Hensley himself died after being bitten in 1955. Renewed controversy came in the summer of 1995 when a young mother died after being bitten while handling snakes in worship.

Debates have ensued as to whether harmful bites result when practitioners lack faith in or are not protected by spiritual anointing. Some who handle by faith alone believe that Scripture only decrees that believers take up serpents; it does not promise that the serpents will not bite.

Controversy has also marked interpretation of the practice. Because biblical scholars question the authenticity of the current ending of Mark, many reject its authority for endorsing the practice. Handlers also use other texts (such as Luke 10:19) to justify their views.

For a time, sociologists linked the practice to deprivation theory. Because practitioners lacked economic, political, and social status, it was assumed that they found in serpent handling a power superior to anything in the larger social order. Few today accept this appraisal.

Freudian interpreters have classified serpent handling as religious psychopathic behavior, suggesting that the serpents represent not only a repressed sexuality because snakes are seen as phallic symbols, but also the power of Satan. This view has also brought controversy.

Those attracted to a Jungian approach recognize that serpents may symbolize both the power of death and resurrection (life). Even analysts who recognize that serpent handling may be part of a coherent religious worldview and affirm its sacramental character insist that the practice symbolizes the confrontation with and triumph over death.

A more recent psychological approach has drawn on attributional theory to explain the plausibility of serpent handling. This understanding also affirms the powerful sexual symbolism in the practice, but emphasizes how the practice is a vivid acting out of the return of the repressed within an acceptable social context.

Yet another approach is to see serpent handling and its cognate practices as manifestations of ecstatic experience, of spiritual possession when one is seized by supernatural power that acts through the individual. When such power takes control, one may speak in tongues, handle serpents, or engage in other extraordinary behavior.

Beginning with Tennessee in 1947, states and communities began to outlaw the practice on the grounds that it endangers the general welfare. Today it is legal only in Georgia and West Virginia. Attempts at prosecution have raised issues of freedom of religious practice, particularly when adults participate willingly.

There is no reliable estimate of the number of serpent handlers in the United States today, but the practice will continue as long as there are believers who are convinced that the supernatural power of Christ will enable them to triumph here and now over the symbols of death and evil. They must act out what they believe.

Bibliography. Burton, T., *Serpent-handling Believers* (Knoxville: University of Tennessee Press, 1993); Daugherty, M. L., "Serpent-Handling as Sacrament," *Theology Today* 33, no. 3 (October 1976): 232–243; Hood, Ralph W., Jr., and D. L. Kimbrough, "Serpent Handling Holiness Sects: Theoretical Considerations," *Journal for the Scientific Study of Religion* 34 (September 1995): 311–322; Kimbrough, D. L., *Taking Up Serpents: Snake Handlers of Eastern Kentucky* (Chapel Hill: University of North Carolina Press, 1995); LaBarre, W., *They Shall Take Up Serpents* (Minneapolis: University of Minnesota Press, 1962).

Charles Lippy

Seventh-Day Adventism. Seventh-Day Adventism is an indigenous American religious movement with a current membership of well over five million, including a vast majority of membership living outside of North America. The controversies associated with Seventh-Day Adventism are rooted in its earliest beginnings as an apocalyptic movement. When William Miller's* predictions concerning the end of the world and the Second Coming of Christ failed to materialize in October 1844, Ellen Harmon White and others reinterpreted Miller's prophecies and nurtured a new religious movement growing out of the despair associated with the so-called Great Disappointment. At the time of its beginning, Adventism* represented a dissident protest to the generally positive 1840s belief in the promise of America to redeem the world. Many Adventists identified America as one of the evil forces opposing the Christian saints described in the Book of Revelation. Thus the movement offered a pessimistic and contradictory alternative to the civil religious optimism so prevalent in America at the time.

Though controversy between the Adventists and civil religious themes in the nation has never been heated, it has arisen on occasion. Presidential appointment of an ambassador to the Vatican, for example, usually caused it to surface. However, by far the most serious controversies in this area have resulted from the national commitment to Sunday as a day of rest. The Adventists' belief in a Saturday Sabbath directly challenged a central tenet of the American civil religion. Seventh-Day Adventists strongly opposed repeated efforts throughout the late nineteenth century, and again during the 1950s, to spread legislation mandating Sunday as a day of rest, legislation commonly referred to as "blue laws." Occasionally dragged into court due to violation of these laws, Adventists have used the First Amendment, often unsuccessfully, to defend their right to deviate from the nation's Sunday laws. The Sabbatarian position of the Adventists has created controversy with Christian groups as well, especially those who have understood the culture's proper Sunday observance as an essential component of efforts to Christianize the American people. Finally, Adventists have generally taken a noncombatant stance toward American conflicts. They formulated this position early in their history as the nation faced the Civil War. Unlike some religious groups, Adventists were not opposed to serving in noncombatant positions. For this reason, controversy associated with noncombatancy never reached serious proportions. The establishment of its highly regarded Medical Cadet Corps Training Program during World War II helped normalize the movement's position on war.

Admired for their contributions to health care in America, the Seventh-Day Adventists faced criticism in 1984 when an Adventist surgeon used a baboon's heart to replace the heart of a dying twelve-day-old girl in a ground-breaking surgery. The baby girl died within three weeks. Media, animal rights activists, and some medical professionals questioned the decision by Loma Linda University Medical Center officials to allow the procedure. Controversy surrounding this event was strengthened by the Adventist tendency to work within closed circles rather than to seek scientific support from other members of the medical community.

Doctrinal controversy within Adventism, between Adventists and evangelicals, and within evangelicalism has arisen in more recent years. Most of this controversy resulted from the increasing dialogue between Adventists and evangelicals since the late 1950s. Before that decade most evangelical Christian groups referred to Seventh-Day Adventism as a cult or, less charitably, as a heresy. Controversy resulted when Walter R. Martin, an evangelical scholar well known for his work on cults, declared Adventism a Christian denomination.

Near the same time, Adventist leadership published a document entitled *Questions on Doctrine* that defended a basic evangelical position on issues like salvation while repudiating traditional Adventist beliefs in other areas, such as the notion that latter-day Christians could achieve a state of sinlessness. While this new form of evangelical Adventism increasingly represents Adventist leadership, controversy remains as traditional and even more liberal factions within Adventism continue to vie for followers.

Bibliography. Bull, M., and K. Lockhart, *Seeking a Sanctuary: Seventh-Day Adventism and the American Dream* (San Francisco: Harper and Row, Publishers, 1989); Gaustad, E. S., *The Rise of Adventism: Religion and Society in Mid-Nineteenth-Century America* (New York: Harper and Row, 1974); Land, Gary, ed, *Adventism in America: A History* (Grand Rapids, MI: William B. Eerdmans Publishing Company, 1986); Martin, W. R., *The Truth about Seventh-Day Adventism* (Grand Rapids, MI: Zondervan, 1960); Numbers, R. L., and J. M. Butler, eds., *The Disappointed: Millerism and Millenarianism in the Nineteenth Century* (Bloomington: Indiana University Press, 1987); Syme, E., *A History of SDA Church-State Relations in the United States* (Mountain View, CA: Pacific Press Publishing Association, 1973).

Mark G. Toulouse

Shakers. Shakers is the popular name for the United Society of Believers in Christ's Second Coming, a charismatic group originating in England in the 1740s, also known as the Millennial Church, Children of Truth, and Alethians (from the Greek word for truth). The group developed a celibate communal lifestyle, downplaying materialism, condemning most ecclesiastical practices, and emphasizing spiritual gifts.

The initial impulse for Shakerism came from the arrival in London in 1706 of several French "prophets" proclaiming an end-time message. From the turmoil that their preaching stirred up emerged a group led by James and Jane Wardley, characterized by noisy meetings in which members were seized by "Ecstatick Fits." By the 1770s an illiterate young woman named Ann Lee was playing a prominent role in this group. Lee and others were arrested several times before she led eight followers to America in 1774.

Shakers revered Lee simply as Mother and regarded her as a second incarnation of Christ. Her revelations and sayings were accorded virtual canonical status. Few of the first generation of Shakers, known as the First Witnesses, were literate, so great stress was placed on oral teaching and its oral transmission. The lack of written sources from this formative period makes it difficult to study the group's origins. Extant biographical accounts and collections of the founders' sayings come from a later period and thus are extremely hagiographic.

Lee settled her group near Albany, New York, where the New Light revival movement was starting. Interest in "spirit-filled" groups ran high, and the Shakers attracted several thousand converts. They also gained enemies because of their opposition to the Revolutionary War (on the basis of their pacifism) and what many saw as their threat to established churches. Lee made several successful missionary journeys through New York and New England. After her death in 1784 Joseph Meacham and Lucy Wright assumed leadership and established the communitarian pattern for which Shakers became famous, formalized in the Millennial Laws of 1821. The entire society was overseen by the central ministry at New Lebanon, New York, a group of two men and two women who appointed ministers to supervise the various villages. Each village typically contained two "families" of thirty persons each. Each family had a large house with separate entrances and sleeping quarters for men and women. The families' business affairs were overseen by deacons and deaconesses responsible to the ministers.

By 1840 the group numbered about six thousand members, with eighteen villages in eight states. With their social and gender egalitarianism, the Shakers drew from all quarters of society. After the Civil War their numbers declined. Frederick Evans and other leaders in the 1870s tried to reverse this trend, beginning the *Shaker* magazine and making speaking tours in America and England, but by 1905 there were only a thousand members. As absolute numbers declined, the percentage of female members rose dramatically, reaching 88 percent in 1936. By the 1990s the number of Shakers was under a dozen, mostly elderly women, living at Sabbathday Lake, Maine, the only surviving village. Friends and admirers help with maintenance chores or offer financial support.

Shakers stressed celibacy, public confession of sins, spiritual gifts, and a spirit of unity. Harmony, however, did not always prevail within the sect. In the 1830s and 1840s, for example, a number of young Shakers, mostly women, began to receive visions in what is called the Era of Manifestations. The central ministry tried to enforce order. Tensions flared between eastern and western villages, between young and old, and between males and females. Even as late as 1965 disagreement broke out between the Sabbathday Lake family and the central ministry in Canterbury, New Hampshire, when the central ministry tried to prohibit any new members from joining the society, in response to the presence at Sabbathday Lake of newcomer Theodore Johnson, who hoped to revive Shakerism. The Shaker legacy is indelibly associated with their craft work. For two centuries they dedicated themselves to a simple, thrifty lifestyle. In addition to a distinctive style of furniture, they invented such things as the circular saw, a threshing machine, and the clothespin. They were the first to package and sell seeds.

Bibliography. Brewer, Priscilla, *Shaker Communities, Shaker Lives* (Hanover, NH: University Press of New England, 1986); Campion, Nardi, *Mother Ann Lee: Morning Star of the Shakers* (Hanover, NH: University Press of New England, 1976); Desroche, Henri, *The American Shakers: From Neo-Christianity to Presocialism* (Amherst, MA: University of Massachusetts Press, 1971); Morse, Flo, *The Shakers and the World's People* (Hanover, NH: University Press of New England, 1980); Stein, Stephen J., *The Shaker Experience in America: A History of the United Society of Believers* (New Haven: Yale University Press, 1992); Whitson, Robley, *The Shakers: Two Centuries of Spiritual Reflection* (New York: Paulist Press, 1983).

Albert A. Bell, Jr.

Sheen, Fulton J. Archbishop, educator, and radio and television personality. Fulton J. Sheen was born in El Paso, Illinois, on May 8, 1895, the son of Newton Morris Sheen and Delia Fulton Sheen. Sheen was baptized Peter but later took the maiden name of his mother. He was educated at local Catholic elementary and high schools in Peoria, received his A.B. degree from St. Viator's College in Bourbonnais, Illinois, and then entered St. Paul's Seminary in St. Paul, Minnesota. He was ordained a priest of the Diocese of Peoria on September 20, 1919. After ordination he continued his studies at the Catholic University of America, the Sorbonne, the Collegio Angelico in Rome, and the Catholic University of Louvain in Belgium, where he earned a doctorate and the prestigious *agrégé en philosophie* in 1925.

After a year of pastoral work in his home diocese of Peoria, in 1926 Sheen joined the faculty of the Catholic University of America, where he remained until 1950, teaching courses on the philosophy of religion. He was also the author of some seventy books, most of them of a devotional or apologetic nature. While a professor at the Catholic University of America, Sheen also became a highly regarded preacher, frequently appearing in the pulpit of St. Patrick's Cathedral in New York City. In 1930 he began a highly popular Sunday-afternoon radio broadcast on the "Catholic Hour" of NBC Radio; in 1951 he repeated that success with an even more popular television series called "Life Is Worth Living." Sheen also became a well-known figure because of the number of prominent people whom he received into the Catholic Church, such as journalist Heywood Broun and Clare Boothe Luce.

In 1950 Sheen left the Catholic University of America to become the national director of the Society for the Propagation of the Faith, a fund-raising organization for Catholic missionary activities. The following year he was made an auxiliary bishop of New York. Sheen was highly successful as a fund-raiser, but he clashed with Francis Cardinal Spellman of New York over the financial policies of the Society for the Propagation of the Faith. In 1966 Sheen was made bishop of Rochester, New York, a post for which he had neither training nor experience. After three unhappy years Sheen resigned and was made the titular archbishop of Newport. He returned to New York City, where he continued to write and preach until his death in that city on December 9, 1979.

Bibliography. Fields, Kathleen Riley, "Bishop Fulton J. Sheen: An American Catholic Response to the Twentieth Century," (Ph.D. diss., University of Notre Dame, 1988); Noona, Daniel P., *The Passion of Fulton Sheen* (New York: Dodd, Mead, 1972); Sheen, Fulton J., *Treasure in Clay: The Autobiography of Fulton J. Sheen* (Garden City, NY: Doubleday, 1980).

Thomas J. Shelley

Shuttlesworth, Fred Lee. Fred Lee Shuttlesworth, born on March 18, 1922, was the controversial civil rights* minister of Birmingham, Alabama, whose organization, the Alabama Christian Movement for Human Rights (ACMHR) set the stage for massive protest demonstrations in 1963. As much as anyone in the national civil rights movement, Shuttlesworth, pastor of the Bethel Baptist

Church, inspired support for the struggle in Birmingham and the South by an almost legendary eagerness to sacrifice his life in defiance of Jim Crow. For this reason Martin Luther King, Jr.,* called him "one of the nation's most courageous freedom fighters." After founding the ACMHR in June 1956, Shuttlesworth survived a Christmas Eve bombing of his home. Thus convinced that God was directing his involvement in civil rights, he insisted that other ministers join the fight. With his visceral impatience with anyone who did not share his commitment or his timetable, he often clashed with black middle-class ministers and professionals, as well as with his principal antagonist, Birmingham's commissioner of public safety, Eugene "Bull" Connor.

Leading up to the 1963 demonstrations, Shuttlesworth provided constant agitation and confrontation to segregation in Birmingham. He urged King to throw a national spotlight on the Magic City through a massive direct-action campaign. King and the Southern Christian Leadership Conference* decided to go to Birmingham because of Shuttlesworth's direct invitation and because of a cadre of available demonstrators Shuttlesworth's organization had developed over the previous seven years. After the demonstrations President John F. Kennedy, introducing national civil rights legislation, said, "If it was not for Birmingham, we would not be here today." But for the combative Shuttlesworth, those demonstrations would likely not have been so successful.

Bibliography. Branch, Taylor, *Parting the Waters: America in the King Years, 1954–1963* (New York: Simon and Schuster, 1987); King, Martin Luther, Jr., *Why We Can't Wait* (New York: Harper, 1964).

Andrew M. Manis

Sixteenth Street Baptist Church. One of the best known African-American churches in Birmingham, Alabama, Sixteenth Street Baptist Church became a symbol for the civil religious conflict over segregation in the South when its edifice was dynamited in 1963. Situated in downtown Birmingham, the church was the spiritual home for a congregation of mostly middle-class, professional persons who participated very little in civil rights* agitation. In fact, its longtime minister, the Reverend Luke Beard, had expressed great caution over the new movement. This changed somewhat under the ministry of John Cross, a younger minister who arrived in Birmingham in 1962. As pastor, he allowed the church to serve as headquarters for massive protest demonstrations against Jim Crow in the spring of 1963. Led by Martin Luther King, Jr.'s,* Southern Christian Leadership Conference* and Fred Shuttlesworth's* Alabama Christian Movement for Human Rights, legions of African Americans launched their protest marches into the downtown business district from Sixteenth Street Baptist Church. Marked by dramatic television footage of segregationist resistance in the form of police dogs and firehoses, the demonstrations precipitated the national Civil Rights Act of 1964, which desegregated public accommodations throughout the country.

Southern segregationist fanaticism ultimately struck in September 1963, one week after white public schools in Birmingham were first integrated. On Sunday morning, September 15, an estimated fifteen sticks of dynamite virtually destroyed the building and killed four young girls as they studied a Sunday school lesson on "The Love That Forgives." From 1951 through 1963 there had been some thirty-one bombings of African-American homes or churches in Birmingham. Such attempts on churches, however, had never occurred during services or had any fatalities. The victims, Denise McNair, aged eleven, and Cynthia Wesley, Carole Robertson, and Addie Mae Collins, all aged fourteen, collectively became martyrs for the civil rights movement. Their deaths sparked further activism among blacks and gradually weakened massive resistance to integration among southern whites. In a celebrated trial twenty-five years later, Ku Klux Klan member Robert E. Chambliss was convicted of the murders.
Bibliography. Branch, Taylor, *Parting the Waters: America in the King Years, 1954–1963* (New York: Simon and Schuster, 1987); King, Martin Luther, Jr., *Why We Can't Wait* (New York: Harper, 1964).

Andrew M. Manis

Smith, Gerald L. K. Gerald Lyman Kenneth Smith was born on February 27, 1898, in Pardeeville, Wisconsin, about thirty-five miles south of Madison. From a devout farm family with a strong Republican background, his father was both a salesman and a preacher. At the age of seven Gerald accepted Christ and five years later announced plans to go into the ministry. Upon leaving high school in 1915, he attended Valparaiso University in Indiana. He graduated in 1918, and volunteered for the army, but the war ended before he reported for duty. He returned to Wisconsin to begin a career as a successful minister of the Christian Church. While pastoring churches, he met Elna Sorenson and eventually persuaded her both to abandon Methodism* and marry him on June 22, 1922. Quite an orator, Smith received appointments at ever-larger churches and in 1929 took an assignment in Shreveport, Louisiana.

He soon fell under the spell of Huey P. Long, Louisiana's political boss. By 1934 Smith's association with Long had cost him his church pulpit. Long appointed Smith the national organizer for his Share Our Wealth Program, a scheme calling for the confiscation of wealth. Smith proved an effective speaker, and Long called him "next to me the greatest rabble rouser in the country." After Long's assassination in 1935, Smith served as the principal eulogist at his funeral. Smith tried to take over Long's machine, but Long's Louisiana cronies blocked this attempt. The next year, Smith joined with Father Charles Coughlin* and Francis Townsend to run an opponent to Franklin Roosevelt. Their candidate won a little less than 2 percent of the vote in a Democratic landslide.

For the next forty years Smith crusaded against American intervention in World War II, labor unions, communism, immigrants, the United Nations, racial equality, and the Jews. Smith failed to capture the Republican nomination for the U.S. Senate in Michigan in 1942. He garnered even fewer votes in his two runs for the presidency in 1944 and 1948. By the 1950s Smith quit the campaign hustings to become a spokesperson for anti-Semitism through his magazine, the *Cross and Flag*, published between 1942 and 1977.

Smith eventually settled in 1964 in Eureka Springs, a small town in the Arkansas Ozarks. There he established what he called his Sacred Projects, a giant statue of Christ of the Ozarks, a passion play, a Christ Only Art Gallery, and a Bible Museum. He died on April 15, 1976, and is buried on Magnetic Mountain, Arkansas.

Bibliography. Jeansonne, Glen, *Gerald L. K. Smith: Minister of Hate* (New Haven, CT: Yale University Press, 1988); Ribuffo, Leo P., *The Old Christian Right: The Protestant Far Right from the Great Depression to the Cold War* (Philadelphia.: Temple University Press, 1983).

James M. Woods

Smith, Henry Preserved. Henry Preserved Smith (1847–1927) was a Presbyterian biblical scholar, theological professor, and librarian. Born at Troy, Ohio, on October 23, 1847, Smith attended Marietta and Amherst colleges, graduating from the latter in 1869. After studying at Lane Theological Seminary,* he did graduate work at the University of Berlin under the mediating theologians Isaak Dorner, Hugo Kleinert, and Karl Semisch; he returned to the United States in 1874 without much change in his New School Presbyterian views. During an additional year (1876–1877) of study in Germany he studied at Leipzig with Franz Delitzsch and Christoph Luthardt. While relatively conservative by German standards, Delitzsch and Luthardt nonetheless awakened in Smith a strong historical sense that led him increasingly into both textual- and historical-critical issues. Having accepted a professorship at Lane, where he taught Old Testament, he began in 1882 to contribute to the emerging debate in the northern Presbyterian Church over biblical criticism. Siding with Charles A. Briggs* of Union Theological Seminary* and other emerging "higher critics," Smith nevertheless avoided direct confrontation with traditionalists in the denomination for a while. When Briggs's inaugural address of January 20, 1891, set off a firestorm among Presbyterians with its attacks on "bibliolatry," verbal inspiration, inerrancy, and prophecy as prediction, Smith sided with Briggs. That soon led to a confrontation with the Presbytery of Cincinnati, which in 1892 charged Smith with heresy. Convicted by the presbytery, Smith lost appeals to the Synod of Ohio (1893) and the General Assembly (1894). When the support of Lane's administration and trustees wavered, Smith resigned. He was without an official position from 1893 until 1898. During this period he wrote the volume on the books of Samuel in the *International Critical Commentary* (1899). In 1898 he joined the faculty of Amherst College and became a Congregationalist minister. From 1907 to 1913 he was on the faculty of the Meadville Theological School, and from 1913 to 1925 he was a member of the faculty and librarian of Union Theological Seminary. Among his better-known writings were *Inspiration and Inerrancy* (1893), *The Bible and Islam* (1897), *Old Testament History* (1903), *The Religion of Israel* (1914), and *Essays in Biblical Interpretation* (1921). He died on February 26, 1927.

Bibliography. Loetscher, Lefferts A., *The Broadening Church: A Study of Theological Issues in the Presbyterian Church since 1869* (Philadelphia: University of Pennsylvania Press, 1954); Smith, Henry Preserved, *The Heretic's Defense: A Footnote to History* (New York: Scribner's, 1926).

Donald L. Huber

Smith, Joseph, Jr. Joseph Smith, Jr., was born in Sharon, Vermont, on December 23, 1805, and died in Carthage, Illinois, on June 27, 1844. He was the son of Joseph Smith, Sr., and Lucy Mack Smith. He was the "translator" and publisher of the Book of Mormon, a sacred history of ancient America, as well as the author of a collection of subsequent revelations and sacred texts. On April 6, 1830, he founded the Church of Christ (later changed to Church of Jesus Christ of Latter-Day Saints*) in Fayette, New York. In a number of moves occasioned by both internal and external conflict, Smith led his followers from New York to Ohio, then to Missouri, and finally to Illinois, where in 1840 they established a thriving city-state, Nauvoo. Conflict with non-Mormon neighbors and internal dissension culminated in the assassination of Smith and his brother Hyrum by a mob on June 27, 1844, and the eventual expulsion of the Mormons from Illinois in 1846.

The controversies engendered by Smith's teachings can be summarized as follows: In its most essential form, conflict was a result of Smith's profoundly antipluralist convictions in a pluralistic age; of the belief that the restored Church of Christ was the only "true" church of Christ, with baptism* performed by all other churches being invalid; that the Book of Mormon was more true than the Bible; that Smith's other revelations were also Scripture, containing radical doctrines such as eternal progression, suggesting that humankind was God in embryo, and implying a plurality of Gods. Plural marriage was seen as a logical corollary of such beliefs. Economic cooperation was another source of conflict in an age of laissez-faire capitalism. Such principles could best be practiced if Mormons lived together and controlled their own society politically. To this end Smith established a theocratic kingdom of God, incompatible with American ideas of political pluralism. Smith's religious, economic, social, and political ideas were perceived as so radical that they led to violent opposition, both within the church and from the surrounding community, ending in his death. Many of these ideas and practices, including the theocratic kingdom and plural marriage, were later realized by Brigham Young and those Mormons who followed him to the Rocky Mountain West, establishing the headquarters of the Church of Jesus Christ of Latter-Day Saints in Salt Lake City. However, a significant number of Joseph Smith's disciples, rejecting theocracy and polygamy, sought alternative expressions of the faith in a number of Mormon churches and or-

ganizations, the most prominent of which is the Reorganized Church of Jesus Christ of Latter Day Saints* with headquarters in Independence, Missouri.
Bibliography. Brodie, Fawn M., *"No Man Knows My History": The Life of Joseph Smith, the Mormon Prophet* (New York: Alfred A. Knopf, 1945; 2nd ed., 1971); Brooke, John L., *The Refiner's Fire: The Making of Mormon Cosmology, 1644–1844* (New York: Cambridge University Press, 1994); Bushman, Richard L., *Joseph Smith and the Beginnings of Mormonism* (Urbana: University of Illinois Press, 1984); Hill, Donna, *Joseph Smith: The First Mormon* (Garden City, NY: Doubleday, 1977); Shipps, Jan, "The Prophet Puzzle: Suggestions Leading to a More Comprehensive Interpretation of Joseph Smith," *Journal of Mormon History* 1 (1974): 3–20.

Klaus J. Hansen

Social Gospel Movement. The Social Gospel movement emerged within American Protestantism during the late nineteenth and early twentieth centuries. It was a response to the harsh social and economic conditions that came with the industrialization and urbanization of American society.

The ideology and social systems of the Gilded Age were challenged as social Darwinism and laissez-faire capitalism were blamed for the human misery that prevailed among American workers. Specifically criticized were the ideology of radical individualism, the preference of capital over labor, and competition as the defining model for human relationships.

The Social Gospel movement also criticized much of the church of its day. With direct and frequent appeals to the Old Testament prophets and the teachings of Christ, the church was challenged to abandon an exclusively inner piety and to proclaim the Kingdom of God as present today in all social institutions.

A primary goal of the Social Gospel movement was to achieve within the economic system the same level of democracy that existed, at least in theory, in the political system. Concrete programs proposed included minimum wages, profit sharing, safe and dignified working conditions, and the elimination of child labor. Beyond these there was a push for equal educational opportunities through public education, public parks and recreational facilities, and international cooperation.

The most significant spokesperson for the movement was Walter Rauschenbusch (1861–1918) whose book *A Theology for the Social Gospel* (1917) was widely acclaimed as definitive. Other important figures were Josiah Strong (1847–1916), Washington Gladden (1836–1918), Shailer Mathews (1863–1941), George D. Herron (1862–1926), and Richard T. Ely (1854–1943), an economist with religious interests.

The two most important influences on the thought of the Social Gospelers seem to have been the "kingdom of God" ideas of nineteenth-century European theology and the spirit and goals of American progressivism. The preaching of Horace Bushnell* was significant. The developments in England's Christian socialism under the leadership of F. D. Maurice had their influence. The example and spirit of the antislavery movement inspired many. In general the "heady" optimism of this era provided a cultural wave that gave impetus to the movement. It is important to note, however, that none of the ideas of these contributors were adopted uncritically. For example, Rauschenbusch was careful to distinguish himself from much of the ideology of Christian socialism and to call for a recognition of human sinfulness.

The Social Gospel movement made significant contributions to the emergence of the American labor movement and the social policies of the New Deal. In addition, the ecumenical movement emerged in large measure around the central issues of and through the efforts of leaders in this movement. The Social Gospelers declined in prominence in the face of World Wars I and II and the emergence of Christian ideologies that put more stress on the sinfulness of humanity, for example, Neo-Orthodoxy and Christian realism.

Bibliography. Carter, Paul A., *The Decline and Revival of the Social Gospel* (Ithaca: Cornell University Press, 1956); Handy, Robert T., ed., *The Social Gospel in America 1870–1920* (New York: Oxford University Press, 1966); Hopkins, Howard Charles, *The Rise of the Social Gospel in American Protestantism 1865–1915* (New Haven, CT: Yale University Press, 1940); Visser 'T Hooft and Willem Adolph, *The Background of the Social Gospel in America* (St. Louis: Bethany Press, 1968).

Daniel B. McGee

Sophia Movement. The Sophia movement is a movement of Christian feminists in the 1990s honoring a female image of divine wisdom. In November 1993 in Minneapolis, a conference was held entitled "Re-Imagining." It was convened at the midpoint of the Ecumenical Decade: Churches in Solidarity with Women, designated by the World Council of Churches to follow the United Nations Decade for Women and call the attention of global religious communities to women's needs. "Re-Imagining" was attended by 2,300 women and men and sponsored by a cluster of Catholic and Protestant groups, including Presbyterians, Methodists, Lutherans, American Baptists, and the United Church of Christ.

According to conference organizers, re-imagining theology was needed to reinvigorate the church and nourish women's and men's spirituality. Over four days, participants attended worship services, workshops, plays, concerts, and plenary sessions. Speakers included well-known womanist, mujerista, feminist, and Asian women theologians. Workshops were held on Jesus, creation, church, language, arts, ethics, ministry, and sexuality. At one session, more than one hundred lesbians received a standing ovation as they gathered on the dais. At another, participants shared a ritual meal of milk and honey and sang chants to Sophia as mother, creator, and guide. Organizers hoped that the conference "will challenge and expand our horizons in undreamed-of ways, will enrich and nurture us spiritually, and will provide the opportunity to dialogue with women and men from around the world."

They were right on one point: the Re-imagining Conference generated an undreamed-of hurricane of controversy. It was attacked as heretical, blasphemous, and destructive of Christian faith. News reports circulated that during the conference a pagan goddess Sophia was worshipped, milk and honey were substituted for the Eucharistic bread and wine, and "lesbian love-making" was openly affirmed. Evangelical coalitions in the Presbyterian Church USA (PCUSA) and the United Methodist Church decried the allocation of denominational funds for sponsorship and threatened to withhold further contributions. They called for denominational employees who attended to be fired. Mary Ann Lundy,* PCUSA executive and conference organizer, was forced to resign, and the 1994 PCUSA General Assembly condemned the conference as violating Reformed theology. Besides the Presbyterians, Methodist, Lutheran, and American Baptist denominational representatives distanced themselves from the conference. The secular press picked up the story.

Although the backlash was a surprise, conference organizers and participants quickly denounced it as inaccurate. They explained that Sophia was no pagan goddess, but an ancient Judeo-Christian concept. In the Hebrew Bible and Apocrypha, Sophia denoted the wisdom aspect of God and was portrayed as a woman; in Christian Scriptures, Jesus was described in similar language as Sophia. Sophia was reclaimed as a liberative, empowering image for women. Participants declared that the conference enabled them to affirm their identities as women, nourish their spiritual lives, and celebrate their oneness in Christ. Stressing that their aim was reformation, not destruction of the church, they suggested that conservatives were threatened by women claiming the authority to re-imagine Christianity. The issue was not heresy, but power. They declared their right to lift up the Christian tradition as healing, just, and opposed to sexism, racism,* violence, and homophobia.

The Sophia movement continues. A second conference, Re-Imagining II, was held in October 1994 in Minneapolis, and another is planned. In June 1995 a group of Presbyterians formed Voices of Sophia to advocate feminist concerns. The Sophia movement symbolizes the mainstreaming of Christian feminism. Feminists have gained increasing visibility and leadership in mainline Euro-American, Protestant denominations. Yet the intense hostility toward it indicates that patriarchy remains well entrenched. Conservatives believe that political and theological liberalism* is rife in mainline Protestantism, an extremism led by women. The Sophia movement is a lightning rod of the conflict between Christian feminism and the New Religious Right.

Bibliography. Dimon, Karen, ed., "Re-Imagining," *Church and Society* 84 (May–June 1994): 5–135; Edwards, James R., "Earthquake in the Mainline," *Christianity Today* 38 (November 14, 1994): 38–43; Heim, David, ed., "Evaluating Re-Imagining," *Christian Century* 111 (April 6, 1994): 339–44; "Re-imagining: The Ecumenical Decade, Churches in Solidarity with Women" (Conference program, Minneapolis, MN, November 4–7, 1993); Wylie-Kellerman, Jeanie, ed., "Women's Spirituality in the Church and Beyond," *Witness* 77 (July 1994): 5–24, 26–29, 32–34, 38–39.

Evelyn A. Kirkley

Southeastern Baptist Theological Seminary. The Seminary of the Southern Baptist Convention (SBC)*, located in Wake Forest, North Carolina, was founded in 1951 and taken over in 1987 by fundamentalists in the denomination.

At first, the Southeastern Baptist Theological Seminary (SEBTS) shared the campus of Wake Forest College. In 1956, when the college moved to new facilities in Winston-Salem, North Carolina, the seminary began to expand under its first president, Sydnor Stealey. Soon SEBTS gained a reputation as an open and progressive seminary. Despite occasional protests from conservatives, the seminary grew to an enrollment of over 1,200 students and a faculty of forty by 1986.

During the fundamentalist takeover of the SBC after 1979 all the seminaries became important targets, but none more than SEBTS. When enough conservative members had been appointed, the seminary's Board of Trustees voted, 15 to 10, in a tumultous meeting in the fall of 1987 to require strict adherence to the principle of biblical inerrancy among future recruits to the faculty and to institute a new hiring procedure. The president, and not a faculty committee, would recommend new faculty to the Board. President Randall Lolley resigned, followed by Morris Ashcraft, Dean of the Faculty. The Board appointed Lewis Drummond as the new president. The faculty responded by organizing an American Association of University Professors (AAUP) chapter and hiring an attorney. Some alumni expressed their dismay over the situation by tearing up their degrees and mailing them back to the school; alumni contributions dropped dramatically.

Other Baptist educational institutions faced similar problems. At the other seminaries, the only schools controlled directly by the SBC, faculty did not object so vigorously to the new requirements. On the state level, some colleges and universities—Baylor and Furman, for example—took steps to dissociate themselves from the state conventions or to amend their bylaws so that a majority of their trustees were appointed by their own boards rather than by the state Baptist Conventions.

Early in 1989 the Southern Association of Colleges and Schools (SACS), an accrediting agency, criticized SEBTS' trustees for ''arbitrarily infringing upon the established traditions of the school.'' The basic issue, in SACS' view, was ''that the procedures for amending the bylaws have not been followed, and that published statements do not accord with present practice.'' The trustees were giving lip service to academic freedom while doing everything in their power to undercut it. The school was given until the year's end to resolve its internal problems without sanctions being imposed. In the spring of 1989 the AAUP voted unanimously to censure SEBTS because the trustees had imposed a creedal stance on the faculty and had excluded them from the hiring of new colleagues. The new Dean of the Faculty, L. Russell Bush III, had even been hired over the faculty's unanimous opposition.

Between 1989–1991, as enrollments declined, the faculty tried to reach some accommodation with the trustees, but without success. In a faculty meeting in March of 1991 President Drummond called for "theological integrity" on the part of the faculty. Soon thereafter the Board of Trustees began an investigation of the faculty's theological positions. A number of faculty resigned or accepted early retirement. Some joined a new seminary started in Richmond by moderate Baptists who had organized as the Alliance of Baptists. Student enrollment at SEBTS dropped by over 50 percent, with fewer than twenty faculty.

By the summer of 1991 both SACS and the Association of Theological Schools (ATS) placed the seminary on "warning" status because the Board of Trustees continued to exclude faculty from the governance and hiring processes. In December of that year SACS placed the school on probation. The ATS took the same action in the fall of 1992.

Paige Patterson, a prime mover in the fundamentalist takeover of the SBC, became president of SEBTS in the summer of 1992. Enough new faculty had been recruited that the tenor of the school had changed and protests diminished. Probations were lifted in 1994, and enrollments began to recover enough that the administration could deny there had been a problem. The seminary's alumni directory merely noted in 1992 that "after 14 years of excellent leadership, Dr. Lolley resigned as president."

Bibliography. Bland, Thomas A., ed., *Servant Songs: Reflections on the History and Mission of Southeastern Baptist Theological Seminary, 1950–1988* (Macon, GA: Smyth and Helwys, 1994); Hester, Richard, "AAUP Censures Southeastern Seminary." *Christian Century* 106 (1989): 742–744; Shurden, Walter, ed., *The Struggle for the Soul of the SBC: Moderate Reponses to the Fundamentalist Movement* (Macon, GA: Mercer University Press, 1993); Willimon, William H., "Southeastern Seminary: Fundamentalists Move In," *Christian Century* 104 (1987): 1020–1021; Wingfield, Mark, "Seminary Given Until December to Correct Hiring Policy," *Christianity Today* 33 (February 3, 1989): 54–55.

Albert A. Bell, Jr.

Southern Baptist Convention. The Southern Baptist Convention (SBC) was founded in 1845 as a direct result of a Baptist controversy over the appointment of slaveholding missionaries. During the early nineteenth century Baptists* in America, who united in various foreign and home missionary societies, sought to remain neutral on the slavery question, insisting that it was a political, not a religious, issue. With the growth of the abolitionist movement and southern defense of certain "sectional" practices, the scene was set for confrontation. In 1845 Georgia Baptists presented the Triennial Convention, the national missionary society of the Baptist denomination in the United States, with the name of James Reeve, a known slaveholder, as a candidate for missionary service. When the missionary society rejected the appointment, Southerners met in Augusta, Georgia, in May 1845 to organize a new convention. The convention implicitly supported the right of Americans to hold slaves and explicitly affirmed the formation of the Confederate States of America.

Controversies over theology, polity, education, and social issues have impacted Southern Baptist life from the beginning. One of the earliest and most far-reaching involved the movement known as Old Landmarkism, evident in the denomination by 1859. Landmarkists, led by J. R. Graves* of Nashville, Tennessee, and J. M. Pendleton of Bowling Green, Kentucky, believed that Baptist churches constituted the only true church of Christ on earth and could trace their lineage in unbroken succession all the way back to Jesus' baptism by John the Baptist in the Jordan River. They insisted that Baptist churches alone possessed the "landmarks" of the true New Testament church, evident in congregational autonomy, immersion baptism of believers, the Lord's Supper as given only to members of a specific local congregation (closed Communion), and a true ministry in the church. Landmarkism itself began in a controversy over whether to invite pedobaptist ministers (those baptized as infants) to participate in Baptist worship services. In rejecting that possibility, Landmarkists set forth their belief that only Baptists could claim complete doctrinal affinity with the New Testament.

Controversy developed in the Southern Baptist Convention (SBC) over several Landmark issues. First, Landmarkers sought to make their doctrines normative for all churches that composed the SBC. They attempted to require Landmark definitions of all who would participate in the denomination. Second, although the convention ultimately rejected Landmarkism as normative for all its churches, significant elements of the movement, particularly ideas about baptism* and Communion, were utilized by many churches. Debates over open Communion, rebaptism of those who came from other Christian traditions, and the relationship of the denomination to the local church created significant controversy and division among Southern Baptists. In 1906, for example, a group of SBC churches in Arkansas left the convention, rejecting denominational organization as unbiblical and denouncing the SBC for failing to require Landmark beliefs of all participating churches.

In related controversies, William Whitsitt, president of the Southern Baptist Theological Seminary,* Louisville, Kentucky, was forced to resign his position in 1898 because his scholarly investigations challenged Landmark doctrines. Whitsitt correctly claimed that Baptists had not discovered immersion until the 1640s, some thirty years after their beginnings in Holland. Landmarkers, who believed that such practices had never been lost, demanded his resignation for heresy. Likewise, Tarlton Perry Crawford,* SBC missionary to China, created controversy with his suggestion that mission boards were not biblical and that only local churches should send out and support missionaries—another Landmark idea.

By the late nineteenth century Southern Baptists were also debating the relationship between personal evangelism and the developing Social Gospel. While most of the constituency promoted the need for personal evangelism as more imperative for the church than changing the social structures, there were some small but significant representatives of Social Christianity in the denomination.

In the early twentieth century controversies related to fundamentalism* and liberalism* also found their way into the SBC. In 1925 the denomination approved its first official confession of faith, the Baptist Faith and Message, as a basic doctrinal statement for its churches. In 1926 an effort was made to require all Baptist-related schools of higher education to reject the teaching of evolution in their classrooms. While a resolution was passed mandating such an action, it was never fully enforced on all (perhaps even most) schools.

Educational institutions frequently have been a battleground for Southern Baptists. Perhaps the most volatile issues centered on whether colleges and universities, supported by the state Baptist conventions, and seminaries, supported by the national denomination, were promoting orthodoxy in the classroom and in the writing and research of the professors. In the 1950s, for example, Ralph Elliott, a professor at Midwestern Baptist Theological Seminary in Kansas City, Missouri, published a book entitled *The Message of Genesis*,* in which he brought methods of biblical criticism to bear on the Genesis text. The book was published by Broadman Press, the national publishing house of the denomination. This led to debates over the issue at the annual meeting of the SBC and a call for a rescission of the work. Broadman Press, ceased publication of the book, and when Elliott refused to agree not to republish the work, he was fired from his position for insubordination.

Controversies accelerated in the denomination in the latter quarter of the twentieth century. Issues included the doctrine of biblical inerrancy as the primary theory of biblical inspiration for SBC schools and churches, the ordination of women* as pastors and deacons in Baptist churches, the denomination's response to abortion* and homosexuality,* and the appointment of trustees to denominational boards and agencies. In 1979 a long-term controversy began between convention fundamentalists and moderates over control of the denominational organization. Fundamentalist dominance of the convention led to numerous moderate reactions such as formation of new missionary agencies, seminaries, and publication houses, and redefining relationships between numerous state colleges and state Baptist conventions. Questions of the ordination of women, while left to the discretion of local churches, often created controversy and dismissal of churches from local associations of Baptist congregations who rejected the ordination of females in the church. While these divisions produced no official schism by the end of the century, the denomination experienced significant fragmentation at almost every level of its organizational life.

Bibliography. Baker, Robert, *The Southern Baptist Convention and Its People* (Nashville: Broadman Press, 1972); Cothen, Grady, *What Happened to the Southern Baptist Convention?* (Macon, GA: Smyth and Helwys, 1993); Fletcher, Jesse, *The Southern Baptist Convention* (Nashville: Broadman and Holman Publishers, 1994); Leonard, Bill J.,

God's Last and Only Hope: The Fragmentation of the Southern Baptist Convention (Grand Rapids: Eerdmans, 1990).

Bill J. Leonard

Southern Baptist Theological Seminary. The Southern Baptist Theological Seminary was the first theological seminary to be founded by the Southern Baptist Convention.* The seminary was founded in 1859 to provide theological training for ministers in the Southern Baptist Convention, a denomination begun in 1845 after a controversy with northern Baptists over slavery and other sectional issues. Throughout its history the school has experienced numerous controversies, most related to the tension between academic investigation and Baptist orthodoxy. One of the earliest controversies surfaced in 1879 when Crawford Toy,* professor of Old Testament, began using certain critical methods of biblical studies in his classes at the seminary. Seminary president James P. Boyce was forced to ask Toy to desist or relinquish his teaching position. Toy resigned and later became professor of oriental languages at Harvard.

A second controversy descended on the seminary as a result of the writing of president and church history professor William Whitsitt. In a brief book entitled *A Question in Baptist History*,* published in 1896, Whitsitt documented his claim that Baptists had not begun to practice baptism* by total immersion until the year 1641, over thirty years after their beginnings in Holland and England. This assertion challenged the popular belief promoted by the Landmark movement that Baptists and Baptist-like churches had preserved immersion in an unbroken succession since the time of Jesus' baptism in the River Jordan. The Baptist constituency was divided in its response to Whitsitt and his findings. Early in the controversy trustees of the seminary supported the president and urged him to remain in his post. As the dispute deepened and some effort was made to eliminate denominational funding of the school, many advised him to resign for the sake of the institution. The divisions soon found their way into the churches, as potential pastors were required to state their position on the Whitsitt matter. Whitsitt resigned in 1898 to accept a position at Richmond College. His views were later accepted by the vast majority of Baptist scholars.

During the early twentieth century debates over the teaching of evolution created new controversy at Southern Baptist Theological Seminary and throughout the convention. In 1926 the convention passed a resolution that forbade the teaching of evolution as a valid perspective at Southern Baptist institutions of higher learning. Theologian E. Y. Mullins, president of the seminary, responded by refusing to accept the resolution. With the coming of the Depression, attention turned elsewhere and the resolution was not enforced.

In 1958 the seminary experienced a major controversy related less to theology than to administration of the school. When Duke K. McCall* became president in 1951 he brought a new administrative style to the office. Prior to McCall's era, seminary presidents were viewed primarily as "chairman of the faculty" with extensive faculty participation in administrative affairs. McCall's leadership style, based on a view of the president as chief executive officer, created controversy among the faculty. In 1958 thirteen faculty members, many of them senior professors, resigned in protest and urged the trustees to dismiss the president. The trustees refused and declared their support of McCall, calling upon the faculty members to return to their positions or be dismissed. When they refused, the thirteen professors were fired. The school confronted a crisis in morale and was placed on probation by its accrediting agency. McCall received extensive financial support from the Southern Baptist Convention and essentially rebuilt the faculty, remaining as president until 1982.

Like other agencies of the Southern Baptist Convention, the seminary was drawn into the controversy over biblical inerrancy and the effort of fundamentalists to gain control of denominational institutions. This conflict began in 1979 when fundamentalists commenced a successful effort to elect convention presidents who would appoint fundamentalists to trustee boards of every denominational agency. Since appointments were made over a period of years and since the southern seminary had over sixty board members, almost twice as many as most other SBC agencies, a fundamentalist majority was not in place until 1989. For years, perhaps since the 1920s, the convention's oldest seminary had been a target of conservatives who believed that it was a seedbed of liberalism* on such diverse issues as race, the Social Gospel, the use of certain methods of biblical criticism in studying Scripture, and the writings of many of its widely published faculty.

When fundamentalist-oriented trustees gained a majority on the board of trustees, they began to promote policies that moved the school toward a more conservative agenda. In 1990 trustee Jerry Johnson issued a document that alleged that certain members of the faculty, including President Roy L. Honeycutt, were guilty of varying heresies including universalism, questioning certain elements of Scripture, and supporting various liberal social agendas. The faculty responded by defending all those charged by Johnson and organizing a Faculty Association to negotiate with trustees. That same year trustees declared that all hiring, tenure, and promotion would be based on conservative responses to certain doctrinal positions. These included the belief that Adam and Eve were real, not mythic, individuals, affirmation of the historicity of Jesus' miracles as recorded in the Gospels, and other conservative doctrinal ideals. Faculty charged that trustees were acting illegally in adding requirements to existing contracts and called upon the Association of Theological Schools, the seminary's accrediting agency, to investigate. A faculty-trustees negotiating committee was organized, and a Covenant of Renewal was developed. The covenant removed the previous trustee mandate while requiring that all new faculty subscribe to conservative dogmas regarding the inerrancy of Scripture.

Controversy continued with Honeycutt's retirement and the election of Albert Mohler as president in 1993. A staunch conservative and advocate of Calvinism,

Mohler worked with trustees in encouraging the departure of less conservative faculty. In 1994 he was instrumental in securing the resignation of Molly Marshall,* associate professor of theology, charging her with violating the school's doctrinal statement, or Abstract of Principles, a charge that Marshall denied. In 1995 he fired Diana Garland, dean of the School of Social Work, in a dispute over hiring new faculty who would be required to repudiate the ordination of women* to pastoral ministry. Garland had argued that specific views of faculty regarding the ordination of women were not required by the Abstract of Principles.

The controversy over fundamentalism* had perhaps the most significant impact on the Southern Baptist Theological Seminary of any in its history. Between 1990 and 1995 the school lost more than 70 percent of its faculty and 40 percent of its student body.

Bibliography. Ammerman, Nancy, *Baptist Battles* (New York: Rutgers University Press, 1990); Leonard, Bill J., *God's Last and Only Hope: The Fragmentation of the Southern Baptist Convention* (Grand Rapids, MI: William Eerdmans Publishing Company, 1990); Mueller, William, *A History of the Southern Baptist Theological Seminary* (Nashville: Broadman Press, 1958).

Bill J. Leonard

Southern Christian Leadership Conference. In light of the success of the Montgomery bus boycott of 1955–1956, Martin Luther King, Jr.,* and several black ministers founded the Southern Christian Leadership Conference (SCLC) in 1957 at Ebenezer Baptist Church in Atlanta. As an organization advocating the nonviolent passive resistance philosophy, SCLC became one of the leading civil rights* organizations during the 1950s and 1960s. With King as president, SCLC rivaled the more established civil rights organizations such as the NAACP* and the National Urban League. Some of its major activities included the March on Washington in 1963 and the march from Selma to Montgomery in 1965. SCLC also was a major force pushing for the passage of the Civil Rights Act in 1964 and the Voting Rights Act in 1965. The organization served as the platform for the rise of several other black leaders such as Andrew Young and Jesse L. Jackson* after King's assassination in 1968.

But a by-product of SCLC's activities as a civil rights organization was its work as the major black ecumenical organization of the period. As early as 1933, Carter G. Woodson had lamented that if there was any area in which African Americans had the opportunity to exercise complete freedom, it was within the black church, because the black church was a completely autonomous entity. Instead, black ministers had chosen to emulate their former white masters in accepting sectarianism. With the start of the civil rights movement in the 1950s, the situation had caused African-American churches still to be split primarily along sectarian lines.

However, there were some black efforts toward ecumenism, which were led by African Methodist Episcopal Bishop Reverdy C. Ransom, who founded the Fraternal Council of Negro Churches in 1934. In the 1940s and 1950s Ransom was succeeded by William H. Jernigan, a prominent Baptist. The Washington Bureau of the Fraternal became an important lobby for the black church's economic and political concerns. Yet in 1950, with the establishment of the National Council of Churches* and the rise of the civil rights movement, the Fraternal Council discontinued operating.

Replacing the Fraternal Council as the leader of black ecumenism in 1957 was SCLC, which served as the primary conduit for coordinating civil rights activities across the South. According to Lincoln and Mamiya, "Though not deliberately organized as such, this midwife of black consciousness clearly was ecumenical in character and consequences," for at the national level SCLC was church oriented, and local affiliates were led by ministers of various denominations who conducted their campaigns through local churches.

In terms of structure, SCLC's board was composed of black ministers. According to Mary R. Sawyer, even the organization's name shows it to have been "a self-conscious religious organization." Likewise, in the various civil rights campaigns across the South, "the lifeblood of SCLC was the Baptist and Methodist and Pentecostal ministers and church members who crossed denominational lines to confront terror and danger in order to be the church."

However, with the agitation for black power in the 1960s, SCLC was unable to respond to the situation. A meeting was called in July 1966 by Benjamin A. Payton, executive of the Commission on Religion and Race of the National Council of Churches, which led to the founding of the National Committee of Negro Churchmen. Composed primarily of black ministers in mainline white denominations, the National Committee took an affirmative position in relation to black power and eventually replaced SCLC as the leading black ecumenical organization.

Bibliography. Lincoln, C. E., and L. H. Mamiya, *The Black Church in the African American Experience* (Durham: Duke University Press, 1990); Sawyer, M. R., "Black Ecumenical Movements: Proponents of Social Change," *Review of Religious Research*, vol. 30, no. 2 (December 1988); Wilmore, G. S., *Black Religion and Black Radicalism* (Maryknoll, New York: Orbis Books, 1983); Woodson, C. G., *Mis-education of the Negro* (Washington, DC: Associated Publishers, 1969).

Lawrence H. Williams

Southwestern Baptist Theological Seminary. A theological seminary funded by the Southern Baptist Convention* (SBC) and located in Fort Worth, Texas, Southwestern Baptist Theological Seminary (SWBTS) has only seldom experienced religious controversy in the more public sense. The genuine or even marginal theological controversies at SWBTS correlate to three major controversial periods in the history of the SBC.

Although never developing into destructive religious controversy, controversial theological circumstances contributed to the establishment of SWBTS. The Whitsitt controversy supplied the immediate backdrop to SWBTS's origin. The trustees of Southern Baptist Theological Seminary* (SBTS) elected William H.

Whitsitt* as president of SBTS in 1895. As early as 1880 Whitsitt had argued both that Baptists had originated in the sixteenth-century European reformations and that prior to 1641 Baptists had baptized new Christians by sprinkling or pouring rather than by immersion. In 1896, when Whitsitt again published these conclusions, Landmarkist Baptists* in many of the western states vehemently attacked Whitsitt as unorthodox. During the Baptist General Convention of Texas (BGCT) in 1896, many messengers to that meeting wanted the BGCT to condemn Whitsitt's views.

Although B. H. Carroll, Texas Baptist leader and Southwestern Baptist Seminary founder, served on the SBTS Board of Trustees, the board refused to investigate Whitsitt's historical conclusions. Because of his defeat and its erosion of the confidence of the supporters in Texas, Carroll took two decisive yet manipulative steps to motivate the removal of Whitsitt from SBTS. First, explicitly refusing to characterize the question in the Whitsitt controversy as either historical or theological, he construed the real issue as the necessity of preserving the SBC's unity at any cost. According to Carroll, because an unsatisfactory resolution to the Whitsitt controversy might fragment the SBC, SBTS was expendable in order to preserve the SBC's unity, especially since it was possible to establish another seminary but impossible to reunify a fragmented SBC. Second, Carroll threatened to introduce a motion to dissolve the SBC's formal relationship to SBTS during the SBC's next meeting in 1899. To avoid the repercussions of this motion on SBTS, Whitsitt resigned in 1898.

Following a long involvement with Baylor University, by 1901 Carroll had influenced the establishment of a Theological Department at Baylor University over which he became the dean. In 1905, during the absence and without the knowledge of the university's president, S. P. Brooks, Carroll influenced Baylor's Board of Trustees to create Baylor Theological Seminary from Baylor's Theological Department. Many people in the SBC and in Texas opposed this new seminary for a variety of reasons, the chief of which revolved around its obvious role as a competitor with SBTS. As late as 1903, however, Carroll had denied both that he intended for Baylor University to compete with SBTS and that the Whitsitt controversy had motivated any of Baylor's policies or actions. Furthermore, in 1907, only two years after the institution of Baylor Theological Seminary, Carroll both successfully led Baylor's trustees to separate the seminary from the university and effectively convinced the BGCT to assume ownership and governance of the seminary. At that time Baylor Theological Seminary received a new name, Southwestern Baptist Theological Seminary, though it was temporarily still located in Waco. The trustees moved SWBTS to Fort Worth, Texas, in 1910, and by 1925 the BGCT had transferred the seminary's ownership to the SBC.

In spite of J. Frank Norris's* enthusiastic and significant contributions in moving SWBTS to Fort Worth, after he began to embrace fundamentalism,* he initiated a series of vitriolic attacks against the new seminary in 1921. Norris had accused Samuel Dow, a professor at Baylor University, of believing in evolution and had attacked the university for its compromising spirit. L. R. Scarborough, SWBTS's second president, among other leaders, defended Baylor against Norris's charges. Shortly thereafter, Norris claimed that W. W. Barnes, a professor of church history at SWBTS, did not believe the narrative account of creation in the book of Genesis. In 1922 Barnes moderated the meeting of Tarrant County Baptist Association at which the association refused to seat the messengers from First Baptist Church of Fort Worth, where Norris served as pastor, for that church's abandonment of historic Baptist polity. Scarborough actively supported this action against Norris. In 1926, during its annual meeting, the SBC adopted an antievolutionary statement from the presidential address of George W. McDaniel. Conscious of Norris's constant efforts to expose SWBTS as supporting evolutionary theory, Scarborough led the trustees of SWBTS to add the SBC's antievolutionary statement to SWBTS's articles of faith. Despite the measures taken against Norris, he continued publicly to attack and to agitate against SWBTS until his death in 1952.

Fundamentalists in the SBC initiated in 1979 the first of numerous coordinated efforts to eliminate nonfundamentalist perspectives from the SBC. By 1994 fundamentalists had virtually completed their conquest of the SBC. As president of SWBTS during these fundamentalist campaigns, Russell Dilday initially resisted the fundamentalist efforts. He opposed the theory of biblical inerrancy, yet strongly advocated the authority of the Christian Scriptures. As the fundamentalists began to dominate SWBTS's Board of Trustees, Dilday assumed a mediating and less combative posture. Nonetheless, constant friction with the trustees over issues related to the SBC's controversy plagued Dilday's administration. Though unsuccessful in 1985, in the fall of 1989 the board effectively censured Dilday's political activity in the SBC. This encounter attracted a large crowd of support for Dilday during his lengthy meeting with the board. In this context, two minor controversial events occurred prior to the board's termination of Dilday's presidency in 1994.

In 1988 the Baptist Sunday School Board (BSSB) commissioned H. Leon McBeth, professor of church history at SWBTS, to write the BSSB's centennial history, for publication in 1990. Although the BSSB had already paid McBeth eighteen thousand dollars, near the end of the editorial process, in 1990, the BSSB canceled the book's publication. According to the BSSB, McBeth had too favorably assessed the moderate leadership of the BSSB, specifically Lloyd Elder, during the SBC's recent controversy. In the fall of 1990 SWBTS's faculty passed a resolution that both affirmed support for McBeth and requested that the BSSB reverse its decision. Nonetheless, the BSSB destroyed all existing copies of McBeth's history. McBeth has never published the book, although SWBTS's library contains copies of the manuscript.

In the spring of 1993 Henry N. Smith, then instructor of missions at SWBTS, published an article on the topic of salvation and religious pluralism in *Southwestern Journal of Theology,* SWBTS's theological journal. Smith criticized Calvinistic soteriology and suggested a more optimistic Christian perspective on the soteriological potential in other religious traditions. In the spring of 1993 someone distributed copies of Smith's article during an evangelism conference in Fort Worth. Immediately SWBTS's administration received negative reactions to the article. Following Smith's interrogation by the administrators, SWBTS offered him two possibilities: (1) Smith could write a second article to clarify and, in essence, to recant the perspective of his first article; or (2) Smith could allow the first article to stand and could take a yearlong paid sabbatical leave as his severance package. Smith chose the latter alternative. Although Smith's manipulation by the administration prevented a public controversy, because of the procedures operative in Smith's case, deep suspicions about both academic freedom* and the trustworthiness of relationships among colleagues intensified in the faculty of SWBTS.

The administrative action against Henry Smith, however, did not increase the board's confidence in Russell Dilday's leadership. On March 9, 1994, the trustees dismissed Dilday. In this way the board hoped to solve its persistent theological and political frustrations with Dilday. This action followed the board's positive evaluation of Dilday on the previous evening, at which time the board also had denied the truth of rumors about his termination.

This event immediately produced a storm at SWBTS that swept across the entire SBC. Reception of news from Dilday's meeting with the board about his impending dismissal disrupted the seminary's classes and elicited large crowds of support for Dilday. Many students joined in a protest against the board's action led principally by Robert P. Jones, a student in the master of divinity program. For a short time Jones edited a student newspaper in which a variety of protests appeared. Baptist state papers published criticisms of and debates about these events. Many of the seminary's professors, during their classes, openly criticized the board's action as unchristian. The faculty issued a statement that affirmed the excellence of Dilday's leadership. As further results of this event, the seminary experienced a sharp decline in student enrollment, the withdrawal of significant financial support, and intensified efforts to provide alternative theological education in Texas. The Association of Theological Schools, one of SWBTS's accrediting agencies, even placed the seminary on academic probation for two years for violating the seminary's established operating procedures and, thereby, for threatening to inhibit the institution's stated academic purposes. By the spring of 1996, although suspicions and tensions remained, an equilibrium had returned to SWBTS, and open protest had ceased.

Bibliography. Baker, Robert A., *Tell the Generations Following: A History of Southwestern Baptist Theological Seminary* (Nashville: Broadman Press, 1983); Fletcher, Jesse C., *The Southern Baptist Convention: A Sesquicentennial History* (Nashville: Broadman and Holman, 1994; Lefever, Alan J., *Fighting the Good Fight: The Life and Work of Benajah Harvey Carroll* (Austin, TX: Eakin Press, 1994); McBeth, H. Leon, *The Baptist Heritage* (Nashville: Broadman Press, 1987); McBeth, H. Leon, "Celebrating Heritage and Hope: The Centennial History of the Baptist Sunday School Board, 1891–1991" (Unpublished manuscript, Roberts Library, Southwestern Baptist Theological Seminary,

Fort Worth, Texas 1990); Scarborough, L. R., *A Modern School of the Prophets: A History of the Southwestern Baptist Theological Seminary—A Project of Christ—A Product of Prayer and Faith—Its First Thirty Years, 1907–1937* (Nashville: Broadman Press, 1939); Smith, Henry N., "Salvation in the Face of Many Faiths: Toward a Hermeneutic of Optimism," *Southwestern Journal of Theology* 35 (Spring 1993): 26–31.

Jeff Pool

Spellman, Francis J. Sixth archbishop of New York and cardinal, Francis J. Spellman was born in Whitman, Massachusetts, on May 4, 1889, the son of William and Ellen Conway Spellman. He was educated in the local public schools, Fordham University, from which he graduated in 1911, and the North American College in Rome, where he was ordained a priest on May 14, 1916. From 1916 to 1925 Spellman served as a priest of the Archdiocese of Boston, where he incurred the displeasure of the autocratic archbishop, William Henry O'Connell. Using his Roman connections, Spellman wrangled an appointment in Rome as the director of the Knights of Columbus playgrounds and (more importantly) as an attaché at the Vatican Secretariat of State.

Spellman's second Roman sojourn lasted from 1925 to 1931. He continued his earlier practice of cultivating influential Roman ecclesiastics, most notably Eugenio Pacelli, who became Vatican secretary of state in 1930. In 1931 Spellman undertook a secret mission to Paris, where he arranged for the publication of Pius XI's anti-Fascist encyclical, *Non Abbiamo Bisogno*. The following year he was appointed an auxiliary bishop of Boston and was consecrated in St. Peter's Basilica by Cardinal Pacelli. From 1932 to 1939 Spellman served as an unwanted auxiliary in Boston to Cardinal O'Connell, who made no secret of his dislike for Spellman. In 1936, however, Spellman achieved national prominence when he acted as host to Cardinal Pacelli on his tour of the United States. On March 2, 1939, Pacelli was elected Pope Pius XII; on April 24, 1939, Spellman was appointed archbishop of New York.

In New York Spellman was a capable administrator. He refinanced the crippling debt of $28,000,000 left by his predecessor, professionalized the central agencies of the archdiocese, spent over $500,000,000 on the construction and renovation of some 370 schools, created a system of diocesan high schools, and expended over $92,000,000 on the expansion of Catholic hospitals and health care facilities.

Spellman also was appointed military vicar for the armed forces on December 8, 1939, a responsibility that he took very seriously. During World War II and after, his highly publicized visits to American troops overseas made him the most prominent American Catholic prelate and a symbol of American Catholic patriotism. On February 18, 1946, he was appointed a cardinal by Pope Pius XII.

In the postwar years Spellman became a controversial figure when he used seminarians to break a strike at diocesan cemeteries that he believed had been organized by Communists. His staunch anticommunism also led him to support

Senator Joseph McCarthy and American involvement in both the Korean War and the Vietnam War. Spellman also tangled with Eleanor Roosevelt over her opposition to federal aid to parochial schools. He showed splendid pastoral leadership, however, in providing for the care of large numbers of Puerto Ricans who emigrated to New York in the 1950s. At Vatican Council II* Spellman was probably the most important American participant. While adopting a conservative stand on liturgical reform, Spellman was responsible for the presence at the Council of John Courtney Murray, S.J., and he vigorously supported the council's declaration on religious freedom. He died in New York City on December 2, 1967.

Bibliography. Cooney, John, *The American Pope* (New York: Times Books, 1984); Fogarty, Gerald P., "Francis J. Spellman, American and Roman," in *Patterns of Episcopal Leadership*, ed. Gerald P. Fogarty (New York: Macmillan, 1989), 216–234; Gannon, Robert I., *The Cardinal Spellman Story* (Garden City, NY: Doubleday, 1962).

Thomas J. Shelley

Spencer, Peter. One of the founders of the Union Church of Africans, the first church in America organized by African Americans and completely under their control, Peter Spencer was born in Kent County, Maryland, in 1782 as a slave; he died in Wilmington, Delaware, on July 25, 1843.

After being emancipated upon his master's death, Spencer moved to Wilmington and joined the Asbury Methodist Episcopal Church, still a small church at that time with a membership of whites and African Americans. As the church grew, African Americans were relegated to second-class status, seated in a gallery and not allowed to take Communion until after the white members. The white members complained about abuse of church property when African-American members held meetings on the main floor of the church. Tensions led in 1805 to a walkout by African-American members, who soon erected their own building, known as Ezion. This church was to be a mission of the Asbury Church, with African-American trustees.

Tensions flared again in 1812, however, over what the Ezion members saw as interference by Asbury Church. Spencer and William Anderson led another separatist group, which soon built its own sanctuary, the Union Church of Africans. This became the mother church for a number of congregations in the Middle Atlantic states and New England. These congregations, though having some degree of autonomy, were ultimately controlled by Spencer and Anderson. The group originally eschewed the term "Methodist" in its title because of resentment over their treatment by Asbury Church. On several points of ecclesiology, such as the stability of the pastorate, they also distinguished themselves from the Methodists.

In 1816 Spencer attended a conference of African Methodists called by Richard Allen* in Philadelphia. Allen hoped to unite all African Americans who had seceded from white Methodist churches into his African Methodist Episcopal Church, but the conference failed to accomplish that aim. Spencer and Anderson continued to work at building their own Union group. The Union Church of Africans had grown to thirty-one congregations by 1843, when both Spencer and Anderson died, many of the congregations were small and poorly financed. Because Union ministers were unpaid, the churches were unable to attract the sort of capable leadership they needed to prosper. The church suffered a major schism in 1850 and, after the Civil War, merged with the First Colored Methodist Protestant Church to form the African Union First Colored Methodist Protestant Church.

Bibliography. Baldwin, Lewis, *"Invisible" Strands in African Methodism: A History of the African Union Methodist Protestant and Union American Methodist Protestant and Union American Methodist Episcopal Churches, 1805–1809* (Metuchen, NJ: Scarecrow Press, 1983); Richardson, Harry, *Dark Salvation: The Story of Methodism As It Developed among Blacks in America* (Garden City, NY: Doubleday, 1976).

Albert A. Bell, Jr.

Spiritualism. Spiritualism is a movement that posits contact with the spirit world. The belief in life after death has long been a cornerstone of Christianity, with the conviction that Jesus of Nazareth was physically resurrected from the dead. Yet the belief that through mediums earthly and spirit worlds can be bridged is a hallmark of Spiritualism, whose advent in the United States is usually dated to 1848. In that year the Fox family heard mysterious rappings in their farmhouse in Hydesville, New York. The Foxes' young daughters Margaret and Kate developed a method of communicating with the rapping spirit, who told them that he had been murdered in the house several years earlier. The "Rochester rappings" convinced Horace Greeley of the *New York Tribune* of their authenticity and captured national attention. Soon the Fox sisters were holding public séances and attracting believers.

Spiritualism grew both as after-dinner diversion and serious religious commitment. Mediums conducted séances in private parlors and on public stages. Spiritualist churches and summer camps were established from New England to California. Spirit communication expanded beyond rappings to include spirit or automatic writing, planchettes and Ouija boards, table tipping and levitation, playing musical instruments, and materialization in ectoplasmic form. Mediums went into trances, screamed, and moaned as the spirits possessed them. As the spirits manifested in more dramatic ways, exposure of fraudulent mediums grew. In 1888 Margaret Fox confessed that she and her sister had produced the Rochester rappings by cracking their toe joints; however, the following year, unable to find other gainful employment, she recanted her confession and despite diminished credibility resumed work as a medium.

Although accusations of fraud weakened the movement, it mushroomed through the end of the nineteenth century. Its popularity peaked in the 1870s and 1880s, when it provided solace to people grieving loved ones lost in the Civil War. Spiritualism attracted Americans of all classes, races, and educational levels. For some, Spiritualism was an alternative to Christianity, while others practiced Christian Spiritualism. Members of the century's most prominent evangelical family, the Beechers, including Harriet Beecher Stowe,* Charles Beecher, and Isabella Beecher Hooker, were involved with Spiritualism. Mary Todd and Abraham Lincoln had séances conducted at the White House after the death of their son. Well-known mediums included Andrew Jackson Davis, Spiritualist theologian; Helena P. Blavatsky, founder of Theosophy; and Victoria Woodhull, 1872 presidential candidate. Initially an amorphous movement, Spiritualism was gradually institutionalized, and the National Spiritualist Association was formed in 1893.

Spiritualists initially aroused controversy because they were involved in radical reform movements, including abolition, vegetarianism, dress reform, and women's rights. They also provided women with unprecedented opportunities for religious leadership. Women were considered especially suited for mediumship because of their greater emotionality, spiritual sensitivity, and passivity than men's. Women more easily emptied themselves to become channels for spirit communication. Drawing on cultural stereotypes of Victorian womanhood, Spiritualism ironically encouraged women to exercise authority denied them in more traditional religious institutions.

Spiritualism was controversial for theoretical as well as practical reasons. Its scientific, progressive theology challenged orthodox Christianity by blurring the line between life and death. Influenced by eighteenth-century Swedish mystic Emanuel Swedenborg and French scientist and hypnotist Anton Mesmer, and later incorporating evolution and reincarnation,* Spiritualism empirically verified life after death. It opposed Calvinist double predestination,* declaring that those who had passed through the gates of death did not writhe in hell, but lived in heavenly paradise. Elizabeth Stuart Phelps's best-selling novels portrayed the afterlife in glowing terms: surrounded by the things that had made them happiest on earth, spirits gradually ascended to higher realms of bliss. Spiritualism's optimism countered Calvinism's harshness.

In the late twentieth century Spiritualism has achieved a degree of respectability in churches and denominations that resemble mainline Protestant organizations. It continues to attract publicity and generate controversy in channelling, the New Age practice of ancient spirits communicating through living people (called channels rather than mediums). Although these ancient spirits preach universal peace, wisdom, and tolerance more often than they bring specific messages to the bereaved, both their message and medium place them squarely in the Spiritualist tradition.

Bibliography. Braude, Ann, *Radical Spirits: Spiritualism and Women's Rights in Nineteenth-Century America* (Boston: Beacon Press, 1989); Caskey, Marie, *Chariot of Fire: Religion and the Beecher Family* (New Haven: Yale University Press, 1978); Davis, Andrew Jackson, *The Great Harmonia*, 4th ed., 4 vols. (New York: Fowler and Wells, 1853); Moore, R. Laurence, *In Search of White Crows: Spiritualism, Parapsychology,* *and American Culture* (New York: Oxford University Press, 1977); Phelps, Elizabeth Stuart, *The Gates Ajar* (Boston: Fields, Osgood, 1869).

Evelyn A. Kirkley

Spong, John Shelby. Episcopal bishop of Newark, New Jersey, since 1976, author of fourteen books and many articles, standard-bearer and prophet to liberals and self-aggrandizing, naïve heretic to conservatives in the church, John Shelby Spong has championed every progressive cause since the first woman was ordained in the Episcopal Church in 1976. He fought religiously sanctioned racism* in his native North Carolina and, in several of his most controversial books, has condemned the sexism of a patriarchalist Bible, defending the ordination of women and arguing for full inclusion of gay and lesbian people in the church fold. He is widely understood to be the actual target in the extraordinary 1996 heresy trial of colleague Walter Righter, who, with Spong, ordained a noncelibate gay man to the diaconate and later to the priesthood.

Equally critical of the irrational literalism of fundamentalists and the ignorant secularism of religious liberals, Spong grounds his critique of contemporary Christianity in a passionate appeal for the Bible to be taken not literally, but seriously. He approaches the Gospels as Christian *midrashim*, legends developed well after the fact to glorify the life of the man Jesus. "Christianity is an Easter event, not a Christmas event," and the often contradictory gospel stories of Jesus' conception, birth, family life, and friendships were attempts by succeeding generations of believers to mythologize the remarkable life and exalted death of a man in whom God was perfectly reflected (*Born of a Woman*, 50). Not Bultman's singular "demythologizing," but for every age a remythologizing is required to answer the question anew: "Who is Christ for us, for our day?" "To freeze the interpretation of the experience [of God] in the words of any era, including our own, would be to guarantee the eventual loss of the truth of the experience," (*Rescuing the Bible*, 231). Scholarly but by his own admission unoriginal, Spong writes to popularize opinions seldom heard in churches, but widely held by modern theologians like Raymond Brown (*Birth of the Messiah*, 1977), Jane Schaberg (*The Illegitimacy of Jesus*, 1987) and Edward Schillebeeckx (*Jesus*, 1981).

Bibliography. Spong, John Shelby, *Born of a Woman* (San Francisco: Harper San Francisco, 1992); Spong, John Shelby, *Living in Sin?* (San Francisco: Harper and Row, 1988); Spong, John Shelby, *Rescuing the Bible from Fundamentalism* (San Francisco: Harper San Francisco, 1991).

Fred Richter

Stagg, Frank. For two days in April 1956, the instruction committee of the Board of Trustees of New Orleans Baptist Theological Seminary questioned Frank Stagg, who was professor of New Testament and Greek at the seminary, in order to determine whether or not to dismiss him from his faculty position on account of his theological views. In 1951 Stagg had read a paper on the atoning work of Christ to a group of ministers in South Carolina. The paper, entitled "The Cross—A Rationale," was well received, and Stagg prepared mimeographed copies for many persons who expressed an interest in it. Among its admirers was the president of the seminary, Roland Z. Leavell, who told the seminary faculty that it was the finest thing he had ever read on the subject. However, others began to express reservations concerning Stagg's view of the atonement.

In 1955 Stagg's commentary on Acts was published; it was entitled *The Book of Acts: The Early Struggle for an Unhindered Gospel.* In it, Stagg drew parallels between the struggle of early Jewish Christians to accept Gentiles as equal members of the church and the struggle of white American Christians to accept black Christians as equal members of the church. He wrote, "To be preoccupied with [the geographical factor in Acts] is to miss a greater one—the very one which Luke seemed most concerned to present. The boundaries most difficult to cross—then as now—were religious, national, and racial, not geographical. It is easier today to send missionaries to Africa than to have fellowship across racial lines at home" (Stagg, *The Book of Acts,* 36).

In early March 1956 four doctoral students at New Orleans Baptist Theological Seminary wrote to President Leavell to inform him that they believed that Frank Stagg was teaching things that were inconsistent with the doctrinal guidelines of the seminary, known as the Articles of Religious Belief. Apparently their action provided an incentive for the trustees to review Stagg's theology. Letters were solicited from students and also from persons outside the seminary. These letters were received by President Leavell; they were typed up in his office; each page of the typed copies was marked "Strictly Confidential"; all names were omitted from the typed copies; and the typed copies were distributed both to Stagg and to members of the Board of Trustees. Some of the letters contained a defense of Stagg and his theology; most contained criticisms of his theology. The letters make it clear that a coordinated effort had been made to get information concerning Stagg's views.

The accusations in these letters were the focus of the two-day meeting in April in which Frank Stagg replied to questions put to him by members of the instruction committee of the trustees. President Leavell was present during the proceedings, which took place at a hotel in New Orleans.

No minutes of the trustee investigation have survived, but some idea of the scope of issues discussed may be gained from the letters that were the focus of the investigation. Six issues were mentioned in the letters.

First, there was the issue of whether Stagg's view of Scripture was acceptable. In particular, he seemed to value the New Testament more than the Old, and he emphasized the human element as well as the divine element in Scripture. Stagg felt that these positions constituted a positive hermeneutic; his critics felt that they constituted a rejection of the inspiration and infallibility of Scripture.

Second, there was the issue of the Trinity. Although Stagg clearly affirmed the deity of Christ and routinely referred to the Father, the Son, and the Spirit, he also pointed out that there is no doctrine of the Trinity in the Bible. He felt that his position was a biblical one; his critics felt that he was rejecting the traditional trinitarian understanding of God in favor of modalism.

Third, there was the issue of the work of Christ. Stagg rejected an understanding of the work of Christ that he described as "transactional." By that term he meant understandings of the atonement that were objective and that called people to believe but failed to call them to take up the cross and follow Christ. Stagg thought that his position was true to the New Testament; his critics thought that he was rejecting part of the New Testament teaching that was also an important part of the theological heritage of Baptists.*

Fourth, there was the issue of the wrath of God. Stagg emphasized that God's wrath is the inevitable consequence of sin, not a vindictive response God makes to sinners. Stagg felt that he was affirming the teaching of passages such as Romans 1 and Galatians 6:7; his critics felt that he was denying the teaching of passages that speak of God as judge.

Fifth, there was the issue of demons. Stagg affirmed the reality of demons, but he did so in such a way as not to exonerate human beings of their own guilt and sin. Stagg believed that his interpretation of demons was warranted; his critics felt that Stagg's interpretation was too psychological in character.

Sixth and finally, there was the issue of interpretation of individual passages in the Bible. A good example of this was Numbers 15:32–36, which tells the story of the Israelites' stoning a man who had picked up sticks on the Sabbath. Stagg felt that Jesus rejected such violence, and he said that no one today really believes that it was God's will for the man to be stoned, since no one today is prepared to stone anyone for such conduct; Stagg's critics felt that Stagg was rejecting the clear teaching of the passage.

After the meeting the trustees of the seminary voted unanimously not to dismiss Stagg from the seminary faculty. For his part, Stagg agreed to provide a clarification of his theology for the seminary at one of its chapel services, which he soon did. Stagg continued as a faculty member at the New Orleans seminary until he accepted an invitation in 1964 to become the James Buchanan Harrison Professor of New Testament Interpretation at his alma mater, Southern Baptist Theological Seminary* in Louisville, Kentucky.

Frank Stagg's theology is no secret. He is a prolific author and a forceful speaker. In more than a dozen books and numerous other writings, Stagg has presented his understanding of the New Testament message. In Stagg's theology the center of gravity is the life and teachings of Jesus. Although Stagg does not like human creeds or confessions, he could with justice claim to have followed consistently a principle offered in the Baptist Faith and Message, a confessional statement adopted by the Southern Baptist Convention* in 1963. That document states, "The criterion by which the Bible is to be interpreted is Jesus Christ."

From the publication of his commentary on Acts in 1955 until his retirement from Southern Baptist Theological Seminary in 1982 and beyond, Stagg was almost certainly one of the most influential Bible scholars in the Southern Baptist

Convention, and his influence continues through his books and through the writing, lecturing, and preaching that he is doing in his very active retirement. Probably his most influential book has been *New Testament Theology* (1962); another very influential book was *The Doctrine of Christ* (1984), which was written to be used as a study book in Southern Baptist churches and which brought great honor (and no criticism) to its author.

Bibliography. St. Amant, Penrose, "A Continuing Pilgrimage: A Biographical Sketch of Frank Stagg," in *The Theological Educator* (New Orleans: New Orleans Baptist Theological Seminary, 1977); Sloan, Robert, "Frank Stagg," in *Baptist Theologians*, ed. Timothy, George, and David S. Dockery (Nashville: Broadman Press, 1990); Stagg, Frank, *The Book of Acts: The Early Struggle for an Unhindered Gospel* (Nashville: Broadman Press, 1955); Stagg, Frank, *The Doctrine of Christ* (Nashville: Convention Press, 1984); Stagg, Frank, *New Testament Theology* (Nashville: Broadman Press, 1962); Tolbert, Malcolm, "Frank Stagg: Teaching Prophet," in *Perspectives in Religious Studies* (Macon: Mercer University Press, 1985).

Fisher Humphreys

Stanton, Elizabeth Cady. Among the foremost feminist leaders of the nineteenth century, Elizabeth Cady Stanton (1815–1902) challenged her contemporaries' notions on women's rights, labor unions, child rearing, birth control, coeducation, and Christianity. Endowed with a feisty spirit and a revolutionary soul, Stanton cultivated the image of a benevolent matron in order to disarm critics who could not imagine a stout grandmother doubling as a radical propagandist.

Growing up, Stanton pursued athletics and academics with an enthusiasm befitting boys of the age. Born into a wealthy family, she attended a female seminary in her teenage years where, after hearing Charles Finney* preach, she experienced a religious conversion. Her father, concerned with the subsequent gloom that sapped Elizabeth's usually high spirits, prescribed rational philosophy as an antidote. Though she initially wavered in her estimation of religion's efficacy, Elizabeth eventually became a skeptic.

In 1840 Elizabeth married reformer Henry Stanton and was introduced to abolitionist circles where she met Lucretia Mott, a Quaker minister, abolitionist, and feminist. In 1848 the two women organized the first women's rights convention in Seneca Falls, New York. Applying natural rights doctrines to women, Stanton argued that they, too, deserved political enfranchisement and full legal rights. Although in subsequent decades the fight for suffrage was subordinated to the struggle to free the slaves, Stanton expected women, along with African Americans, to receive the vote. When politicians decided to enfranchise only black men, suffragists split into two camps. The more radical group, the National Woman Suffrage Association, led by Stanton, advocated divorce reform, birth control, and labor unions along with suffrage. The American Woman Suffrage Association, organized by Lucy Stone, her husband Henry Blackwell, and Julia Ward Howe, sought only the vote. In 1890 the two groups united, but Stanton's outspoken stances continued to antagonize single-issue suffragists.

While Elizabeth Cady Stanton raised seven children, she continued to collaborate with Susan B. Anthony to further women's rights. A graceful writer and inspiring speaker, she compelled crowds—even when they did not fully agree with her far-reaching platform. Age did not diminish her crusading spirit. Soon after her eightieth birthday she published *The Woman's Bible*, a critique of the church's teaching on women. Biographer Elisabeth Griffith argues that attacks by antisuffrage forces on Stanton's "allegedly antichurch, antifamily, and pro-labor stance" caused the younger generation of suffragists to downplay her influence and importance.

Bibliography. Banner, Lois W, *Elizabeth Cady Stanton, a Radical for Woman's Rights* (Boston: Little, Brown, 1980); Griffith, Elisabeth, *In Her Own Right: The Life of Elizabeth Cady Stanton* (New York: Oxford University Press, 1984); Stanton, Elizabeth Cady, *Eighty Years and More: Reminiscences, 1815–1897* (Boston: Northeastern University Press, 1993); Stanton, Elizabeth Cady, Susan B. Anthony, *The Elizabeth Cady Stanton–Susan B. Anthony Reader* (Boston: Northeastern University Press, 1992).

Diane Winston

Stone, Barton. Barton Stone, the only one of the four "founders" of the Christian Church–Disciple movement to be born in America, was born in Maryland in 1772. After having moved to southern Virginia with his family following the death of his father, he enrolled in a Presbyterian log college (frontier school) operated by David Caldwell with the intention of becoming a lawyer. Caught up in the revivalistic fervor of the college, he decided instead to become a minister.

During this formative period he was impressed by associates who believed strongly that each person should have the right to investigate and develop one's own understanding of faith, apart from creedal statements. He was also introduced to the notion that each congregation should speak for itself apart from hierarchical constraints.

When he received his license to preach, he became a Presbyterian minister in 1796 to two churches in Kentucky, one being at Cane Ridge. His ordination by the Transylvania Presbytery occurred in the afterglow of the American Revolution when the country was basking in freedom from civil domination.

Like other ministers on the American frontier, Stone used the revivalistic technique of persuasion to attract people to his churches and to stimulate religious fervor. Largely through his organizing efforts, the Cane Ridge Camp Meeting was held in August 1801. Thousands attended, and many were converted by the preaching of Presbyterian, Methodist, and Baptist ministers. Stone was impressed with the results and began to question the Calvinistic emphasis on the absolute sovereignty of God and divine election.

In 1803 Stone and four other Presbyterian ministers who had been preaching that Christ died for all people formed the independent Springfield Presbytery. Within a year these ministers, plus one other, dissolved the new presbytery and began a group that they called the "Christian" churches. The foundational beliefs of this new association of churches were set forth in ''The Last Will and Testament of the Springfield Presbytery.'' The beliefs centered around the Scripture as the sole authority for faith, a suspicion of established religious authority, local congregational autonomy with the authority to select a minister, and opposition to divisions within the Body of Christ. Stone's ''Christian'' movement grew and merged in 1832 with Alexander Campbell's* ''Disciple movement'' to form what is now known as the Christian Church (Disciples of Christ).

Bibliography. Dunnavant, Anthony L., and Richard L. Harrison, Jr., eds., *Explorations in the Stone-Campbell Traditions* (Nashville: Disciples of Christ Historical Society, 1995); McAllister, Lester G., and William E. Tucker, *Journey in Faith: A History of the Christian Church (Disciples of Christ)* (St. Louis: Bethany Press, 1975); Rogers, John, ed., *Biography of Eld. Barton Warren Stone, Written by Himself, with Additions and Reflections by Eld. John Rogers* (Cincinnati: Published for the Author by J. A. and U. P. James, 1847); Toulouse, Mark G., *Joined in Discipleship* (St. Louis: Chalice Press, 1992); Ware, Charles C., *Barton Warren Stone: Pathfinder of Christian Union* (St. Louis: Bethany Press, 1932).

Coleman Markham

Stowe, Harriet Elizabeth Beecher. Harriet Elizabeth Beecher Stowe (1811–1896), member of a prominent Calvinist New England family, is most remembered for authoring the very influential *Uncle Tom's Cabin,* a work that considerably heightened antislavery sentiment in the 1850s. Stowe was born in Litchfield, Connecticut, daughter of the prominent religious leader Lyman Beecher* and a sister of a major American preacher, Henry Ward Beecher,* and seven other children. In 1832 her father assumed the presidency of Lane Seminary* in Cincinnati, Ohio, an area of abolitionist sentiment. There in 1836 Harriet married Calvin E. Stowe, a professor of the school. To this union seven children were born. After living near slaveholding areas for a number of years, the Stowes in the 1850s moved to New England, first to Bowdoin, Maine, and later to Andover, Massachusetts. It was in New England that she composed *Uncle Tom's Cabin,* a best-seller and a moving statement about the brutality of American slavery, the power of Christian faith and love in adversity, the humanity of African Americans, and the heroic nature of black Christianity. Stowe wrote this book during a very difficult decade for black Americans and those fighting enslavement, that is, after the passage of the federal Fugitive Slave Law that obligated those in free states to return escaped blacks to chattel bondage and several years prior to the U.S. Supreme Court's *Dred Scott* decision that not only upheld the principles of the Fugitive Slave Law but nullified African-American citizenship. Indeed, Stowe envisioned her book as a contribution to the cause of abolishing slavery. The defenders of slavery and enemies of the black race regarded her name with disdain. Stowe produced additional works, including thirty fictional works focused on the themes of Christian love, faith, duty, and battling against adversity, but none equaled *Uncle Tom's Cabin.* Stowe had her own share of troubles in the areas of finance, health, death, and depression. In her later years she embraced the Episcopal Church. Stowe's contribution to one of the most significant religious and civil controversies of the modern world has shone brilliantly through the years.

Bibliography. Ahlstrom, Sydney E., *A Religious History of the American People* (New Haven: Yale University Press, 1972); Bowden, Henry H., *Dictionary of American Religious Biography* (Westport: Greenwood Publishing, 1976); Brauer, Jerald C., *The Westminster Dictionary of Church History* (1971); *Dictionary of Christianity in America* (Downers Grove: InterVarsity Press, 1990).

Sandy Dwayne Martin

Strang, James Jesse. James Jesse Strang (1813–1856) was one of several major contenders (with Brigham Young and Sidney Rigdon) for the leadership of the Mormon Church after the death of Joseph Smith,* who was murdered by a mob on June 27, 1844. Strang produced a letter of appointment as Smith's successor (regarded as a forgery by most scholars), but could not prevail against Brigham Young, who succeeded in convincing the majority of Mormons in Illinois to follow him to the Rocky Mountains. Armed with a companion volume to the Book of Mormon, the Book of the Law of the Lord—a purported translation of the "Plates of Laban"—Strang set up the Church of Jesus Christ of Latter Day Saints in Voree, Wisconsin, in 1846 and was able to convince a significant number of Mormons outside the Illinois heartland of the authenticity of his claims to be Smith's successor, including some prominent Mormons such as William Smith (a brother of Joseph), Apostle John E. Page, and William E. Marks, president of the Nauvoo stake (a major ecclesiastical unit). In 1847 he moved his headquarters to Beaver Island in Lake Michigan, where he established a theocratic kingdom in 1850, with himself as king, surrounded by a royal "Order of Illuminati"—somewhat in emulation of Joseph Smith's theocracy in Nauvoo, Illinois, including the practice of polygamy. As in the case of Joseph Smith, such radical ideas and practices led to internal dissension as well as outside opposition, culminating in Strang's murder in 1856. After his martyrdom Strang's magnetism continued to exert its attraction on loyal followers, with a few disciples in Wisconsin and New Mexico preserving his church and his memory to this day.

Bibliography. Foster, W. Lawrence, "James J. Strang: The Prophet Who Failed," *Church History* 50 (1981): 182–92; Hansen, Klaus J., "The Making of King Strang: A Re-examination," *Michigan History* 46 (1962): 201–19; Quaife, Milo M., *The Kingdom of Saint James: A Narrative of the Mormons* (New Haven: Yale University Press, 1930); Strang, Mark A., ed., *The Diary of James J. Strang* (East Lansing: Michigan State University Press, 1961); Van Noord, Roger, *King of Beaver Island: The Life and Assassination of James Jesse Strang* (Urbana and Chicago: University of Illinois Press, 1988).

Klaus J. Hansen

Suicide. Moral questions associated with suicide (literally self-killing) go back to the earliest traditions of Western civilization. Pythagoras, Plato, and Aristotle held suicide to be a crime against the community, and Plato even argued that it was tantamount to a crime against God. In the classical world of Greece and Rome, suicide was often idealized as a noble form of death, but from the second century onwards Christian teaching has condemned it. Judaism condemns any active and deliberate hastening of death as equivalent to murder; and suicide is regarded as "worse than murder in some respects" inasmuch as there can be no atonement by repentance for killing oneself. Cyprian, Ambrose, Irenaeus, and Athanasius all contributed to a Christian doctrine, but it was Augustine who succinctly formulated the Christian position and, specifically addressing the "nobility of suicide" argument, named the three grounds on which suicide is renounced: it violates the commandment "Thou shalt not kill"; it precludes any opportunity for repentance; and it is a cowardly act. St. Thomas coined the classical formula for Christians in the thirteenth century, very like the Jewish reason for proscribing suicide: "Suicide is the most fatal of sins, because it cannot be repented of." Richard Hooker and Jeremy Taylor added the conviction that no one can claim a right to death because human life belongs to God. None of the Christian churches endorses suicide.

Issues associated with "mercy killing" (popularly but mistakenly called "euthanasia") arose in the modern period with the infamous T4 *Gnadentod* program instituted by Adolf Hitler and his chief physician, Karl Brandt. Despite advocacy by some religious persons— among them John Donne, Dean Inge, and Joseph Fletcher—both Judaism and Christianity sternly condemn this practice. The current religious controversies most closely aligned with this topic focus on physician-assisted suicide, which some have proposed as appropriate in the face of medical futility. The Hippocratic pledge, however, is that "I will give no deadly drug to any, though it be asked of me, nor will I counsel such." Further, among the ancient moral traditions of Western medicine is the maxim that obligates physicians to preserve (some versions say "prolong") life and to relieve pain (some versions include "suffering"). Nowadays these duties appear sometimes not complementary but antagonistic—life may be preserved only with great personal distress, or intractable pain can be relieved only at the expense of life itself.

With the advent of "living wills," "durable power of attorney for health care decisions," and other procedures intended to address end-of-life issues, several churches have adopted position papers. Some of these speak generally of "death with dignity" and individual prerogative. The United Methodist Church "asserts the right of every person to die in dignity"; the United Church of Christ affirms additionally the right of individuals to "not have their lives unnecessarily prolonged"; and the Presbyterian Church USA concurs, adding that "it is best to safeguard autonomy in medical decision-making by whatever means." Other churches, like the Roman Catholic Church, the Episcopal Church, the Evangelical Lutheran Church in America, and the Assemblies of God, say plainly that a clear distinction is to be made between actions that halt life-support systems and actions that directly cause death: while there is no duty to continue the

former in treatments that are nonbeneficial, "it is morally wrong and unacceptable to take a human life in order to relieve the suffering caused by incurable
illness." Still others, like the Presbyterian Church in America and the Lutheran
Church–Missouri Synod, address only the matter of physician-assisted suicide
and condemn it as "an affront to the Lord who gives life" and which "opens
the door for future abuse."

The North American context is fertile ground for individualism, self-
determination, and autonomy. In the absence of virtually any shared vision about
the good life, it is inevitable that disputes will arise about what constitutes a
good death. Suicide, together with physician-assisted suicide, raises serious
questions for religionists about the limits of self-determination and whether,
when we have almost no shared vision of common good, the skills of a profession like medicine should be available to help individuals achieve their private
vision of good life and good death.

Bibliography. Judicatory position papers are available from the appropriate church commission or its headquarters. Feldman, David M., *Birth Control in Jewish Law* (New York:
New York University Press, 1968); Jakobovits, Immanuel, *Jewish Medical Ethics*, new
ed. (New York: Bloch Publishing Co., 1975); *The Pastoral Constitution on the Church
in the Modern World*, in *The Documents of Vatican II*, ed. Walter M. Abbott (New York:
Guild Press, Association Press, and American Press, 1966), no. 27; Rosner, Fred, *Modern
Medicine and Jewish Law* (New York: Yeshiva University, 1972); Smith, Harmon L.,
"Physician-assisted Suicide: Both Physicians and Christians Should Know That This is
Not an Idea Whose Time Has Come," *North Carolina Medical Journal* 1993, 54, no. 8
378–82; Vatican Congregation for the Doctrine of the the the Faith, *Declaration on Eutha-
nasia* (1980).

Harmon L. Smith

Sunday, William (Billy) Ashley. Billy Sunday (1862–1835) was one of the
best-known evangelists of early-twentieth-century America. Born in Ames,
Iowa, he established something of a reputation as a professional baseball player
for the Chicago White Stockings. He was converted at Chicago's Pacific Gospel
Mission. His evangelistic work began through work with the Young Man's
Christian Association (YMCA) and later as an associate of revivalist J. Wilbur
Chapman. A revival campaign in Garner, Iowa, in 1896 represented the start of
his career as a populist preacher. His revivals were organized by a well-ordered
company of "advance men" and a multitalented team of associates. Every effort
was made to involve area churches as well as civic and religious leaders. Publicity was extensive, and announcements of colorful "Sundayisms"—pithy and
provocative comments—were aimed at attracting a crowd.

Sunday's revivalism sparked numerous controversies in the communities
where he held forth. First, many religious leaders criticized his populist style
and the circuslike atmosphere of his revival campaigns. Some were concerned
about the coarseness of Sunday's language, his criticism of religious formalism,
and his pulpit antics. For example, he sometimes railed against "those ossified,

petrified, mildewed, dyed-in-the-wool, stamped-in-the-cork, blown-in-the-bottle, horizontal, perpendicular Presbyterians.'' He declared: ''Ladies, do you want to look pretty? If some of you women would spend less on dope and cold cream and get down on your knees and pray, God would make you prettier.''

Sunday's use of slang and expletives (damnation and hellfire) scandalized many in more refined Protestant society. Likewise, his mannerisms, including racing up the aisles, sliding into home plate, and leaping on top of the pulpit itself, were equally offensive to those who preferred ministerial decorum. Others defended them as colorful and populist methods of attracting the unchurched.

In his revival campaigns Sunday courted controversy, particularly when it brought him into public conflict with what he viewed as infidel philosophy and godless living. He did not hesitate to attack local liberals, particularly ministers and educators who accepted historical-critical theories in biblical studies or who questioned cardinal doctrines of the faith. During a campaign in Dixon, Illinois, in 1905, Sunday and Joseph Fort Newton, pastor of the Liberal Christian Church, carried on a running battle from their respective pulpits over the meaning of faith and the nature of Christianity. Sunday's greatest enemy, however, was liquor, or, as he called it, booze. His revivals included the call both to Christian conversion and to renounce the use of all alcohol. In every campaign he preached his famous ''booze sermon'' attacking the ''liquor-crowd'' and demanding that Christians fight against them.

Critics charged that Sunday was sometimes a naïve pawn of big business, used in some places to distract workers from unionizing or to offer them religion to keep them in their place. Writing for *Harper's Weekly* in 1915, George Creel charged that business leaders who invited Sunday to conduct revivals in Colorado had done so to break strikes against coal mines and to elect a governor who was a ''coal company man.'' Creel believed that Sunday was duped by the businessmen. One of Carl Sandburg's ''Chicago Poems'' contains a denunciation of Sunday that includes the line ''You, Billy Sunday, put a smut on every human blossom.'' A 1916 article by Joseph Berry entitled ''Criticisms of Present Day Evangelism'' criticized preachers like Sunday for their attacks on other ministers, the lack of recognition of local ministers, the ''shake-my-hand'' method of inviting people to conversion, the misuse of statistics on attendance and conversion, and the use of pressure tactics to secure offerings. Sunday himself seemed to thrive on the controversies and responded in kind to his critics. His brand of revivalism was an appeal to Christian conversion linked closely to American patriotism, antiliquor diatribes, and middle-class values.

Bibliography. Dorsett, Lyle W., *Billy Sunday and the Redemption of Urban America* (Grand Rapids, MI: Eerdmans Publishing Company, 1991); Ellis, William T., *''Billy'' Sunday: The Man and His Message* (New York: John C. Winston, 1914); McLoughlin, William G., *Billy Sunday Was His Real Name* (Chicago: University of Chicago Press, 1955).

Bill J. Leonard

Swing, David. David Swing, born in Cincinnati in 1830, took a leading role in promoting an evangelical brand of theological liberalism.* After teaching in the Philosophy Department at Miami University in Oxford, Ohio, he accepted a pastoral position at Westminster Presbyterian Church in Chicago. He associated with New School Presbyterianism, placing great emphasis on the love of Christ. His insistence on a gospel of love, along with his lyrical style of preaching, earned him the nickname "the Poet-Preacher."

Enormously popular in his parish, Swing worked closely with other Chicago clerics regardless of their denominational affiliation. Such details mattered little to Swing, who believed that the love taught by the gospel would show forth more fully if denominations cooperated rather than competed. His unconcerned attitude with what he considered insignificant details also surfaced in his approach to confessional and creedal statements. That penchant for promoting the gospel of love over the language of confessional statements eventually brought Swing into conflict with members of his own Presbyterian denomination.

By 1874 Swing enjoyed unquestionable popularity in his adopted home, but his views attracted critics. One of those critics, an ardent Princeton graduate and recent immigrant to Chicago, finally came to consider Swing's emphasis on love too great a departure from the teachings of the Westminster Confession. From his teaching position at McCormick Theological Seminary, Francis Landey Patton read Swing's sermons and the articles he published in his newspaper, the Chicago *Alliance*, with great concern. In March 1874 Patton preferred charges of heresy against Swing, resulting in a sensational heresy trial before the Chicago Presbytery.

Positions taken in Swing's trial indicated that the reunion of New School and Old School Presbyterians in 1868 effected the formal reunification of the denomination, but did not completely resolve the differences between the two parties. Swing was tried on two charges of heresy, supported by some twenty-nine specifications. The Chicago Presbytery, despite clear evidence supporting Patton's charges, asserted its independence from Princeton orthodoxy by finding Swing not guilty of heresy. Patton, however, refused to let the matter die and promised to press the case against Swing to the larger Synod of Northern Illinois. Although Swing firmly believed that he had done nothing more than responsibly preach the gospel of Jesus Christ, he resigned his Presbyterian pulpit rather than submit to further ecclesial proceedings.

The trial for heresy scarcely affected Swing's popularity in Chicago. Upon leaving the Presbyterian Church, Swing helped to create an independent congregation that frequently met in the newly constructed Chicago Music Hall. Swing continued to propound a gospel of love that emphasized the goodness of humanity and the perfectability of the human race.

Bibliography. Hutchison, William R., "Disapproval of Chicago: The Symbolic Trial of David Swing," *Journal of American History* 59 (June 1972): 30–47; Johnson, David, Francis L. Patton, George C. Noyes, *The Trial of the Rev. David Swing* (Chicago: Jansen, McClurg and Co., 1874); Newton, Joseph Fort, *David Swing: Poet-Preacher* (Chicago:

Unity Pub. Co., 1909); Swing, David, *David Swing's Sermons* (Chicago: W. B. Keen, Cooke, and Co., 1874); Swing, David, *Truths for Today: Spoken in the Past Winter* (Chicago: Jansen, McClurg, and Co., 1874).

Russell Congleton

T

Teilhard de Chardin, Pierre. Born the fourth of eleven children in the Auvergne district of central France in 1881, Pierre Teilhard de Chardin died on Easter Sunday, April 10, 1955, in New York City and is buried at St. Andrew's on the Hudson just sixty miles upriver from New York City. At the age of seventeen he entered the Jesuit Novitiate at Aix-en-Provence. After four years of theological education at Hastings, England, he was ordained a priest in 1911. In World War I he served as a medical orderly and stretcher bearer in addition to being a chaplain to the troops. In 1922 he completed his doctorate at the Sorbonne in Natural Science and then set off to China to commence a career of scientific investigation and interpretation. After World War II he returned to Paris for a brief stay and in 1951 came to New York City to work during the final years of his life with the Wenner-Gren Foundation.

Though he was a prolific writer, none of his works were allowed publication by the Roman Catholic Church during his lifetime. After his death in 1955, non-Catholic and Catholic presses made his works available. As late as June 30, 1962, however, a *Monitum* concerning Teilhard was issued by the Supreme Congregation of the Holy Office urging bishops, religious superiors, and rectors of clerical training institutions "to protect minds, especially young minds against the dangers of the works of Father Teilhard de Chardin and of his supporters," with references also being made to "inaccuracies and even serious errors" in philosophical and theological matters with which these works "teem."

Teilhard was often maligned by his critics as having contradicted practically every traditional dogma—no original sin, no necessity of redemption, a natural ending of the world, no particular creative act for the animal species and even less for humans, no Adam and no Eve. Actually, Teilhard was trying to reconcile science and religion as well as faith in the world and faith in God; he became a bridge builder between the idea of God interested in and involved in direction and meaning and a world in evolution. In his effort he related world (cosmos) to God (theos) by Christ (Christos). Evolution to Teilhard was not a hypothesis about human origins but an all-inclusive term that spoke to the totality of human experience. To him, everything in time was in process of transformation. He projected the termination of evolution to be Point Omega and believed that the God-Forward of history would bring creation to that point.

Needless to say, he was an innovator with a terribly unique style and was considered as a dangerous thinker in many circles. Four decades following his death he is widely read and appreciated by Catholics, Protestants, and others. He certainly set forth a theology of universal reconciliation and hope.

Bibliography. Crespy, Georges, *From Science to Theology* (Nashville: Abingdon Press, 1968); Rideau, Emile, *The Thought of Teilhard de Chardin* (New York: Harper and Row, 1967); Speaight, Robert, *The Life of Teilhard de Chardin* (New York: Harper and Row, 1968); Teilhard de Chardin, Pierre, *Building the Earth* (New York: Dimension Books, 1965); Teilhard de Chardin, Pierre, *The Divine Milieu* (New York: Harper and Row, 1960); Teilhard de Chardin, Pierre, *The Future of Man* (New York: Harper and Row, 1964); Teilhard de Chardin, Pierre, *Man's Place in Nature* (New York: Harper and Row, 1966); Teilhard de Chardin, Pierre, *The Phenomenon of Man* (New York: Harper and Row, 1959).

George H. Shriver

Tennent, Gilbert. Gilbert Tennent (1703–1764) was born in County Armagh, Ireland, the eldest of four sons of William and Catharine Tennent. He was educated by his father, and Yale College conferred an A.M. degree upon him in 1725. He served as minister at New Castle, Delaware (1725–1726); New Brunswick, New Jersey (1726–1743); and Second Presbyterian Church, Philadelphia, Pennsylvania (1743–1764). Married three times, he was survived by three children. Among the leaders of the Great Awakening* he ranks with Jonathan Edwards* and George Whitefield.

Having assisted his father in Log College, Gilbert was licensed by the Philadelphia Presbytery in 1725 and ordained in 1726. In New Brunswick he became acquainted with Theodorus Jacobus Frelinghuysen, a Dutch Reformed minister in the Raritan Valley, who encouraged his evangelistic tendencies. His preaching seemingly affected many who were suspected of being unconverted. He and his brothers William, John, and Charles, along with John Blair and Samuel Finley— all associated with Log College—were a major source of the Great Awakening that George Whitefield climaxed in his visit to America in 1739–1740. Whitefield visited Gilbert Tennent on November 13, 1739, while making an evangelistic tour. By mid-December 1740 Whitefield's preaching was acknowledged to have had "great effect," especially in New England.

The perspective that Gilbert Tennent represented was labeled "New Light." While the synod required of all candidates for the ministry assent to the Westminster Confession of Faith, the "New Side" wanted candidates examined about their experience of sanctifying grace and that none be admitted who were not determined to be conscientious Christians. Gilbert Tennent and his associates ignored a rule that members of one presbytery not preach in another without proper authorization. When a requirement was instituted that candidates for the ministry present a diploma from a New England or European college, or a certificate of acceptable scholarship from a committee of the synod, Tennent and his associates viewed it as an attack on Log College, whereupon the schism of 1741 occurred in which Tennent and members of the New Brunswick Presbytery withdrew. The division lasted seventeen years.

After Tennent became minister of Second Presbyterian Church, Philadelphia, his ministry became less controversial. By 1749 he was working for reunion. When the charter for the College of New Jersey was issued in 1746, Gilbert Tennent and his Log College associates were members of the Board of Trustees. From the fall of 1753 to February 1755, Tennent accompanied Samuel Davies of Virginia on a fund-raising tour for the College of New Jersey in Great Britain. **Bibliography.** Coalter, M. J., Jr., *Gilbert Tennent, Son of Thunder* (New York: Greenwood Press, 1986); Harper, M. D., Jr., "Gilbert Tennent: Theologian of the 'New Light' " (Ph.D. diss., Duke University, 1958); Tennent, Gilbert, *Sermons on Important Subjects* (Philadelphia: James Chattin, 1758); Sprague, W. B, *Annuals of the American Pulpit,* 9 vols. (New York: Robert Carter and Brothers, 1858) 3: 35–41; Tennent, Gilbert, *The Danger of an Unconverted Ministry, Considered in a Sermon on Mark vi. 34,* 2nd ed. (Philadelphia: B. Franklin, 1740).

Frederick V. Mills, Sr.

Tietjen, John H. President of Concordia Seminary (St. Louis) of the Lutheran Church–Missouri Synod beginning in 1969, John H. Tietjen was removed from that post in 1974 after a protracted battle with conservatives in the synod who had charged him with permitting the teaching of false doctrine in the seminary. Born in New York City in 1928, Tietjen was the son of German immigrant parents who had come to America in the aftermath of World War I. He studied for the ministry at Concordia Seminary, graduating in 1953. From 1953 to 1966 he was a parish pastor in New Jersey. In 1959 he received the Th.D. degree from Union Theological Seminary,* New York. His dissertation was published under the title *Which Way to Lutheran Unity? A History of Efforts to Unite the Lutherans of America* (Concordia, 1966). From 1966 to 1969 he was executive secretary of the Lutheran Council in the USA, a cooperative agency for several American Lutheran denominations, including the Missouri Synod. After his dismissal from Concordia Seminary he became president of Christ Seminary–Seminex,* an independent Lutheran seminary formed by former faculty and students of Concordia Seminary. He served in this post from 1975 until 1987, when Seminex was merged into three existing seminaries at the time of the formation of the Evangelical Lutheran Church in America (ELCA). Resigning shortly after his election as bishop of the ELCA's Metropolitan Chicago Synod in 1987, Tietjen became a parish pastor in Texas.

Bibliography. Tietjen, John H., *Memoirs in Exile: Confessional Hope and Institutional Conflict* (Minneapolis: Fortress Press, 1990).

Donald L. Huber

Toy, Crawford Howell. Crawford Howell Toy (1836–1919), Baptist scholar and educator, was born in Norfolk, Virginia. He graduated in 1856 with honors from the University of Virginia, taught English for three years at the Albemarle Female Institute, Charlottesville, Virginia, and studied theology for one year at the Southern Baptist Theological Seminary,* then in Greenville, South Carolina, with the intention of becoming a missionary to Japan. In 1861 he joined the Confederate army as a private and later became a chaplain. After the war he taught Greek for a year in the University of Virginia. For two years he studied theology and Semitic languages at the University of Berlin. In 1869 he was appointed professor of Old Testament interpretation in the Southern Baptist Theological Seminary, which in 1877 was moved to Louisville, Kentucky.

Toy's views on the inspiration of the Bible began to reflect the results of his Berlin studies and ongoing biblical scholarship. Specifically, they led him to interpret the Bible in the light of its own times and not literally. He gave up efforts to harmonize the first chapters of Genesis and science, concluding that the Genesis chapters represented the crude cosmogonic ideas of the Israelites who borrowed them from the Babylonians. He believed that God permitted his servants to "convey truth in the form proper to the time." The proper approach to the Bible was to "take the kernel of truth from its outer covering of myth." He believed that the Servant mentioned in Isaiah 42:1–4 and 53:1–12 referred to Israel, though there was a final fulfillment in Christ. He believed that the Bible was wholly divine and wholly human and that the Scripture was the truth of God communicated by him to the human soul, appropriated by it, and then given out with free, human energy as the sincere, real conviction of the soul. The writers of Scripture had received messages from God and uttered them under purely free, human conditions. They spoke in their own language, not another's, and wrote under the conditions of their own age, not under those of some other age. Toy believed that the Scriptures declared the fact of God's divine inspiration but said nothing of the manner of his action. Regarding the New Testament, he said that finding a historical or other inaccuracy did not affect the divine teachings of these books, since the center of the New Testament was Christ and salvation was in him. Historical errors could not affect the fact of his existence and teachings.

When the seminary moved to Louisville, Kentucky, in 1877, it faced a financial crisis. Encountering opposition to his views and sensitive to the seminary's financial conditions and fund-raising efforts now perhaps hurt by his views, Toy submitted a letter of resignation to the Board of Trustees in May 1879 presenting his views and stating that they did not conflict with the "Fundamental Principles of the Seminary,'' a document seminary professors signed. The board accepted his resignation.

The controversy between Toy and his opponents rested on differences in his view of inspiration from those held by Baptists* generally. The message was clear to professors in Baptist seminaries. They were supposed to teach only views acceptable to Southern Baptists. Biblical scholarship must take a second place to denominational orthodoxy. Financial exigency and expediency took precedence over academic freedom.* There were two understandings of ''Truth.'' Toy was never tried for heresy; indeed, he chose not to push his views to a heresy trial, and his opponents did not persist in bringing him to trial. He moved to New York, where he became literary editor of the *Independent*. In 1880 he was called to Harvard as Hancock Professor of Hebrew and other Oriental languages, a position he held with distinction and scholarly success until his retirement in 1909.

Bibliography. Lyon, David C. ''Crawford Howell Toy,'' *Harvard Theological Review* 13 (January 1920); Shriver, G. H., ed., *American Religious Heretics* (Nashville: Abingdon Press, 1966); Toy, C. H., *History of the Religions of Israel* (Boston: Unitarian Sunday-School Society, 1882); Toy, C. H., ''Toy's Letter of Resignation to the Board of Trustees'' (Library, Southern Baptist Theological Seminary; a copy is in Shriver's work).

Donald L. Huber

Transcendentalism. From the Hebrew Scriptures and Eastern religions to Plato and Plotinus, Augustine and medieval scholasticism, the Cambridge Platonists, Immanuel Kant, Emerson, and Thoreau, transcendentalism (literally, the study of that which is ''beyond'') has occupied a prominent place in the history of humanity's search for religious and philosophical knowledge. In American religious history transcendentalism experienced its greatest prominence among a group of New England writers, ministers, and intellectuals between 1830 and 1860. Centered in and around Concord, Massachusetts, these transcendentalists eventually formed a most heterogeneous ''club,'' but not without sharing a number of romantic attitudes and beliefs concerning various religious, philosophical, and social ideas. As children of a New England Unitarianism that during the early decades of the nineteenth century largely rejected the bulk of its Calvinistic heritage, the transcendentalists revolted against the vestiges of rationalism, materialism, and mechanism derived from Locke, Paley, and Enlightenment philosophy still present in the Unitarianism of the 1830s. The two Concordites who gained the most enduring legacy as transcendentalists were Ralph Waldo Emerson (1803–1882), a former Unitarian minister turned essayist, lecturer, and poet, whose seminal works *Nature* (1836), ''The American Scholar'' (1837), and ''The Divinity School Address'' (1838) provided a definite shape and context for American transcendentalism; and Henry David Thoreau (1817–1862), Emerson's eccentric disciple and noted naturalist whose *Walden* (1854) and *A Week on the Concord and Merrimack Rivers* (1849), as well as such essays as

"Resistance to Civil Government" (1849) and "Life without Principle" (1863), provided a practical demonstration of transcendental idealism. Other leading voices of American transcendentalism included William Ellery Channing (1780–1842), an outspoken anti-Calvinist Unitarian minister whose sermon "Unitarian Christianity" (1819) provided a foundation for the "liberal" beliefs the transcendentalists would build upon; Amos Bronson Alcott (1799–1888), political and educational reformer and father of Louisa May Alcott; George Ripley (1802–1880), militant reformer and founder of Brook Farm, the grand transcendental social experiment, as well as the *Dial*, transcendentalism's short-lived periodical; Orestes Augustus Brownson* (1803–1876), whose search for "true" religious experience eventually led him from the dormant creedalism of Unitarianism to the living institutional creedalism of Roman Catholicism; Frederic Henry Hedge (1805–1890), founder in 1836 of the Transcendental Club; Margaret Fuller* (1810–1850), outspoken feminist, literary critic, journalist, and first editor of the *Dial* (1840–1844); Theodore Parker* (1810–1860), dissenting Unitarian minister whose heterodox views on inspiration of Scripture and miracles were made famous in his 1841 sermon "The Transient and Permanent in Christianity"; and Jones Very (1813–1880), whose poetry exhibits one of the most eccentric voices within transcendentalism. Walt Whitman should be added to this list as well; though not from New England, he nevertheless voiced the concerns and attitudes of transcendentalism throughout his poetry and prose.

Though as a group these transcendentalists never arrived at a truly informative definition of transcendentalism, Emerson was right when he asserted in "The Transcendentalist" (1842) that "what is popularly called Transcendentalism among us is Idealism." It was an idealism grounded largely on a Neoplatonic foundation, modified by the epistemological idealism of Kant, Fichte, and Schelling, and then filtered through the romantic idealism of Goethe, Wordsworth, Coleridge, and Carlyle and even Mme. de Stael and Victor Cousin. Its adherents sought to reverse the Lockean emphasis upon sense experience as well as Calvinism's doctrine of man's bondage to sin by proclaiming the supremacy of "intuitive thought" and the "divine spark" within each person. As Charles Mayo Ellis noted in *An Essay on Transcendentalism* (1842), transcendentalism "maintains that man has ideas, that come not through the five senses, or the powers of reasoning; but are either the result of direct revelation from God, his immediate inspiration, or his immanent presence in the spiritual world" (Miller, 23). In every facet of life and thought they sought to liberate the self from any view of religion, philosophy, literature, and society that fostered spiritual servitude, intellectual conformity, and material dependence.

Though best known for its literary legacy, American transcendentalism began primarily as an "unorganized" movement among a group of Unitarian ministers determined to dispense with a religion of stale dogma and clichéd cultural pieties in favor of a truly "religious" experience based upon an immediate awareness of one's relation to the divine. Whereas the Calvinistic view of man looks within and sees total depravity, the transcendentalists looked within and saw innate divinity. Theirs was a celebration of universalism and the ultimate human ability to become godlike ("I am part and particle of God," Emerson said in *Nature*) that stood in stark contrast to Calvin's doctrine of limited atonement for "the elect" alone and man's inability to approach God. To the transcendentalists, man's point of connection with the divine came not through God's prevenient grace derived from an inspired Scripture but by way of man's innate intuitive powers, present within a creative imagination that mirrored God's mind itself, working organically through man and nature in a manner that transformed the transparent material world through its power to perceive the transcendental spiritual realities that lay beyond. As a consequence, Christ was no longer necessary as the mediator between man and God, for "self-reliant" man could now serve as his own mediator. Christ was man's savior, not because his death as the "God-man" propitiated God's judgment upon sin, but because his life as a "man-God" served as the supreme example for all humanity of one man's recognition of his innate divinity and relation to God. To the transcendentalists, Christ was more fully divine than any other human being not because he was the incarnate God performing miracles on earth but because he was a man participating fully in the miracle of divine immanence, so that his declaration "I and my Father are one" (John 10:30) was a statement to be appropriated by all men, not just himself.

Such a view of man and his divinity was bound to have ramifications in all areas of life and thought. The majority of the transcendentalist ministers allowed these views to modify but by no means extinguish an already-liberal Christian theology, but some of the more radical transcendentalists soon found themselves either completely outside the bounds of the church and traditional orthodoxy (such as Ripley and Emerson) or at extreme odds with the Unitarianism of the 1840s and 1850s (such as Theodore Parker). Parker never left the Unitarian Church, despite efforts by the Boston Association to have him removed. What the transcendentalist controversy did force from the Unitarians was an attempt (though reluctant and feeble) at the barest of creeds, but a creed nevertheless that attempted to retain the essence of transcendentalism (the intuitive awareness of God within man as a result of his "divine spark") without its most radical (what the conservative Unitarians considered "non-Christian") tenets—the denial of the supernatural origins of Christianity and the Scriptures, with the accompanying dismissal of miracles and the "unique" deity and sacrifice of Christ. Whether they became religious mavericks seeking spiritual experience apart from ecclesiastical constraints or liberals not willing to relinquish all their "Christian" distinctives, the American transcendentalists were convinced that both man and society needed a transcendental cleansing. As a result, between 1830 and 1860 they maintained, in their pulpits and with their pens, a militant opposition to slavery, imperialism (such as the Mexican War), and the increasing tendency toward bureaucratization in government and "philistinism" in American culture. By exalting self-reliance and intuitive experience, the transcendentalists, as Whitman noted in *Democratic Vistas,* argued for a humane democracy, whether in religion, government, or belles lettres, driven by an exalted individualism grounded upon the innate goodness of man, the necessity for freedom of expression, and the ultimate reality of man's oneness with his fellow human beings, the natural world, and the divine.

Bibliography. Albanese, Catherine L., *Corresponding Motion: Transcendental Religion and the New America* (Philadelphia: Temple University Press, 1977); Boller, Paul F., *American Transcendentalism, 1830–1860: An Intellectual Inquiry* (New York: Putnam, 1974); Gura, Philip F., and Joel Myerson, eds, *Critical Essays on American Transcendentalism* (Boston: G. K. Hall, 1982); Hutchison, William R., *The Transcendentalist Ministers: Church Reform in the New England Renaissance* (New Haven: Yale University Press, 1959); Miller, Perry, *The Transcendentalists, an Anthology* (Cambridge: Harvard University Press, 1960).

Timothy D. Whelan

Transubstantiation. In eucharistic theology, transubstantiation is the conversion of the whole substance of the bread and wine into the whole substance of the body and blood of Christ, with only the appearances (also called species or accidents) remaining. Belief in transubstantiation was defined as part of Catholic faith in the Fourth Lateran Council (1215). Further elaboration of the idea in Scholastic theology received its classic formulation in the thought of Thomas Aquinas in the thirteenth century.

All the sixteenth-century Protestant reformers repudiated transubstantiation, substituting alternative notions such as consubstantiation (Luther), impanation (Osiander), virtualism (Calvin), or symbolism (Zwingli). In response to such challenges, the Council of Trent (1551) condemned Protestant variations and reaffirmed the traditional Catholic teaching. Catholics and Protestants in America continued these arguments in tracts, books, religious periodicals, and public debates. The pragmatic and reductionist tendencies of American revivalism* made the mystery and subtleties of Catholic eucharistic dogma highly suspect to evangelical Protestants especially.

Yet even Catholics themselves began to argue over the finer points of Scholastic terminology in the early twentieth century as advances in modern physics raised questions about the process of eucharistic conversion. What happens at the atomic or even subatomic level when bread and wine are transubstantiated? The most visible contenders in these latter controversies have been Europeans, but their arguments have been followed closely and defended or challenged in the United States as well.

One midcentury debate focused on the meaning of the term "substance" in the definition of transubstantiation. On the one side were claims that the substance of bread and wine can be identified with the particles of modern physics (molecules, atoms, protons, electrons, and so on), which cease to exist when converted into the body and blood of Christ, leaving only their accidents, such as extension, mass, and electrical charges. On the other side lay the claim that substance is a strictly metaphysical reality; the change effected through transubstantiation lies beyond any reality open to physical experience or the science of physics. From this perspective, the particles identifiable by science all lie in the realm of accidents.

More recent debates have left the Scholastic tradition altogether and drawn their philosophical assumptions from phenomenology and existentialism instead, offering such terms as "transignification" or "transfinalization" to describe the eucharistic event. For some theorists, the substance of a thing is its meaning and final destination, which are ultimately assigned by God. If God, in the Eucharist, designates bread and wine as Christ's body and blood, then their substance has been transformed, because "things are what God wants them to be." Others speak of a "relational ontology" in which a reality is constituted through its relational connections. Though the bread and wine remain unchanged as physical realities, they change as they are placed by Christ within his relation to his community.

These notions have themselves been dismissed by some as artificial and no more intelligible than the medieval teachings they seek to replace. These critics insist that all attempts, medieval or modern, to divorce reality from appearances only lead to skepticism. Instead, the Eucharist must be approached primarily as ritual, along a path that directs us to the mystery of the real presence of Christ.

A few ecumenists have found these developments promising, but official Catholic response to the newer speculations has been disapproving. Pope Pius XII's encyclical *Humani Generis* (1950) complained that some Catholic theologians were reducing the eucharistic presence to a mere symbolism. Similar criticisms were further developed in Paul VI's *Mysterium Fidei* (1965), which insisted that theories of the eucharistic conversion must recognize it as nothing less than an ontological change. Meanwhile, as theologians and church officials debate the implications of transubstantiation, the broader traditional meaning of the Eucharist seems to be fading in the church at large: A 1994 national opinion poll of American Catholics showed that only 34 percent believe that "the bread and wine are changed into the body and blood of Christ"; a full 63 percent saw the elements only as "symbolic reminders."

Bibliography. FitzPatrick, P. J., *In Breaking of Bread: The Eucharist and Ritual* (Cambridge: Cambridge University Press, 1993); Kilmartin, E. J., "Sacramental Theology: The Eucharist in Recent Literature," *Theological Studies* 32 (1971): 233–77; Vollert, C., "The Eucharist: Controversy on Transubstantiation," *Theological Studies* 22 (1961): 391–425.

                                                                                                          T. Paul Thigpen

Trusteeism. Within the context of American Catholicism, trusteeism is the name given to an effort to place parishes under the control, through civil law, of the lay trustees, who will then hire and fire the local pastor and own the church property. Lay intrusion into church affairs has a long history within Catholicism, and trusteeism is its American episode. Trusteeism emerged primarily as a problem in the East and South and lasted for almost a century after the American Revolution. The roots of this movement are within the over-whelmingly Protestant milieu of American Catholicism during the colonial, rev-olutionary, and antebellum eras. Since Protestant churches had lay trustees or churchwardens who operated and owned the local church, local Catholic churches should be operated in the same manner.

Trusteeism appeared first in New York City's pioneer Catholic parish of St. Peter's. Father. John Carroll, then prefect apostolic for the United States, ap-pointed Father Charles Whelan, O.F.M., Capuchin, as New York's first resident Catholic priest in June 1785. Another Franciscan Capuchin, Irishman Andrew Nugent, arrived and became his assistant. By January 1786 the two clerics were at loggerheads, with Father Nugent vying to become paster. St. Peter's Board of Trustees invoked the civil law of incorporation to dismiss Whelan and retain Nugent as their pastor. Carroll rejected this assumption of civil powers against his authority and told the board that if he accepted it, "the unity and Catholicity of the Church is at an end; it would be formed into distinct and independent Societies; nearly in the same manner, as the Congregational Presbyterians of your neighboring New England States." The trustees defied Carroll, fired Whe-lan, and retained Nugent as pastor. Nugent then alienated the trustees, who initiated civil action to remove him. Father Nugent was eventually suspended from the priesthood and died in schism. By 1790 St. Peter's was operating under Carroll's authority.

During the first six decades of the nineteenth century, trusteeism spread to other parishes and arose for various reasons. In New Orleans the French *mar-guilliers* refused to accept the authority of Bishop Carroll in 1805 and appointed their own pastor. This kept St. Louis parish, later Cathedral, in schism for almost forty years. Similiar situations occurred in Philadelphia, Baltimore, Buffalo, Norfolk, and Charleston, South Carolina. American bishops appealed to Rome, and two popes issued decrees in 1822 and 1828 that reiterated the policy that church property and control belonged to the hierarchy. Bishop John England of Charleston went around civil law concerning trustees by demanding the property deed for any church being built in his diocese. This policy was adopted over the next few decades.

This issue entered politics during the nativistic, anti-Catholic uproar of the 1850s. When New York Archbishop John Hughes had a Catholic assemblyman introduce a bill giving the Catholic hierarchy control over church affairs and property in 1851, this was portrayed as an attempt to allow an undemocratic, foreign prince to manipulate church affairs in America. Hughes's bill was de-feated, and similar actions by Catholic bishops in Connecticut, Pennsylvania, New Jersey, and Arkansas failed to pass between 1849 and 1855. In states like Pennsylvania and New York laws were passed stating that church property could only be owned by a lay board of trustees. Although the Pennsylvania law was repealed soon, the New York law was not revised until 1863, allowing for church property to be controlled by the Catholic hierarchy. A decision by the U.S. Supreme Court in 1872 also upheld church authorities in litigation over church properties. By the time of the Third Plenary Council in 1884, the trustee controversy was over for most American Catholic churches.

Trusteeism did not totally die, appearing after 1884 in ethnic disputes over local parishes. This led to the creation of such groups as the Polish National Church or the Ukrainian National Church. Given the overwhelmingly Protestant religious culture in America, it was perhaps inevitable that a form of Catholic congregationalism, under the name of trusteeism, would arise. By halting this process and maintaining hierarchical control over church property, the bishops preserved a distinct Catholic church structure, although this type of system would be viewed with suspicion by many other Americans well into the twentieth century.

Bibliography. Dignan, Patrick J., *A History of the Legal Incorporation of Catholic Church Properties in the United States, 1784–1932* (Washington, DC: Catholic University of America Press, 1933); McNamara, Robert F., "Trusteeism," *New Catholic Encyclopedia,* 15 vols. (New York: McGraw-Hill, 1967), 14:323–25; Hennesey, James J., *American Catholics: A History of the Roman Catholic Community in the United States* (New York: Oxford University Press, 1981).

James M. Woods

Truth, Sojourner. Born to slave parents in 1797 in Ulster County, New York, Sojourner Truth was first named Isabella. Early in life she was separated from her parents and was owned by a Dutch family. She labored for these rural elite, who specialized in lumber, grain, and commerce. Living with several families, she suffered beatings and abuse. When her owner refused to free her as he had promised, she walked to freedom, carrying her youngest child with her. She changed her name to Sojourner Truth when she was instructed by a voice in 1843 to travel and preach the truth of God.

Sojourner Truth devoted her life to the antislavery movement and the rights of women, attracting the attention of abolitionists such as Bishop Daniel Payne, Frederick Douglass, and Harriet Beecher Stowe.* Before the Civil War she traveled extensively from New England to Michigan, where she eventually made her headquarters at Battle Creek.

Although she was illiterate, her fiery speeches were filled with quotations from the Bible, vivid metaphors, and mystical references. She was inspired by her family bonds as well as by her beliefs. She was taught how to cope with the disruptive forces she experienced both as a child and as an adult, forging an identity rooted both in African traditions and in Christianity. Through memory and oral tradition molded by a vivid awareness of the spiritual presence of God, she was empowered to attack both slavery and the treatment of women. She was one of the first freedom riders when public transportation was desegregated in Washington and northern Virginia.

Truth was an astute observer of people and was a master at addressing people and confronting critical issues relating to self-determination and human rights of African-American people. After the Civil War Sojourner Truth worked diligently on behalf of freed people despite her age, urging the government to address poverty and violence among the African-American communities of the North and South.

Bibliography. Mabee, Carlton, with Susan Mabee Newhouse, *Sojourner Truth: Slave, Prophet, Legend* (New York: New York University Press, 1993); Sterling, Dorothy, *We Are Your Sisters: Black Women in the Nineteenth Century* (New York: Norton, 1985); Truth, Sojourner, *Narrative of Sojourner Truth*, edited with an introduction by Margaret Washington (New York: Vintage Books, 1993).

Coleman Markham

Turner, Henry McNeal. Henry McNeal Turner (1834–1915), a prominent African Methodist Episcopal Church (AME) bishop and race and political leader, was born in Newberry Courthouse, South Carolina, and died in Windsor, Canada. Largely privately educated and self-taught, Turner joined the Methodist Episcopal Church, South, in 1848, received a preacher's license in 1853, and served as an evangelist (1853–1857). In 1858 he embraced the AME Church, an African-American denomination, served as an evangelist (1858–1862), and pastored Israel AME Church in Washington, D.C. (1862–1863). While in Washington, he recruited African-American army troops and became the first black army chaplain (1863–1865). Accompanying troops to the South (1863–1865), he also worked as a missionary and church organizer, one of the greatest among white and black northern Methodist contenders for the alliance of southern black Christians. His most successful work, the Georgia conference became the connection's largest prior to 1876. Active in Georgia Reconstruction politics, Turner served as Macon postmaster (1869) and in the state House of Representatives (1868, 1870). Additionally, Turner was presiding elder (1865–1867), connectional newspaper founder of the *Southern Christian Recorder* (1889) and the *Voice of Missions* (1892), general manager of the AME Book Concern (1876–1880), bishop (1880–1915), and supporter of the Methodist Holiness movement, prohibition, and African missions.

With increased mistreatment of African Americans in the post-Reconstruction South, Turner, a proud race spokesperson, became involved in a number of political controversies by advocating African emigration as the only means to black freedom, using armed self-defense against lynchings, and voting for certain Democratic presidential candidates because of the Republicans' neglect of blacks. In the 1880s Turner, almost igniting a connectional schism, ordained Sarah Hughes deacon in South Carolina, an action later abrogated by the denomination. Sometimes seen as halting proposed unification (1880s) of the AME and the AME Zion, Turner insisted on retaining the name ''African'' in the new church title. His essay ''God Is a Negro'' spoke eloquently about affirming the African heritage in religious thinking and art, but caused a stir in some denominational circles.

Bibliography. Angell, Stephen, *Bishop Henry McNeal Turner and African American Religion in the South* (1992); *Dictionary of Christianity in America*, Hill, Samuel S., ed.

(Downers Grove: InterVarsity Press, 1990); *Encyclopedia of Religion in the South* (Macon, GA: Mercer University Press, 1984).

Sandy Dwayne Martin

Turner, Nat. The revolt staged by Baptist preacher Nat Turner from Southampton, Virginia, confirmed the worst fears of the southern white people. Nat Turner was a deeply religious man, evangelical and morally well-disciplined. He was taught by his parents and grandmother that he was destined for a great purpose. They were convinced that he had special knowledge. He knew the stories from the Bible and songs from the African-American community, many of which protested against the injustices of slavery.

In his spiritual encounters with the Spirit of God, he became convinced that God wanted him to lead the establishment of a Kingdom of Righteousness in which slavery would be abolished. Turner increasingly saw visions and waited for signs. For Turner, Christ would soon return to the earth in the midst of a battle of white and black spirits. He was convinced that he was being called by God to lead the way in ushering in the new Kingdom. He only had to wait for the sign, and he would then take up the sword against the enemy.

After 1825 he began having a series of visions that lasted until 1831 and that he interpreted as signs of the appearing of Christ. During that period he and his friends organized the final revolt against the white enemy. After a solar eclipse in the winter of 1831 and unusual atmospheric occurrences in the summer, he was convinced that it was time for the revolt.

The revolt began on August 21, 1831. Although numerous white people were killed during the early days, Turner's group was overwhelmed by the militia and soldiers. He escaped but was captured on October 30. Following a trial, he was hanged on November 11, 1831.

Turner was convinced that the revolt was ordained by a just God who was on the African-American side in the struggle for freedom. Although the rebels did not achieve their goal, the quest for justice was gaining momentum.

Bibliography. Aptheker, Herbert, *American Negro Slave Revolts* (1943. Reprint. New York: International Publishers, 1963); Aptheker, Herbert, *Nat Turner's Slave Rebellion* (New York: Humanities Press, 1966); Harding, Vincent, *There Is a River* (New York: Harcourt Brace Jovanovich, 1981); Oates, Stephen B., *The Fires of Justice* (New York: Harper and Row, 1975); Tragle, Henry I., ed., *The Southampton Slave Revolt of 1831* (Amherst: University of Massachusetts Press, 1971).

Coleman Markham

U

Unification Church. The terms "the Moonies" and "Reverend Moon" attained nearly universal recognition in America after 1974 for about a decade. These referred to a religious group and its founder, a movement whose reputation was far from savory. The means by which it was alleged to attract a few thousand followers, mostly young adult children from society's better classes, were commonly attributed to deceit, high-pressure tactics, and even "brainwashing." The Unification Church's founder was viewed with suspicion, and its teachings were regarded as weird at best. Observers were hard pressed to recall such a sudden dramatic burst onto the American scene by a movement with such small numbers, in particular one that evoked such an incendiary reaction.

Rooted in Korean history, the Unification Church is properly identified with its founder, the Reverend Sun Myung Moon, his life, and his spiritual vision and teachings. This young (1954) body's official name is revealing: the Holy Spirit Association for the Unification of World Christianity.

Reverend Sun Myung Moon, or "Father," was born in 1920 in Korea to parents who converted to Presbyterianism when he was ten. Always deeply religious, he experienced an appearance of Jesus at age sixteen. During his student days he became politically active, first participating in the Korean independence movement. Following the end of World War II, he continued both his spiritual quest and his political involvement, activities that landed him in Communist prisons several times. During one stretch, 1948–1950, the treatment he received was notably harsh and oppressive. His profound opposition to communism as both political system and economic theory, an enduring dedication that has informed him and the church's policies, stems from these very difficult years.

Moon's composition of *Divine Principle*, the Unificationist sacred text that supplements the Bible, began in 1951. The book was completed the next year, and the church was founded three years later. Suspicion and sharp criticism greeted its emergence, one feature of which was a brief imprisonment for Moon and a few others. A second momentous event along Moon's spiritual journey occurred in 1960 with his marriage to Hak Ja Han. It was indeed momentous inasmuch as family is the central metaphor and value in Unification Church life. No Church teaching is more distinctive or determinative than the conviction that Rev. and Mrs. Moon are True Parents; rather than being just inspiring, that term stands as a theological claim.

Being married and having and rearing children properly is more than a convention or a healthy way to live. Such behavior is a virtual definition of godly living. Placing such a high value on family—from True Parents to one's own generation of a family—occasions and justifies the highly eccentric Unificationist means for identifying one's marriage partner. The selection is not made by the couple; indeed, each marriage, referred to as "the Blessing," is prearranged. On the conviction that God has preordained every mate selection, a Blessing Committee made up of older Blessed wives examines the credentials of young members applying for marriage. The information gathered is provided to Rev. Moon, who then does the selecting. Divorce is strictly forbidden, as are, of course, any extramarital sexual relations.

Rev. Moon has been sent into the world to complete the unfinished mission of Jesus. Members do not equivocate in their confession to be Christian. Yet they have a special vocation: to unify the worldwide, diversified Christian movement around the enlarging and fulfilling messianic mission of Rev. Sun Myung Moon. The revelation to and through him brings about the Completed Testament era, the age that began in 1960, superseding the biblical era. He is the Lord of the Second Advent who came to heal the division between man and God.

The Church of Rev. Moon founded in Korea has spread broadly, having some measure of presence in well over one hundred nations. Membership in the United States never has reached ten thousand, while figures for Korean and Japanese membership stand near half a million. The movement's notoriety has dimmed greatly, and its presence in America is far less visible than in its 1970s heyday. Even if it expands considerably, we may doubt that the Unification Church will ever attract American notice as it did then. Still, it remains active in political and educational endeavors, sponsoring high-level conferences devoted to world unity and peace, supported by Moon's and the church's extensive investments and commercial operations.

Bibliography. Barker, Eileen, *The Making of a Moonie* (Oxford: Basil Blackwell, 1984); Biermans, John T., *The Odyssey of New Religious Movements* (Lewiston, NY: Edwin Mellen Press, 1986); Bromley, David G., and Anson D. Shupe, Jr., *"Moonies" in America* (Beverly Hills, CA: Sage Publications, 1979); *Divine Principle* (Terrytown, NY: Holy

Spirit Association for the Unification of World Christianity, 1973); Mickler, Michael L., *A History of the Unification Church in America, 1959–1974* (New York: Garland, 1993).

Samuel S. Hill

Union Theological Seminary. A small group of New York Presbyterians founded Union Theological Seminary as an alternative to the intense theological controversies that dominated antebellum American theology and theological education. In addition to the battle between Trinitarians and Unitarians that raged from 1800 onward, American Congregationalists struggled over the theology of Nathaniel Taylor of Yale. This particular battle was so passionate that conservatives established a counterseminary, the Theological Institute of Connecticut at East Windsor, to teach their doctrines. Many orthodox Congregationalists were also fearful that the revivalism* of Charles G. Finney,* often called the New Measures, might lead the denomination into heresy.

Theological issues divided Presbyterians even more deeply. The Second Great Awakening* had two primary emphases. Part of the awakening was a significant ingathering of members by the American churches. Led by the Baptists* and the Methodists, a large number of people experienced an emotional conversion that led them to resolve to live holy and respectable lives. Although many of the new saints entered the church in time-honored ways, the thrust of the revival was toward the belief that individuals could decide whether they wished salvation or not. In other words, neither original sin nor predestination* was a bar to taking effective spiritual action to secure one's own salvation. These new theological emphases entered the Presbyterian Church through such revivalists as Charles G. Finney. Not only did Finney use many Methodist techniques, including the altar call and popular "gospel music," but he also accepted much of their theology. For Finney, there was no reason why an individual could not make himself or herself a new heart. Salvation was available to all. In less blatant ways, such Presbyterian leaders as Albert Barnes, the popular pastor of Philadelphia's First Presbyterian Church, said much the same thing. Barnes was tried for heresy twice. The first time was for what he said in a published sermon, "The Way of Salvation," and the second time was for his commentary on Romans. In both, Barnes affirmed the importance of human decision in conversion.

Theology was not the only offense. The leaders of the Second Great Awakening had established a number of voluntary societies to convert the world and the nation. Beginning with the American Board of Commissioners in 1810, they had established the American Sunday School Union, the American Home Missionary Society, the American Bible Society, the American Educational Society, and the American Tract Society. Although these societies invited Christians of all denominations to join, they were predominantly Congregational and Presbyterian. Despite agreement with the goals of these voluntary agencies, their extraecclesiastical status worried many strict Presbyterians. One of the premises of Presbyterianism is that the church should control its ministries through its own church courts and that all of the church's ministries should be responsible to the General Assembly. Strict Presbyterians, led by ministers in the area of Pittsburgh, wanted to replace the societies with boards organized under the General Assembly.

The founders of Union Theological Seminary represented those who supported the revival and the societies. Their hope was to establish a school that would stand above these battles. In their own words, they wanted a theological seminary "around which all men, of moderate views and feelings, who desire to live free from party strife, and to stand aloof from all the extremes of doctrinal speculation, practical radicalism, and ecclesiastical domination may cordially and affectionately rally." The school later accepted a limited oversight by the New School Presbyterian General Assembly and, after 1868, the General Assembly of the United Presbyterian Church. Nonetheless, it retained its original independence. Union's Board of Directors was self-governing, with full authority to determine its own membership.

The name Union was given to the seminary in 1839 in its act of incorporation by the New York State legislature. The sources give varying reasons for the name. These range from the need to distinguish the school from the General Theological Seminary (Episcopal) to the desire of the founders to protest the 1837–1838 division of the Presbyterian Church into Old and New School denominations. Others have seen the name as an expression of the original desire to stand above theological divisions.

One way that Union worked to fulfill its unique mandate was through the promotion of theological scholarship. German-trained Edward Robinson, the seminary's first Bible professor, had a worldwide reputation as a student of biblical geography. His *Researches in Palestine* (1841) was the first American book simultaneously published in a German translation. Henry Boynton Smith and Philip Schaff,* both church historians, continued to advance Union's position as a center of advanced scholarship based on continental models.

Union's scholarly commitments were seriously threatened in the 1890s when the Presbyterian Church tried and convicted Charles Augustus Briggs,* the seminary's Old Testament professor, for heresy. Briggs was one of the most eminent scholars of his generation. His book *Biblical Studies,* published in 1883, summarized much of the advanced biblical study of his generation. Briggs, whose theological interests were encyclopedic, also published widely in Presbyterian history and produced a theological encyclopedia. Briggs had also taken a leading role in the drive to revise the Presbyterian standards. His pamphlet "Whither" was a tightly reasoned argument for a creed that was in closer harmony with modern thought than the Westminster Confession and Catechism.

Briggs's trial stemmed from remarks that he made at his inauguration as Edward Robinson Professor of Biblical Theology in 1891. The trustees had recently established the chair to honor Robinson, and Briggs was a natural choice to be its first occupant. Briggs's chosen theme was the authority of the Bible, and he sought to show how traditional understandings of the Bible actually hindered people from understanding the text. Among these were, he said, verbal inspiration, inerrancy, the violation of the laws of nature or miracle, and belief in predictive prophecy. The address immediately raised controversy, which was probably Briggs's intention.

The intensity of the controversy, however, was more than Briggs or anyone else had anticipated. The Presbyterian Church tried and convicted him of heresy and ordered him removed from the ministry. Union's Board of Directors faced a hard choice. The school had voluntarily allowed the Presbyterian Church to superintend its teaching and its faculty. In the main, this had been a useful relationship for both the school and the church. The trial of Professor Briggs put things in a different light. Although Union continued to consider itself a Presbyterian school, the seminary's Board of Directors officially withdrew from its agreements with the denomination. The effects of this decision were not immediately felt, but the directors' action set a direction for the school. Over the years, Union would become progressively more ecumenical in its faculty and student body.

Bibliography. Handy, Robert T., *A History of Union Theological Seminary in New York* (New York: Columbia University Press, 1987); Loetscher, Lefferts, *The Broadening Church: A Study of Theological Issues in the Presbyterian Church since 1869* (Philadelphia: University of Pennsylvania Press, 1972); Rogers, Max Gray, "Charles Augustus Briggs: Heresy at Union," in *American Religious Heretics,* ed. George Shriver (New York: Abingdon Press, 1966).

Glenn Miller

Unitarianism/Universalism. Unitarianism and Universalism are two liberal religious reactions to Calvinist orthodoxy with different origins and emphases but significant commonalities. Universalism—the doctrine that all people will ultimately be saved—first took shape as an identifiable American movement under the leadership of John Murray (1741–1815), an itinerant English preacher who arrived in New Jersey in 1770. Challenging the Reformed doctrines of unconditional election and limited atonement, he preached throughout the colonies, and the first Universalist Church in America was founded in Gloucester, Massachusetts, in 1779.

In 1803 the New England convention of Universalists (formed in 1792) adopted the Winchester Profession of Faith, affirming their belief in biblical revelation, the moral necessity of good works, and the certainty of eventual salvation for all. But this consensus was shattered by debate over the teaching of Hosea Ballou (1771–1852), who in 1817 became pastor of Second Universalist Church in Boston. Ballou's "ultra-Universalism" held that the consequences of sin manifest themselves only in the present life; all are saved immediately after death. Ballou's opponents, the "Restorationists," insisted instead on a limited, purgative punishment after death.

Later controversies in the denomination were provoked by the encounter with German-English rationalism, biblical criticism, evolutionary theory, the Social

Gospel movement,* and humanism. These movements influenced many Universalists to view the Bible as fallible and non-Christian religions as equally valid roads to the universal goal of realizing human potential.

Unitarianism emerged more gradually in the early nineteenth century among the heirs of New England's Puritan founders. For some, Enlightenment assumptions were beginning to replace traditional religious certainties; they scandalized their more conservative colleagues by rejecting fundamental Calvinist doctrines such as total human depravity. The controversy captured public attention in 1805 when the liberal Henry Ware (1764–1845) was chosen the Hollis Professor of Divinity at Harvard. A war of theological pamphlets later ensued. As many of the established churches split between the orthodox and the innovators, the latter often gained legal control of church properties, bringing a number of Massachusetts's Puritan churches into the Unitarian fold.

In 1819 William Ellery Channing (1780–1842), pastor of the Federal Street Church in Boston, preached the sermon "Unitarian Christianity," the definitive statement of the movement. Channing championed the "rational" nature of Christianity, and though he affirmed that the Bible contained divine revelation, he called for the rejection of any interpretations that failed to satisfy the demands of human reason. Channing and his colleagues adopted the label "Unitarian" because the Christian doctrine of the Trinity—traditionally understood as a mystery inaccessible to human reason alone—was deemed unworthy of rational belief.

Questioning all religious tradition in the light of individual reason, Unitarians soon were denying the deity of Christ and the unique authority of the Bible as well. The American Unitarian Association was formed in 1825, but just as the movement seemed to be solidifying, Channing's rationalism was challenged by the new romanticism of the transcendentalists. Chief among these was Ralph Waldo Emerson (1803–1882), who drew from pantheistic Eastern sources to propose a religion received through intuition rather than reason.

When denominational leaders worked to organize Unitarians more effectively in the later nineteenth century, many suspected the imposition of a new orthodoxy. Some left to form the Free Religious Association in 1867, but others remained to push Unitarianism toward a completely noncreedal and essentially post-Christian stance. In the twentieth century the emerging Humanist wing of the movement spurred new debates by reformulating Unitarian theology on nontheistic grounds.

Meanwhile, seeking an ethical rather than dogmatic basis of religion, Unitarians came to emphasize a more social interpretation of religion, a move that harmonized with similar changes among the Universalists. The 1961 merger of the American Unitarian Association and the Universalist Church of America brought under the same roof a wide diversity of beliefs with a common ancestry of revolt against established ways of religious thought and practice.

Bibliography. Miller, R. E., *Larger Hope: The First Century of the Universalist Church in America, 1770–1870* (Boston: Unitarian Universalist Association, 1979); Robinson,

D., *The Unitarians and the Universalists* (Westport, CT: Greenwood Press, 1985); Wright, C., ed., *A Stream of Light: A Sesquicentennial History of American Unitarianism* (Boston: Unitarian Universalist Association, 1975).

T. Paul Thigpen

V

Varick, James. One of the founders of African-American Methodism, James Varick was born somewhere near Newburgh, New York, around 1750 and died in New York City on July 22, 1827. The son of a slave, he was a shoemaker by trade.

Varick and other African Americans in New York were in the habit of attending the John Street Methodist Church, sitting in a gallery. By 1796 the number of those attending had grown so large that Bishop Francis Asbury gave them permission to meet as a group in the church when it was not being used. In 1799 Varick led a group that built their own building, Zion Church. At first there was some debate about who should lead services at the church. Asbury ordained Varick in 1806. Several other congregations, from Connecticut to Pennsylvania, grew out of Zion Church.

In 1820 several Zion congregations allied themselves with another African-American church leader, Bishop Richard Allen* of Philadelphia. Varick's group responded by formally organizing themselves in 1821 as the African Methodist Episcopal Church. The word Zion was added to the title in 1848. Throughout his life Varick continued to work for improvements in the lot of African-Americans by founding schools and self-help associations.

Bibliography. Baldwin, Lewis, *"Invisible" Strands in African Methodism: A History of the African Union Methodist Protestant and Union American Methodist Protestant and Union American Methodist Episcopal Churches, 1805–1809* (Metuchen, NJ: Scarecrow Press, 1983); Turner, Smith, "A Man Named James Varick," *American Methodist Episcopal Zion Quarterly Review* 107 (1995): 29–33.

Albert A. Bell, Jr.

Vatican Council I. On June 29, 1867, Pope Pius IX announced that a General Council of the church would be convened at the Vatican, the first in three centuries. On December 8, 1869, this council opened with 689 prelates, most of whom were from Europe. Representing the American church were 6 archbishops, 40 bishops. By January it became clear that the main question being considered was papal infallibility.* Bishops from Italy, France, Spain, and Latin America favored a formal declaration of this doctrine. In opposition generally were prelates from nations where Catholics were a minority, Germany, England, and the United States. There were exceptions to this, as a small minority of French prelates were in opposition, while Archbishop Henry Manning of England was strongly in favor of the declaration.

American prelates were deeply divided. Archbishops Eugene Blanchet of Portland and Jean Odin of New Orleans and Bishops Michael Heiss of La Cross, William Elder of Natchez, Auguste Martin of Natchitoches, Claude Dubuis of Galveston, and Eugene O'Connell of Sacramento all advocated a formal declaration. Three archbishops and seventeen bishops signed a petition on January 12, 1870, stating that they believed in the doctrine, yet questioned the wisdom of such a declaration, as it might damage evangelization efforts. Actually, opposition bishops were not all that unified. Some, like Thaddeus Amat of Monterrey, California, and Edward Fitzgerald* of Little Rock, did not think that the time was opportune. Others, like Archbishop Peter Kenrick of St. Louis and Bishops Augustin Verot of Savannah, Michael Domenec of Pittsburgh, and Bernard McQuaid of Rochester, did not believe that the doctrine could be maintained either in Scripture or in tradition. Archbishops John Purcell of Cincinnati and Richard Whelan of Wheeling believed that the papacy must get universal consent from the bishops before declaring a new dogma for the church. Bishop Verot spoke so vociferously against the doctrine that certain French prelates dubbed him *l'enfant terrible*.

While the dissenters' position would not be accepted by the council, the assembly did alter the document in certain ways. The pontiff could only make statements on faith and morals, and he must explicitly state that he was speaking *ex cathedra*, from the throne of St. Peter. The pronouncement must be to the universal church, not just a particular region, and the pontiff must clearly state that he bound all the faithful to accept it. The pope's position, however, was not in any way dependent upon the consent of the bishops; they might be consulted, but this was not required.

On July 13, 1870, the first vote was taken, and 451 prelates voted *placet*, or "it pleases," 88 voted *non placet* or "it does not please," 62 prelates voted *placet juxta modum*, or "it pleases with modification," and 70 members of the council absented themselves. Pope Pius IX then ordered another vote on which the prelates must take a *placet* or *non placet* position.

The final vote was conducted on Monday, July 18, 1870. The 18 American prelates who had voted *placet* earlier came and repeated their vote. Of the 3 American prelates who had voted *placet juxta modum*, all now voted *placet*.

Three American members who had been absent earlier arrived and voted for the declaration, including the future prominent prelate James Gibbons. Of the 7 who had voted *non placet* five days earlier, 1 changed his mind, Bishop William McCloskey of Louisville, and thus 25 American bishops supported the declaration. Five of the other 7 refused to appear: Archbishop Kenrick and Bishops Verot, Domenec, McQuaid, and Ignatius Mrak of Marquette, Michigan. Only Bishop Fitzgerald returned and repeated his *non placet* vote, the Arkansas bishop stating his opinion after 491 successive affirmations. Eventually, 533 prelates voted for the declaration, and only 1 other person, Bishop Luigi Riccio of Cajazzo in Sicily, joined Fitzgerald in opposition. At the vote's conclusion, Bishop Fitzgerald went before the assembly and submitted to its decision.

All the American bishops eventually made public submission to the declaration, and most of the faithful accepted it as well. In Germany a major schism occurred as opponents founded the Old Catholic Church, believing that this new doctrine had deviated from earlier beliefs. While some Catholic theologians late in the twentieth century have challenged papal infallibility, it remains one of the officially declared doctrines of the Catholic Church.

Bibliography. Daniel-Rops, Henri, *The Church in the Age of Revolution, 1789–1870* (New York: E. P Dutton and Company, 1965); Hennesey, James J., *American Catholics: A History of the Roman Catholic Community in the United States* (New York: Oxford University Press, 1981); Hennesey, James J., *The First Council of the Vatican: The American Experience* (New York: Herder and Herder, 1963); McAvoy, Thomas T., *A History of the Catholic Church in the United States* (Notre Dame: University of Notre Dame Press, 1969); O'Gara, Margaret, *Triumph in Defeat: Infallibility, Vatican I, and the French Minority Bishops* (Washington, DC: Catholic University Press, 1988).

James M. Woods

Vatican Council II. The Second Vatican Council, or Vatican II, took place from 1962 to 1965. This council and the documents emerging out of it transformed the Catholic Church. The struggle over Vatican II's legacy has dominated the Catholic Church over the past thirty years. It was not clear, however, during the preparation for, and the beginning of, the council that any dramatic transformation would take place. As in any such gathering, the outcome was determined very much by personalities and interaction among participants.

Numerous specific features of Catholicism were addressed and then changed during Vatican II. Participants chose to reassert the concept, appearing often in the New Testament, of the "People of God." This new emphasis placed responsibility and power in the hands of the laity. Vatican II also emphasized the Eucharist as central to the presence of the church, even where the hierarchical presence was limited. This change also empowered local, grassroots religious leaders, devolving power from Rome. Related to this development was a new emphasis on Scripture. Vatican II represented movement away from obscure theological reasoning and in the direction of the more accessible language of the Bible. Vatican II also advocated easy access to sacred Scripture. Catholics subsequently played an active role in translating the Bible into a wide variety of languages. In the same spirit, Vatican II took the dramatic step of permitting the use of local vernacular in the place of Latin during mass.

Vatican II also emphasized the importance of tolerating and even celebrating religious diversity, both within Christianity and among the world's other religions. Vatican II noted the complementary nature of differing theological interpretations and the existence of "churches" (rather than one church) for virtually the first time in the history of Catholicism.

Vatican II's most significant legacy was articulated in the section known as *Gaudium et Spes,* which focused on the relationship between the Catholic Church and the modern world. The somewhat blunt language of *Gaudium et Spes* stated that it was the responsibility of the church to "foster progress in needy regions and social justice on the international scene." It also went so far as to comment on certain specific issues: for example, it condemned political corruption and the arms race and asserted the right of workers to organize. The more general goal of this specific document was to apply Christianity to glaring injustice and to press for "the dignity of the human person" in this world.

Like many religious reappraisals, the influence of Vatican II reflects the work of those Catholics who took the council (and the documents that came out of it) seriously and acted on these newly articulated ideas. An entirely new version of Christianity, commonly known as liberation theology,* came from Catholics working in regions of the world, especially Latin America, marked by the suffering emphasized in Vatican II.

A central goal of Vatican II was to increase Catholicism's relevance in the "modern" world. There is little question that the Catholic Church succeeded in this regard. With this success, however, has come renewed debate about the legacy of Vatican II. The lengthy tenure of Pope John Paul II has been marked by increased adherence to some aspects of Vatican II. For example, the spirit of Vatican II was evident in John Paul II's crucial role in subverting political authority in Eastern Europe. But in other areas John Paul II seemed more intent on opposing the spirit of Vatican II. This pope was vocal in his opposition to priests who openly supported revolution and participated in revolutionary movements and regimes in Latin America.

Bibliography. Boff, Leonardo, *Trinity and Society* (New York: Orbis, 1988); Hastings, Adrian, ed., *Modern Catholicism: Vatican II and After* (New York: Oxford University Press, 1991); Latourelle, Rene, *Vatican II: Assessments and Perspectives* vols. 1–3 (New York: Paulist Press, 1989); O'Connell, Timothy E., *Vatican II and Its Documents: An American Reappraisal* (Collegeville, MN: Liturgical Press, 1991).

Frederick M. Shepherd

Vesey, Denmark. In 1800 Denmark Vesey purchased his freedom from Captain Joseph Vesey, for whom he had been a personal servant with an unusual degree of freedom. He traveled extensively with the captain throughout the Caribbean and perhaps even to Africa.

After he gained his freedom, he lived in Charleston, accumulating a sizable savings from his trade as a skilled carpenter. Through his extensive contacts and keen intelligence, he was regarded as a leader in the African-American community. He was outspoken in his opposition to oppression and injustice, even refusing to bow to white people on the street.

Charleston was a center of independent African-American religious expression, particularly among Methodists. In 1818 some of the African-American Methodists formed the independent African Church of Charleston, with Morris Brown as the bishop. Both the African-American and white communities recognized the potential of such an independent spirit.

Vesey and a number of his friends, including Gullah Jack Pritchard and Peter Poyas, began to meet privately when white suppression of their public religious activity increased. Vesey was inspired by the apocalyptic message of Zechariah and the story of Joshua at Jericho. He saw parallels between the situation of his people and those of ancient Israel in their opposition to an escape from slavery.

In addition to biblical inspiration for overt action, he was motivated by the courage of the freedom fighters in Santo Domingo and Haiti. Vesey blended American and African motifs in his quest for his people's freedom. Gullah Jack Pritchard, a conjurer, infused the group with the belief that African spirits would make them invulnerable.

Vesey and his friends carefully organized a rebellion that was to take place in Charleston and the surrounding countryside in July 1822. One of the slaves who was recruited to participate in the rebellion revealed the secret to his master, so the plan was foiled. Vesey, Pritchard, and Poyas were arrested and executed. All of them died in silence without revealing the names of any of their recruits. While the Charleston conspiracy failed to achieve its goal, the event inspired an increased African-American opposition to injustice.

Bibliography. Carroll, Joseph C., *Slave Insurrections in the United States, 1800-1865* (Boston: Chapman and Graves, 1938); Harding, Vincent, *There Is a River* (New York: Harcourt Brace Jovanovich, 1981); Killens, John O., ed., *The Trial of Denmark Vesey* (Boston: Beacon Press, 1970); Lofton, John, *Insurrection in South Carolina* (Yellow Springs, OH: Antioch Press, 1964); Wilmore, Gayraud S., *Black Religion and Black Radicalism*, 2nd rev. ed. (Maryknoll, NY: Orbis Books, 1983).

Coleman Markham

Vick, George Beauchamp. Though George Beauchamp Vick never attended college or seminary or received ordination, he possessed a keen business sense and extraordinary motivational skills that, within the Baptist Bible Fellowship* (BBF), more than made up for his lack of formal education. Undoubtedly the most important figure in the history of the BBF, Vick was born on February 5, 1901, in Russellville, Kentucky, but spent most of his early years in Louisville, Kentucky. After graduation from Louisville Male High School, he began working for the railroad, eventually taking a position in 1920 with the Fort Worth and Denver Railroad in Fort Worth, Texas. Almost immediately he joined J.

Frank Norris's* First Baptist Church of Fort Worth, becoming a Sunday school teacher and eventually superintendent of the Junior Department. In 1924 he quit the railroad and began working full-time for Norris at First Baptist, thus beginning a working relationship with the fundamentalist giant that would span more than twenty-five years and a church ministry that would last for over fifty years. By 1930 Vick's Junior High, High School, and Young Married departments were averaging over 2,000 in attendance each Sunday. Norris was so pleased with his young protégé that he once told him, "You do everything the way I like—only better." In his ten years at First Baptist Vick gained invaluable experience in every aspect of church work while observing firsthand the great master motivator and innovator, Norris himself. In 1930, however, despite his great success, Vick left Norris and spent the next six years working with several leading evangelists of the day. He returned to Norris in 1936, only this time in Detroit, Michigan, to serve as general superintendent (de facto pastor) of Norris's other church, Temple Baptist. Pastoring two churches 1,300 miles apart in the 1930s was a task only a Norris would conceive of attempting, but even for Norris the task was too much to handle alone. Unlike Norris, the charismatic pulpiteer and sensational controversialist, Vick was the gentle motivator and brilliant organizational man, building Temple Baptist in twelve years from an attendance in the low hundreds to over 3,000 by 1948, making it and First Baptist in Fort Worth the two largest Baptist churches in America at that time (with a combined membership of over 25,000). Just as Norris had done at Fort Worth, Vick stressed extensive and vigorous church visitation, numerous Sunday school classes for adults, and indigenous Sunday school literature using the Bible only (no outside quarterlies). In 1948 Vick became copastor with Norris and in 1950 sole pastor.

The greatest controversy of Vick's life came in 1950, and it directly involved his long-time mentor, Norris. In 1948 Norris, recognizing a general dissension among the ranks of his World Fundamental Baptist Missionary Fellowship (WFBMF) concerning the financial stability of the Bible Baptist Seminary, Norris's school housed on church property in Fort Worth, persuaded Vick to take over as president of the seminary. Vick at first rejected the offer, primarily because he knew himself and Norris too well; if he was to become president, he would have to have absolute authority over the school, and this he was convinced Norris would never relinquish. Norris, however, in a letter dated April 18, 1948, assured Vick that he would indeed have "liberty of action" in all matters concerning the seminary.

Having been promised in writing a "place of first responsibility and with it, absolute freedom," Vick accepted and began making changes immediately. Within two years he had streamlined the operations of the seminary dramatically, cutting the outstanding debt in half, eliminating inept teachers, strengthening the curriculum, and raising salaries. He restored the credibility of the school within the ranks of the WFBMF and developed a substantial and loyal following as a result. Unfortunately, every correction was an admission of failure on the part of the previous administration, which was essentially Norris and his right-hand man in Fort Worth, the aging Louis Entzminger. Norris would simply not have been Norris if he had allowed Vick, despite Norris's previous claims of "noninterference," to upstage Norris in his own backyard. Hence in the spring of 1950 Norris reasserted himself, first by making changes in the personnel of the seminary without Vick's approval, and then by suggesting to the student body that Vick was trying to fire Entzminger (when it had really been Norris who had wanted the ailing Entzminger removed). Norris drummed up enough support to have a new set of bylaws passed by the student body and then proceeded to remove Vick as president.

Vick attended the May meeting of the WFBMF as planned and defended himself so well that the majority of the students and pastors sided with him, not Norris. Visibly shaken by this rebuff, Norris tried every tactic to silence his critics and maintain power. Since he controlled the property of the seminary, he had the upper hand, and most knew that. They also knew that once you found yourself on the wrong side of J. Frank Norris, you could rarely, if ever, reestablish a working relationship. The break had occurred, and it would have to be played out. Vick was the man the splinter group looked to for leadership, and he indeed provided it, although reluctantly at first. Vick was an intensely loyal man himself, and to break with Norris, his spiritual father, was a momentous decision indeed. But on May 24, 1950, the Baptist Bible Fellowship arose out of the WFBMF, with Vick the first president of the new school, Baptist Bible College, which would be located in Springfield, Missouri, along with the new headquarters of the fellowship. Vick remained as president of the college and pastor of Temple Baptist Church of Detroit until his death in 1975, exerting a powerful influence over thousands of pastors and missionaries throughout the world by means of the Baptist Bible Fellowship and its college. During these years the student body increased from 107 to over 2,400 (at that time the largest "Bible school" of its type in the world), the number of missionaries approached 450, and Vick's church was one of the twenty-five largest in America.

Bibliography. Bartlett, Billy Vick, *The Beginnings: A Pictorial History of the Baptist Bible Fellowship* vol. 1 (Springfield, MO: Baptist Bible College, 1975); Bartlett, Billy Vick, "G. B. Vick: Organizer, Leader, Teacher, Preacher," *Fundamentalist Journal*, September 1983, 32–34; Randall, Mike, *G. B. Vick* (Springfield, MO: Baptist Bible College, 1987).

Timothy D. Whelan

Virgin Birth. The doctrine of the Virgin Birth holds that Jesus was born of a virgin mother without the agency of a human father. It is an article in all of the oldest creeds of the church, and as Raymond Brown says, "for some 1600 years of Christian existence (A.D. 200–1800) the virginal conception of Jesus, in a biological sense, was universally believed by Christians" (Brown, 35). In the first two centuries of the church the doctrine was rarely mentioned. In the last two centuries it has become, for some, a touchstone of true orthodoxy, a transcendent mystery, and, for others, an inconvenient claim best understood mythically.

There has not been a specific "Virgin Birth controversy" in American religious history. Rather, the doctrine has become an issue from time to time in larger conflicts between conservative and liberal Christians, and Americans have often followed the lead of European theologians in their discussion of this doctrine. When the fundamentalists formalized their creed shortly before World War I, belief in the Virgin Birth ranked as one of their ten essential components of the faith. A flurry of publications occurred in the first two decades of the twentieth century when the results of biblical criticism were beginning to permeate to the level of laypersons' awareness, and they saw the doctrine as being "fiercely assailed." Vincent Taylor's *Historical Evidence for the Virgin Birth* was probably the most objective study of that period.

Many would downplay the importance of the doctrine of the Virgin Birth because it is mentioned in only two New Testament passages. It might be seen as a stage in the development of Christology. In Romans 1, Paul stresses the resurrection as the proof of Christ's divinity; Mark emphasizes the outpouring of the Spirit at the baptism. Matthew and Luke move the crucial moment back to the birth, while John makes of Jesus the preexistent Logos.

The Virgin Birth can be interpreted in a number of ways. The most literal view (more accurately, the virginal conception) would hold that Jesus was conceived by Mary with the miraculous intervention of the Holy Spirit and that sperm from Joseph (or any other man) was not involved. This view has led to such embellishments as the perpetual virginity of Mary. On the other hand, it is possible to dismiss the story as having been introduced as a way of affirming the humanity of Jesus over against Gnostic and Docetic ideas that he only appeared to be human. Some would even argue that since in Jewish thought of the time God was thought to be present in every act of human conception, the promise that the Holy Spirit will come upon Mary implies nothing more than that God would bless her (normal) act of conception.

The doctrine of the Virgin Birth assumes importance today because for many Christians, it is inextricably linked with the doctrine of Christ's divinity. Others, more comfortable with the principles of modern biblical criticism, recognize that the Virgin Birth story was an ancient way of asserting a fundamental truth, but that one can assent to that truth without being bound by the form in which prescientific minds cast it.

Bibliography. Barrett, Edward, "Can Scholars Take the Virgin Birth Seriously?" *Bible Review* 6, no. 3 (October 1988): 10–15, 29; Boslooper, Thomas, *The Virgin Birth* (Philadelphia: Westminster Press, 1962); Brown, Raymond, *The Virginial Conception and Bodily Resurrection of Jesus* (New York: Paulist Press, 1973); Crouch, James, "How Early Christians Viewed the Birth of Christ" *Bible Review* 9 (October 1991): 34–38; Taylor, Vincent, *The Historical Evidence for the Virgin Birth* (Oxford: Clarendon Press, 1920).

Albert A. Bell, Jr.

Voluntaryism. Not to be confused with philosophical concepts related to freedom of the human will, the term "voluntaryism" concerns the reliance of religious groups on voluntary contributions for their support rather than on government funds. While it is difficult for anyone in modern America to realize it adequately, the separation of church and state* two hundred years ago and the voluntaryism among American churches resulting from it were not unanimously embraced. Many disapproved of the experiment and feared its possible consequences.

For the timid, a simple break with tradition was enough to have them oppose it. Western European countries had functioned with legitimate states supporting a preferred ecclesiastical system within a single realm, and the church in turn sanctioning governmental policy. This interdependency predominated in both Protestant and Catholic lands, with differences only in the type of church receiving government protection and subsidy. Those who called for an end to this monopoly saw freedom for themselves in relying on voluntary support alone; traditionalists saw threats to a stable relationship that had proved itself for a millennium.

Others opposed voluntaryism because it would, in their view, remove the basis for morality in civil life. If religious tests were not required of candidates for office and all enfranchised to vote for them, scoundrels with dangerous opinions might be elected. If jurors were not limited to members of the official church, the results of court proceedings might fail to reflect the high standards that God expected of Christian nations. Voluntaryism would remove the religious basis for a godly society and ruin the foundations of social propriety. Further, if state churches were left to themselves for maintaining clergy, buildings, and public functions, most people would refuse to contribute, and state churches would collapse due to general indifference if not hostility. To prevent this, states had a duty to sustain the official structure, financially through taxes and culturally by legislating morals.

By the late eighteenth century some advocates of voluntaryism argued that state churches should be abolished because they interfered with government. Taxes for clerical salaries and laws derived from confessional sources were not the proper touchstones for civil life, they held, and such hindrances to the common weal should be avoided. Most religious questions were too unimportant to have public significance. Other advocates of voluntaryism argued that state support of one church ought to be abolished because government interfered with religious affirmations that were too important for outside interference. Secular strictures on beliefs, worship, and ethical standards violated private conscience and tried to impose restrictions where they could never be enforced. Most religious questions of ultimate significance could not be regulated by a political apparatus and then applied uniformly to the whole population.

These two basic arguments for separation of church and state, plus the urgings of many sectarian groups that had been supporting themselves on a voluntary basis for decades, came to fruition in the early national period of the United

States. By 1791 states in the new American republic agreed that the national Congress could not favor any church or prevent one from conducting its affairs alongside others. A few states continued the old policy of supporting one group over others, but they eventually adopted voluntaryism too—New Hampshire in 1817, Connecticut in 1818, and Massachusetts in 1833. The usual consequence of this momentous experiment has been a healthy competition among religious denominations. Lack of favoritism has given all groups an equal voice and opportunity to recruit adherents. It has removed artificial barriers and allowed for growth or decline based on the appeal of different gospels and the zeal of their advocates. Once controversial, this arrangement is now deeply ingrained in the American perspective.

Bibliography. Ban, Joseph D., and Paul R. Dekar, eds., *In the Great Tradition* (Valley Forge, PA: Judson Press, 1982); Hudson, Winthrop S., *The Great Tradition of the American Churches* (New York: Harper, 1953).

Henry Warner Bowden

W

War. War is usually defined as armed conflict between states. The most distinguishing feature of war is the widespread, prolonged, and intense level of violence. It has always and everywhere been a part of human history. In Judeo-Christian history the three most common moral evaluations of war are found in the pacifist, holy-war, and just-war traditions.

The pacifist tradition brands warfare as morally unacceptable. While there are many variations on this basic stance, there are two different approaches that are important to distinguish. Vocational pacifists such as the early Christians only claim that the violence of warfare is inconsistent with the life of the one committed to Christ's love. They do not promote pacifism as a national strategy but plead that they cannot participate in war because of their distinctive moral commitments. Pragmatic pacifists propose that their strategy of nonviolence is appropriate for all people of good will and is an appropriate governmental strategy. Resting upon an optimistic view of human nature, the claim is that nonviolence will, in the long run, win over the hearts of the aggressors with the result that less harm will be done by not answering violence with violence.

The polar-opposite position from pacifism is the holy-war or crusading tradition, which views warfare as a holy activity by which God's Kingdom is established and evildoers punished. God bids the faithful to take up arms as a divine calling. In this effort no sacrifice is too great to achieve victory. No restraint is placed upon the means of warfare, and all issues or parties in a war are viewed in absolutist terms. There were clear expressions of this attitude toward war in Israel's history and in the period of the Crusades in Christian history. In the modern era the spirit of nationalism demands absolute loyalty to the state and creates a secular version of holy war that some have called the "total-war" position.

The just-war tradition proposes that while war is a moral tragedy, it is sometimes the lesser of two evils. Yielding to the reality of human sinfulness, war is entered into as a last resort, for limited purposes, and with great restraint. Seminal formulation of this view is found in Ambrose but it is fully developed by Augustine, Thomas Aquinas, Vitoria, and Suarez. As the most widely held position on warfare in Christian history, it holds that war is morally justified only when it is (1) declared by a legitimate authority; (2) for a just cause; (3) fought as a last resort; (4) fought with a just intention; (5) and fought in a just or restrained manner.

In recent years there has been within the church a growing sense that the massive and indiscriminate destructiveness of modern weapons and the absolutist claims of modern nationalism break all the restraints that just-war theory places upon warmaking. In different ways, many are seeking to formulate a Christian response that embraces the pacifist goal of peace and the just-war tradition's struggle to find practical ways to recognize and deal with the reality of human sinfulness.

Bibliography. Bainton, Roland H., *Christian Attitudes toward War and Peace* (New York: Abingdon Press, 1960); Long, Edward Leroy, Jr, *Peace Thinking in a Warring World* (Philadelphia: Westminster Press, 1983); Ramsey, Paul, *The Just War* (New York: Charles Scribner's Sons, 1968); Stassen, Glen H., *Just Peacemaking: Transforming Initiatives for Justice and Peace* (Louisville: Westminster/John Knox Press, 1992).

Daniel B. McGee

Warfield, Benjamin Breckinridge. Benjamin Breckinridge Warfield (1851–1921) occupied the pivotal chair in theology at Princeton Theological Seminary in the contentious years between 1887 and 1918. From that position Warfield propounded and to a degree redefined the Princeton Theology developed by Archibald Alexander, Charles Hodge,* and Archibald Alexander Hodge.* Working with his colleague, Archibald Alexander Hodge, Warfield outlined a theory of biblical inerrancy against those in the church who argued that the Bible existed simply as one of many human documents. The Warfield-Hodge inerrancy theory remains popular among conservative Protestants in the United States today.

Warfield received the classical nineteenth-century theological education, including graduate study in Germany. He returned to Princeton at a time when Protestants in the United States struggled mightily with questions concerning the viability of traditional Protestantism in the face of modernity. While Warfield deplored the internecine strife among Protestants in general and Presbyterians in particular, he made clear that accommodations of historic Christian orthodoxy to modernity had distinct limits. True to his rationalist heritage, Warfield sought to win his opponents with logic rather than bludgeon them with polemics.

Warfield firmly believed in the value of apologetic theology as a means of convincing reasonable, rational men and women to accept the truth of the gospel. His insistence on rational Christianity often placed Warfield at odds with proponents of experiential Christianity, such as those supporting the "Higher Life" movement. His theology made even less room for experience than did that of Charles Hodge. At the same time Warfield sharply criticized "modern rationalists" who refused to take up his starting point, namely, that theology was the science of the study of God and that Scripture was authoritative.

While critical of theories of biblical inspiration less nuanced than his own, Warfield insisted that the doctrine of inerrancy could not be compromised. His theory of inerrancy rested on the proposition that the original "autographs" of the canonical books bore the marks of "immediate inspiration" by God. The subsequent translations of these documents took place under the supervision of the Holy Spirit, thus assuring that God's word was preserved. Warfield's theory left room for mistakes in transcription, but he steadfastly maintained that the autographic texts of the Scriptures indeed came to us. He distinguished the autographic texts (the words) from the autographic codex (the material on which the text was written) in an attempt to deflect the criticism that his original-autograph argument was specious. Instead, he argued that we had the autographic texts due to the superintending providence of God despite the fact that the autographic codex may never be found.

Bibliography. Hoffecker, W. Andrew, *Piety and the Princeton Theologians* (Phillipsburg, NJ, and Grand Rapids, MI: Presbyterian and Reformed and Baker, 1981); Meeter, John E., and Roger Nicole, *A Bibliography of Benjamin Breckenridge Warfield, 1851–1921* (Nutley, NJ: Presbyterian and Reformed, 1974); Noll, Mark A., ed., *The Princeton Theology 1812–1921* (Grand Rapids, MI: Baker, 1983), 241–316; Warfield, Benjamin B., *Selected Shorter Writings of B. B. Warfield*, ed. John E. Meeter, 2 vols. (Phillipsburg, NJ: Reformed and Presbyterian, 1970, 1973); Warfield, Benjamin B., *The Works of Benjamin B. Warfield*, 10 vols. (Grand Rapids, MI: Baker, 1981).

Russell Congleton

Weld, Theodore Dwight. Theodore Dwight Weld (1803–1895), evangelist, abolitionist, and temperance advocate, was born in Hampton, Connecticut, came of age in New York State, and died in Hyde Park, Massachusetts. From a background of conservative Calvinistic Congregationalism, Weld studied at Hamilton College (1825), Oneida Institute (1829–1831), Lane Seminary* (1832–1834), and Oberlin College. He married Angelina Grimké,* a South Carolina–born reform leader in her own right. Converted by Charles G. Finney,* he became a revivalist. Soon, however, his attention turned to the cause of temperance and the brutalities of African-American enslavement. Bringing his revivalist skills and techniques, such as the use of the altar call and extended meetings, to the abolitionist crusade, Weld successfully converted many to the antislavery position, including Harriet Beecher Stowe,* the author of *Uncle Tom's Cabin*. In 1834 Weld and a number of other students were expelled from Lane Seminary

because they violated the school's strictures against abolitionist activities by conducting the "Lane Debates," whereupon they transferred to the recently organized Oberlin College. An agent of the American Anti-Slavery Society, Weld eschewed opportunities to hold prominent positions and offices in reform associations. Instead, he followed a more modest approach that included writing and editing abolitionist literature; for example, he published anonymously two very important antislavery pieces, *The Bible against Slavery* (1837) and *Slavery As It Is* (1839). A combination of a voice injury and disdain for political activity caused Weld and his wife to withdraw from heavy public exposure. For a time (1838–1841) Weld did engage in antislavery lobbying in Washington, D.C., working with the abolitionist section of the Whig party. Between 1840 and 1867 Weld taught school in New Jersey and Massachusetts. While he made occasional appearances in support of reform issues such as education after 1867, he officially retired from public life that year. Because he so persistently avoided highlighting his public presence, Weld's contribution to the most significant religious and social controversies of American history was long forgotten or overlooked.
Bibliography. Bowden, Henry H., *Dictionary of American Religious Biography* (Westport: Greenwood Publishing, 1977); *Dictionary of Christianity in America* (Downers Grove: InterVarsity Press, 1990); Brauer, Jerald C., *The Westminster Dictionary of Church History* (1971).

Sandy Dwayne Martin

White, Andrew D. Born of Episcopal parents in Homer, New York, Andrew D. White (1832–1918) soon moved with his family to Syracuse. Higher education at Geneva College (now Hobart) was despised, and he transferred to Yale, graduating in 1853. Studies abroad in Paris and Berlin preceded his return to Yale for the A.M. degree. By the time he was twenty-five, White was teaching history at the University of Michigan, where he became one of the most respected and popular professors. There he developed a dream of founding a university himself (in 1860 he had inherited a large amount of money) that would search for truth unfettered by any religious orthodoxy and would appeal to liberal-minded men of learning.

In 1864 White entered politics, was elected to the New York Senate, and was soon chair of the Committee on Literature (involved with all educational legislation). Turning down an offer to teach at Yale, he accepted the presidency of the newly founded Cornell University. He insisted that Cornell be nonsectarian and that the Board of Trustees never include a majority of any one religious denomination. Reminding his critics that nonsectarian did not mean irreligious, at every turn he emphasized the religious aspects of the university. Though some fierce attacks labeled the school as "godless" (since no religious body controlled it), White won wide support for his new university with its novel methods. Launching the university on a positive note, he also taught European history. Mixing roles, White gained a strong reputation in political and diplomatic circles, serving briefly as minister to Germany and later to Russia. In 1884

White was elected as the first president of the American Historical Association and the next year resigned as president of Cornell in order to travel, write, and be involved as a diplomat.

Certainly one of his greatest contributions to literature and thought was his two-volume *A History of the Warfare of Science with Theology in Christendom* in 1896. This work had consumed his scholarly efforts for some twenty years. White certainly did not oppose religion in this watershed work; he was a deeply religious man who sought to live by and preserve the religious truths at the heart of Christianity. He was opposed, however, to tunnel-visioned theologians who hardened dogma and scriptural texts. Religion itself did not conflict with science; rather, certain theologians and sects waged needless wars. To White, religion should be freed from enforced dogma in its search to set forth the truth. The strongest opposition to his work came from Roman Catholics and fundamentalists. The secular press and liberal Protestants praised the volumes as among the greatest of the century. Though misunderstood by many, White's true aim was to show, in fact, that contemporary science had really left the essence of Christianity undisturbed. He closed his own *Autobiography* with this cogent reflection:

> The best way of aiding in a healthful evolution would seem to consist in firmly but decisively resisting all ecclesiastical efforts to control or thwart the legitimate work of science and education; in letting the light of modern research and thought into the religious atmosphere; and in cultivating, each for himself, obedience to ''the first and great commandment, and the second which is like unto it,'' as given by the Blessed Founder of Christianity. (2: 573)

Bibliography. Altschuler, Glenn C., *Andrew D. White: Educator, Historian, Diplomat* (Ithaca: Cornell University Press, 1979); White, Andrew D., *Autobiography* 2 vols. (New York: Century Co., 1914); White, Andrew D., *A History of the Warfare of Science with Theology in Christendom,* 2 vols. (New York: D. Appleton and Co., 1896).

George H. Shriver

Wicca. Wicca is a gynocentric religion also known as witchcraft. The word ''wicca'' derives from an Anglo-Saxon root meaning to bend or shape. Wiccans, more commonly called witches, bend unseen powers to their will through magic. Modern Wicca dates to 1951 when the last of British antiwitchcraft laws was repealed, and Gerald Gardner began writing on and teaching Wicca. Gardner's students Sybil Leek and Raymond and Rosemary Buckland introduced witchcraft to the United States. The movement spread across the country in the 1960s, especially in New York and California, as a result of growing interest in alternative religions. Most witches were converts from other religious traditions. A number of variations developed besides Gardnerian, including Alexandrian, Druidic, and Dianic witchcraft.

Wiccans, however, trace their history far before 1951. They believe that Wicca descended from prehistoric matriarchal cultures that worshipped the Mother Goddess and honored women and childbirth. This ancient tradition of women's wisdom, they claim, survived the dawn of patriarchy and Judeo-Christianity by going underground. In scattered groups, women and some men practiced witchcraft in secret until the church attempted to root it out through the Inquisition. During the Burning Times, as witches call the Middle Ages, millions of Wiccans were massacred as worshippers of Satan. This interpretation is disputed by historians. Evidence for an ancient, woman-honoring Goddess religion is scanty, and many historians argue that medieval witchcraft persecutions reflected the church's misogyny rather than attempts to eliminate a rival religious tradition.

In the United States today, Wiccans sharply distinguish themselves from Satanism, black magic, and devil worship. They view Wicca as a global religious tradition alongside Islam, Judaism, and Christianity. Although witches hold diverse beliefs, most worship the Horned God and the Goddess in three aspects: maiden, mother, crone. They attune themselves to natural rhythms and to shifting cosmic, psychic, and sacred energies. Their ethical system is based on magic, the harnessing of these energies through spells, trances, herbs, and amulets. Witches cast spells for healing, success, and empowerment for themselves and others. Because they believe that the energies they send will be returned threefold, they rarely use magic to harm.

While many Wiccans practice alone, witchcraft's primary organizational unit is the coven. Optimally composed of thirteen, covens meet to practice magic and to celebrate Wiccan holidays or sabbats. There are eight annual seasonal festivals: four minor sabbats at autumnal and vernal equinoxes and summer and winter solstices, and four major ones, Candlemas (February 2), Beltane (April 30), Lammas (August 1), and the best-known Wiccan holiday, Halloween (October 31). Covens also meet to initiate new witches. Some covens perform rituals skyclad (in the nude), while others wear ceremonial robes.

A significant strain of the tradition is feminist Wicca. It stresses women's community building, justice, liberation, and overcoming sexism. Starhawk, Zsuzsanna Budapest, Margot Adler, Carol Christ, Charlene Spretnak, and others affirm Wicca's value for women since it celebrates nature, sexuality, and a female deity. Feminist covens often exclude men. Whether they practice feminist Wicca or not, many Wiccans are politically involved in feminist and environmental causes as well as defending their own civil rights and tax-exempt status as a religious organization.

Wicca is controversial because many Christians consider it heathen, blasphemous, and offensive to Christianity. They associate Wicca with Satanism and the New Age movement,* claiming that witches worship Satan, cast evil spells, and engage in sexual abuse and child pornography. Wicca's polytheism, emphasis on nature and sensuality, and empowerment of women do counter much Christian belief and practice. Yet while some Wiccans are self-consciously hostile to Christianity, many are not. They seek merely to practice their religion in peace and freedom.

Bibliography. Adler, Margot, *Drawing Down the Moon* (Boston: Beacon, 1979); Eller, Cynthia, *Living in the Lap of the Goddess* (New York: Crossroad, 1993); Spretnak, Charlene, *The Politics of Women's Spirituality* (Garden City, NY: Anchor, 1982); Starhawk, *The Spiral Dance* (San Francisco: Harper and Row, 1979); Stone, Merlin, *When God Was a Woman* (New York: Dial Press, 1976).

Evelyn A. Kirkley

Williams, Roger. Roger Williams (1603–1683) was educated at Pembroke College, Cambridge University (B.A., 1627) and was episcopally ordained in 1629. He did postgraduate work at Cambridge University (1627–1629). He was Anglican chaplain to the Esse family (1629–1630); minister in Plymouth Colony (1631–1633); minister in Salem (1634–1635); and founder and resident of Providence (later Rhode Island) (1636–1683).

Controversy over Roger Williams's views stalked him from the time he set foot in the United States until his death. Elements of the controversy still persist. He migrated to Boston in 1631 and refused to accept the call of the Boston Church because he had become a Separatist and the Boston Church had not separated from the Church of England. He also denied the rights of magistrates to punish any infraction of the commandments that prescribed the duties between God and man. Moreover, he championed the separation of church and state.* Clearly unpopular in Boston, he accepted a call to the Salem Church, which was at odds with Boston. Williams's unpopular views continued when he disputed the colonists' rights (actually the king's patents) to claim Indian lands. He denounced Plymouth for not being separatist. Back in Salem, the Boston authorities brought and then dropped the following charges against him: (1) that he wrote treatises denying royal patents to Puritan claims on property; (2) that he declared that King James had lied when the king said that he was the first Christian prince to discover New England; (3) that he declared that Europe was not Christian even though it was so stated by the king.

The storm grew in Salem, where Williams continued his opposition to the tax imposed on every man for the support of public worship. He opposed compulsory church attendance and refused to take a new oath imposed by the magistrates. He denied the right of the General Court to impose oaths or to legislate for the church. At long last the General Court brought Williams to trial in 1635, but the particulars forming the bases of their charges were not legally or formally presented. His Separatist views were not hidden, nor did he back away from his belief in the separation of church and state. Specifically he was charged with denying the legality of royal patents to give Indian land to the colonists. He was also charged with saying that it was unlawful to hear any of the parish ministers from the Church of England, since they had no rights there, and with saying the power of civil magistrates extended only to the bodies and goods of men and not to religion. Williams was banished.

In January 1636 he left home and remained with the Narragansett Indians, whom he had befriended. He bought land from the Indians to found Providence. From the outset he established religious freedom, desiring it to be a shelter for persons distressed for conscience and loving friends desiring to take refuge with him. He believed and so stated in his *The Bloudy Tenent of Persecution** that God did not require the enactment or enforcement of religion. Such enforced uniformity caused civil wars. Moreover, this document allowed religious freedom to "the most paganish Jewish, Turkish, or Anti-Christian consciences and worships." Any battle against them would be by the Sword of the Spirit, that is, God's Spirit and the Word of God. It was his belief that "true civility and Christianity may both flourish in a state or Kingdom, notwithstanding the permission of diverse and contrary consciences, either of Jew or Gentile."

After changing from Anglican priest to Separatist preacher, by 1639 he was immersed (probably) as a Baptist, only to move beyond them to dissatisfaction with all sects. He was critical of the accommodation of the church to the state brought about during the time of Constantine. He was known for four decades as a "Seeker." As a "Seeker" he maintained a radically purist conception of the church and criticized ministers who received remuneration. While despairing of ever finding the true church on earth, he continued to search for it diligently.

Bibliography. Miller, Perry, *Roger Williams: His Contributions to the American Tradition* (1953. Reprint. New York: Atheneum, 1962); Williams, Roger, *The Complete Works of Roger Williams*, 7 vols. (New York: Bobbs-Merrill Company, 1963).

Robert K. Gustafson

Woman's Christian Temperance Movement. The Woman's Christian Temperance Movement was the first mass movement of American women controlled exclusively by women, led by reformer leader and feminist Frances Willard (1839–1898). It was initially organized in 1874 to support temperance, although it later added issues of social justice and women's suffrage. The early beginnings were in Hillsborough, Ohio, when a group of women led spontaneous crusades against saloons and retail liquor stores after hearing professional lecturer Diocletian Lewis speak on the evils of drink. Women marched in large groups to local saloons, singing gospel songs and swinging axes through the air, aiming at barrels of gin. Drug stores ceased selling liquor except on prescription, and saloons closed their doors.

In August 1874 women assembled at Lake Chautauqua, New York, to participate in the first national Sunday school teachers' institute sponsored by Methodist bishop John Heyl Vincent. While they were sitting around evening campfires describing their temperance activities of the previous months, someone suggested that they should take steps toward national organization. Vincent offered his assistance. Women took the leadership in designing an effective grassroots organization where no two members came from the same state and where membership ranged from the East to the West. The women from Freedonia, New York, gave the group their own name, and the movement was called Woman's Christian Temperance Union (WCTU).

On Wednesday, November 18, 1874, the first national convention of the Woman's Christian Temperance Union was held in Cleveland, Ohio, at the Second Presbyterian Church. Sixteen states were represented, with over 135 registered women. Men were not allowed to vote, although they could participate as guests. Women at this meeting pledged total abstinence, promoted temperance education in public schools, and supported evangelical methods for their cause, such as mass meetings and prayer services. Annie Wittenmyer, founder of the Methodist Home Missionary Society and editor of the *Christian Woman*, was elected the first national president. Frances Willard, who later would become president in 1879 at the sixth annual convention, was chosen as corresponding secretary.

By 1880 the Woman's Christian Temperance Union had grown larger than any other existing women's organization. Twelve hundred local unions with over 27,000 members focused on gospel temperance, seeking to close down saloons and warning men of the dangers of drink and loss of their souls. Women were visiting jails, almshouses, and prisons to care for those fallen by drink. Soon the union's focus extended to concern for evils of the prison system.

In the late 1870s the leadership split over suffrage. Willard, who had worked with evangelist Dwight Moody in Chicago, thought that temperance could be aided by the ballot, but Wittenmyer feared that women's suffrage added to their platform would weaken their temperance cause. Willard, however, could not resist and made her commitment public at a camp meeting at Old Orchard, Maine, in 1874, declaring "that Woman, who is truest to God and our country by instinct and education, should have a voice at the polls." When Willard was elected president in 1879, the goals of the Woman's Christian Temperance Union extended from gospel temperance to social activism, including what Willard called "the home protection ballot."

Sallie Chapin became instrumental in organizing southern women for the cause as superintendent of the Department of Southern Work. Chapin, a friend of Robert E. Lee and widow of a merchant from Charleston, South Carolina, lectured in every southern state until 1889, when the department was no longer needed. With Willard in the North and Chapin in the South, the WCTU worked to change attitudes toward women, providing speaking opportunities and outlets for social activism, as well as demonstrating solidarity during Reconstruction. When the WCTU began working in the South, Southerners and Northerners had not worked together in religious voluntary associations for nearly two generations.

Not just an exclusively white organization, the WCTU was concerned about organizing other groups. African-American women, Native American women, and immigrant women were encouraged to form their own organizations. In 1883 the WCTU employed a Swedish woman, Anna Lindahl, to meet immigrants when they landed in New York and distribute literature. In 1884 Mary

Clement Leavitt was sent to organize the world. When she returned home in 1891, she had traveled over 100,000 miles in 43 countries, had worked with 229 interpreters in 47 languages, and had organized 130 temperance societies around the world, spending only $8,000 that she raised herself.

The *Union Signal*, the largest women's paper in the world, was the official journal of the organization. The publication project, directed by Matilda Carse, developed women as well, employing women as writers, proofreaders, and binders.

By 1896 the gospel temperance concerns grew less, alcoholism was seen more as a disease rather than a sin, and the women turned their attention to the issues of urban poverty. Working in Chicago, in the same neighborhood as Jane Addams's Hull House, the WCTU sponsored two nurseries, two Sunday schools, an industrial school, a homeless mission, a free medical dispensary, and a low-cost restaurant. The union studied diet and the hazards of smoking and advocated sensible dress styles for women. As women became involved in the public sphere, the right to vote became even more crucial.

Willard died in 1898 at the age of 59. After her death the WCTU weakened. Financial troubles, changes in society, competition from the growing General Federation of Women's Clubs, and lack of leadership contributed to its diminished growth from 1892 to 1900. Lillian Stevens, president from 1898 to 1914, reinstated the union's singular focus on temperance issues.

Bibliography. Bordin, Ruth, *Frances Willard: A Biography* (Chapel Hill: University of North Carolina Press, 1986); Bordin, Ruth, *Woman and Temperance: The Quest for Power and Liberty, 1873–1900* (Philadelphia: Temple University Press, 1981); Gifford, Carolyn De Swarte, *Writing Out My Heart: Selections from the Journal of Frances E. Willard, 1855–1896* (Chicago: University of Illinois Press, 1995); Hardwick, Dana, *Oh Thou Woman That Bringest Good Tidings: The Life and Work of Katharine C. Bushnell* (Kearney, NE: Morris Publishing, 1995).

Linda McKinnish Bridges

Woman's Rights Convention. Two women, Lucretia Mott and Elizabeth Cady Stanton,* were the leaders of the first women's rights convention in the United States, held on July 19, 1848, in a small Wesleyan chapel in Seneca Falls, New York. This convention began the long and arduous struggle for women's right to vote, which was finally achieved in 1920. This convention was the formal beginning of the women's rights movement still in progress today.

The World Anti-Slavery convention held in London in 1840 may have been a direct influence on the Seneca Falls Convention, for Mott and Stanton joined an American delegation to participate in this meeting. After arriving in London, however, the women discovered that only men were allowed to be seated as delegates. The women, including Mott and Stanton, were required to sit in the galleries during the ten-day conference. During this conference on slavery, these two women were also discussing social injustice and women and began to consider a plan of action.

Mott, born in 1793 in New England, was ordained as a Quaker minister at the age of twenty-eight, and was an active abolitionist and founder of the first Female Anti-Slavery Society. She married James Mott and settled in Philadelphia as a teacher and important public abolitionist leader. Stanton, born in 1815 near Albany, New York, was educated and, like Mott, was active in the abolitionist movement. With her husband and large family, Stanton moved to Seneca Falls and was contacted by Mott. Lucretia, while visiting Jane Hunt, a friend in Waterloo, New York, not far from Seneca Falls, invited Elizabeth to join them for tea. While they were drinking tea around a mahogany table on July 9, 1848, the first seeds for a revolutionary movement were planted.

Jane Hunt, Mott's hostess, Martha Wright, Mott's sister, and Mary Ann McClintock joined the conversation as these five women decided to call a meeting to discuss the social, civil, and religious rights of women. The article in the local paper, the *Seneca County Courier*, on July 14, 1848, invited the public to attend a convention to discuss women's rights on July 19–20, 1848, at the Wesleyan Chapel in Seneca Falls, New York. The first day of the convention was for women only, although men could attend on the second day.

A few days before the convention, the five women met again, this time at the home of Mary Ann McClintock, to draft their grievances into a Declaration of Sentiments modeled on the Declaration of Independence. The document called for the right to vote and declared that "all men and women are created equal." The declaration was read and signed at the convention.

Over 300 people came that day from a radius of over fifty miles, including personal friend and abolitionist leader Frederick Douglass. At the end of the two-day meeting, however, only 68 signed the declaration, including 32 men. Only one signer, Charlotte Woodward, lived to participate in a presidential election. The slight gains made on July 14, 1848, would not be seen until 1920 when women were given the right to vote. It was a long struggle. In 1980 the Women's Rights National Historical Park was created in Seneca Falls, belonging to the National Park Service.

Bibliography. Flexner, Eleanor, *Century of Struggle: The Woman's Rights Movement in the United States* (Cambridge, MA: Belknap Press of the Harvard University Press, 1959); Sherr, Lynn, *Failure Is Impossible: Susan B. Anthony in Her Own Words* (New York: Times Books, 1995); Stanton, Elizabeth Cady, Susan B. Anthony, and Matilda Joslyn Gage, *History of Woman Suffrage*, 3 vols. (New York: Arno Press and the New York Times, 1969).

Linda McKinnish Bridges

Women-Church. A profound crisis in women's relationship to a primarily masculine version of Christianity has spurred a recent liturgical movement called "women-church." Displaying an ambivalent relationship to biblical origins and historic Christian creeds and confessions, this ecclesial movement that interfaces Christian tradition and feminist theory seeks to construct a community of faith no longer shackled to patriarchal interpretations. Women-church realizes that the spiritual insight and vitality necessary for the work of justice cannot be replenished by sheer activism alone; worship that connects with the Holy and with like-minded community is necessary sustenance. Participants in this movement are no longer willing to wait for the institutional churches to reform themselves sufficiently that women feel fully welcomed. Recalcitrance on the part of the church over the ordination of women,* inclusive liturgy, and advocacy for those on the margins has contributed to the momentum of women-church over the past decade.

Those participating in women-church, a loose configuration of communities of prayer and worship, distinguish themselves from secular feminists who find Christianity hopelessly irredeemable. Women-church seeks a critical retrieval of the liberating tradition within the church as well as constructing new conceptual patterns for interpreting the significance of women's relationship to the divine. Christianity's historic privileging of maleness, both in attributes ascribed to God and the priority of men over women, has distanced women from "God the Father" and from full inclusion as equal humans. Women-church, by contrast, provides a sanctuary for those who have been bombarded with dominant male imagery for God and nourishment for those who are suffering "eucharistic famine" (R. R. Ruether's term).

Criticized for being "separatist" or for revisionist theology that allegedly bears little resemblance to historic Christian faith, women-church nevertheless continues its improvisatory work in helping women participate in the trajectories of Christianity. The burgeoning literature in the fields of liturgics, hymnody, and feminist homiletical theory gives evidence of the current reformation in structures of worship. Ideally, women-church is a remediating impulse that will not need to remain a discrete ecclesial communion alongside the institutional church; however, because it provides a welcoming spiritual nurture that many find lacking in traditional worship, women-church continues to foster experimental patterns of worship that identify and resonate with the distinctiveness of women's experience.

Bibliography. Ruether, Rosemary Radford, *Women-Church: Theology and Practice of Feminist Liturgical Communities* (San Francisco: Harper and Row, 1985); Russell, Letty M., *The Liberating Word: A Guide to Non-sexist Interpretation of the Bible* (Philadelphia: Westminster Press, 1976); Schaffran, Janet, and Pat Kozak, *More Than Words: Prayer and Ritual for Inclusive Communities* (Bloomington, IN: Meyer/Stone Books, 1986).

Molly Marshall

Woodrow, James. Born in Carlisle, England, to Scottish parents, Reverend Thomas and Marion Williamson Woodrow, James Woodrow (1828–1907) immigrated to America as a child and grew up in Ohio, receiving a rigorous home education with some studies outside the home. He graduated from Jefferson College in Pennsylvania in 1849. He studied in the Lawrence Scientific School at Harvard University in the summer of 1852. After teaching in academies in Alabama and being a headmaster, he became a professor of science at Oglethorpe University in Georgia in 1853. He took leave from Oglethorpe to study at the University of Heidelberg, where he received his Ph.D. in chemistry in 1856. While there, he seized the opportunity to study geology and visit sites in Europe. He returned to Oglethorpe to continue his teachings and take theological studies. He was ordained to the ministry in 1860. In 1861 he inaugurated a unique chair in theological education at Columbia Theological Seminary, the Perkins Professorship of Natural Science in Connection with Revelation. His position there was designed "to evince the harmony of science with the records of our faith, and to refute the objections of infidel naturalists" (Gustafson, 58). Just after he gave his inaugural address, the Civil War started, and he became the chief chemist of the Columbia, South Carolina, laboratory for the Confederacy (1861–1865). A devout churchman and minister, he became the editor and proprietor of the quarterly *Southern Presbyterian Review* in 1861 when the Presbyterian Church in the South was suddenly cut off from its church publications.

When Columbia Theological Seminary reopened in September 1865 after the war, Woodrow resumed his teaching. The seminary was small, and Woodrow also became a science professor at South Carolina College (now the University of South Carolina). He taught there from 1869 to 1872, and from 1880 to 1897. From 1891 to 1897 he was president of the college.

Not until 1884 was any question openly raised about Woodrow's teaching and views—twenty-three years after his appointment to the chair and after his address in which he gave an outline of what he intended to teach. Woodrow set out to find harmony between science and Scripture; however, he later assumed the position that the absence of discord (noncontradiction) rather than harmony was the preferred position. Woodrow was adamant that the Bible did not teach science and that science was incompetent to answer theological questions.

Suddenly Woodrow found himself at the center of the evolution controversy in the Presbyterian Church (1884–1889). He was accused of teaching evolution in the seminary, including views that his opponents claimed changed the interpretation of many Scripture passages then received by the church. Woodrow held that a proper definition of evolution excludes all references to the origin of the forces and laws by which it works, and therefore it is neither Christian nor non-Christian and does not affect the belief in God or in religion. His opposition argued that the Bible was supreme in revelation and in science and that where there was conflict, science must be rejected.

Accused of heresy, Woodrow asked for a trial to clear him from false accusations or, if he were found guilty, to institute process against him in accordance with the Book of Discipline of the church. His opponents preferred to convict him and remove him from his teaching position at the seminary through pronouncements and directives of church courts without a trial, which they feared they might be unable to win. In September 1884 the Board of Directors of the seminary approved Woodrow's views of the relations between the teachings of Scripture and natural science, believing that nothing in the doctrine of evolution as defined and limited by Woodrow was inconsistent with perfect soundness. In

December of the same year a reconstituted Board of Trustees voted to request Woodrow's resignation.

Woodrow refused to resign. He charged that the board's resolutions condemning his teaching as being unscriptural and contrary to the standards of the church had been made without judicial investigation, by which alone such matters in the government of the church must be authoritatively determined. He asked for a trial. The board refused the request and dismissed him.

In April 1885 Woodrow requested that Augusta Presbytery try him. Augusta Presbytery took up the matter and found nothing that warranted a trial for heresy. No one would make charges; therefore, no process could be instituted. Woodrow took the next step to appeal to the four synods who appointed to the board to act as their agent. The terms of his employment were that he should not be removed except for unfaithfulness to his trust or incompetency in the discharge of his duties; he could, however, be temporarily suspended by the board until the case could be fully tried.

The board, a year after dismissing Woodrow, asked him if he would comply with the synods' wishes that evolution not be taught. Woodrow acknowledged the right of the synods to prescribe what subjects should be taught in the seminary and stated that he would omit evolution from the subjects taught if the synods so directed. Even with Woodrow's promise of compliance, the board in a split vote (8–5) requested him to resign in order to stop agitation and promote the highest interests of the seminary. Woodrow said that he was not ready to reply. A motion was again made to remove him, but it lost (7–6).

The trial was scheduled for Augusta Presbytery in August, after the General Assembly of the church was to meet in May. Opponents of Woodrow led the assembly to approve a statement that the Scriptures, expounded in the Confession of Faith and Catechisms, taught that ''Adam and Eve were created, body and soul, by immediate acts of Almighty Power, thereby preserving a perfect race unity; [and] That Adam's body was directly fashioned by Almighty God without any natural animal parentage of any kind, out of matter previously created from nothing'' (Gustafson, 209–10). Woodrow tried in vain to keep the assembly from making any statements that would inject into the word of God something that was not there—nothing said that creation was immediate. The General Assembly's action was in essence an *in thesi* deliverance with a trial pending before Augusta Presbytery. The safeguards assuring a Presbyterian minister a lawful hearing without a high court's prejudicial actions weighing in the balance had not been preserved. The assembly, adding to the confusion, went one step further; it assumed immediate jurisdiction over all seminaries and recommended that the synods dismiss Woodrow and appoint another professor in his place.

Augusta Presbytery, meeting in August before the seminary opened, held the trial of Woodrow and found him not guilty. Immediately the Reverend William Adams, who had brought the charges, appealed the verdict to the next meeting of the Synod of Georgia. Expressing reluctance to teach in the seminary until the appeal was settled, Woodrow was granted a leave of absence in September 1886. The Synod of Georgia annulled the action of Augusta Presbytery and ordered Woodrow's dismissal, which the board approved at its December 1886 meeting.

Woodrow protested the actions to the May 1887 General Assembly, but illness kept him from attending. Instead, the 1888 General Assembly considered the complaint. By a vote of 109–34 the assembly did not sustain Woodrow's complaint, but it did adopt a statement containing some of Woodrow's thinking, including the idea that God did not reveal his mode of creation—a statement in contradiction to its previous statement.

Woodrow maintained his scientific and religious views as articulated throughout the long ordeal. He kept his positions at the University of South Carolina. He was elected and appointed to positions of honor and responsibility by the synod and subsequent General Assemblies. Only in 1969 did the General Assembly of the Presbyterian Church in the United States reverse its former decisions and assume a position that vindicated Woodrow. Before Woodrow's death on January 17, 1907, he was honored by a resolution from the Board of Directors of Columbia Theological Seminary that removed any and all aspersions that might be drawn from any actions of the board.

Bibliography. Gustafson, R. K., *James Woodrow (1828–1907): Scientist: Theologian, Intellectual Leader* (Lewiston, NY: Edwin Mellen Press, 1995); Presbyterian Church in the United States, General Assembly Minutes, 1861–1944, 1969; Woodrow, Marion, ed., *Dr. James Woodrow as Seen by His Friends: Character Sketches and His Teachings* (Columbia, SC: R. L. Bryan, 1909).

Robert K. Gustafson

Woolman, John. An American-Quaker preacher and abolitionist, who was born in Rancocas, New Jersey, on October 19, 1720, Woolman was the fourth of thirteen children of a moderately wealthy farmer.

In his late teens Woolman began to experience troubling spiritual conflicts that led him to begin speaking in the First Day worship of local Friends' meetings. He became a "recommended minister" and traveled around New England and into the southern colonies. His journeys were usually of short duration because he felt a strong obligation to his family, but he exercised enormous influence over all who heard him. He urged his fellow Quakers to deemphasize materialism in their lives. True to his own message, he gave up a prosperous retail merchandising business and supported himself as a tailor and part-time teacher and surveyor.

On a visit to Virginia in 1746 Woolman was struck by the injustice of slavery and spent the rest of his life attacking the institution vigorously. He refused to profit from the work of slaves and, when visiting friends who owned them, would pay the slaves for their labors on his behalf. In 1754 he published one of his most important essays, *Some Considerations on the Keeping of Negroes.* This document led the London Yearly Meeting of 1758 to condemn the slave trade. In 1760 Woolman confronted a number of wealthy Quaker slave-owners after the Society's Yearly Meeting in Rhode Island. In 1762 he published *Some Considerations on the Keeping of Negroes: Part Second*, which stated his case even more forcefully than the first essay. Many Quakers began manumitting their slaves. By 1776 the Philadelphia Yearly Meeting had banned the ownership of slaves, and other Quaker meetings in the colonies soon adopted the same stance.

Woolman also took a strong stand on pacifism, even negotiating between Indians and colonial settlers and urging Quakers not to pay taxes levied by England to support the French and Indian War. His *Journal* was a revered piece of reading for the Transcendentalists and for many English intellectuals. Charles Lamb called it the only American book he had read twice. Woolman died of smallpox while on an anti-slavery visit to England on October 7, 1772.

Bibliography. Cady, Edwin H., *John Woolman: The Mind of the Quaker Saint* (New York: Washington Square Press, 1966); Gummere, Amelia M., ed., *The Journal and Essays of John Woolman* (New York: Macmillan, 1922); Moulton, Phillips, *The Journal and Major Essays of John Woolman* (New York, Oxford University Press, 1971); Whitney, Janet, *John Woolman: American Quaker* (Boston: Little, Brown, 1942).

Albert A. Bell, Jr.

Z

Zionism. The term "Zionism" refers to Mt. Zion, one of the mountains overlooking the city of Jerusalem. Its origins as a religious phenomenon go back to the destruction of the First Temple and the Babylonian exile in the year 586 B.C.E. The prophets and, later in history, the rabbinic leadership evoked visions of an end to the Exile and a return to Zion as a sign of messianic redemption. References to Zion are abundant in Jewish liturgy. Throughout the millennia of Jewish Diaspora, a return to Zion was always uppermost in Jewish thought.

Combining this religious vision with nineteenth-century European nationalist movements provided the beginning of the modern movement today called Zionism. In 1881 virulent and violent pogroms against the Jewish people erupted throughout Russia, causing some Jewish intellectuals to despair of Jews ever finding acceptance in Russia or among the nations of Europe. Leon Pinsker, a Russian-Jewish intellectual, wrote in his famous tract *Autoemancipation* that no matter how the Jews assimilated into modern culture, they would still be despised and oppressed. The "Judophobia" exhibited by European nations was due to the perception of the Jewish minority as being a "ghost nation." In every country, Jews were "guests" and in no country were they "hosts." A Jewish return to a national homeland would relieve the world of its anti-Semitism and return the Jewish people to a condition of normalcy.

Subsequent to Pinsker's work, a young Viennese journalist, Theodore Herzl, wrote a book in German, *Der Judenstaat* (the Jewish state). Herzl was influenced by the rise of anti-Semitism in German- and French-speaking Europe. Herzl covered the Dreyfus affair in France. He called for the nations of Europe to assist the Jewish people in creating a worldwide movement to create a political entity for Jews to escape anti-Semitism. More than a theoretician, Herzl organized the Zionist movements throughout the world to be a significant political force. He organized the First Zionist Congress in 1897, which met in Basle, Switzerland, and traveled to the capitals of Europe to meet with non-Jewish dignitaries and organize the Jewish communities.

While the land of Israel was never without a Jewish presence, Jews had begun to immigrate to the land of Israel to create a modern Jewish presence as early as the 1860s. They established some Jewish settlements there. These pioneers were motivated more for spiritual reasons than for political concerns. Many of these early settlements were unsuccessful and had to be abandoned. Later settlements learned from the failures of the earlier immigrants, and by the late nineteenth century permanent and viable Jewish settlement took root in the soil of the land of Israel after nearly two thousand years of exile.

Zionism was seen by many in the Jewish world as an opportunity for spiritual renewal. Asher Ginsburg, whose pen name Ahad Ha'Am meant ''one of the people,'' wrote extensively about creating in the land of Israel a spiritual center for the Jewish people. Many Jews were motivated by socialism, which had a large following among Jewish idealists from Eastern Europe. A. D. Gordon wrote about the importance of restructuring the Jewish people by returning them to the land as farmers. Eliezer Ben-Yehuda viewed the creation of a Jewish homeland as an opportunity to resurrect Hebrew as a modern spoken language of a modern living people, instead of being simply the language of prayer and ancient texts.

Zionism was not without its Jewish detractors. Reform Judaism* opposed Zionism and the creation of a Jewish homeland in the land of Israel for two complementary reasons. In theory, they perceived the dispersion of the Jewish people to the Diaspora as a positive force for world redemption and not as a punishment by God. Reform Jews were infatuated with patriotism for their countries and were anxious about perceptions of dual loyalty. They opposed Zionism's view of the Jewish people as a nation among nations, defining themselves instead as a people united by their faith. The most extreme expression of this anti-Zionism was embodied in the American Council for Judaism, which today is a movement of no significance among American Jewry. However, it should be noted that the most prominent American Zionist leaders, Abba Hillel Silver and Stephen S. Wise, were Reform rabbis. By the 1930s, most Reform Jews had sympathy for the aims of the Zionist settlers and lent their active support to Zionist causes. Following the Holocaust, Reform Jews were counted among Israel's most ardent supporters.

Opposition to Zionism could also be found among the most religiously traditional elements of the Jewish people. According to some, the founding of a Jewish homeland on the land of Israel can only come about with the coming of the Messiah. All political activity demonstrates a lack of faith in God. For them, the current State of Israel has no legitimate existence, since it was created by people and not by God. Even today there are elements among traditional Jews who deny the validity of the Jewish state. However, it should be noted that today the vast majority of traditional Jews do actively support the modern State of Israel. Most Orthodox rabbis and leaders found the opportunity to live as Jews without the burdens of being a minority to be a blessing.

Bibliography. Avineri, Shlomo, *The Making of Modern Zionism: The Intellectual Origins of the Jewish State* (New York: Basic Books, 1981); Halpern, Ben, *The Idea of the Jewish State*, 2nd ed. (Cambridge, MA: Harvard University Press, 1969); Hertzberg, Arthur, *The Zionist Idea* (New York: Atheneum, 1973); Laqueur, Walter, *A History of Zionism* (New York: Schocken Books, 1976).

Jonathan Miller

BIBLIOGRAPHY

AAUP Policy Documents and Reports. Washington, DC: AAUP, 1990.

Abernathy, R. D. *And the Walls Came Tumbling Down.* New York: Harper and Row, 1989.

Adams, James E. *Preus of Missouri and the Great Lutheran Civil War.* New York: Harper and Row, 1977.

Ahlstrom, Sydney E. *A Religious History of the American People.* New Haven: Yale University Press, 1972.

Albanse, Catherine L. *Corresponding Motion: Transcendental Religion and the New America.* Philadelphia: Temple University Press, 1977.

Allen, Margaret V. *The Achievement of Margaret Fuller.* University Park: Pennsylvania State University Press, 1979.

Allen, Richard. *The Life Experience and Gospel Labors of the Rt. Rev. Richard Allen.* New York: Abingdon Press, 1960.

Alley, Robert S. *School Prayer: The Court, the Congress, and the First Amendment.* Buffalo: Prometheus Books, 1994.

Alley, Robert S. *Without a Prayer.* Amherst, NY: Prometheus Books, 1996.

Altizer, Thomas J. J. *The Gospel of Christian Atheism.* Philadelphia: Westminster Press, 1996.

Ammerman, Nancy. *Baptist Battles.* New Brunswick, NJ: Rutgers University Press, 1990.

Anbinder, Tyler. *Nativism and Slavery.* New York: Oxford University Press, 1992.

Anderson, R. M. *Vision of the Disinherited.* New York: Oxford University Press, 1979.

Aptheker, Herbert. *Nat Turner's Slave Rebellion.* New York: Humanities Press, 1966.

Arndt, Karl J. R. *George Rapp's Harmony Society, 1785–1847.* Rev. ed. Rutherford, NJ: Fairleigh Dickinson University Press, 1972.

Baepler, Walter A. *A Century of Grace: Missouri Synod, 1847–1947.* St. Louis: Concordia, 1947.

Bainton, Roland H. *Christian Attitudes toward War and Peace*. New York: Abingdon Press, 1960.

Baker, Robert A. *Tell the Generations Following*. Nashville: Broadman Press, 1983.

Baldwin, L. *To Make the Wounded Whole*. Minneapolis: Fortress Press, 1992.

Balmer, Randall and John R. Fitzmier. *The Presbyterians*. Westport, CT: Greenwood Press, 1993.

Ban, Joseph D., and Paul R. Dekar, eds. *In the Great Tradition*. Valley Forge, PA: Judson Press, 1982.

Banning, Lance. *The Sacred Fire of Liberty*. Ithaca: Cornell University Press, 1995.

Barnette, Henlee H. *Clarence Jordan*. Macon: Smyth and Helwys, 1992.

Barr, James. *Holy Scripture: Canon, Authority, Criticism*. Philadelphia: Westminster Press, 1983.

Barry, Colman J. *The Catholic Church and German Americans*. Milwaukee: Bruce, 1953.

Bawer, Bruce. *A Place at the Table*. New York: Poseidon Press, 1993.

Beaver, R. Pierce, ed. *American Missions in Bicentennial Perspective*. South Pasadena, CA: Carey Press, 1977.

Bedau, Hugo A., and Chester Pierce, eds. *Capital Punishment in the United States*. New York: AMS Press, 1976.

Bellah, Robert N., and Phillip E Hammond. *Varieties of Civil Religion*. San Francisco: Harper and Row, 1980.

Bennett, John C., ed. *Christian Values and Economic Life*. New York: Harper and Bros., 1954.

Berrigan, Daniel. *To Dwell in Peace: An Autobiography*. San Francisco: Harper and Row, 1987.

Berrigan, Philip. *Widen the Prison Gates*. New York: Simon and Schuster, 1973.

Berryman, Phillip. *Liberation Theology*. Bloomington: Meyer/Stone Books, 1987.

Biermans, John T. *The Odyssey of New Religious Movements*. Lewiston, New York: Edwin Mellen Press, 1986.

Blocker, Jack S., Jr. *American Temperance Movements*. Boston: Twayne Publishers, 1989.

Blumhofer, Edith L. *Aimee Semple McPherson*. Grand Rapids, MI: Eerdmans, 1993.

Boettner, Loraine. *The Reformed Doctrine of Predestination*. Phillipsburg, NJ: Presbyterian and Reformed Publishing Co., 1932.

Boff, Leonardo. *When Theology Listens to the Poor*. San Francisco: Harper and Row, 1988.

Bordin, Ruth. *Woman and Temperance*. Philadelphia: Temple University Press, 1981.

Boslooper, Thomas. *The Virgin Birth*. Philadelphia: Westminster Press, 1962.

Boston, Robert. *The Most Dangerous Man in America?* Amherst, NY: Prometheus Books, 1996.

Boston, Robert. *Why the Religious Right Is Wrong about Separation of Church and State*. Buffalo: Prometheus Books, 1995.

Boswell, John. *Christianity, Social Tolerance, and Homosexuality*. Chicago: University of Chicago Press, 1980.

Bowden, Henry W. *Dictionary of American Religious Biography*. Westport, CT: Greenwood Press, 1977.

Bowden, Henry W. *American Indians and Christian Missions*. Chicago: University of Chicago Press, 1981.

Boyd, Gregory A. *Oneness Pentecostals and the Trinity*. Grand Rapids, MI: Baker, 1992.

Boyd, Malcolm. *Gay Priest: An Inner Journey.* New York: St. Martin's Press, 1986.

Brackney, W. H. *The Baptists.* Westport, CT: Greenwood Press, 1988.

Braude, Ann. *Radical Spirits.* Boston: Beacon Press, 1989.

Bridge, Donald, and David Phypers. *The Water That Divides: The Baptism Debate.* Downers Grove, IL: InterVarsity Press, 1977.

Brodie, Fawn M. *"No Man Knows My History": The Life of Joseph Smith, the Mormon Prophet.* New York: Alfred A. Knopf, 1945.

Brooks, Hays, and John E. Steely. *The Baptist Way of Life,* 2nd rev. ed. Macon: Mercer University Press, 1981.

Brotz, H. *The Black Jews of Harlem.* New York: Schocken Books, 1964.

Brown, Dale W. *Understanding Pietism.* Grand Rapids, MI: Eerdmans, 1978.

Burgess, Stanley, and Gary B. McGee, eds. *Dictionary of Pentecostal and Charismatic Movements.* Grand Rapids, MI: Zondervan, 1988.

Burnham, Kenneth E. *God Comes to America: Father Divine and the Peace Mission Movement.* Boston: Lambeth Press, 1979.

Burton, T. *Serpent-handling Believers.* Knoxville: University of Tennessee Press, 1993.

Bushman, Richard L. *Joseph Smith and the Beginnings of Mormonism.* Urbana: University of Illinois Press, 1984.

Butterfield, L. H. *Elder John Leland, Jeffersonian Itinerant.* Worcester, MA: Davis Press, 1953.

Carey, Patrick W., ed. *Orestes A. Brownson: Selected Writings.* New York: Paulist Press, 1991.

Cauthen, Kenneth. *The Impact of American Religious Liberalism.* New York: Harper and Row, 1962.

Cavert, Samuel McCrea. *Church Cooperation and Unity in America: A Historical Review: 1900–1970.* New York: Association Press, 1970.

Cazden, Elizabeth. *Antoinette Brown Blackwell: A Biography.* Old Westbury, NY: Feminist Press, 1983.

Cheney, Charles Edward. *What Reformed Episcopalians Believe.* N.p.: Christian Education Committee, Reformed Episcopal Church, 1961.

Chevannes, Barry. *Rastafari: Roots and Ideology.* Syracuse: Syracuse University Press, 1994.

Chidester, David S. *Salvation and Suicide: An Interpretation of Jim Jones, the Peoples Temple, and Jonestown.* Bloomington: Indiana University Press, 1988.

Chryssides, George D. *The Advent of Sun Myung Moon.* New York: St. Martin's Press, 1991.

Cimino, Dick. *The Book.* Harlingen, TX: Wonderful Word, 1975.

Clapp, Rodney. *The Reconstructionists.* Downer's Grove, IL: InterVarsity Press, 1990.

Clark, Clifford E., Jr. *Henry Ward Beecher: Spokesman for a Middle-Class America.* Urbana: University of Illinois Press, 1978.

Clark, Theodore R. *Saved by His Life.* New York: Macmillan, 1959.

Cleage, A. B., Jr. *Black Christian Nationalism.* New York: William Morrow and Co., 1972.

Cleage, A. B., Jr. *The Black Messiah.* New York: Sheed and Ward, 1968.

Coalter, M. J., Jr. *Gilbert Tennent, Son of Thunder.* New York: Greenwood Press, 1986.

Cone, J. H. *Black Theology and Black Power.* New York: Seabury Press, 1969.

Cone, J. H. *A Black Theology of Liberation.* Philadelphia: J. B. Lippincott, 1970.

Cone, J. H. *Martin and Malcolm and America.* Maryknoll, New York: Orbis Books, 1991.

Cone, J. H. *The Spirituals and the Blues.* New York: Seabury Press, 1972.

Conforti, Joseph A. *Jonathan Edwards, Religious Tradition, and American Culture.* Chapel Hill: University of North Carolina Press, 1995.

Conforti, Joseph A. *Samuel Hopkins and the New Divinity Movement.* Grand Rapids, MI: Christian University Press, 1981.

Coser, Lewis. *The Functions of Social Conflict.* Glencoe, IL: Free Press, 1956.

Cox, Harvey G., ed. *The Situation Ethics Debate.* Philadelphia: Westminster Press, 1968.

Crapsey, Algernon Sidney. *The Last of the Heretics.* New York: Alfred A. Knopf, 1924.

Crapsey, Algernon Sidney. *Religion and Politics.* New York: Thomas Whittaker, 1905.

Crespy, Georges. *From Science to Theology.* Nashville: Abingdon Press, 1968.

Crews, Clyde F. *An American Holy Land.* Wilmington: Glazier Press, 1987.

Crews, Mickey. *The Church of God: A Social History.* Knoxville: University of Tennessee Press, 1990.

Crim, Keith, ed. *Abingdon Dictionary of Living Religions.* Nashville: Abingdon Press, 1981.

Criswell, W. A. *Why I Preach That the Bible Is Literally True.* Nashville: Broadman Press, 1969.

Crittenden, Ann. *Sanctuary: A Story of American Conscience and the Law in Collision.* New York: Weidenfeld and Nicolson, 1988.

Crockett, W., ed. *Four Views on Hell.* Grand Rapids, MI: Zondervan, 1992.

Daly, Mary. *Gyn/Ecology: The Metaethics of Radical Feminism.* Boston: Beacon Press, 1978.

Davidson, William F. *The Free Will Baptists in America, 1727–1984.* Nashville: Randall House Publications, 1985.

Dayton, Donald. *Theological Roots of Pentecostalism.* Grand Rapids, MI: Francis Asbury Press, 1987.

Dear, John, ed. *Apostle of Peace: Essays in Honor of Daniel Berrigan.* Maryknoll, New York: Orbis, 1996.

de Camp, L. Sprague. *The Great Monkey Trial.* Garden City, NY: Doubleday, 1968.

Deck, Allan Figueroa. *The Second Wave.* New York: Paulist Press, 1989.

Deloria, Vine V., Jr. *God Is Red.* New York: Dell Publishing, 1983.

Deloria, Vine V., Jr., and Clifford M. Lytle. *American Indians, American Justice.* Austin: University of Texas Press, 1983.

Divine Principle. Terrytown, NY: Holy Spirit Association for the Unification of World Christianity, 1973.

Dollar, George W. *The Fight for Fundamentalism.* Sarasota, FL: Daniels Publishing, 1983.

Dorgan, Howard. *Giving Glory to God in Appalachia.* Knoxville: University of Tennessee Press, 1987.

Dowell, W. E. *The Birthpangs of the Baptist Bible Fellowship.* Springfield, MO: Temple Press, 1977

D'Souza, Dinesh. *Falwell, before the Millennium: A Critical Biography.* Chicago: Regnery, 1984.

Dunnavant, Anthony L., and Richard L. Harrison, Jr., eds. *Explorations in the Stone-Campbell Traditions.* Nashville: Disciples of Christ Historical Society, 1995.

Easter, O. P. *Nannie Helen Burroughs.* New York: Garland Publishing, 1995.

Edwards, Paul M. *Our Legacy of Faith: A Brief History of the Reorganized Church of Jesus Christ of Latter-Day Saints.* Independence, MO: Herald House, 1991.

Eller, Cynthia. *Living in the Lap of the Goddess.* New York Crossroad Press, 1993.

Ellis, John Tracy. *American Catholics and the Intellectual Life.* Chicago: Heritage Foundation, 1956.

Ellwood, R. S., Jr., *One Way: The Jesus Movement and Its Meaning.* Englewood Cliffs, NJ: Prentice-Hall, 1973.

Eve, Raymond A., and Francis B. Harrold. *The Creationist Movement in Modern America.* Boston: Twayne, 1991.

Fackre, Gabriel. *The Religious Right and Christian Faith.* Grand Rapids, MI: Eerdmans, 1982.

Fairclough, A. *Martin Luther King, Jr.* Athens: University of Georgia Press, 1995.

Falwell, Jerry. *Listen, America!* Garden City, NY: Doubleday, 1980.

Fenn, R. K. *The Persistence of Purgatory.* Cambridge: Cambridge University Press, 1995.

FitzPatrick, P. J. *In Breaking of Bread: The Eucharist and Ritual.* Cambridge: Cambridge University Press, 1993.

Fogarty, R. S., ed. *Special Love/Special Sex: An Oneida Community Diary.* Syracuse: Syracuse University Press, 1994.

Forest, Jim. *Living with Wisdom: A Life of Thomas Merton.* Maryknoll, NY: Orbis, 1991.

Fosdick, H. E. *The Living of These Days.* New York: Harper and Row, 1956.

Foster, Frank Hugh. *A Genetic History of the New England Theology.* Chicago: University of Chicago Press, 1907.

Foster, L. *Women, Family, and Utopia: Communal Experiments of the Shakers, the Oneida Community, and the Mormons.* Syracuse: Syracuse University Press, 1991.

Frerichs, Ernest S., ed. *The Bible and Bibles in America.* Atlanta: Scholars Press, 1988.

Friedly, Michael. *Malcolm X: The Assassination.* New York: Carroll and Graf, 1992.

The Fundamentals: A Testimony to Truth. eds. R. A. Torrey, A. C. Dixon. 4 vols. Los Angeles: Bible Institute of Los Angeles, 1917.

Gannon, Robert I. *The Cardinal Spellman Story.* Garden City, NY: Doubleday, 1962.

Gaustad, E. S. *Dissent in American Religion.* Chicago: University of Chicago Press, 1973.

Gaustad, E. S. *The Great Awakening in New England.* New York: Harper and Row, 1957.

Gaustad, E. S. *Sworn on the Altar of God.* Grand Rapids, MI: Eerdmans, 1996.

George, John, and Laird Wilcox. *Nazis, Communists, Klansmen, and Others on the Fringe: Political Extremism in America.* Buffalo: Prometheus Books, 1992.

Gleason, Philip. *Keeping the Faith.* Notre Dame: University of Notre Dame Press, 1987.

Goen, C. C. *Revivalism and Separatism in New England, 1740–1800.* Middletown, CT: Wesleyan University Press, 1987.

Goldberg, David, ed. *Anatomy of Racism.* Minneapolis: University of Minnesota Press, 1990.

Goldman, P. *The Death and Life of Malcolm X.* 2nd ed. Urbana: University of Illinois Press, 1979.

Gottschalk, Stephen. *The Emergence of Christian Science in American Religious Life.* Berkeley: University of California Press, 1973.

Graef, H. *Mary: A History of Doctrine and Devotion: 1963–1965.* 2 vols. New York: Sheed and Ward, 1965.

Graves, J. R. *Old Landmarkism: What Is It?* Memphis: Baptist Book House, 1880.

Gregory, Joel. *Too Great a Temptation.* Fort Worth: Summit Group, 1994.

Griffith, Elisabeth. *In Her Own Right: The Life of Elizabeth Cady Stanton.* New York: Oxford University Press, 1984.

Grimké, Francis J. *The Works of Francis J. Grimké.* 4 vols. Washington, DC: Associated Publishers, 1942.

Guelzo, Allen. *For the Union of Evangelical Christendom: The Irony of the Reformed Episcopalians.* University Park: Pennsylvania State University Press, 1994.

Gustafson, R. K. *James Woodrow: (1828–1907) Scientist, Theologian, Intellectual Leader.* Lewiston, NY: Edwin Mellen Press, 1995.

Haddad, Y. Y., and J. I. Smith. *Mission to America.* Gainesville: University of Florida Press, 1993.

Haddad, Y. Y., and J. I. Smith, eds. *Muslim Communities in North America.* Albany: State University of New York Press, 1994.

Hadden, Jeffrey K., and Anson Shupe. *Televangelism, Power, and Politics on God's Frontier.* New York: Holt, 1988.

Hall, David. *The Antinomian Controversy 1636–1638: A Documentary History,* 2nd ed. Durham: Duke University Press, 1990.

Ham, E. E. *50 Years on the Battle Front with Christ: A Biography of Mordecai F. Ham.* N.p.: Old Kentucky Home Revivalist Press, 1950.

Handy, Robert T. *A History of Union Theological Seminary in New York.* New York: Columbia University Press, 1987.

Hansen, Klaus J. *Mormonism and the American Experience.* Chicago: University of Chicago Press, 1981.

Hardman, Keith J. *Charles Grandison Finney, 1792–1875: Revivalist and Reformer.* Syracuse: Syracuse University Press, 1987.

Hargis, Billy James. *My Great Mistake.* Tulsa: Christian Crusade, 1986.

Harper, William Rainey. *Religion and the Higher Life: Talks to Students.* Chicago: University of Chicago Press, 1904.

Harrell, D. E. *Oral Roberts.* Bloomington: Indiana University Press, 1985.

Hart, D. G. *Defending the Faith: J. Gresham Machen and the Crisis of Conservative Protestantism in Modern America.* Baltimore: Johns Hopkins University Press, 1994.

Hawkesworth, M. E. *Beyond Oppression: Feminist Theory and Political Strategy.* New York: Continuum, 1990.

Haygood, W. *King of the Cats: The Life and Times of Adam Clayton Powell, Jr.* Boston: Houghton Mifflin, 1993.

Hennesey, James J. *American Catholics.* New York: Oxford University Press, 1981.

Henry, Stuart. *Unvanquished Puritan.* Grand Rapids, MI: Eerdmans, 1973.

Higham, John. *Strangers in the Land: Patterns of American Nativism, 1860–1925.* New Brunswick, NJ: Rutgers University Press, 1988.

Hill, Robert A., ed., and Barbara Bair, assoc. ed. *Marcus Garvey: Life and Lessons.* Berkeley: University of California Press, 1987.

Hill, Samuel S., ed. *Encyclopedia of Religion in the South.* Macon: Mercer University Press, 1984.

Hill, Samuel S. *Handbook of Denominations in the United States.* 10th ed. Nashville: Abingdon Press, 1995.

Holder, Vincent F. *The Yankee Paul: Isaac Thomas Hecker.* Milwaukee: Bruce Publishing Co., 1958.

Holmes, David L. *A Brief History of the Episcopal Church.* Valley Forge, PA: Trinity Press International, 1993.

Hopkins, Charles Howard. *The Rise of the Social Gospel in American Protestantism, 1865–1915.* New Haven: Yale University Press, 1940.

Howe, Claude L., Jr. *Seventy-Five Years of Providence and Prayer: An Illustrated History of New Orleans Baptist Theological Seminary.* New Orleans: NOBTS, 1993.

Hudson, Winthrop S. *Baptist Concepts of the Church.* Chicago: Judson Press, 1959.

Hudson, Winthrop S. *The Great Tradition of the American Churches.* New York: Harper, 1953.

Hudson, Winthrop S. *Religion in America.* 3rd ed. New York: Scribner's, 1981.

Hutchison, William R. *The Modernist Impulse in American Protestantism.* Cambridge: Harvard University Press, 1976.

Ice, Jackson Lee, and John J. Carey. *The Death of God Debate.* Philadelphia: Westminster Press, 1967.

Jacobson, Simon. *Toward a Meaningful Life: The Wisdom of the Rebbe.* New York: William Morrow and Co., 1995.

Jeansonne, Glen. *Gerald L. K. Smith: Minister of Hate.* New Haven: Yale University Press, 1988.

Johnson, David S., Francis L. Patton, and George C. Noyes. *The Trial of the Rev. David Swing before the Presbytery of Chicago.* Chicago: Jansen and Co., 1874.

Jordan, Clarence. *The Substance of Faith.* New York: Association Press, 1972.

Kaplan, M. M. *Judaism as a Civilization.* New York: Macmillan, 1934.

Kayal, Philip M. *Bearing Witness.* Boulder, CO: Westview Press, 1993.

Kephart, William M. *Extraordinary Groups: The Sociology of Unconventional Lifestyles.* New York: St. Martin's Press, 1976.

Kilcourse, George. *Ace of Freedoms: Thomas Merton's Christ.* Notre Dame: University of Notre Dame Press, 1993.

Killens, John O., ed. *The Trial of Denmark Vesey.* Boston: Beacon Press, 1970.

Kimbrough, D. L. *Taking Up Serpents: Snake Handlers of Eastern Kentucky.* Chapel Hill: University of North Carolina Press, 1995.

King, M. L., Jr. *Stride toward Freedom.* New York: Harper and Row, 1958.

Klaw, S. *Without Sin: The Life and Death of the Oneida Community.* New York: Viking Penguin, 1993.

Knee, Stuart E. *Christian Science in the Age of Mary Baker Eddy.* Westport, CT: Greenwood Press, 1994.

Kraus, Norman C. *Dispensationalism in America.* Richmond: Mennonite Publishing, 1958.

Kuenning, Paul P. *The Rise and Fall of American Lutheran Pietism.* Macon: Mercer University Press, 1988.

Kuklick, Bruce. *Churchmen and Philosophers.* New Haven: Yale University Press, 1985.

Lacy, C. *The Word-carrying Giant: The Growth of the American Bible Society.* South Pasadena, CA: William Carey Library, 1977.

Land, Gary, ed. *Adventism in America.* Grand Rapids, MI: Eerdmans, 1986.

Langmuir, Gavin I. *History, Religion, and Antisemitism.* Berkeley: University of California Press, 1990.

Larson, Orvin. *American Infidel: Robert G. Ingersoll.* New York: Citadel Press, 1962.

Lean, Garth. *On the Tail of a Comet: The Life of Frank Buchman.* Colorado Springs: Helmers and Howard, 1988.

Lee, Dallas. *The Cotton Patch Evidence.* New York: Harper and Row, 1971.

Leonard, Bill J., ed. *Dictionary of Baptists in America.* Downers Grove, IL: InterVarsity Press, 1994.

Levine, Lawrence. *Defender of the Faith: William Jennings Bryan, the Last Decade, 1915–1925.* New York: Oxford University Press, 1965.

Levy, Leonard. *The Establishment Clause.* New York: Macmillan, 1986.

Lewis, James R., ed. *From the Ashes: Making Sense of Waco.* London: Rowman and Littlefield, 1994.

Lincoln, C. E. *The Black Muslims in America.* Boston: Beacon Press, 1961.

Lincoln, C. E., ed. *The Black Experience in Religion.* Garden City, New York: Anchor Books, 1974.

Lincoln, C. E., and L. H. Mamiya. *The Black Church in the African-American Experience.* Durham: Duke University Press, 1990.

Lippy, Charles H., and Peter W. Williams. *Encyclopedia of the American Religious Experience.* 3 vols. New York: Scribner's, 1988.

Loetscher, Lefferts A. *The Broadening Church.* Philadelphia: University of Pennsylvania Press, 1954.

Longfield, Bradley J. *The Presbyterian Controversy: Fundamentalists, Modernists, and Moderates.* New York: Oxford University Press, 1991.

Lumpkin, Katharine Du Pre. *The Emancipation of Angelina Grimké.* Chapel Hill: University of North Carolina Press, 1974.

Mabee, Carlton, with Susan M. Newhouse. *Sojourner Truth: Slave, Prophet, Legend.* New York: New York University Press, 1993.

Malcolm X, with A. Haley. *The Autobiography of Malcolm X.* New York: Grove Press, 1965.

Marsden, George M. *Reforming Fundamentalism.* Grand Rapids, MI: Eerdmans, 1987.

Marsh, C. E. *From Black Muslims to Muslims.* Metuchen, NJ: Scarecrow Press, 1984.

Marshall, Molly. *What It Means to Be Human.* Macon: Smyth and Helwys, 1995.

Martin, William. *A Prophet with Honor: The Billy Graham Story.* New York: William Morrow, 1991.

Massa, Mark S. *Charles Augustus Briggs and the Crisis of Historical Criticism.* Minneapolis: Fortress Press, 1990.

McAvoy, Thomas T. *The Americanist Heresy in Roman Catholicism, 1895–1900.* Notre Dame: University of Notre Dame Press, 1963.

McCaffrey, Lawrence J. *The Irish Diaspora in America.* Bloomington: Indiana University Press, 1976.

McCulloh, Gerald, ed. *Man's Faith and Freedom: The Theological Influence of Jacobus Arminius.* New York: Abingdon Press, 1962.

McGann, Agnes Geraldine. *Nativism in Kentucky to 1860.* Washington, DC: Catholic University of America Press, 1944.

McLoughlin, W. G., Jr. *Modern Revivalism.* New York: Ronald Press, 1959.

McNeill, John J. *The Church and the Homosexual.* Kansas City: Sheed Andrews and McMeel, 1976.

Melton, J. Gordon. *The Encyclopedia of American Religions*. Detroit: Gale Research Co., 1978.

Melton, J. Gordon, ed. *Religious Leaders of America*. Detroit: Gale Research, 1991.

Merton, Thomas. *Faith and Violence*. Notre Dame: University of Notre Dame Press, 1968.

Metzger, Walter. *Academic Freedom in the Age of the University*. New York: Columbia University Press, 1961.

Mickler, Michael L. *A History of the Unification Church in America, 1959–1974*. New York: Garland, 1993.

Miller, Neil. *Out of the Past*. New York: Vintage Books, 1995.

Miller, Perry, ed. *The American Transcendentalists*. Garden City, NY: Doubleday and Co., 1957.

Miller, Perry. *Jonathan Edwards*. New York: William Sloane, 1949.

Miller, Perry. *Roger Williams: His Contribution to American Culture*. New York: Atheneum, 1962.

Miller, Perry. *The Transcendentalists*. Cambridge, MA: Harvard University Press, 1960.

Miller, Robert Moats. *Harry Emerson Fosdick: Preacher, Pastor, Prophet*. New York: Oxford University Press, 1985.

Monk, Maria. *Awful Disclosures of the Hotel Dieu Nunnery of Montreal*. New York: Howe and Bates, 1836.

Moore, R. Laurence. *In Search of White Crows: Spiritualism, Parapsychology, and American Culture*. New York: Oxford University Press, 1977.

Morey, Robert A. *Reincarnation and Christianity*. Minneapolis: Bethany, 1980.

Moulton, Phillips P., ed. *The Journal and Major Essays of John Woolman*. New York: Oxford University Press, 1971.

Mulder, John M., and John F. Wilson, eds. *Religion in American History*. Englewood Cliffs, NJ: Prentice-Hall, 1978.

Murdoch, Norman H. *Origins of the Salvation Army*. Knoxville: University of Tennessee Press, 1994.

Murphy, L. G., ed. *Encyclopedia of African American Religions*. New York: Garland Publishing, 1993.

Murray, Iain H. *Spurgeon v. Hyper-Calvinism: The Battle for Gospel Preaching*. Edinburgh: Banner of Truth Trust, 1995.

Myrdal, Gunnar. *An American Dilemma*. 2 vols. New York: Harper and Bros., 1944.

Nauman, St. Elmo, Jr., ed. *Exorcism through the Ages*. New York: Philosophical Library, 1974.

Nelson, E. Clifford, ed. *The Lutherans in North America*. Philadelphia: Fortress Press, 1975.

New Scofield Reference Bible. New York: Oxford University Press, 1967.

Noll, Mark A., ed. *The Princeton Theology, 1812–1921*. Grand Rapids, MI: Baker, 1983.

Noll, Mark A., ed. *Religion and American Politics*. New York: Oxford University Press, 1990.

Nichols, James H. *Romanticism in American Theology*. Chicago: University of Chicago Press, 1961.

Noonan, J. T., Jr. *Contraception*. New York: Mentor-Omega Books, 1967.

Norwood, F. A. *The Story of American Methodism*. Nashville: Abingdon Press, 1974.

Noyes, J. H. *Religious Experience of John Humphrey Noyes*. Reprint. Manchester, NH: Ayer, 1977.

Numbers, Ronald L. *The Creationists: The Evolution of Scientific Creationism.* New York: Alfred A. Knopf, 1992.

Nutt, Rick. *Contending for the Faith.* Cincinnati: Presbytery of Cincinnati, 1991.

O'Brien, D. *Isaac Hecker: An American Catholic.* New York: Paulist Press, 1992.

Ogletree, Thomas W. *The Death of God Controversy.* Nashville: Abingdon Press, 1966.

Payne, W. J., ed. *Directory of African American Religious Bodies.* Washington, DC: Research Center on Black Religious Bodies, Howard University School of Theology, 1991.

Peterson, Merrill. *Thomas Jefferson: Writings.* New York: Library of America, 1984.

Pickering, Ernest. *Biblical Separation: The Struggle for a Pure Church.* Schaumberg, IL: Regular Baptist Press, 1979.

Pike, Diane Kennedy. *Search: The Personal Story of a Wilderness Journey.* Garden City, NY: Doubleday, 1970.

Plimpton, Ruth Talbot. *Mary Dyer: Biography of a Rebel Quaker.* Boston: Branden, 1994.

Poch, Robert K. *Academic Freedom in American Higher Education.* Washington, DC: ASHE-ERIC Higher Education Report no. 4, 1993.

Quimby, Phineas Parkhurst. *The Complete Writings.* Ed. Ervin Seale. 3 vols. Marina del Rey, CA: DeVorss, 1988.

Quinn, D. Michael. *The Mormon Hierarchy: Origins of Power.* Salt Lake City: Signature Books, 1994.

Raab, Earl. *Religious Conflict in America.* Garden City, New York: Anchor Books, 1964.

Randall, Mike. *G. B. Vick.* Springfield, MO: Baptist Bible College, 1987.

Rankin, Richard. *Ambivalent Churchmen and Evangelical Churchwomen.* Columbia: University of South Carolina Press, 1993.

Raser, Harold E. *Phoebe Palmer.* Lewiston, NY: Edwin Mellen Press, 1987.

Reimers, David M. *White Protestantism and the Negro.* New York: Oxford University Press, 1965.

Reinhard, James Arnold. *Personal and Sociological Factors in the Formation of the Free Methodist Church, 1852–1860.* Iowa City: University of Iowa Press, 1971.

Reventlow, Henning Graf. *The Authority of the Bible and the Rise of the Modern World.* Philadelphia: Fortress Press, 1985.

Richards, W. Wiley. *Winds of Doctrines.* Lanham, MD: University Press of America, 1991.

Richardson, Harry. *Dark Salvation: The Story of Methodism As It Developed among Blacks in America.* Garden City, NY: Doubleday, 1976.

Rideau, Emile. *The Thought of Teilhard de Chardin.* New York: Harper and Row, 1967.

Ritchie, Homer G. *The Life and Legend of J. Frank Norris.* Fort Worth: Homer G. Ritchie, 1991.

Robinson, D. *The Unitarians and the Universalists.* Westport, CT: Greenwood Press, 1985.

Robinson, James M., ed. *The Beginnings of Dialectic Theology.* Richmond: John Knox Press, 1968.

Rogers, Jack, and Donald McKim. *The Authority and Interpretation of the Bible: An Historical Approach.* San Francisco: Harper and Row, 1979.

Ruether, Rosemary Radford. *Sexism and God-Talk: Toward a Feminist Theology.* Boston: Beacon Press, 1983.

Ruether, Rosemary Radford. *Women-Church: Theology and Practice of Feminist Liturgical Communities.* San Francisco: Harper and Row, 1985.

Rutland, Robert A., ed. *James Madison and the American Nation, 1751–1836: An Encyclopedia.* New York: Simon and Schuster, 1985.

Ryan, Thomas. *Orestes A. Brownson: A Definitive Biography.* Huntington, IN: Our Sunday Visitor Press, 1976.

Ryrie, Charles. *Dispensationalism Today.* Chicago: Moody Press, 1965.

Sandeen, Ernest R. *The Roots of Fundamentalism.* Chicago: University of Chicago Press, 1970.

Sawyer, M. R. *Black Ecumenism.* Valley Forge, PA: Trinity Press, 1994.

Scanzoni, Letha, and Virginia Mollenkott. *Is the Homosexual My Neighbor?* San Francisco: HarperSanFrancisco, 1994.

Schillebeeckx, E. *Celibacy.* New York: Sheed and Ward, 1968.

Schlesinger, Arthur, Jr. *A Pilgrim's Progress: Orestes A. Brownson.* Boston: Little Brown, and Co., 1966.

Sheen, Fulton J. *Treasure in Clay.* Garden City, NY: Doubleday, 1980.

Sherr, Lynn. *Failure Is Impossible: Susan B. Anthony in Her Own Words.* New York: Times Books, 1995.

Shipps, Jan. *Mormonism: The Story of a New Religious Tradition.* Urbana: University of Illinois Press, 1985.

Shriver, George H., ed. *American Religious Heretics.* Nashville: Abingdon Press, 1966.

Shurden, Walter. *Not a Silent People.* Nashville: Broadman Press, 1972.

Smith, Ebbie C. *Balanced Church Growth.* Nashville: Broadman Press, 1984.

Smith, H. Shelton, Robert Handy, and Lefferts Loetscher. *American Christianity.* 2 vols. New York: Scribner's, 1960.

Smith, Harmon L. *Ethics and the New Medicine.* Nashville: Abingdon Press, 1970.

Sontag, Frederick. *Sun Myung Moon and the Unification Church.* Nashville: Abingdon Press, 1977.

Sontag, Susan. *AIDS and Its Metaphors.* New York: Farrar, Straus and Giroux, 1989.

Speaight, Robert. *The Life of Teilhard de Chardin.* New York: Harper and Row, 1967.

Stagg, Frank. *The Book of Acts.* Nashville: Broadman Press, 1955.

Stassen, Glen H. *Just Peacemaking: Transforming Initiatives for Justice and Peace.* Louisville: Westminster/John Knox Press, 1992.

Stein, Stephen J. *The Shaker Experience in America.* New Haven: Yale University Press, 1992.

Stewart, Omer C. *Peyote Religion: A History.* Norman: University of Oklahoma Press, 1987.

Stone, Merlin. *When God Was a Woman.* New York: Dial Press, 1976.

Strang, Mark A., ed. *The Diary of James J. Strang.* East Lansing: Michigan State University Press, 1961.

Streiker, Lowell D. *New Age Comes to Main Street.* Nashville: Abingdon Press, 1990.

Stringfellow, William, and Anthony Towne. *The Bishop Pike Affair: Scandals of Conscience and Heresy, Relevance and Solemnity in the Contemporary Church.* New York: Harper and Row, 1967.

Sumner, Robert L. *Man Sent from God: A Biography of Dr. John R. Rice.* Murfreesboro, TN: Sword of the Lord, 1959.

Synan, Vinson. *The Holiness-Pentecostal Movement in the United States.* Grand Rapids, MI: Eerdmans, 1971.

Teilhard de Chardin, Pierre. *Man's Place in Nature*. New York: Harper and Row, 1966.
Teilhard de Chardin, Pierre. *The Phenomenon of Man*. New York: Harper and Row, 1959.
Thompson, Ernest Trice. *Presbyterians in the South*. 3 vols. Richmond: John Knox Press, 1963–1973.
Tietjen, John H. *Memoirs in Exile*. Minneapolis: Fortress Press, 1990.
Torbet, Robert G. *A History of the Baptists*. 3rd ed. Valley Forge, PA: Judson Press, 1973.
Toulouse, Mark G. *Joined in Discipleship*. St. Louis: Chalice Press, 1992.
Trumbull, C. G. *The Life Story of C. I. Scofield*. New York: Oxford University Press, 1920.
Tull, James E. *Shapers of Baptist Thought*. Valley Forge, PA: Judson Press, 1972.
Vahanian, G., ed. *The Death of God*. New York: Braziller, 1961.
Van Noord, Roger. *King of Beaver Island: The Life and Assassination of James Jesse Strang*. Urbana: University of Illinois Press, 1988.
Vaughn, William P. *The Antimasonic Party in the United States, 1826–1843*. Lexington: University Press of Kentucky, 1983.
Wallace, Dewey D., Jr. *Puritans and Predestination*. Chapel Hill: University of North Carolina Press, 1982.
Ward, L. B. *Father Charles E. Coughlin: An Authorized Biography*. Detroit: Tower Publications, 1933.
Washington, J. R., Jr. *Black Sects and Cults*. Garden City, NY: Doubleday, 1972.
Washington, James M., ed. *A Testament of Hope: The Essential Writings of Martin Luther King, Jr.* New York: Harper and Row, 1986.
Watts, M. *The Dissenters*. Oxford: Clarendon Press, 1978.
Webb, George. *The Evolution Controversy in America*. Lexington: University Press of Kentucky, 1994.
Wenger, John C. *What Mennonites Believe*. Rev. ed. Scottdale, PA: Herald Press, 1991.
White, Andrew D. *A History of the Warfare of Science with Theology in Christendom*. 2 vols. New York: D. Appleton and Co., 1896.
Williams, Selma R. *Divine Rebel: The Life of Anne Marbury Hutchinson*. New York: Holt, Rinehart and Winston, 1981.
Williamson, Geoffrey. *Inside Buchmanism*. New York: Philosophical Library, 1955.
Wilmore, Gayraud S. *Black Religion and Black Radicalism*. 2nd rev. ed. Maryknoll, New York: Orbis Books, 1983.
Wind, James P. *The Bible and the University: The Messianic Vision of William Rainey Harper*. Atlanta: Scholars Press, 1987.
Winston, Diane. "Boozers, Brass Bands, and Hallelujah Lassies." Ph.D. diss., Princeton University, 1996.
Wright, Melton. *Fortress of Faith: The Story of Bob Jones University*. Greenville, SC: BJU Press, 1984.
Wright, Stuart A. ed. *Armageddon in Waco*. Chicago: University of Chicago Press, 1995.

INDEX

Boldface page numbers indicate location of main entries.

CONTRIBUTORS

ALLEY, ROBERT S. Ph.D., Princeton University. Professor Emeritus of Humanities, University of Richmond.

BELL, ALBERT A., JR. Ph.D., University of North Carolina at Chapel Hill. Professor and Chair, Department of History, Hope College, Holland, Michigan.

BOWDEN, HENRY WARNER. Ph.D., Princeton University. Chair and Professor, Department of Religion, Rutgers University.

BRANCH, ROGER G. Ph.D., University of Georgia. Chair and Professor, Department of Anthropology and Sociology, Georgia Southern University.

BRIDGES, LINDA MCKINNISH. Ph.D., Southern Baptist Theological Seminary. Associate Professor of New Testament and Greek, Baptist Theological Seminary, Richmond, Virginia.

COCHRAN, BERNARD H. Ph.D., Duke University. Chair and Professor, Department of Philosophy and Religion, Meredith College.

CONGLETON, RUSSELL. Ph.D. candidate, Duke University.

CREWS, CLYDE F. Ph.D, Fordham University. Professor of Religion, Bellarmine College.

DAVIS, THOMAS J. Ph.D., University of Chicago. Assistant Professor of Religious Studies, Indiana University–Purdue University at Indianapolis.

DUNNAVANT, ANTHONY L. Ph.D., Vanderbilt University. Associate Professor of Church History, Lexington Theological Seminary.

EGGER, VERNON. Ph.D., University of Michigan. Associate Professor of History, Georgia Southern University.

GRAHAM, STEPHEN R. Ph.D., University of Chicago. Assistant Professor of Church History, North Park Theological Seminary.

GUSTAFSON, ROBERT K. Th.D., Union Theological Seminary, Richmond. Professor Emeritus, University of North Carolina at Pembroke. Deceased, November 1995.

HANSEN, KLAUS J. Ph.D., Wayne State University. Professor of History, Queen's University, Kingston, Canada.

HILL, SAMUEL S. Ph.D., Duke University. Emeritus Professor of Religion, University of Florida.

HUBER, DONALD L. Ph.D., Duke University. Professor of Church History, Trinity Lutheran Seminary, Columbus, Ohio.

HUMPHREYS, FISHER. Th.D., New Orleans Baptist Theological Seminary. Professor of Divinity, Beeson Divinity School, Samford University.

KILCOURSE, GEORGE. Ph.D., Fordham University. Professor of Theology, Bellarmine College.

KIRKLEY, EVELYN A. Ph.D., Duke University. Assistant Professor of Theological and Religious Studies, University of San Diego.

LEONARD, BILL J. Ph.D., Boston University. Dean, Divinity School, Wake Forest University.

LIPPY, CHARLES. Ph.D, Princeton University. Professor of Religion, University of Tennessee at Chattanooga.

LONGFIELD, BRADLEY J. Ph.D., Duke University. Associate Professor of Church History, University of Dubuque Theological Seminary.

LUCAS, PHILLIP. Ph.D., University of California at Santa Barbara. Assistant Professor of Religious Studies, Stetson University.

MANIS, ANDREW M. Ph.D., Southern Baptist Theological Seminary. Associate Editor, Mercer University Press.

MARKHAM, COLEMAN. Ph.D., Vanderbilt University. Professor of Religion, Barton College.

MARSHALL, MOLLY. Ph.D., Southern Baptist Theological Seminary. Professor of Theology, Central Baptist Theological Seminary.

MARTIN, SANDY DWAYNE. Ph.D., Union Theological Seminary, New York City. Associate Professor of Religion, University of Georgia.

MCCARTHY, DAVID B. Ph.D. candidate, Duke University.

MCGEE, DANIEL B. Ph.D., Duke University. Professor of Religion, Baylor University.

MILLER, GLENN. Ph.D., Union Theological Seminary, NYC. Dean and Professor, Bangor Theological Seminary.

MILLER, JONATHAN. M.Div., Hebrew Union Seminary. Rabbi Temple Emanu-El, Birmingham, Alabama.

MILLS, FREDERICK V., SR. Ph.D., University of Pennsylvania. Professor of History, LaGrange College, LaGrange, Georgia.

NASH, ROBERT N., JR. Ph.D., Southern Baptist Theological Seminary. Professor of Religion, Shorter College, Rome, Georgia.

PINSON, J. MATTHEW. Ph.D. candidate in history, Florida State University.

POOL, JEFF. Ph.D., University of Chicago. Assistant Professor of Systematic Theology, Southwestern Baptist Theological Seminary.

PORTERFIELD, AMANDA. Ph.D., Stanford University. Professor of Religious Studies, Indiana University–Purdue University at Indianapolis.

PRATT, ANDREW. Ph.D., Southern Baptist Theological Seminary. Instructor of Religion, Southeast Missouri State University.

RICHTER, FRED. Ph.D., Auburn University. Associate Professor of English, Georgia Southern University.

ROSSING, JOHN P. Ph.D. candidate, Emory University. Pastor, Dalton, Georgia.

SHELLEY, THOMAS J. Ph.D., Catholic University of America. Professor of Church History, St. Joseph's Seminary, New York.

SHEPHERD, FREDERICK M. Ph.D., Georgetown University. Assistant Professor of Political Science and History, Samford University.

SHRIVER, GEORGE H. Ph.D., Duke University. Professor of History, Georgia Southern University.

SLOAT, JOHN W. Th.M., Pittsburgh Theological Seminary. Pastor Emeritus, Northminster Presbyterian Church, New Castle, Pennsylvania.

SMITH, HARMON L. Ph.D., Duke University. Professor of Moral Theology (Divinity School) and Professor of Community and Family Medicine (Medical School), Duke University.

THIGPEN, T. PAUL. Ph.D., Emory University. Assistant Professor of Religious Studies, Southwest Missouri State University.

TOULOUSE, MARK G. Ph.D., University of Chicago. Associate Professor of Church History, Brite Divinity School, Texas Christian University.

TURNER, HELEN LEE. Ph.D., University of Virginia, Associate Professor of Religion, Furman University.

VANDALE, ROBERT L. Ph.D., University of Iowa. Professor of Religion, Westminster College, New Wilmington, Pennsylvania.

WEAVER, DOUGLAS. Ph.D., Southern Baptist Theological Seminary. Associate Professor of Christianity and Chair, Division of Religion and Philosophical Studies, Brewton-Parker College, Mt. Vernon, Georgia.

WHELAN, TIMOTHY D. Ph.D., University of Maryland. Assistant Professor of English, Georgia Southern University.

WILLIAMS, LAWRENCE H. Ph.D., University of Iowa. Associate Professor of African-American Studies and History, Luther College, Decorah, Iowa.

WINSTON, DIANE. Ph.D., Princeton University. Fellow at the Center for the Study of American Religion, Princeton University.

WOODS, JAMES M. Ph.D., Tulane University. Associate Professor of History, Georgia Southern University.

ISBN 0-313-29691-X

9 780313 296918

90000>

EAN

HARDCOVER BAR CODE